Linguistic Expeditions

KLEAR-RILI Studies in Korean Language and Linguistics

THE KOREAN LANGUAGE EDUCATION AND RESEARCH CENTER &
THE RESEARCH INSTITUTE OF LANGUAGE AND INFORMATION

LINGUISTIC EXPEDITIONS

Ho-min Sohn

고려대학교출판부
KOREA UNIVERSITY PRESS

Acknowledgments

Grateful acknowledgment is hereby made for permission to reprint in this volume the author's papers from journals and books published by:

Bunka Hyoron Company, Hiroshima, Japan
Center for Korean Studies of the University of Hawaii, Honolulu
Chungnam National University Press, Taejon, Korea
Department of Linguistics of the University of Hawaii, Honolulu
English Literary Society of Korea, Seoul
Hankuk University of Foreign Studies Press, Seoul
Hornbeam Press, Columbia, U.S.A.
Indiana University Press, Bloomington
International Circle of Korean Linguistics
Korean Language Society, Seoul
Korean National Commission for UNESCO, Seoul
Language Research Institute, Seoul National University, Seoul
Linguistic Research, Inc., Edmonton, Canada
Linguistic Society of Korea, Seoul
North-Holland Publishing Company, Amsterdam
Pacific Linguistics, Australian National University, Canberra
Seoul National University Press, Seoul
University of Hawaii Press, Honolulu

Korea University Press
82-2-3290-4230 (Tel.) 82-2-923-6311 (Fax)
http://www.kupress.com kupress@korea.ac.kr
145, Anam-Ro, Seongbuk-Gu, Seoul, 136-701 Korea

Published January 2014

ISBN 978-89-7641-836-4 93710

KRW 30,000

To my wife Sook-hi and
children James, Julie, Jeannie & Andrew

Preface to the KUP Edition

Linguistic Expeditions was first published by the Hanshin Publishing Company in Seoul in 1986 and subsequently reprinted a couple of times before going out of print in the mid-1990s. As indicated in the preface of the original edition, it is an anthology of twenty-five selected papers (of which four are co-authored) that I wrote in English between 1971 and 1985. It encompasses my linguistic analyses of many intriguing issues that had transpired in Micronesian and Melanesian languages as well as Korean and comparative Korean-Japanese-English. In order to address the issues in these languages, I applied methods and theories of phonological, graphical, syntactic, semantic, pragmatic, historical-comparative, sociolinguistic, and pedagogical analysis.

Linguistic Expeditions was thoroughly and perceptively reviewed by Professor Lewis S. Josephs for *Korean Studies*, vol. 12(1), pp. 91-94 (1988), University of Hawaii Press (retrieved January 26, 2013 from Project MUSE database http://muse.jhu.edu/). Aside from the specific evaluations of individual chapters (papers), some general remarks the reviewer made in this four-page review are: "Sohn ⋯ has put together a superb collection of his writing that will provide general linguists, linguistic specialists, and students of the Korean language with a vast wealth of interesting and serviceable data and with many challenging ideas of a theoretical nature ⋯ Those interested in controversial theoretical issues but in need of sufficient linguistic data to test hypotheses will find much to their satisfaction in the papers of this collection. It is clear that Sohn does not hesitate to reanalyze the raw linguistic data in radical though insightful ways, leaving the earlier, more traditional analyses stale and static by comparison." The review concluded with the following remarks: "While reading through Sohn's monograph, I made a general evaluation of each paper in terms of three criteria: interest, to generalist or specialist; insightfulness; and clarity of presentation. For those with limited time who wish only to sample articles at the top of the scale, the following are strongly recommended: Papers 4, 5, 6, 9, 11, 16, 17, 22, and 23. These papers set the standard for a volume of works that will have a marked influence on the evolution of Korean and Micronesian linguistics for many years to come."

After some twenty years since its last print run, I am glad to see the book photo printed and published through the Korea University Press(KUP) in the series *KLEAR and RILI studies in Korean Language and Linguistics*, a joint academic endeavor between KLEAR(Korean Language Education & Research Center, incorporated with the State of Hawaii, USA) and RILI (Research Institute of Language Information at Korea University). I am indeed happy to be given the golden opportunity to share my earlier ideas and findings with a new generation of scholars and students in the spirit of the time-honored Eastern adage "*On-go-ji-sin*(reviewing the old and learning the new)".

I am greatly indebted to Seok-Hoon You at Korea University, without whose initiative to have the monograph photocopied and published by the KUP, this volume would never have reappeared.

Ho-min Sohn
Honolulu
January 2014

PREFACE

This book is a collection of twenty-five selected papers (of which four are co-authored) that I have written in English since 1971. The main reason for putting them together as a monograph is that many of them are dispersed among a wide variety of books and journals which are not easily accessible to the audience. It is hoped that this volume will be of modest service to those who are interested to learn about linguistic facts of some languages less known to the Western world.

The languages covered in this collection include English, Japanese, Korean, Kwara'ae (a Melanesian language spoken in the Solomon Islands), and many Micronesian languages including Ulithian and Woleaian. In particular, Ulithian and Woleaian were hardly studied before I explored their structure and vocabulary and designed their orthography. Rather comprehensive descriptions of these two languages are found in *A Ulithian Grammar* (by Ho-min Sohn & B. W. Bender, Australian National University Press, 1973), *Woleaian Reference Grammar* (by Ho-min Sohn, University of Hawaii Press, 1975), and *Woleaian-English Dictionary* (by Ho-min Sohn & A. Tawerilmang, University of Hawaii Press, 1976). For the analysis of Ulithian and Kwara'ae, I conducted "linguistic expeditions" in Micronesia for five months in 1968 (for Ulithian) and in New Zealand and the Solomon Islands for ten months in 1971-1972 (for Kwara'ae). For Woleaian and some other Micronesian languages. I worked in Honolulu with the native speakers from Micronesia for many years. For the study of Korean, I have made several research trips to Korea since 1971 in order to collect field data as well as library materials. Most analyses and accompanying discussions in this book are predominantly data-based, without extensive involvement in the matters of abstract theoretical polemics. This emphasis on facts and data has largely been due to my belief that theory construction based on a limited amount of data is as shaky as a house built on sand and well-collected data are of utmost and eternal value to linguists. Thus, some of the theoretical varieties and approaches I adopted or discussed may no longer be as fashionable among linguists as they once were, but nonetheless I believe the data I provided for analysis remain no less important than before.

Although this monograph is necessarily very limited in the topics chosen, reflecting my own interests, it nevertheless covers a wide range of linguistic areas, so that the papers are arranged under four broad chapters for the convenience of the readers: (1) phonology and writing systems; (2) syntax, semantics, and pragmatics; (3) historical and comparative studies; and (4) sociolinguistics and language pedagogy. Although there are doubtless many errors and inadequacies that remain in the papers, I have not rewritten any of them, limiting myself to the correction of typographical errors, a minimum of editing, some essential additions and deletions, and the grouping of references at the end of the book.

I cannot leave this preface without mentioning two people to whom I have owed most in growing as a student of linguistics - Professor Sheon Gi Gim in Korea and Professor Byron W. Bender in the United States. The former encouraged and led me to pursue linguistics when I went astray as a student at Seoul National University, while the latter helped and guided me to be a successful student of linguistics at the University of Hawaii. My debt to Bender will be apparent in many of the papers in this volume. I respect and thank them at all times. Another person I should mention is my close colleague Dong Jae Lee, who, ever since 1971, has shared joys and sufferings with me at the Department of East Asian Languages and Literatures of the University of Hawaii. Needless to say, there are many other teachers, colleagues, and students whose teaching, advice, and cooperation have had direct and indirect impact on my career and scholarship. Space does not allow me to spell them out here.

This book is dedicated to my wife and four children who have suffered enormously and willingly submitted to so much sacrifice ever since I was a graduate student. I sincerely thank the love and indefatigable support and cooperation that they have always given me.

I wish to express my gratitude to the journal and book editors and publishers, as well as my co-authors, for their generous permission for me to reprint the papers in this volume. Many thanks also go to Mr. Tae-geun Park, President of Hanshin Publishing Company, who has kindly offered to publish this collection despite its enormous financial burden. Finally, I would like to extend my thanks to Hankuk University of Foreign Studies in Seoul and my colleagues there without whose thoughtful invitation to me as a visiting professor I would not have been able to be involved in the publication process in person.

Ho-min Sohn
Seoul
June 1986

CONTENTS

CHAPTER 1
PHONOLOGY AND WRITING SYSTEMS

1. METATHESIS IN KWARA'AE

Unlike most languages, Kwara'ae has a powerful synchronic phonological rule of metathesis, which feeds most other phonological rules in the language. This paper establishes some justification for the rule, presenting forms and alternations that motivate metathesis and providing some evidence that the rule is psychologically real. The paper further examines the interaction of the rule with other major phonological rules, and reviews Ultan's hypotheses on the nature of metathesis, concluding that Kwara'ae evidence does not support them. Kwara'ae metathesis is characterized as a process of minimizing the number of syllables by converting open to closed syllables, with a minimum loss of phonological features as well as of communication.

Most descriptions of systematic or isolated metathesis in languages have been made on the diachronic perspective whether they concern individual languages or typological comparisons, or whether they consider grammatical devices or purely phonological changes (e.g. Sievers 1901; Grammont 1950; Martinet 1955; Lehmann 1962; Biggs 1965; Thompson and Thompson 1969; Bailey 1970; Malone 1971; Ultan 1971; Underhill 1972; Silva 1973; Langdon 1976). Recent observations of metathesis as a synchronic process were usually based on a few sporadic phenomena (e.g. Chomsky and Halle 1968; Schane 1971; Semiloff-Zelasko 1973). While many generative phonologists appear to view metathesis as a common phonological process (e.g. Chomsky and Halle 1968: 361), Webb (1976), after examining some frequently cited examples from Kasem, Zoque, Korean, Old English, Jamaican Creole, and Classical Arabic, concludes that (a) synchronic examples of systematic metathesis are very rare and (b) even the few apparent cases are best handled suppletively, and not in terms of metathesis (i.e. permutation of phonological segments), and thus argues against metathesis as a phonological process.[1]

Through my work on Kwara'ae I have found that metathesis in the language is a regular synchronic process of a purely phonological nature and that it has a central role according to which most other significant phonological rules are motivated.[2] The aims of this paper are (1) to present the facts and the rule associated with Kwara'ae metathesis, (2) to show the interaction of the metathesis with other phonological processes, and (3) to discuss the nature of Kwara'ae metathesis in connection with Ultan's (1971) putatively universal hypothesis.

The phonology described in this paper of Kwara'ae is based on systematic (or underlying) phonemicization because it greatly simplifies the otherwise complicated description of the language, captures greater underlying generality of the facts of the language, and reveals the internalized linguistic knowledge of native speakers. As a result of the application of this principle to Kwara'ae, the following points enable us to clearly comprehend the phonological structure. Some ten surface (or taxonomic) vowels are unambiguously derived from five underlying vowels by a set of general, as well as natural, synchronic rules.[3] No underlying consonant clusters exist in the syntagmatic relation of segments. This then contributes to a simpler canonical structure. There is no distributional constraint in the occurrence of underlying vowels and consonants. Native speakers have no difficulty in converting underlying to surface and surface to underlying phonemicization. Biggs (1965) reports that the short form of a Rotuman base (i.e. the metathesized form) is predictable from the corresponding long form (i.e. the unmetathesized form), though the reverse does not apply. But in Kwara'ae the relationship is biconditional in that long forms are also uniquely reconstructable from their short form counterparts.

I postulate the following underlying consonant and vowel phonemes for Kwara'ae:

(1)

Consonants					*Vowels*		
		t	k	’	i		u
b		d	g		e		o
	f	s				a	
m		n	ŋ				
		l					
		r					

Ivens (1931) and Deck (1933-34) set up three additional consonants, k^{w}, g^{w}, and *ŋ*ʷ, from such examples respectively as [kwi] ‘dog’, [gwəu] ‘head’, and [ŋwɛ’$lu·] ‘intestine’. However, there is no contrast between [o/uV_i]

and [wV$_i$] such as [oa] and [wa], [ui] and [wi], [oe] and [we], [ue] and [we], etc. [kw], [gw], and [ŋw] do not appear in the word-final position and they and a vowel following them are not metathesized. As Deck (ibid.: 36-39) points out, these three velarized consonants precede *a, e,* and *i* only. As will be seen, [w] is derived from *o* or *u,* which also suggests that [Cw] can be derived from *Co* or *Cu*. It is proposed therefore that the three consonants, along with [w], be described phonologically as a result of glide formation (see Rule 3 below) and thus simply surface manifestations, before a vowel, of *k* + *o/u, g* + *o/u,* and ŋ + *o/u*. This analysis on the phonological level will explain the above-mentioned sequential constraints that [kw], [gw], and [ŋw] have.

There are five underlying vowels which are all short and may occur in geminate. There are long vowels like [ö·], [œ·], [æ·], and [ɛ·] which appear only before a consonant and do not have short counterparts except before a glottal stop, as in [mö·l] 'lemon', [sœ·k] 'lie', and ['æ·b$ɛ·n] 'to help'. Each of these vowels is viewed as a sequence of two underlying simple vowels, as in [ö·] = *oi,* [œ·] = *oe,* [æ·] = *ae,* and [ɛ·] = *ai.* Phonetic similarity and the lack of contrast between each paired terms, as well as pattern congruity and native speakers' intuitive judgment, all support this analysis. Shortening before a glottal stop, as in [mɛ'] 'hither', does not affect the underlying cluster solution, because it is phonetically predictable.

There are no underlying semivowels, although we observe surface [w]s, as in [waŋg] 'to want' which should be derived from *oga.* Stress is not so conspicuous. In general, it occurs on the initial syllable in surface forms. No minimal pair differentiated only by stress has been found, a fact indicating that stress is not phonemic.

As direct evidence which motivates the reconstruction of unmetathesized forms and justifies the metathesis rule as a synchronic process, there are innumerable sets of allomorphs whose alternation indicates metathesis. Observe the forms in (2), where $ is a phonetic syllable boundary.

(2)	A		B	
(a)	[da$luəm]	'bailer, to bail'	[dəul$ma·]	'bail it'
(b)	['æ·b$ɛ·n]	'to help'	['æ·b$a$nia]	'help it'

The B-form of each alternating pair is made up of the A-form followed by the third person object suffix [a], which is confirmed by native speakers. [a·] in (2aB) is a slightly contracted form of [a:], which has resulted from the stem-final [a] and the suffix [a]. This suggests that [əm] in (2aA) is a metathesized counterpart of the stem-final [ma] in (2aB), [a] being raised to [ə] in the neighborhood of [u]. Similarly, [da$lu] and [dəul] show another metathesis alternation. In (2b) [ɛ·n] alternates with [a$ni] which occurs before the suffix [a], revealing that [ɛ·] is a merger of [a] and [i]. Further, observe the alternation in (3).

(3)	A		B	
(a)	[an$doal]	'pubic area'	[aond$ləum]	'your pubic area'
(b)	[sa·t]	'name'	[sa$ta·nd̑]	'their name'
(c)	[ba·b̆$li·ĭ]	'cheek'	[ba·b$lĭ$lĭiuk]	'my cheek'

Again, B-forms consist of A-forms plus a possessive suffix: [uk] 'my', [um] 'your', or [and̑] 'their'. Metathesis alternation is observable in [an$do] vs. [aond] and [al] vs. [lə] in (3a), [sa·t] vs. [sata] in (3b), and [lĭ·ĭ] vs. [lĭ$lĭ] in (3c).

In order to systematically capture the obvious relationship existing in each pair of alternants, it is necessary to give one representation to each morpheme and derive the interrelated allomorphs from it through a set of general phonological rules. Incidentally, establishment of such base forms justifies the need for a systematic phonological level distinct from a phonetic one.

It is unmistakably clear that the formal type of Kwara'ae metathesis is a transposition of two contiguous segments, a consonant and a vowel. There is every reason to believe that CV is the base structure from which VC is derived. For one thing, by postulating the CV base, we get a simpler underlying canonical shape of syllables, i.e. (C)V, CV being the unmarked and optimal syllable type (cf. Hyman 1975: 161 and 188). Suppose, contrary to our claim that (2aA) be derived from *daluma,* that we derive it from *daulam* by changing *ul* to *lu*. Since the base form in this case ends in a consonant, the syllable structure would be of the form (C)V(C). Thus, the underlying word or syllable structure would be the same as the surface one in its complexity. With CV as the base, on the other hand, we can get greater underlying simplicity. A natural question one may pose at this point is why a simpler, unmarked syllable structure must be disrupted resulting in a more or less marked structure like CVC. One might think that this is a counter-tendency because a natural process is to preserve or create preferred syllable structures. However, the consideration of word structure outweighs that of syllable structure, as observed immediately below.

Second, CV→VC is a natural or plausible phonological process in the language. For instance, while there is no conceivable phonetic motivation to change *daulam* to [da$luəm], conversion of *daluma* to [da$luəm] results in a change in the syllable structure from three phonetic syllables

[CVCVCV] to two [CV$CVVC]. This is a natural process because its function is to reduce the number of underlying syllables. Furthermore, word-final weakening is a universal phenomenon. Deletion, devoicing, or permutation of a word-final simple vowel is attested in many other languages as natural processes (e.g. Sohn 1975a: 26-28; Sohn and Bender 1973: 22-34, and fn. 7 for some Micronesian cases). Postulation of word-final strengthening by converting the preconsonantal vowel to the postconsonantal one, as hypothesized in *daulama* to [dəul$ma·], is against such phonetic naturalness, especially because this language does not have any word-final stress.

Third, CV→VC is a much more general process than VC→CV in the language. Under the latter alternative, we would not be able to explain why metathesis is blocked in certain base forms. For instance, something like *aebain* and *aebaina* must be postulated for ['æ·b$ε·n] 'to help' and ['æ·b$a$nia] 'help it', respectively. The question is why *eb* does not become *be* and the word-final *in* does not become *ni,* while *ina* should become *nia.* If we postulate *abeani* and *abeania,* on the other hand, we can simply say that all CVs become VCs, except a word-initial one, which is unmarked or optimal, and one which is followed (or protected) by a word-final vowel. Thus, postulation of the CV base contributes to predictability, one of the important criteria in determining underlying forms. At the same time, we can easily imagine that many nonalternating surface forms such as [mö·l] 'lemon', [sœ·k] 'lie', and [məu'] 'fear' are outputs of metathesis. We saw in (3b) that there is an alternation between the independent form [sa·t] and its contextual variant [sata] 'name', from which we can reconstruct the base form *sata* in view of the foregoing arguments. This structural pressure leads us to suppose such nonalternating forms as those given just above as derived from *moli, soke,* and *ma'u,* respectively, all having a CVCV canonical structure. This allows great generality to the metathesis rule.

Finally, postulation of CV→VC is also supported by historical evidence. Proto-Oceanic words consist of open syllables (e.g. Grace 1969). Thus, for example, Kwara'ae [uk] 'my', [um] 'your', and [an̯d] 'their' correspond to Proto-Oceanic *ku, mu,* and *da,* respectively.

Based on the above observations, we can establish the base forms of (2) and (3) as shown in (4).

(4)	*daluma*	'bailer, to bail'	*dalumaa*	'bail it'
	'abeani	'to help'	*'abeania*	'help it'
	adola	'pubic area'	*adolamu*	'your pubic area'
	sata	'name'	*satada*	'their name'
	babalili	'cheek'	*babaliliku*	'my cheek'

The process that converts CV to VC reflects native speakers' knowledge of the language. In addition to synchronic alternations such as given in (2) and (3), there is some other clear evidence that metathesis is psychologically or synchronically real. First, while always pronouncing sentences in metathesized forms in actual speech situations, native speakers are able to cite individual words in both metathesized and unmetathesized forms. That is, speakers are aware of underlying phonological, i.e. unmetathesized, forms and capable of producing them as citation forms.

Second, as in a citation situation, one may call a person by his name in an unmetathesized form when he is in a relaxed and leisured situation (e.g. [sabe]), whereas he uses a metathesized form in a normal or imminent situation (e.g. [sæ·b]).

Third, those who are familiar with romanization mostly use unmetathesized spellings, deliberately converting, word by word, the spoken sentences into written forms.[4] For instance, they spell [liəm] 'five' as *lima,* thus not in terms of the actual sounds and syllables but in terms of a theoretically real but actually unnatural form. This means that speakers have knowledge of the underlying two-syllable structure of this word.

Finally, native speakers apply metathesis to foreign words in their pronunciation. Thus, *Peter* is pronunced as [piət] and *Lisa* as [liəs]. All this supports that the present analysis is valid and synchronically real, because it captures the native competence of speakers.

I propose the following rule to account for Kwara'ae metathesis.

(5) *Rule 1: Metathesis*

$C_iV_i \rightarrow V_iC_i$ \$ / (A) V_1______ #

(B) # (C)V_1______

Conditions: (1) The rule applies in the order of (A) and (B).

(2) If V_i is a vowel to which a metathesized vowel is attached, the rule does not apply.

Rule 1 is obligatory in that speakers pronounce only metathesized forms for communicative purposes in either slow, normal or allegro speech. As mentioned earlier, base forms are used in citing words, in writing, and in songs, but not in speech communication.

Rule 1 does not need any grammatical information, hence it is purely phonological. The general morpheme boundary (+) is not needed either, because metathesis occurs across morpheme boundaries, as in *sata* + *da* [sata·nd̂] 'their names'. Only the word boundry (#), either internal or external, is necessary to refer to for the process to take place. Thus, in compound words including reduplicated ones, where one or more word boundaries appear, metathesis takes place in each stem independent of the others. For instance, *kaidai # kaidai* [kɛ·n$dɛ·$kɛ·n$dɛ·] 'o'clock' does not undergo any metathesis because each stem, i.e., *kaidai* 'time', is allowed by a word boundary and does not satisfy either of the two environments.

A phonetic syllable boundary ($) is formed at the place vacated by V_i. This syllable boundary is characterized by a slight phonetic juncture. Due to this juncture, no further metathesis takes place between a consonant and a vowel on both sides of the juncture. Thus, [b$a] in ['æ·b$ania] 'help it', which is derived from *'abeania,* cannot further be permuted.[5] Without metathesis, a normal syllable boundary should fall before a CV, not between C and V (see Rule 13).

There is a constraint that a consonant which is not preceded by a vowel is never metathesized with the following vowel, as in *sa* [sa] (person marker) and *sulia* [su$ĭia] 'because'. Thus, a vowel cannot participate in metathesis if the preceding consonant is preceded by another consonant due to a metathesis process that vacates the vowel position. For instance, the second *o* in *boel$bolea* [bœ·l$bo$lea] (from *bolebolea* 'crazy') cannot be metathesized with the preceding consonant *b* because an earlier metathesis has moved the first *e* to the position before *l.* All this means that there must be a vowel before a consonant which attracts the vowel following the consonant. The above constraint is expressed by V_1 in the two environments of the rule.

Metathesis does not occur between a consonant and a vowel sequence (including a double vowel) that ends a word, as observed in *baruu* [ba$ru·] 'few' and *olofoloa* [o·lfoloa] 'channel'. This constraint, which we may call 'final V_2 constraint' is incorporated in the environment (A) of the rule.

As described in condition 1, metathesis applies to a word in a fixed order.[6] The first order is word-final, as in *daluma* [da$luəm] 'bailer' and *ma'i* [mɛ'] 'hither'. The second order is word-initial, as in *atamemeo* [a·tmemeo] 'spider' and *dalumaa* [dəul$ma·] 'bail it'. Any change of order would produce unacceptable sequences.[7] The application of the second order first to *daluma* 'bailer' [da$luəm] would derive *[dəul$ma]. If we do not set up the second order, *atamemeo* 'spider' would also be realized as *[a$tæ·m$meo]. At the moment, we do not have words of the length to justify the third order, i.e. word-medial. Compounds like *balioloolo* [bɛ·l$o·l$o·l] 'right hand' and *ma'eta'eelo* [mæ'$tæ'$eol] 'doorway', if fossilized as simple words in the future, will serve as examples of such an order.

As stated in condition 2, a simple vowel which has attracted another vowel through metathesis cannot participate in metathesis with the preceding consonant even though other conditions are met. Figuratively speaking, a vowel which has attracted another vowel as a sister cannot be attracted by another vowel. For instance, *gogola* 'octopus' is changed to *gogoal* by metathesis, but now the second *g* and the second *o* cannot be metathesized due to this condition. One might say that this condition is nothing but an extension of the 'final V_2 constraint' mentioned above and that modification of environment (B) as # (C)V_1____C would deal with this word-medial phenomenon. However, condition 2 is motivated by the existence of such examples as *'abeania* ['æ·b$a$nia] where *e* takes part in metathesis in spite of the following underlying vowel. If we take historical word boundaries into account in underlying representations, as in *'abe#ania,* condition 2 would certainly be dispensed with. It appears, however, that historical word boundaries are not learned by native speakers as boundaries. This lack of psychological reality leads us to postulate condition 2 instead of setting up historical word boundaries as underlying elements.

The application of Rule 1 is illustrated in (6).

(6)	*daluma* 'bailer'	*dalumaa* 'bail it'	*'abeani* 'to help'
(a)	daluam	–	'abeain
(b)	–	daul$maa	'aeb$ain

In (6), the phonetic juncture or syllable boundary is not specified in the word-final position, where the juncture comes anyway.

The types of metathesis that Kwara'ae is sensitive to may be grouped into the following six general sets in view of the structure of words.

(7)

Type 1: $(C)VC_iV_i \rightarrow (C)VV_iC_i$

ma'u	[məu']	'fear'
oga	[waŋg̑]	'to want'

Type 2: $(C)V(C)VC_iV_i \rightarrow (C)V(C)VV_iC_i$

mauri	[məuir̥]	'alive'
satada	[sa$ta·nḍ]	'their names'
alage	[a$læ·ŋg̑]	'seaweed'

Type 3: $(C)VC_iV_iCVV \rightarrow (C)VV_iC_iCVV$

dalumaa	[dəul$ma·]	'bail it'
talaŋai	[ta·l$ŋɛi]	'100'
ogatiu	[waŋ$tiu]	'stomach'

Type 4: $(C)VC_iV_i(C)VCVV \rightarrow (C)VV_iC_i(C)VCVV$

atamemeo	[a·tmemeo]	'spider'
olofoloa	[o·lfoloa]	'pass, channel'
bolebolea	[bœ·lbolea]	'crazy'

Type 5: $(C)VC_iV_i(C)VC_jV_j \rightarrow (C)VV_iC_i(C)VV_jC_j$

fa'itani	[fɛ'$tɛ·n]	'to turn over'
adolamu	[aond$ləum]	'your pubic area'

Type 6: $(C)VC_iV_i(C)V(C)VC_jV_j \rightarrow (C)VV_iC_i(C)V(C)VV_jC_j$

abaabaku	[a·mbambəuk]	'your shoulder, wing'

baboula	[baob$wəl]	'thick'	*abufaŋa'a*	[əubfaŋa']	'fast (giving up of food)'
u'iani	[wi'$ɛ·n]	'to throw'			

The following type of words do not undergo metathesis in that they do not satisfy the environmental requirements.

(8) *ki*	[ki]	(plural marker)
geo	[geo]	'megapod'
magaa	[maŋ$ga·]	'to destroy'
abui	[a$bui]	'to climb'
'ua	['uə]	'ancient'
iu	[iu]	'yes'
kirio	[ki$rio]	'porpoise'

Kiparsky (1968) draws the distinction between feeding and bleeding rule ordering. Rule 1 feeds most other Kwara'ae phonological rules, if not absolutely. Below are given, without much elaboration, the major phonological rules, most of which describe allophonic reductions and are triggered by metathesis. Rules are ordered, each applying once in a derivation, and are obligatory unless marked as optional.

(9) *Rule 2*: simple Vowel *a* Raising

$$\text{a} \rightarrow \begin{bmatrix} \text{ə} \\ \text{ɛ} \end{bmatrix} \Big/ \begin{bmatrix} \begin{Bmatrix} \text{(u)}\_\_\_\_\text{(u)} \\ \text{i}\ \_\_\_\_\ \text{C} \end{Bmatrix} \\ \_\_\_\_\ \text{i} \end{bmatrix}$$

When two or more vowels occur contiguously, they are subject to weakening, rendering the sequence of vowels a single phonetic peak: *a* is raised to [ə] in the environment of *u* or after *i* if followed by a consonant and to [ɛ] before *i*. When the simple vowel *a* occurs at the end and is preceded by *i*, it is not subject to being raised, as in *sulia* [su$ľia] 'because'. The rule does not apply to the long vowel *aa* either, as in *ta'iruaa* [tɛ'$rua·] 'itchy'. While examples like *mauri* [məuir̯] 'alive' do not presuppose metathesis for the raising, examples like *daluma* [da$luəm] must undergo Rule 1 before the raising. Some more examples follow.

(10) *laua* 'plant'→(R2)→ləuə [ləuə]
lima 'five'→(R1, R2) → liəm [liəm]
tiai 'other'→(R2) → tiɛi [tiɛi]
ma'i 'hither'→(R1, R2) → mɛi' [mɛ']

(11) *Rule 3*: [w] glide Formation

$$\begin{bmatrix} \text{o} \\ \text{u} \end{bmatrix} \rightarrow \text{w} \Bigg/ \left\{ \begin{matrix} \$ \\ \# \\ \begin{bmatrix} +\ \text{cons} \\ +\ \text{velar} \end{bmatrix} \end{matrix} \right\} \underline{\quad\quad} \begin{bmatrix} \text{a} \\ V_i \end{bmatrix}$$

Condition: V_i does not include *u* or *o*.

When preceded by a juncture (a syllable or word boundary) or a velar consonant (*k, g,* or *η*), *o* and *u* are reduced to the semivowel [w] if a vowel other than *u* and *o* follows. This rule is illustrated in (12).

(12) *oga* 'to want'→(R1, R3)→wag [waŋg]
baboula 'thick'→(R1, R2, R3)→baob$wəl [baob̑$wəl]
koao 'white'→(R3)→kwao [kwao]
u'iani 'to throw'→(R1, R2, R3)→wi'$ɛin [wi'$ɛin]
goagoae 'armpit'→(R3) → gwagwae [gwa$gwae]

(13) *Rule 4*: Vowel Fusion

$$\begin{bmatrix} \text{oi} \\ \text{oe} \\ \text{ae} \end{bmatrix} \rightarrow \begin{bmatrix} \text{ö}\cdot \\ \text{œ}\cdot \\ \text{æ}\cdot \end{bmatrix} \Bigg/ \underline{\quad\quad\quad} \text{C}$$

As a process of vocalic weakening, Rule 4 monophthongizes or coalesces vowel clusters with a compensatory mora length. This rule does not apply unless there is a consonant following the vowel sequence. For example, in word-final position *ae* does not change to [æ·], as in *ogaŋoae* [waŋ$ŋwae] 'belly', and *oi* does not change to [ö·], as in *fa'iloi* [fɛ'$loi] 'snake'.

(14) *moli* 'lemon'→(R1, R4)→mö·l [mö·l]
nominomi 'sand-fly'→(R1, R4)→nö·m$nö·m [nö·m$nö·m]
soke 'lie'→(R1, R4)→sœ·k[sœ·k]
asofe 'rat'→(R1, R4)→asœ·f [asœ·f]
ma'eta'eelo 'doorway'→(R1, R4)→mæ·'$tæ·'$eol [mæ'$tæ'$eol]

(15) *Rule 5*: *i*-truncation (optional)
i→·/ɛ______

[ɛi] is optionally reduced to [ɛ·], as illustrated in (16).

(16) *dami* 'gum'→(R1, R2, R5)→dɛ·m [dɛim/dɛ·m]
aliali 'fast'→(R1, R2, R5) →ɛ·l$ɛ·l[ɛil$ɛil/ɛ·l$ɛ·l]

(17) *Rule 6*: Geminate Shortening
$V_iV_i \rightarrow V_i\cdot$

Two identical vowels are shortened by a mora length, as shown below.

(18) *soro* 'a kind of canoe'→(R1, R6)→so·r [so·r]
dalumaa 'bail it'→ (R1, R2, R6)→dəul$ma· [dəul$ma·]

(19) *Rule 7*: Further Vowel Shortening

$$\begin{Bmatrix} \cdot \\ \text{i} \end{Bmatrix} \rightarrow \varnothing \; / \; \text{V} \_\_\_\_\_ \, '$$

A long vowel which is contracted by Rule 6 and *i* after another vowel (e.g. [ɛi] are further shortened before a glottal stop, ending up with a single vowel. Notice that this rule is strictly ordered after Rules 3 and 4 which convert *ui* to [wi] and *oi* to [ö·], respectively, thus bleeding Rule 7. Examples follow.

(20) *fi'itatali* 'hibiscus'→(R1, R2, R5, R6, R7)→fi'$tatɛ·l [fi'$ta$tɛil/fi'$ta$tɛ·l]
ma'eta'eelo 'doorway'→(R1, R4, R7)→mæ'$tæ'$eol [mæ'$tæ'$eol]
ŋoa'iluu 'intestine'→(R1, R2, R3, R5, R6, R7)→ŋwɛ'$lu· [ŋwɛ'$lu·]

(21) *Rule 8*: Palatalization

$$\begin{bmatrix} \text{d} \\ \begin{Bmatrix} \text{l} \\ \text{s} \end{Bmatrix} \end{bmatrix} \rightarrow [+\text{palatal}] / \_\_\_\_\_ \begin{bmatrix} \text{i} \\ \begin{Bmatrix} \text{eV} \\ \text{i} \end{Bmatrix} \end{bmatrix}$$

Although slight palatalization of a consonant before a high front vowel is universal, Kwara'ae has phonologized or 'exaggerated' this phonetic variation, with *d, l,* and *s* receiving particularly noticeable palatalization.

(22) *ŋorimadiko* 'edible grub'→(R1, R4, R8)→ŋö·r$mad̆iok [ŋö·r$ma$d̆iok]
babaliliku 'my cheek'→(R1, R6, R8)→ba·b$l̆il̆iuk [ba·b$l̆i$l̆iuk]
bale'o 'breadfruit'→(R1, R8)→bal̆eo' [ba$l̆eo']
asila 'salt'→(R1, R2, R8)→ašiəl [a$šiəl]
selo 'sail'→(R1, R8)→šeol [šeol]

(23) *Rule 9*: Prenasalization (optional)

$$\begin{Bmatrix} \text{b} \\ \text{d} \\ \text{g} \end{Bmatrix} \rightarrow [+\text{nasal}]/\text{V}\_\_\_\_\_$$

The phonemes *b, d,* and *g* are optionally prenasalized after a vowel within the same syllable. Thus, nasalization does not occur in word-initial position and after another consonant or a juncture. Degree of prenasalization is correlated with the sonorance of the neighboring vowels and the kinds of consonants themselves. *b* is the least prone to prenasalization, usually absent in fast speech except between two vowels. The nasal consonants produced in this way cannot be interpreted as a separate phoneme, because, above all, the nasal and the accompanying oral consonant function as a unit in metathesis, as in *adolamu* [aond$ləum] 'your pubic area'.

(24) *labua* 'to pound'→(R2, R9)→lambuə [la(m)$buə]
'abeani 'to help'→(R1, R2, R4, R5, R9)→'æ·mb$ɛ·n ['æ·(m)b$ɛ·n]
lade 'gravel'→(R1, R4, R9)→læ·nd [læ·(n)ḓ]
ago 'shelter'→(R1, R9)→aoŋg [ao(ŋ)g̭]

The lack of prenasalization in words like *daudau* [dəu$dəu] 'pole' and *du'uguau* [du'$gwəu] 'hat' is due to the juncture immediately preceding each consonant in question.

(25) *Rule 10*: Consonant Devoicing

$$\left\{\begin{matrix} b \\ d \\ g \\ r \end{matrix}\right\} \rightarrow [-\text{voice}] / \_\_\_\_ \left\{\begin{matrix} [-\text{voice}] \\ \# \end{matrix}\right\}$$

This rule is absolutely fed by the metathesis rule in that the latter creates all of the inputs to this rule. It does not apply when the following sound is voiced, as in *ogala'a* [waŋg$la'] 'selfish'.

(26) *abatoro* 'clothes'→(R1, R6, R10)→a·b$to·ɾ̥̭ [a·b$to·ɾ̥̭]
kado 'thin'→(R1, R9, R10)→kaond̥ [kaond̥/kaod̥]
alage 'seaweed'→(R1, R4, R9, R10)→alæ·ŋg̭ [alæ·ŋg̭/alæ·g̭]

(27) *Rule 11*: [g] deletion
$g \rightarrow \varnothing \; / \; ŋ\_\_\_\_\$C$

Due to this process, *g* is neutralized to *ŋ* in a preconsonantal position. Reconstruction of *g* is possible because [g] is retained before a word boundary, as in *oga* [waŋg̭] 'empty space' (cf. *ogatiu* [waŋ$tiu] 'stomach').

(28) *rule 12*: *f* alternation (optional)
f→h

The phoneme *f* [f] has a dialectally or idiolectally conditioned allophone [h]. In general, the speakers of the coastal area use [f] and those of the middle bush use [h]. To some these two sounds are free variants.

(29) *Rule 13*: Syllabification
$\varnothing \rightarrow \$ \; / \; V(C)\_\_\_\_C$

Viewing a phonetic syllable as correlating with a chest pulse, a phonetic syllable boundary (a slight juncture) is placed before a consonant unless there is one already assigned by Rule 1. This syllabification manifests a parallelism between word structure and syllable structure. For instance, a word never begins with more than one consonant and likewise nor does a syllable. The surface structure of Kwara'ae is $(C)(w)V_i(N)(C)$, with the peak V_i consisting of a monoph-, diph-, or triph-thong in that order of naturalness. That is, two or more unlike vowels in sequence are pronounced as a monosyllabic peak, as in [məuir̯] (*mauri* 'alive'). The coda C may be preceded by a nasal consonant (N), as in [aond$ləum] (*adolamu* 'your pubic area'). The nasal consonant created by prenasalization can become the only coda element, as in [waŋ$tiu] (*ogatiu* 'stomach'). Examples of (C)w include [kwi] (*kui* 'dog') and [wi'$ɛ·n] (*u'iani* 'to throw').

Kisseberth (1970) observes that some rules of a language are functionally related in that they 'conspire' to produce the same output. Schane (1972) and Hyman (1975: 164) point out that the function of certain rules is to retain or form desired syllable structures. Most of the phonological rules given above and the constraints associated with them are, directly or indirectly, pointed to the optimal surface syllable structure (C)V(C). Thus, for example, if there is a phonetic nasal created before an onset consonant by Rule 9, a syllable boundary falls between the two consonants, as in *labua*→[lam$buə] 'to pound'. Thus, Rule 13 resyllabifies in case a syllable would otherwise begin with two consonants. Some further examples of the outputs of Rule 13 are given below.

(30) *olofoloa* 'channel'→(R1, R6, R13)→o·lfoloa [o·lfoloa]
bale'o 'breadfruit'→(R1, R8, R13)→ba$leo' [ba$leo']
kirio 'porpoise'→(R13)→ki$rio [ki$rio]

The phonological analysis of Kwara'ae that has been presented thus far, and which is regarded as having psychological reality, is not abstract at all in that there is nothing 'imaginary' in underlying segments. Also, the rules are all phonetically natural and plausible.

In his extensive typological study of metathesis, including Kwara'ae, Ultan (1971) has come to the following three putatively universal hypotheses regarding the function of metathesis processes:

(1) Metathesis is a conservative process. "It serves to preserve phonological elements, or familiar patterns, that otherwise might be lost, merged with other elements or changed in shape due to the workings of other processes... In this respect it differs fundamentally from most other

processes: assimilation, dissimilation, syncope, epenthesis, and so on''.

(2) Metathesis is a recessive process. ''It tends to be inhibited or counteracted by other, more dominant processes... This characteristic also helps to explain why instances of all-pervasive metathesis are so rare and why... some scholars look upon all or most cases of metathesis as sporadic.''

(3) ''The proneness of different phonetic classes to metathesize tends to stand in direct correlation with a hierarchy of resonance: mutatis mutandis, the more resonant a sound the more susceptible it is to metathesis.''

Ultan's first hypothesis is not substantiated because Kwara'ae metathesis is not necessarily a mechanism to preserve segments or familiar patterns. It occurs not only word-finally but word-medially also which has nothing to do with the prevention of vowels from being lost. Notice, for instance, *dalumaa*→[dəul$ma·] 'bail it', where *daluma* is a single morpheme and undergoes morpheme-internal metathesis. There is no evidence that aphaeresis or syncope is a tendency that would be operative in the language, although apocope is a common phenomenon in Oceanic languages. The CVCV...-canon is a long-sustained original pattern of Oceanic languages including Kwara'ae. Kwara'ae metathesis is a strong force that disrupts this familiar pattern drastically, forming a new phonotactic pattern on the surface. Kwara'ae metathesis does not contribute to the prevention of phonological segments from merging with one another or changing in shape. Instead, it provides for such sound changes as we have seen. I have not observed any 'fundamental' difference of metathesis from most other phonological processes.

Ultan's second hypothesis is not supported by Kwara'ae evidence either, because no process is more dominant than metathesis in this language. As we have observed, metathesis in Kwara'ae is by no means sporadic, but a full-fledged powerful synchronic process which does not allow any exception.

Ultan's third hypothesis is not provable by means of Kwara'ae metathesis whose type is $C_iV_i \rightarrow V_iC_i$, i.e. the process occurs between any consonant and any vowel.

How can we characterize Kwara'ae metathesis? In view of the environment and conditions associated with the process, we may say that it is a process of conversion from open to closed syllables, while minimizing the number of syllables with a minimum loss of phonological features. It takes place only when the output reduces the number of the underlying syllables. Separated vowels tend to stick together and contract to form a syllable nucleus. A vowel always pulls the following vowel over a consonant unless the latter vowel is a member of the final V_2 or a vowel which already has a sister vowel pulled by it. The whole mechanism is simply a tendency toward Martinet's (1972) classical principle that phonological processes and changes are directed toward economizing speech efforts with a minimum of communication hindrance or perceptual loss. The reduction of the number of syllables in a word by means of metathesis tends to follow such a principle. We are not clear about the direct cause that led to such an all-pervasive process in Kwara'ae.[8]

As we have seen, metathesis has a tremendous impact on the whole phonological system of Kwara'ae. The surface canonical form is entirely different from the underlying one, allowing consonant clusters and more surface vowels. Although the process is synchronic at the moment, I anticipate that the process will eventually turn to a historical remnant when exceptions start to occur and the speakers no longer have the unmetathesized forms as their psychological reality. This anticipation is bolstered partly by the widely attested linguistic fact that the phonological rules at the top of an ordered set are more vulnerable to morphologization or restructuring than the lower level rules which tend to be more productive and more phonetic, and partly by the actuality that at least some people have already started to write Kwara'ae in metathesized forms.[9]

Notes

1. This study is based on the data I collected in Auckland, New Zealand, and on Malaita, the Solomon Islands, in 1971-72 when I was associated with the Anthropology Department of the University of Auckland as a post-doctoral research fellow. In Auckland, I was assisted by Brother Colin Baura from Malaita for six months. On Malaita, I stayed in a village called Laugwata for two months and was assisted by Headman Ismael Oso.

I gratefully thank Bruce Biggs and Byron Bender for the kindness they extended to me in obtaining the fellowship and for their consistent encouragement. Special thanks are given to Andrew Pawley who kindly helped me in many ways, including with my research, during my stay in New Zealand.

An earlier version of this paper was presented at the 1977 LSA Symposium on Austronesian Linguistics, Honolulu, summer 1977. I would like to thank George Grace for his helpful comments.

2. Kwara'ae is a Melanesian language, one of some thirteen interrelated languages of Malaita. It is bounded on the north by the Fataleka language and on the south by the Kwaio language.

   Two grammatical descriptions of Kwara'ae are available, both by missionaries (Ivens 1931 and Deck 1933-34). These grammars include only minimal phonological information, such as vowels and consonants with their rough comparisons with English sounds. Deck's extensive grammar touches on metathesis only by the following remark: "The outstanding peculiarity of Kwara'ae lies in the extraordinary metathesis of the final especially, and other, syllables of words... This applies to rapid speech only. Thus, *leka* becomes *leak; aabu, aub; 'aemu, 'aeum; aliali, ailail; likotai, lioktai; Peter, Piat; kusi, kuis...*" (ibid.: 38-39).
3. It is interesting to note that Biggs (1965: 386-389) reports a very similar phenomenon of metathesis in the language of Rotuma, an isolated island 250 miles north of Vanua Levu, the most northerly Fijian Island. In connection with proposals over the number of Rotuman vowels, Biggs presents the following statistics:

Hocart: 12	Churchward: 10 or 14
Codrington: 7	Haudricourt: 14
Wesleyan missionaries: 5	Grace: 12
Roman Catholics: 10	Biggs: 10 (i, e, æ, a, ü, ö, œ, u, o, ɔ)

   Postulating ten phonemic vowels. Biggs adds that /i, e, u, o, ɔ, a/ occur in all positions, /æ/ initially and medially, and /ü, ö, œ/ medially only and that almost every base has long (unmetathesized) and short (metathesized) forms. He considers the metathesis a historical innovation of the language, and concludes that the ten phonemic vowels have been derived from the five vowels of Proto-Central-Oceanic as a result of metathesis and subsequent syllable reduction. The later includes (1) reduction of the less sonorous of the two vowels to a semi-vowel (e.g. **trio* > **tior* > *tyor*), (2) coalescence of two similar vowels in the quality of one of them (e.g. **laji* > **lœej* > lœ*j*), and (3) coalescence of two unlike vowels and retaining features of the quality of each (e.g. **'uli* > **'uil* > *'ül*).
4. Native speakers do not write exactly the same base forms that I reconstruct, but in most cases the forms they write clearly represent base forms. For instance, they do not write the glottal stop which is phonemic and leave out one of the geminate vowels. Thus, the base for *ma'eta'eelo* 'doorway' is written as *maetaelo* [mæ'$tæ'$eol], that of *ba'eeko* 'shark' as *baeko* [bæ'$eok], and that of *gu'uuta* 'stopper' as *guuta* [gu'$wət].
5. Metathesis is thus not cyclic in that it applies only once to given segments. To the extent that it is not cyclical, it cannot be called directional in the sense of Howard (1972) although it applies in a fixed order.
6. In view of the Proto-Oceanic word structure which is mostly of two or three syllables (Grace 1969), Kwara'ae metathesis must initially have worked from right to left, as, for instance, Woleaian dissimilatory *a*-raising does (Sohn 1971; Howard 1972: 45). If all the stems of long compounds could be identified, a directional constraint of rule application, in the sense of Howard (ibid.), would be more appropriate. Since many historical stem boundaries in compounds are not morphemically identifiable any longer, it is inevitable to postulate the order constraint.
7. Bender reports, in a Micronesian seminar in 1977 at LSA Institute, that the historical source of one of his Marshallese mid-high vowels discussed in Bender (1968), i.e. *e*, may be due to the metathesis of the final vowel with the preceding consonant, the first order metathesis in this paper. He illustrates this as follows:

   lé̈b from lebi — 'grave'

béq from beqi — 'bladder'
yém from yime — 'house'
yék from yike — 'fish'

8. One conjecture I advanced in the original version of this paper was that the speakers of Kwara'ae (and also Rotuman and other languages) might have been heavily influenced by the word structure of English which has predominantly closed syllables in contrast to the written shapes which reflect the former open syllable canon, e.g. *make, take, bite, tube, tide, force, able, globe,* etc. This conjecture was largely due to the fact that the majority of Melanesians are bilingual in their vernaculars and (Pidgin) English. George Grace (personal communication), however, suspects that is not true, thinking that the earliest reports on Rotuman indicate metathesized forms.
9. According to Andrew Taylor (personal communication) of the United States Bible Societies, London, words are written in their metathesized form in the recently printed New Testament which he says seems much easier for people to read. This at least implies that the future generation may no longer recover the unmetathesized forms in an easily predictable way. As a hint of possible future morphologization, we may refer to Biggs (1975:388), in which Rotuman metathesis is reported to have certain grammatical functions.

Reprinted from *Lingua* 52:305-323 (1980).

2. SURFACE AND DEEP CONTRASTS IN ULITHIAN PHONOLOGY

(*with Byron W. Bender*)

One of the major problems in Ulithian (ULI) phonology is that there are many asymmetrical and limited phonetic contrasts. The aim of the paper is to present some conspicuous contrast patterns of such limited distribution and associated problems in Section 1, to suggest solutions to them in Section 2, to discuss a problem concerning the third person singular object suffix forms in Section 3, and to illustrate underlying contrasts in Section 4.

As will be seen, we propose to set up 'base forms' of morphemes and words, which have been decided upon in light of the general phonological characteristics observable in various morphophonemic changes in the surface forms of ULI.[1] Such phonological characteristics are mostly synchronic, but occasionally diachronic evidence is taken into account in cases of indeterminacy.

There are several definite advantages to this approach in which phonemicisation is determined by base form contrasts. For example, various asymmetrical and limited phonetic contrasts can be accounted for in terms of environmental conditioning; the alternation of stem-final vowels may be explained by general phonetic rules; and the maximum uniformity thereby attained in base forms facilitates syntactic description, because a given grammatical or lexical item generally has one and only one phonemic shape.

1. Surface Form Contrasts

1.1. A superficial non-contrast might be noticed between the velarised bilabial stop *mw* and its plain counterpart *m* when they are unreleased, i.e. before a pause or a homorganic consonant. Consider, however, the following pair:

(1) a. [lɑ:m] 'mosquito'
b. [la:m] 'lamp; clear'

Spectrographic analysis indicates that the second formant of the vowel in (1a) falls rapidly to a back [u] or [o] position, showing the velarisation of the following consonant, while the vowel in (1b) shows a smooth transition to a plain [m] position. This evidence and the distributional limitation of [ɑ(:)] have led us to the conclusion that the significant contrast is between the two final nasals, and that the backing of the vowel [ɑ:] in (1a) is caused by the [+back] feature of the final nasal.

1.2. Two [l]'s of different quality contrast in certain limited environments. In the first place, the so-called 'construct suffix' morpheme [l] 'of' (referred to as Cs-ℓ) and the third person singular possessive suffix morpheme [l] 'his' (3s-ℓ) contrast in many instances. In such contrasts, Cs-ℓ is light and relatively fronted, while 3s-ℓ is dark and retracted. The different qualities of the two [l]'s may be reflected in preceding stem vowels (see below), which fact might lead one to suppose that the grammatical difference between the two morphemes concerned is manifested by the stem vowels, and that there are different allophones of *l* following these vowels.[2] Consider for example the following:

(2)				
[uƀʷel<]	'chest of'	:	[uƀʷɑl>]	'his chest'
[tapal<]	'cheek of'	:	[tɑpɑl>]	'his cheek'
[sogoˆl<]	'stick of'	:	[sogoˇl>]	'his stick'

No contrasts are found if the vowel preceding [l] is a single (short) [i], [e], [u], or [ə]. However, long vowel [e:] does show a contrast before the two suffixes.

(3)				
[ŋi:l<]	'teeth of'	:	[ŋi:l<]	'his teeth'
[rexel<]	'age of'	:	[raxel<]	'his age'
[lurul<]	'shade of'	:	[lurul<]	'his shade'
[ƀʷɔ:đəl<]	'nose of'	:	[ƀʷɔ:đəl<]	'his nose'
[pece:ˆl<]	'foot of'	:	[pece:ˇl>]	'his foot'

Regarding the [l]'s of the two morphemes as phonemically identical would require one to set up a number of new vowel phonemes, e.g. *a* in contrast with *a*ˇ , *e* in contrast with *e*ˇ , etc. Besides, no regularity could be captured in the alternation between the two series of stem vowels:

(4) [e] + Cs-ℓ vs. [ɑ] + 3s-ℓ
[e] + Cs-ℓ vs. [e] + 3s-ℓ
[a] + Cs-ℓ vs. [ɑ] + 3s-ℓ, etc.

As an alternative to such a treatment, which would set up a number of additional vowel phonemes of limited distribution, two distinct *l* phonemes might be postulated, with the vowel contrasts accounted for as allophonic variants conditioned by the *l*'s. But the two *l*'s would actually contrast only in these two morphemes (Cs and 3s) after certain vowels; in all other positions (with the possible exception of (6) below) they would be in complementary distribution, varying mechanically according to the neighbouring vowels. One could emphasise this limitation in a transcription by using an *l* archiphoneme in the non-contrastive positions — using, for example, *l*'s with fronting and backing diacritics for the fully specified *l*'s, and an *l* without any diacritic for the archiphoneme.

(5) wubʷel< 'chest to' wubʷal> 'his chest'
tapal< 'cheek of' tapal> 'his cheek'
raxel 'age of' raxel 'his age'

This solution implies the existence of two allomorphs for each of the two suffix morphemes. Or one could follow the principle 'once a phoneme, always a phoneme' (Householder 1964:25) and extend the contrast to the many non-contrastive positions in which *l* may occur, but this would introduce a great deal of unnecessary redundancy and tend to obscure the severely limited distribution of the *l*-contrast. None of the solutions discussed thus far would provide a basis for any simple generalisation concerning the vowel alternations before the two suffixes in some forms but not in others.

A second instance of the *l*-contrast may be found in the following examples:

(6) (a) [xađal< + ƀʷo] 'to walk in line because'
(b) [xɑđɑl>ƀʷo] 'supposedly'
(c) [xɑƀʷl<e] 'we (excl.) will...'
(d) [xɑƀʷl>e] 'to miss him'

(6a) and (6b) differ from each other in several respects: (i) the quality of the [l]'s, (ii) the quality of the low vowels, and (iii) the presence of a pause juncture (+) in (6a). (6c) and (6d), on the other hand, differ only in the quality of the [l]'s. This suggests that the difference in the low vowels preceding the different [l]'s in (6a) and (6b) is conditioned by the latter, rather than the other way around. There being no indication that the quality of *l* is determined by the presence or absence of pause, one would have to conclude from the evidence of the forms in (6) that there would seem to be no other solution than to set up two underlying *l*'s.

1.3. In word-final position, there is a contrast between a sequence consisting of the voiceless [x] followed by a [+back] voiceless vowel (i.e. [o̥,ɑ̥, u̥), the same [x] followed by ∅, and the sequence of the voiced velar fricative [g] followed by a corresponding voiced vowel:

(7)	[ƀʷurɑxo̥]	'smoke'	:	[malekɑ:xo̥]	'travel'
	[xɑ:xo̥]	'helm'	:	[đoxo̥]	'to get'
	[kəlɔxo̥]	'hungry'	:	[ƀʷarəxo̥]	'dance'
	[ƀʷulɑxɑ̥]	'taro'	:	[fɑsɑmɑxɑ̥]	'pebble'
	[mɑŋɑ:xu̥]	'clothes'	:	[ƀʷuxu̥]	'knot'
	[tet:erax]	'sailing'	:	[bʷarex]	'pain'
	[ləƀʷa:x]	'to hide'	:	[tɔgɔx]	'coconut shell'
	[kɑgo]	'box'	:	[tɑmɑgo]	'cigarette'

The most conspicuous occurrence of this kind is associated with the second person singular object suffix, which has the phonetic form [xo̥] and its allomorph [xu̥]. The latter occurs after a high vowel (e.g. *i* or *u*) and the former elsewhere.

(8) [pɑ:luxu̥] 'to lead you'
  cf. [pa:liyei] 'to lead me'
[tɑvɑxo̥] 'to cut you'
  cf. [tɑvayei] 'to cut me'
[đɑƀʷoxo̥] 'to follow you'
  cf. [đaƀʷeyei] 'to follow me'

The above surface information might lead one to postulate a set of voiceless vowels of extremely limited distribution (finally after *x*), or else a *g* phoneme (in partial complementation with *x*) to account for the final vowels that do not devoice.

1.4. There is a contrast of high frequency of occurrence between the two low vowels [a] and [ɑ]. They contrast not only before the two morphemic [l]'s (Cs -*ℓ* and 3s -*ℓ*) as in (9) but also in many independent forms as in (10).

(9) short	[wagal<]	'vein of'	:	[wɑgɑl>]	'his vein'
	[tal<]	'rope of'	:	[tɑl>]	'its rope'
	[tapal<]	'cheek of'	:	[tɑpɑl>]	'his cheek'

	long	[wa:l<]	'canoe of'	: [wɑ:l>]	'his canoe'
		[ifa:l<]	'underside of'	: [ifɑ:l>]	'its underside'
(10)	short	[maθ]	'sated'	: [mɑθ]	'cooked'
		[ƀʷal<]	'to inspect'	: [ƀʷɑl>]	'stuck'
	long	[ya:f]	'fire'	: [yɑ:f]	'swimming'
		[ta:l<]	'rope'	: [tɑ:l>]	'well versed'
		[fa:s]	'stone'	: [fɑ:s]	'penis'

In spite of the high frequency of the contrast, several points may be noted against the establishment of the two vowels as separate phonemes. In the first place, there is no contrast in the environment C__#. Observe the following examples of low and front vowel contrasts:

(11)	[ri]	'spouse'	[li]	'to kill'	[ƀ^{2}i]	'sides of vagina'
	[re]	'they'	[le]	'this'	[ƀ^{2}e]	'fortune-telling'
	[ræ]	'side	[læ]	'as'	[ƀʷæ]	'to find out'
	[rɑ]	'branch'	[lɑ]	'that'	[ƀ^{2}ɑ]	'rotten'
	*[ra]		*[la]		*[ƀ^{2}a]	

Secondly, [ɑ] in C__# is differentiated into front and retracted varieties when the Cs-ℓ and 3s-ℓ suffixes follow, which suggests that the contrast may not be inherent but conditioned by the suffixal environment.

(12)

[rɑ] 'branch' → [ra:l<] 'branch of'

[rɑ] 'branch' → [rɑ:l>] 'its branch'

Thirdly, no contrast has been found in the environment X__Y in which X is non-null and Y is a syllable, though both the fronted and retracted low vowels may occur in this position. That is, their occurrences are perfectly predictable according to X and Y. Observe that the quality of the first vowel in each word in (13) can be predicted from the vowel in the following syllable, i.e. fronted if the following vowel is one classed as non-back (i.e. [i, e, æ, ə, a]), and retracted elsewhere.

(13)	[madep]	'a part'
	[mɑdɑr]	'to disperse'
	[madel<]	'being stated of'
	[mɑdɑl>]	'its being cooked'

In short, the contrast between [a] and [ɑ] is limited to the environment__C#.

1.5. A final problem regarding surface contrasts is raised by the existence of two different monophthongal vowel qualities in the mid-central area that contrast only when long. For the moment, the two qualities are transcribed as [ə] and [ë]:

(14) [tə:s] 'truch' : [të:s] 'porcupine fish'
[ɖə:r] 'lavalava' : [ɖë:r] 'indebtedness'
[pə:l] 'emptiness of' : [pë:l] 'arm of'

The vowel in the first column is common, while the vowel in the second is rare but also occurs in a few other forms such as:

(15) [yë:r] 'accustomed; name of an island'
[më:l] 'name of a star'
[më:r] 'fresh (tree, vegetables)'
[cë:l] 'leaf of'

Sound spectrographs show that both vowels are monophthongal, and that Fl of the vowel in [tə:s] = 450 and F2 = 1600; F1 of the vowel in [të:s] = 550 and F2 = 1400. The above formants indicate that the two sounds [ə] and [ë] are very close to the French vowels [ø] and [œ] respectively (Delattre et al. 1952:198). [ə] seems to have more lip rounding than [ë].

Several problems are involved in the phonemic interpretation of the two sounds. First of all, the number of forms containing [ë] is small. Secondly, the contrast between the two is limited to long segments. Thirdly, [ë:] in C__C is not shortened before a suffix, while [ə:] may be:

(16) [ɖə:r] 'lavalava' : [ɖərəl] 'lavalava of'
[ɖë:r] 'indebtedness' : [ɖë:rəl] 'indebtedness of'
[tə:s] 'truth' : [tə:səl] 'truth of'
[të:s] 'porcupine fish' : [të:səl] 'porcupine fish of'

These limitations make one hesitant to set up two mid-central vowel phonemes.

2. Suggested Solutions

2.1. Most of the problems raised in the preceding section can be solved simply, straightforwardly, and with greater generality by introducing non-*ad hoc* base forms in the phonology. Then, as will be seen, superficial contrasts of limited distribution turn out to be allophonic variants conditioned by material present in the base forms but not readily observable on the surface, or the result of geminates versus non-identical vowel qualities. Such base and surface forms will be directly related by a series of ordered phonological rules. The approach followed here not only solves the problem of limited distribution but also contributes to regularising most of the irregular morphophonemic alternations.

2.2. A solution to the problem of surface vowel contrasts before bilabial nasals (see 1.1.) has already been implied in the earlier discussion; the consonants can be said to contrast as *mw* and *m* in base forms, conditioning vowel allophones that in some cases constitute their chief stigmata. Thus, for example, the base forms of the items in (1) are established in (17).

(17) a.	lamwo	‘mosquito’	(cf. [lɑmʷol<]	‘mosquito of’)
b.	lama	‘lamp; clear’	(cf. [lamal<]	‘lamp of’)

Phonological rules will impose the [+back] feature of *mw* onto the preceding vowel, lengthen the non-final vowels, and delete the final vowels.

With regard to the problem of two [l]’s of different quality, the Cs and 3s morphemes may be set up as *li* and *la* respectively. Seemingly contrasting stem vowels before the two morphemes can then both be derived from the same basic stem vowel as the result of the conditioning of the two contrasting basic vowels *i* and *a* in the suffix morphemes *-li* and *-la*. Although *-li* and *-la* lost their final vowels, as do most other lexical base forms, they still carry features of the vowels such as [+high, −back, −low] from *i*, and [−high, +back, +low] from *a*, which cause the alternations of the stem vowels. Thus the process is active, i.e. synchronic. The fronted and retracted *l*’s thereby conditioned do not affect the basic stem vowels *i*, *u*, ə, or short *e*. Rather, the *l*’s are assimilated in quality to these mid or high vowels. These four basic stem vowels happen to correspond to Sonsorolese (SNS) high vowels in most instances (Bender 1967 and Quackenbush 1968).[3]

(18) ULI base forms			SNS surface forms	
taŋi	[taŋ]		[taŋi̥]	‘to cry’
cf. [taŋil<]		(+ Cs)		
lutu	[lut]		[rutu̥]	‘to jump’
cf. [lutul<]		(+ Cs)		
maulu	[mɑul]		[mauru̥]	‘war’
cf. [mɑulul<]		(+ Cs)		
yađe	[ya:θ]		[ya:ti̥]	‘gall bladder’
cf. [yađel<]		(+ Cs)		
taxuru	[tɑgur]		[talɨxɨ̥]	‘back’

cf. [tɑgurəl<] (+ Cs)
fađə [fa:θ] [fa:ti̥] 'eyebrow'
cf. [fađəl<] (+ Cs)

From this comparative evidence, we tentatively conclude that only those vowels which were historically high vowels are resistant to the influence from the following *l*'s of different quality. This may be supported by the fact that SNS (and also Woleaian (WOL)) preserves many reflexes of original forms. For WOL reflexes, see Tawerilmang and Sohn 1984.

The irregular alternation of the stem vowels before the two morphemes Cs and 3s, as illustrated in (4), turns out to be regular if we set up well-motivated basic stem vowels covering all relevant lexical items and develop an appropriate set of morphophonemic rules to map the base forms onto surface manifestations. Thus, for example, the following are proposed as the basic stem vowels underlying (4):

(19)
a → [e] : [ɑ]
a → [a] : [ɑ]
e [e] : [e]

The difference in alternation between [e] : [ɑ] and [a] : [ɑ] is due to the influence of the vowel in the preceding syllable, i.e. [e] : [ɑ] only when the preceding vowel is high.[4] (20) gives the base forms corresponding to (2) and (3).

(20) uba-li	'chest of'	:	uba-la	'his chest'
tapa-li	'cheek of'	:	tapa-la	'his cheek'
soxo-li	'stick of'	:	soxo-la	'his stick'
ŋii-li	'teeth of'	:	ŋii-la	'his teeth'
raxe-li	'age of'	:	raxe-la	'his age'
luru-li	'shade of'	:	luru-la	'his shade'
bɔɔđə-li	'nose of'	:	bɔɔđə-la	'his nose'
pecee-li	'foot of'	:	pecee-la	'his foot'

The reconstruction of base forms for stems as well as for *-li* and *-la* is synchronic but largely corresponds to the forms of PMC (Proto-Micronesian), WOL, and SNS. Thus the reconstructed stem vowels not only have historical and comparative significance, but they also indicate the traditional declensional classes to which the nouns belong. A sample set of ULI, WOL, and SNS forms follows, in which the similarity between the ULI base forms and the corresponding SNS independent forms should be noted.[5]

(21)		base form	ind. form	+ Cs	+ 3s
	ULI	yafara	[yɑfɑr]	[yafaral<]	[yɑfɑrɑl>]
	WOL	---	[yefare̥]	[yaferali̥]	[yaferale̥]
	SNS	---	[yafalḁ]	[yafalari̥]	[yafalarḁ]
		'shoulder'			
	ULI	imwa	[i:ɨm]	[imʷel<]	[imʷɑl>]
	WOL	---	[i:mʷe̥]	[imʷeli̥]	[imʷale̥]
	SNS	---	[i:mʷḁ]	[imʷeri̥]	[imʷarḁ]
		'house'			

The second instance of contrasting *l*'s (6) can also be resolved by setting up proper base forms. Again, the two *l*'s are allophones of a single underlying *l*. The processes involved are as follows:

(22) base			
xađale#bo	→	xađal<e#bo	
	→	xađal< + bo	
		[xađal< + bʷo]	'to walk in line because ....'
xađalboo	→	xađal>bo	
		[xɑđɑl>bʷo]	'supposedly'
xa#be#le	→	xa#be#l<e	
	→	xabl<e	
		[xɑƀʷl<e]	'we (excl.) will'
xabɔle + ya	→	xabɔley	
	→	xable	
		[xɑƀʷl>e]	'to miss him'

2.3. The problematic contrasts among final-syllable velar fricatives and their following vowel (or lack thereof) (see (7) and (8)) can be resolved most efficiently by setting up base forms in such a way that surface voiceless vowels are represented as [+back] single vowels and surface voiced vowels as geminates, while Ø vowels which in this position are [−back] are set up in the same way as are all other final vowels that delete. This treatment is well motivated in that (a) no words end in a double vowel on the surface, and (b) when suffixes are added, voiceless vowels and Ø vowels are realised as single voiced vowels, while voiced vowels are realised as geminate vowels. These two points are basic for the establishing of all ULI base forms. Thus the phonetic manifestations of independent base forms are effected by simply devoicing single [+back] vowels after *x* but dropping single vowels otherwise in word-final position, including the position *x*__#. The examples in (7) can be phonemicised as the following base forms. The corresponding phonetic forms followed by Cs-ℓ are also given for reference.

(23)	buraxo	'smoke'	[ƀʷuragol<]
	malekaaxo	'travel'	[malekɑ:gol<]
	xaaxo	'helm'	[xɑ:gol<]
	đoxo	'to get'	[đogol<]
	kəlɔxo	'hungry'	[kəlɔgol<]
	barəxo	'dance'	[ƀʷarəgol<]
	bulaxa	'taro'	[ƀʷulagal<]
	fasamaxa	'pebble'	[fasamagal<]
	maŋaaxu	'clothes'	[mɑŋɑ:gul<]
	buxu	'knot'	[ƀʷugul<]
	tetteraxe	'sailing'	[tet:eragel<]
	bbarexe	'pain'	[ƀʷ:aregel<]
	ləbaaxe	'to hide'	[ləƀʷa:gel<]
	tɔxɔxə	'coconut shell'	[tɔgɔgəl<]
	kaxoo	'box'	[kɑgo:l<]
	tamaxoo	'cigarette'	[tɑmɑgo:l<]

In the same way, the examples in (8) are the surface forms derived from the base forms in (24). Notice the morphophonemic changes effected in the environment of the morpheme boundaries.

(24)	paali + yei	'to lead me'	:	paali + xo	'to lead you'
	tafa + yei	'to cut me'	:	tafa + xo	'to cut you'
	đabe + yei	'to follow me'	:	đabe + xo	'to follow you'

2.4. That the low vowel qualities [a] and [ɑ] turn out to be predictable within the general framework adopted here should come as no surprise in light of the previous discussions, which indicated that the contrast between them was limited to the environment __C#, and that certain contrasts in this environment could be conditioned by deleted final stem vowels set up following the consonant in base forms. Thus, [a] and [ɑ] prove to be conditioned variants of *a*. Some of the examples in (9) and (10) are phonemicised as (25).

(25)	waxa-li	'vein of'	waxa-la	'his vein'
	waa-li	'canoe of'	waa-la	'his canoe'
	mađe	'stated'	mađa	'cooked'
	yafe	'fire'	yafa	'swimming'

2.5. With regard to the two mid-central vowel contrasts, the problem lies in the interpretation of [ë:]. It turns out that words containing this sound correspond to words that have a vowel cluster rather than a long monophthongal vowel in other TK languages.

(26) To	ULI	[pë:] 'arm' and [pë:l] 'arm of' correspond:
	SNS:	paai and paɨrI
	Tobi (TBI):	paa and paɨr
	WOL:	paaů and paůlI
	Ifaluk:	paa and pawul
To	ULI	[ca:y] 'leaf' and [cë:l] 'leaf of' correspond:
	SNS:	saaɨ and saaɨrI
	TBI:	caaɨ and caaɨr
	WOL:	šəə and šəəlI
To	ULI	[të:s] 'porcupine fish' correspond:
	SNS:	taɨθI
	TBI:	taɨs

We are reluctant to establish [ë:] as a new phoneme for the distributional reasons indicated in the preceding section, and this comparative evidence suggests that we may be able to interpret it as a cluster of already established phonemes instead. Internal evidence such as the alternation between the independent and construct forms of 'leaf' also point in this same direction. For this item the base form can be established as *cayə* and then the independent form will be derived by dropping the final vowel and lengthening the remaining vowel, i.e., [ca:y].

[pë:] and [pë:l] should be handled differently because they do not show parallel alternation. ULI æ corresponds in many cases to *a* of other TK languages, and ULI *u* to *ɨ*. Thus the base form of [pë:] will be set up as *pæu*. (We cannot set it up as *pau* because of the existence of forms such as [mɑul] 'war,' for which the basic cluster *au* is needed). The other examples such as [të:s['porcupine fish' and [dë:r] 'indebtedness' may be handled in the same way as [pë:]. A later phonetic rule should specify the phonetic quality of these phoneme composites.

3. Third Person Object Suffixes

One matter particularly difficult to decide upon was the base form of the third person singular object suffix, which corresponds to the surface forms (*y*) or ∅ in the following examples.

(27) [lli-(y)] 'kill him'
[fə:ru-(y)] 'make it'
[fɑgo-(y)] 'miss him'
[xɑmɑđɑvɑ-∅] 'explain it'
[đaƀwe-(y)] 'follow him'

That is, the suffix is realised on the surface as an optional [y] except for the position after [a] where it is zero. There is some evidence, however, in support of the assumption that the base form of the suffix is *-ya*.[6]

Although *ya* never appears phonetically as [yV] when the verb to which it is suffixed functions as the main verb, it does appear as such if the verb is nominalised before an attributive suffix.

(28) [lliyei] 'what I killed'
[lliyəmʷ] 'what you killed'
[lliyal>] 'what he killed'
[lliyel<se mal<] 'what someone killed'
[lliyac] 'what we (incl.) killed'
[lliyæ:r] 'what they killed'
[xamađavayey] 'what I explained'
[xamađavayəmʷ] 'what you explained'
[xɑmɑđɑvɑyɑl>] 'what he explained'
[xamađavayel<se mal<] 'what someone explained'
[xɑmɑđɑvɑyɑc] 'what we (incl.) explained'
[xamađavayæ:r] 'what they explained'

If in (28) the forms (e.g. [ye], [yə] and [yɑ]) between a verb stem (i.e. [lli], [xɑmɑđɑvɑ]) and an attributive suffix (e.g. [y], [mʷ], [l>], [l<], [c]) are reduced to the base form *-ya*, then general morphophonemic rules will derive all the forms related to the base *-ya* unambiguously and without exception.

Exactly the same morphophonemic behavior may be observed in many words which are not transitive verbs. For example, [fɑlu(y)] 'island' and [cu(y)] 'to disappear' retain the optional [y] in their independent form, and if attributive suffixes are added, the following phonetic forms are obtained:

(29) [fɑluyey] 'my island'
[fɑluyəmʷ] 'your island'
[fɑluyɑl>] 'his island'
[faluyel< se mal<] 'someone's island'

[fɑluyæ:r]	'their island'
[cuyey]	'my disappearance'
[cuyəm^w]	'your disappearance'
[cuyɑl>]	'his disappearance'
[cuyel< se mal<]	'someone's disappearance'
[cuyæ:r]	'their disappearance'

Since the base forms of [fɑlu(y)] and [cu(y)] have been set up as *faluya* and *cuya*, the parallelism between (28) and (29) leads to the reconstruction of the forms in (27) except for [xɑmɑđɑvɑ] as follows.

(30)	lli-ya	'kill him'
	fəəru-ya	'make it'
	faxo-ya	'miss him'
	đabe-ya	'follow him'

Thus the final vowel deletion rule and the rule of optional deletion of semi-vowels may connect (30) to (27). On the other hand, [y] simply does not occur on the surface in the environment *a__#*.

4. Examples of Contrasts in Base Form Segments

Minimal pairs have not been found in sufficient number to make phoneme attestation easy, but the following examples may suffice to show the contrasts:

consonants

p	pare	'a kind of fruit'	tapa	'cheek'
t	tale	'rope'	tata	'a kind of fish'
c	cale	'water'	faca	'pandanus fruit'
k	kakka	'to carry'	piskaa	'spear'
b	bađe	'scar'	taba	'taboo'
f	fase	'stone'	yafa	'swimming'
đ	đaa	'intestine'	fađe	'string'
s	sare	'big knife'	fasa	'penis'
x	xapi	'bottom, hip'	waxa	'vein'
mw	mwale	'man'	mweemwee	'to look for'
m	male	'animal, bird'	lama	'light bulb'
n	naanaa	'mummy'	sukuunu	'school'
ŋ	ŋaaŋe	'I'	faŋa	'to permit'
l	laŋe	'sky'	cale	'water'
r	rale	'day'	baro	'box'

y	yala	'sun'	xaya	'fish hook'
w	waa	'canoe'	wawa	'stick dance'

short vs. long consonants

Defective are (i) quasi-native *n* which has the lowest frequency of occurrence; (ii) *x* whose doubling results in *kk;* and (iii) *y* and *w*.

p : pp	pale	'dry'	ppale	'light'
	capi	'ancestor'	cappa	'turning over'
c : cc	caŋa	'short of reach'	ccaŋa	'skinny'
k : kk	makili	'sugar cane'	makkala	'comb (Falalop)'
b : bb	barexe	'hot (taste)'	bbarexe	'pain'
	bece	'hot'	bbece	'white'
	uba	'chest'	bubbu	'fish spec.'
f : ff	fisi	'star'	ffisi	'lightning'
	yafe	'fire'	yaffe	'land crab'
đ : đđ	đare	'to walk'	đđare	'to run'
s : ss	soŋo	'mangrove'	ssoŋo	'angry'
mw : mmw	mwɔlo	'desire'	mmwolo	'generous, kind'
	mwixilici	'miser'	mmwixi	'pepper'
m : mm	mata	'eye'	mmata	'to wake up'
	mađare	'to disperse'	mmađare	'to burst'
ŋ : ŋŋ	ŋata	'hole'	ŋŋata	'hurry''
	fayelaŋa	'world'	faiŋŋa	'itchy feeling'
l : ll	loyo	'perfume'	lloyo	'wet'
r : rr	ro-	'all'	rro-	'string-bound bundle'
	raxe	'year, age'	rrai	'happy'

vowels

i	lli	'to kill'	cibe	'scissors'		
e	lee	'this'	pecee	'leg'		
æ	læ	'as, which'	pæce	'sexual lust'		
a	laa	'that'	capi	'lavalava'	paca	'tail'
ɔ	cɔɔ	'people'	llɔyo	'sweet'	bɔlo	'feather'
u	cuu	'to meet'	lloyo	'wet'	bolo	'soil'
ə	tə	'for a moment'	ləŋə	'ant'	bbələ	'filthy'

short vs. long vowels

In the base form phonemicisation, many superficial length contrasts are suppressed. For example, [pix] 'to play ball' (*v.*) and [pi:x] 'ball' (*n.*) have no contrast in length in the base. Both are derived from the same base *pixi*, but the noun form is lengthened while the verb is not, and final vowels are dropped from both.

i : ii	cima	'head'	ciifeli	'nail'
e : ee	fedexe	'fight'	feefele	'woman'
æ : ææ	bæxi	'to float (Vt)'	xææetaa	'to do what'
a : aa	xaamami	'we (excl.)'	xaamaama	'to practice'
	fale	'food pounder'	faale	'cynical'
ɔ : ɔɔ	bɔŋu	'feast'	bɔɔdə	'nose'
o : oo	bolo	'soil'	booto	'boat'
u : uu	lutu	'to jump'	luutu	'soft wood'
	buru	'high tide'	duuduu	'to bathe'
ə : əə	dəra	'lavalava'	təəsə	'truth'
	fəlaŋa	'ashes'	irəətə	'village'

Notes

1. Some of the traditional principles of so-called taxonomic phonemics (see Chomsky 1964: 75ff) such as biuniqueness and invariance are disregarded in the base form phonemicisation. On the other hand, concepts like contrast and complementary distribution are relevant only at the level of underlying base forms. Bender (1968) also attempted a rigorous base form phonemicisation of Marshallese, where skewed surface distributions are of a different sort.
2. Dyen (1965:33ff) seems to be following such a hypothesis in his description of a partially parallel phenomenon in Trukese.
3. The corresponding WOL stem vowels are also high, as pointed out and illustrated in Sohn and Bender (1973:Preface).
4. In ULI, WOL, and SNS, the basic vowel *a* is raised to *e* when it occurs between two high (basic) vowels (Bender 1973 and Sohn 1971 and 1975a).
5. The SNS data were provided by Celestine Yangilmau and the WOL by Anthony Tawerilmang. For a description of WOL phonology, see Sohn (1975a:Ch.1).
6. An alternative analysis would lead us to end up with the base form *-a* as the object suffix. In this case, the semivowel *y* must be introduced by a rule, as proposed for WOL in Tawerilmang and Sohn 1984.

Reprinted from *Studies in Micronesian Linguistics,* ed. by Byron W. Bender. 201-213 (1984). Canberra: Australian National University.

3. *a*-RAISING IN WOLEAIAN

1. Some recent studies on Micronesian languages are aimed at internally reconstructing morpheme base forms by checking various distributional limitations and 'morphophonemic' alternations and, at the same time, discovering the most general processes (rules) to relate the reconstructed base forms to the forms actually pronounced by ideal native speakers (Bender 1968, Benton 1968, Hsu 1969, and Sohn 1969).[1] The procedural assumption underlying such efforts is that the different 'allomorphic' forms of any given morpheme may be derived from a single (or minimum number of) base form(s) by means of those rules which should express the generalizations of the language concerned, and phonemes should be set up not through contrasts on the surface but within the framework of reconstructed base forms. It has been found that this line of work has certain definite advantages. It contributes to lexical economy in that all the 'allomorphs' which can be derivable by rules need not be incorporated in the lexicon. It may also lead to a reduced phoneme inventory as in the case of Marshallese three vowel system (Bender 1968:23-4), since many distributionally limited superficial contrasts are ascribable to environmental conditioning in base forms. It may further lead to fuller distributions for all consonants and vowels (e.g., ibid.: 23). Other advantages are that most of the irregular surface alternations of stem final vowels turn out to be regular in base forms and a greater symmetry is attained in the canonical structure of morphemes, as will be noticed in the Woleaian examples below (for details see the works cited above).

2. The present report is a brief addition to the foregoing studies by way of certain phonological evidence from Woleaian. This will be concerned with *a*-raising as indicated in the following tentative vowel inventory of Woleaian:

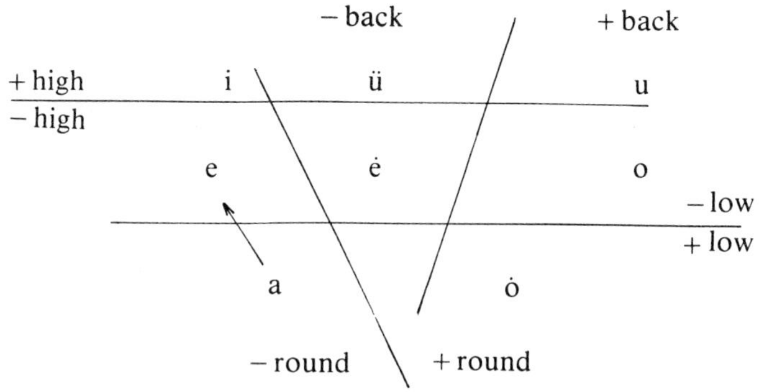

The discussion shall proceed in the order of: an observation of distributional limitations of *a* and a/e alternations 3, reconstruction of base forms 4, relevant rule formulation 5, and a case of irregular alternations 6.

3. A conspicuous phenomenon in Woleaian phonology is the process of raising of *a* to *e* in certain definable syntagmatic environments. This process, which involves two types of 'morphophonemic' changes, dissimilation and assimilation, is clued in the superficial non-occurrence of the sequences CaC_oa and VhC_oaC_oVh where Vh, a high vowel, may either be superficial or only underlying. The definite evidence for the working of this process is given by the following sets of examples in which *a* alternates with *e* consistently.[2]

3.1. Observe the following possessive paradigms:

	'eye'	'drinking object'
ind. form	ma:t	ü:l[3]
1. sg.	m*e*taj[4]	ülüm*e*j
2. sg.	m*e*tam^{w}	ülüm*e*m^{w}
3. sg.	m*e*tal	ülümal
1. pl. incl.	m*e*taš	ülümaš
1. pl. excl.	mat*e*mam	ülüm*e*mam
2. pl.	m*e*tami	ülüm*e*mi
3. pl.	m*e*ta:r	ülüm*e*:r

In the first paradigm the vowel of the independent form (*a*:) differs from those of the possessive forms (*e*'s) except in the 1. pl. excl. form where *a* is maintained but the second vowel is changed to *e* as different from all the other members of the paradigm. The interpretation such as "*a* becomes *e* before a possessive suffix" or "*a* becomes *e* when shortened" would immediately be counterevidenced by the form in 1. pl. excl. What seems to be the only possible explanation for these alternations is that dissimilation in the language (as in Marshallese) converting a single low vowel *a* into a mid vowel *e* before another *a* in the following syllable and this process works in reverse order, from right to left recursively. Thus in the 1. pl. excl. form (base forms: *mata* + *mami*) dissimilation changes the second *a* to *e* in the first place, so another application of the process is blocked because now the initial *a* is not followed by another *a*. In all the other members of the paradigm, the initial *a* changes to *e* before another *a* since there is no third *a* following. In the second paradigm above (base form: *wülüma*) the change of *a* to *e* in the third syllable of the 1. pl. excl. form is also accounted for by the process of dissimilation. What about the other a/e alternations in the paradigm where there is no *a* following? The most reasonable interpretation is that the alternations are the direct result of an assimilation converting *a* to *e* between two high vowels whether the second high vowel is either overt as in the 2. pl. form or covert as in the other forms except for the 3. sg. and 1. pl. incl. forms where the covert second vowel is *a*. The covert high vowels are underlying ones reconstructed in the light of 'morphophonemic' generalizations of the language as may be observed in the (tentative) base forms of the possessive suffixes below (cf. Sohn 1969: 274 for Ulithian equivalents):

1. sg.	*2. sg.*	*3. sg.*	*1. pl. incl.*	*1. pl. excl.*	*2. pl.*	*3. pl.*
-ji	-mu	-la	-ca	-mami	-mii	-jire

It should be noted at this point that one of the important differences between the dissimilation and the assimilation is that the former does not take the final underlying vowel into account as an environmental condition while the latter does. This implies that the former process is rather superficial compared with the latter.

3.2. Other paradigms including numerative compounds and transitive verbs show both types of a/e alternations. For example, such alternations in the following numerative compounds (*ruwa* '2' + a numerative classifier) are self-explanatory.

dissimilation		*assimilation*	
ruwetab^w	'2 halves'	ruwefijE[5]	'2 handfuls'
ruweŋaf	'2 arm-lengths'	ruwetip	'2 flat pieces'
ruwefaü	'2 round things'	ruweül	'2 handfuls of leaves'

cf.	ruwagofetI	'2 pieces'
	ruwam^{w}eü	'2 groups'
	ruwa:lI	'2 skinny things'

3.3. Both types of raising are also observable in such reduplicated forms as the following.

dissimilation			*assimilation*		
a.	kekkaŋi	'to be eating'	b.	raxirexI	'to line up'
a′.	m^{w}arem^{w}ar	'lei'	b′.	laüleü	'to deliver babies'
			b″.	fitijetijE	'to marry each other'

It may be assumed that the vowels in one part of a reduplicated form are, in principle, the same as those in the other in the base whatever the superficial difference may be. Obviously *e* is derived from *a* in a, b and b′. As regards a′ and b″, that the underlying form of the reduced final vowel is *a* can be demonstrated by adding the construct suffix *-li* yielding *m^{w}arem^{w}erall* 'lei of' and *fitijetijalI* 'the marrying each other of'. Therefore the *e*'s in a′ and b″ may also be considered the result of *a*-raising.

3.4. The causative prefix in Woleaian is *xa-* with all stems but those whose first syllable contains *a* in which case *xe-* appears:

a.	xab^{w}u:togo	'to make him go'
	xatem^{w}a:üwė	'to make him sick'
b.	xelago	'to make him come'
	xemm^{w}ašü	'to hold him'

The variant *xe-* can best be accounted for in terms of dissimilation.

3.5. The a/e alternations in the following sets of related forms of complex morphological structure constitute further definite evidence that the process of dissimilation is operating, although these examples involve two problems that will be taken up in 4 and 6.

raŋeraŋ	'yellow'			
xeraŋeraŋ	'make yellow'	(xe- causative	raŋeraŋ)	
xeraŋereŋa	'make it yellow'	(xe-	raŋereŋa	*-ja*[6]) obj. suffix
xeraŋereŋalI / xareŋereŋalI	'making yellow of'	(xe-	raŋereŋa	-lI) construct suffix
tepaŋi	'to help it'	(tepa	-ŋi[7]	*-ja*)

xetapetap	'to support'	(xe-	tape	-redup.)	
xetapetepa	'to support it'	(xe-	tape	-redup.	*-ja*)
xatepetepalI	'supporting of'	(xa-	tepe	-redup.	-lI)

Whenever some morphemes are affixed to the stem, there follow some rearrangements that prevent two *a*'s from lining up in sequence. In spite of the multiple a/e alternations apparent in the above examples, the dissimilation (as well as assimilation) process seems to be unidirectional, i.e., from *a* to *e* and not vice versa. That is, no justification may be made in favor of a possible hypothesis that underlying *e* becomes *a*.

3.6. The last supporting evidence that *a*-raising works in Woleaian comes from the comparative angle. Observe the following examples in which Woleaian *e* corresponds with *a* in PO indicating that original *a* may be (or may have been) dissimilated to *e* (PO data: Biggs 1965 and Grace 1969). Whether these dissimilations are historical or active will be discussed shortly.

Woleaian	*PO*	
jefar	*qapaRa	'shoulder'
jennap } ja:l }	*sala(n)	'road'
meram	*marama	'moon'
metawE	*masawa	'sea'
metaxO	*mataku(t)	'to be afraid'
temwa:ü	*masaki(t)	'to be sick'

The examples given thus far seem to be sufficient to show that *a*-raising is a general process going on widely in Woleaian. As a matter of fact, this process is so general that no exception is found. Even the two Japanese loanwords cited in Bender 1969b do not show up as exceptions since the initial vowels are pronounced long, in which case dissimilation does not operate:

ka:ma	'kettle'	ta:ma	'light bulb'
ka:ma:lI	'kettle of'	ta:ma:lI	'light bulb of'

4. The next question is how to reconstruct the base form of each occurrence of CeC_oa and VhC_oeC_oVh, i.e., whether the *e* should be represented as *a* or *e* in the base.

4.1. In the first place, *e* should be represented as *a* in the base when *a*, instead of *e,* appears in other variants of the same lexical item in an environment where there is no such vowel to or from which it is to be assimilated or dissimilated. Such are obviously cases of synchronic process. Thus, for example, in the examples given in 3.1 the first vowel of *metaj* is *a* in the base because *ma:t* and *matemam* have *a* as the first vowel in an environment where there is no *a* in the following syllable. On the other hand, *e* in *ülümej* should be *a* in the base in that *ülümal,* etc. preserve *a* on the surface. The underlying forms of the examples in 3.1, 3.2 and 3.4 are thus represented respectively as follows:

(3.1)	ind. form	*mata*	*wülü*[8]
	1. sg.	*mata-ji*	*wülüma-ji*
	2. sg.	*mata-mu*	*wülüma-mu*
	3. sg.	*mata-la*	*wülüma-la*
	1. pl. incl.	*mata-ca*	*wülüma-ca*
	1. pl. excl.	*mata-mami*	*wülüma-mami*
	2. pl.	*mata-mii*	*wülüma-mii*
	3. pl.	*mata-iire*	*wülüma-iire*
(3.2)	*ruwa-tabo*	*ruwa-fija*	
	ruwa-ŋafa	*ruwa-tipa*	
	ruwa-fawü	*ruwa-wülü*	
(3.4)	*xalaxo-ja*		
	xamm^{w}acu-ja		

In order to check out whether *a* looms up in certain environments or not, it may be useful to apply the reduplication or construct (*-li* attachment) tests, although there are certain limitations.[9] For example:

redup. test: tepaŋi 'to help it' base: *tapaŋi-ja*
(xet*a*pet*a*p 'to make help')

construct test: meram 'moon' base: *marama*
(m*a*remalI 'moon of')

4.2. Our next concern is with the handling of the *e* that appears in such reduplicated forms as those in 3.3. Although *e* in the examples never alternates with *a,* it is still preferable to have *a* in the base in that the second half of each reduplication ends in *a* in the base and such a treatment can contribute to simpler formulation of reduplication rules.[10] Thus there is no problem in representing the base forms of the examples in 3.3 as follows (except for *m^{w}arem^{w}ar*):

kakkaŋi-ja *raxiraxi*
fitijatija
lawülawü

One serious problem is associated with the representation of $C_iV_iC_je$-$C_iV_iC_ja$ type reduplication. Compare the related forms below:

m^{w}ar*e*m^{w}ar	'lei'
m^{w}ar*e*m^w*e*raII	'lei of'
xem^{w}ar*e*m^{w}ar	'to put leis on'
xem^{w}ar*e*m^w*e*ra	'to put the lei on him'

(See also the examples given in 3.5.)

It should be noticed that the first half of the reduplicated form always ends in *e* regardless of the following vowel. If, in spite of this fact, we set up *a* instead of *e* in view of the second half of reduplication which ends in *a,* one problem will be how to derive *e* from *a* where there is no *a* in the following syllable. One might want to talk about 'progressive' dissimilation in this case, as the preceding *a* could influence the following *a.* However, existence of such forms as xa:r*e*wer*e*waII 'greenness of' in which the *e* in question has *e*'s on both sides immediately refutes such a hypothesis. There may be three different approaches toward the solution of this problem, none of which seems completely satisfactory at the moment. The first would be to set up *e* in the base, assuming that *e* has been dissimilated historically and that the reduplicated form has been fossilized as such. However, I would be hesitant to consider, for example, the third vowel in xetap*e*tepa 'to support him' to be historically fossilized in view of such forms as tep*a*ŋi 'to help him' where *a* always occurs, although this approach would say that the connection between the two forms just cited is purely etymological, perhaps some sort of mental association outside of the grammar, or possibly part of what Householder (1959:232) has termed the 'idiom grammar'. This treatment, furthermore, would constitute an exception to otherwise regular reduplications in which both halves of reduplicated forms should, in principle, be identical early in the derivation, having been derived from one and the same unreduplicated base. By distinguishing between 'fossilized' and 'functioning' reduplication it would necessarily bring certain complications to the formulation of reduplication rules. But the strongest counterevidence is the fact that corresponding forms in Ulithian, a mutually intelligible neighboring dialect, always reveal *a* in the position in question where Woleaian has *e*.

A second not especially attractive alternative would be to set up *a* in order to deal with the assumed historical dissimilation completely within a synchronic framework. This consideration would keep regularity in the underlying form, but require some manipulation by way of a rule or condition so that the semi-fossilized *e* could be derived from *a*. At the moment I have no way of knowing how this rule could be worked out explicitly. Possibly a diacritic feature could be used to distinguish *a*'s which always raise to *e* in the first half of reduplication from those that are open to the full functioning of all rules.

The third alternative would be to set up *a*, but with the assumption that this raising of *a* to *e* is not historical but a synchronic process of prejunctural weakening which changes a single *a* to *e* before a juncture. If this should prove true, it would constitute a third process, together with assimilation and dissimilation, affecting the raising of *a*. Thus it may be assumed that an internal juncture falls between the two parts of every reduplication. This treatment is supported by the fact that before such a boundary *a* never occurs on the surface, as may be observed below:

te=tepaŋi 'to be helping' base: *ta=tapaŋi-ja*
cf. xe-tape=tepa 'to support him'
were=wer 'thunder' base: *wera=wera*
cf. werewerall 'thunder of'

Unless prejunctural weakening is taken into account, it would not be easy to adequately explain the appearance of *te-*, instead of *ta-*, and *were-*, instead of *wera-*. Appearance of word-final voiceless *e* [E], after certain consonants, in the position where the base vowel is *a* furnishes further justification for the above treatment:

pa:bʷijE	'pig'	base: *paabʷija*
bʷuguwE	'knee'	*bʷuxuwa*
wa:xE	'vein'	*waxa*
jalüsE	'sideburns'	*jalüsa*

The processes assumed to be involved are:

$$a \xrightarrow[\text{raising}]{} e \;/\; C\_\_\_ \begin{Bmatrix} = \\ \# \end{Bmatrix} \begin{cases} \xrightarrow[\text{devoicing}]{} & E \;/\; Cx\_\_\_\# \\ \xrightarrow[\text{apocope}]{} & \emptyset \;/\; \tilde{C}x\_\_\_\# \end{cases}$$

where Cx is a class of consonants which prevent apocope.

The Ulithian cognates already mentioned which show *a* in correspondence with *e* in Woleaian also stand in favor of the foregoing synchronic treatment.

If all instances of 'exceptional *e'* were clearly prejunctural, the last solution would be by far the most convincing so far as it goes. One problem which makes us hesitant in adopting this solution definitely, however, is related to the following type of examples.

jar*e*mat	'person'	cf. Ulithian: jaramat
		Trukese: jaramas
jar*e*m*e*talI	'person of'	

Such words probably had bimorphemic stems at one time, but do not have two clearly separate meanings synchronically, although they function phonologically in the same way as *m^{w}arem^{w}ar* and other reduplicated forms of the same syllable structure (see the examples given in 3.5). The question here is whether we would be justified in positing an internal juncture (=) at the historical or hypothetical morpheme boundary to account for the consistent raising of a basic *a*.

4.3. The next question is how to decide the base forms of those words which are not covered by 4.1 or 4.2 above. At this point, resort may be made to comparative evidence, in particular to Ulithian (and Trukese) counterparts, as in these dialects dissimilation (not assimilation) seems to have been mostly historical, with only sporadic active operation.[11] For example, all the forms but *metaxO* and *tem^{w}a:ü* in the examples in 3.6 have *a* as the first vowel in the base as judged from the reduplication/construct tests mentioned in 4.1 above. These tests are not effective in the said two words because their final vowels could not possibly be *a* and the dissimilation operates backward. Now Ulithian and Trukese forms furnish evidence for the justification that the underlying vowel is *e* and not *a*:

(3.6)	*Woleaian*	*Ulithian*	*Trukese*	*W. base forms*
	jefar	jafar	jafar	*jafara*
	jennap	{ jellap jallap		*jala-lapa*
	ja:l	ja:l	ja:n	*jala*
	meram	maram	maram	*marama*
	metawE	{ madaw medaw	madaw	*madawa*
	metaxO	metaxO	mesėk	*metaxo*
	tem^{w}a:ü	tem^{w}aj	semm^{w}en	*tem^{w}aawü*

Further forms which are indeterminate by Woleaian evidence alone are given below:

W.	*U.*	*W. base form*	
weri-xemam	weri-xamam	*weri-xamami*	'see us (excl.)'
tera	se:r	*teraa*	'adze'
m̩eŋa:xO	maŋaxO	*maŋaaxo*	'clothes'
xareŋap	xaraŋap	*xaraŋapa*	'bonito'

Incidentally this will lead to the possibility of establishing the bases common to Ulithian and Woleaian when they differ only in a/e alternations, since the difference can simply be handled by the dissimilation rule applicable only to Woleaian.

If no comparative or other etymological evidence is available, there will be no harm in picking up *e* as a basic vowel since this is the pronounced one.

The discussions made thus far may also be applicable to the assimilation phenomenon, although this will not be elaborated.

5. The above observation naturally leads to the last question: how to formalize the rules of *a*-raising. The rule of assimilation is straightforward:[12]

PR1. $a \longrightarrow e \ / VhC_0\_\_C_0Vh$

As the conditioning environment should involve the underlying final vowel, the rule must be applied before final vowel reduction. On the other hand, the dissimilation must work only after final single vowel *a* is changed or reduced. Following the third alternative solution, which was discussed in 4.2 above, the rule of prejunctural weakening of *a* may be as follows:

PR2. $a \longrightarrow e \ / C \_\_ \begin{Bmatrix} = \\ \# \end{Bmatrix}$

Now, the dissimilation operates only on a single vowel *a* and is regressive, working (mainly) from right to left recursively. This fact must be specified in this rule, as suggested below:

PR3. $a \longrightarrow e \ / \ C\_\_C_0a \ (C_0\tilde{a}X)\#$
where X = null or one or more segments

The above three rules may be combined on the condition that dissimilation works later than prejunctural weakening (which fact is indicated by numerals in the following). So far as the process of final *a* weakening to *e* is admitted, there is no need to place the assimilation before the dissimilation in rule ordering. (This modifies my earlier statement that dissimilation is rather superficial (3.1). Ordering is relevant only between PR2 and PR3.

$$\text{PR}(a\text{-raising}) \qquad a \longrightarrow e \;/\; \left\{\begin{array}{l} \text{VhC}_o\_\_\text{C}_o\text{Vh} \\ \text{C}\_\_ \left\{\begin{array}{c} = \\ \# \end{array}\right\} \cdots\cdots\cdots (1) \\ \text{C}\_\_\text{C}_o\text{a}(\text{C}_o\tilde{\text{a}}\text{X})\# \cdots\cdot (2) \end{array}\right.$$

An example of rule-working is given below:

rules[13]	2-arm-length	in-belly-of-sky
	ruwa-ŋafa	*le-ssaxa-li laŋi*
1. assimilation		ė
2. prejunctural *a*-raising	e	
3. dissimilation	e	e
4. devoicing/apocope	Ø	I I
5. vowel dropping between C's[14]		Ø
6. nasalization[15]		nn
7. voicing		g
	ruweŋaf	lesseganneŋI
	'two arm-lengths'	'in the middle of the sky'

6. One final problem which has not been touched upon is the appearance of the following forms (see example set 3.5) where the initial part of each word seemed to me to undergo 'progressive' dissimilation, optional in certain words and obligatory in others.

x*a*reŋereŋalI	'making yellow of'
(=x*e*r*a*ŋereŋalI)	
x*a*t*e*petepalI	'supporting of'
(*x*e*t*a*petepalI)	
x*a*p*e*lepelalI	'sarong of'
(*x*e*p*a*lepelalI;	cf. xepalepal 'sarong')

One reasonable possible explanation for these irregular dissimilations suggested by Professor Bender is to consider such variants the results of obligatory or optional switches in the ordering of PR2 (prejunctural weakening) and PR3 (dissimilation). This solution seems far more attractive than my original consideration in terms of switches in direction on dissimilation, in that it would not necessitate any additional rule or condition on an existing rule to deal with the 'exceptional' phenomenon, while nothing would be lost in terms of simplicity of the lexicon since in either case (rule switching or dissimilatory direction switching), those forms permitting the switch would have to be specially marked in the lexicon. One possible way of marking the base forms of such irregular variants, following the rule-switching solution, may be something like the following in which the underlying representations of such forms should be accompanied by information of rule applications indicating whether given forms are regular (unmarked) or irregular (marked) with regard to a/e alternations (+ means obligatory and ± optional).

raŋa = raŋa 'yellow' [if *xa-* : ± PR3 ⟶ 2]
for { xareŋereŋalI (PR3 ⟶ PR2)
xeraŋereŋalI (PR2 ⟶ PR3)

tapa 'help' [if redup. and *xa-* : + PR3 ⟶ 2]
for { xatepetepalI (PR3 ⟶ PR2)
*xetapetepalI

cf. *mʷara = mʷara* *(unmarked with regard to rule order)*
for { *xemʷ*aremʷera 'to put leis on him'
*xamʷeremʷera

The irregular variants of the above kind will require further checking.

Notes

1. The language data are provided by Tony Tawerilmang from Western Woleai. I appreciate the comments Byron Bender has made throughout this report.
2. Similar processes in Marshallese are discussed in Bender 1968 and Bender 1969b.
3. The lengthening manifest in surface forms of monosyllabic nouns is regular. *ülüm* would be the expected independent form under the rules formulated to date. However, the loss of additional segments (final *üm* in this case) is not completely idiosyncratic, and this phenomenon may yet prove to be regular.
4. *j* (ofter spelled *y*) is a high front semivowel.
5. Certain voiceless vowels appear after a class of consonants. Single base vowel *a* becomes E finally after these consonants (see 4.3 for related discussion).
6. The motivations for (tentatively) postulating *ja* as the underlying object suffix will not concern us here.

7. Transitive forms of many verbs in the language contain 'thematic' material which is present in base forms but dropped from reduplicated forms.
8. [ü] and [wü] are in free variation. The motivation for setting up *w* will not be elaborated here.
9. One limitation is discussed in 4.3.
10. Much the same treatment is suggested in Bender 1969b: 24 in connection with the difference between two vowels in such Marshallese reduplicated words as ṁakṁ&k where & represents a higher mid surface quality derived from a mid *e* when a following *i* is dropped. Positing a high stem vowel in the base forms and an assimilation rule similar to our PR1 (see 5.), Bender derives & from underlying *a* as in {ṁaki} + redup. > ṁakiṁaki > ṁakiṁeki which form then undergoes the raising of *e* with the loss of final *i*.
11. Reconstruction through such comparative evidence is motivated by the fact that Woleaian is linguistically (as well as geographically) lying between Ulithian and Trukese in the dialect chain, forming a closer relation with Ulithian. It seems reasonable, therefore, to set up W. basic *a* or *e* according to whether U. and T. have *a* or *e* on the surface. If U. and T. show different vowels, it may be suggested that W. basic vowel be identified with the U. form in view of the closeness between the two dialects (with excellent mutual intelligibility).
12. *a*-raising seems to be very general among Micronesian languages. It operates widely in Ulithian. Quackenbush 1968 contains evidence that Sonsorol is another dialect where this process is working consistently. The Marshallese case has already been mentioned (see footnote 10).
13. Rules 4-7 are not relevant to the present discussion.
14. Between certain identical consonants (such as nasals, laterals, fricatives) a single vowel drops.
15. *l* and *n* are separate phonemes in Woleaian (e.g., saite*n* 'sword', *n*a:*n*a 'mother', b^wu*nn* 'heart', xi*l*ej 'my skin', *l*a:ŋO 'house fly') with such distributional limitations as **ll* and **lVl*. These non-occurring sequences are considered as having undergone (a) vowel dropping in the second case and (b) nasalization of *ll* for both. For example:

   b^w*ulla* $\xrightarrow[(b)]{}$ b^wunn 'heart'

   calü-li $\xrightarrow[(a)]{}$ šallI $\xrightarrow[(b)]{}$ šannI 'water of'

Reprinted from *Working Papers in Linguistics* (University of Hawaii) 3.8:15-35 (1971).

4. AN ORTHOGRAPHIC DESIGN FOR WOLEAIAN

The following discussion is concerned mainly with orthographic recommendations for Woleaian (WOL), but I hope it will also contribute to the solution of similar problems for neighbouring languages including Ulithian (ULI), Satawalese (STW), and Lamotrek, and more importantly, to the design of a unified orthography for all of the Yap Outer Islands. The present discussions will cover (1) some basic concepts of an orthography, (2) the sound system of WOL, (3) the proposed alphabet, and (4) the proposed spelling conventions. The last two constitute the proposed orthography of WOL.[1]

At the end of this paper, an appendix is provided to briefly present the orthography adopted in Sohn (1975a) and Sohn and Tawerilmang (1976) since the recommendations in this paper were made.

1. Basic Concepts

1. Speech and Writing. The people of Woleai need a standard way of writing that everyone can use since writing is very important in our use of language, especially in our modern society where living becomes more complex day by day. The main role of a writing system is to represent speech, thus enabling communication across time and space. Thus, speaking and hearing correspond respectively to writing and reading.

Three typical types of writing systems are in use in the world today. These are alphabets, ideographies, and syllabaries. Most of our familiar writing systems, including that of English, are alphabets. If a writing system uses symbols or letters, each of which directly corresponds to an individual sound, and not to a word or word meaning, it is called an alphabet. Thus, for example, *k* in the alphabet of English represents a sound and not a meaning. If a writing system uses symbols or characters each of which directly corresponds to a word or word meaning, it is called ideographic. Thus, for example, the Chinese character 我 [wǒ] represents the meaning 'I'. If a writing system uses symbols or letters each of which corresponds neither to an individual sound nor to a word, but to a syllable, it is called a syllabary. Thus, for example, the Japanese letter カ represents the syllable [ka] which indicates neither one sound nor a meaning but a syllable consisting of a consonant and a vowel. Ideographies have the grave disadvantage that there must be a great number of symbols, because every language has tens of thousands of words, and the users of such a writing system are subjected to a much heavier burden on their memories than are those whose languages are represented alphabetically. For example, a dictionary of Chinese includes more than 50,000 different symbols or characters. On the other hand, syllabaries are adequate only in such a language as Japanese where there are a relatively small number of different syllables. The number of syllables depends on the number of vowels and consonants and the type of syllable structure. For example, Japanese has only fifty-one basic letters representing all possible syllables in the language, because the number of vowels and consonants is very small and the syllable structure is of the form of a consonant only (C-type), a vowel only (V-type), or a consonant followed by a vowel (CV-type).

WOL has a syllable structure as simple as Japanese, but has many more vowels and consonants. This fact makes it disadvantageous for Woleaians to have a syllabary. In fact, WOL was represented by various types of syllabary in the past (Riesenberg and Kaneshiro 1960). These syllabaries apparently originated as ideographic pictures, but they were syllabaries in that the symbols thus created were used to represent any syllables of the same sounds, regardless of the original meaning. It is important to note that in spite of their large number, the symbols given in Figure 26 in Riesenberg and Kaneshiro (278) are far from adequate to represent all WOL words and sentences correctly and unambiguously.

Alphabets have an advantage over the other systems, in that only a handful of letters are used to represent an infinite number of words and sentences in a language. Since the number is small (for example, English has twenty-six basic letter symbols), it is easy to learn, write, and read the letters.

For this reason, we propose adopting an alphabetic writing system for the representation of the WOL language.

2. Relation between Sound and Letter. An ideal alphabet writing system should serve not only for native speakers who already know the language but also for those who either partly know the language or want to learn or work on it. If an orthography is to be devised only for those who have native

control of the language, we do not need any strict correspondence between sound and letter, because a loose correspondence can also give the ordinary speaker enough indication of what has been said so that he can supply the rest. In any language, a great deal can be omitted without a corresponding loss in the transmittal of messages from one person to another. For example, if we use the traditional spelling *shuh* to mean both 'mountain' and 'basket' in spite of the difference in pronunciation, there is not much difficulty in the conveyance of messages, since native speakers would pronounce them correctly if given the context. However, for non-native speakers who want to learn a language or are in the process of learning, or even for those native speakers who are not mature in the language, a strict correspondence between sound and letter is important, for it will make language learning easier and faster if they can learn how to pronounce each written word and sentence correctly. Strict sound-letter correspondence is also desirable not only for the benefit of native speakers who are in the initial stage of reading, but also because writing has to be a correct representation of speech. We could devise a totally separate set of phonetic symbols instead of alphabetic letters as in English, but if the alphabetic letters can be used as phonetic symbols, as they are, nothing could be more efficient.

Furthermore, strict sound-letter correspondence will contribute to the economy of language users' efforts. Loose correspondence forces speakers to memorise spellings of individual words with much effort, because their pronunciation does not automatically provide correct spellings, as is obvious to users of English. Finally, strict sound-letter correspondence will lead easily to the standardisation of writing, since it provides native speakers with a norm in writing their language, i.e. the norm "Follow your pronunciation."

I consider an orthography to be ideal, then, if it is useful for both mature speakers and language learners, and if it is subject to easy learning and correct reading and writing. One basic requirement for such an orthography is that sound and letter must match as unambiguously as possible. The WOL orthography proposed here is devised with such objectives in mind.

2. The WOL Sound System

The most important prerequisite for an orthographic device based on an alphabet is an intensive linguistic analysis in order to reveal the sound system of the language. A poor knowledge of a sound system often leads one to devise an orthography which contains too many or too few symbols on the one hand, and includes useless spelling conventions or misses important sounds on the other. The spelling proposed by Smith (1951), which is an alphabetic writing, is an example of an orthography based on a poorly analysed sound system, in which Smith sets up too many letters and poor spelling conventions.

My intensive analysis of WOL, with the help of Tony Tawerilmang from Woleai, has revealed that WOL has fifteen short and eleven long significant consonants, six short and eight long significant vowels, and two significant semi-vowels, significant in the sense that any interchange of them in words will necessarily be accompanied by a change in meaning of the words involved. For example, replacement of [i] with [a] in [rixi̥] 'run' and [raxi̥] 'year' results in the change of meaning. (The square brackets mean the actual pronunciation of the forms. For the pronunciation of each symbol see the pages following. The small circle under a symbol indicates voicelessness of the sound.)

There are many non-significant sounds also, non-significant in the sense that they have no power to change meanings even if they were interchanged. Their differences, entirely automatic, are caused by their sound environments. For example, in [rixi̥], exchange of the two sounds [i] and [i̥], even if it were made, would not bring about any change in the meaning of the word. Their difference is quite automatic, [i̥] appearing at word-final position and [i] between consonants or at word-initial position. Such non-significant sounds as [i] and [i̥] are grouped into a significant sound /i/ for orthographic purposes. The significant sounds are technically called 'phonemes' and are transcribed in slashes.

(1) WOL Consonants

WOL consonant phonemes are either single or double. The fifteen single consonants of WOL are classified in the following page according to manner and place of articulation.

The phonemes /p/, /t/, /c/, and /k/ are voiceless unaspirated stop consonants, pronounced approximately as *p*, *t*, *ch*, and *k* in the Eng. words 'spy', 'strong', 'matches', and 'sky' respectively. Single /c/ and /k/ occur only in loanwords. The phonemes /f/, /s/, and /x/ are voiceless fricative consonants, pronounced like *f*, *s*, and *ch* in Eng. 'five' and 'sun' and Ger. *ich* 'I', respectively. /x/ is voiced between two voiced vowels.

The phoneme /ᵽ/ is also a voiceless fricative consonant, produced as if one were blowing a candle while pulling the tongue backward. Between two

manner of articulation			place of articulation				
voice	mode	tongue shape	lips	lip-teeth	teeth-gum	hard palate	soft palate
voiceless	stop	plain	/p/		/t/	/c/	/k/
	fricative	plain		/f/	/s/		/x/
		pulled back	/ᵽ/				
		curled back				/š/	
voiced		curled back				/r/	
	nasal	plain	/m/		/n/		/ŋ/
		pulled back	/ṁ/				
	flap	plain			/l/		

voiced vowels, it tends to be voiced. /š/ is another voiceless fricative, produced in the same way as the initial sound of Eng. 'shepherd' but with the tongue curled backward. /r/ is a voiced fricative pronounced with the same tongue position as /š/. It is similar to the initial sound of Eng. 'read' except that for WOL /r/ the tongue is curled backward. While /š/ has a noticeable hissing sound, produced by squeezing the air through a narrow slit between the tongue tip and the palate, /r/ lacks such hissing because there is a wide groove between the tongue tip and the palate which allows the air to flow out freely.

The phonemes /m/, /n/, and /ŋ/ have the same sound quality as the Eng. sounds. Simple /n/ occurs only in loanwords. /ṁ/ is pronounced in the same way as /m/ but with the tongue pulled back. WOL /l/ is a flap sound more or less like the *r* in British 'very'. /l/ is pronounced with much less pressure than in the case of /t/. Although /l/ is not a lateral sound in WOL, it corresponds to the lateral /l/ in neighbouring languages including Ulithian. It is for this reason that the symbol /l/ is used to represent the sound.

Observe the following words in which the consonants discussed above are italicised. The examples are given in both phonemic and phonetic transcriptions. The wedge (̬) under a symbol indicates voicing.

/paapaa/	[p̣aapa]	‘to count’
/metai/	[metai]	‘my eyes’
/icii/	[ici]	‘one (from Jp.)’
/kacitoo/	[kacito]	‘movie (from Jp.)’
/yaafi/	[yaafi̥]	‘fire’
/silei/	[silei̥]	‘my mother’
/iixe/	[iixe̥]	‘fish’
/wexare/	[wex̬are̥]	‘root’
/taaꝑu/	[taaꝑu̥]	‘taboo’
/taꝑeeye/	[taꝑeeye̥]	‘follow him’
/šoo/	[šǒ]	‘copra’
/rixi/	[rixi̥]	‘to run’
/yaremate/	[yaremate̥]	‘person’
/sensei/	[sensei]	‘teacher (from Jp.)’
/ŋii/	[ŋi]	‘tooth’
/ṁaale/	[ṁaale̥]	‘man’
/yaalo/	[yaalo̥]	‘sun’

There are eleven double consonants as shown below.

manner of articulation			place of articulation				
voice	mode	tongue shape	lips	lip-teeth	teeth-gum	hard palate	soft palate
voiceless	stop	plain	/pp/		/tt/	/cc/	/kk̇/
		pulled black	/ṗṗ/				
	fricative	plain		/ff/	/ss/		
voiced	nasal	plain	/mm/		/nn/		/ŋŋ/
		pulled back	/ṁṁ/				

All double consonants and their corresponding simple consonants share the same sound qualities except that double ones are stronger and longer than their simple counterparts. /ṗṗ/ is the only consonant which does not have a simple counterpart /ṗ/ but corresponds instead to /ꝑ/. It is not only stronger and longer than /ꝑ/, but it is also different in that it is a stop sound while /ᵽ/ is a fricative. On the other hand, the five simple consonants /ᵽ, x, š, r, l/ do not have corresponding double consonants. When /c/, /k/, and /n/ occur in native words, they are always pronounced as double consonants. Observe the following examples in which double consonants are italicised.

/*pp*iye/	[ppiye̥]	'sand'
/*tt*iri/	[ttiri̥]	'fast'
/*cc*aa/	[cca]	'blood'
/*kk*aŋi/	[kkaŋi̥]	'sharp'
/*ṗṗ*eše/	[ṗṗeše̥]	'white'
/*ff*axe/	[ffaxe̥]	'to cough'
/*ss*aaᵽu/	[ssaaᵽu̥]	'fishing kit'
/*mm*ate/	[mmạte̥]	'to awake'
/*ᵽunno*/	[ᵽunno̥]	'heart'
/*ŋŋ*awe/	[ŋŋawe̥]	'bad'
/*ṁṁ*uto/	[ṁṁuto̥]	'to vomit'

A double consonant is slightly weakened if it occurs in word-initial position and is followed by a vowel and a second occurrence of the same double consonant. For instance, /ṁṁoṁṁoŋoo/ 'to be eating' is pronounced as [ṁoṁṁoŋo] and /kkekkeᵽate/ 'to be barking' as [kekkeᵽate̥].

(2) WOL Vowels

WOL vowel phonemes are either single or double. The six single vowels of WOL may be arranged according to tongue height, tongue frontness or backness, and lip shape, as follows:

tongue	front	central		back
	(flat lips)	(plain lips)	(round lips)	(round lips)
high	/i/		/u̇/	/u/
mid	/e/			/o/
low		/a/		

The phoneme /i/ is similar to a short variety of English *ee* as in 'meet', /e/ to English *e* in 'bed', /a/ to English *a* as in 'park', /u̇/ to German *ü* in *müssen* 'must', /u/ to the short variety of English *oo* in 'pool', and /o/ to English *o* in 'short'. /e/ is pronounced with slight lip rounding when it occurs before a round vowel, e.g. /iteu̇/ [iteu̇] 'who?'

Simple vowels are pronounced as voiceless when they occur in word-final position after a consonant or semivowel, e.g. /maate/ [maate̥] 'eyes'. The only exception is words of the shape (C)V (optional simple consonant + obligatory vowel) in which case no devoicing occurs, e.g. /me/ [me] 'and', /xo/ [xo] 'you', and /ᵽe/ [ᵽe] 'will' all of which are function words. Except for /a/, all the simple vowels may occur in word-final position. The voiceless /e/, i.e. [e̥], is pronounced with slight lip rounding when it occurs after a round vowel, e.g. /u̇u̇we/ [u̇u̇we̥] 'neck'.

Although native speakers are reluctant to spell word-final voiceless vowels, these vowels are significant in distinguishing words with different meanings. For instance, the two members in each of the following pairs are pronounced differently. Their meanings are different too, indicating that they are distinct words.

a.	/peeši/	[peeši̥]	'hotness'
	/peeše/	[peeše̥]	'lime'
b.	/xu̇u̇su̇/	[xu̇u̇su̥̇]	'louse'
	/xu̇u̇se/	[xu̇u̇se̥]	'octopus'
c.	/laaṁu/	[laaṁu̥]	'mosquito'
	/laaṁo/	[laaṁo̥]	'lagoon'
d.	/xaccu̇/	[xaccu̥̇]	'good'
	/xacce/	[xacce̥]	'fish smell'
e.	/metaxi/	[metaxi̥]	'pain'
	/metaxu̇/	[metaxu̥̇]	'fear'
f.	/laaŋi/	[laaŋi̥]	'sky'
	/laaŋo/	[laaŋo̥]	'house fly'

Word-final voiceless vowels are also significant in that they affect the sound quality of the preceding vowel. For instance, the *a*'s and *e*'s preceding a final round voiceless vowel (i.e. [o̥], [u̥̇], [u̥]) are pronounced with the lips quite rounded, as illustrated by the rounded *a* [ɒ] or rounded *e* [ə] in each word below:

/ṁalo/	[ṁɒlo̥]	'to hide'
/mešaro/	[mešɒro̥]	'dirt'
/ssexu̇/	[ssəxu̥̇]	'full'
/ᵽᵽelu̇/	[ᵽᵽəlu̥̇]	'dirt'
/leweṁu/	[lewəṁu̥]	'your tongue'

Voiceless word-final vowels are sensitive to the sound environment. If a word follows them closely in the same phrase, they become voiced. In the following expressions, notice the italicised symbols which are voiced vowels.

/iṁe kkaa/ [iṁe kka]	[iṁ*e* kka]	‘these houses’
/rixi laxo/	[rix̯*i* laxo̥]	‘to run away’
/ꝑunno xaccu̇/	[ꝑunn*o* x̯accu̥̇]	‘good heart’
/xotɔɔto laa/	[xotɔɔto la]	‘that crack’
/ꝑušo xemase/	[ꝑuš*o* x̯emase̥]	‘very stupid’
/yalu̇su̇lu̇ yaape/	[yalu̇su̇l*u̇* yaape̥]	‘ghost of Yap’

There are eight double vowels in WOL which may be arranged as follows:

tongue	front	central		back
	(flat lips)	(plain lips)	(round lips)	(round lips)
high	/ii/		/u̇u̇/	/uu/
mid	/ee/		/əə/	/oo/
low		/aa/		/ɔɔ/

A double vowel is about twice as long as a simple vowel. Notice in the above table that there are two double vowels, /əə/ and /ɔɔ/, which do not correspond to any simple vowel phonemes. These two double vowels were historically each a sequence of two different simple vowels, but in modern WOL, they are simply long vowels. /əə/ is similar to French *oeu* in *coeur* 'heart', pronounced with the lips rounded. It is the sound made by simultaneous pronunciation of /ee/ and /oo/. /ɔɔ/ is similar to Eng. *aw* in *law*. All the other double vowels are simply lengthened varieties of the corresponding simple ones. While simple vowels in word-final position are devoiced after a consonant or semivowel, double vowels are slightly shortened, with voicing retained, in the same position. Thus, in the following examples, word-final (short) voiced vowels which occur after a consonant or semivowel are actually ‘allophones’ of double vowels.

/*ii*y*aa*/	[iiya]	‘where?’
/leelix*uu*/	[leelix̯u]	‘a taro sp.’
/y*aa*i/	[yaai]	‘mine’
/l*u̇u̇*l*u̇u̇*/	[lu̇u̇lu̇]	‘to chew’
/ləələə/	[ləələ]	‘to fill with liquid’
/t*uu*loŋo/	[tuuloŋo̥]	‘to dive in’

/ᵽooti/	[ᵽooti̥]	'nose'
/lɔɔlɔɔ/	[lɔɔlɔ]	'wavy'

(3) WOL Semivowels

There are two semivowels, /w/ and /y/. They are glides in that the tongue starts at a position slightly higher than for /u/ and /i/, respectively, and approaches the position for the vowel that immediately follows. /w/ and /y/ are phonemes in that they serve to differentiate meanings, as shown in the following minimal pairs.

/waai/	[waai]	'my canoe'
/yaai/	[yaai]	'mine'
/woo/	[wo]	'bunch'
/yoo/	[yo]	'to sneak'

(4) Phoneme Alternations

While there are non-significant (allophonic) variations in sounds, as between [i] and [i̥], there are also alternations between phonemes. As in allophonic variations, phoneme alternations are caused in many cases by the sound environment in which they occur. In what follows, let us briefly observe such phoneme alternations in WOL.

As already stated, the five simple consonants /ᵽ/, /x/, /š/, /r/, and /l/ do not have corresponding double consonants. If, for some grammatical purpose such as the formation of the progressive form of a verb, these consonants are doubled, a doubled /ᵽ/ becomes /ṗṗ/, doubled /x/ becomes /kk/, doubled /š/ and /r/ both become /cc/, and doubled /l/ becomes /nn/, as illustrated below.

/ᵽuxaa/	[ᵽux̬a]	'boil it':
/*ṗṗ*u*ṗṗ*uxaa/	[ṗuṗṗux̬a]	'be boiling it'
/*x*aŋii/	[xaŋi]	'eat it':
/*kk*e*kk*aŋiiye/	[kekkaŋiiye̥]	'be eating it'
/*š*aalu̇/	[šaalu̥̇]	'water':
/*cc*e*cc*al u̇u̇we/	[ceccal u̇u̇we̥]	'fill it with water'
/*r*aaŋe/	[raaŋe̥]	'yellow powder':
/*cc*e*cc*aŋe/	[ceccaŋe̥]	'apply yellow power'
/*l*u̇tu̇/	[lu̇tu̥̇]	'to jump':
/*nn*u̇tu̇/	[nnu̇tu̥̇]	'to be jumping'

There are other types of boundary phenomena in which phoneme alternations take place. For instance, /mannů/ [mannů̥] 'bird of' results from /malů/ 'bird' + /li/ 'of' with the deletion of the vowel /ů/ before a morpheme boundary and between /l/'s. With the deletion of /ů/, two /l/'s are automatically changed to /nn/. Also it is clear that /ů/ causes the following vowel /i/ to be changed to /ů/ before it is deleted, hence /mannů/. Thus, we can say that /malů-li/ is the 'base form' from which /mannů/ is derived. Base forms will be preceded by an asterisk in what follows e.g. **malů-li* 'bird of'. Observe the following examples.

**xala-la* /xanne/ [xanne̥] 'his food'

**tapo-li-šůů-lapa* /tapoccůůlape/ [tapoccůůlape̥] 'tip of the backbone'

Notice in the second example that, with the deletion of *i*, the consonants *l* and *s* are collapsed to /cc/. In the same way, *l* + *r* = /cc/, *l* + *t* = /tt/, and *l* + *s* = /ss/. Vowel deletions will be discussed shortly under vowel alternations.

Rather extensive phoneme alternations may be observed in vowels. For instance, the word which means 'name' is phonemically represented in three different ways, /iite/, /ite/, and /ita/. The form /iite/ shows up when the word is pronounced without any modifying element following. The form /ite/ appears in three different environments: (i) before a modifying word, as in /ite xaccuů/ 'good name'; (ii) before a suffix whose initial vowel is high, as in /itei/ 'my name'; and (iii) before a suffix whose initial vowel is /a/, as in /itemami/ 'our (excl.) name'. The form /ita/ appears in all other environments not mentioned above, as in /itale/ 'his name'. Since the different realisations of the word 'name' are due to sound environments such as neighbouring vowels, the word boundary, and the presence or absence of a modifying word, we can easily imagine that there is a 'base form' for each word which is free from environmental influence, and that the different forms associated with each word are predictable from the base form in terms of their sound environments. For instance, suppose we set up /ita/ as the base form for 'name'. Then /iite/ and /ite/ are derivable from the base form **ita* by means of a few general phonological rules which will be given shortly. We cannot adopt /iite/, /ite/, or any other form as the base form, because none of them can explain the derivation of the other forms.

Technical details aside, the following simple procedures may be used to obtain base form vowels of WOL words.

a. If there is an alternation between /a/ and other vowels, choose /a/ as the base form vowel. For instance, between /e/ and /a/ in /itei/ 'my name' and /itale/ 'his name', /a/ should be the base form vowel, hence **ita* 'name'.

b. If a long first vowel of an independently pronounced word, e.g. /iite/ 'name', alternates with the corresponding short vowel contained in a larger word, e.g. /itale/ 'his name', the short vowel should be taken for the base form, e.g. **ita* 'name'. If a long vowel does not have a short alternate vowel, the long one is the base form vowel. For instance, in /pooti/ 'nose' and /pootile/ 'his nose', the first vowel is consistently long, hence **pooti* 'nose'.
c. While a voiced final vowel of a content word is represented as long in both base and phonemic form, e.g. **waa* /waa/ 'canoe', a voiced final vowel of a function word of (C)V type is represented as short, e.g. **i* /i/ 'I', **xo* /xo/ 'you', **ye* /ye/ 'he, she, it', and **ŋe* /ŋe/ 'and'. This is because a final vowel of a content word is slightly longer than that of a function word even when pronounced in isolation, and the former is definitely lengthened when followed by some other element, e.g. [waale̥] 'his canoe', but the latter remains always short, whatever environment it may occur in.
d. If there is no phoneme alternation, base form vowels should be based on the pronunciation, e.g., **yase* /yaase/ [yaase̥] 'liver', **yalůsů* /yalůs ů/ [yalůsů̥] 'ghost', and **taai* /taai/ [taai] 'no longer'.
e. Many words and parts of words do not allow any element to be attached after them, preventing us from observing the alternation of final voiceless vowels. The general rule in such cases is simply to set up the voiced counterparts of the voiceless vowels for the base forms. Thus, for instance, the base forms of /šaxů/ [šaxů̥] 'just', /xaaŋů/ [xaaŋů̥] 'I', /ṁu/ [ṁu̥] 'your', and /li/ [li̥] 'of' are respectively **šaxů*, **xaaŋů*, **ṁu*, and **li*. One exception to this rule is that the base form vowel of a final /e/ [e̥] is *a*, e.g. **la* /le/ [le̥] 'his'. This exception is based not only on historical and comparative evidence but on the fact that all other final *a*'s are realised as /e/ anyway.

Once base forms for all WOL morphemes are determined, the following major phonological rules, among others, will derive the phonemic vowels from base form vowels. None of the following rules applies to base forms of (C)V type.

(a) A simple word-final *a* becomes /o/ after *o*, *ɔɔ*, or *u* + consonant. Examples: **punna* /punno/ [punno̥] 'heart' *punna xaccú* /punno xaccú/ [punno x̯accų̊] 'good heart'

(b) In all the other environments, a simple word-final *a* becomes /e/.
Examples: **mata* /maate/ [maatḙ] 'eye'
**mata xaccú* /mate xaccú/ [mate x̯accų̊] 'good eye'

(c) A simple word-final *i* becomes /ú/ after *ú*, and /*u*/ after *u*.
Examples: *yalúsú-li /yalúsúlú/ [yalúsú-lų̊] 'ghost of'
*meŋaaxu-li Tonii /**meŋaaxu-li Tonii*[meŋaaxulu toni] 'Tony's clothes'

(d) The first simple vowel of a base form becomes doubled (or lengthened) when there is no modifier following and when both of the following conditions are met:
   i. The base form must consist of only two simple vowels, with one or two simple consonants or semivowels. Thus, the first vowels of **punna* 'heart', **falúwa* 'island', **pee* 'divination', do not undergo doubling.
   ii. The base form must be used as a noun. For instance, the first vowels of the verb **úlú* 'to drink' and the adverb **šaxú* 'just' do not undergo doubling.

Examples: **faú* /faaú/ [faaú] 'stone'
**ita* /iite/ [iitḙ] 'name'
**úwa* /úúwe/ [úúwḙ] 'neck'
**mata* /maate/ [maatḙ] 'eye'

(e) A simple *a* becomes /e/ between high vowels. This rule applies across word boundaries as long as the word boundary is not accompanied by a breath pause.
Examples: **itai* /itei/ [itei] 'my name'
**raxiraxi* /raxirexi/ [rax̯irexi̥] 'to line up'
**malú kkaila* /malú kkeile/ [malúkkeilḙ] 'strong man'
**xaaú ŋalii* /xaaú ŋelii/ [xaaúŋeli̥] 'to say to him'
**i maŋimaŋi* /i meŋimeŋi/ [imeŋimeŋi̥] 'I think'

(f) When the simple vowel *a* occurs before a low vowel (i.e. /a/ or /ɔ/), it becomes /e/. This rule operates from right to left (Sohn 1971).[2]
Examples: **mata-i* /metai/ [metai] 'my eyes'
**marama* /merame/ [meramḙ] 'moon'
**xamɔɔa* /xemɔɔwe/ [xemɔɔwḙ] 'erase it'

(g) Before a morpheme boundary, a simple vowel drops obligatorily between two identical consonants and optionally between *l* and a teeth-gum or palatal consonant.
Examples: **malú-li* /mannú/ [mannų̊] 'bird of'

sila-la /sinne/ [sinne̥] 'his mother'
lima-malů /limmelů/ [limmelů̥] 'five animate objects'
tama-li-tama-i /temattemai/ [temattemai] 'my grandfather'
yaů-li-rale /yaůccale/ [yaůccale̥] 'wather'
tapo-li-šůů /tapoccůů/ [tapocců] 'bone tip'

(h) Before the third person plural possessive suffix *ra* /re/, a simple vowel is always lengthened and, moreover, if the vowel is *a* preceded by a high vowel, it goes to /ee/, not /aa/.
Examples: *yawa-ra* /yewaare/ [yewaare̥] 'their mouths'
upa-ra /upeere/ [upeere̥] 'their chests'
lewe-ra /leweere/ [leweere̥] 'their tongues'
sila-ra /sileere/ [sileere̥] 'their mother'

Phoneme alternation is also observable in semivowels. There are certain morphemes which in their initial position have /w/ in one environment, /y/ in another, and zero in the third, without any change in meaning. This alternation is perfectly predictable, given the base forms of the meaning units and the environments in which they occur. That is, /w/ appears if the preceding vowel is round, /y/ appears if the preceding vowel is unrounded, and nothing appears if the preceding vowel is the same simple vowel as the following one. For instance, the base form of the unit meaning 'me' is **ai* and that of the unit meaning 'it' is **a*. The base form **ai* 'me' corresponds to the four alternant forms /wei/, /wai/, /yei/, and /yai/. The base form **a* 'it' corresponds to /we/, /ye/, and /a/.[3] The /w/-/y/-zero alternation is due to the environments stated just above. The alternation /e/-/a/ is due to the environments mentioned with regard to vowel alternations. Examples follow.

xamasůrůů-ai /xemasůrůůwei/ [xemasůrůůwei] 'make me sleep'
xam̊oŋoo-ai /xam̊oŋoowai/ [xam̊oŋoowai] 'feed me'
weri-ai /weriyei/ [weriyei] 'see me'
xůlaa-ai /xůlaayai/ [xůlaayai] 'know me'
xasůů-a /xasůůwe/ [xasůůwe̥] 'build it'
lii-a /liiye/ [liiye̥] 'kill it'
nůůwa-a /nůůwaa/ [nůůwa] 'wash it'

3. The Proposed WOL Alphabet

An orthography has two aspects, paradigmatic (systematic) and syntagmatic (combinatorial). The two aspects correspond respectively to sound systems and sound combinations. The paradigmatic aspect, to be discussed in this section, is associated with a set of graphic symbols or letters, whereas the syntagmatic aspect, which will be taken up in Section 4, is associated with spellings or spelling conventions.

1. the following alphabetic and other relevant symbols are proposed.

Consonants

simple	alphabetic symbols	double	alphabetic symbols
/p/	p	/pp/	pp
/t/	t	/tt/	tt
/c/	c	/cc/	cc
/k/	k	/kk/	kk
/f/	f	/ṗṗ/	bb
/s/	s	/ff/	ff
/x/	h	/ss/	ss
/ᵽ/	b	/mm/	mm
/š/	sh	/nn/	nn
/r/	r	/ŋŋ/	nng
/m/	m	/mm/	mmw
/n/	n		
/ŋ/	ng		
/ṁ/	mw		
/l/	l		

Vowels

simple	alphabetic symbols	double	alphabetic symbols
/i/	i	/ii/	ii
/e/	e	/ee/	ee
/a/	a	/aa/	aa
/u̇/	iu	/u̇u̇/	iiu
/u/	u	/əə/	eo
/o/	o	/uu/	uu
		/oo/	oo
		/ɔɔ/	ao

Semivowels

/w/	w
/y/	y

Other symbols

- . period
- , comma
- ? question mark
- ! exclamation mark
- ( ) parentheses
- " " or ' ' quotation marks
- - hyphen

Arabic numerals are used to indicate numbers.

Mathematical symbols like +, −, and ÷ are used.

Capital letters are used for the first letters in sentences and proper nouns.

2. All the symbols given above are borrowed from the alphabetic and other symbols used in writing Eng. By borrowing them from Eng., time and labour will be saved in learning to read and write, not only due to our familiarity with them but also due to their simplicity in comparison with other alphabets existing in the present-day world. Furthermore, adoption of the letters from the Eng. alphabet allows us to use machines for the graphic representation of Eng., including typewriters.

The letters of the Eng. alphabet, however, do not provide all the symbols required by the significant WOL sounds. In order to get around such a situation, it is a common practice to use two letters to indicate other sounds, or to introduce some kind of superscript such as (′) (″), and (-). The former we call digraphs and the latter, diacritic marks. In general, learning to discriminate digraphs (consisting of two existing symbols) is easier than learning to discriminate diacritics which are entirely new symbols, since digraphs are mnemonically much better. Moreover, digraphs are easier to type than diacritics. One serious drawback of digraphs, however, is that ambiguities may occur as in English *ph* ('ha*ph*azard' vs. '*ph*oto'). If such ambiguities are suppressed, digraphs are preferred. In WOL, it is proposed not to include diacritic marks. Digraphs are allowed to the extent that they do not bring in ambiguity. The digraphs are *iu*, *iiu*, *eo*, *ao*, *sh*, *mw*, *mmw*, *ng*, and *nng*. The reasons for proposing these symbols are summarised below. Throughout this section, asterisked morphemes or words represent spellings.

The digraph *iu* for /u̇/ (as in **faiu* /faau̇/ 'stone') is introduced to distinguish the vowel from /i/ and /u/. The fact that the phonetic quality of /u̇/ is ambivalent between those of /i/ and /u/ justifies the composition of the digraph. An alternative might be to set up *u* for /u̇/ and *wu* for /u/, since it is more economical in terms of time, space, and labour in reading and writing to assign complex symbols to those sounds like /u/ which occur rarely, and simple symbols to frequently appearing sounds like /u̇/. Another supporting reason for this alternative might be that the original /u/ of the Oceanic languages corresponds to WOL /u̇/, whereas WOL /u/ is a later development. This alternative is not adopted, however, because then **mwu* would be ambiguous between **m-wu* /mu/ and **mw-u* /ṁu̇/. Actually, /mu/ does not occur in WOL while /ṁu̇/ does (e.g. /ṁu̇ccu̇/ '*to* complete'), which would allow us to establish a convention to the effect that, in such sequences, *w* always goes with *u*. Even in that case, writing /ṁu/ 'your' as **mwwu* would look very inelegant.

Both *eo* and *ao* (as in **leoleo* /ləələə/ 'fill with liquid' and **laolao* /lɔɔlɔɔ/ 'wavy') represent single long vowels. There is no short counterpart of either. The use of two vowel symbols is justified by the fact that they are long. Selection of the composite symbols *a* and *o* for *ao* and *e* and *o* for *eo* is motivated by the fact that the sound represented by *eo* is pronounced with the tongue in a position intermediate between that for *e* and that for *o*, while the sound represented by *ao* is pronounced with the tongue low as for *a*, but with the lips rounded as for *o*. *eo* and *ao*, wherever they appear, are each pronounced in only one way, and therefore there is no ambiguity. The WOL sound pattern does not permit sequences *e* and *o*, or *a* and *o*, without an intervening consonant or semivowel.

An alternative might be to reverse the letters as in *oa* instead of *ao* and *oe* instead of *eo*. This has to be decided upon during the upcoming orthography meeting.

The choice of the symbol *sh* is motivated by tradition as well as by similarity to the sound *sh* in the Eng. word 'shoes'. However, there are other alternatives that are equally plausible. It is strongly recommended that we use the same symbols for all the dialects of the Outer Islands so far as the sounds represented by *sh* and *cc* (or *c*) are concerned, because the interisland pronunciation differences are quite regular and predictable as shown below in:

			Alternative Spellings						
WOL	ULI	Satawal	I	II	III	IV	V	VI	VII
[š]	[c]	[r̥]	sh	sh	sh	sh	c	ch	ch
[cc]	[cc]	[cc]	cc	cc	c	ch	cc	cch	cc
([c])			(c)						

As already mentioned, WOL /c/ occurs only in loanwords. The decision has to be made at the orthography meeting.

mw which is pronounced with the tongue back approaching the velum is distinguished from plain *m*. Tradition favours the digraph, too.

As regards *ng*, our alphabet follows tradition, because the alternative *g* is commonly understood as indicating a non-nasal sound and sometimes people use *g* for the sound represented by *h* (as in **laho* 'to go').

Double sounds related to the above digraphs are represented by doubling the first symbol, as in *iiu*, *mmw*, and *nng*.

Besides the above digraphs, selection of simple symbols has also been given careful attention, particularly the following:

h. According to tradition, both *h* and *g* have been used for the same sound. Sometimes, one person may use both indiscriminately. The reason for proposing *h* is simply that the sound is fricative and basically voiceless, although it becomes voiced between two voiced vowels.

b and *bb*. The sound represented by *b* /ᵱ/ is basically a voiceless fricative, but it becomes voiced between voiced vowels. While this sound is a fricative, its long counterpart, *bb* /ṗṗ/ is a stop. There are several other alternative spellings to consider:

	Short	Long
1.	b	pw
2.	pw	ppw
3.	fw	ffw
4.	bw	bbw

Choice of *b* and *bb* is motivated by simplicity.

l. Although the sound is more or less like a flap [r] as already mentioned, we adopted the symbol *l* in view of the fact that the sound corresponds to [l] in the neighbouring languages and there is a separate sound, the resonant [r], to which the symbol *r* is more appropriately assigned.

4. Spelling Conventions

(1) Basic Principles

The next consideration is how to spell WOL words and sentences by means of the abovementioned alphabetic letters. In the first place, we have to decide in what manner sounds and letters are to be matched in actual words. There may be several alternatives.

One is to write down words in letters corresponding to their actual pronunciation. Since, for instance, the word for 'name' is pronounced as [iitę̞], this phonetic transcription would be used as the spelling for the word. This type of writing may be called the phonetic spelling. However, phonetic spelling would require the writer spelling in this way to pay an inordinate amount of attention to purely automatic allophonic variations which may be predicted from the sound environment in which they occur.

A second alternative is to spell words in letters corresponding to their phonemic representation. Since, for instance, the word for 'name' is represented phonemically as /iite/, the sequence **iite* would be used as the spelling. In the same way, 'my name' is **itei*, 'his name' **itale*, and 'our (excl.) names' **itemami*. This type of spelling convention may be called phonemic spelling.

A third alternative is to write down words in letters corresponding to their base form representation. For instance, the word for 'name' would be represented as **ita*. In the same way, 'my name' would be **itai*, 'his name' **itala* and 'our (excl.) names' **itamami*. As we have seen, base forms of words are set up by reducing any sounds caused by environments to their source sounds, that is, to those sounds which would be pronounced if no sound environment were present. This type of writing may be called base form spelling.

Other alternatives include combinations of the above three types of spelling, which will not be discussed here. Let us compare the phonemic and base form spellings to observe their merits and shortcomings.

As we saw in the examples just above, phonemic spelling is more faithful to actual pronunciation than base form spelling is. On the other hand, base form spelling is very neat in that, in general, one morpheme may be spelled in only one way, which is not the case with phonemic spelling. One of the most serious drawbacks of the latter system is that there must be two or three or more spellings for a great many WOL morphemes. Our example 'name' must be spelled as three different ways,**iite*, **ite*, and**ita* in spite of the fact that the differences are entirely predictable from the sound environment. The causative prefix must also have two different spellings, he- and ha- although the first variant may be derived from the second by the *a*-raising that is conditioned by a low vowel in the following syllable.

In general, a writing system need not reflect what native speakers can predict by general phonological rules (c.f. Lester 1974:141). This is tantamount to saying that a writing system should be a base form spelling, in which one morpheme is represented only by one spelling. Even English, in spite of so many irregular correspondences between sound and letter, has adopted an extensive degree of base form spelling (e.g. Chomsky and Halle 1968:48).

Compare the two types of spelling below and notice how the actual practice follows the base forms.

rough pronunciation	phonemic spelling	base form spelling
[pæts]	pat*s*	*pats*
[boyz]	boy*z*	*boys*
[æksɨz]	ax*ɨz*	*axes*
[peintid]	peint*id*	*painted*
[workt]	work*t*	*worked*
[pleid]	plei*d*	*played*
[politik]	politi*k*	*politic*
[politišən]	politi*sh*ian	*politician*

The one-morpheme one-spelling principle of the base form spelling has the following advantages among others.

(a) Reading and writing for meaning will be greatly facilitated, since one-morpheme one-shape contributes to quick word-recognition as well as to quick memorisation of spellings. This applies both to native speakers and to language learners. Observe the 'plural' suffix *-s* in the above Eng. examples. It has three different pronunciations [s], [z], and [ɨz], yet all of them are spelled the same way, i.e. *s*. As it is spelled in only one way, it allows a more rapid translation from spelling to meaning and vice versa than would spelling it in three different ways, say, *s*, *z*, and *iz*. One might say that this kind of one-morpheme one-shape spelling is a hindrance to those who are in the initial stages of learning to read. However, there is no evidence that such a system is a barrier to learning to read, even in the initial stages. Once a few simple general rules of pronunciation are observed, together with instructions as to how each letter is to be pronounced, it will be easy for the reader to pronounce each word correctly. Moreover, the ultimate goal of reading is not rapid pronunciation but quick recognition of meanings of words and sentences, to which one-morpheme one-spelling definitely contributes, since such a system will maintain a close correspondence between morphemes and their orthographic representations.

(b) The one-morpheme one-spelling principle will contribute to the simplicity of dictionaries. Instead of listing different forms of one word as two, three, or four separate entries, we need list only one form, and the rules of predictable pronunciations can be given in a few lines at the beginning of the dictionary. It would be pointless and clumsy for the orthography to indicate such predictable forms and include them in the dictionary as separate entries.

(c) Furthermore, in many cases the base form spelling allows different dialects to have the same or very similar spellings in spite of considerable differences in pronunciation. Predictable sound changes are in many cases limited to certain dialects and not to others. If such predictable sounds are not represented in spellings, the same spellings can be used for many dialectally different words. For example, observe the difference in phonemic representation in the following words:

ULI	WOL		Spelling
/maram/	/merame/	'moon'	marama
/maramal/	/maremali/	'moon of'	maramali

If we spell /e/ in WOL dialect as *a* in view of the predictability of /e/ from *a*, the same spelling can be used for both ULI and WOL dialects in spite of the difference in pronunciation. One important consequence of this is that speakers of one dialect can read texts written in the other dialect easily because they recognise many words which are spelled the same way in spite of different pronunciations. This situation exists in many other languages, including English and Chinese. For example, English is spoken in many different parts of the world, and speakers from one place, say Texas, may not at first understand easily the English spoken by a farmer in New Zealand. In spite of that, written English is easily understood by everyone. What this implies is that if the Administration of Yap District were to make written announcements, say, in the ULI dialect, then the Woleaian and Satawalese people would have no difficulty in reading them because of the many words spelled in the same way as in their own dialect.

Word boundaries will be marked by spaces. What constitutes a word for spelling purposes is dtermined by the sound patterns and grammatical structures of WOL (see Sohn 1975a for details). However, traditional practices will also have to be taken into account so far as options are allowed. In principle, each content or function word with or without affixes is considered a spelling unit, as shown below.

**Paangali yaremata nge re ccapara be re laho teramiya.*
/paaŋali yaremate ŋe re ccepare ꝑe re laxo teramiye/
'Everybody believes that he will go to heaven'.
**Semaliu maliumwashoho ye liia me lanni ruumwu wee yaala.*
/semalů malůṁašoxo ye liiye me lanni ruuṁ wee yaale/
'A thief killed him in his room'.

If two or more geographical or social dialects have different pronunciations for the same meaning, two cases may arise. First, the pronunciations may not be related at all, as in the use of WOL **ranga* and Faraulep *taiho* for 'turmeric'. Second, the pronunciations are so related that the general phonological rules we mentioned are able to reduce them to the same spelling, then they are automatically spelled the same way as in the case of ULI /maram/ and WOL /merame/ both as **marama* 'moon'. If they cannot be reduced to the same spelling, they have to be spelled differently:

Eastern WOL **peleehisi* 'blanket'
Western WOL **pelaihiti* 'blanket'

Which dialect of the Outer Islands is to be used for 'standard' or 'official' purposes should be decided by the speakers of the dialects taking into consideration political structure, geographical locations, population, etc.

(2) Examples

In view of the advantages discussed above, I propose that the WOL spelling conventions follow, in principle, the base form spelling. Relegating some other spelling-related conventions to the appendix, let us observe some examples of base form spellings below.

pronunciation	glosses	phonemic representation	proposed spelling
[u̇u̇we̥]	'neck'	/u̇u̇we/	iuwa
[u̇wei]	'my neck'	/u̇wei/	iuwai
[u̇wale̥]	'his neck'	/u̇wale/	iuwala
[walu̇welu̥̇]	'plant'	/walu̇welu̇/	waliuwaliu
[iteilaxo̥]	'I don't go.'	/i tei laxo/	I tai laho.
[yetailaxo̥]	'He doesn't go.'	/ye tai laxo/	Ye tai laho.
[merame̥]	'moon'	/merame/	marama
[maremali̥]	'moon of'	/maremali/	maramali
[tepaŋi]	'help him'	/tepaŋii/	tapangii
[xetapetape̥]	'to help'	/xetapetape/	hatapatapa
[xatə]	'make (him) climb'	/xatəə/	hateo
[xemɔɔwe̥]	'erase it'	/xemɔɔwe/	hamaoa
[ᵽunno̥]	'heart'	/ᵽunno/	bunna
[ᵽunnale̥]	'his heart'	/ᵽunnale/	bunnala
[kku̥̇]	'fingernail'	/kku̇/	kkiu
[kku̇]	'my fingernail'	/kku̇u̇/	kkiui
[kkutu]	'my spit'	/kkutuu/	kkutui

pronunciation	glosses	phonemic representation	proposed spelling
[meŋaax̯ulu̥]	'clothes of'	/meŋaaxulu/	mengaahuli
[peše]	'foot'	/pešee/	peshee
[i]	'I'	/i/	i
[si]	'we (incl.)'	/si/	si
[xaaŋu̥̇]	'I (ind. form)'	/xaaŋu̇/	haangiu
[še̥] (suffix)	'our (incl.)'	/še/	sha
[re̥] (suffix)	'their'	/re/	ra
[yai] (suffix)	'me'	/yai/	ai
[yei] (suffix)		/yei/	
[wai] (suffix)		/wai/	
[wei] (suffix)		/wei/	
[ye̥] (suffix)	'him, her, it'	/ye/	a
[we̥] (suffix)		/we/	
[(a)] (suffix)		/a/	
[tap̵eeye̥]	'follow him'	/tap̵eeye/	tabeea
[ya̮awe̥]	'mouth'	/yaawe/	yawa
[yewaare̥]	'their mouths'	/yewaare/	yawara
[siile̥]	'mother'	/siile/	sila
[silale̥]	'his mother'	/silale/	silala
[sileere̥]	'their mother'	/sileere/	silara
[limmelu̥̇]	'five animate objects'	/limmelu̇/	limamaliu
[iṁettaṁolu̥̇]	'the chief's house'	/iṁettaṁolu̇/	imwalitamwoliu
[wessilei]	'my mothers'	/wessilei/	welisilai
[weccapi̥]	'ancestors'	/weccapi/	welishapi
[yaúccale̥]	'weather'	/yaúccale/	yaiulirala

APPENDIX

Following the general recommendations of the Yap Outer Islands Orthography Committee (Kuroiwa 1973), I adopted the following alphabet and spelling conventions for a reference grammar of Woleaian (Sohn 1975a and Woleaian-English dictionary (Sohn and Tawerilmang 1976). For related discussions, see Sohn (1975a: Chapter 2).

(1) The WOL Alphabet

Consonants

simple	alphabetic symbols	double	alphabetic symbols
/p/	p	/pp/	pp
/t/	t	/tt/	tt
/c/	ch	/cc/	ch
/k/	k	/kk/	k
/f/	f	/ᵽᵽ/	bb
/s	s	/ff/	ff
/x/	g	/ss/	ss
/ᵽ/	b	/mm/	mm
/š/	sh	/nn/	n
/r/	r	/ŋŋ/	nng
/m/	m	/ṁṁ/	mmw
/n/	n		
/ŋ/	ng		
/ṁ/	mw		
/l/	l		

Vowels

/i/	i	/ii/	ii
/e/	e	/ee/	ee
/a/	a	/aa/	aa
/u̇/	iu	/u̇u̇/	iu
		/əə/	eo
/u/	u	/uu/	uu
/o/	o	/oo/	oo
		/ɔɔ/	oa

Semivowels

/w/	w
/y/	y

(2) Spelling Conventions

Almost all native speakers seem to prefer tradition and convenience to linguistic simplicity and clarity, at least at this stage of linguistic sophistication. This is quite understandable when we take into account the popular notion that writing systems are only for those who know the language. Some major conventions are as follows.

a. Final simple vowels which become voiceless in independent forms are not spelled. Thus, for instance, the following three words are to be spelled identically in spite of the differences in pronunciation.

[xaccu̥]	'good'	gach
[xacco̥]	'tickle'	gach
[xacce̥]	'fish smell'	gach

Moreover, in base form spelling, the third person singular object suffix would be represented as *a,* as in **giulaa* [xúla] 'know it', **liia* [liiye̥] 'kill it', and **gasiiua*]xasúúwe̥] 'erect it'. In the spelling adopted, these words are represented as **giula*, **liiy*, and **gasiuw*, respectively, thus entirely obscuring the formal identity of the grammatical morpheme

b. The vowel lengthening that occurs in nouns of certain sound combinations is disregarded in spelling, as in [iite̥] /iite/ 'name' **it*.

c. Except for (a) and (b) above, all sounds are, in principle, spelled as they are pronounced, as in [itei] 'my name' **itei*, [itale̥] 'his name' **ital*, [peše] 'foot' **peshe*, and [me] 'and' **me*. However, if a word consists only of a double consonant followed by a voiceless vowel, that vowel is spelled, as in [tti̥] 'to close' **tti*. Thus, spellings of [tti̥] and [tti] 'tea' **tti* are not distinguished.

d. The unit of spelling is the word, including compounds. Each word is preceded and followed by a space. If two words, one of which is a modifier, are phonologically close-knit and one cannot occur without the other, like a numeral and a classifier ([semalu̥] 'one animate object' **semal*), they form a compound.

(3) Examples

The examples given in Section 4 (2) are respelled as follows according to the conventions adopted.

**iuw* 'neck', **iuwei* 'my neck', **iuwal* 'his neck', **waliuwel* 'plant', **I tei lag* 'I don't go', **Ye tai lag* 'He doesn't go', **meram* 'moon', **maremal* 'moon of', **tepangi* 'help him', **getapetap* 'to help', **gateo* 'make (him) climb', **gemoaw* 'erase it', **bun* 'heart', **bunal* 'his heart', **kiu* fingernail, **kiu* 'my finger-nail', **kutu* 'my spit', **mengaagul* *'clothes of', **peshe* 'foot', **i* 'I', **si* 'we' (incl.), **gaang* 'I' (ind. form), **sh* 'our' (incl.), **r* 'their', **yai*, **yei*, **wai*, **wei* 'me', **y*, **w*, **zero* 'him, her, it', **tabeey* 'follow him', **yaw* 'mouth', **yewaar* 'their mouths', **sil* 'mother', **silal* *'his mother'*, **sileer* 'their mother', **limmel* 'five animate objects', **imwettamwol* 'the chief's house', **wessilei* 'my mothers', **wechap* 'ancestors', **yaiuchal* 'weather'.

Since the spelling conventions we have adopted are not those of the base form spelling, we have included a base form after each headword in the Woleaian-English dictionary (Sohn and Tawerilmang 1976).

Notes

1. This paper is a revised version of the one originally prepared for the Yap Outer Islands Orthography Committee which met in Colonia, Yap, from December 26, 1972 through January 5, 1973.
2. In Sohn (1971), which is reprinted in this volume, only /a/ was postulated as the conditioning factor for the dissimilative /a/ to /e/ raising. It has been found, however, that another low vowel, /ɔ/, also conditions the raising.
3. In Sohn (1971) for Woleaian and Sohn and Bender (1984) for Ulithian, **ya* is proposed for the third person object suffix. This, however, appears to be less satisfactory than the postulation of **a* as proposed in this paper.

Reprinted from *Studies in Micronesian Linguistics,* ed. by Byron W. Bender. 215-236 (1984). Canberra: Australian National University.

5. ROMANIZATION OF KOREAN: A CROSS-PHONEMIC APPROACH

1. A common practice in designing an alphabetic orthography is to comply with one of the following principles: (a) phonetic, usually broad, (b) phonemic, and (c) morphophonemic (or systematic phonemic).[1] While phonetic transcription is based more or less on the universal sound qualities of the phones the language in question happens to have, phonemic and morphophonemic transcriptions are entirely language-specific in that they are determined by the unique sound patterns of that particular language. The latter two transcriptions are more or less deviant from the actual pronunciations because phonemes, to a lesser degree, and morphophonemes, to a considerable degree, are abstractions devoid of neighboring phonological influence.

Hangŭl is a morphophonemic system in which, for example, 'the Yalu River' is transcribed as 압록강 whose phonemic transcription would be 암노깡 . In devising an orthography of an unwritten language, phonemic or morphophonemic transcription is preferred to phonetic transcription for the reason that it reflects much better the native speaker's psychological reality regarding the sound patterns of his language. For example, native speakers of Korean usually do not realize that there are differences between the two ㅂ sounds in 부부 [pubu] 'husband and wife', which are clearly distinctive to the speakers of some other languages such as English and Japanese. In general, a morphophonemic orthography is regarded as superior to a phonemic one. For one thing, one-morpheme one-shape contributes to quick morpheme- and word-recognition as well as to quick memory of spellings. This applies both to native speakers and to language learners. Observe the spelling of the 'plural' suffix -(*e*)*s* in English which is associated with three different phonemic forms /-s/, and /-z/, and /-ɨz/ as respectively in *books, cows,* and *buses/houses.* Also observe the Korean spelling 옷 'clothes' which is associated with such phonemic forms as /os/ (before a vowel), /ot/ (before a non-nasal consonant or pause), /on/ (before /n/), and /om/ (before /m/, as a variant). Second, as alluded to in the above, the one-morpheme one-spelling principle contributes to the simplicity of dictionaries. Instead of listing different phonemic forms of a morpheme as two, three or four entries, we can list only one form, and the phonological rules that enable the reader to predict the correct pronunciations can be given at the beginning of the dictionary. Furthermore, in many cases a morphophonemic orthography allows different dialects to have the same or very similar spellings in spite of large phonemic gaps. Predictable sound changes are in many cases limited to certain dialects and not to others. Observe, for example, the spelling 'ear' which is associated dialectally with such phonemic forms as /kwi/, /kü/, and /ki/. One important consequence of this is that speakers of one dialect can read texts written in the morphophonemic spellings of another (standard) dialect easily because they recognize many commonly spelled words in spite of different pronunciation. English is spoken in a wide area and speakers of one dialect, say Texas, may not at first understand easily the English spoken by a farmer in New Zealand. In spite of that, written English is easily understood by everyone in that it is, to a large extent, a morphophonemic writing system from which dialectally variant pronunciations can be derived by dialect-specific phonological rules.[2]

2. The concept of orthographic representation and that of romanization should not be identified, in that the former is primarily for the native speaker's writing and reading of his language whereas the latter is for the convenience of the foreigner who is not familiar with the language. That is, although the writer of romanization may be either the native speaker of the language or the foreigner, *it is intended for the foreigner to read* the words, phrases, and sentences of the language. While the speaker of the language has mastered the phonological rules to freely convert the orthography to speech and vice versa, the foreigner is totally ignorant of such language-specific phonolgical rules. Except in the case of phonetic transcription, therefore, there is no reasonable argument we could possibly advance in favor of the claim that romanization be in one-to-one correspondence with the orthography of the language which is a graphic representation of the native speaker's internalized knowledge of his sound patterns as well as of the morphemes and their combinations. As we are well aware, morphophonemic representation, whether in orthography or in romanization, requires the user of the system to master the rules of the complex phonemic alternations existing in the language, and

phonemic representation requires him to master the rules of allophonic variations.

It is improper and absured, therefore, to impose morphophonemic romanization on the foreigner who does not have any knowledge of the complicated sound patterns of the language. For example, Korean has such morphophonemic rules as neutralization of consonants (e.g., *pich* → /pit/ 'light'), nasalization (e.g., *cip-mun* → /cimmun/ 'house door'), liquidation (e.g., pan-lan → /pallan/ 'rebellion'), bilabialization/velarization (e.g., sin-mun →/simmun/'newspaper'; *sin-kan* →/singkan/'a new publication'), metathesis (e.g., *noh-ta*→/notha/ 'to place'), assibilation (e.g., *coh-so*→/cosso/'it's good'), palatalization (e.g., *kath-i* → /kachi/ 'together'), tensification (e.g., mith-patak → /mitppatak/ 'bottom'), *h*-weakening (e.g., *ahop* → /aop/ 'nine'), cluster simplification (e.g., *kaps* → /kap/ 'price'), vowel shortening (e.g., *hin-n*ūn → /hinnun/ 'white snow'), and *l/n* addition (e.g., *mul-yak* → /mullyak/ 'liquid medicine'; kkoch-iph → /kkonnip/ 'flower pedal'). How long would a foreigner have to learn such morphophonemic rules of Korean before he could possibly convert morphophonemic transcription into approximate pronunciation (i.e., phonetic representation). Thus, when spellings written in morphophonemic romanization are pronounced by a foreigner, they are frequently unintelligible to the native speaker. How many native speakers of Korean would understand what they mean when 'the Yalu River' is pronounced as [abloggang] and 'the Independence Gate' as [doglibmun] by a foreigner, who has no way of knowing how to convert them into the sensible pronunciations respectively of [amnokkang] and [tongnimmun].

It is frequently claimed that the morphophonemic romanization of Korean is advantageous in that it can easily be converted into *Hangǔl* at the expense of the convenience of the foreigner for whom romanization has its raison d'être. Suppose Koreans do not read English spellings well and English is to be hangǔrized, as in hangǔrization of English loanwords. Now as foreigners, do Koreans want to have, for their practical purposes, a transcription system which is faithful to the pronunciations of English written expressions or one which can be converted to English spellings? Do we want *knife* to be written as 크니페, instead of 나이프, *late night* to be written as 라테니 그흐트, instead of 레이트나이트 in order to serve the convenience of the English speaker to convert hangǔrization to English spellings and vice versa? Unfortunately, naive Koreans who do not know anything about English would have no way to recover approximate sounds of the words. How would they be expected to know such English pronunciation rules as those that [k] becomes silent in the initial position before *n* while it is actualized in non-initial position, as in *acknowledge*, *acne*, and *picnic*; *iCe#* is pronounced as [ayC]; *ɑCe#* is pronounced as [eyC]; and *igh* is pronounced as [ay]?

One might claim that morphophonemic romanization is useful for visual or silent reading as a mnemonic device, since the same morpheme is represented as the same form no matter where it appears. However, the naive foreigner is neither sensitive to the notion of morphemes, nor interested in morpheme analysis. For example, the foreigner, unless taught, would not be able to associate *dog* in *doglibmun* 'the Independence Gate' with the *dog* in *dogtang* 'a private bath'. Even if he did, what practical purposes, except for some scholarly reasons such as linguistic analysis of data, would it serve? It is precisely for the above-mentioned reasons that foreigners, scholars and laymen alike, vehemently refuse to use the existing romanization system of the Korean Government Ministry of Education, which is essentially morphophonemic (except for the use of *r* and *l*, which is phonetic).

To a much lesser degree, purely phonemic romanization of Korean is also not very desirable, if not unworkable, for the reason that users of the Roman alphabet have their own phonemic interdistinctions quite different from those of Koreans, thus perceiving certain different Korean phonemes as the same sounds and the same phonemes as different. Thus, for example, Americans perceive 불 'fire' and 풀 'grass' as the same *pul*, while perceiving the same phoneme ㄱ in 가극 'opera' as two different significant sounds, as in *kagŭk*. I propose, therefore, that romanization should not be based on language-specific, uni-phonemic principles but on the cross-linguistic perspective, i.e., on cross-phonemic principles.

English is an international language and most educated people in the present-day world know English to a variety of degrees. In designing Korean romanization, therefore, the English sound patterns and pronunciations associated with Roman letters and spellings should be the primary reference among all the languages using the Roman alphabet. It is my firm belief that an ideal romanization of Korean should at least take the bi-phonemic principles of Korean and English into account, not just one of them. This is particularly the case because our long-cherished desire is to have a unified system of romanization that will be acceptable to both Koreans and non-Koreans at the same time for both academic and general purposes.

3. Out of some two dozens of romanization systems of Korean that have appeared in print (cf. Martin, et. al 1967 and Klein 1979: 195-197), the most widely used ones are the McCune-Reischauer (hereafter, M-R) system, the Korean Government Ministry of Education (hereafter, MOE) system,

and the Yale-Martin (hereafter Y-M) system.[3] Being a morphophonemic romanization which adheres closely to the *Hangŭl* spelling, the Y-M system purports, like *Hangŭl*, to retain all relevant morphophonemic information in words. Since it is linguistically very rigorous, does not employ diacritics, and is convenient for linguists of Korean to write and read, it has become the most popular among recent linguists involved in the structural analysis of the Korean language such as for dictionaries, grammars, and linguistic papers. However, it has never been diffused to the general public, Korean or non-Korean, due mainly to the unfamiliar use of certain symbols (e.g., *e* for 어, *u* for 으, *c* for ㅈ) and deviation from the actual pronunciation of Korean expressions.

The MOE system, which is also essentially morphophonemic, has been used for the past twenty-five years mainly by Korean government agencies. Although it is convenient for the native speaker of Korean to use, it has never been popular among foreigners due to the weaknesses of the following sort (quoted from Austerlitz, et al. 1980):

(1) The values assigned to some of the symbols in the system differ from the values that Koreans have learned to apply to the same symbols when writing English words.
(2) The choice of the letter symbols *b*, *d*, *g* seems unfortunate, since romanized forms often clash with English words having quite different meanings and sometimes unpleasant connotations: *bag*, *bug*, *gag*, *gab*, *jug*, *dog-rib*.
(3) It often requires considerable effort for the English speaker to learn how to pronounce intelligibly Korean words written according to the Ministry of Education system.

Since they are transliterations of the *Hangŭl* spelling, both the Y-M system and the MOE system of romanization have the advantage of being easily reduced to *Hangŭl* and vice versa. These systems, however, require the writer to have a good command of *Hangŭl* and the reader to have a good knowledge of the complicated set of phonological rules in order to arrive at the phonetic representations. This may not be a problem at all to the speaker of Korean because all he has to do is to learn the Roman letter symbols corresponding, one-to-one, to the *Hangŭl* letters, but is extremely painstaking for general non-Koreans because they must learn them all, including the phonological rules. As mentioned earlier, the goal of romanizing Korean should be for the convenience of non-Koreans, for they are the ones who need romanization.

It is for the above-mentioned reasons that, being primarily phonetic, the M-R system, in spite of some obvious defects, has widely been used by and for non-Koreans for the past forty some years. It is being employed by such a wide variety of people (Koreans as well as non-Koreans) as library cataloguers, humanists, social scientists, natural scientists, various other professionals, as well as those involved in the tourist industry and the general public. One intrinsic weakness this system has, however, is the proliferation of diacritical marks (e.g., *ŏ* for 어, *ŭ* for 으, *ch'* for ㅊ, *p'* for ㅍ, *han'gŭl* for 한글). A serious but unavoidable difficulty posed by this system for the native speaker of Korean is, as has been pointed out by many, that it "prescribes writing phonetic distinctions that are outside the linguistic awareness of the native speaker, who must learn to overdifferentiate elements in the sound system of his own language; to produce correctly the romanized form of the word *pubu* 'husband and wife' a Korean must learn to write the first syllable differently from the second, though to him they sound identical" (Austerlitz, et al. 1980). Since it is based on (broad) phonetic transcription, the M-R system is unable, in many cases, to provide details of morphophonemic information in multi-morphemic words, as in *Tongnimmun* 'the Independence Gate' which does not reveal the word *tongnip* 'indepencence', nor *tok* 'isolation' and *rip* 'standing'. As previously pointed out, morphophonemic information in a word is far less important than the word itself to general non-Koreans, just as we would not want such English homonyms as *meat/meet*, *tail/tale*, and *knight/night* to be hangŭrized differently and such multi-morphemic words as *politician to be hang*ŭrized morphemically as 포리틱이안. In the same vein, the fact that the M-R system cannot easily be reduced to the *Hangŭl* spelling and vice versa should not be a serious problem at all either to the reader or writer of the system. Such reduction would be meaningless to those who do not know Korean, whereas reduction can easily be done anyway by those who speak and write Korean. Furthermore, since the *Hangŭl* spelling contains some inherent difficulties (e.g., unwritten *sai siot*) and even educated native speakers frequently make *Hangŭl* spelling mistakes, the convertibility criterion does not seem to be very revealing.

At this time when a unified system of romanization of Korean is lacking, it is very encouraging to note that modifications to both the MOE system and the M-R system have recently been proposed, the former in 1978 by the Ministry of Education itself and the latter in 1981 by a group of scholars in the United States of which I am a part (Austerlitz, et al. ibid.).

The changes proposed by the Ministry of Education (MOE), i.e., writing the vowels in the same way as the M-R system and easing their strict morphophonemic spelling convention to a considerable extent, are a great step forward to the prospect of having a unified standard romanization of Korean. The MOE recommended no change to the romanization of the symbols *b*, *d*, *g*, and *j* for the lax consonants ㅂ, ㄷ, ㄱ, and ㅈ, respectively, with which non-Koreans are not satisfied when they appear in non-medial positions. As pointed out by H. Lee (1979:149), the MOE proposal is a compromise, especially in the transcription of consonants, between phonemic and morphophonemic spellings. This, however, would not be of much benefit either to Koreans or to non-Koreans, because such a system can be reduced neither to the Korean *Hangůl* spelling nor to the Korean pronunciation, as in *sognisan* for 속리산, which is written *soglisan* under the existing MOE system and *songnisan* under the M-R system.

The M-R system and its applications were examined at the Workshop Conference on Korean Romanization held at the Center for Korean Studies of the University of Hawaii in June 1981. The outcome of the conference is reported in Austerlitz, et al. (ibid.). Accepting the basic principles of the M-R system, such as the phonetic representation of Korean words and the choice of letters, and realizing that users of romanization differ in their need for precision, we made a variety of suggestions and proposed possible options, including the following, among other things.

(1) We suggested that the diacritic ˘ be replaced by a dot (or a single tick ', in typing), pointing out that it can actually be omitted when no confusion would be resulted.
(2) We saw no compelling reason to retain the apostrophe in *a'e*, *o'e*, and *n'g* to set the sounds apart.
(3) We invited consideration of substituting the letter *h* for the apostrophe to mark the aspirate consonants (*ph*, *th*, *kh*, *chh*, instead of *p'*, *t'*, *k'*, *ch'*).
(4) We recommended symbols for certain obsolete *Hangůl* letters.
(5) Recognizing some inconsistencies in the M-R system, we recommended the unified practice of representing both the "hidden" *sai siot* and the written *sai siot* (e.g., *sakȯn* for 삿건, *yongkȯn* for 용건).
(6) We recommended that dialect forms explicitly recognized in the *Hangůl* spelling be preserved in romanization (e.g., North Korean *rodong* and *nyȯja*).
(7) We recommended that *shwi* be simplified to *swi*.

(8) through (33). We made extensive proposals which address questions of word division, capitalization, and punctuation. In (8), for example, we recommended that, contrary to *Hangŭl* conventions, the particle be written separately (e.g., *mul i* 'water (as subject)', *nŏ to* 'you too', *nŏ rŭl* 'you (as object)', *i kŏt i* 'this (as subject)').

4. Realizing that the goal of romanization is to help non-Koreans read Korean and that a cross-phonemic approach is an essential method for an ideal romanization, I would like to propose the following alternative for consideration toward a unified standard romanization. The experiments I have conducted support my proposal to a considerable extent.[4]

(1) Vowel Symbols

Since the vowel symbols proposed by the MOE in 1978 are the same as those of the M-R system, I have nothing to add except suggesting that, as proposed by Austerlitz, et al., the breve (˘) be replaced with a dot (·) (or ' in typing) and the diacritic may be dispensed with in less official transcriptions such as in personal names:[5]

i		u̇		u
e		ȯ		o
	ae		a	

Since both diacritics and digraphs have good points and bad points, it is hard to weigh their relative merits.[6] One serious drawback of diacritics is that they do not carry any conventionalized sound quality. Another minor weakness is the inconvenience in typing. As regards digraphs, English speakers usually pronounce them not as monophthongs but as diphthongs or a sequence of two vowels. Another difficulty digraphs have is associated with the problem of sound division, if not homophone clashes, as in *geueola*, *mueos*, and *geeuleun*. Even the speakers of Korean may have some difficulty in immediately pronouncing them correctly.

I tend to favor the diacritical practice for 어 and 으, but not for 애, because (a) it has become a long tradition among non-Koreans; (b) a diacritic mark indicates the monophthongal nature of the vowels; (c) non-Koreans can guess that the sound values of *ȯ* and *u̇* are similar at least to those of *o* and *u*, respectively; and (d) the diacritical mark can easily be left out when deemed unessential, without losing information. A further support to my preference of the diacritical mark for 어 and 으 and the digraph for 애 comes from one of my experiments.[7] The majority of the subjects prefer *ŭ* to *u* or *eu* for 으, *ŏ* to *eo*, *e*, or *o* for 어, and *ae* to *e*, *ă*, or *ay* for 애.

(2) Consonant Symbols

The 1978 MOE proposal still prefers to maintain *b*, *d*, *j*, *g* for ㅂ, ㄷ, ㅈ, ㄱ, respectively, and spell them according to the uni-phonemic principle, i.e., regardless of allophonic variations in Korean (unless they become other phonemes as a result of morphophonemic alternations). Non-Koreans, on the other hand, still, in general, prefer the M-R spelling where, for example, the initial and final ㅂ (*p*) is distinguished from the intervocalic ㅂ (*b*) in that voicing is distinctive to English speakers.[8]

In spite of the anticipated initial resistance from many naive non-Koreans, I propose to use the same voiced consonant for the word-initial (I) and word-medial intervocalic (M) position and the voiceless consonant for the word-final and pre-consonantal (F) position. Observe the following comparison table.

	ㅂ			ㄷ			ㅈ			ㄱ		
	I	*M*	*F*	*I*	*M*	*F*	*I*	*M*	*F*	*I*	*M*	*F*
MOE	b	b	b	d	d	d	j	j	j	g	g	g
M-R	p	b	p	t	d	t	ch	j	(t)	k	g	k
PROPOSED	b	b	p	d	d	t	j	j	(t)	g	g	k

The following points are the rationale behind the above proposal.

(a) As pointed out earlier, the M-R system is very difficult for Koreans to use unless they get some training, because it requires using different Roman letters for one and the same Korean phoneme or *Hangŭl* letter. This is particularly the case with the initial lax consonants which are spelled *p*, *t*, *k*, *ch* and the medial counterparts which are spelled *b*, *d*, *g*, *j*. By spelling the initial and intervocalic consonants in the same way (e.g., *b-b*), we can relieve the MOE's reasonable concern that Koreans, as major writers (not readers) of the romanization, are unable to perceive the distinction between the two different sound qualities.[9]

(b) English speakers perceive Korean lax consonants as identical with their own voiceless aspirated phonemes, pronouncing the initial *p*, *t*, *k*, *ch* in the M-R system always like ㅍ, ㅌ, ㅋ, ㅊ, respectively. Thus, for example, the family name 변, when spelled as *Pyŏn*, is pronounced by an English speaker as unwanted 편, which is another family name in Korea. By using *b* for ㅂ, such undesirable homophone clashes can be averted.

(c) Initial lax consonants become voiced after another word when they occur in the same phrase. For example, [tal] 'moon' becomes [dal] after [k^hɨn] 'big', as in [k^hɨn dal] 'a big moon'. This phenomenon also supports the suggestion that the initial and medial lax consonants be spelled identically.[10]

(d) One very unsatisfactory practice of the M-R system is the use of *ch* for the lax consonant ㅈ and *ch'* for the aspirate ㅊ, in spite of the fact that *h* is used as aspiration in the writings of many languages. The present proposal would remove such dissatisfaction, eliminating pronunciation confusion, for example, in the family names *Chŏn* 전 (全) and *Ch'ŏn* 천(千) as spelled according to the M-R system. To my surprise, all the five Korean-English bilingual students I tested wrote *j* for the initial sound of the personal name 전명희.[11] Also notice in footnote 7 (Table 2) that five Americans prefer *j* and four *ch* for the initial consonant of 정.

(e) The phonetic distinction between a lax consonant (e.g., ㅂ) and the corresponding aspirated consonant (e.g., ㅍ) is one of the hardest part for an English speaker to recognize and produce, since aspiration is not distinctive to him.[12] The best way to have an English speaker recognize ㅂ and ㅍ as distinct is to have him use *b* and *p*, respectively, since voicing is distinctive to him.

(f) Similarly, the phonetic distinction between a lax consonant (e.g., ㅂ) and the corresponding voiced consonant (e.g., *b*) in the initial position is very hard for a Korean to perceive, since voicing is not distinctive to him. When an English speaker pronounces ㅂ in the initial position like English *b*, therefore, no Korean would fail to immediately recognize it as ㅂ (probably along with some foreignism), but not as any other Korean consonant. We hangurize *b* as ㅂ and *p* as ㅍ, as in *Bible* 바이블 and *Peter* 피터. Why can't we do the reverse?

(g) Word-final consonants seem to be perceived by Koreans differently from the initial and medial consonants. According to my experiment with five Korean-English bilingual students, all five spelled 바보 as *babo*, not as *pabo*. However, no one used a voiced consonant at the word-final position. For example, 강현숙 is spelled as *Kang Hyun Suk, Gang Hyon Sook, Ghang Hyun Sook, Gang hyun suk,* and *Gang Hyun Sook*. Notice that *g* is used for the initial ㄱ sound in four cases but all of them used *k* for the final ㄱ sound. The same five bilingual students plus one American student who did not know any Korean writing all agreed that they would spell the Korean word 밥 'rice' as *bap* or *pap* (in that order of preference) but not *bab* or *pab*. None of the nine American students I experimented with used a voiced consonant symbol for Korean word-final or pre-consonantal lax consonants.

(h) As in Korean, English voiceless stops are hardly released in word-final position, whereas English voiced consonants are usually released in the same position. In this respect also, a voiceless consonant (e.g., *p*) is preferable to a voiced consonant (e.g., *b*) in word-final position.

(i) Using a voiceless consonant at the final position would prevent clashes with English words having unpleasant connotations: *bak* instead of *bag*, *buk* instead of *bug*, *gak* instead of *gag*, *dongnip* instead of *doglib*, etc. While *bag*, for example, is pronounced as it is in English, *bak* is often pronounced by an English speaker as it is in Korean.

(j) The MOE's hitherto imbalanced treatment of ㄹ by spelling *r*(I)-*r*(M)-*l*(F) would now be regularized along with the proposed pattern *b*-*b*-*p*, etc.

Once the above proposal regarding the lax consonants is accepted, the aspirate and tense consonants will not cause any difficulty. One suggestion may be to retain the MOE symbols. A slightly more reasonable idea is to retain the MOE symbols for the aspirate consonants and the palatal tense stop (i.e., *jj*) while adopting the M-R symbols for the other tense consonants (i.e., *pp*, *tt*, and *kk*). The reason is that a tense consonant is not voiced under any circumstances. The symbol *jj* appears unavoidable, however, because the M-R system uses a trigraph (i.e., *tch*) which must be avoided if possible.[13] One might propose to use *h* for the aspiration, as in *ph*, *th*, *kh*, in line with *ch*, especially because *p* (ㅍ), *t* (ㅌ), *k* (ㅋ) and the word-final *p* (ㅂ), *t* (ㄷ), *k* (ㄱ) are graphically identical.[14] I don't think *h* is quite necessary, however. For one thing, aspirate consonants never occur in word-final position, thus they are in complementary distribution with the corresponding word-final lax consonants. Second, as noticed in many varieties of the hangǔrization of English loanwords, Koreans relate Korean lax consonants to English voiced consonants and word-final voiceless consonants.[15] English non-final voiceless consonants are, on the other hand, transcribed with Korean aspirate consonants. Examples are: *body* 보디, *tube* 튜브, *gap* 갭, *block* 블록, *epic* 에픽, *attack* 아택, *step* 스텝, snap 스냅, *stop* 스톱. The situation can be shown more explicitly as follows, taking the bilabial consonants as an example:

Current Hangŭrization			*Proposed Romanization*	
English	*Korean*		*Korean*	*English*
final *b* ⟶	브	(ㅂ in 브 is non-final.)	non-final ㅂ ⟶	*b*
non-final *b* ⟶	ㅂ			
final *p* ⟶	ㅂ		final ㅂ ⟶	*p*
non-final *p* ⟶	ㅍ		non-final ㅍ ⟶	*p*

(There is no final ㅍ in Korean.)

The present proposal, therefore, is essentially to reverse the currently used hangŭrization to romanization as far as the bilabial and velar consonants go. Third, use of *ph* and *th* is not favorable because English speakers usually pronounce them as [f] and [θ]/[ð], respectively, as in *philosophy* and *thing/this*. Finally, other things being equal, we should honor the tradition, in this case the MOE practice. Neither MOE nor M-R uses *h* for aspirate stops.

Based on the above observations, the aspirate and tense series are proposed to be transcribed as follows:

	ㅍ	ㅃ	ㅌ	ㄸ	ㅊ	ㅉ	ㅋ	ㄲ
MOE	p	bb	t	dd	ch	jj	k	gg
M-R	p'	pp	t'	tt	ch'	tch	k'	kk
PROPOSED	*p*	*pp*	*t*	*tt*	*ch*	*jj*	*k*	*kk*

For the rest of the symbols, MOE and M-R are in complete agreement:

MOE/M-R/	ㅅ	ㅆ	ㅎ	ㅁ	ㄴ	ㅇ	ㄹ (I,M)	ㄹ (F)
PROPOSED	s	ss	h	m	n	ng	r	l

(3) Spelling Convention

As previously pointed out, the more significant difference between MOE and M-R is in the spelling convention than in the selection of symbols, with MOE being morphophonemic and M-R (broad) phonetic. It is proposed that we essentially follow the M-R spelling convention, i.e., spell as they are pronounced, but (a) within the constraint of the letter symbols proposed above with cross-phonemic considerations, and (b) according, in principle, to the word-divisions proposed in Austerlitz, et al. (ibid.), which stipulates that "sound changes are written within a solid word, but not across a space or a hyphen".[16] These are illustrated below.

	부부 'husband & wife'	가극 'opera'	거북 'turtle'	전주 (place name)
MOE	bubu	gageug	geobug	Jeonju
M-R	pubu	kagŭk	kŏbuk	Chŏnju
PROPOSED	bubu	gagu̇k	gȯbuk	Jȯnju

	목포 (place name)	압록강 'the Yalu River'	충청북도 'North Chungchong Province'
MOE	Mogpo	Abroggang	Chungcheongbuk-do
M-R	Mokp'o	Amnokkang	Ch'ungchŏngbuk-to
PROPOSED	Mokpo	Amnok-gang	Chungchȯng buk-do

	공짜 'free charge'	날자 'a date'	한글 'the Korean alphabet'	대한민국 'Republic of Korea'
MOE	gongjja	nalja	hangeul	Daehanmingug
M-R	gongtcha	nalcha	han'gŭl	Taehanmin'guk
PROPOSED	gongjja	naljja	hangu̇l	Daehan minguk

	법률을 'regulations (as object)'	새집 'a new house'	한국과 'Korea and ...'	종로구 'Jongno Ward'
MOE	beobryureul	sae jib	Hanguggwa	Jongro-gu
M-R	pŏmyurŭl	sae chip	Han'gukkwa	Chongno-gu
PROPOSED	bȯmyul u̇l	sae jip	Hanguk gwa	Jongno-gu

	공산측의 주장 'the assertions of the Communist side'
MOE	gongsancheugeui jujang
M-R	kongsanch'ŭgŭi chujang
PROPOSED	gongsanchu̇k u̇i jujang

Needless to say, the proposals I have advanced in this paper are neither exhaustive nor completely consistent (e.g., use of *jj* for ㅈㅈ). I have brought them up as a possible candidate for a unified system. Use of romanization has recently been accelerated both in Korea and abroad, in Korea with the MOE system and abroad with the M-R system. It is deplorable to see, for example, the same maps with entirely different Roman symbols and spellings. It is strongly suggested, therefore, that a unified romanization system be worked out through joint efforts between Korean soholars and government officials in Korea on one hand and linguists and other professionals in the United States on the other. This is not an easy job, of course, because our compromise should be not only between the MOE system and the M-R system but with our long romanization traditions of the users as well. Once we have an ideal system incorporating the best features of the existing systems and, thus, satisfying Koreans and non-Koreans alike, all existing major and minor systems will naturally be in disuse, except perhaps for the Y-M system for linguistic purposes.

Notes

1. I presented a part of the proposal discussed in this paper at the opening session of the Workshop Conference on Korean Romanization held on June 3-6, 1981 at the University of Hawaii Center for Korean Studies. I am grateful to my colleague Dong Jae Lee for allowing me to experiment with his students and for providing me with helpful comments on this paper.
2. In 1972 I designed a morphophonemically oriented alphabetic orthography for Woleaian, a hitherto unwritten Micronesian language. When my draft proposal was presented to the Yap Orthography Committee, the native speakers of the language showed considerable dissatisfaction not with the symbols but with the spelling conventions. They were not linguistically sophisticated enough to be bothered by a set of morphophonemic rules which they had to follow in order to spell and read their words. As a result, I ended up with a phonemic orthography, which is being used by the speakers of the language. In Sohn and Tawerilmang (1976), however, each headword is written in the phonemic spelling followed in parentheses by the corresponding morphophonemic spelling.
3. C. B. Kim (1978) has examined the three systems plus the 1978 MOE draft proposal on the basis of his five criteria, concluding that Y-M and M-R are the best systems among them, MOE (1978) the next, and the existing MOE (1959) the worst. Similarly, Klein (1979) has also compared the three systems by way of experiments, the result being that M-R (for general purposes) and M-Y (for linguistic purposes) are better systems than MOE.
4. I have conducted two experiments with University of Hawaii students in Honolulu, the first one in May 1981 with five Korean-English bilingual students who immigrated to Hawaii over ten years ago, and the second one in April 1982 with nine American students in the Elementary Korean class, who have learned Korean for only two semesters. As a matter of convenience, the former will be called Experiment I and the latter Experiment II. The

students in Experiment I were not familiar with any romanization systems, whereas the students in Experiment II had some familiarity with the M-R system but were hardly able to use them.

5. The symbols *u̇* and *ȯ* are used in some Micronesian orthographies (including the Trukese one) to represent the central vowels. Moreover, the breve (˘) may be misunderstood as indicating a short vowel.
6. As an evaluation device for the adequacy of a romanization system, Koo (1975) set up the following hierarchical categories: phonological rules, phonetic symbols, diacritics, and digraphs, saying that the system that employs fewer in each category and in a lower hierarchy should be evaluated as better. This means that, in principle, digraphs are better than diacritics. In designing the romanized orthography of Woleaian, I employed the digraph *iu* for the central high vowel, *oa* for the low back vowel, and *eo* for the midcentral vowel (Sohn 1975a and Sohn and Tawerilmang 1976). This was prompted by the inherent length of these vowels and their roundness feature.
7. In Experiment II, I asked the nine American students to choose the best spelling for each Korean word given in Table 1. The result is given in Table 2.

Table 1

은	Eun	Ŭn	Un		
정	Jeong	Jŏng	Jong	Chŏng	Chong
권	Kwŏn	Gweon	Gwŏn	Kwen	Kwon
애	ae	e	ă	ay	

Table 2

Hangul	STUDENTS 1	2	3	4	5	6	7	8	9
은	Ŭn	Ŭn	Ŭn	Un	Eun	Un	Ŭn	Ŭn	Un
정	Chŏng	Jŏng	Chŏng	Jeong	Chŏng	Jeong	Chŏng	Jeong	Jeong
권	Gwŏn	Gwŏn	Kwŏn	Kwŏn	Kwŏn	Kwŏn	Kwŏn	Kwŏn	Kwŏn
애	ae	ae	e	ae	?	ae	e	ae	?

The following statistics is obtained from Table 2:

으 :	ŭ	5 students	u	3 students	eu	1 student		
어 :	ŏ	14	eo	4	e	0	o	0
애 :	ae	5	e	2	ă	0	ay	0

8. In transcribing my pronunciations in Experiment II, students were inconsistent in initial and intervocalic positions, but generally speaking, they perceived Korean lax consonants in a way essentially supportive of the M-R system. Some examples are given below:

Table 3

	1	2	3	4
경기도	kyŭng gi do	kyung gi do	kyong *k*i do	kyung *k*i do
동대문구	tong dae mun gu	*d*ong dae mun *k*uk	tong dae mun gook	to dae mungu
바보	pa bo	*b*aa bo	pabo	pabo
권구택	kwŏn *k*u tĕk	kwaun goo tăk	won *p*u tack	hwon bu tek
조정춘	cho *ch*ŭng chun	*j*o jung choon	cho *ch*ung cheung	cho *ch*ŭng ch'ung

5	*6*	*7*	*8*
kyonggi-do	chun *k*ee do	kyung *k*i *t*o	kyun gi do
*d*ongdaemun-gu	*d*ongdaemoongoo	pun *t*e mun gu	*d*ong de mûn *k*û
pabo	*b*ah bo	pa-bo	pabo
kwon bu taek	quon goo tek	quan *p*u tek	kwon *k*u tehk
cho *ch*ung choon	*jo ch*ung choon	cho *ch*u chun	cho *ch*ung choong

9
chong i *t*ok
tong *t*aen nun guk
pa*p*o
kwon *p*u tack
cho *ch*un chun

Notice in the italic consonants in Table 3 that, in eight cases, voiced consonants are used where voiceless ones are expected, while, in twenty four cases, voiceless consonants are given where voiced ones are expected.

9. As observed in the examples given in footnotes 7 and 8, even some English speakers have difficulty in distinguishing them in running speech.
10. The final lax consonants are also voiced when followed by a vowel within the same phrase, as in 밥 이인분 'two serves of rice'. One difference, however, is that an initial lax consonant never becomes a part of the preceding syllable, thus maintaining the phonological identity of the word, whereas the final one, if and when voiced, must be a part of the following syllable, no longer functioning phonologically as a word-final ㅂ. As proposed in Austerlitz, et al. (1980), only phonological units of words are to be taken into account for romanization.
11. In Experiment I, the personal name in question was transcribed by the students as follows: *Jon Myong Hee, Jung Myung Hi, Jon myong hee, Jhun Meung Hee,* and *jun myong hi.*
12. Data from Experiment II shows that English speakers, even after having studied Korean for two semesters, can hardly distinguish between Korean lax and aspirate series. Some transcription examples are given below.

	1	*2*	*3*	*4*	*5*	*6*	*7*	*8*	*9*
최	*Chae*	*Chwe*	*Chwe*	*Ch'oe*	*Chwae*	*Chwa*	*chew*	*Chwe*	*Chae*
조	*Cho*	*Jo*	*Cho*	*Chô*	Cho	Jo	Cho	Cho	Cho
피	Pi	Pi	Pi	P'i	Bi	Pee	Pi	Phi	Pi
변	Pyŭn	Byun	Pyun	P'yun	Pyun	Byun	Byun	Pyon	Pyon

In order to help students compare the two sounds, I pronounced the word with an aspirate consonant first followed by the word with a lax consonant.

13. Besides, as observed previously, the symbol *j* is somewhat liked by English speakers for the sound ㅈ even in initial positions. My pronunciation of 장석진 in Experiment II, where 진 was uttered as tensed 찐, was transcribed by the nine American students as: *chang sŏk jin, jahng sauk jin, sun sock chin, chang sŏt ch'in, chang sŏk jin, chung suk jin, chang sot chin, chang suk jin*, and *chang sot chin*. It will not be terribly bad to use *jj* for ㅉ which is a low-frequency sound in Korean anyway.

14. As a matter of fact, the Y-M system of romanization uses *ph*, *th*, *ch*, *kh* for ㅍ, ㅌ, ㅊ, ㅋ, respectively.
15. The use of ㅂ and ㄱ for English final *p* and *k* may have been motivated by the fact that they (ㅂ and ㄱ) become voiced allophonically when followed by a vowel. The current hangŭrization uses ㅅ for English word-final *t*, as in *cerdit* 크레딧 and *cabinet* 캐비넷, due obviously to Koreans' morphophonemic habit to pronounce ㅅ as *t* in word-final position and as *s* before a vowel (e.g., 크레딧이 'credit (as subject)' and 크레딧을 'credit (as object)'.
16. Austerlitz, et al.'s overriding principle regarding word division and hyphenation is: "when in doubt, close up the word in question", requiring the rules to specify when to insert spaces and when to hyphenate the word in question.

Reprinted from *Korea Journal* 22.8:49-60 (1982).
Seoul: Korean National Commission for UNESCO.

CHAPTER 2
SYNTAX, SEMANTICS, AND PRAGMATICS

6. A RE-EXAMINATION OF 'AUXILIARY' VERB CONSTRUCTIONS IN KOREAN

1. Traditional grammars and dictionaries distinguish between 'main' and 'auxiliary' verbs in Korean. For example, *sal* 'lives' and *silh* 'is undesirable, is hateful' in (1) and (2) are 'main' verbs, wherease *siph* 'is desirable' is called an 'auxiliary' verb (e.g., Martin et al. 1967: 1060 and 1066).[1]

(1) na-nun tosi-eyse *sal*-ki *silh*-ta. 'I hate to live in cities.'
(2) na-nun tosi-eyse *sal*-ko *siph*-ta. 'I want to live in cities.

Choi (1965:244-45) classifies verbs as 'main' vs. 'auxiliary', depending on whether a verb can stand by itself in a predicative function or whether it necessarily follows another verb, thereby 'helping' it. When one applies this 'stand-by-itself' test to the above three verbs, as in (3) to (5), *siph* turns out to be 'auxiliary', because only (5) is ungrammatical.

(3) na-nun tosi-eyse sal-ass-ta. 'I lived in cities.'
(4) na-nun tosi-ka silh-ta. 'I hate cities.'
(5) *na-nun tosi-ka siph-ta. 'I like cities.'

Thus, in connection with 'auxiliary' verb constructions, by which I mean those constructions where an 'auxiliary' verb appears, we may say, in traditional terms, that in "*compound verb expressions*, ... the *main verb* merely tells what action or quality is under discussion ... and is otherwise frozen; the *auxiliary verb* completes the expression and fits it into the sentence with appropriate endings" (Martin and Lee 1969:133).

2. Many recent generative linguists, however, do not distinguish between the two classes of verbs, claiming implicitly or explicitly that the so-called 'auxiliary' verbs in Korean are nothing but 'main' verbs.[2] The major reason for this claim is that both of them have the same general syntactic behavior.

In the first place, both classes of verbs are dominated by the main verb node in deep structure. The framework for such deep structures is provided by the notion of sentence embedding called complementation. Within this framework, (1) and (2) are considered to have been derived from exactly the same deep structure sketched roughly as in (6).

(6)

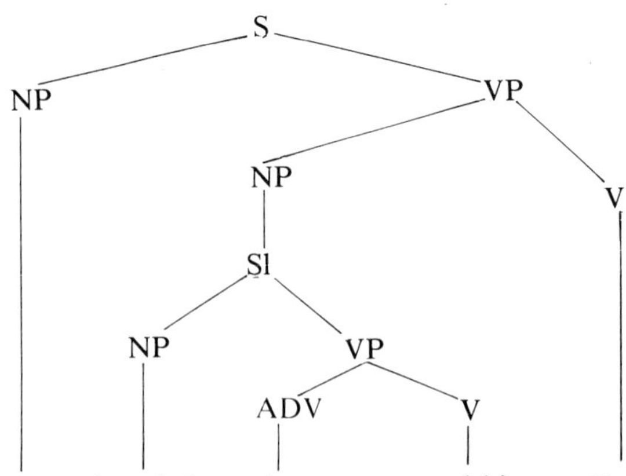

(1) na-nun (nay-ka) tosi-eyse sal-ki silh-ta.
(2) na-nun (nay-ka) tosi-eyse sal-ko siph-ta.

(6) shows that both *silh* and *siph* are dominated by the node V which stands for the main verb of the matrix sentence S and that *sal* is the verb of the embedded or complement sentence Sl. Thus, sentences like (1) and (2) are handled in the same framework of complementation as the sentences in (7), where the reflexes of the complement sentences (italicized) show up a little more clearly on the surface.[3]

(7) na-nun kupun-eykey *o-si-la*-ko malhay-ss-ta.
'I told him to come.'
na-nun *kupun-i o-si*-nun kes-ul a-n-ta.
'I know that he is coming.'
na-nun *kupun-i ka-si-ess*-ki-lul pala-n-ta.
'I hope that he has gone.'

The complementation treatment of an 'auxiliary' verb construction and the resultant claim that there is no such thing as 'auxiliary' verbs in Korean are quite in accord with recent linguistic efforts to search for conceptual structures underlying complex surface manifestations. A somewhat related treatment for English auxiliary verbs is made by Ross (1967), who argues that

(8) has five 'main' verbs (italicized), saying that each of these verbs is directly dominated by VP in deep structure.

(8) Boris *must have been being examined* by the captain.

One of the sources of his argument that 'auxiliary' verbs are 'main' verbs in English is Japanese 'auxiliary' constructions such as (9).

(9) Biru-ga tegami-o kai-te *ita*.
'Bill was writing a letter.'

Assigning to (9) the same underlying structure as (6) given above for Korean, Ross argues that the fact that *tegami-o kai-te* precedes the 'auxiliary' *ita* is the same as the fact that *tegami-o* precedes the 'main' *kaite*, that is, all objects precede their verbs in Japanese, while in English the same thing applies in reverse order. Thus, Ross considers that his hypothesis "auxiliaries are main verbs" can *explain* Greenberg's note that in SOV languages an 'auxiliary' verb follows the verb, while in SVO languages an 'auxiliary' precedes the verb.

Another type of syntactic characteristic, in addition to complementation, that both 'main' and 'auxiliary' verbs share is that they are subclassified in much the same way in terms of their inherent and selectional features. For example, almost all grammars and dictionaries of Korean distinguish between transitives, intransitives and adjectives as subsets of both 'main' and 'auxiliary' verbs, as illustrated in (10).

(10)

	main	*auxiliary*
transitive	mek 'eats'	po 'tries ... ing'
intransitive	sal 'lives'	ci 'gets to be'
adjective	celm 'is young'	siph 'is desirable'

Certain 'main' and 'auxiliary' verbs share the selectional property that they do not take any agent subject, as in *silh* 'is hateful' and *siph* 'is desirable', while others share the property that they take only an agent subject, as in *mek* and *po*. Certain 'main' and 'auxiliary' verbs share the property that they allow only verbs of action to be embedded in their complements, as in *sicakha* 'begins' (e.g., *pi-ka o-ki sickhan-ta* 'it starts raining') and *peli* 'finishes' (e.g., *pap-ul mek-e peli-ess-ta* 'I finished eating (rice)').

3. The intention of the present paper is to show that there is a strong syntactic and semantic cohesion between a 'main' verb and the cooccurring 'auxiliary' verb [4 and 5], and on this basis, to propose some reinterpretation

of and possible modifications to certain existing deep structure postulations for Korean 'auxiliary' constructions [6]. The non-technical term 'cohesion' here means the state of sticking together between two elements more tightly than either with a third, as in molecular attraction or in the husband-wife relation. The relevance of the term in this paper will be made clear as the discussion proceeds.

Three types of 'auxiliary' verbs as illustrated in (ll) will be discussed here. This means that I am excluding from the discussion the following types of compounds which are traditionally considered 'auxiliary': (a) defective noun + 'auxiliary' verb such as *chey-ha* 'pretends to', *cik-ha* 'is possible' and *ka-siph* 'seems like', and (b) negative particle + verb such as *ani-ha* 'does not do' and *mos-ha* 'cannot do'.[4]

(11) a. *A-type* (those following the 'infinitive suffix' *a*, *e*, or ∅)[5]

ci	a. gets to be, becomes b. gets (is) done
cwu	does as a favor for (a person)
ha	(transitivizes adjectives of human feeling)
iss	is in a state resulting from, is done
mek	(gives a strong derogatory flavor to the preceding word)
na	keeps (doing), does again and again
nay	does all the way
noh	does for later use
o	gradually (comes to do), keeps growing
peli	finishes, does completely
po	tries (doing to see how it will be), experiences
poi	looks (seems) like
ppaci	gets to be (old, rotten, bad, etc.) through and through
ssah	does to a great extent, extremely
talla/tao	please do (as a favor) for me
tay	does terribly, awfully, a lot
ttuli	(intensifies a transitive; makes an intransitive transitive)
tul/tuli	does into
tuli	does as a favor for a superior
twu	does something to get it out of the way, gets it done

b. *ko-type* (those following the 'gerund' *ko*)

iss	is doing
mal	finishes up doing
na	has just finished (doing)
siph	is desirable

c. *key-type* (those following the 'adverbial' *key*)
   ha causes, makes, permits
   mantul makes, causes, sets, forces
   toy turns out, gets to be, comes to pass

4. Syntactic Characteristics

The first characteristic property that all Korean 'auxiliary' verbs share is that they must be accompanied by a preceding verb. In generative terms, they obligatorily have a sentential complement in deep structure. This means that they cannot be the main verb of the most deeply embedded sentence. In this sense, 'auxiliary' verbs are the only pure 'complement' verbs. This constraint, which is tantamount to Choi's definition that a verb never functioning as an independent predicate is 'auxiliary', is the primary property for identifying the set of 'auxiliary' verbs within the larger class of verbs. The syntactico-semantic properties to be discussed below seem to be due more or less to the above primary constraint and can serve as supporting evidence for the existence of the 'auxiliary' set in Korean. In other words, such properties are closely related to the cohesion, both syntactic and semantic, existing between the verb of the sentential complement and the following 'auxiliary' verb. Such cohesion is evidently due to the very nature of the pure 'complement' verb.

The second property is that each 'auxiliary' verb is obligatorily preceded by its own fixed complementizer, *A*, *ko* or *key*, with the 'infinitival' *A* having an absolute majority of members. The 'auxiliary' verb *iss* appears with both *A* and *ko* with different resulting meanings, as will be seen in [6]. No 'main' complement verb takes any of these complementizers. In general, 'main' complement verbs have more freedom in taking different complementizers, as observed in (12).

(12) a. ku pun-i ka-n *kes*-ul moll-ass-ta.
   'I didn't know *that* he went.'
  a'. ku pun-i ka-ss-*um*-ul moll-ass-ta.
   (similar to the above)
  a''. ku pun-i ka-n *ci*-lul moll-ass-ta.
   'I didn't know if he went.'
  b. na-nun cwi-lul cap-*ki* silh-ta.
   'I hate to catch rats.'
  b'. na-nun cwi-lul cap-nun-*kes*-i silh-ta.
   'I hate the work of catching rats.'

The third property is that, in 'auxiliary' verb construction, the optional 'accusative' case marker *lul* is placed between the embedded verb and the 'auxiliary' verb if any case marker is allowed at all. This happens regardless of the transitive or intransitive nature of the 'auxiliary' verb and the kind of cooccurring complementizer. Observe (13).

(13) a. na-nun pap-ul mek-ko (-lul) iss-ess-ta.
'I was eating rice.'
b. na-nun keki-ey ka-ko (-lul *or* -ka) siph-ess-ta.
c. John-i o-key (-lul *or* -ka) toy-n-ta.
'John is expected to come.'
d. John-un wus-e (-lul) po-ass-ta.
'John tried laughing.'

In (13a), the 'auxiliary' verb *iss* is intransitive but no case marker except 'accusative' is allowed. In (13b), the 'adjective' verb *siph* allows both the 'nominative' *ka* and 'accusative' *lul*. So does the intransitive *toy* in (13c). The transitive *po* in (13d) of course allows only *lul*. 'Main' verb constructions do not have such a "*lul* constraint", as in (14).

(14) John-i ka-ss-ta nun kes-i (*-lul) nappu-ta.
'It is bad that John went.'
ku il-un ayssu-ki-ey (*-lul) talli-e iss-ta.
'It depends on (our) efforts.'
na-nun keki-ey ka-ki-ka (*-lul) silh-ta.
'I don't like to go there.'
ku kkoch-i po-ki-ka (*-lul) coh-ta.
'The flower is nice to look at.'

I boldly assume that the *lul* constraint is another outcome of the cohesion between an embedded verb and the associated 'auxiliary' verb. The case marker *lul* has the most varied functions of all the case markers, such as object, goal, location, purpose, duration, instrument (Cf. Martin et al. 1967:1295-6). It is a kind of 'elsewhere', 'unmarked' or 'neutral' case marker. The use of such a semantically quite neutral case marker, instead of other more marked ones, and the replaceability of *lul* for *ka* plus the complete optionality of a case marker (either *lul* or *ka*) in (13) before an 'auxiliary' verb all seem to indicate an aspect of the aforementioned cohesion.

The fourth property is that there are phenomena of assimilation in transitivity and causativity from an embedded verb to the following 'auxiliary' verb. Consider (15) and notice that the 'adjective' verb *coh* 'is good' occurs with the 'nominative' form of *Mary* in (15a) but with the 'accusative' form in (15b) suggesting that there is an assimilation of transitivity from *coh* to *ha*.

(15) a. na-nun Mary-*ka* coh-ta. 'I like Mary.'
(Lit. For me Mary is good.)
b. na-nun Mary-*lul* (but *-*ka*) coh-a (-*lul* but *-*ka*) ha-n-ta.
'I like Mary.'

None of the 'main' complement verbs reveal such a complete assimilation. At best, they allow optional intrusion of *lul* in certain limited cases, as observed in (16).

(16) a. John-i ka-n kes-i nappu-ta. 'It is bad that John went.'
a′. John-i (but *-ul) ka-n kes-ul a-n-ta.
'I know that John went.'
b. pi-ka o-n-ta. 'It rains.'
b′. pi-ka (*or marginally* -lul) o-ki (-lul) pala-n-ta.
'I hope it will rain.'
c. Mary-ka papo-ta. 'Mary is stupid.'
c′. Mary-ka (*or* -lul) papo-lako mit-nun-ta.
'I believe that Mary is stupid.'

For discussions of the Japanese equivalent to the (16c) type where the quotative complementizer *ko* is followed by a verb of 'thinking' or 'feeling', see Kuno (1972b). As for the assimilation from transitive to intransitive, observe the sentences in (17).

(17) a. na-nun kongpu-lul (*but* *ka) ha-n-ta. 'I study.'
b. na-nun kongpu-lul (*or* -ka) ha-ko (-lul *or* -ka) siph-ta.
'I want to study.'

This incomplete transitive-to-intransitive assimilation is also shared by 'main' verbs with syntactico-semantic features similar to *siph*, as in (18).

(18) na-nun kongpu-lul (*or* ka) ha-ki (-ka) *silh*-ta.
'I don't like to study.'

The causative sentence in (19) shows a similar phenomenon. The intransitive *ka* 'goes' is assimilated in causativity to the causative 'auxiliary' *ha,* allowing its subject *John* to take the 'accusative' or 'dative' case marker.

(19) na-nun John-i (*or* -ul *or* -eykey) ka-key (-lul) hay-ss-ta.
'I let (*or* made) John go.'

The fifth property is the assimilation of certain inherent syntactico-semantic features of the 'main' embedded verb to those of the following 'auxiliary' verb. In (20a), the verb *al* 'knows' has [−process] feature and its occurrence as the 'main' verb in an imperative or propositive sentence of simplex type is unnatural to me. However, as soon as it is followed by a [+process] 'auxiliary' verb, the sentences become perfectly natural as in (20b).

(20) a. ?ku muncey-lul a-sey-yo! '*Know the problem.'
?ku muncey-lul a-psi-ta. '*Let's know the problem.'
b. ku mun-cey-lul al-a po-se-yo! 'Try to understand the problem.'
ku muncey-lul al-a po-psi-ta. 'Let's try to understand the problem.'

This syntactic cohesion does not seem to appear in 'non-auxiliary' constructions, as illustrated in (21) where the 'main' [+process] verb *sicakha* 'starts' leaves the [−process] feature of *al* intact, hence the sentences remain ungrammatical.

(21) ?ku muncey-lul al-ki sicakha-sey-yo!
'*Start to know the problem.'
?ku muncey-lul al-ki sicakha-psi-ta.
'*Let's start to know the problem.'

The sixth property is that an embedded verb and the following 'auxiliary' matrix verb are inseparable in free scrambling forming a close-knit unit in movement (Cf. Yang 1972:121). Compare the 'non-auxiliary' construction in (22a), where all the scramblings are acceptable, with the 'auxiliary' construction in (22b), where no scrambling is allowed unless 2 and 3 go together in that order.

(22) a. na-nun ka-ki-ka silh-e-yo. 'I don't like to go.'
1 2 3
132, 213, 231, 312, 321
b. na-nun ka-ko-ka siph-e-yo. 'I would like to go.'
1 2 3
231, *132, *213, *312, *321

The seventh property is that almost all adverbs including manner and negative are not allowed to be inserted between an embedded verb and the following 'auxiliary' verb, as illustrated in (23b). This is not generally the case with 'non-auxiliary' constructions, as in (24).

(23) a. John-i {mopsi / an} po-ko siph-ta.
'I miss John indeed' and
'I do not miss John.'
b. *John-i po-ko {mopsi / an} siph-ta.

(24) John-i o-ki-lul {mopsi / an} kitali-n-ta.
'I am eagerly waiting for John to come' and
'I am not waiting for John to come.'

The eighth property is that no verbal suffixes, except for voice (passive or causative) and honorific (*si*), may be attached to an embedded verb before a complementizer + 'auxiliary' verb. Compare the 'auxiliary' constructions in (25) with the 'non-auxiliary' ones in (26), where the bracketed parts indicate complements and the italicized parts, verbal suffixes.

(25) na-nun [keki-ey ka] -A po-ass-ta. 'I went there (and found out...).'
na-nun [wul] -ko siph-ess-ta. 'I wanted to cry.'
na-nun Mary-lul [o] -key hay-ss-ta. 'I let (*or* made) Mary come.'

(26) na-nun [Mary-ka ka-*ss-e-ss*] -ki pala-ss-ta.
'I wished that Mary had gone.'
na-nun [Mary-ka ka-*ss-ta*-nun] kes-ul a-n-ta.
'I know that Mary went.'
[Mary-ka o-*ass-te-nya*] -ko mul-ess-ta.
'He asked me whether Mary came.'

Some 'main' complement verbs have the same property as 'auxiliary' ones with regard to the lack of verbal suffixes. Such 'main' verbs share with 'auxiliary' ones some other properties too, as noticed throughout this paper, implying that they constitute a sister set closest to the 'auxiliary' set in terms of complementation. (27) illustrates such 'main' verbs.

(27) pi-ka o-ki *sicakhay*-ss-ta. 'It started to rain.'
na-nun ka-ki *silh*-ess-ta. 'I hated to go.'

The ninth and last property is the so-called Equi-NP constraint which is operative between an embedded complement and the matrix 'auxiliary' sentence. Except in the causative *key ha* (e.g., *nay-ka ku-pun-i ka-key hay-ss-ta* 'I caused him to go'), at least one noun phrase associated with an embedded verb must be coreferential with a noun phrase associated with an 'auxiliary' verb, thus being deleted on the surface. In (28) the deleted noun phrases are given in parentheses.

(28) a. John-un [(John-i) talli] -e po-ass-ta. 'John tried running.'
b. na-nun [(nay-ka) cwuk] -ko siph-ess-ta. 'I wanted to die.'
c. ku pun-un na-lul [(nay-ka ku pun-eykey) coh] -a ha-n-ta. 'He likes me.'
d. ku congi-ka [(X-ka ku congi-lul) ccic] -e ci-ess-ta. 'The paper is torn.'

Most often, coreferentiality holds between the subject of the embedded verb and that of the 'auxiliary' verb as in (28a). This is another aspect of the cohesion between the embedded verb and the associated 'auxiliary' verb, in that the closeness in the relation between the two verbs is such that they tend to have one and the same subject. Here again, certain 'non-auxiliary' complement verbs go with the 'auxiliary' set, as in (29).

(29) ku pun-i [(ku pun-i) kongpuha] -ki sicakhay-ss-ta.
'He started to study.'
na-nun [(nay-ka) ka] -ki sih-ess-ta.
I hated to go.'

I do not claim that the above properties are exhaustive. One could present more on various grounds.

5. Semantic Characteristics

We have observed nine syntactic properties in the preceding section, all of which indicate in one way or another the fact that there is a close syntactic tie between the two verbs constituting an 'auxiliary' construction. It seems to me that all the above syntactic properties are not purely superficial but somehow reflect or are correlated with certain semantic cohesion between the two verbs. In the following, I will limit myself to the discussion of three cases where semantic cohesion is observable.

Let us begin with the three sentences in (30). Whether the three sentences differ only superficially, having one and the same meaning, or differ even in meaning, is a problem yet to be solved.

(30) a. na-nun ku pun-i o-key hay-ss-ta.
b. na-nun ku pun-ul o-key hay-ss-ta.
c. na-nun ku pun-eykey o-key hay-ss-ta.
'I made (*or* let) him come.'

In spite of the existing proposal that the three sentences are synonymous and therefore transformationally related to each other, my own position is that they are not the same in meaning, and that, although there is an equal semantic cohesion between *o* and *hay* in all three sentences, the closeness of the tie between *ku pun* and *o* is not the same in all of them. In the first place, (30a) has only a causative meaning, whereas (30b) and (30c) have both a causative and permissive meaning. I cannot think of any occasion in which (30a) is used as permission. If this is true, (30b) and (30c) are not derivable from (30a) unless we assign permissive meaning to the transformational process. Notice that the English translations given in (30) are merely rough approximations to the three sentences. Secondly, *ku pun* 'he' is the agent of *o* alone in (30a) without any direct semantic relation with *hay* whose agent is *na* 'I'. In (30b), *ku pun* is the patient of the compound *o-key hay* 'causes to come *or* permits to come'. The action referred to by the compound directly affects the patient *ku pun.* In (30c) on the other hand, *ku pun* is the experiencer of the compound *o-key hay,* which implies that the action indicated by the compound affects *ku pun* indirectly. Finally, it seems to me that there is a close semantic tie between *ku pun* and *o* in (30a), which is not the case with the other two sentences where the close tie lies only between the two verbs in relation to *ku pun.* This observation is supported partly by the following three sets of examples.

(31) a. *na-nun ku pun-i # o-key hay-ss-ta.
b. na-nun ku pun-ul # o-key hay-ss-ta.
c. na-nun ku pun-eykey # o-key hay-ss-ta.

(32) a. *ku pun-i na-nun o-key hay-ss-ta.
b. ku pun-ul na-nun o-key hay-ss-ta.
c. ku pun-eykey na-nun o-key hay-ss-ta.

(33) a. *na-nun ku pun-i caknyen-puthe o-key hay-ss-ta.
b. na-nun ku pun-ul caknyen-puthe o-key hay-ss-ta.
c. na-nun ku pun-eykey caknyen-puthe o-key hay-ss-ta.
'Since last year I have caused (*or* let) him to come.'

(31a) is unacceptable due to the phonological juncture separating *ku pun* and *o,* but (31b) and (31c) are perfectly acceptable because here the semantic compound *o* and *hay* functions as a unit in relation to the rest of the sentence. The ungrammaticality of (32a), where *ku pun* is detached from *o* and placed before *na,* implies that *ku pun* and *o* are again inseparably related and the boundary of free scrambling is not allowed between the two, which is not the case with the other two sentences. (33a) is not acceptable because the temporal adverbial *caknyen-puthe* 'since last year' goes with the higher verb *hay* only, while the tie between *ku pun* and *o* is not breakable by any higher adverbial.

All the above indicates that, first, there is semantic cohesion between *o* and *hay;* secondly, this cohesion makes *o* and *hay* function as a compound semantic unit; thirdly, this compound may have its own object in (30b) or experiencer in (30c) and, finally therefore, the three sentences are not synonymous. The kind of semantic cohesion observed between *o* and *hay* is rare with 'non-auxiliary' complement verbs, as illustrated in (34) where *kitali* 'waits' is a transitive complement verb. (34b) and (34c) are unacceptable to me.

(34) a. na-nun ku pun-i o-ki-lul kitali-ess-ta.
b. ?na-nun ku pun-ul o-ki-lul kitali-ess-ta.
c. *na-nun ku pun-eykey o-ki-lul kitali-ess-ta.
'I waited for him to come.'

An argument similar to the above could be made for the claim that syntactic assimilation in transitivity as observed in (15) through (18) is correlated with semantic assimilation.

The second case of semantic cohesion between an embedded and an 'auxiliary' verb may be observed through a sophisticated semantic judgment. Observe (35) and notice the two possible readings.

(35) kaykwuli-lul mek-e po-ass-ta.
a. I [tried] [eating frogs].
b. I [tried eating] [frogs].

To my knowledge, no one has proposed different deep structures for the possible two readings, probably assuming that there is no semantic difference between the two (Cf. H. Lee 1970:52; K. Lee 1970:21 and I. Yang 1972:117). A common practice is to construct a deep structure based on the readings like (35a). A close examination of (35), however, reveals that (35a) and (35b) are respectively the answers to (36a) and (36b) for example.

(36) a. mues-ul hay-ss-ni? *or* mues-ul hay po-ass-ni?
'What did you do?' or 'What did you try doing?'
b. mues-ul mek-e po-ass-ni? 'What did you try eating?'

Thus, as the respective answers to (36), (35b) may be shortened to *kaykwuli-lul* but (35a) may not. (35a) may at most be shortened to *kaykwuli-lul mek-e-lul.* The contrastive sentences (37a) and (37b) also illustrate the existence of (35a) and (35b).

(37) a. talun il-ul hay-ss-ul ppun ani-la kaykwuli-lul mek-e-to po-ass-ta.
'I did not only other things but also tried eating frogs.'
b. say-ppun ani-la kaykwuli-to mek-e po-ass-ta.
'I tried eating not only birds but also frogs.'

Insertion of the phonological juncture (#) after *kaykwuli-lul* in (35) results always in the (35b) reading, while the lack of juncture gives the ambiguity. This fact seems to constitute another piece of evidence that there exist the two readings. Existence of (35b) along with (35a) reflects another aspect of semantic cohesion in 'auxiliary' constructions.

The third case of semantic cohesion between an embedded verb and the matrix 'auxiliary' verb is observable in connection with Karttunen's (1971) theory of 'implicative' verbs.[6] Most of the Korean 'auxiliary' verbs given in (11) are implicative verbs in Karttunen's sense. The exceptions are *ha* 'causes, permits', *mantul* 'causes', *toy* 'turns out' (these are *key*-type), *siph* 'is desirable' (*ko*-type), *ha* (transitivizer) and *poi* 'looks' (these are *A*-type). Such exceptional ones have their own unique syntactico-semantic characteristics within the 'auxiliary' set that may justify their exceptionality, but I will not go into the discussion here.

Karttunen observes a semantic distinction, 'implicative' vs. 'non-implicative', among predicates that take infinitive complements in English. Verbs like *remember, manage, bother* and *happen* are called 'implicative' in that there is truth value implication between a main sentence with such a verb as predicate (i.e., matrix verb) and the complement embedded in it. For example, the assertion of (38a) implies belief in the truth of (38b) which is the complement of (38a).

(38) a. John remembered to lock his door.
b. John locked his door.

On the other hand, verbs like *hope, agree, decide, promise* and *plan* are 'non-implicative' because there is no such implicative relationship between a main sentence that contains such a verb and the embedded complement. For example, the assertion of (39a) does not imply the truth of (39b).

(39) a. John hoped to solve the problem.
b. John solved the problem.

Karttunen demonstrates that such an implicative relationship also holds in negation, question, command, modality, tense, adverbials and others.

Most of the Korean 'auxiliary' verbs behave the same way as (38), while 'non-auxiliary' verbs are rarely 'implicative'. One verb of the latter type is *sicakha* 'begins' only if it appears after the complementizer *ki* as in (40).

(40) a. pi-ka o-ki sicakhay-ss-ta. 'It started to rain.'
b. pi-ka o-ass-ta. 'It rained.'

Existence of 'non-auxiliary' implicative verbs like *sicakha,* however small the number is, plus the existence of non-implicative 'auxiliary' verbs like *siph* prevent us from claiming that 'implication' is a necessary or sufficient condition for a verb to be 'auxiliary'. However, the fact that most of the implicative verbs in Korean are 'auxiliary' ones is of significance to the present discussion because implication is an aspect of semantic cohesion between an embedded verb and the cooccurring matrix verb. In the following, two 'auxiliary' verbs *po* (implicative) and *siph* (non-implicative) will be taken up for illustration. The sentence (41c) is the complement of (41a) and (41b). Notice that (41a) implies the truth of (41c), whereas (41b) has no implication as to the truth of the proposition expressed by its complement (41c). This fact is clearly evidenced in (42), where (42a) is ungrammatical but (42b) is grammatical.

(41) a. John-un hankwuk umsik-ul mek-e po-ass-ta.
'John tried some Korean food.'
b. John-un hankwuk umsik-ul mek-ko siph-ess-ta.
'John wanted to eat Korean food.'
c. John-un hankwuk umsik-ul mek-ess-ta.
'John ate Korean food.'

(42) a. *John-un hankwuk umsik-ul mek-e po-ass-una, an mek-ess-ta.
b. John-un hankwuk umsik-ul mek-ko siph-ess-una, an mek-ess-ta.
'John wanted to eat Korean food, but didn't.'

The same implicative relationship holds in the sentences in (43), which is the negation of (41). (43a) implies (43c) but (43b) does not.

(43) a. John-un hankwuk umsik-ul mek-e po-ci anh-ass-ta.
'John didn't try any Korean food.'
b. John-un hankwuk umsik-ul mek-ko siph-ci anh-ass-ta.
'John didn't want to eat Korean food.'
c. John-un hankwuk umsik-ul mek-ci anh-ass-ta.
'John didn't eat any Korean food.'

At this point, it is clear that implicative verbs like the 'auxiliary' *po* are different from such 'factive' verbs like the 'main' *al* 'knows', in Kiparsky-Kiparsky's (1970) sense, since in 'factive' verbs negation in the main sentence does not affect the presupposition represented in the complement sentence, as observed in (44a) and (44b).

(44) a. ku-pun-i ka-n kes-ul al-ci mos-hay-ss-ta.
'I didn't know that he went.'
b. ku-pun-i ka-ss-ta.
'He went.'

The sentences in (45) and (46) all show the same implicative relationship.

(45) a. ka po-ass-ni? 'Did you go (and find anything out)?'
b. ka-ko siph-ess-ni? 'Did you want to go?'
c. ka-ss-ni? 'Did you go?'

(46) a. {ecey / *nayil} mek-e po-ass-ta. 'I tried eating yesterday.' / *'I tried eating tomorrow.'
b. {ecey / nayil} mek-ko siph-ess-ta. 'I wanted to eat yesterday.' / 'I wanted to eat tomorrow.'
c. {ecey / *nayil} mek-ess-ta. 'I ate yesterday.' / *'I ate tomorrow.'

Exactly the same thing happens when we test with locative and passivization. The equi-subject constraint is another case.[7] One noticeable fact is that, in a long sequence of 'auxiliary' construction, implication breaks down if there is a non-implicative 'auxiliary' verb included in the sequence, as we see in (47).

(47) *ecey-nun nayil* mek-e *po*-ko *siph*-e *ci*-ess-ta.
'Yesterday I came to the point where I want to eat (it) tomorrow.'

It seems that the common semantic feature shared by all implicative verbs in Korean is the simultaneity or inseparability of the two events represented by the embedded verb and the matrix verb, which is not the case with non-implicative verbs. In general, simultaneity applies not only to time but to space, the agent, manner, reason, and many other relevant factors. Most of the Korean 'auxiliary' verbs have such a property in relation to the preceding embedded 'main' verb, which reflects semantic cohesion between the two.

6. Deep Structure Shape

In this section I will comment on a few of the current proposals involving a generative treatment of Korean 'auxiliary' verb constructions. My discussion will be limited to four topics, namely, justification for complementation, complementizer treatment, Equi-constraint and the node dominating the sentential complement. No rule formalism, either for constituent structure or for transformations, will be discussed.

As has been implied thus far, I am in favor of postulating a sentential complement for each 'auxiliary' verb construction. I. Yang's (1972:124-26) only explicit justification for complementation treatment, rather than lexical derivation, of his 'compound verbs' (which include 'auxiliary' verbs) is that otherwise there would be no explanation for the occurrence of the case marker *lul* and 'delimiters' like *nun, to, ya, man* between the two verbs constituting a 'compound verb' (e.g., *ka-ko-lul siph-ta* 'I want to go' and *ka-ko-to siph-ta* 'I want to go also'). I have some additional reasons for preferring complementation. Observe (48) for example.

(48)

tosi-eyse-nun	sikol-eyse	sal-ko	siph-ko	sikol-eyse-nun	tosi-eyse
1	2	A	B	3	4
sal-ko	siph-ta.				
C	D				

'In the city, I want to live in the country and in the country I want to live in the city.'

Here, 1, 2, 3 and 4 are locatives, while A, B, C and D are verbs (B and D are 'auxiliary' verbs). It is intuitively clear that 1 goes with B, 2 goes with A, 3 with D and 4 with C. Suppose we postulate only two sentences, instead of four, in the deep structure. We would have great difficulty in accounting for the strict cooccurrence restriction between the locatives and the verbs since each locative is exclusively associated with one of the verbs. Furthermore, we would have two locative cases (1 and 2; 3 and 4) in each simplex sentence in the deep structure of (48), which has to be avoided in grammatical description (Cf. Fillmore 1971:248). This difficulty will be eliminated if we postulate underlying sentential complements for 2A and 4C. Similarly, (49) includes a matrix time adverb (*caknyen-ey* 'last year') which goes with the 'main' verb *ka*. Notice, in particular, the tense agreement between the past form of *siph* and *caknyen* and between the tenseless (future) form of *ka* and *naynyen*. Unless we postulate two sentences in deep structure, we have no simple way of accounting for such tense agreement within the generative framework.

(49) na-nun caknyen-ey-nun naynyen-ey Seoul-ey ka-ko siph-ess-ta.
'Last year I wanted to go to Seoul next year.'

Other tests such as double subject constructions (e.g., *John-i Mary-ka ka-key hay-ss-ta* 'John made Mary go'), non-synonymity between, for example, *an nemeci-key toy-ta* 'becomes not to fall' and *nemeci-key an toy-ta* 'does not become to fall' and double honorifices (e.g., *ka-si-e po-si-ess-ta* 'tried going (honorific)' provide further evidence that an 'auxiliary' verb construction is to be handled by postulating an embedded sentence for the first verb and a matrix sentence for the 'auxiliary' verb.

My second comment is concerned with the way of introducing such complementizers as *key, ko* and *A*. There are two lines of argument on this: one is that such complementizers have their own semantic content and therefore must be so represented in deep structure (e.g., I. Yang 1972:13-19) and the other is that they have no semantic content and therefore must be introduced by transformation (e.g., H. Lee 1970:130-32 and K. Lee 1970:8). As regards *ko* and *A*, I. Yang (ibid.) presents the minimal pair *ka-ko iss-ta* 'is going' which involves durative aspect and *ka-A iss-ta* 'has gone' which involves perfective aspect and concludes that the source for such a semantic difference is the difference between the complementizers *ko* and *A*. K. Lee recognizes two different lexical items associated with *iss:* one which means 'is in the process of' appears automatically with *ko* and one which means 'is in the state of' appears automatically with *A*.

In order to see the case more clearly, let us first compare the verb *ka* with *ip* 'dresses' as in (50).

(50) ka-ko iss-ta 'is going' vs. ip-ko iss-ta 'is dressing'
ka-A iss-ta 'has gone' vs. ip-ko (*-A) iss-ta 'has dressed'

Notice that in the *ka* set the durative-processive and perfective-stative difference is manifested by the *ko* and *A* difference but in the *ip* set the semantic difference is not formally realized but only *ko* appears in both cases.

What (50) implies is that the semantic difference mentioned does not always correspond to the complementizer difference, that *ko* also provides perfective-stative meaning after certain embedded verbs, and that both embedded and matrix verbs are relevant to complementizers. The so-called *A*-series (Cf. Na 1971:18) such as *cwuk* 'dies', *phi* 'blooms', *ssek* 'is rotten', *nok* 'melts', *su* 'stands', and *swum* 'hides' go with the *ka* set, while many of the so-called *ko* series (usually transitive verbs) such as *pis* 'combs', *ci* 'carries on back', *sin* 'wears (shoes)' and *cha* 'carries on side' go with the *ip* set. Next, let us examine if similar semantic distinction with the two complementizers *ko* and *A* appears before other verbs than *iss*.

(51)	a.	koki-lul mul-*ko* ka-n-ta.	'goes with meat in its mouth' (action going on)
		koki-lul mul-*A* ka-n-ta.	'carries meat away'
	b.	wus-*ko* (*-A) sal-ass-ta.	'lived with smile'
		nol-ko (*-A) tani-n-ta.	'is fooling around'
	c.	coh-*A* (*-ko) cinay-ss-ta.	'got along in good terms'
		swum-*A* (*-ko) sal-ass-ta.	'lived in the state of hiding'
		cwuk-*A* (*-ko) cinay-n-ta.	'lives oppressed'
	d.	mek-*A* (*-ko) peli-ess-ta.	'finished eating'
		nok-*A* (*-ko) ka-n-ta.	'is melting' (Lit. goes on in the state of melting)
	e.	ka-*ko* (*-A) siph-ta.	'wants to go'

Details aside, all the examples given in (51), whether the second verbs are 'main' (a-c) or 'auxiliary' (d,e), show that constructions with the complementizer *ko* have durative-processive meaning and, in addition, stative meaning where *A* is not allowed syntactically, whereas those with *A* have only stative meaning in its broad sense. With *A,* the 'perfective' meaning does not necessarily appear in (51). *ko* in (e) does not seem to provide the durative-stative meaning but only stative meaning. In order words, durative-processive meaning is 'latent' before *siph,* if we assume that *ko* in (e) is the same *ko* as those in the other examples. Thus, my (tentative) conclusion is that the complementizer *ko* has the simultaneous action feature plus the 'state' feature, while *A* has only the 'state' feature. The two features of *ko* do not always show up. They are activated in some contexts and suppressed in others (Cf. Kempson and Quirk 1971). Before certain *ko*-series, both appear (e.g., *ip-ko iss-ta*); before the *A*-series only the 'simultaneous action' feature appears while 'state' is latent; and before *siph* only 'state' is activated. Other secondary meanings like 'perfective' with *A* are derived as a result of the semantic combination between the preceding and the following verb.

With respect to the *key*-type of 'auxiliary' verbs, it is often claimed that *key* is devoid of meaning and should be introduced by transformation. I believe, however, that *key* has the meaning 'in a way that' or 'so that' whenever it occurs. The sentence in (52) has two readings. (52a) contains the 'auxiliary' *hay* 'causes' and (52b) the 'main' *hay* 'does'. Intuitively, the difference in the two readings is due to the difference between the two *hay*'s while the complementizer *key* retains the same meaning in both cases.

(52) ku il-ul nam-i mol-u-key hay-ss-ta.
  a. I made the work secret to others.
   (Lit. I arranged the work in such a way that nobody may know it.)
  b. I did the work secretly.
   (Lit. I did the work in a way that nobody may know it.)

Furthermore, (53) shows that *key* can be replaced by the adverb *tolok* 'to the point where, so that' and by the compound *key-kkum* 'so that indeed' with a slight difference in meaning resulting. This means that the appearance of *key* is not predictable.

(53) na-nun John-ul ka-key (*or* tolok *or* key-kkum) hay-ss-ta.
   'I made (*or* let) John go.'

Since the three complementizers under discussion have their own semantic content and their appearance is not entirely predictable, they should be inserted in the deep structure.

Another brief comment concerns the so-called Equi-NP, or more narrowly Equi-Subject constraint, which has frequently been proposed in connection with 'auxiliary' verb constructions in Korean. As we have observed, most of the Korean 'auxiliary' verbs are 'implicative' verbs and an implicative relationship holds between the complement and the matrix sentence in affirmative and negative statements, questions and commands. Furthermore, identity is observable not only in the subjects but also in the tenses, and all kinds of adverbials. Thus, the traditional Equi-NP constraint is nothing more than a part of the more general Equi Constraint. If we should recognize Equi-NP deletion as a useful grammatical process, then we should also recognize such other processes as Equi-negative deletion, Equi-temporal deletion, Equi-spacial deletion, Equi-manner deletion, Equi-tense deletion, etc. Such processes should be relevant to 'implicative auxiliary' verb constructions, if Equi-NP deletion is relevant to them. For example, (54a) is considered to be an outcome of the application of such deletion processes to (54b).

(54) a. na-nun caknyen-kkaci mikwuk-eyse Washington-ey an ka po-ass-ta.
'Until last year, I had not been to Washington in the U.S.'
b. na-nun caknyen-kkaci mikwuk-eyse (na-ka caknyen-kkaci
1 2 3 1 2
mikwuk-eyse Washington-ey an ka-ss-ta) an po-ass-ta.
3 4 5 4 5

Let us take a look at the negative adverb *an* for example. It is clear that in the deep structure the matrix sentence in (54) is negative in that *na* 'I' did not *po* 'try *or* experience'. It is also clear that the embedded sentence is negative in that *na* 'I' did not *ka* 'go'. The negative adverb *an* may not simply be attached to either the matrix or embedded sentence, because in such a case implicational relationship of negation would not be indicated and the significant difference between 'factive' and 'implicative' verbs could not be specified in the deep structure. Thus, *an* before *ka-ss-ta* and *an* before *po-ass-ta* are identical in reference and the second *an* is obligatorily deleted accordingly. There is no such identity of reference between, for example, the two negatives in *an ka-ci anh-ass-ta* 'it is not the case that I did not go', where the embedded negation is negated. Similar arguments could be made for the other elements postulated with numbers in (54b). For example, if we do not postulate *caknyen-kkaci* in the complement, implicational relationship does not hold because (54) does not imply 'I did not go to Washington' but 'I did not go to Washington until last year' which is the correct meaning intended by the complement. There is still another justification for the embedded *caknyen-kkaci*. Such non-implicative verbs as *siph* may have its own temporal adverb which is different from that of the embedded verb. Thus, recall the classical justification for postulating an embedded subject, as indicated in the parentheses in (55b), in view of the surface parallel, as indicated in (55a). (56) is an analogous treatment for *caknyen-kkaci*.

(55) a. I want for him to go.
b. I want (for me) to go.

(56) a. caknyen-kkaci-nun [naynyen-kkaci ka]-ko siph-ess-ta.
'Until last year, I had wanted to go until next year.'
b. caknyen-kkaci-nun [(caknyen-kkaci) ka]-A po-ass-ta.
'I had been (there) until last year.'

My final comment will be on some existing proposals involving the deep structure configuration of 'auxiliary' constructions. One common practice in case grammar treatment of Korean 'auxiliary' verb constructions is to place the sentential complement under the domination of the Object Case NP. What I question is whether this practice is really well motivated and whether it could be modified in a certain way.

One difficulty with the Object Case domination is already apparent, that is, the clash of two object cases as observed in (30b). In order to get around the clash, we would have to assume that the surface object *ku pun-ul* is nothing but the underlying agent *ku pun-i* or experiencer *ku pun-eykey*. This has to be based on another assumption that either (30a) and (30b) or (30b) and (30c) or all three sentences have exactly the same meaning and therefore must be derived from the same deep structure. This assumption that all three are synonymous has already been denied in this paper. That is, the three case markers *i, eykey* and *lul* in (30) are not free variants. Suppose we detach the sentential complement from the Object Case node and assign it under the Complement NP dominated by VP. We would be able to differentiate the three sentences in (30) as follows:

(57) a. D.S. of (30a)

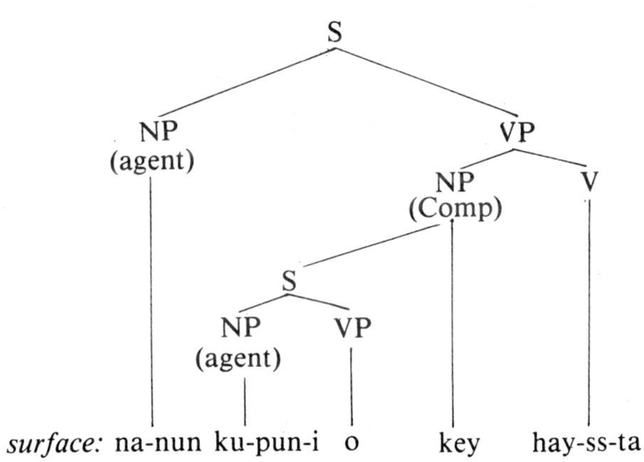

b. D.S. of (30b)

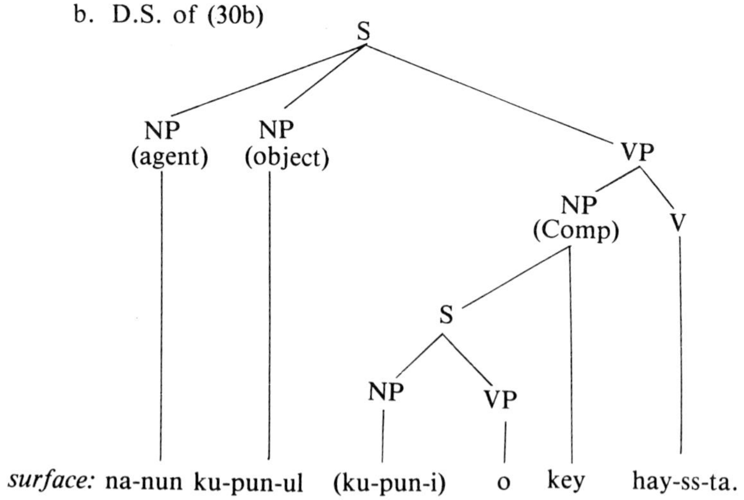

c. D.S. of (30c)

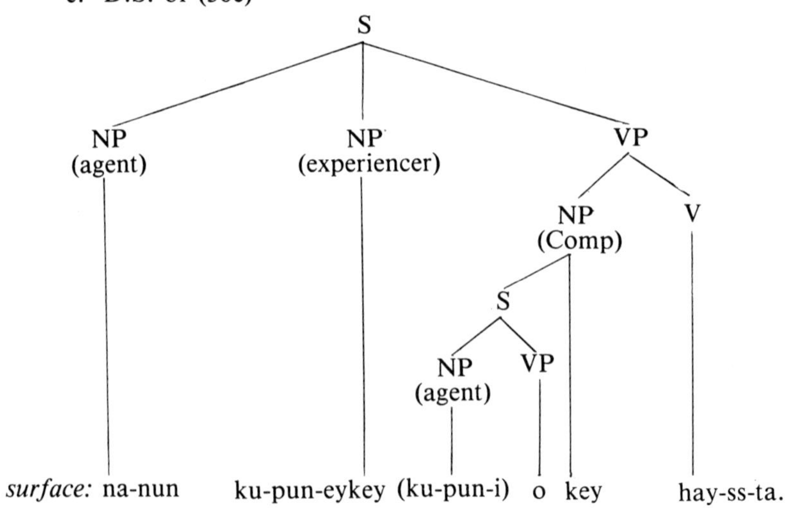

The parentheses in the above indicate obligatory deletion on the surface. It is not important for the present discussion whether the VP domination is compatible with the current case grammar framework or not. My point is that the Object Case domination shows certain weaknesses.

Secondly, by detaching the complement from under the Object Case node and attaching it under VP in the deep structure, such transformational mechanisms as NP-raising, case marker changing (*ka* to *lul*) and attachment of the predicate to the main VP would be unnecessary. For a comparison, observe (58a) which is based on VP domination and (58b) which is based on Object Case domination, for the sentence (15b) *na-nun Mary-lul coh-A ha-n-ta* 'I like Mary.'

(58) a.

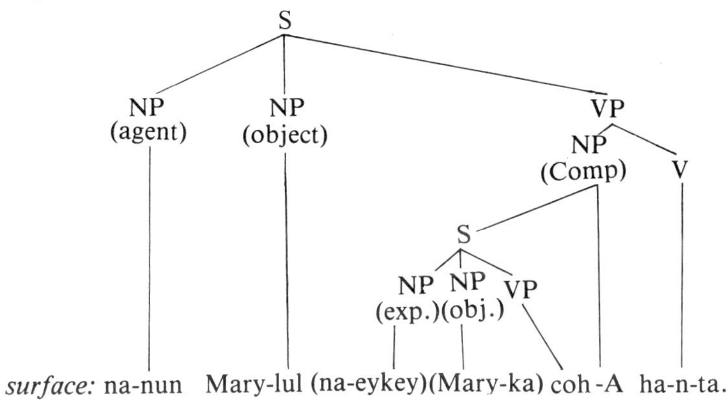

b.

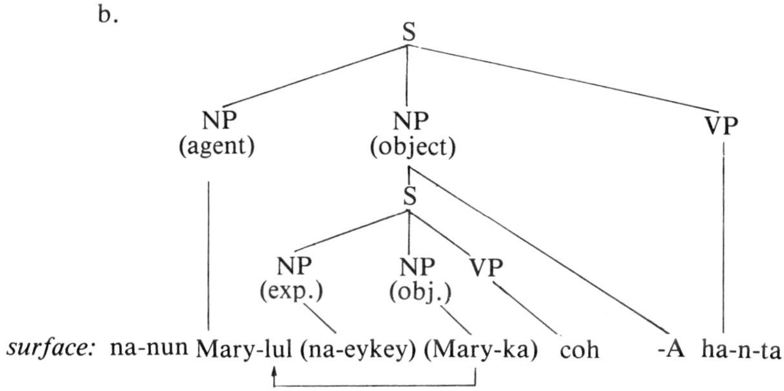

In order to derive (15b) from (58b), we have to raise the embedded Object Case NP (*Mary*) to the higher S, changing *ka* to *lul*, while attaching the embedded VP, the complementizer and others, if any, to the higher VP. (58a) is definitely more economical, since such processes are not needed. Furthermore, it seems clumsy in view of a symmetrical description to raise the embedded *Mary* and delete the embedded *na*, instead of either raising both *Mary* and *na* or deleting both of them, since both *Mary* and *na* appear on the surface in any case.

Thirdly, the proposed VP domination will also be useful in handling free scrambling (Cf. (22)) and adverb constraint (Cf. (23)), since they do not have to be later rules which are applicable only after NP raising, Predicate raising, etc. have applied. The VP domination allows such processes to be applicable to the relevant deep constituent structure as the structural description.

Fourthly, we have already touched upon different case relations and their associated meanings. Observe (15b) again. The subject *na* 'I' likes *Mary,* who is the patient (hence object) of *ha.* The action affects *Mary* directly and has nothing to do with the fact that *Mary* is good to *na* which should be the case in (58b). In the deep structure (58a), semantic cohesion, with correlated syntactic cohesion, of the 'auxiliary' construction is expressed. In the deep structure (58b), however, no semantic cohesion is assumed and any syntactic cohesion is relegated to transformational processes. As observed, however, there *is* semantic cohesion in Korean 'auxiliary' verb constructions.

Fifthly, the relation between a complement and an 'auxiliary' verb and that between a complement and a 'non-auxiliary' verb are generally not the same in semantic nature (see (61b) for the treatment of exceptions). Compare (59a) and (59b).

(59) a. John-i ka-ko-lul iss-ta.
  'John is going.'
 b. John-i ka-n-kes-ul a-n-ta.
  'I know that John went.'

Notice that both sentences contain the accusative marker *lul/ul.* The complement *John-i ka-n-kes* is certainly the object of the transitive verb *al* 'knows' in (59b), but the complement *ka-ko* is neither the agent, goal, or traditional subject, nor an object or any other specifiable case.[8] It is a pure 'complement' which describes (or 'modifies') the intransitive verb *iss* in relation to *John.* It seems to be unreasonable to view these entirely different semantic relations as derived from the same semantic or deep structure. As already discussed (Cf. sentences in (13)), the appearance of *lul/ul* after an embedded verb in 'auxiliary' constructions does not indicate that the complement is necessarily an object. The two sentences in question seem to have (60a) and (60b) as deep structures.

(60) a.

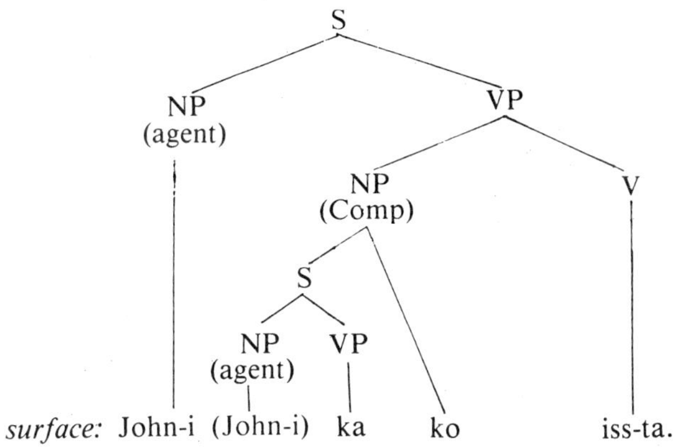

b.

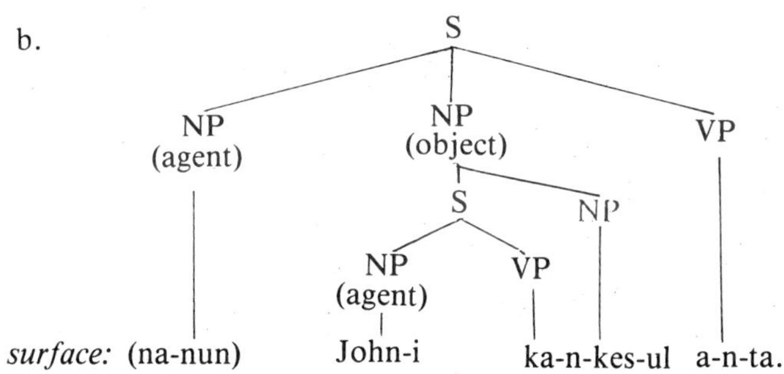

In the same way, the semantic relation between *coh* and *ha* in (15b) does not seem to be the same as that existing in (59b). *coh* is simply 'complemental' to *ha*.

Finally, the proposed VP domination gives allowance for the treatment of such ambiguous sentences as (35) if the ambiguity is not a false one. That is, (35a) may be handled like (57a) and (35b) like (57b). Furthermore, VP domination can accommodate such 'non-auxiliary' complement constructions as (61b) which I think has a meaning different from (61a). Thus, (61a) can be handled like (60b) and (61b) like (57b). As has been observed so far, some 'non-auxiliary' verbs like *kitali* 'waits' have some properties in common with 'auxiliary' verbs. (61b) certainly deserves to be handled in the same way as an 'auxiliary' construction. Besides, *pi* 'rain' in (61b) seems to be the object of the whole compound *o-ki-lul kitali* where *o* is 'complemental' to *kitali, just as ka* is 'complemental' to *iss* in (59a).

(61) a. na-nun [pi-ka o-ki] -lul kitali-n-ta.
'I am waiting for rain-falling.'
b. na-nun [pi] -lul [o-ki-lul kitali] -n-ta.
'I am waiting for rain that it falls.'
c. *na-nun [pi-lul o]-ki-lul kitali-n-ta.
d. *na-nun [pi]-ka [o-ki-lul kitali]-n-ta.

Notes

1. The term 'verbs' covers what have traditionally been called adjectives and the copula in addition to 'true' verbs. Throughout this paper, Yale Romanization is followed. English definitions of the Korean words cited are based mainly on Martin et al. 1967.
2. H. Lee 1970, K. Lee 1970 and I. Yang 1972, among others, are wholly or partly devoted to the discussion of 'auxiliary' verbs within the generative framework of complementation. Yang makes a distinction between verbal and nominal complementations. The former roughly correspond to the 'auxiliary' verb constructions that will be taken up in this paper. Yang (12-13) identifies verbal complementations based on (a) non-applicability of 'modality adjustment,' (b) 'verbal compounding' and (c) predicate raising. It seems to me, however, that some 'non-auxiliary' verbs also satisfy these constraints partly or wholly. For example, *silh* seems to satisfy all the above constraints in the following sentence:
   na-nun ku ay-ka po-ki silh-ta. 'I don't like the child.'
   (Cf. na-nun ku ay-lul po-ki silh-ta.)
3. 'Main' verbs such as *malha* 'tells', *al* 'knows' and *mut/mul* 'asks' in (7) and 'auxiliary' verbs such as *siph* have the same property of 'complement' verbs in Binnick's (1970:558) terminology, as against such simple 'main' verbs as *celm* 'is young', *ka* 'goes' and *ttayli* 'hits'. Thus, complement verbs are those verbs which may have an embedded sentential complement. The term 'auxiliary' is certainly a misnomer. A better name, although sophisticated, would be 'pure complement' verbs for the reasons to be discussed in Section 4.
4. Choi (1965) and most dictionaries of Korean contain quite a large number of 'auxiliary' verbs. For certain items, however, scholars do not always agree on the classification. In addition to *chey-ha, cik-ha* and *ka-siph,* the following are traditionally classed as 'auxiliary', although Martin et al. treat them as compounds: *ka-po* 'seems to', *kes-kath* 'seems like', *man-ha* 'is sufficient to', *na-po* 'seems like', *na-siph* 'is likely to', *pep-ha* 'has good reason to', *ppen-ha* 'is near, almost', *sang-siph* 'appears', *tus-ha* 'seems like' and *tus-siph* 'gives the impression of'. It seems to me that each compound in this class can be handled as appositive complementation, with the defective noun (e.g., *chey* 'pretending') as the complementizer, the clause preceding it (e.g., *ca-n* in *ca-n chey* 'pretending to sleep') as the complement and the verb, which is basically of 'auxiliary' type, (e.g., *ha* 'assumes, takes') as the matrix verb of the higher sentence. This treatment is motivated by the fact

that such a construction (see (a) below) involves clausal coreferentiality between the complementizer and the whole embedded sentence. For example, (b) seems to underlie (a), with details omitted.

(a) John-un ca-n-chey hay-ss-ta.
'John pretended to be sleeping.'

(b) $[[\text{John}]\text{-un}]_{NP}$ $[[[\text{John-i ca-ta}]_S$ $[\text{chey}]_N]_{NP}$ $[\text{hay-ss-ta}]_V]_{VP}]_S$

The negative compounds appear after the complementizer *ci.* The prohibitive *mal* 'don't' which also appears after *ci,* is traditionally classed as an 'auxiliary'. It seems to me that *ha/hay* (in *ani ha* and *mos ha*) is to be classed as a main verb if we follow Choi's definition of 'auxiliary' verbs based on the 'stand-by-itself' principle as in (c) and (d). *ha/hay* remains the same in meaning in (c) and (d).

(c) ku il-ul ani-hay-ss-ta. 'I didn't do the work.'
ku il-ul mos-hay-ss-ta. 'I couldn't do the work.'

(d) ku il-ul kkuth-nay-ci ani-hay-ss-ta.
'I didn't finish the work.'
(Lit. I didn't do finishing the work.)
ku il-ul kkuth-nay-ci mos-hay-ss-ta.
'I couldn't finish the work.'
(Lit. I couldn't do finishing the work.)

In addition, *ha/hay* in such compounds as *ya ha* 'must do', *ki-to ha* 'also does' and *ki-nun ha* 'does (topicalized)' is classed traditionally as an 'auxiliary'. This *ha/hay* does not seem to be different from the *ha/hay* mentioned in (c) and (d).

Notice that many 'auxiliary' verbs given in (11) have corresponding 'main' verbs with the identical form and somewhat related meaning, as in *ha/hay* 'does' vs. *ha/hay* 'causes, permits' and *po* 'sees, looks at' vs. *po* 'tries ...ing'. Their semantic (as well as syntactic) difference, however, is great enough that their status as separate lexical items is warranted.

5. *A* here is a 'morphophoneme' symbol. It is realized as *a* after *a* and *o* and as *e* elsewhere. It is, however, realized as Ø (zero) if there is no consonant between it and the preceding *a*. After the verb *hay* (*hai*) 'does', *e* or Ø appears, giving the combination *haye* or *hay*.
6. I am indebted to L. Josephs who first drew my attention to Karttunen's theory in a seminar led by him in 1971.
7. In connection with (20), syntactic cohesion between *al* 'knows' and *po* was indicated in the command and propositive sentences. Although the sentences in (20a) are unnatural, I tend to think that implicational relationship still holds between the embedded and the matrix sentences in (20b).
8. In this connection, Josephs 1972 demonstrates that the two Japanese complementizers *koto* and *no* are semantically different. *koto* and *no* are not formally differentiated as such in Korean, but both are reflected as *kes* 'the fact that, that', a common complementizer for non-auxiliary verbs.

Reprinted from *Working Papers in Linguistics* (University of Hawaii) 5.3: 63-88 (1973).

7. MODALS AND SPEAKER-HEARER PERSPECTIVES IN KOREAN

The aim of this paper is to observe certain Korean modals which are inherently related to the speaker or the hearer and to propose possible underlying structures involving them.[1] The discussion will be concentrated not so much on involved formalism as on the nature of such modals.

1. Korean has developed rich affixal, for the most part, suffixal, slots of verbs. These slots are filled by such morphemes as follows: the negative (*ani-*), passive (*-i/-hi/-li/-ki*), causative (*-i/-hi/-u/-li/-ki*), honorific (*-(u)si*), purposive (*-lye*), past (*-ess*), past-past (*-(e)ss-ess*), volitional (*-keyss*), presumptive (*-keyss*), prospective (*-(u)l*), activitive (*-n-/nun*), formal deference (*-sup/-up/-p*), retrospective (*-ti/-te*), indicative (*-ni*), suspective (*-ci*), apperceptive (*-kwun*), promise (*-ma, -lkkey*), reportive (*-ta/-la, -ney, -e*), interrogative (*-ni, -kka*), propositive (*-ca, -sey, -sita*), imperative (*-la, -key, -siyo, -o*) and polite (*-yo*).[2] Certain affixes form single-member slots, while others may share the same slots. Some of them have extremely limited distribution; others appear freely. There are intricate co-occurrence restrictions among them, but they will not be a matter of concern in this discussion.

These morphemes are often called auxiliaries, verbal affixes, verbal endings, or modality elements. The term 'modals' is used in this paper in view of their affixal nature on the surface structure and their predicative nature in the deep structure, along with the generally shared meaning that they represent the speaker's attitude or 'view of potential' (Marino 1973: 312) with respect to the propositional content. In other words, these affixes modify the associated propositional content in one way or another, directly or indirectly.[3]

2. Five post-verbal slots are particularly relevant to the affixes which are uniquely related to the speaker, or the hearer, the speaker and the hearer,

or the speaker and the human referent. These five slots are filled, among others, by the honorific suffix (-(*u*)*si*), the homophonous presumptive and volitional suffixes (-*keyss*), the formal deference suffix (-*sup*/-(*u*)*p*), the retrospective (-*ti*/-*te*), indicative (-*ni*) or directive (-*si*) suffixes, and the formal reportive suffix (-*ta*/-*la*) in that order. Although the last slot is represented by the formal reportive suffix (to which the discussion will be limited), there are a large number of mutually exclusive morphemes, such as those indicating statement, question, promise, command, and proposition of various degrees of formality, each involving the speaker and hearer in its underlying grammatical relationships. These suffixes, which will be called 'person-sensitive modals', are illustrated in the sentences in (1) in which all the slots happen to be filled.

(1) a. Kim-sensayng-nim-i Korea-ey an-ka-*si*-ess-*keyss-sup-ti-ta*.
Kim-Mr.-hon.title-SM Korea-to not-go-(1)-past-(2)-(3)-(4)-(5)
'According to my observation, it seemed to me that Mr. Kim had not gone to Korea.'

b. Kim-sensayng-nim-i Korea-ey an-ka-si-ess-keyss-sup-ti-kka?
'According to your observation, did it seem to you that Mr. Kim had not gone to Korea?'

The possible underlying grammatical relationships that are supposed to exist in the above-mentioned person-sensitive modals are illustrated in (2).

(2)

slots	*suffixes*	*underlying grammatical relationships*	*remarks*
(1)	-(u)si	(x, z, DEFER)	x = speaker y = hearer z = subject person (3rd per. or hearer)
(2)	-keyss	($\begin{Bmatrix}x\\y\end{Bmatrix}$, S, PRESUME)	
	-keyss	($\begin{Bmatrix}x\\y\end{Bmatrix}$, S, INTEND)	$\begin{Bmatrix}x\\y\end{Bmatrix}=\begin{cases}\text{x in the statement}\\\text{y in the question}\end{cases}$
(3)	-sup/-(u)p	(x, y, DEFER)	
(4)	-ti/-te	($\begin{Bmatrix}x\\y\end{Bmatrix}$, S, OBSERVED)	
(5)	-ta/-la	(x, y, S, REPORT)	

3. Some general meanings and syntactic behaviors of the individual modals in question are briefly described as follows. The suffix -(*u*)*si* appears when the speaker shows deference to the subject person referent in view of

age, social status, kinship, closeness and certain social norms. Social norms may be illustrated by such situations as: (a) one should not express deference in referring to one's husband in front of one's elders, (b) one should not express deference in referring to one's brother in front of one's father, or (c) one may express deference in referring to one's son or junior in front of the latter' son for educational purposes.

In certain definable instances, the *suffix -(u)si* occurs when the person referent who is shown deference is in a locative case, as in (3), or the possessor of an inanimate subject, as in (4).

(3) a. Kim-sensayng-nim-kkey ton-i manh-*usi*-ta.
-at money-SM much-(1)- (5)
'Mr. Kim has a lot of money.'
(Lit. money is a lot at Mr. Kim)
b. Sensayng-nim-kkey pok-i nayli-si-ki-lul pala-p-ni-ta.
you-hon. title-to blessing-SM befall-(1)-that-OM hope-(3)-(4)-(5)
'I hope that blessings will befall you.'

(4) a. Kim-sensayng-nim-uy nwun-i khu-si-ta.
-of eyes-SM big-(1)-(5)
'Mr. Kim's eyes are big.'
b. sensayng-nim-uy tayk-i i kunche-si-p-ni-kka?
house this nearby-(1)-(3)-(4)-(5)
'Is your house near here?'

If the person shown deference does not have the above function, -(*u*)*si* never appears. For instance, compare the two (nearly) synonymous sentences in (5), where the active sentence (5a) does not contain -(*u*)*si*, while the passive sentence (5b) does, although the speaker's deference to *Kim-sensayng* is constant.

(5) a. kay-ka Kim-sensayng-nim-ul mul-ess-ta.
dog-SM OM bite-past-(5)
'A dog bit Mr. Kim.'
b. Kim-sensayng-nim-i kay-hanthey mul-li -*si*-ess-ta.
dog-by bite-passive-(1)-past-(5)
'Mr. Kim was bit by a dog.'

Thus the appearance of -(*u*)*si* is a surface phenomenon. It has to be introduced, for instance, after the subject is selected.

The suffix *-keyss* is traditionally called the future tense marker.

However, recent studies have revealed the fact that this suffix has two distinct meanings, i.e. volition and presumption (or conjecture), relegating the futurity meaning to a secondary position (e.g. I. Yang 1972:23, 26 and C. Lee 1973a:53-55).

The volitional *-keyss* signifies the speaker's intention at the time of utterance. Due to its very meaning of 'volition' in the present state of mind, the action denoted by the verb that precedes it should naturally take place in the future, as in the case of the English verb *intend*. Because of the meaning 'present volition', only a non-past verb may occur before the volitional *-keyss*. Non-past action verbs in Korean refer to both future and present time. Observe the sentences in (6) where (6a) indicates both the present and the future, while (6b) only the future. In (6b) the noun *nayil* 'tomorrow' suppresses the present time meaning.

(6) a. nay-ka ka-n-ta. (i) 'I will go.'
(ii) 'I go.' or 'I am going.'
b. nayil nay-ka ka-n-ta. 'I will go tomorrow.'

In a parallel way, if a verb occurs with the volitional *-keyss*, which necessarily contains certain features such as 'anticipative' (the term is defined in Chafe 1973:177), the present time reference is suppressed.

(7) Nay-ka ka-keyss-ta. 'I intend to go.'
(Lit. I intend that I will go.)

The volitional *-keyss*, therefore, does not impose any futurity meaning on the propositional content, but only suppresses the 'present' meaning, leaving the 'future' intact. Thus, it is not a future tense marker.

In addition to the constraint that only non-past verbs may occur before the volitional *-keyss*, it has two more restrictions. First, it occurs only with action verbs. One noteworthy fact is that the verb *al* 'to know', which is commonly classified as an action verb in view of its being transitive, taking the activitive suffix *-n* and occurring with the so-called progressive aspect (e.g., *al-ko iss-ta* '*to be knowing'), is different from the other action verbs in at least two respects. When *al* is followed by *-keyss*, only the meaning of presumption appears, just like an adjective as in (8).

(8) al-keyss- sup-ni- ta. 'I presume that I know it.'
know-(2)-(3)- (4)-(5) or 'I understand it.'

Also, like an adjective, *al* does not occur in an imperative or propositive sentence. Thus we may classify the verb *al* as a *stative* verb.

Another constraint of the volitional *-keyss* is that it requires referential identity between the speaker and the subject of the propositional content. If this requirement is not met, then only the presumptive meaning appears. For instance, (9a) is ambiguous, but (9b) is not.

(9) a. nay-ka cwuk-keyss-ta.
I-SM die- (2)- (5) (i) 'I intend to die.'
(ii) 'I presume that I will die.'
b. kui-ka cwuk-kyess-ta.
he-SM die-(2)-(5) 'I presume that he will die.'

On the other hand, the presumptive *-keyss* which represents the speaker's presumption at the time of utterance, occurs with all types of verbs and adjectives regardless of different tenses or aspects. Identical reference between the speaker and the subject is not required. Observe the sentences in (10).

(10) a. nayil pi-ka o-*keyss*-ta. 'I presume that it will
tomorrow rain-SM come-(2)-(5) rain tomorrow.'
b. cikum pakk-ey pi-ka o-*keyss*-ta.
now outside-at 'I presume that it is raining (Lit. it rains) outside.'
c. Chicago-ey pi-ka o -ko-iss -*keyss*-ta.
come-progr.-exist-(2)-(5)
'I presume that it is raining in Chicago.'
d. pi-ka wa -ss-*keyss*-ta.
come-past-(2)-(5)

Notice in (10) that *-keyss* indicates the speaker's present presumption of the content denoted by whatever elements precede it in each sentence. Notice further that *-keyss* does not carry any inherent futurity meaning, nor is it future-oriented in any case regardless of the kind of verbs or tenses. (10d) is often called 'past-future' or 'subjunctive mood', but in fact it is simply a present presumption of the speaker regarding a past event.

Both the volitional and presumptive *-keyss* are associated only with the speaker in the statement and only with the hearer in the question sentence. (11) illustrates this fact.

(11) a. nay-ka ka-keyss-ta.
I-SM go-(2)-(5)
'I intend that I will go.'

b. ney-ka ka-keyss-ni?
   you-SM go-(2)-(5)
   'Do you intend that you will go?'
c. kui-ka ka-keyss-ni?
   he-SM go-(2)-(5)
   'I presume that he will go.'
d. kui-ka ka-keyss-ni?
   he-SM go-(2)-(5)
   'Do you presume that he will go?

Another feature common to both the volitional and the presumptive *-keyss* is that they occur only in statement and question sentences, but not in other types of sentences (e.g. command or proposition). This is partly due to the fact that in a command, for example, the hearer must be the subject, while *-keyss* requires the hearer only in the question sentence.

The suffix *-sup/-(u)p* indicates the speaker's formal deference toward the hearer when performing the act of speaking. Korean has intricate speech levels that reflect the speaker's attitude toward the hearer in terms of deference, formality and politeness. In general, these levels are expressed by means of the nouns or pronouns that are used to denote the hearer as the subject, by the presence or absence of *-sup/-(u)p*, and by different forms of sentence-type suffixes. Among the several speech levels (e.g. Martin 1954 and Martin and Lee 1969 set up six levels), only the formal deference level is responsible for the appearance of the suffix *-sup/-(u)p*. Unlike *-keyss*, the speaker-hearer relationship with regard to the honorific suffix and the formal deference suffix is not affected by sentence types.

The suffix *-ti/-te* has various terms such as: the retrospective tense, the retrospective aspect, and the retrospective mood. The basic meaning is that the speaker in statements or the hearer in questions, personally observed or perceived the content denoted by the elements that precede the suffix. This suffix inherently contains the past feature in addition to the speaker's personal observation or perception. For instance, in (12), the main verb *o* 'to come' is non-past, but the suffix *-te* imposes the past feature on the propositional content.

(12) pi-ka o *-te*-la.
     rain-SM come-(4)-(5)
     'I observed that it rained.'

The presence of the past feature is also observable from the fact that the volitional *-keyss* which requires the propositional content to be realized in the future is incompatible with *-ti/-te*. Thus the sentence in (13) is grammatical only in the sense of presumption.

(13) nay-ka ka-*keyss-te*-la.
I- SM go-(2)-(4)-(5)
(i) *I perceived that I intended to go.
(ii) I perceived that I could go.
(Lit. I perceived that I presumed that I would go.)

Unless the presumptive *-keyss* is inserted between a main verb and *-ti/-te*, as in (13), the subject of the main verb followed by the retrospective suffix cannot be the speaker in normal situations because the verbal expression of the speaker's own observation or perception of his own action or description is unnatural. The sentence (14) is acceptable only when a person talk about his dream, or a movie, in which case he views himself as the third person.

(14) nay-ka ka-te-la.
I-SM go-(4)-(5)
'I observed that I went.'

If the presumptive *-keyss* precedes the retrospective suffix, the above constraint is removed in that one's perception of one's 'feeling' (i.e. presumption) is naturally expressed. In the same way, the sentences in (15) are grammatical in that the main verb *kippu* 'to be happy' in (15a) and the auxiliary verb *-siph* 'to wish' in (15b) are 'feeling' verbs.

(15) a. nay-ka kippu-*te*-la.
I-SM happy-(4)-(5)
(Lit. I perceived that I was happy.)
b. nay-ka ka-ko-siph-*te*-la.
I-SM go-that-wish-(4)-(5)
(Lit. I perceived that I wished to go.)

The suffix *-ti/-te* is parallel to the suffix *-keyss* in that (a) neither the hearer nor the subject person is involved in the statement, (b) the speaker perspective is changed to the hearer perspective in question sentences, and (c) it occurs exclusively in statement and question sentences.

Finally, the sentence-type suffix *-ta/-la* represents the speaker's *formal* report of the content of the whole sentence to the hearer. In casual or informal reports, this suffix is replaced by other suffixes such as the infinitive *-e/-a* and the intimate *-ney*. In other sentence types, including question, command, proposition and promise, *-ta/-la* is replaced by relevant suffix morphemes. In all the different sentence-type suffixes, the speaker-hearer relationship is constant, with the speaker as the abstract agent and the hearer as the goal or indirect object of the predicates as indicated by such suffixes.

4. The discussion will now focus on the question concerning what kind of underlying structures may be postulated regarding the person-sensitive modals discussed thus far. Two general types of description are available in the framework of generative grammar: one which does not admit, as arguments in the underlying structure, the speaker-hearer perspectives involved in the modals and the other which includes them as arguments, at least in dealing with the honorific suffix and the formal deference suffix. The former type is observable in such works as S. Song (1967), S. Kim (1967), Cook (1968), and I. Yang (1972). For instance, I. Yang (1972:3-4) provides the relevant rules as in (16).

(16) S → P (Pre M) M (conj)
  Pre M → (Adv) (Neg) (Hon)
  M → Tns (keyss) SL—Md—S-type

The Pre M (pre-modality)-M (modality) distinction is motivated by the fact that modality deletion is applicable only to the M node. Yang further expands SL (speech levels), Md (mood), and S (sentence)-type, each into disjunctive constituents so that the formal deference suffix, the retrospective suffix and the reportive suffix may be derived, respectively.

The other type of description is more abstract and is represented by H. Lee (1970) and C. Lee (1973a). Following Ross's (1970) idea of performative sentences, H. Lee derives sentence-type suffixes such as *-ta* from a topmost performative sentence. He then proceeds to assign such semantic features as [+Humble], [+Honorific], and [+Respect] to personal nouns and pronouns, claiming that such features in the speaker and hearer of a performative sentence are responsible for the formal deference suffix, whereas such features between the performative sentence subject, i.e. the speaker, and the embedded subject NP are responsible for the derivation of the honorific suffix *-usi*. The derivation of the suffixes is formalized by means of transformational rules (H. Lee 1970:87-100).

C. Lee (1973a:43-49), on the other hand, regards both the honorific and the formal deference suffixes as reflexes of abstract higher two place predicates superordinating the performative predicate. He points out that the assignment of such semantic fatures as [+Honorific], etc. to nouns is not well motivated because the same person may become [−Honorific], etc. in different interpersonal situations. In his formula, as shown in (17), DEFER is an abstract verb meaning 'be deferential to', 'respect,' etc., P representing the propositional content.

(17) DEFER (x, y (STATE (x, y (P))))

The performative verb STATE is said to be responsible for the 'declarative marker' *-ta* and DEFER for the formal deference suffix. According to C. Lee, the higher deference predicate modifies the immediately lower performative predicate. For a sentence in which *-usi* and *-sup/-(u)p* both occur, C. Lee proposes that the two abstract predicates be conjoined on the same higher level partly because the speaker is available on that level and partly because deference expression is not a content proposition of an illocutionary act.

If I understand C. Lee correctly, he wants to describe the Korean honorific and formal deference suffixes in a way parallel to such English embedded performative sentences as those in (18) (ibid.: 38-43):

(18) 'May I suggest that you run for the Presidency this time?'

in which *May I* functions simply as a sign of deference, and not as a request for permission from the hearer. He contends that the central force of the utterance is expressed by the embedded performative in this type of sentence and a response to such utterances would be directly related to the embedded performative rather than to the modal construction.

5. Which of the two types of grammar mentioned above would describe Korean modals in a better way? Both have their own strengths and weaknesses. For instance, the first type of grammar has its strength in that the deep structures are easily and straightforwardly related to the corresponding surface manifestations, while its weakness lies in the fact that it does not capture the underlying nature of the language better than the second type of grammar.[4] On the other hand, the latter type of grammar has the reverse strengths and weaknesses.

In the following, a proposal concerning the underlying structure of the modals under discussion will be made by utilizing the second type of grammar, i.e. the line of generative semantics. Relevant arguments in favor of higher sentence approach concerning English modals are found in such works as Ross (1967), McCawley (1971) and Huddleston (1974). A number of further justifications may be made in favor of this approach on the basis of Korean evidence. The interpersonal relationships with respect to the honorific and deference system will be shown explicitly, as correctly pointed out by C. Lee (1973a). The speaker or hearer perspective involved in the other modals mentioned will also be revealed clearly. Moreover, certain important semantic and syntactic relations existing between a modal and the associated propositional content or between the modals themselves will be explained further. A few concrete illustrations follow. Observe the sentences in (19).

(19) a. nay-ka ka-keyss-ta. (i) I intend to go.
    I-SM Vol/Prs (ii) I presume that I will go.
  a′. nay-ka ka-keyss-ni? 'Do you presume that I will go?'
    Prs
  b. ney-ka ka-keyss-ta. 'I presume that you will go.'
    you Prs
  b′. ney-ka ka-keyss-ni? (i) Do you intend to go?
    Vol/Prs (ii) Do you presume that you will go?

Without postulating higher grammatical relations that have the speaker or hearer as the agent it would be very hard to account for the presence or absence of volitional meaning in (19), because its presence is conditioned by the identity of reference between the speaker or hearer and the surface subject.

Secondly, the sentence in (20) contains the suffix *-keyss* which indicates the speaker's presumption of the two combined propositional contents that are conjunctively related.

(20) nay-ka ka-myen Mary-to ka-*keyss*-ta.
  I-SM go-if Mary-also go-presume-reportive
  'I presume that if I go Mary will also go.'

Within the framework in which the speaker appears as an argument in a higher sentence, the meaning of (20) may be correctly represented, which would not be true with the other type of grammar. What this implies is that a modal like *-keyss, -ti/-te,* or *-ta* modifies or semantically dominates not merely the verb of the propositional core it is associated with on the surface, but the entire content denoted by the sentential elements that precede the modal.

Thirdly, the hierarchical relationship among the modals may be revealed satisfactorily only in the type of grammar in which higher predicates are postulated. The sentences in (13) and (14) provide an example. The verb of a propositional core cannot immediately precede the retrospective modal if the subject is the speaker, but it can if the presumptive *-keyss* intervenes. What this signifies is that the modal *-ti/-te* immediately dominates the modal *-keyss* which in turn dominates the propositional content. Furthermore, the fact that the past feature in *-ti/-te* moves the present time of *-keyss* to the past is another example of the domination relationship between *-keyss* and *-ti/-te*. Conversely, no example can be found in which *-keyss* dominates *-ti/-te* semantically. This domination of the retrospective modal over the presumptive modal is partly endorsed by the syntactic correlation, in that, in general, the dominating modal follows the one dominated.[5] Another example of domination relation is found in the fact that *-keyss* and *-ti/-te* are both dominated by the sentence type modals including *-ta*. As has already been mentioned, the speaker perspective is replaced by the hearer perspective as soon as the statement sentence is changed to the question sentence. As will be observed, the person-sensitive modals dominate negation or tense, this fact requiring the former set to superordinate the latter.

6. In view of the foregoing observations, together with the discussion that follows, it is proposed that the underlying structure of (1a) be something like (21).

(21) Proposed underlying structure for (1a)

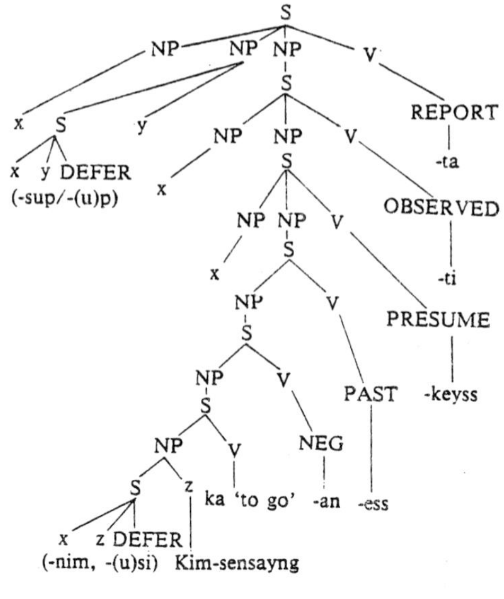

The following discussion will be limited to the three modals, *-ta*, *-(u)si* and *-sup/-(u)p*, since it seems that the others (*-keyss* and *-ti/-te*) will be less problematic.

It should be initially noticed that the formal reportive suffix *-ta* occurs regardless of the performative or non-performative nature of the verb it occurs with. Observe the sentences in (22) and (23).

(22) a. pi-ka o-*p*-ni-*ta*.
'It is raining'
(reporting with formal deference)
b. cuksi ka-l-kes-ul myenghay-ss-*sup*-ni-*ta*.
'I ordered (them) to go immediately.'
(reporting with formal deference)

(23) cuksi ka-l-kes-ul myengha-*p*-ni-*ta*.
'I order you to go immediately.'
(ordering with formal deference)

The sentences in (22) show that the verbs (*o* 'to come' and *myengha* 'to order') occurring with *-ta* are non-performative, whereas the verb *myengha* 'to order' in (23) is performative but is followed by the suffix *-ta*. It should be noticed further that the formal deference modal occurs only before *-ta* both in (22) and (23), regardless of whether the verb preceding it is performative or not. What then is *-ta?* We may consider it consistently as a reflex of a statement performative verb. If so, (23) would be viewed as containing double performative verbs, command followed by statement. Or we might consider it as a performative verb reflex in (22) but semantically empty in (23). This latter interpretation is counter-intuitive to me, because *-ta* has a consistent meaning 'the speaker's formal report to the hearer'. Whether *-ta* is a performative reflex or not is a matter of interpretation. Furthermore, the consistent appearance of the formal deference modal before *-ta* leads us to view *-ta* as a homogeneous unit. Thus, for instance, the English sentence 'I order you to go' is expressed in Korean as 'I report to you that I order you to go.' In the same way, the sentence *May I suggest that you run for the Presidency this time?* should be expressed in Korean as something similar to 'I *report* to you with my deference to you that I suggest that you run for the Presidency this time' as can be inferred from (23).

Thus, it is true that in (23) the higher sentence for the formal deference should be somewhere above the performative sentence whose predicate is *myengha* 'to order'. However, there is no reason to view the deference sentence as higher than the reportive sentence associated with *-ta*. Rather, the former must come under the domain or scope of the latter. In the first place, the deference modal *-sup/-(u)p* is not simply the speaker's deference attitude, but a verbal expression of the attitude. So far as it is a verbal expression, it has to be conveyed by the speaker's *report* to the hearer. Thus, the report dominates the deference. If, conversely, the deference were to be on top of the report, my introspection would force me to interpret the deference as a simple gesture of deference such as bowing or hesitancy.

Secondly, the formal deference modal never follows the reportive modal on the surface, while in the English sentence, *May I . . .*, the modal indicating deference is the sentence-initial element. As previously mentioned, it is a general phenomenon that the dominating element follows the one dominated in Korean, which is an SOV or verb-final language. The same is true with other sentence types. For instance, (24a) may be translated into (24b) or (24c). Notice that the deference modal always precedes the sentence-type suffix.

(24) a. Will you pass the salt?
b. sokum com cwu-si-keyss-*sup*-ni-kka?
salt just give -Question
c. sokum com cwu-si-*p*-siyo.
-Imperative

Thus, the surface manifestation of the modals leads one to postulate the abstract deference sentence as an embedded construction, rather than a topmost one.

This paper further proposes to deal with the honorific and formal deference modals, i.e., *-(u)si* and *-sup,* on different levels in view of their characteristic syntactic differences.[6] For instance, *-sup* (including its allomorphs) has nothing to do with the propositional content, while *-(u)si* is always directly associated with the propositional core. *-sup* is related to the *indirect object* of the performative sentence, while *-(u)si* is related to the *subject* of the propositional core. *-sup* appears only once in a sentence, while *-(u)si* occurs as many times as needed. *-sup* is placed outside the syntactic domain of negation or tense, while *-(u)si* is inside it. *-sup* never appears in an embedded construction, while *-(u)si* does. *-sup* is immune to such transformations as subject choice or passivization, while *-(u)si* is sensitive to them. On the surface, *-sup* appears near *-ta*, the sentence-final element, while *(u)si* is found only immediately after the verb of the propositional core. All these observations indicate that quite different syntactic rules are associated with the derivation of *-sup* and that of *-(u)si*, and furthermore that the proper place for *-sup* should be in the reportive (as well as in the question, imperative or propositive) higher sentence where the speaker and the hearer are interpersonally related, while the proper place for *-(u)si* is in the propositional core where the subject of the sentence is located.

A further proposal is that the interpersonal relationships including various speech levels and the honorific expression be specified as a relative clause with the hearer or the subject as the antecedent, as in (21). Thus, for instance, 'you whom I am deferential to', 'you whom I am intimate with', 'you whom I am familiar with', etc. would derive different speech level endings. Once we accept *-sup* and *-(u)si* as reflexes of two place predicates, as C. Lee has proposed, it is reasonable to relate the underlying sentences involving the predicates to the proper word (i.e., the hearer or the subject) in the relevant tree as a modifier rather than to the whole tree. First, it can be observed that the interpersonal relationships do not have any underlying connection with verbs. Secondly, the sentence involving such an abstract predicate (i. e. a reflex of *-sup* or *(u)si*) contains the argument which is co-referential to the hearer or the subject of the propositional core, which is simply accounted for by the already available relativization mechanism. Thirdly, C. Lee's concern that the deference expression is not a content proposition of the illocutionary act may be dispensed with by the proposed relativization treatment. Fourthly, H. Lee's direct association between the speaker in the performative sentence and the subject of an embedded sentence is rather unnatural in that the interpersonal relationship is certainly to be represented in the same proposition. For instance, in (25), H. Lee's description would relate the semantic feature [+Humble] in the performative subject in S1 directly to the feature [+Respect] in *sensayng* which appears in S4 in order to obtain *-si*.

(25) $_{S1}$[$_{S2}$[ikes-i $_{S3}$[$_{S4}$[sensayng-nim-i cwu-*si*-n]$_{S4}$ ton-ulo
this-SM teacher give money -with
sa-n]$_{S3}$ chayk i]$_{S2}$ ta.]$_{S1}$
buy book is
'This is the book I bought with the money given by the teacher.'

According to the treatment proposed here, a relative clause consisting of the arguments 'I' and 'the teacher' and the predicate 'DEFER' modifies *sensayng* 'the teacher' in S4. Finally, the proposed relativization also reflects the absence (or looseness) of the domination relationship between *-sup* or

-(*u*)*si* and the other modals, person-sensitive or not. For example, the retrospective modal *-ti/-te,* while changing the tense of the main verb or *-keyss,* does not affect *-sup* or -(*u*)*si* although on the surface *-sup* and -(*u*)*si* always precede it. In a reverse manner, neither *-sup* nor -(*u*)*si* affects the other modals semantically. This clearly indicates that the human relationships involved are not something that goes into an immediate domination relationship with the other predicates in the deep structure.

Viewed in this way, it is easy to postulate the underlying structures for the other person-sensitive modals, as observed in (21). The volitional *-keyss,* the presumptive *-keyss,* the retrospective *-ti/-te,* and the reportive *-ta* are similar in that all of them involve a sentence as one of their arguments. Among these, *-ta* is unique in that it is an abstract three place predicate. All the abstract modal propositions will eventually be deleted after they have performed their proper roles for the derivation of surface forms.[7] In particular, the sentence related to -(*u*)*si* is responsible for the honorific title *-nim* and other non-modal effects which are not a matter of concern here.

7. In spite of the postulation of the underlying structures as in (21), it is by no means claimed that modals in Korean are the same predicates as main or auxiliary verbs. A brief summary that follows will indicate my findings on the characteristics of person-sensitive modals that are not, in general, shared by verbs. Some of these apply to the other modals as well.

First, as has been repeatedly mentioned, all these modals reflect the speaker and/or hearer perspectives. Incidentally, this is a strong piece of evidence that we cannot interpret them as one place predicates with a sentence as the only argument in underlying structure (Cf. Langendoen 1970:186-88 for the treatment of english modals as one place predicates). They are all transitive. An implication of the person-sensitiveness of these modals is that their frequent occurrence partly contributes to the structural pressure that allows Korean sentences to do without their predictable subjects.

Secondly, they are never used as a propositional core. They must have a propositional core to modify.[8]

Thirdly, not one of them can be negated in any way. For example, passive or causative suffixes may be negated, but the scope of negation never extends to any of the modals. This fact is also supported by syntactic manifestation. In Korean, we have short and long form negation. (1a) is a sentence with short form negation. Its long form counterpart is (26).

(26) Kim-sensayng-nim-i ka-si-*ci-anh*-ess-keyss-sup-ni-ta.

The italicized part cannot be moved in any position after *-keyss*. Although *-si* is before the negative suffix, it is never negated. Its presence there is motivated by other reasons as have already been stated. For the nagativizability of some German modals, see Bouma (1973:35-36 and ch. 7).

Fourthly, none of them can be passivized or causativized, although all of them are underlying transitive verbs. If there is any passivization or causativization involved in a sentence, it is related only to the propositional content. Moreover, no adverbial can modify them.

Fifthly, none of them may have past or past-past suffixes or aspects of their own within the underlying proposition to which they belong. For example, the presumptive *-keyss* occurs with all the tenses and aspects, but these are always related to the propositional content, not to *-keyss*.

Finally, on the surface, all of them are verbal suffixes. This indicates that the predicates associated with them are all abstract. This further means that they are bound. In English, the modals may appear by themselves, as in *You may,* which is not the case in Korean.

Notes

1. The original version of this paper was reported at the Korean-Japanese Syntactic Festival sponsored by the Linguistic Society of Hawaii on September 26, 1974 at the University of Hawaii.

   The Yale romanization is followed in representing Korean forms in this paper. Abbreviations used are: SM = subject marker; OM = object maker; Nom = nominalizer; Hon = honorific suffix.
2. For the moment, I simply follow some linguists for the terms of these morphemes. Remember, however, that scholars are not in agreement at all, not only on the terminology but also on the identification of such morphemes.
3. Incidentally, the exact equivalents of the so-called English modals such as *may*, *can*, *must*, *will* are not found in Korean. The suppositional *should* and the inferential *must* are somewhat close semantically to the presumptive *keyss* and the volitional *will* to the volitional *keyss*, whereas most other English modals are equivalent to Korean embedding constructions. Thus, the root sense of *may* (i.e., permission) is expressed in Korean by something like 'to be O.K. if ...', as in

   ka-to coh-ta. '(You) may go.'
   go-if O.K.-reportive
4. Grammarians belonging to this group also have either implied or noticed the possibility of abstract analysis of certain modals. For instance, S. Song (1967:26-27) points out that

the constituent 'Hon' may be correctly attached as an optional element after animate subject nouns rather than after verbs although it is to be realized as a verbal suffix. I Yang (1972:22, 236) indicates that the performative analysis as conducted by H. Lee (1970) would predict some modality elements and that 'the retrospective mood' may be predictable if a higher sentence is postulated, although he does not elaborate any further on these.

5. We cannot, however, take this syntactic phenomenon as a generalization in accounting for semantic domination relationships. For example, the formal deference modal and the retrospective modal have no semantically significant domination relationship. Rather, the former is closely related to the sentence-type modals such as *-ta*. In spite of this, the formal deference modal precedes the retrospective modal which in turn precedes the sentence-type modal *-ta* or *-kka*, as we saw in (1).
6. Strictly speaking, the two modals are not the same in their semantic ranges. For instance, recall that among Martin's six speech levels only the formal deference is associated with *-sup*. *-(u)si*, on the other hand, does not always require 'formal deference' and is also subject to various social norms, as already discussed. Notice that *pi-ka o-si-n-ta* 'It is raining' (Lit. The esteemed rain falls) is a common expression.
7. The very presence of an abstract predicate triggers an obligatory transformation, i.e. deletion of the proposition in this case. For the discussion of case incorporation transformations which are to be triggered by abstract predicates, see Sohn 1974b.
8. Modals and 'auxiliary' verbs share this particular characteristic. In many other respects, however, 'auxiliary' verbs are similar neither to modals nor to 'main' verbs. For a detailed discussion of Korean 'auxiliary' verbs, see Sohn 1973b.

Reprinted from *Papers in Linguistics* 7.3/4:493-520 (1974).

8. RETROSPECTION IN KOREAN

It is argued in Sohn (1974a) that Korean verbal suffixes like the honorific *-si*, the formal deferential *-sup*, and the performative elements such as *-ta* (reportive) and *-kka* (question) are all underlyingly transitive sentences with the speaker or hearer as the agent. The present paper is an attempt to push the frontier forward and reveal some fundamental semantic properties (the semantic structure, the semantic units, and the interactions of these units) associated with the retrospective suffix.[1]

1. Korean has developed a productive verbal suffix which involves the semantic range that most linguists christen as 'retrospective'. This suffix, which has such variants as *-te* (dialectally *-tu*), *-ti* and *-t* (representable morphophonemically as -TE), occurs in constructions such as the following.[2]

(1) a. John-i ka-*te*-nya? 'Did you see John going?'
John-SM go-R-Q
b. John-i ka-*t*-ey. 'I saw John going.'
John-SM go-R-Int.
c. John-i ka-ss-keyss-up-*ti*-kka?
John-SM go-Prf.-Pre.-Fd.-R-Q
d. John-i *ka-te*-la-ko ha-*te*-la.
John-SM go-R-Rep.-Quo. say-R-Rep.
'I heard him saying that he had seen John going.'
e. John-i ka-*te*-n-ka molu-keyss-ta.
John-SM go-R-M-Qi. unaware-Pre.-Rep.
'I wonder if I observed John going.'
f. ikes-i nay-ka ilk-*te*-n chayk-i-ta.
this-SM I-SM read-R-M book-Cop.-Rep.

Probably due to the lack of its comparable form in other languages, plus the sensitivity of its meaning to the syntactic and semantic environments, there is no agreement among scholars as to the term designating the category the retrospective suffix is supposed to belong to, called variously a tense (e.g. Choi 1965:348), an aspect (e.g. Martin 1954:37), a mood (e.g. I. Yang 1972:4), or a manner (e.g. S. Chang 1973a:40). If such traditional grammatical terms are to be used, it may be claimed that -TE cuts across the distinction ot mood and tense, in that it refers not only to the past but also to the speaker's perceiving of a propositional content.[3] This will be elaborated upon shortly.

As regards the lexical meaning of the suffix, Martin (forthcoming:356) defines it roughly as 'it has been observed', stating that 'the observation can be that of the speaker, that of someone else, or a purely grammatical device'. The 'observation' here is, of course, a cover term, which should include such detailed meanings as 'find', 'see', 'notice', 'witness', 'perceive', 'watch', 'hear', 'recall' and many others (e.g. Martin et al. 1967, I. Yang 1972:234).

2. The structure underlying -TE that I should like to postulate is of the shape in (2).

(2)

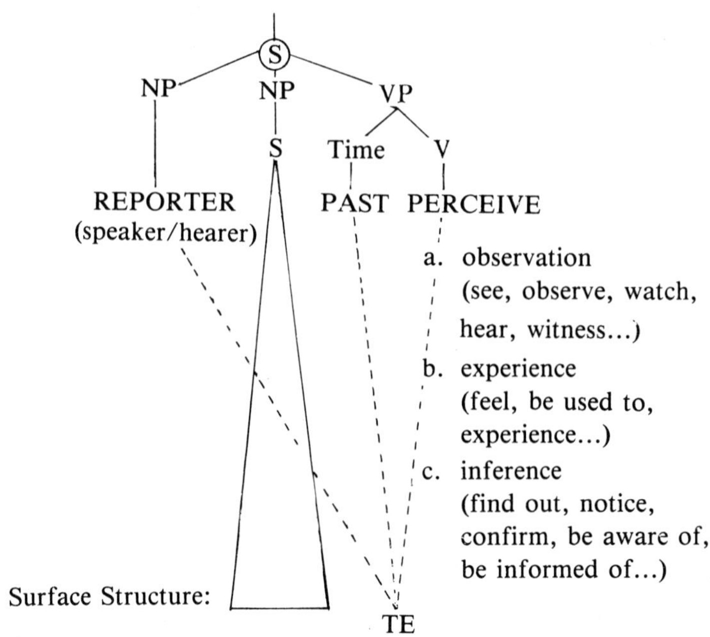

The syntactic verbal suffix -TE is viewed as being derived from the semantic structure sketched in (2), which has the semantic units REPORTER, PAST, and PERCEIVE, with PERCEIVE being the abstract predicate. These three semantic units are realized as -TE in the actual sentence, with the underlying meanings retained. The only element external to -TE is the complement sentence (S) which is an obligatory propositional content and the object of the transitive predicate PERCEIVE. The structure in (2) is further superordinated either by a performative sentence (in the case of non-embedded sentences) or by a noun phrase (in the case of embedded sentences). Thus, one reading of the sentence *John-i ka-te-nya*? is something like 'I request that you report to me whether you observed (in the past) John going'. In separate sections I will further elaborate on some details regarding the postulation of an underlying sentence for -TE (Section 3), the NP node dominating REPORTER (Section 4), the Time node dominating PAST (Section 5), the V node dominating PERCEIVE (Section 6), and a brief conclusion (Section 7).

3. There are many reasons to prefer postulating a superordinate sentence in (2) for -TE to an auxiliary or suffixal treatment of the Chomskyan type. For one thing, -TE requires an agent argument, i.e. the REPORTER, who PERCEIVES a propositional content. Needless to say, such a structural relation is characteristic of a sentence in that the minimum requirement of a sentence is a predicate occurring with an argument. Moreover, a sentential complement postulated in (2) shows an embedding phenomenon for a complex sentence, which is universal in human language. -TE requires such a complement sentence as another argument related to the predicate PERCEIVE.

Secondly, all adverbials of the sentence where -TE occurs are dominated semantically by -TE. In *John-i ecey ka-ss-te-la* 'I noticed that John went yesterday', for example, what the speaker noticed is not the completed action of going, but 'John's having gone yesterday'. The adverb *ecey* refers to the time when the action of going took place, and does not specify the time of the speaker's notice of the event. The speaker may have noticed it a few minutes ago. Since *ecey* goes with *ka-ss*, 'notice' should not take the same underlying level as they do. Even a more transparent time disparity between the action of going and the action of notice may be observed in *John-i molay ka-te-la* 'I noticed that John would go the day after tomorrow'. Noticing took place in the past, whereas John's going will take place in the future. All this means that the proper structure of -TE should be a superordinate sentence.

Thirdly, a sequence of conjunctive sentences may also be dominated by -TE, forcing the postulation of a higher sentence for -TE inevitable. Observe (3a) where the two clauses are jointly the objects of the speaker's observation. One might claim that (3a) is derived from something like (3b), which is obviously false in view of the meanings involved.

(3) a. John-un kongpuha-myense coffee-lul masi-*te*-la
John-T study-while coffee-OM drink-R-Rep.
'I observed John drinking coffee while studying.'
b. (John-un kongpuha-*te*-la)-myense John-un coffee-lul masi-*te*-la.

(3a) asserts one observed fact, whereas (3b) asserts two. That is, the parenthesized sentence in (3b) is not asserted at all in (3a).

Fourthly, the immunity of -TE from the scope of negation is another argument for the superordination. Observe the sentences in (4).

(4) a. John-i ka-*te*-nya? 'Did you see John going?'
John-SM go-R-Q
Aniyo. 'No.'
No
b. John-i an-ka-ss-*te*-la.
John-SM not-go-Prf.-R-Rep.
'I noticed that John had not gone.'
c. John-i ka-ci-an-ass-*te*-la.
John-SM go-N-not-Prf.-R-Rep.
'I noticed that John had not gone.'

In (4a) the negative answer, *aniyo*, means that 'John did not go' rather than 'I did not see'. (4b) never means 'I did not notice the fact that John had gone' in which case -TE would be in the scope of negation. Notice in (4c) which is the long form negation of (4b) that the negative suffix *-an* precedes -TE, which provides a syntactic support for the higher level of -TE on top of negation. In general, the higher an abstract structure is presumed to be, the later it comes in a linear surface structure in consistent SOV languages (e.g. Korean and Japanese). It is widely claimed that the negative element of a sentence in any language is an underlying higher predicate. If this is true, it is still more the case with the retrospective suffix, because this suffix dominates negation underlyingly.

Finally, even the genericness of a sentence is not affected by -TE.

(5)	a.	inkan-un cwuk-nun-ta. man-T die-Pr.-Rep.	'Man is mortal.'
	b.	*inkan-un cwuk-ess-ta. man-T die-Prf.-Rep.	*'Man is dead.'
	c.	inkan-un cwuk-*te*-la. man-T die-R-Rep.	'I confirmed that man is mortal.'

(5a) is a generic expression, in which both the subject and the predicate are generic, whereas (5b) is awkward because the generic subject is followed by a non-generic verbal expression (due to the perfective *-ess*). In (5c) the genericness is intact even though the verb is followed by -TE. The speaker's confirmation of the generic proposition in (5c) is another piece of evidence that -TE is related to a higher sentence in the conceptual structure.[4]

4. Since we have postulated an underlying sentence for -TE, let us now look at the semantic units which are interrelated in this sentence. As indicated in (2), -TE is uniquely associated with the REPORTER, which may be either the speaker or the hearer or somebody else. In any case, he is the one who PERCEIVES an event and at the same time is in a position to report on his PERCEIVING. In other words, the agent of PERCEIVING and the immediately higher REPORTER should be coreferential. In sentence-final position, the REPORTER is the speaker if the -TE structure is superordinated by a reportive performative, as in (6). The reading of (6a), for example, is something like '*I report* to you that *I* observed John going.' If the -TE structure is dominated by a question performative construction, the potential REPORTER is the hearer, as in (7). The reading of (7a), for example, is something like 'I request that you report to me whether *you* observed John going.' (Cf. Dahl 1970, Gordon and G. Lakoff 1971).

(6)	a.	John-i ka-*te*-la. John-SM go-R-Rep.	'I saw John going.'
	b.	na-nun kippu-p-*ti*-ta. I-T gland-Fd.-R-Rep.	'I felt that I was happy.'
(7)	a.	John-i ka-*te*-nya? John-SM go-R-Q	'Did you see John going?'
	b.	tangsin-un kippu-p-*ti*-kka? you-T glad-Fd.-R-Q	'Did you feel that you were happy?'

The same is true when the -TE construction is quoted by a sentence where the main verb is a communicative verb. In (8a) it is *Mary* who is the 'speaker' or REPORTER of the quoted sentence, and therefore it is the 'speaker' and REPORTER *Mary* who is the agent of the predicate *observed.* In (8b), on the other hand, the quoted construction is that of a question and, therefore, it is the 'hearer' and potential REPORTER 'I' (the speaker of the entire sentence) who is the agent of the predicate *observed.*

(8) a. John-i ka-*te*-la-ko Mary-ka malhay-ss-ta.
John-SM go-R-Rep.-Quo. Mary-SM say-Prf.-Rep.
(I report to you that *Mary reported* to me that *she* had observed John going.)

b. John-i ka-*te*-nya-ko Mary-ka mul-ess-ta.
John-SM go-R-Q-Quo. Mary-SM ask-Prf.-Rep.
(I report to you that Mary requested that *I report* to her whether *I* had observed John going.)

This sort of speaker-hearer correlation may also be observable in English modals. For instance, Jespersen (1955:261) states that the use of *shall* is restricted to the first person in statements and to the second person in questions, though in some subordinate clauses it is used in all three persons.

As we have seen in the examples in (6)-(8), the agent speaker in statements and the agent hearer in question are *exclusive* in the sense that the agent perceiving an event cannot be both the speaker and the hearer at the same time. Needless to say, this is because the -TE construction is dominated by a performative sentence and, thus, is the content proposition of an illocutionary act. That is, the event perceived is new information reported (in statement) or requested (in question) between speaker and hearer; this fact makes the simultaneous involvement of both speaker and hearer as the agent impossible. In contrast with this strict exclusiveness of the agent in the performative-dominated -TE, there is no such constraint in -TE appearing in other positions, although the agent must always include the REPORTER, actual (speaker) or potential (hearer). Observe the following examples.

(9) a. ikes-i John-i ilk-*te*-n chayk-i-ta.
this-SM John-SM read-R-M book-Cop.-Rep.
'This is a book which I (*or* you and I) observed John reading.'

b. pi-ka o-*te*-ni nalssi-ka chwup-ta.

rain-SM come-R-as weather-SM cold-Rep.
'I (*or* you and I) observed it raining, and now it is cold.'

(10) a. ikes-i John-i ilk-*te*n chayk-i-ni?
this-SM John-SM read-R-M book-Cop.-Q
'Is this a book which you (*or* you and I) observed John reading?'

b. pi-ka o-*te*-ni nalssi-ka chwup-ni?
rain-SM come-R-as weather-SM cold-Q
'Is it cold as a result of the rain that you (*or* you and I) observed?'

Thus, in non-performative environment the exclusiveness becomes opaque allowing 'inclusive' agents, since the -TE construction is not directly questioned.

It is often claimed that when dominated by a performative sentence the speaker or hearer agent involved in -TE must not be coreferential with the subject of the next lower sentence in order for the whole sentence to be grammatical (I. Yang 1972:234, S. Chang 1973a:51). This so-called 'non-equi-subject constraint' is based on such rather unnatural sentences as *nay-ka ka-te-la* 'I observed myself going'. The unnaturalness of such expressions (i.e., reporting the observation of one's own progressive event or requesting the hearer to report the observation of his own progressive event) is universal, and not unique to -TE constructions. Therefore, such a 'constraint' has to be dealt with in connection with empirical matters of fact in human experiences. Moreover, the above expressions are perfectly allowable in a possible or imaginary world, such as a dream or a movie, as S. Chang (1973a) also pointed out. In this case, the lower speaker or hearer is extremely objectivized, as if it were a third person. Even in a real world, the 'non-equi-subject constraint' does not hold, if an adequate modifier is used (11a), if certain suffixes (such as the perfective and the presumptive) precede -TE (11b), or if the lower subject is an Experiencer in relation to the verb (11c).

(11) a. na-honca-*man* ka-*te*-la. 'I found out that *I* was the only one who was going.'
I-alone-only go-R-Rep.
Ney-ka *ceyil* celm-te-nya? 'Did *you* find that *you* were the most young of all?'
you-SM most young-R-Q

b. ney-ka ka-*ss*-*te*-nya? 'Did *you* experience (*your*) going?'
you-SM go-Prf. -R-Q

nay-ka cwuk-*keyss-te*-la. '*I* felt that *I* would die.'
I-SM die-Pre.-R-Rep.

c. nay-ka *chwiha-te*-la. '*I* felt *myself* intoxicated'
I-SM drunk-R-Re.

nay-ka *kippu-te*-la '*I* felt that *I* was happy.'
I-SM glad-R-Rep.

Again, when the -TE construction is not dominated by a performative sentence, there is no restriction whatsoever. Thus, for instance, *nay-ka ka-te-n ku cip* 'the house I experienced to go to' is perfectly natural in the real world. As we will see in Section 6, this is because the observation reading is suppressed in embedded position when the two subjects in question are identical.

5. A common description of the retrospective suffix is that a sentence with the suffix expresses a past event as observed or recalled by the speaker or the hearer (e.g. Choi 1965:433). -TE is not restricted to past events alone, however, as illustrated in (12).

(12) a. nay sayngil-i nay-tal i-*te*-la.
my birthday-SM next-month Cop.-R-Rep.
'I found that my birthday will be next month.'

b. John-i nayil ka-*te*-la.
John-SM tomorrow go-R-Rep.
'I noticed that John will go tomorrow.'

c. ce salam-i nwukwu-*te*-la!?
that person-SM who-R-Rep.
'I wonder whom I observed him to be.'

d. John-i cikum-to ku cip-eyse sal-*te*-la.
John-SM now-also that house-at live-R-Rep.
'I noticed that John is still living in that house.'

(12 a,b) illustrate future events, whereas (12 c,d) show that the events are those of the present. In all the sentences in (12), the action of the speaker's PERCEIVING each event took place in the past. Thus, PAST is a necessary semantic unit contained in -TE. It is this PAST that does not allow an imperative or propositive sentence to carry -TE. This PAST is not inherently related to the time of an event, although naturally past PERCEIVING is more frequently associated with past events.

The PAST in -TE indicates any time prior to the time of utterance, which is inherently the present. One might claim that the time in -TE in an embedded position is the past with reference to the time of the matrix event in such examples as given in (13).

(13) John-i mek-*te*-n pap-ul Mary-ka mek-ess-ta.
John-SM eat-R-M rice-OM Mary-SM eat-Prf.-Rep.
'Mary ate the rice that, I observed, John had eaten (*or* had been eating).'

I hold the view that the time sequence between events in (13) is so fixed not because the matrix time is the reference point in relation to which the time of PERCEIVING the embedded event is PAST, but because the empirical world forces the events to be arranged only in that temporal order. For instance, while it is natural for *Mary* to finish eating the rice which *John* has not finished eating, it is impossible for *John* to be eating the rice which *Mary* has finished eating. This view is supported by the sentence in (14) where the matrix time precedes the embedded time and by the sentence in (15) where the events are simultaneous.'[5]

(14) John-i mek-*te*-n pap-ul Mary-ka ci-ess-ta.
John-SM eat-R-M rice-OM Mary-SM cook-Prf. Rep.
'Mary had made the rice which, I observed, John was eating.

(15) John-i salangha-*te*-n yeca-lul na-to salanghay-ss-ta.
John-SM love-R-M girl-OM I-also love-Prf.-Rep.
'I loved the girl whom, I observed, John loved.'

All this means that the matrix time cannot be the reference point for the PAST contained in the retrospective suffix. Consider further the sentence in (16) which is the same as (13) except that it carries the embedded time adverb *kucey* 'day before yesterday' and the matrix time adverb *ecey* 'yesterday'.

(16) John-i kucey mek-*te*-n pap-ul Mary-ka
John-SM day-before-yesterday eat-R-M rice-OM Mary-SM
ecey mek-ess-ta.
yesterday eat-Prf.-Rep.
'Mary ate the rice yesterday which I observed John eating the day before yesterday.'

Both time adverbs are used only in relation to the utterance time, and not to the time of Mary's eating, i.e. 'yesterday'.

Only in imaginary future events may the reference point be moved to a time in the future which is in the speaker's imagination, as illustrated in (17).

(17) pi-ka o-myen ka-*te*-n cha-ka su-l-kes-i-ta.
rain-SM come-if go-R-M car-SM stop-Pros.-fact-Cop.-Rep.
'If it rains, the car, which we will observe going, may stop.'

Notice that the reference point in (17) is in the imaginary future and the speaker's imaginary observation in the future is prior to this reference point.[6]

The event time and the time of PERCEIVING the event do not have to be the same for a grammatical expression, as illustrated in (18).

(18) a. John-i ecey ka-*te*-la.
John-SM yesterday go-R-Rep.
i. I observed John going yesterday.
ii. I noticed that John was to go yesterday.

b. John-i nayil ka-*te*-la.
John-SM tomorrow go-R-Rep.
ii. I noticed that John will go tomorrow.

In (18 ai) the time of observation and that of the event are the same whereas in (18 aii) and (18 bii) they are different. The underlying structures of (18 ai), (18 aii) and (18 bii) are roughly as (19).

(19)

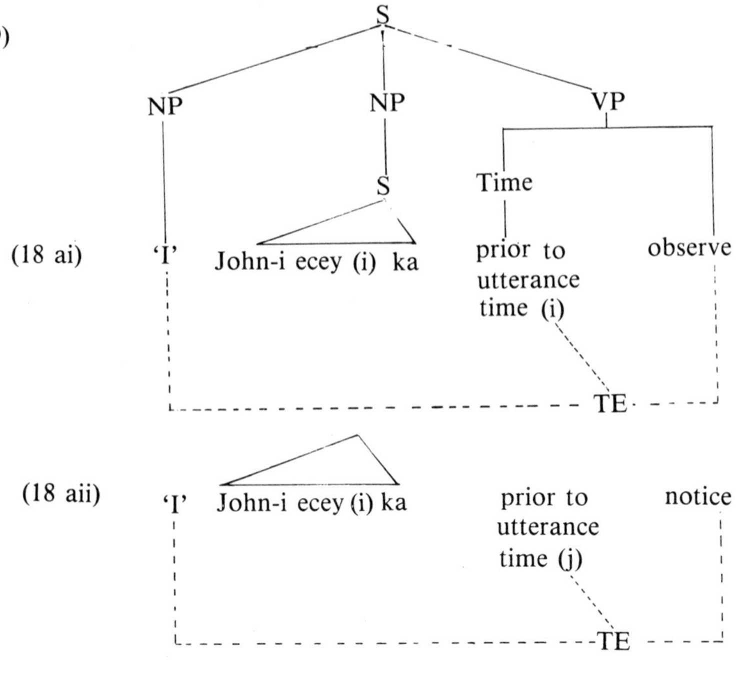

(18 bii)

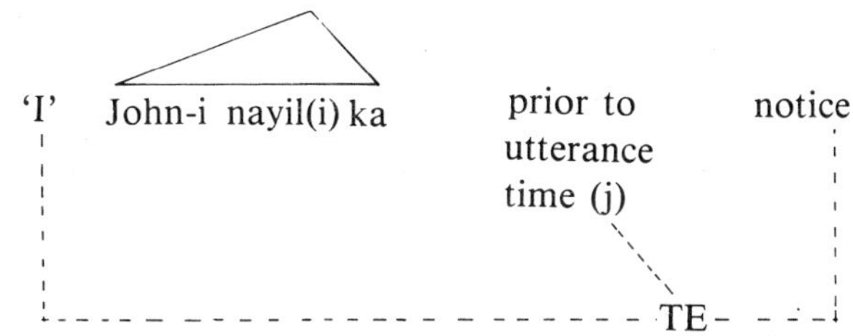

It has frequently been claimed that -TE (especially in a relative clause) contains the meaning 'progressive' (e.g. Na 1971:24), 'unfinished action' (e.g. H.S. Lee 1957:72), or 'durative' (I. Yang 1972:239). Such meanings may be noticeable in the sentences in (20).

(20) a. John-i ka-*te*-la. 'I saw John *going*.'
John-SM go-R-Rep.

b. ip-*te*-n os-ul pes-ess-ta.
put on-R-M clothes-OM take off-Prf.-Rep.
'I took off the clothes which I started *putting on*.'

c. yeki twu-*te*-n khal-i epseci-ess-ta.
here put-R-M knife-SM disappear-Prf.-Rep.
'The knife which I *used to* put here has disappeared.'

Again, existence of such a meaning may be justified by the sentences in (21).

(21) a. Ecey {ha-*te*-n / *ha-n} il-ul onul kkuthmachi-ess-ta.
yesterday {do-R-M / do-Per.M} work-OM today finish-Prf.-Rep.
'I finished the work, today, which {I was doing / *I finished doing} yesterday.'

b. chayk-ul {ilk-*te*-n / *ta ilk-*te*-n} salam-i pakk-ulo na-ka-ss-ta.
book-OM {read-R-M / all read-R-M} person-SM outside-to out-go-Prf.-Rep.
'The person who {was reading a book / *was reading a book completely} went out.'

This paper claims that such imperfective meaning is not a part (or inherent feature) of -TE, but belongs to the zero filler which contrasts with the perfective -*(a)ss* or -*(u)n*. In the first place, the imperfective meaning does not appear if the perfective suffix occurs.

(22) a. John-i ka-*ss-te*-la. 'I noticed that John had gone.'
John-SM go-Prf.-R-Rep. (perfective)
b. John-i mek-*ess-te*-n pap 'the rice that I noticed John had
John-SM eat-Prf.-R-M rice eaten' (perfective)

Secondly, the imperfective meaning appears even if there is no retrospective suffix, as observed in (23).

(23) a. John-i ka-n-ta. 'John is going.'
John-SM go-Pr.-Rep.
b. John-i mek-nun pap 'the rice John is eating'
John-SM eat-Pr. rice
c. John-i ka-myen pull-ela. 'Call John if he is going.'
John-SM go-if call-Im.

6. Let us now look at the abstract predicate which underlies the retrospective suffix. It is well known that meanings are elusive in relation to their associated forms, which is also the case with the predicate underlying -TE. However slippery meanings may be, we can distinguish three broad meaning classes that function as the predicate, i.e., OBSERVE, EXPERIENCE, and INFER each of which has a number of members, definable mainly in terms of the nature of cooccurring main verbs. It can be said that the three meaning classes belong to a higher semantic class which represents human perception. Since the three meaning classes are mutually exclusive, being conditioned by the underlying structural environment, let us view them as constituting a 'natural' semantic class (or one might want to call it a sememe), to be represented as PERCEIVE. Note that PERCEIVE is relevant only to -TE, in that there are many non-affixal perception verbs. Like other perception verbs (see, for example, Givón (1972) for a discussion of English perception/knowledge verbs), PERCEIVE takes a sentential complement and does not require identity of its subject with that of the lower verb, as we have observed.

The meaning of inference always appears when the time (or place) of PERCEIVING and the time (or place) of the event expressed by the immediately lower sentence are not the same. There are many situations in which one can perceive an event through inference. In *John-i hankwuk-ey ka-ss-te-la* 'I found out that John had gone to Korea', for instance, the time of John's going and that of the speaker's PERCEIVING of the fact are not the same. The speaker may have contacted John's wife, seen a newspaper or a passenger list, or heard from someone in Korea before arriving at the assertion.

When equi-time (plus equi-place) is held, either the meaning of observation or the meaning of experience shows up, and the two meanings are again mutually exclusive. When the subject of the -TE structure (i.e. the agent of PERCEIVING) and the immediately lower subject are not the same, the meaning of observation always appears, as in *John-i ka-te-la* 'I saw John going,' *John-i ka-te-ni* 'as a result of John's going (which I saw),' and *John-i ka-te-n nal* 'the day when I observed John going'. When the two subjects are the same, two things happen. If -TE is not dominated by a performative sentence, the meaning of experience always holds. If -TE is dominated by a performative sentence, the meaning of experience occurs when the verb preceding -TE is one of experiencing or when -TE is preceded by the perfective suffix; otherwise the observation meaning appears. These may be represented schematically as follows.

(24)

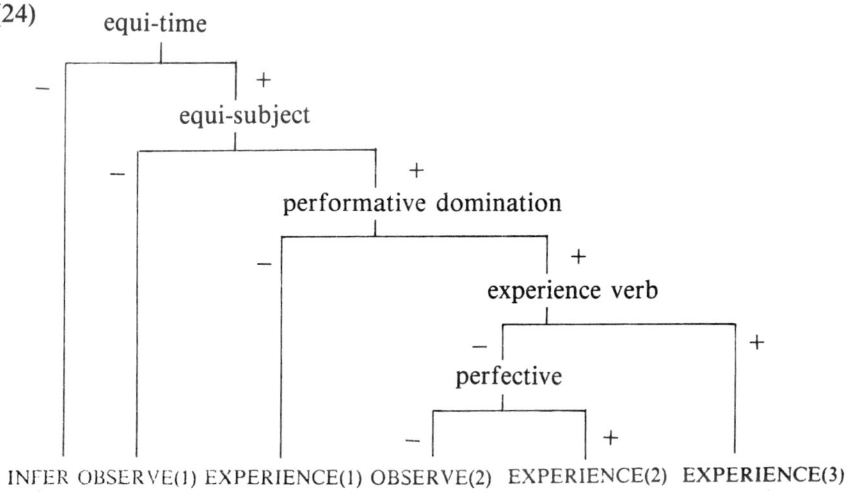

(25) examples

INFER: John-i nayil ka-*te-la*.
John-SM tomorrow go-R-Rep.
'I found out that John would go tomorrow.'
yengkwuk-eyes sal-*te*-n John-i wa-ss-ta.
England-in live-R-M John-SM come-Prf.-Rep.

'John, who, I heard, had lived in England, came.'
John-i ka-ss-*te*-nya?
John-SM go-Prf.-R-Q
'Did you notice whether John had gone?'
nay-ka twusi-kan ca-ss-*te*-la.
I-SM two hours-for sleep-Prf.-R-Rep.
'I found myself having slept for two hours.'

OBSERVE (1): John-i pakk-eyse nol-*te*-la.
John-SM outside-at play-R-Rep.
'I saw John playing outside.'
John-i ka-*te*-ni an-o-n-ta.
John-SM go-R-but not-come-Pr.-Rep.
'I saw John going, but he hasn't come.'
yengkwuk-eyse sal-*te*-n John-i wa-ss-ta.
England-in live-R-M John-SM come-Prf.-Rep.
'John, whom I saw living in England, came.'

EXPERIENCE(1): ikes-i nay-ka ilk-ess-*te*-n chayk-i-ta.
this-SM I-SM read-Prf.-R-M book-Cop.-Rep.
'This is the book I experienced to have read.'
ney-ka sal-*te*-n cip-un enu-kes-i-nya?
you-SM live-R-M house-T which-thing-Corp.-Q
'Which house is the one you lived in?'

OBSERVE(2): na-honca ka-*te*-la.
I-alone go-R-Rep.
'I observed that only I was going.'
ney-ka ceyil celm-*te*-nya?
you-SM most young-R-Q
'Did you observe that you were the youngest?'

EXPERIENCE(2): ney-ka ka-ss-*te*-nya?
you-SM go-Prf.-R-Q
'Did you go yourself?'
nay-ka nolayhay-ss-*te*-ni motwu cohahay-ss-ta.
I-SM sing-Prf.-R-as all be happy-Prf.-Rep.
'As I sang (which I experienced), everybody was happy.'

EXPERIENCE(3): nay-ka kippu-*te*-la.
I-SM glad-R-Rep.
'I felt that I was glad.'
ney-ka chwiha-*te*-nya?

you-SM drunk-R-Q
'Did you feel intoxicated?'
nay-ka colli-*te*-la.
I-SM drowsy-R-Rep.
'I felt I was drowsy.'
ney-ka cwuk-ko siph-*te*-nya?
you-SM die-Com wish-R-Q
'Did you feel that you wished to die?'
nay-ka ka-keyss-*te*-la.
I-SM go-Pre.-R-Rep.
'I felt that I could go.'

The same sentence may have at least two readings depending on whether the speaker has equi-time (and equi-place) or non-equi-time (or non-equi-place) in mind, as illustrated in (26).

(26) a. John-i hankwuk-ey sal-*te*-la.
John-SM Korea-in live-R-Rep.
i. I saw John living in Korea. (OBSERVE (1))
ii. I found out that John is living in Korea. (INFER)
b. ne-nun ka-ss-*te*-nya?
you-T go-Prf.-R-Q
i. Did you go? (Lit. Did you experience of having gone?) (EXPERIENCE (2))
ii. Did you notice that you had gone? (INFER)

If the verb preceding -TE has both experience and non-experience features, the meanings in -TE also diverge, as in (27).

(27) a. John-i *aphu-te*-la.
John-SM sick-R-Rep.
'I saw John sick (talking about the whole body).' (OBSERVE (1))
b. nay-ka *aphu-te*-la.
I-SM hurt-R-Rep.
'I felt I was hurt (talking about a part of the body).' (EXPERIENCE (3))

Obviously the reason is that in (27a) *aphu* 'to be sick' is not an experience verb, while *aphu* 'to be hurt' in (27b) is.

As we saw in (24), OBSERVE (2) is detrimental to the otherwise neat system. In other words, if OBSERVE (2) were to give in to EXPERIENCE, we would need only ±equi-time and ±equi-subject as the conditioning features for the distinction between the three meanings of PERCEIVING. We may ascribe this phenomenon to the primacy of the observation meaning in -TE. That is, the other meanings are viewed as being derived from the observation meaning due to such constraints as the non-equi-time which makes direct observation impossible, the equi-subject which changes 'observation' of oneself to 'experience' in non-performative environments, and the experience verbs which are resistant to observation. Aside from these constraints, -TE retains its primary and dominant meaning of observation, including OBSERVE (2) which occurs when the -TE structure is a content proposition of an illocutionary act. In this case, as we have seen in Section 4, the tenacity of observation is so strong that the first person (in statement) or the second person (in question) subject is extremely objectivized, as if the body were detached from the soul to become the object of observation. Because of this tenacity of observation in performative-dominated position, sentences like those in (28) are acceptable only in an imaginary world, whereas corresponding embedded sentences as shown in (29) where observation gives in to inference or experience belong to common daily speech.

(28) a. Washington-i i cip-eyse sal-*te*-la.
Washington-SM this house-in live-R-Rep.
'I observed Washington living in this house.' (OBSERVE (1))

b. nay-ka i cip-eyse sal-*te*-la.
I-SM this house-in live-R-Rep.
'I saw myself living in this house.' (OBSERVE (2))

(29) a. ikes-un Washington-i sal-*te*-n cip-i-ta
this-T Washington-SM live-R-M house-Cop.-Rep.
'This is a house where (I was informed) Washington lived.' (INFER)

b. ikes-un nay-ka sal-*te*-n cip-i-ta.
this-T I-SM live-R-M house-Cop.-Rep.
'This is a house where (I was informed) Washington lived.'

It is obvious that any grammar which tries to postulate the sentences in (28) as the underlying structures for the embedded sentences in (29) will fail, because the latter lacks the superordination of a performative sentence. That is, an embedded sentence is by no means the same as the corresponding unembedded sentence. It is a defective sentence, as it were.

7. Summary. I have tried to characterize the semantic side of the retrospective suffix -TE by presenting the following proposals among others.

(1) The conceptual structure underlying -TE is that of a transitive sentence of the shape 'Agent + S + Time + Predicate'. The REPORTER (speaker/hearer) functioning as the Agent, PAST functioning as Time, and PERCEIVE functioning as Predicate converge into the suffix -TE in their surface realization, leaving the complement S intact.

(2) The performative sentence or the matrix sentence of a quotative construction is responsible for the selection of the REPORTER (speaker, hearer, or somebody else), exclusiveness of the REPORTER, and tenacity of the observation meaning.

(3) The so-called 'non-equi-subject constraint' is not especially relevent to -TE. What is relevant to -TE in this connection is the tenacity of the observation meaning.

(4) -TE is not restricted to past events alone. The event time and the time or PERCEIVING the event do not have to be the same for a grammatical expression.

(5) The reference point of the PAST in -TE is always the utterance time, except in imaginary situations in which case the reference point may be in the future.

(6) Time sequence between an embedded -TE event and the matrix event is constrained largely by the rules of the empirical world of experience.

(7) The common claim that -TE contains an imperfective meaning is not true. The imperfective meaning comes from the unmarked counterpart of the perfective.

(8) The abstract predicate PERCEIVE is a 'natural' semantic class that consists of OBSERVE, EXPERIENCE, and INFER, which are mutually exclusive, being conditioned by underlying structural relations. These conditioning factors are equi-time, equi-subject, performative domination, experience verb, and the perfective.

(9) An embedded sentence (with or without -TE) and the corresponding unembedded sentence do not have the same underlying structure, because the former lacks the performative sentence which carries an illocutionary force.

Notes

1. The present research was supported by a University of Hawaii Intramural grant and the travel for the presentation of the initial version of this paper at the 27th Annual Meeting of the Association for Asian Studies (San Francisco, March 24, 1975) was made possible by the Center for Korean Studies at the University of Hawaii. I gratefully acknowledge Byron Bender, Choon Hak Cho, David Ashworth, Dong Jae Lee, Hsin-I Hsieh, Jang H. Koo, Joe Ree, Samuel Martin, Seok C. Song, and Yutaka Kusanagi for their valuable comments.
2. The Yale romanization is followed in representing Korean forms in this paper. The abbreviations used are:

Com (complementizer)	Cop. (copula)
Fd. (formal deference)	Im (imperative)
Int. (intimate speech level)	M (modifier suffix)
N (nominalizer)	OM (object marker)
Pr. (processive)	Pre. (presumptive)
Prf. (perfective)	Pros. (prospective)
Q (question)	Qi. (indirect question)
Quo. (quotative)	R (retrospective suffix)
Rep. (reportive)	SM (subject marker)
T (topic marker)	

The variants of -TE are morphologically conditioned. Included here are also somewhat archaic *-le-*, *-ley*, and *-l*, as discussed in Na 1971 and I. M. Lee 1971. The basic morphological slot of the retrospective suffix is immediately before the slot of the sentence ending 'mood' (e.g. Martin 1954:37). For the various syntactic cooccurrence restrictions, see Choi (1965:360).

3. In English also, *will* and *shall* are said to be as much a matter of mood as of tense (e.g. Lyons 1968:310). In Sohn (1974a) -TE is tentatively called a modal.
4. The postulation of a superordinating structure for -TE was briefly attemped in I. Yang (1972:236), S. Chang (1973a:50) and Sohn (1974a) without much justification.
5. I. Yang (1972:234) brought out the question of gapped and immediate time sequence between a relative event where -TE appears and the matrix event. Here again, it is my view that any time sequence including gapped, immediate or simultaneous is allowable unless the empirical world of experience or time words suppress one or another sequence, as illustrated in the following.

   John-un Mary-ka sal-te-n cip-ulo isa-hay-ss-ta.

   i. John moved to the house I saw Mary living in.
   ii. John moved to the house I saw Mary once living in.
   iii. John had moved to the house I saw Mary living in.
6. In connection with reference points, Kusanagi (1972:52-68) made an interesting observation on Japanese tense on the basis of the concept of 'time focus' of the speaker. R. Lakoff (1970:841-43) put importance on the speaker's point of view of the sentence in determining the superficial tense to be assigned to the verb.

Reprinted from *Language Research* (Seoul National University) 11.1:87-103 (1975).

9. TENSE IN KOREAN

Tense is defined as the grammatical feature of the verb phrase that expresses relations of simultaneity of time (present) or relations of "before" (past) or 'after' (future) in time.[1] In this respect, it is often said that the semantic function of time adverbials like 'now', 'yesterday', and 'next week' is partially duplicated by the verb phrase (e.g., Leech 1969:134). For example, observe sentence (1), in which *ecey* 'yesterday' and the suffix *-ss* share the semantic feature 'past'.

(1) John-i ecey ttena-*ss*-ta.
John-SM yesterday leave-ss-Rep.[1]
'John left yesterday.'

A common description of Korean tense is in terms of past, present, and future. Observe the sentences in (2)-(4).

(2) a. pi-ka o-*ass*-ta.
rain-SM come-*ass*-Rep.
'It rained.'
b. mul-i kiph-*ess*-ta.
water-SM deep-*ess*-Rep.
'The water was deep.'

(3) a. pi-ka o-*n*-ta.
rain-SM come-*n*-Rep.
'It is raining.'
b. mul-i kiph-ta.
water-SM deep-Rep.
'The water is deep.'

(4) a. pi-ka o-{*keyss*-ta. / *li*-la.}

rain-SM come-{keyss / li}-Rep.

'It may/will rain.'[2]

b. muli- kiph-{*keyss*-tà. / *uli*-la.}

water-SM deep-{keyss / uli} -Rep.

'The water may/will be deep.'

Most scholars associate *-ss/-ass/-ess* (hereafter -ASS) as they appear in sentences (1) and (2) with past tense. However, *-n* (*-nun* after a consonant) in sentence (3a) is called variously present or present progressive tense (Choi 1965:348, S. Kim 1967:24-28, and many other traditional Korean grammarians), processive aspect (Martin 1954:37 and Forthcoming), indicative aspect (e.g., S. Song 1967:241, Cook 1971:82-83), or a combination (i.e., a portmanteau) of progressive aspect, indicative mood, and present tense (Na 1971:129). Notice that *-n/-nun* does not appear after a stative verb, as in sentence (3b). *-keyss* and *-(u)li* in sentence (4) have also received many different interpretations. For example, Martin, S. Song, S. Kim, and many others call *-keyss* a future tense marker, whereas Cook and Sohn (1974a) call it a modal. Na calls both *-keyss* and *-(u)li* subjunctive moods. I. Yang (1972:4, 23-26) does not assign any grammatical category to *-keyss* on the grounds that "It contains heterogeneous functions such as the future tense, volition, and conjecture". He does not discuss *-(u)li* but assigns the category 'future' to *-(u)l* (e.g., John-*i o-l kes i-ta* 'John will come'), which I believe is related to *-(u)li* both syntactically and semantically. Martin (1954:37) assigns the term 'prospective aspect' modifier to *-(u)l.* He considers *-(u)li* the combination of the 'prospective' *-(u)l* and the nominal marker *i* (Martin: personal communication). Choi (1965:353) states that *-keyss* and *-(u)li* are future tense markers, while setting up two additional morphemes which are homophonous with his future tense *-keyss*, i.e., the possibility *-keyss* and the conjecture *-keyss.*

Korean has also developed the suffix cluster -ASS-ASS, which is called past-past tense by many linguists. Traditional grammarians like Choi (1965:441-442) consider -ASS-ASS the past perfective. Na (1971:100-101) analyzes the first -ASS as the perfective aspect and the second -ASS as a past tense. In his view, the second -ASS and the retrospective suffix (discussed below) constitute the category of past tense. Linguists like Cook (1971:83) call it a remote past. Martin (1954:35) says that "the action or state of past-past is more remote or more definitely completed than that of past, ...''.

(5) nay-ka ka-ss-ul-ttay John-un imi cwuk-*ess-ess*-ta.
I-SM go-ASS-M-time John-TM already die-ASS-ASS-Rep.
'When I went there, John had already died.'

Very recently N. Kim (1975) insightfully challenged the 'double past' treatment of -ASS-ASS, claiming that the second -ASS is the 'experiential-contrastive' aspect, while viewing the first -ASS as a true past. Kim presents a number of interesting pieces of evidence to support his claim, some of which, I think, will need further clarification.[3] I will not engage further in the discussion of 'double past' constructions in this paper, since I am not yet ready to present my own definite views.

In addition, Korean has another productive verbal suffix, -TE (*-te, -tu, -ti, -t,* etc.), which has the 'retrospective' meaning. This suffix is called again variously a tense (e.g., Choi 1965:348), and aspect (e.g., Martin 1954:37), a mood (e.g., I. Yang 1972:4), a manner (e.g., S. Chang 1973a:40), etc. Scholars like Na (1971:129) regard -TE as a genuine past-tense morpheme in Korean.

(6) pi-ka o-*te*-la.
rain-SM come-TE-Rep.
'I observed that it was raining.'

The aim of this paper is to present my own view regarding how time relations such as past, present, and future are reflected in such Korean verbal suffixes (or in their absence) as those we have seen thus far. This paper will also clarify the concepts of past, present, and future especially in relation to their reference points of time, for example, past in relation to when? The view presented in this paper is drastically different from the popular understanding of Korean tense as discussed above. Let me elaborate point by point below, making broader generalizations at the end.

My first claim is that, contrary to the common belief that *-keyss* and *-(u)li* refer to future time either primarily or secondarily, both suffixes contain always and only present time as one of their semantic features, and never future or past. Observe the sentences in (7).

(7) a. pi-ka o-$\left\{\begin{matrix}\text{keyss-ta.}\\\text{li-la.}\end{matrix}\right\}$
rain-SM come-$\left\{\begin{matrix}\text{keyss}\\\text{li}\end{matrix}\right\}$-Rep.

'I conjecture or presume that it will rain (e.g., tomorrow)/it is raining (e.g., in Seoul now).'

b. nay-ka ka- {keyss-ta. / li-la.}

I-SM go- {keyss / li} -Rep.

(i) 'I intend to go.'
(ii) 'I may go.'
(iii) 'I am able to go.'

In (7a) the event of raining may be present or future but it has nothing to do with *-keyss* or *-(u)li*, which refers only to the speaker's conjecture or presumption at the time of utterance, i.e., at 'present'.[4] In (7b) *-keyss* and *-li* indicate the speaker's volition (i), conjecture (ii), and ability (iii), again at the time of utterance, i.e., at 'present'. The 'present' time status of these morphemes does not change in sentence (8), where the event refers to past time.

(8) Pi-ka o-ass- {keyss-ta. / uli-la.}

rain-SM come-ASS- {keyss / uli} -Rep.

'I conjecture (or presume) that it (has) rained.'

Thus we cannot say that sentence (8) includes past-future, although the term past-future is commonly used to describe such sentences.

My second claim is that the retrospective suffix -TE as it appears in sentence (6) inherently contains past time, never future or present, as one of its semantic features. In other words, its semantic content is the speaker's observation, experience, or inference in the past. Since this point is made clear in Sohn (1975c) I will not dwell on it here. Na's (1971:129) statement that it is a genuine past marker comes close to my claim, but he does not present the other, more important, semantic features in -TE explicitly.

My third claim is that the major semantic features of -ASS as they appear in sentences (1) and (2) are perfective (or completive) and past, not just past (i.e., completed in the past). Observe the sentences in (9).

(9) a. ecey-puthe ilha-*n*-ta.
yesterday-from work-n-Rep.
'I have been working since yesterday.'

b. inkan-un cwuk-*nun*-ta.

man-TM die-nun-Rep.
'Man is mortal.'

In (9a) the event ranges over past (yesterday) and present, whereas in (9b) the event covers eternity, which of course includes eternal past. Yet, -ASS cannot be used; it is used only when the speaker describes an event already completed or, following Kusanagi's (1972) term, 'focuses' his attention on that portion of an event which has been completed, as we have already observed in the sentences in (1) and (2).[5] On the other hand, -ASS must be used whenever an event is perfected, even if the event has some sort of current relevance (cf. Palmer 1968:74). Observe the sentences in (10).

(10) a. cikum-kkaci ilhay-*ss*-ta.
now-until work-ASS-Rep.
'I've worked until now.'
b. son-ul pi-*ess*-ta.
hand-OM cut-ASS-Rep.
'I've cut my hand.' (It's still bleeding.)

Thus 'current or present relevance' is not distinctive in the tense of Korean. The important thing is whether a perfected event is in the mind of the speaker. In this respect, I prefer the category term 'perfective' to 'past' for -ASS. As we saw in the sentences in (9), past time is also covered even when there is no -ASS. Besides, we use, for example, the term 'modal' instead of present for *-keyss* and *-(u)li,* and we use the term 'retrospective' instead of past for -TE. Use of 'perfective' instead of past contributes to the symmetry. Moreover, in sentence (11), the past meaning is almost suppressed while the perfective meaning is exceptionally conspicuous, even if we assume a future 'reference' time.

(11) ne-nun cwuk-*ess*-ta.
you-TM die-ASS-Rep.
'You have died.' (meaning 'I or somebody will kill you.')

Incidentally, -ASS obtains some associated semantic features while retaining the perfective and past as definitional in sentences like those in (12), where the rough associated meanings are italicized. Conceptually, such additional meanings can be viewed as higher sentences.

(12) a. nay sayngil-i nayil i-*ess*-ta.
My birthday-SM tomorrow is-ASS-Rep.
'I noticed that my birthday is tomorrow.'
b. hayngyel-i nayil iss-*ess*-ta.

parade-SM tomorrow exist-ASS-Rep.
'I noticed that the parade will take place tomorrow.'

c. na-nun cange-lul mek-*ess*-ta.
I-TM eel-OM eat-ASS-Rep.
'I have decided to eat eel.' (in ordering an eel dish)

One might think that, so far as the perfective feature is distinctive, the past time is redundant. I don't think this will hold, because we cannot say, for example, **nayil-kkaci ka-ss-ta* in the sense 'He will have gone by tomorrow'. Thus, -ASS is strictly limited to the past time.

My fourth claim is that we should set up an important unmarked category (zero) which contrasts with -ASS, i.e., non-perfective and non-past. While the non-presence of *-keyss/-(u)li* or -TE simply means the lack of the meanings they carry, non-presence of -ASS does not merely mean the non-existence of perfective, but positively means that an event is going on at present, e.g., (3a, b), will take place in the future, takes place habitually, e.g., (9a), or takes place timelessly or eternally, e.g., (9b). The non-perfective category is more contentful than the perfective, in that the latter covers only past, whereas the former ranges over present, future, and past.[6] It is indeed an unmarked category in this sense. Many people must erroneously call *-keyss* and *-(u)li* future tense markers because they do not recognize this important unmarked category which is associated with the time reference future. The semantic ranges of the perfective and non-perfective are overlapped in 'past'. The distinctive feature in this case is whether the speaker describes a completed event (or 'focuses' his attention on the completed portion of an event), i.e., perfective, or an incomplete event, i.e., non-perfective, as seen in the sentences in (13).

(13) a. cikum-kkaci mek-*ess*-ta.
now-until eat-Ass-Rep.
'He has eaten until now.' (perfective)

b. cikun-kkaci mek-Ø-*nun*-ta.
now-until eat-Ø-nun-Rep.
'He has been eating until now.' (non-perfective)

Since the non-perfective inherently carries the meaning that the speaker describes the 'present' incompletion of an event, it cannot be used, in a normal situation, with an adverb which inherently carries only past (e.g., **John-i ecey ka-n-ta* *'John is going yesterday'). Na (1971:129) also distinguishes between perfective aspect (-ASS) and progressive aspect (-Ø), but, as we have seen, the counterpart of perfective is much more than simply progressive.

My fifth claim is that the description of *-n/-nun* (after a consonant), as it appears in sentence (14), as present tense or present progressive (in contrast with -ASS) or processive aspect (in contrast with the indicative *-ni/nu* etc.) is not correct.

(14) pi-ka o-*n*-ta.
rain-SM come-n-Rep.
(a) 'It is raining (now).'
(b) 'It will rain (e.g., tomorrow).'
(c) 'It rains (e.g., often).'

(14b) immediately refutes all the categories proposed above. Moreover, *-n/-nun*, whatever its category may be, certainly does not fill the same slot as the perfective -ASS, although *-n/-nun* is in complementary distribution with both -ASS and -TE in simple sentences. Observe the sentences in (15).

(15) a. inkan-un cwuk-*nun*-ta.
man-TM die-nun-Rep.
'Man is mortal.'
b. inkan-un cwuk-*te*-la.
man-TM die-TE-Rep.
'I observed that man is mortal.'
c. *inkan-un cwuk-*ess*-ta.
man-TM die-ASS-Rep.
*'Man died.'

Both -TE and -ASS contain past time as one of their semantic features, but (15a), where *-nun* occurs, goes with (15b), where -TE occurs, in grammaticality, and not with the unacceptable (15c), where -ASS occurs.[7] This and other pieces of evidence indicate that *-n/-nun* and -TE share the same slot.[8] This happens to support Martin (1954:37), who assigns his 'processive' *-n/-nun* to the same aspect slot together with the retrospective, although, as I mentioned above, *-n/-nun* is not a processive element. I certainly agree with S. Song (1967:23, 241), who probably on phonological and intuitive grounds, treats the suffix *-n/-nun* as an indicative element. I do not understand why Song calls it an aspect, however (Song 1967:20, 242).

To my knowledge, no one has ever clearly described the semantic content of the Korean indicative, although, for distributional reasons, many linguists correctly put it in the same slot as the retrospective.[9] What I should like to claim is that the indicative suffix has a semantic content very similar to that of the retrospective suffix as described in Sohn (1975c), except that the former inherently carries present, whereas the latter inherently carries past. That is, the indicative suffix (*-n/-nun/-ni/-nu/-Ø*) refers to the speaker's (in statement) or hearer's (in question) observation, experience, and inference. These three meanings are mutually exclusive, being conditioned by whether the subject of the main event is the speaker or hearer himself (±identical subject) and whether the event time overlaps the time of observation/experience/inference (±identical time). Observation meaning shows up when (−identical subject) and (+identical time) hold, experience meaning when (+identical subject) and (+identical time) are met, and inference meaning (i.e., judgement on the basis of concrete facts) in the case of (−identical time).[10]

(16) a. pi-ka o-Ø-*n*-ta.
rain-SM come-Ø-n-Rep.
(i) observation: 'It is raining.'
(ii) inference: 'It will rain.' 'It rains (habitually).'

b. nay-ka ka-Ø-*p*-*ni*-ta.
I-SM go-Ø-DF-ni-Rep.
(i) experience: 'I am going (i.e., in the process of going).'
(ii) inference: 'I am going (e.g., tomorrow).'
'I (habitually) go.'

Notice that the meaning, 'It will rain' in (16a) does not appear unless the speaker has some inferential knowledge about the weather, say, through radio broadcasting.

Now let me propose a broader generalization: every marked verbal suffix has an inherent time reference, past or present. The unmarked verbal suffix, i.e., the non-perfective, has present, future, and past reference. Remember that past alone does not occur in the non-perfective without present. Even all the performative suffixes, including the formal reportive *-ta*, have the present reference as an inherent semantic feature. From the foregoing discussions, the surface linear arrangement of those suffixes discussed thus far is as shown in (17) (omitting those which have not been taken up). For comparison, see Choi (1965:352), Martin (1954:37), S. Song (1967:241), S. Kim (1967:24-28), Cook (1971:83), I. Yang (1972:4), and Na (1971:129).

(17) $$\text{Modality} \rightarrow \begin{Bmatrix} \text{Perf.} \\ \text{Non-perf.} \end{Bmatrix} \text{(Modal)} \begin{Bmatrix} \text{Indicative} \\ \text{Retrospective} \\ \cdots\cdots\cdots \end{Bmatrix} \begin{Bmatrix} \text{Reportive} \\ \cdots\cdots\cdots \end{Bmatrix}$$

Perf. = -ASS [+perfective, +past]
Non-perf. = Ø [−perfective, +present, +future, +past/present/(future)]
Modal = *-keyss*, *-(u)li* [+conjecture, +volition, +ability, +present]
Indicative = *-n/-nun/-nu/-ni/-Ø* [+observation, +experience, +inference, +present]
Retrospective = -TE [+observation, +experience, +inference, +past]
Reportive = -ta, etc. [+report, +present]

What (17) means is that a time reference like present, past, or future is not itself a category term but one of the semantic features associated with each verbal suffix. The structure underlying (17) is conceptually hierarchical, but I will not discuss that here.

Finally, let me propose another important generalization. What are the reference points against which we say present, past, or future? That is, past is the time prior to when? To my knowledge, no one has even raised this question, most probably because people assume that the reference point for all time relations in a simple sentence is always the time of utterance. I strongly deny this assumption and claim that all the time references mentioned above (17) are relative to each other in such a way that a time reference (i.e., past, present, or future) is prior to, simultaneous with, or after the time of the event referred to by the immediately dominating suffix. For example, in sentence (18), it is obvious that the non-perfective present or future (-Ø) is not simultaneous with or after the utterance time but simultaneous with or after the time of the speaker's presumption (*-keyss*). Now, the present time in *-keyss* is simultaneous not with the utterance time but simultaneous with the time of the speaker's experience (-TE), which is in turn past with reference to the time of the speaker's report (*-ta/la*). The present time in the reportive *-ta/la* is the utturance time, which is the top-most absolute time in (18).

(18) [[[[pi-ka ecey o-Ø] *-keyss*] -te] -la].
rain-SM yesterday come-non-perf. -modal-R-Rep.
'I (previously) noticed that it would rain yesterday.'

Notes

1. This paper was supported by a University of Hawaii intramural grant for 1974-75. The Yale romanization system is followed in representing Korean forms. The following abbreviations are used in this paper:

DF deferential marker
M modifier ending
OM object marker
P polite marker
R retrospective suffix
Rep. reportive suffix
SM subject marker
TM topic marker

2. *-keyss* and *-(u)li* are very close in meaning and syntagmatic distribution, but are not exactly the same. I will not go into the differences here. Suffice it to point out that the use of *-(u)li* in sentence-final position tends to be out-dated, but it is quite common in quotative sentences (e.g., *Pi-ka o-li la-ko sayngkak hay-yo* 'I think it will probably rain'). *-(u)li* does not appear with any speech levels but the plain one and cannot be followed by the retrospective suffix.
3. Although N. Kim (1975:530) claims that every sentence containing the double past has contrastive meaning, sentences like (5), where -ASS-ASS occurs, do not carry any contrastive meaning. Besides, sentence (5) does not carry experiential meaning either, although the subject is animate (John).

   My second question is with regard to Kim's (ibid.) statement that the experiential meaning shows up only when the subject is animate. Observe the following sentences.

   (i) ku salam-i nemeci-ess-ess-ta.
   That person-SM fall-ASS-ASS-Rep.
   'He has once fallen down.'

   (ii) ku mal-i nemeci-ess-ess-ta.
   that horse-SM fall-ASS-ASS-Rep.
   'The horse has once fallen down.''

   (iii) ku kitwung-i nemeci-ess-ess-ta.
   that pillar-SM fall-ASS-ASS-Rep.
   'The pillar has once fallen down.'

   As far as the -ASS-ASS part is concerned, the three sentences are semantically identical to me. Following Kim's analysis, however, the second -ASS in (i) and (ii) has experiential meaning, whereas that in (iii) does not. My own feeling for the moment is that the -ASS in question is related not to the subject's experience but to the speaker's perception of some sort which is equally applicable to the above three sentences.

   My third question is related to Kim's (ibid.:534-536) analysis of *ten* as an adnominal form of the experiential-contrast aspect. If we should equate -TE underlyingly with the -ASS in question in such constructions as *ku-ka mek-ess-te-n umsik* 'the food he ate', I wonder how we could account for *ku-ka mek-ess-ess-te-n umsik* 'the food he has (or had) once eaten' where both the second -ASS and -TE show up. Moreover, the ambiguity existing in *cwuk-ess-te-n ku salam* 'the person who had died/the person who had been dead' does not seem to consitute a strong piece of evidence in favor of the existence of experiential-contrast in *ten*. This is becuase we find the same ambiguity in *cwuk-un,* as in *cwuk-un salam-i nay chinkwu ta* 'The one who died is my friend' and in *cwuk-un salam-i tasi sala-na-ss-ta* 'The one who was dead has become alive'.
4. Cook (1968:73fn.) correctly points out that *-keyss* is not a tense but a modal. He assigns *-keyss* the meanings volition and presumption. Furthermore, Cook (ibid.:78) states that

-keyss and *-(u)li* are two different realizations on the surface of the same modal category.

5. For the relevance of the speaker's focusing his attention in tenses, see Lakoff (1970) and Kusanagi (1972).
6. Such semantic features as progressive, repetition, and habituality are shared by both -ASS and Ø. They are not differentiated (hence not distinctive) in formal terms.
7. Joe Ree drew my attention to the fact that sentence (15c) would be acceptable if it was delivered by an omniscient being. This fact does not alter my argument, however. First, both (15a) and (15b) do not require the presupposition that the speaker is an omniscient being. Second, acceptability of (15c) presupposes the loss of its genericness of the act of dying, which is not the case with (15a) and (15b).
8. *-n/-nun* alternates with *-nu* which occurs before a noun (e.g., *ka-nu-n salam* 'a man who is going/who will go/who goes'). Before such defective nouns as *-tey* 'a fact, a circumstance,' *-nu* may follow -ASS, while it occurs in complementary distribution with -TE.

    John-i o-*nu-n*-tey-yo.
    John-SM come-nu-M-tey-P
    'John is coming.'
    John-i o-ass-*nu-n*-tey-yo.
    John-SM come-ASS-nu-M-tey-P
    'John has arrived.'
    John-i o-te-*n*-tey-yo.
    John-SM come-TE-M-tey-P
    'I saw John coming.'
    John-i o-ass-te-*n*-tey-yo.
    John-SM come-ASS-TE-M-tey-P
    'I noticed that John had arrived.'

9. For example, Cook (1971:83) attaches *-ni* to the deferential suffix *-p,* calling them together a formal aspect, probably because it is hard to isolate the semantic content of *-ni.* He treats *-n/-nun* as the informal counterpart of *-pni.*
10. One important difference between -TE and the indicative suffix in this connection is that in a simple sentence -TE has the observation meaning instead of experience, even if (+identical subject) and (+identical time) hold. See Sohn (1975c).

    nay-ka ka-te-la
    I-SM go-TE-Rep.
    'I saw myself going.'

Reprinted from *The Korean Language: Its Structure and Social Projection,* ed. by Ho-min Sohn. 47-61 (1975). Honolulu: Center for Korean Studies of the University of Hawaii.

10. CONTRACTIONS AS A MECHANISM OF POLYSEMIC BREEDING: A DEVICE FOR SPEAKER INVOLVEMENT IN KOREAN

The aim of this paper is to observe the syntactic mechanisms of a few common types of contraction in the final position of Korean complex sentences, and explain how and why the speaker comes into the newly developed sense or polysemy which such contractions trigger.

The term 'polysemy' is usually associated with words which have a set of related senses, but a wider latitude will be given to it to accommodate affixes or even a sequence of affixes.[1] In order to see what is meant by 'polysemic breeding', since no one has ever used such a term, let us look at the sentences (1) for illustrations.[2]

(1) a. John-un kongpuha-n-ta-n-ta.
TP study -IN-SE-IN-SE
i. They (someone or John) say(s) that John is studying.
ii. I say that John is studying.
b. John-un kongpuha-n-ta *ko ha* -n-ta.
TP study -IN-SE QT say-IN-SE
i. They (someone or John) say(s) that John is studying.
ii. *I say that John is studying.

Obviously, sentence (la) is a contracted form of (lb) through the process of the well-known *ko* (quotative) *ha* 'say' deletion, which is optional and usually unconditional. Any mature native speaker of contemporary Korean has internalized this automatic deletion. The fact that (la) is an optional contraction of (lb) is more clearly observable by analogy through the interrogative counterparts of the sentences in (2), where (2a) and (2b) have exactly the same meaning.

(2) a. John un kongpuha-n-ta-ni?
TP study -IN-SE-QE
i. Do(es) they (anyone or John) say that John is studying?
ii. *Do you say that John is studying?
b. John un kongpuha-n-ta *ko ha* -ni?
TP study IN-SE QT say-QE
i. Do(es) they (anyone or John) say that John is studying?
ii. *Do you say that John is studying?

It is often the case that deletion of a certain form which is responsible for the contraction of a construction results in the loss of the relevant information, or else the deleted form can be recovered from the textual or situational context without the loss of any information carried by the form. In sentence (la), however, the contraction which results from *ko ha* deletion not only retains the original reading (lai) but also has developed an additional reading which contains the speaker as the higher subject. Pending coinage of a better term, I will use 'polysemic breeding' to refer to the cases like (laii).

How has polysemic breeding come about in sentences like (la)? With the deletion of *ko ha*, which consists of the quotative complementizer *ko* and the matrix verb *ha*, the suffixes that were attached to the verb *ha* are doomed to be 'stranded' or 'orphaned' [following Martin's (1976) terms which he uses in describing certain Japanese object constructions]. These stranded suffixes are naturally adopted by the embedded verb phrase, i.e., *kongpuhan-ta* 'is studying' in (la). Now the embedded verb becomes the only verb in the whole sentence with an extended verbal suffix cluster. We still relate (la) to (lb) in our conceptual process, in which case we only have the reading (lai). We also utter sentence (la) as a simple sentence without any conceptualization of an embedded sentence, in which case the reading (laii) is allowed with the sentence-final suffixes *-n-ta* containing the meaning 'I say'. In other words, one *-n-ta* is the contracted version of *ko ha-n-ta* 'they (someone or John) say(s)' and the other *-n-ta* is intrinsically 'I say', although both have been developed from *ko ha-n-ta*. In the latter case, syntactical restructuring or reanalysis is involved in that the new sense is bred with the synchronic estrangement from its historical source of derivation.[3] The restructuring seems to be in progress in view of the existence of sentence (2a), in which no polysemic breeding has yet developed and no restructuring has been made.

Let us examine another example (3) where again the *ko ha* deletion is involved.

(3) a. John-un kongpuha-n-ta-nikka.
TP study -IN-SE-because
i. because (or when) they (someone or John) say(s)/said that John is studying
ii. I (*they, *someone, *John) told you that John is studying.
b. John-un knogpuha-n-ta *ko ha*-nikka.
TP study -IN-SE QT say-because
i. because (or when) they (someone or John) say(s)/ said that John is studying
ii. *I (they, someone, John) told you that John is studying.

The conjunctive verbal suffix *-nikka* means 'reason' or 'time'. When *ko ha* is deleted and the main sentence is not expressed, (3a) obtains the (ii) reading (with a slight rising intonation), another case of polysemic breeding. In (3aii), syntactic restructuring is involved as in (laii): *-nikka* is adopted by the embedded verb phrase *kongpuha-n-ta* as its extended suffix, which has obtained the meaning 'I told you'. (3ai) is the reading of the sentence which is a contracted counterpart of (3b).

How can we account for the fact that polysemic breeding in sentences like (la) and (3a) involves the *speaker* as the underlying higher subject? Korean is well known as a verb-final language, and the sentence-final verbal suffixes represent various attitudes of the speaker toward either the propositional content or the hearer. For instance, the suffix *-(u)si* represents the speaker's respect to a subject or locative human referent; the suffix *-keyss*, the speaker's volition or conjecture toward the propositional content; the suffix *-te/-ti*, the speaker's past observation, experience or inference regarding the propositional content; the suffix *-((s)u)p*, the speaker's respect toward the hearer; the suffix *-kwun*, the speaker's confirmation of the propositional content; the suffix *-ma*, the speaker's promise to the hearer; the suffix *-ca*, the speaker's suggestion to the hearer; and so on. In the underlying structure, we may be able to postulate the speaker as the subject in these cases, as in 'I respect X; I intend X; I conjecture X; I observed X; I confirm X; I promise X; I propose X; etc.', where X is either a sentence, the hearer, or a referent. All these suffixes are modality elements which cannot be negated in any way and thus cannot be assigned any truth value.

The fact that the so-called auxiliary verbs generally represent the speaker's 'evaluative viewpoints' (K. Lee 1976b) partly supports the present claim that the sentence-final position in Korean, and for that matter in SOV languages in general, is the territory of the speaker's subtle attitudes. Further notice in (4) that the complement verb *pota* 'to look' cannot be negated in any way, nor can it be made perfective.

(4) a. pi -ka o -nun ka po -ta.
rain NM come-IN likelihood look-SE
'I guess it is raining.'
b. pi -ka an o -nun ka po -ta.
rain NM not come-IN likelihood look-SE
'I guess it is not raining.'
c. *pi -ka o -nun ka an po -ta.
rain NM come-IN likelihood not look-SE
*'I don't guess it is raining.'
d. *pi -ka o -nun ka po -ass-ta.
rain NM come-IN likelihood look-PR-SE
*'I guessed it was raining.'

Obviously, the sequence consisting of the defective noun *ka* 'likelihood, assumed fact' and the matrix verb *po* 'look' has been syntactically fossilized and functions as a sequence of verbal suffixes which are attached to the embedded verb *o* 'come', indicating exclusively the speaker's guessing of the propositional content at the time of utterance. That no case marker, limiter, or adverbial element can be placed after the noun *ka* is a piece of additional evidence for such syntactic fossilization.

It is my view that the strong force that interlinks sentence-final verbal affixes to the speaker's attitudes in Korean naturally tends to push in the speaker as the only underlying higher subject, whenever certain syntactic restructuring, including contractions, changes a complex sentence to a simple sentence where the original matrix verbal elements function as embedded verbal suffixes. The higher abstract verb that functions as the predicate of the newly bred higher speaker subject is derived, with or without semantic change, from the deleted elements, the remaining elements, or an interaction of both sets of elements. For instance, the higher verb SAY in the (ii) reading in sentence (la) seems to be due to the deleted element *ha* 'say'. So does the verb TOLD in the (ii) reading in sentence (3a).

The abstract verb GUESS in (4) has simply derived from the expressed elements with the meanings 'to look' and 'likelihood, assumed fact'. Some other examples that follow will illustrate different processes of derivation of higher verbs, including the interaction of deleted and remaining elements.

The claim I made at the beginning of the preceding paragraph is supported by the grammaticality of (5a) and the ungrammaticality of (5b) and (5c).

(5)	a.	nay-ka ka-l-lay. I NM go-intend-do 'I intend to go.'	nay-ka ka-lye-ko hay. I NM go-intend-to do 'I intend to go.'
	b.	*John-i ka-l-lay. NM go-intend-do	John-i ka-lye-ko hay. NM go-intend-to do 'John intends to go.'
	c.	*pi -ka o-l-lay. rain NM come-about-to-do	pi -ka o-lye-ko hay. rain NM come-about-to do 'It's about to rain.'

The construction *-lye-ko ha-ta* indicates the human subject's intention when the verb is agentive, whereas it denotes the subject's impendence when the verb is not agentive. When this construction is contracted due to the *-ko ha* deletion, only the speaker subject in a statement (or the hearer subject in a question) is acceptable with the intentional sense. (5b) gives us the non-sensical reading, 'I am going to for John to go', and (5c) the non-sensical 'I am going to for it to rain'. In other words, the restructured *-l-lay* completely falls under the domain or territory of the speaker's attitude, i.e., his intention toward the proposition. Naturally, the speaker cannot intend to do the action that belongs inherently to somebody else or something else, hence the ungrammaticality of (5b) and (5c).

A similar case can be observed in (6).

(6)	a.	nay-ka ka-l -kkey. I NM go-will-promise 'I promise to go.'	nay-ka ka-l ke(s i)-ya. I NM go-will fact is-ISE 'I will (probably) go.'
	b.	*John i ka-l -kkey. NM go-will-promise	John-i ka-l ke(s i)-ya. NM go-will fact is-ISE 'John will probably go.'

The construction *-l kes i-ya*, which comprises the embedded elements *-l kes* and the matrix elements *i-ya*, indicates the speaker's prediction. When the defective noun *kes* 'fact, the fact that, case', the copula *i*, and the intimate style suffix -(*y*)*a* are extremely contracted to *kkey* and reanalyzed as a suffix of the verb *ka* 'go', the speaker's 'promise' sense breeds, and the original prediction sense is completely suppressed. (6) is different from (5) in that in the latter the original sense of intention is intact. The sincere promising action, as a performative action at the time of utterance can be made only by the speaker himself. While the source sentences can be made as perfective, the derived ones with *-kkey* 'I promise' cannot be perfectivized, nor negated, due to the illocutionary force associated with *-kkey*. (6b) is not acceptable in the same way as 'I promise that John will go' or 'I promise for John to go' is not semantically plausible. Incidentally, we may say that the speaker's prediction sense and promise sense form a natural semantic class in view of the observed semantic breeding that results from the restructured syntactic contraction.[4]

Another difference between (5) and (6) is that, as mentioned earlier, (5) allows the speaker's intention in statement to be shifted to the hearer's intention in question but (6) does not permit this kind of shift, as observed in (7). The first sentence of (7b) is totally ungrammatical and non-sensical.

(7)	a.	ney-ka ka-l-lay? you NM go-intend-do 'Do you intend to go?'	ney-ka ka-lye-ko hay? you NM go-intend-to do 'Do you intend to go?'
	b.	*ney-ka ka-l -kkey? you NM go-will-promise	ney-ka ka-l ke(s i)-ya? you NM go-will fact is-ISE 'Will you go?'

The contracted form of (7a) is parallel to the sentences with such verbal suffixes as *-te* (retrospective) and *-keyss* (volition, conjecture) which allow the shift between the speaker and the hearer depending on the statement and question respectively. The contracted form of (7b) is parallel to the sentences with suffixes like *-ma* (promise), *-ca* (suggestion), and *-kwun* (confirmation) which do not allow such a shift.

Let us consider another common type of polysemic breeding which occurs by way of syntactic contraction. As briefly alluded to in (3), Korean has a powerful syntactic mechanism that deletes the whole main clause, restructuring the subordinate clause as the main sentence. The newly analyzed sentence carries various degrees of illocutionary force, with polysemic breeding manifested. Examine the sentences in (8).

(8) a. John-i ka-l kka -yo?

NM go-will whether-PSE
i. Do you think John will go? (doubt or rhetorical)
ii. (?)May I suggest that John go?

b. nay-ka ka-l kka -yo?
I NM go-will whether-PSE
i. Do you think I will go? (doubt or rhetorical)
ii. Shall I go? (= May I suggest that I go?)

c. wuli-ka ka-l kka -yo?
we NM go-will whether-PSE
i. Do you think we will go? (doubt or rhetorical)
ii. Shall we go? (= May I suggest that we go?)

d. sensayng-nim -i ka-si-l kka -yo?
you -HT NM go-HS-will whether-PSE
i. Do you think you will go? (doubt or rhetorical)
ii. May I suggest that you go?

The original function of the defective noun *kka/ka* 'likelihood, assumed fact' is as an indirect question marker or complementizer, as shown in sentences in (9) which are considered the rough sources of the sentences in (8) respectively.

(9) a. John-i ka-l kka moll -ayo.
NM go-will whether not-know-PSE
'I wonder if John will go.'

b. nay-ka ka-l kka moll -ayo.
I NM go-will whether not-know-PSE
'I wonder if I will go.'

c. wuli-ka ka-l kka moll -ayo.
we NM go-will whether not-know-PSE
'I wonder if we will go.'

d. sensayng-nim -i ka-si-l kka moll -ayo.
you -HT NM go-HS-will whether not-know-PSE
'I wonder if you will go.'

With the deletion of the main information clause and the addition of the polite style suffix *-yo* to *kka*, together with the question intonation, we obtain the sentences in (8). The indirect questions in (9) become the direct questions in (8), as the meanings that the sentences in (8) carry partly reflect these contraction processes. As a result of the contractions, new senses are bred, in particular the sense of the speaker's suggestion. Notice that the noun *kka* has now become a suffix of the sentence final verb and falls under the domain or territory of the speaker's attitude. Since this is the case, it is reasonable to speculate that the most felicitous polysemic mechanism has led to the breeding of such senses as the speaker's suggestion, offer, asking about the hearer's intention (e.g., do you want me to ...?), etc.[5]

One may naturally ask why sentence (8aii) has the sense of the speaker's suggestion only marginally and what kind of condition makes this reading acceptable. My answer is that the illocutionary force of the speaker's attitude associated with *-l kka-yo* normally refers to an action which is controllable by the speaker. When a third person's action is in question as in (8a), his action must be controllable by the speaker for readings like (8aii) to be acceptable. The point I am making is more clearly shown in sentences in (10), where the presupposition is that the third persons have an in-group relation to the speaker.

(10) a. wuli ay -ka ka-l kka -yo?
my son NM go-will whether-PSE
i. Do you think my son is going? (doubt or rhetorical)
ii. May I suggest that my son go? *or* Shall I send my son?
b. nay-ka ka-l kka -yo, John -i ka-l kka -yo?
I NM go-will whether-PSE NM go-will whether-PSE
i. Do you think I am going or John is going?
ii. Shall I go or shall I send John?

The uniqueness of (8a) vis-à-vis (8b) through (8d) may be further substantiated by (11), the negative counterparts of the sentences in (8).

(11) a. John -i ka-ci {A. anh-ul / B. (?)mal} kka -yo?
NM go-CM whether-PSE
i. Do you think John is not going?
ii. Shall John not go?
b. nay-ka ka-ci {A. anh-ul / B. mal} kka -yo?
I NM go-CM whether-PSE
i. Do you think I am not going?
ii. Shall I not go? (= May I suggest that I don't go?)
c. wuli -ka ka-ci {A. anh-ul / B. mal} kka -yo?
we NM go-CM whether-PSE

i. Do you think we are not going?
ii. Shall we not go? (= May I suggest that we don't go?)

d. sensayng-nim-i ka-si-ci {A. anh-ul / B. mal} kka -yo?
you -HT NM go-HS-CM whether-PSE
i. Do you think you are not going?
ii. May I suggest that you don't go?

The negative verb *malta* is usually used with suggestion or command and *anhta* with statement and question, e.g., *ka-ci mal-ca* 'Let's not go', *ka-ci mal-ela* 'Don't go', *ka-ci anh-nun-ta* 'He is not going', *ka-ci anh-ni?* 'Is he not going?', **ka-ci anh-ca* 'Let's not go', **ka-ci mal-ni?* 'Is he not going?'. (11a) allows *malta* marginally, only when the subject's (John's) action can be controlled pragmatically by the speaker.

One final set of examples which is of the type similar to (8) and which provides further support for my claim regarding speaker involvement is what Martin and Lee (1969:361-363) call circumstantial/exclamatory constructions. In (12), *tey* is a defective noun with the basic meaning 'place, circumstance'.

(12) a. pi -ka w -ass-nun tey ka-si-keyss -eyo?
rain NM come-PR-IN cir. go-HS-intend-PSE
'In the circumstance that it rained, are you going to go?'

b. pi -ka w -ass-nun tey -yo.
rain NM come-PR-IN cir.-PSE
i. In the circumstance that it rained ...
ii. My, it rained!

In (12a) we have only the circumstantial reading, whereas, in (12b) both circumstantial (i) and exclamatory (ii) readings are possible. In (12bi), added meanings like 'What shall you do?' are easily detectable depending on the pragmatic or discourse situation. The so-called principle of 'avoid confrontations' or 'leave options to the hearer' (cf. Dillon (1977:133)) seems to have relevance to the pragmatics of (12bi) in that (12b) may be used as a strategy of indirection in regard to politeness. (12bii) is a case of polysemic breeding. By now, it should not be hard to imagine why the speaker's attitude gets involved in (12bii), where the original noun *tey* is restructured as a verbal suffix that gives birth to the sense of the speaker's exclamation of what Martin and Lee (1969:363) call 'intense reaction'.

In summary, I have tried to show that the strong force interlinking sentence-final verbal suffixes to the speaker's mood in Korean (an SOV language) tends to put the speaker as the only underlying higher subject whenever a certain contraction causes a complex sentence to be restructured as a simple one where the original matrix verbal elements now function as embedded verbal suffixes. I have also attempted to account for the syntactic and semantic ramifications that have arisen in connection with the above major claim.

Notes

1. The research reported in this paper was supported by a University of Hawaii research grant. The following abbreviations are used for the Korean function morphemes:

CM	= complementizer	PR	= perfective suffix
HS	= honorific suffix	PSE	= polite-level sentence ending
HT	= honorific title	QE	= question ending
IN	= indicative suffix	QT	= quotative particle
ISE	= intimate-level sentence ending	SE	= statement ending
NM	= nominative particle	TP	= topic particle

2. I. Yang (1971) calls sentences like those given in (la) double modality constructions.
3. An alternative approach to this phenomenon might be interpretive semantics, in which case restructuring would not come into the picture and the reading of (laii) would be obtained by a synchronic interpretive rule. It is not an easy job to tell whether a certain syntactic rearrangement like a contraction is a synchronic process or a diachronic fossilization when there is a concomitant semantic change. This is especially the case when such a rearrangement is, like an on-going phonological change or dialectal diffusion, still vivid in the psychological reality of native speakers. Unable, for the moment, to formulate any well-motivated interpretive rules that are generally applicable to all the cases brought up in this paper, I follow, in principle, the generative semantic approach, taking syntactic restructuring into account. The polysemic divergences envisaged in this paper cannot be accounted for by such conversational postulates as those elaborated by Gordon and Lakoff (1975), in that the newly bred senses are always there and not entailed only under certain circumstances. There is no convincing evidence that Cole's (1975) diachronic approach of conversational implicature is particularly useful in the analysis of our data.
4. The phenomenon is more or less similar, for example, to the polysemic divergence between *conjecture* and *volition* in the Korean verbal suffix *-keyss*, between the root sense *permission* and the epistemic sense *possibility* in English *may*, and between the root sense *ability* and the epistemic sense *possibility* in English *can* (e.g., Jackendoff 1972:100).
5. For further discussions of *-l kka*, see C. Lee (1973a:58-59) and I. Yang (1976b:25-26).

Reprinted from *Papers in Korean Linguistics*, ed. by Chin-W. Kim, 197-205 (1978). Columbia: Hornbeam Press.

11. THEME-PROMINENCE IN KOREAN

1. **Introduction.** The term 'theme' or 'topic' in this paper is viewed broadly as 'what the speaker is talking about (now)' (Halliday 1967:212) or more specifically as a spatial, temporal, or individual frame (denoted by a noun phrase) within which the sentence holds, with the applicability of the main predication limited to the domain of that frame (cf. Chafe 1976:50-51).[1] In any case, its notion is taken as being independent of givenness or old information. A more popular definition of theme or topic is in terms of either givenness (e.g. Vachek 1966:89-90; Chafe 1970:211-212; Gundel 1974:38; Gundel 1978:2; Bak 1977:63) or the lowest degree of communicative dynamism within a sentence (Firbas 1966:270; Firbas and Pala 1971:92). This informationally oriented definition seems to me to serve only a secondary purpose in Korean, revealing little significant syntactic correlation. For instance, a widely held belief in the literature which, to my knowledge, has never been challenged is that the particle (*n*)*un* marks theme in Korean. If theme is inherently correlated with given or old information, how can we account for the fact that the answer to (la) allows (*n*)*un* as the most natural particle despite the new information of the referent that the noun it occurs with denotes?

(1) a. wenswungi-ka salam-uy cosang i-ni?
'Are monkeys the ancestors of human beings?'

b. {*etten salam-un* / *wuli hyeng-un*} kulehkey sayngkak-hay.
{'Some people / 'My brother} think(s) that way.''

Furthermore, attribution of givenness to theme would compel us, contrary to the common belief, to regard *John-i* as theme in (3a) in that it carries old information and fits the definition of theme stated earlier.[2]

(2) John-i ettehkey tway-ss-ess-ni?
'What happened to John?'

(3) a. *John-i* aph-ass-e.
b. *John-un* aph-ass-e.
c. Aph-ass-e.
'John was sick.'

(3a) and its contracted (3c) are natural answers to (2), whereas (3b) is acceptable only when John is contrasted with someone else.[3] Only when we strip theme of the yoke of givenness can we describe thematic constructions with great generality.

Theme is a notion distinct from case. The former, largely a discourse or situation-sensitive notion, is related syntactically and semantically to the rest of the sentence as a whole. The latter is a sentence-internal notion, indicating the role of a noun phrase in relation to its directly associated verb (or, in the case of genitive, to another noun phrase), be it Fillmorean semantic case, relational-grammar case, or surface case.

With theme defined as above, I advance the following proposals:

(a) Korean is a theme-prominent language in that theme plays a major role in Korean syntax, just as in Chinese which is viewed as a typical theme-prominent language (e.g. Li and Thompson 1976).
(b) Theme is as basic as case in the description of Korean, and therefore, both should be postulated in underlying structure. The thematization or topicalization process which has been proposed by many generative linguists is seriously handicapped and hard to maintain.
(c) Contrary to what many traditional, structural, and generative grammarians claim, the so-called subject particle *ka/i* is also relevant to thematic constructions with its own semantic content, just like any other limiters such as *(n)un* 'as for', *to* 'also', and *man* 'only'.

These proposals are elaborated in what follows.

2. **Korean: A Theme-Prominent Language.** Generative studies of Korean have erroneously been under significant influence from works on English, which manifests a typology quite distinct from Korean. In dealing with theme in Korean, therefore, it is essential to peruse what some recent

typologists say about similar phenomena shown in various languages, so that Korean constructions can be studied more effectively in a broad typological perspective.

Li and Thompson (1976:459), for example, recognize four basic types of languages: (a) subject-prominent languages for whose descriptions the subject-predicate relation plays a major role (e.g. Indo-European, Indonesian, Finno-Ugric); (b) topic-prominent languages which can be more efficiently described in terms of the concept of topic-and-comment (e.g. Chinese, Lahu, Lisu); (c) languages that are both subject-prominent and topic-prominent, in which there are two distinct sentence types of equal importance (e.g. Japanese, Korean); and (d) languages that are neither subject-prominent nor topic-prominent, in which the subject and the topic are not distinguishable in all sentence types (e.g. Tagalog, Ilocano). A number of distinguishing characteristics of typical topic-prominent languages as opposed to subject-prominent languages that Li and Thompson (hereafter L&T) advance may be summarized as follows:

TOPIC-prominent languages	*SUBJECT-prominent languages*
1. Topics are coded in the surface structure, either by being placed in sentence-initial position or by a morphological marker, or by both.	1. [*no discussion*]
2. Passivization either does not occur at all or appears as a marginal construction (sometimes carrying a special meaning).	2. Passivization is very common.
3. 'Dummy' subjects (e.g. English: 'it', 'there') do not occur.	3. 'Dummy' subjects are common.
4. Topic-oriented "double subject" constructions are very common.	4. "Double subject" constructions are rare or non-existent.
5. The topic, not the subject, tends to control co-referentiality.	5. The subject controls co-referentiality.
6. These languages tend to be verb-final.	6. These languages are not verb-final.
7. There are no constraints on what may be the topic.	7. The topic-comment type of sentence is highly constrained in terms of what can serve as the

	topic constituent.
8. Topic-comment structures are basic sentence types.	8. Subject-predicate structures are basic sentence types.

As mentioned above, L&T classify Korean (and Japanese) as both topic-prominent and subject-prominent on the grounds that the languages give equal importance to the two distinct sentence types. In order for this claim to be justifiable, it should meet both sets of the above distinguishing characteristics. As for coding topic and subject, they (ibid.: 466) assert that in J(apanese) and K(orean) there is an element marking the topic (J *wa* and K (*n*)*un*) and one marking the subject (J *ga* and K *ka/i*). As will be made clear in Section 4, however, the particle *ka/i* is not only an optional subject marker but, to all intents and purposes, also relevant to thematic constructions with its own semantic content, just like any limiters including (*n*)*un*. The particle *ka/i* is losing ground as a pure case marker.

Secondly, regular passive constructions based on affixation of a passive suffix are not productive in Korean. There is a rather small set of transitive verbs which allow a passive suffix, as in *mek-hi* 'to be eaten', *cap-hi* 'to be caught', *po-i* 'to be seen', *kel-li* 'to be hung'. A larger number of verbs, including those ending in *-ha* 'to do', cannot be passivized through affixation, e.g. *ponay* 'to send', *kaci* 'to take', *wumciki* 'to move', *kongpu-ha* 'to study', *salang-ha* 'to love'. L&T (p. 467) attribute the non-productivity of the passive construction in topic-prominent languages to the fact that any noun phrase in such languages can be the topic of a sentence without registering anything on the verb. Korean corresponds with this characterization. Thus, for example, *totwuk* 'a thief' in (4a) can be topicalized as in (4b), with the verb intact.

(4) a. swunkyeng-i ku totwuk-ul cap-ass-ta.
'A policeman caught the thief.'
b. ku totwuk-un swunkyeng-i cap-ass-ta.
'The thief was caught by a policeman.'
(Lit. 'As for the thief, the policeman caught him.')

Besides, in many cases, passive constructions reveal special meanings such as psychological potentiality (C. Lee 1973a:157-161), as illustrated in (5).

(5) a. kaul-ey-nun pap-i cal mek-*hi*-n-ta.
'In autumn, people have a good appetite.'
b. mun-i cecello yel-*li*-ess-ta.

'The door opened of itself.'
(Lit. 'The door was opened of itself.')

Thirdly, 'dummy' subjects do not occur in Korean. The nonoccurrence of dummy subjects in topic-prominent languages is ascribed by L&T (p. 467) to the fact that in such languages, where the notion of subject does not play a prominent role, a subject can simply be dispensed with if it is not called for, whereas in a subject-prominent language, a subject may be required regardless of whether it plays a semantic role. The more important reason seems to be the verb-final nature of topic-prominent languages. All the elements being predicated occur in pre-verbal positions, and that makes it quite redundant to have a dummy subject side by side with a real subject. Another source of dummy subjects in English is discussed in Sohn (1974b) in terms of case incorporation in English verbs. Thus, for instance, *rains* in *it rains* incorporates the semantic concept 'rain' together with its predicate, which requires a dummy in the subject position. In Korean, where no case incorporation is operative, the notion 'rain' is expressed as the subject in *pi-ka o-n-ta* 'it rains'.

Fourth, double or multiple 'subject' constructions are extremely pervasive in Korean. As L&T (p. 468) point out, such constructions are the clearest instances of thematic constructions, in that the theme and the cases (especially that of the subject) can both occur and can be distinguished easily; there is generally no selectional relationship between the theme and the verb; these sentences could not be derived through thematization from some other sentence type, as will be discussed in Section 3; and no pure subject-prominent languages have sentences of this type.

Fifth, theme tends to control co-referentiality in Korean. Observe the examples in (6) and (7), where co-referential constituent deletion is controlled by the theme.

(6) *ce namu-nun* iph-i khe-se [X] silh-ta.
[X] = ce namu-ka/*iph-i
'As for that tree, its leaves are big, so I don't like it/*them.'

(7) a. haksayng-tul-i ppalli talli-ese [X] phikon-hay-ss-ta.
[X] = haksayng-tul-i
'The students were tired because they ran fast.'

b. **ku kyengki-nun* haksayng-tul-i ppalli talli-ese
[X] phikon-hay-ss-ta.
[X] = ku kyengki-ka/*haksayng-tul-i
*'That race was tired, because the students ran fast.'

(7a) is acceptable because the deleted subject is in co-reference to the subject of the main clause, whereas (7b) is out because the deleted subject is controlled by the theme which is inanimate and cannot co-occur with an animate verb. The theme in Korean is so strong that it even controls honorification under certain definable conditions, as illustrated in (8).

(8) *sensayng-nim*-un ton-i manh-*usi*-ta.
'The professor has a lot of money.'
(Lit. As for the professor, there is a lot of money.)

Sensayng-nim 'the professor' does not have any case relationship with the verb, but the honorific suffix *-usi* is attached to the verb whose subject is *ton* 'money'.

Sixth, Korean is a typical verb-final language. The verb-final constraint is strict not only in simple sentences but in conjunctive and embedded constructions too. This constraint is more tenacious in Korean than in Chinese, which is regarded as a typical topic-prominent language.

Seventh, in principle any nominal element in a sentence can be made the theme of the sentence in Korean, although there exists some semantic constraints on what may be the theme. In (9), the italicized elements are themes.[4]

(9) a. *John-uy kho-nun* khu-ta.
'As for John's nose, it is big.'
b. *John-un* kho-ka khu-ta.
'As for John, his nose is big.'
c. *kho-nun* John-i khu-ta.
'As for noses, John's is big.'

Finally, thematic structures are basic sentence types in Korean, and that is the concern of Section 3. Then, how about subject-predicate structures? I claim here that it does more harm than good to postulate subject-predicate, in addition to theme-rheme, in underlying structures. Subject-predicate structures do not exist independently of theme-rheme structures but are incorporated in the latter. The underlying structure I have in mind is something like (10a), and not something like (10b) or (10c) where theme and subject have separate existences.

(10) a. $S \rightarrow NP + \begin{Bmatrix} S \\ VP \end{Bmatrix}$
where NP is a theme and also functions as a subject if

followed by VP.

b. $S \rightarrow \begin{Bmatrix} NP_1 \\ NP_2 \end{Bmatrix} + \begin{Bmatrix} S \\ VP \end{Bmatrix}$

where NP_1 is a theme; NP_2 is a subject.

c. $S \rightarrow \begin{Bmatrix} NP_1 + S \\ NP_2 + VP \end{Bmatrix}$

where NP_1 is a theme; NP_2 is a subject.

For an illustration, let us observe the sentences in (11).

(11) a. John-un kho-ka khu-ta.
'John has a big nose.'
a′. John-un cip-eyse pap-ul mek-ess-ta.
'John had his meal at home.'
b. John-i kho-ka khu-ta.
'John has a big nose.'
b′. John-i cip-eyse pap-ul mek-ess-ta.
'John had his meal at home.'

A widely followed practice is to regard *John-un* as theme and *John-i* as subject in (11). If this is true, (10b) or (10c) should be more adequate and we would have to claim that both theme-rheme and subject-predicate must have a separate existence in underlying structures. As will be discussed in detail in Section 4, however, I consider both *John-un* in (11a) and *John-i* in (11b) to be equally themes on various syntactic and semantic grounds. In the same vein, I also consider both *John-un* in (11a′) and *John-i* in (11b′) to be themes as well as subjects in their sentences, in that they meet the definition of theme as given in the beginning of this paper. That is, any subject is a theme in relation to the rest of the sentence, but not vice versa. As will be seen in Section 4, themes exist hierarchically in Korean; this in fact is built into (10a) by means of the recursiveness of S(entence). All this means that theme-rheme is predominant in Korean, while subject-predicate is secondary and parasitic to the former.

Korean is markedly different from subject-predicate languages such as English. First of all, (10a) is not applicable to English in that there is no rhematic sentence in English. This means that there is always a subject in any sentence, whether it is also a theme or not. The subject in English is syntactically separated by the verb from the rest of the cases. Basically, there is only one significant position before the verb, which must be filled by the subject, real or dummy. In Korean, on the other hand, all cases including subject come before the verb, and can be scrambled, as in (12).

(12) a. John-i cip-eyse pap-ul
cip-eyse John-i pap-ul } mek-ess-ta.
pap-ul John-i cip-eyse
....
'John had his meal at home.'

Secondly, the subject in English figures prominently with regard to grammatical processes in that the verb usually determines and agrees with the subject and only the subject is normally sensitive to such processes as reflexivization, Equi-NP deletion, and imperativization. It was observed earlier that Equi-NP deletion in Korean is controlled by the theme. If more than one theme occurs, the left-most takes precedence in controlling deletion. Besides, all cases including subject are freely deleted whenever their information is situationally or contextually redundant, whether the sentence involved is a satement, a question, an imperative, or a suggestive. It has frequently been claimed that a Korean subject is sensitive to honorification and reflexivization (e.g. Shibatani 1976a). As noticed in sentence (8), the verb receives the honorific suffix *-usi* not because of its subject (*ton* 'money') but because what deserves the speaker's deference is the theme (*sensayng-nim* 'professor'). The underlying grammatical relation existing between the verb and the theme is that of verb-locative, not that of verb-subject. As regards reflexivization, observe the example in (13).

(13) *John*-un *Mary*-lul *caki* pang-eyse kkwucic-ess-ta.
'John scolded Mary in his/her room.'

It is true that the reflexive pronoun *caki* may refer to the subject *John* with higher probability than the object *Mary*. However, there is not the slightest unnaturalness if we use (13) to refer to the event in which *John* scolded *Mary* in the latter's room. All this indicates that the subject does not have any such strong syntactic privilege as to warrant its separate postulation along with theme in Korean.

Finally, Mandarin Chinese is claimed to be a theme-prominent language in spite of the fact that the notion of subject also clearly plays a role in certain sentence structures (e.g. Householder and Cheng 1971, L&T 1976). As has been observed, Korean enjoys a variety of characteristics that are shared by theme-prominent languages, but not by subject-prominent languages. In short, Korean is a theme-prominent language in that the thematic function is systematically built into the syntactic structure of the sentence. Precisely for this reason, Korean abounds in sentence types which are acceptable only when they are used in thematic constructions, as illustrated in (14).

(14) a. na-nun John-i pulep-ta.
'I envy John.'
b. *na-hanthey John-i pulep-ta.
*'To me John is envied.'

Some scholars postulate such unacceptable sentences as (14b) as the non-thematic source of sentences like (14a). Why should we hesitate to regard (14a) as a basic construction?

I suspect that most of what has been mentioned about Korean is also applicable to Japanese. One of the four basic types of languages that L&T set up, i.e. the type in which a language is simultaneously subject-prominent and topic-prominent, is based solely on Korean and Japanese. If my proposal that these languages be grouped together with Chinese is correct, the type in question will be vacuous unless other languages are found to fit into it.

3. Basicness of Thematic Sentences in Korean. In this section, I will claim that thematic constructions in Korean are to be viewed as basic, not as derived from any other structures through the process of thematization or topicalization.[5] First, observe the sentences in (15).

(15) a. *i chayk-un* John-uy kes i-ta.
'As for this book, it is John's.'
b. *i chayk-un* moyang-i coh-ta.
'As for this book, its design is good.'
c. *i chayk-un* John-i sa-ss-ta.
'As for this book, John bought it.'
d. *i chayk-un* sacin-i manh-ta.
'As for this book, there are many pictures in it.'

In uttering the sentences in (15), the speaker's conception/intention is to have 'this book' as the frame about which the rest of the sentence makes a comment. Upon hearing *i chayk-un,* the hearer perceives it as a theme, roughly with the meaning 'as regards *or* concerning this book', equally in all the sentences in (15). Given an identical discourse context, the informational content of 'this book' is exactly the same in all the four sentences. As regards the grammatical cases to which the theme refers with regard to the rest of the sentences, the theme refers to the subject in (15a), to the genitive in (15b), to the object in (15c), and to the locative in (15d). If the underlying structure is to be a semantic structure, it will be absurd to derive themes from different grammatical cases, introducing the semantic content of theme by transformation. There are no sentences more basic than those with a theme in terms of which their meaning can be specified (cf. Keenan 1976 for the notion of basicness). Postulating theme in underlying structure, we can simply say that the underlying cases mentioned above are deleted in co-reference to the themes.

Second, as mentioned earlier, a usual claim is that a theme carries old information in that it refers back to a unit of the preceding sentence in the discourse. What the process of thematization would do, therefore, is to degrade an element to the lowest degree of 'communicative dynamism'. Viewed from the perspective of informational theory, informational contents are bound to be changed upon thematization.

Third, the referent of the theme is affected semantically by the event denoted by the rheme as a whole, since the rhematic predication applies within the thematic domain. The semantic affection is particularly conspicuous in such constructions as self-judgment (or subjective) verb sentences, where the theme is an experiencer as in (14). Also observe the sentences in (16) and (17).

(16) a. na-nun pap-i cal mek-hi-n-ta.
'I have a good appetite.'
b. ?pap-i na-hanthey cal mek-hi-n-ta.
?'The rice is eaten well by me.'

Due to the affective meaning a thematic construction may have, (16a) has the reading in which the thematic referent, as the experiencer, is affected by the event expressed by the rest of the sentence. This is not the case in (16b) where *na* 'I' is simply the agent. Also, in the possessive paraphrase of a thematic construction, the possessor has no semantic bearing on the event expressed by the rest of the sentence. (17a) may be an answer to 'What happened to John?', while (17b) can only be an answer to 'What happened to John's brother?'.

(17) a. John-un hyeng-i cwuk-ess-ta.
'As for John, his brother died.'
b. John-uy hyeng-i cwuk-ess-ta.
'John's brother died.'

The affective meaning is more clearly discernible in conjunctive sentences like those in (18).

(18) a. John-un hyeng-i cwuk-ese sulph-e-ha-n-ta.
'As for John, his brother died, so he is sad.'
b. John-uy hyeng-i cwuk-ese sulph-e-ha-n-ta.
'John's brother died, so (somebody else) is sad.'

Notice that in (18a) the unspecified subject of *sulphuta* 'to be sad' is necessarily *John*, whereas it is not *John* but someone else in (18b). In other words, *John* in (18a) has the two conjoined clauses as its rheme, but *John* in (18b) is related only to *hyeng* and has nothing to do with any other part of the sentence semantically. Incidentally, this semantic phenomenon, along with the others discussed in this section, constitutes a piece of evidence in favor of the syntactic division between the theme and the rhematic part in the initial expansion of a sentence.

Fourth, there are presuppositional differences between a thematic construction and its non-thematic counterpart. As also pointed out by Teng (1974:465) with regard to Chinese, *John*, the theme, is presupposed to be alive in (17a) but there is no such presupposition in (17b). The presupposition seems to be correlated with the affective meaning. Thus, while (19b) is natural, (19a) sounds extremely awkward.

(19) a. ??caknyen-ey cwuk-un John-un hyeng-i cwuk-ess-ta.
'As for John who died last year, his brother died.'
b. caknyen-ey cwuk-un John-uy hyeng-i cwuk-ess-ta.
'A brother of John, who died last year, died.'

Moreover, insertion of limiters or adverbials reveals some other presuppositional difference, as observed in (20) through (22).

(20) a. John-un hyeng-i tto cwuk-ess-ta.
'As for John, his brother also died.' or
'As for John, another brother of his died.'
b. John-uy hyeng-i tto cwuk-ess-ta.
'John's brother also died.' or
'Another brother of John's died.'
(21) a. John-un hyeng-man cwuk-ess-ta.
'As for John, only his brother died.'
b. John-uy hyeng-man cwuk-ess-ta.
'Only John's brother died.'
(22) a. hankwuk-un kaul-i ceyil coh-ta.

'As for Korea, autumn is the best.'

b. hankwuk-uy kaul-i ceyil coh-ta.
'Korean autumn is the best.'

The sentence (20a) necessarily presupposes prior death of a relative, whereas the presupposition underlying (20b) includes the death of someone who is not related to *John* at all. In the same way, (21a) presupposes that no one among John's relatives died except his brother, but (21b) does not have such a narrow range of presupposition. Similarly in (22a), the presupposition is that autumn is better than any other season in Korea, without any other country drawn into the picture. In (22b), however, the comparison is between the Korean autumn and that of other countries. As is apparent in these sentences, one important semantic fact is that the semantic range of the rheme is always within the domain of the theme, which is not the case with non-thematic constructions. All this supports the division between the theme and the rest of the sentence in underlying structure. This also implies that deriving *a*-sentences from *b*-sentences in the above examples is unjustifiable. How could we, for example, handle the obvious presuppositional difference between (22a) and (22b)? Sentence (22a) is uttered only when the speaker compares autumn with the other seasons in terms of Korea, while (22b) is used only when the speaker compares Korea with other countries in terms of autumn.

Fifth, those who are in favor of the transformational approach would say that (23a) and (24a) are derived from (23b) and (24b) respectively.

(23) a. na-nun pay-ka pulu-ta.
'I am full.'

b. na-uy pay-ka pulu-ta.
'My stomach bulges out.'

(24) a. John-un Mary-ka coh-ta.
'John likes Mary.' (speaker's authoritative judgment)

b. Mary-ka John-hanthey coh-ta.
'Mary is good to John.'

Verbs like *puluta* 'full' and *cohta* 'good' are ambivalent between + and − subjective verbs (à la B. Park 1972) or self-judgment verbs (à la I. Yang 1972). When they are used as subjective verbs, their semantic case frame is [Experiencer, Patient ___] and the Experiencer is usually the first person. If the Experiencer is other than the first person, the sentence carries the speaker's authoritative judgment, as in (24a). This is because such verbs denote the internal feelings of the person denoted by the Experiencer and the speaker cannot directly observe the feelings of others without some kind of indirct clues. When the speaker uses such verbs with the Experiencer that denotes other than himself, it means that the speaker authoritatively asserts his knowledge of the referent's internal feelings. When such verbs are used in the non-subjective sense, the Experiencer is not necessary, as shown in (23b) and (24b). Now, if we derive *a*-sentences from *b*-sentences, how could we account for the difference in case frames, the difference in the meanings of the verbs, and the appearance of the authoritative meaning?

Observe further the sentences in (25) where now the verb is a pure subjective verb. According to the transformational approach, the three sentences are to be derived from the same source, i.e. from a structure underlying (25c).

(25) a. na-nun John-i mip-ta.
 'As for me, I hate John.'
 b. ??na-hanthey-nun John-i mip-ta.
 c. ??John-i na-hanthey mip-ta.

How could we account for the fact that a natural sentence (25a) is derived from an unacceptable (or marginally acceptable) sentence through the *optional* process of thematization?

Sixth, the particle *(n)un*, which has usually been regarded as the only theme marker, shares the same morphological and syntactic behavior as the other limiters, as illustrated in (26).

(26) John- { a. un / b. to / c. man } hyeng-i cwuk-ess-ta.

a. 'As for John, / b. 'As for John also, / c. 'As for only John, } his brother died.'

All these limiters have their own definable semantic contents (e.g. I. Yang 1973). Moreover, all of them manifest the same presuppositions as discussed above, which fact justifies that such limiters are all relevant to thematic constructions. Suppose we derive NP + *nun* in (26) from the genitive source (NP + *uy*) through thematization. How about NP + *to*, NP + *man*, etc.? We certainly could not leave them as deep structure elements in view of the syntactic and semantic parallelism between these and *nun*. Then, could we derive them by transformation in any simple way that is linguistically useful?

Seventh, as alluded to in (14) and (16) and as some linguists have also pointed out, there are thematic sentences which do not have a clearcut non-thematic source where the theme can be identified as a case. Such sentences constitute a significant piece of evidence against the process of thematization (e.g. I. Yang 1972; B. Park 1972; D. Yang 1973a; Teng 1974; Bak 1977). Some more examples are given in (27).

(27) a. cha-nun cak-un kes-i coh-ta.
'As for cars, small ones are better.'
b. i chayk-un caymi-ka iss-ta.
'This book is interesting.'
c. John-un caki-ka an ka-ss-ta.
'As for John, he didn't go himself.'
d. John-un salam-i coh-ta.
'John has a good personality.'
e. nayil nalssi-nun pi-ka o-keyss-ta.
'As for tomorrow's weather, it is going to rain.'

So far as the verb does not have any selectional restriction with the theme and the case frame of the verb does not require, as an actant, an NP that refers to the theme, there is no gain in postulating such a dubious element as a clause-mate of the verb in underlying structure.

Eighth, transformational derivation of thematic sentences faces some difficulty in accounting for different controls of co-referential noun phrase deletion (cf. L&T 1976:481 for Chinese).

(28) a. ku yeca-uy son-i numu khe-se [X] silh-ta.
[X] = ku yeca uy son
'Her hands are too big, so I don't like *them*.'
b. ku yeca-nun son-i nemu khe-se [X] silh-ta.
[X] = ku yeca
'As for her, her hands are too big, so I don't like *her*.'

Since the controller of the interpretation of the deleted constituent is the theme *ku yeca* 'she' in (28b), not *ku yeca-uy son* 'her hands', we would need some kind of constraint in the deletion processes if we were to follow the thematization approach. A related case may be observed in (29).

(29) a. ??hankwuk-ey ssal-i manh-ko alumtap-ta.

*'In Korea, there is lots of rice and is pretty.'

b. hankwuk-un ssal-i manh-ko alumtap-ta.
'Korea has lots of rice and is pretty.'

The reason that (29a) sounds unnatural is because the locative cannot control the deletion of the subject of *alumtapta* 'to be pretty'. In (29b), on the other hand, the controller is the theme *hankwuk* 'Korea'. To derive both sentences from the same source would cause unnecessary syntactic complication, in addition to the problem of semantic differences.

Finally, those linguists who make use of thematization would derive, for example, (30a) from (30b), assuming that *ka/i* is the subject marker and *nun* the theme marker.

(30) a. na-*nun* haksaying i-ta.
'As for me, I am a student.'

b. nay-*ka* haksayng i-ta.
'I am a student.'

One insuperable problem with this proposal is how to account for the fact that, upon thematization, the exclusiveness meaning (and usually the new information) that the *ka/i* construction has, is replaced by the thematic/contrastiveness meaning (and usually the old information) that the *nun* construction has. More will be said on this in the following section.

I believe that the foregoing syntactic and semantic arguments are sufficient to warrant the validity of the claim that Korean thematic constructions are basic, not derived.

4. **ka/i in Themes.** The thesis that the post-nominal particle *ka/i* is the subject marker had rarely been disputed among the grammarians of Korean until scholars such as Im (1972, 1974), Shin (1975), and Shibatani (1976) questioned its validity by pointing out that certain occurrences of *ka/i* do not refer to subjects. Mathias (1978:129, 131), for instance, schematizes the relation between *(n)un* and *ka/i* succinctly as shown in (31).

(31) Communication → Context + Assertion
Assertion → Topic + Comment
Comment → Subject + Predicate
Topic → (Korean) NP-*nun*, (Japanese) NP-*wa*
Subject → (Korean) NP-*ka*, (Japanese) NP-*ga*

In this section, I propose that *ka/i*, *(n)un*, and the other limiters are all relevent to theme with their own distinct semantic contents. Observe, for example, sentence (32a) whose underlying structure is viewed as something like (32b).

(32) a. John-i hyeng-i cwuk-ess-ta.
'It is John whose brother died.'

b.

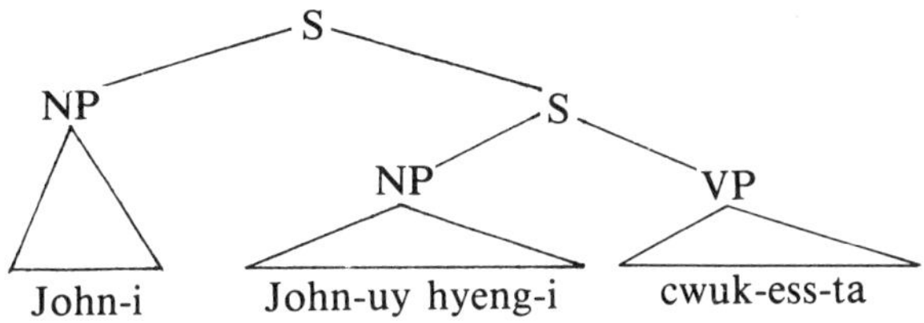

The postulation of (32b), with *John-i* as the theme, is justifiable in many ways. Semantically, *John-i* is the domain within which the rest of the sentence makes the comment on it, just as in *(n)un* constructions. Thus, all the semantic arguments, such as affective meaning, presupposition, and assertiveness, presented in Section 3 in connection with *(n)un* are equally applicable to *ka/i* constructions. Syntactically also, in (32) *John* has no case relationship with the verb and scrambling between *John* and *hyeng* is not permissible. Moreover, the syntactic arguments, such as controls of deletion and lack of identifiable sources, that were advanced in Section 3 in connection with *(n)un* are equally applicable to *ka/i* constructions. All this means that *John-i* must be placed in a higher node as the theme, as shown in (32b), and is not to be derived from any other structure such as that underlying *John-uy hyeng-i cwuk-ess-ta*. 'John's brother died'.

The parallelism between *ka/i* and *(n)un* constructions is illustrated in (33) where *ka/i* and *(n)un* are equally allowed so that they have the same thematic and syntactic relation vis-à-vis the rest of the sentence. Note that all the other limiters (*man* 'only', *to* 'also', *kkaci* 'even', etc.) may occur in the same position with the same thematic function as those of *ka/i* and *(n)un*.

(33) a. $\left.\begin{matrix}\text{nay-ka}\\ \text{na-nun}\end{matrix}\right\}$ pap-i cal mek-hi-n-ta. (Cf. (16a).)
'I have a good appetite.'

b. John-$\left\{\begin{matrix}\text{i}\\ \text{un}\end{matrix}\right\}$ hyeng-i cwuk-ese sulph-e-ha-n-ta.
(Cf. (18a).)
'As for John, he is sad because his brother died.'

c. ??caknyen-ey cwuk-un John- {i / un} hyeng-i cwuk-ess-ta. (Cf. (19a).)
'As for John who died last year, his brother died.'

d. hankwuk- {i / un} kaul-i ceyil coh-ta.
(Cf. (22a).)
'As for Korea, autumn is the best.'

e. {nay-ka / na-nun} John-i mip-ta. (Cf. (25a).)
'I hate John'.

f. cha- {ka / nun} cak-un kes-i coh-ta. (Cf. (27a).)
'As for cars, small ones are better.'

g. John- {i / un} caki-ka an ka-ss-ta. (Cf. (27c).)
'John didn't go himself.'

h. ku yeca- {ka / nun} son-i nemu khe-se [X] silh-ta.
(Cf. (28b).)
[X] = ku yeca/*son
'As for her, her hands are too big, so I don't like *her*.'

i. hankwuk- {i / un} ssal-i manh-ko alumtap-ta.
(Cf. (29b).)
'Korea has plenty rice and is pretty.'

For each of the paired sentences in (33), the only difference is in the lexical meanings of *ka/i* and *(n)un*, with the thematic meaning intact.

Basically, *ka/i* has a meaning of 'exclusiveness' ('exhaustive listing' or 'uniqueness'), whether it is simply a neutral description or focused as the only new (or activated) information in the sentence. The basic meaning of *(n)un* is 'contrastiveness', with Kuno's so-called 'thematic' sense as its proper subset. Discourse contexts and sentential positions are responsible for various degrees of contrastiveness. I will not go into the details of the semantics of the two particles in this paper, but one point I want to make is that exclusiveness and contrastiveness are semantically complementary.[6] That is, it is semantically and logically impossible to describe something contrastively and exclusively at the same time. This paradigmatic relation of the two semantic notions leads us to postulate their corresponding NP *-ka/i* and NP*-(n)un* as belonging to the same paradigm, i.e. the paradigm of themes in our case.

The semantic complementarity of *ka/i* and *(n)un* is clearly observable in sentences like those in (34).

(34) wuli- {a. ka / b. nun / c. Ø} ka-p-si-ta.
'Let's go.'

Sentence (34a) is used when the subject is to be exclusively selected, (34b) when the subject is contrasted with somebody else, and (34c) when the subject is neither exclusively specified nor contrasted, i.e. completely neutrally stated. This semantic fact obviates a common (transformationalists') claim to derive, for example, (34b) from (34a) or derive *wuli-nun* from *wuli-ka -nun*.

There are many additional parallelisms between *ka/i* and *(n)un*. Suffice it here to illustrate a few syntactic parallels. First, both can be multiplied, as in (35).

(35) John- {i / un} kho- {ka / nun} khu-ta.
'John has a big nose.'

Second, paraphrase relations are identical in both, as shown in (36).

(36) a. John-uy kho- {ka / nun} khu-ta.
'John has a big nose.'
b. Kho- {ka / nun} John- {i / un} khu-ta.
'John has a big nose.'

Third, ungrammaticality due to scrambling is also shared by both, as in (37).

(37) a. nalssi- {ka / nun} pi- {ka / nun} o-keyss-ta.
b. *pi- {ka / nun} nalssi- {ka / nun} o-keyss-ta.
'As for the weather, it is going to rain.'

One might say that non-occurrence of *ka/i* in such sentences as (38) constitutes evidence against the claim that *ka/i* is relevant to theme.

(38) mikwuk-{*i / un} Alaska-ka khu-ta.
'As for America, Alaska is big.'

The reason that *ka/i* is not accepted in (38) is, however, due to the tenacious semantic content of the particle, i.e. exclusiveness. If *ka/i* were a pure subject marker without exclusiveness meaning, there would be no reason why (38) with *i* should not be acceptable. Since Alaska is nowhere else except in America, there is no point to exclusively specify America in order to describe the largeness of Alaska. We can say *mikwuk-i ttang-i khu-ta* 'It is America whose land is big' or 'America has a big land' because land exists in any country. The 'contrastive' sense in (38) with *un* is minimal, with the 'thematic' sense outstanding, by virtue of the sentence initial position.

A popular claim is that *(n)un*, especially the 'thematic' *(n)un*, does not occur in embedded sentences, while *ka/i* freely occurs in any position (e.g. Oh 1972:638). The non-occurrence of 'thematic' *(n)un* in embedding can be accounted for by the fact that the 'thematic' (but not the 'contrastive') sense is associated only with the initial position of a main sentence. In its 'contrastive' sense, *(n)un* may occur rather freely in any position. On the other hand, *ka/i* is not entirely free to occur even in subject positions, as observed in (39).

(39) a. John-{i / man / to / ?un} po-n ay-ka ce ay-ta.
'The child ... John ... saw is that one.'

b. John-{*i / *man / *to / un} po-ass-ciman Mary-{ka / nun} an po-n ay-ka ce ay-ta.
'The child that John saw but Mary didn't is that one.'

Notice in (39a) that in the natural reading out of context, *un* is usually not allowed because contrastiveness is rather exceptional in an expression with such a structure. In the apparent contrastive sentence (39b), *un* is the only allowable particle in the first NP. The reason that *i* is not allowed in the first NP is because it has an 'exclusiveness' meaning. Naturally, exclusiveness is not permitted where contrastiveness is called for.

Furthermore, observe the sentence in (40).

(40) a. John-{i / un} hyeng-i cwuk-ess-ta.
'As for John, his brother died.'
b. *John-{i / un} cwuk-un hyeng ...

(40a) allows both *i* and *un* in the first NP. When it is embedded as a relative clause with the second NP co-referential to the head noun, the whole construction becomes ungrammatical whether the first NP occurs with *i* or *un*. Being the theme, the first NP in a multiple 'subject' sentence cannot surface in an embedded construction whether it is accompanied by *i, un,* or any other limiters. All this suggests that *ka/i* and (*n*)*un* behave in a similar way in relation to theme.

As briefly touched on at the outset of this paper, some linguists deal with theme in terms of informational load and ascribe *ka/i* to new and *(n)un* to old information, claiming that only the latter is the theme marker. To substantiate the invalidity of this claim, observe the sentence in (41).

(41) Hawaii-{ka / nun} san-i phulu-kwun-yo!
'As for Hawaii, the mountains are green!'

In (41), both *Hawaii-ka* and *Hawaii-nun* indicate new information, when the speaker utters them overlooking Hawaii from the airplane, whereas both indicate old information when the speaker utters them as a response to *yeki-ka Hawaii yeyyo* 'This is Hawaii'. Obviously, defining theme on the basis of old information will get us nowhere.

So far we have seen a wide variety of structural and semantic parallelisms between NP-*ka/i* and NP-*(n)un*, enough to claim that both can be themes. There is one significant syntactic difference between them, however, as illustrated in (42).

(42) a. *John-*{*i* / *un*} caki-ka ka-ss-ta.
'John went himself.'
b. *John-*{*i* / *un*} hyeng-i cha-lul sa-ss-ta.
'As for John, his brother bought a car.'

c. *John-* $\left\{\begin{array}{l} *i \\ un \end{array}\right\}$ *nay-ka po-ass-ta.*

'As for John, I saw him.'

d. *John-* $\left\{\begin{array}{l} i \\ un \end{array}\right\}$ ton-i manh-ta.

'John has much money.'

The italicized part in (42a) refers to the subjcct; that in (42b), the genitive; that in (42c), the object; and that in (42d), the locative. Notice that, unlike *(n)un* and other limiters, *ka/i* cannot refer to the object case.[7] This sensitivity of *ka/i* to (object) case can be attributable to the ambivalence in its relevance between (subject) case and theme. That is, when an NP-*ka/i* occurs as a clausemate of a verb, *ka/i* functions as the subject marker. This subject-like nature remains loosely intact even when an NP-*ka/i* occurs on a higher node as theme, thus its referential force is unable to reach such an opposite case as that of the object. This functional ambivalence of *ka/i* is partly reflected in the morphological restriction that it hardly ever occurs with a limiter or with a case marker.[8] Furthermore, the ambivalence seems to be rather natural in view of the semantic closeness of subject to theme, as alluded to in Chafe's (1976:43, 51) definitions of subject as "what the sentence is about" and of theme as "the frame within which the sentence holds".[9] On the other hand, *(n)un* and the other limiters never function as case markers, thus being indifferent to cases wherever they occur. We may summarize the foregoing discussions loosely as in (43).

(43)

	ka/i	*(n)un*
theme relevance	+	+
case sensitivity	+	–
contrastiveness	–	+
exclusiveness	+	–

Finally, as alluded to in (10a), I propose that themes exist hierarchically in Korean, as clearly evidenced in sentences like (44).

(44) Ku sin- $\left\{\begin{array}{l} \text{i} \\ \text{un} \end{array}\right\}$ patak- $\left\{\begin{array}{l} \text{i} \\ \text{un} \end{array}\right\}$ kwumeng- $\left\{\begin{array}{l} \text{i} \\ \text{un} \end{array}\right\}$ na-ss-ta.

'That shoe has a hole in the bottom.'

ku sin is the highest theme with the rest of the sentence as its rheme. Within the rheme, *patak* is again a theme vis-à-vis the remaining part. Rule (10a) takes care of this hierarchical existence of themes, in that the S(entence) is recursive. I also regard *kwumeng* as the lowest level of theme as well as the subject of the verb because it is a topic about which the verbal predicate makes a comment. I. Yang (1972) discusses the macro-micro relation with regard to Korean noun phrases. I would rather claim that the relation holds in thematic constructions.[10]

Notes

1. This is a modified version of a paper presented at the 1979 Meeting of the International Circle of Korean Linguistics held at the University of Alaska, Fairbanks. I gratefully acknowledge the discussions I had with Sung Yun Bak and Dong Jae Lee on this paper.
2. The particles *i* and *un* occur after a vowel and *ka* and *nun* after a consonant.
3. Unlike Japanese *ga* (Kuno 1972a:279), Korean *ka/i* can be deleted when it carries old information and can be uniquely recoverable. (3c) can only be equated with (3a) in view of their shared meanings, and not with (3b).
4. A case similar to (9) involves sentences like the following, which are often taken up as a piece of evidence against the transformational approach on the grounds that their non-thematic counterparts are hard to determine (e.g. Bak 1977).

   (i) a. swuyeng-un Waikiki-ka coh-ta.
   'For swimming, Waikiki is good.'
   b. ssal-un hankwuksan-i coh-ta.
   'As for rice, the Korean product is good.'
   c. TV-nun Zenith-ka thunthun-ha-ta.
   'As for TV, Zenith is durable.'

   It seems to me that sentences (ii) may be considered the counterparts of those in (i), although I don't think they are transformationally related.

   (ii) a. Waikiki-uy swuyeng-i coh-ta.
   'Swimming at Waikiki is good.'
   b. hankwuksan-uy ssal-i coh-ta.
   'Korean rice is good.'
   c. Zenith-uy TV-ka thunthun-ha-ta.
   'Zenith TV is durable.'

   The sentences in (ii) can be paraphrased also as in (iii).

   (iii) a. Waikiki-ka swuyeng-i coh-ta.
   'Swimming at Waikiki is good.'
   b. hankwuksan-i ssal-i coh-ta.
   'Korean rice is good.'
   c. Zenith-ka TV-ka thunthun-ha-ta.
   'Zenith TV is durable.'

   Since, in principle, any nominal can be made the theme, we obtain (i) by replacing *ka/i* of the second NPs in (iii) with *(n)un* and place them at the beginning of the sentences, while we obtain (iv) by replacing *ka/i* of the first NPs in (iii) with *(n)un*.

(iv) a. Waikiki-nun swuyeng-i coh-ta.
'As for Waikiki, swimming is good.'
b. hankwuksan-un ssal-i coh-ta.
'As for Korean products, rice is good.'
c. Zenith-nun TV-ka thunthun-ha-ta.
'As for Zenith, TV is durable.'

Incidentally, there is yet another set of paraphrases of (i), as given in (v), which I consider is the most cogent derivational source of (i).

(v) a. swuyeng-un waikiki-uy swuyeng-i coh-ta.
'For swimming, Waikiki is good.'
b. ssal-un hank'wuksan-uy ssal-i coh-ta.
'As for rice, the Korean product is good.'
c. TV-nun Zenith-uy TV-ka thunthun-ha-ta.
'As for TV, Zenith is durable.'

5. As in many other aspects of Korean syntax, studies on theme have been divided into transformational approaches (e.g. S. Song 1967; Ree 1969; Oh 1971, 1972; C. Lee 1973a) and phrase-structure approaches (e.g. D. Yang 1973a; Mathias 1978; Bak 1977).
6. For various claims regarding the semantics of *ka/i* (J *ga*) and *(n)un* (J *wa*), see Kuno (1972a, 1973:37-95), Im (1972, 1974), Oh (1972), D. Yang (1973a:115-118), I. Yang (1973), Shin (1975), Mathias (1977, 1978), Bak (1977, 1978), etc.
7. The object is normally indicated by the particle *(l)ul* which is in complementary distribution with *ka/i,* but whether the nominal it occurs with is to be considered a theme or not is a moot question which requires further study.
8. An example in which *ka/i* does occur with a (locative) case marker is:

(i) cip-*ey*- {ka / nun} amu-to eps-ni?
'Isn't there anyone at home?'

in which *ka/i* is completely estranged from the notion of case just like *(n)un*. Another example where *ka/i* functions just like a limiter is:

(ii) ku-i-*man*- {i / un} ka-n-ta.
'Only he will go.'

in which both *ka/i* and *(n)un* occur after a limiter (*man*).

9. The diachronic relatedness between subject and theme in Indo-European is discussed in Lehmann (1976).
10. The conclusion that both NP-*ka/i* and NP-*(n)un* are relevant to theme will, it is hoped, provide an answer to the problem raised in L&T's (p. 488) statement: "We are aware that subject markers (*ga* and *ka*) sometimes occur with the topics in 'double subject' constructions in Japanese and Korean respectively. It appears that subject markers can appear with topics in certain discourse situations, but we do not at present understand this phenomenon well enough to be more precise."

Reprinted from *Korean Linguistics* (International Circle of Korean Linguistics) 2:1-19 (1980).

12. MULTIPLE TOPIC CONSTRUCTIONS IN KOREAN

How to characterize the so-called double or multiple subject constructions that are predominant in such SOV languages as Chinese, Japanese, and Korean is one of the most controversial and time-honored issues among linguists of such languages (for some recent studies on the subject, see Mikami 1960; Kuroda 1965; Householder and Cheng 1967; S. Kim 1970; I. Yang 1972; Im 1972 and 1974; B. Park 1973; Kuno 1973; Teng 1974; Shibatani 1977; Shibatani and Cotton 1976-77; Masuoka 1979; Haig 1979; Sohn 1980; and Bak 1981; among others.)[1]

Observe, for instance, the Korean sentences in (1).[2]

(1) a. John-KA nwun-KA khu-ta.
          NM eye NM big
   'John has big eyes.'
   b. John-NUN nwun-KA khu-ta.
          TP eye NM big
   'John has big eyes.'
   c. John-uy nwun-KA khu-ta.
          's eye NM big
   'John's eyes are big.'

As compared with single subject constructions like (1c), sentences like (1a) and (1b) are frequently called double subject constructions, and, in particular, those like (1b), where the 'thematic/contrastive' particle NUN appears, are called topic-comment constructions.

Many linguists of Korean tend to associate the particle NUN (equivalent more or less to Japanese *wa*) directly to the notion of topic, claiming that only the NUN occurring with the sentence-initial, unstressed, and definite or generic noun phrase marks topic in Korean (cf. Ree 1969, Kuno 1972a and 1973, D. Yang 1974, Mathias 1978). Taking it axiomatic that topic is what the speaker is talking about, Bak (1981:284) claims that the optimal topichood in Korean is realized, syntactically, in the 'higher NP' position, morphologically, in the particle NUN, and semantically, in definiteness.

In this paper I will propose that topic be redefined in terms of sentence structure in Korean and, like any other limiters (such as *to* 'also, even', *man* 'only') and the nominative particle KA (equivalent more or less to Japanese *ga*), NUN is an independent functional unit with its own basic lexical meaning (CONTRASTIVENESS) and its own syntactic and semantic constraints, and should be detached from the notion of topic. Thus, all the three sentences in (1) are viewed as topic-comment constructions in our sense of the term 'topic', the first two being double topic and the third a single topic.

Needless to say, a NUN-attached element which is definite or generic and unstressed tends to reveal a high degree of 'thematicity' in the sentence-initial position, especially when the predicate of the sentence denotes a more or less generic event. I regard the appearance of such thematicity as due to the weakening of the contrastiveness of NUN in that particular environment, where the unexpressed domain of the sentence is semantically boundless unless delimited by the speech situation, presuppositions, or stress placement. When the unexpressed domain is limited in this way, even the sentence-initial NUN-attached element manifests strong contrastiveness as in any other position. The prevalent notion that only the so-called thematic NUN marks topic in Korean seems to me to be misled by weakened or diluted contrastiveness, i.e., by the boundless contrastiveness that NUN denotes.

In the following I will argue that topic in Korean, an SOV language, may be defined unequivocally as an S-dominated NP in the constituent structure $S \rightarrow NP + \begin{Bmatrix} S \\ VP \end{Bmatrix}$.[3] The S or VP following an NP is the comment of that NP. Since S is recursive, Korean topic is assumed to exist hierarchically, hence the notion of multiple topic constructions. A topic NP may be a bare noun phrase or marked by a limiter, including the particles NUN and KA, as schematically illustrated roughly in (2) in the following page. This syntactic and sentential definition of topic in Korean is based on the following observations.

First, topic, as defined above, has strong semantic correlations in that it never fails to constitute or set a domain for something to be talked about. This domain-setting meaning satisfies such existing semantic definitions of

(2)

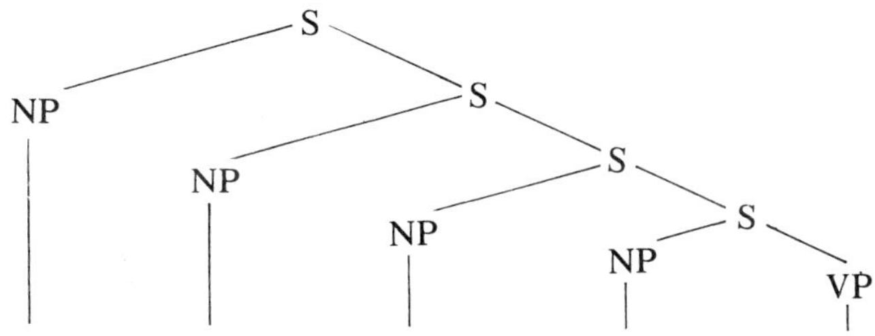

wuli cip-NUN chipung-man twu-kwuntey-KA kwumeng-KA na-ss-ta.
'Our house has holes in two places only on the roof.'

topic as the element of which something is asserted or what the speaker is talking about (e.g. Jespersen 1924:146; Halliday 1967:212; Hornby 1971: 1976; and Bak 1981). This semantic fact provides evidence that a higher NP and a lower NP do not form a syntactic constituent in multiple topic constructions, although semantically the two NP's may have the relationship of macro-micro (I. Yang 1972) or universe-scope (Householder and Cheng 1967).

Referring to the Chinese style of topics which is somewhat close to the Korean style, Chafe (1976:50-1, 55) defines topic as "a spatial, temporal, or personal frame or domain for an assertion which follows". Chafe thinks that the 'what the sentence is about' notion of topic applies better to subjects like 'eyes' in (1) in that what bigness is predicated of is not 'John' but 'eyes'. In the same vein, however, there is no question that 'John' in (1a) and (1b) is what the sentence 'eyes are big' is about. Chafe further considers such a temporal adverb as *Tuesday* in the English sentence *Tuesday I went to the dentist* somewhat equivalent to the Chinese topic. In a corresponding Korean sentence, *hwayoil-ey-NUN na-NUN chikwa-ey ka-ss-ta* (Tuesday-on-TP I-TP dentist-to went), 'Tuesday' is not regarded as a topic in our sense in that, despite the occurrence of NUN, the rest of the sentence does not assert of 'Tuesday' as its domain, nor does 'Tuesday' satisfy various syntactic characteristics of a topic in our sense. It is simply a temporal adverbial with various degrees of contrastiveness.[4] Although Chafe's semantic definition of topic is close to ours, it is a little too broad to capture significant linguistic generalization in Korean.

Similarly in (2), 'our house' is the primary domain which the rest of the sentence comments on; 'the roof' is a smaller domain within the comment, of which the following sentence is asserted; and so forth. The semantic relationship holding between *wuli cip* 'our house' and the rest on its right, that between *cipung* 'the roof' and the rest on its right; that between *twukwuntey* 'two places' and the rest on its right, and that between *kwumeng* 'holes' and the rest on its right are all exactly the same. Notice also the gradual narrowing down of the semantic scope of the successive domains as the NP's move to the right. All this, together with the other facts to be discussed, suggests the existence of the hierarchical topic structure of underlying sentences.

The meaning of 'domain-setting' is more vivid when we compare a more topical sentence with its less topical paraphrase, as illustrated in (3).

(3) a. John$_i$- {KA / NUN} nwun-KA khe-se [X]$_i$ kep-KA manh-ta.
eye big-so fear much
'John has big eyes, so he is timid.'
b. *John-uy nwun$_i$-KA khe-se [X]$_i$ kep-KA manh-ta.
's eye big-so fear much
*'John's eyes are big, so his eyes are timid.'

In (3a) the understood topic [X] is necessarily 'John', whereas it is not 'John' but 'John's eyes' in (3b), rendering the sentence semantically unacceptable. In other words, 'John' in (3a) has two conjoined sentences as its comment, but 'John' in (3b) is related only to 'eyes' and otherwise has no semantic bearing on the event denoted by the rest of the sentence. In short, the consistent meaning of domain-setting for an assertion is significant and must be recognized and captured linguistically as such. Such domains are identified as topics and such topics exist hierarchically.

Second, evidence shows that Korean multiple topic constructions as defined above exist in the constituent structure, i.e. are basic, and not derived from a single subject (which is also a topic in our sense) construction. Indeed, in a great many cases, multiple topic constructions are relatable to a corresponding single topic (or subject) structure, as observed in (1). Many generative grammarians of Korean (e.g. S. Song 1967; Ree 1969; Oh 1961; C. Lee 1973a) propose to derive sentences like (1a,b) from those like (1c) transformationally. Frequently such transformational processes are called 'topicalization' for NUN (e.g. (1b)) and 'subjectivization' for KA (e.g. (1a)). For a similar treatment in Japanese, see Kuno (1973:71).

As I discussed in detail in Sohn (1980), the transformational approach, although insightful, is encumbered with many difficult problems. One of the problems is how to handle the meaning differences, as noticed thus far. Differences exist not only in the basic meaning of 'domain-setting', but in various affective meanings, presuppositions, controls of co-referential deletion, and sometimes even underlying case frames. From the discoursal point of view, difference shows up also in informational contents such as old and new. All this would render any attempt to have recourse to surface interpretive rules very costly, if not impossible. Syntactically also, the transformational approach would not be able to easily handle limiter-attached NP's and many multiple topic sentences whose single topic (or subject) counterparts are not clearly identifiable, as illustrated in (4).

(4) a. John-*to* nwun-KA khu-ta.
also eye big
'John also has big eyes.'
b. John-man caki-KA an ka-ss-ta.
only self not went
'Only John didn't go in person.'
c. i chayk-KA caymi-KA eps-ta.
this book interest lack
'This book is not interesting.'
d. nalssi-KA pi -KA o-keyss-ta.
weather rain come-probably
'As for the weather, it will probably rain.'
e. kupun nolay-NUN sok -KA siwenha-ta.
his song heart refreshed
'His song makes me feel great.'
f. na-NUN John-KA pulep-ta.
I enviable
'I envy John.'
g. wul-ki-NUN way wu-ni?
crying why cry
'Of all things, why are you crying?'

Recently there has been some endeavor to derive all sentences from underlying abstract topic-comment structure which is informationally oriented. This approach is based on the definition of topic in terms of givenness (e.g. Vachek 1966:89-90; Chafe 1970:211-212; Gundel 1974:38; Gundel 1978:2; Bak 1977:63).[5] Ingenious as it may be, this approach seems to serve only a secondary purpose in Korean, as it stands now, revealing little apparent syntactic correlation. Although NUN more frequently indicates old information and KA tends to be associated with new information due to their basic lexical contents including presupposition and assertion, there are many instances in which that is not the case, as illustrated in (5).

(5) a. Speaker A: John-KA eti-KA aphu-ni?
where ache
'Where does John have trouble?'
Speaker B: John-KA meli-KA aph-a. (John = old)
head ache
'John has a headache.'
b. Speaker A: chentang-KA iss-ni?
heaven exist
'Does heaven exist?'
Speaker B: etten salam-NUN kulehkey mit-e.
some people so believe
(etten salam = new)
'Some people believe so.'

Chomsky's (1965:221) definition of topic as the leftmost major category NP which is dominated by S in the surface structure is somewhat similar to ours. For instance, Chomsky regards both the 'topicalized' NP (comparable to Korean NP-NUN) and the clefted NP (comparable to Korean NP-KA) as topics of the respective sentences. The main difference is that he views topic as a surface phenomenon. If we apply this more or less English-based definition to Korean, we would be compelled to equate topic to all and only the initial nouns in (6) which do not share any significant commonality, syntactic or semantic, except for their appearance in the surface sentence-initial position.

(6) a. John-NUN Mary-eykey latio -lul cwu-ess-ta.
to radio AC gave
b. Mary-eykey John-NUN latio-lul cwu-ess-ta.
c. latio-lul John-NUN Mary-eykey cwu-ess-ta.
'John gave a radio to Mary.'

According to our definition, only 'John' is the topic in all the sentences. Preposing or scrambling of cases for focus or stylistic purposes or various ellipses do not affect topicness in our sense. This point is demonstrated efficiently in Bak (1981).

Third, the proposed definition of topic seems to be supported in view of human mental or cognitive processes. Let us assume that the structure of natural language reflects human cognition or mentality. It seems to be universal that in order to attain maximally effective and smooth communication, human beings tend to place a topic in the general sense in the sentence-initial position, other things being equal, and add the predication after it (cf. Chomsky 1965; D. Yang 1974; Li and Thompson 1976; Magretta 1977; Givon 1978; Bak 1981, etc.). This way the hearer is provided with a frame of reference against which to perceive the whole sentence or discourse with a minimum of effort. In almost all languages, therefore, a topic is placed on the left of a sentence (cf. Newmeyer 1980:233). An analysis of topic/comment based solely on old/new information or on the particle NUN is unable to capture this universal fact.

It is also easy to assume that human cognition and mentality make extensive use of the notion of hierarchical relationships in all areas of human life, including communication. Observe various man-made social hierarchical systems such as government agencies, schools, and companies! Hierarchical notion applies not only to human mentality but to the nature of the universe of which human mentality is a part. Observe the anatomical structure of organisms and the composition of the solar system! Needless to say, this hierarchical notion is built into all the aspects of natural language. One salient difference between SVO and SOV languages seems to be that the former allow only the primary topic to be syntacticized as the subject because there is only one major nominal slot before the verb, whereas the latter SOV languages allow all the hierarchical topics to be 'packaged' in a sentence because there are multiple nominal slots before the verb, as in *na-NUN ku umsik-KA mas-KA cho-ta* (I, the food, taste is good) 'I like the taste of the food'. The constituent structure rule proposed earlier, i.e. $S \rightarrow NP + \left\{ \begin{matrix} S \\ VP \end{matrix} \right\}$ accommodates the hierarchical multiplicity of topics most naturally. In SVO languages like English, the S on the left side of the rule is simply lacking. We may call Korean a topic-prominent language and English a subject-prominent language not because of the occurrence of the particle NUN in Korean which basically denotes CONTRASTIVENESS but because of the prevalence of the hierarchical multiplicity of topical NP's in Korean, but not in English. The reason is that, as Kuno (1972a:269) illustrates, English sentences also carry, although not coded on the surface, the thematicity and contrastiveness that Japanese *wa* (and Korean NUN) denotes. For example, the English sentence *John kissed Mary* may be interpreted as thematic, contrastive, exhaustive, and neutral in Kuno's sense. On the other hand, there is no evidence that hierarchical multiplicity of topics is conceptualized as such by English speakers. To them, only the primary (and, at most, secondary) topic appears to be conceptually essential in a given simple sentence. The real significant difference between Korean and English is, therefore, the presence in the former and absence in the latter of the hierarchical multiple recursiveness of topic-comment in both basic syntactic structure and cognitive processes.

Fourth, the proposed definition of topic well characterizes the typology of 'topic-comment languages'. Li and Thompson (1976) distinguish four basic language types (i.e. subject prominent, topic prominent, subject/topic prominent, and non-subject/non-topic prominent). They present Korean and Japanese as the examples of the languages that are both subject-prominent and topic-prominent, stating that there are two distinct sentence types of equal importance in these languages, i.e. the NP-NUN type ('topic-prominent') and the NP-KA type ('subject-prominent'). In Sohn (1980), however, I argued that Korean (and Japanese for that matter) must be a topic-prominent language in that topic, not subject, in their sense, plays the major role in Korean syntax, just as in Chinese which they view as a typical topic-prominent language. Korean meets all the distinguishing characteristics Li and Thompson advance for typical topic-prominent languages, such as unproductive passivization, lack of 'dummy' subjects, productive topic-oriented 'double subject' constructions, topic's controllability of co-referentiality, verb-final nature, relative freedom on what may be the topic, and the basicness of topic-comment structures. In particular, Li and Thompson (p. 468) point out that 'double subject' constructions are the clearest instances of topic constructions, in that the topic and the subject can both occur and be distinguished easily. They further state (p. 488): "we are aware that subject markers (*ga* and *ka*) sometimes occur with the topics in 'double subject' constructions in Japanese and Korean respectively. It appears that subject markers can appear with topics in certain discourse situations, but we do not at present understand this phenomenon well enough to be more precise." The structural definition of topic, the notion of multiple topic constructions, and the denial of NUN as the topic marker, as proposed in this paper, will clear out the above dilemma Li and Thompson are in.

Fifth, the structural definition of topic as an S-dominated NP captures the generality that there are a number of shared behaviors among all the limiters including the particles NUN and KA. Obviously, these particles constitute a syntactic and semantic natural class. Topic viewed only as a

NUN-attached element with the so-called thematic sense belittles such an important generality. Observe the sentences in (7).

(7) a. Korea- { NUN / *to* / *man* / KA } kaul- { NUN / *to* / *man* / KA } coh-ta.
autumn good

'...Korea, ... autumn is good.' (*to* 'also', *man* 'only')

b. Korea-uy kaul- { NUN / *to* / *man* / KA } coh-ta.
's autumn good

'... Korean autumn is good.'

Notice that the different particles appear in the first and second NP's in (7a) and the second NP in (7b). Semantically, all these particles function as limiters or restrictives, having their own lexical meanings, including presuppositions and assertions, and semantic and syntactic constraints (cf. I. Yang 1973).[6] Notice also that the three NP's in question in (7) function as domains of which the rest of the sentence on their right makes assertion. This topical meaning is persistent regardless of the particles used. As a result, the assertion in (7a) is that autumn is good in comparison with the other seasons *in Korea* (which is the primary domain of this sentence). On the other hand, in (7b) the comparison is between the *Korean autumn* (which is the only domain in the sentence) and that of other countries, again regardless of the particles used. All this means that topic in our sense is one thing and limiters another; there is no inherent correlation between them. Furthermore, all limiters may occur with indefinite nouns, which fact implies that the so-called thematic sense the particle NUN reveals in sentence-initial position when the NP is definite or generic is not the inherent feature of NUN, but is derived from its inherent contrastiveness meaning in that particular syntactic environment. What sense can we get if some definite or generic entity is contrasted with the domainless universe? The traditional notion of 'topic' is precisely what we get. Thus, we suspect that the traditional definition of Korean topic has captured a derived sense of the contrastiveness that NUN inherently has, while our definition captures a more fundamental nature of language.

Finally, as regards the term 'topic'. The term topic, rather than say 'subject', appears more appropriate for the S-dominated NP. There is generally no selectional relationship between a higher NP and the main verb. For instance, in sentence (8a) it is a fire which broke out, not John nor his house.

(8) a. John-{NUN / Ka} cip -KA pul-KA na-ss-ta.
house fire broke out
'As for John, his house caught a fire.'

b. John-uy cip -ey pul -KA na-ss-ta.
's house at fire broke out
'A fire broke out at John's house.'

Thus, all such higher NP's are stranded or orphaned, so to speak, from the clause-mate case frame of the verb, which is rarely the case with such SVO languages as English, where the subject is always selectionally related to the verb. The only significant function of these stranded NP's is as topic in our sense of the word. The fact that such NP's are syntactically higher (and semantically wider in domain) than the subject of the verb and that such NP's (including the subject) are mutually hierarchical is easily observable in (9a), where, unlike (9b), scrambling is not allowed, revealing that the NP's are not clause-mates.

(9) a. *cip-KA John-{NUN / KA} pul-KA na-ss-ta.
*John-{NUN / KA} pul-KA cip-KA na-ss-ta.
*pul-KA John-{NUN / KA} cip-KA na-ss-ta.

b. pul-KA John-uy cip-ey na-ss-ta.

Furthermore, unlike *pul* 'fire', *John* in (8a) is comparable to the genitive in (8b) and *cip* in (8a) to the locative in (8b), hence the inadequacy of the term 'subject' for *John* and *cip*. Also, certain higher NP's cannot be followed by the nominative particle KA at all, although this particle is frequently equated with the notion of subject in Korean. Observe the sentences in (10), for example.

(10) a. John-{NUN / *to* / *man* / *KA} Mary-KA po-ass-ta.
saw
'... John, Mary saw him.'

b. Korea- { NUN / *to* / *man* / *KA } John-KA ka-ss-ta.
went

'... Korea, John went there.'

KA has the dual function of limiter and case marker. Because of this latter function, it is constrained in such a way that it cannot occur when a topic is coreferential to the object, as in (10a), or goal, as in (10b), of the main verb. Instead, the accusative particle LUL may occur in this position.[7] This fact provides additional evidence that it is more appropriate to employ the term 'topic' than '(sentential) subject' (cf. B. Park 1973) even if we allow Chafe's (1976:43-44) notion of 'subject' as the 'adding-knowledge-about' and the ancient notion of subject as 'what we are talking about'.

The reanalysis proposed in this paper is assumed to capture some significant generalizations pertaining to the structure of Korean, and for that matter, all the topic-comment languages in general.

Notes

1. This is a revised version of the paper prepared for the 55th Annual Meeting of the Linguistic Society of America held in San Antonio, Texas, December 28-30, 1980.
2. The Yale romanization system is followed in this paper. The abbreviations used are: NM = nominative particle; TP = thematic/contrastive particle;; AC = accusative particle; KA = *ka* after a vowel and *i* after a consonant: NUN = *nun* after a vowel and *un* after a consonant.
3. This idea was briefly touched upon in Sohn (1980:5)
4. Similarly, observe the following sentences:

   i. ecey-NUN nalssi-KA coh-ass-ta.
   yesterday weather good
   'Yesterday's weather was good.'

   ii. ecey-NUN apeci-KA o-si-ess-ta.
   father came
   'Father came yesterday.'

   As a domain for the following comment, *ecey-NUN* in (i) is viewed here as a higher topic NP denoting contrastiveness. However, *ecey-NUN* in (ii) may not be viewed as the domain for the following predication. Rather, it is a time adverbial with the meaning of contrastiveness. *Nalssi* is a lower topic (and the subject) in (i) whereas *apeci* is the only topic (and the subject) in (ii).

5. Bak (1981) has abandoned this informationlly based approach.
6. For example, notice the similar behavior that all the limiters follow in not generally appearing in the subject position of an embedded sentence.

   na- {*NUN / **to* / **man* / *KA (1) / KA (2)} po-n salam-NUN Kim sensayng i-ess-ta.
   I saw person Mr. was

   Here, KA (1) is a limiter with exclusive meaning, while KA (2) is viewed as a case marker with neutral meaning. All these limiters presuppose sister members, among other things.
7. However, LUL-attached NP's are not topics in our sense but preposed elements in that they do not constitute a domain. On the other hand, KA-attached elements, when they are allowed to occur in multiple topic constructions, may refer to the possessor of the following topic or the locative of the main verb, as well as its subject, just as any other limiter-attached elements.

Reprinted from *Hangeul* (Korean Languge Society) 173/174:669-686 (1981).

13. SEMANTICS OF COMPOUND VERBS IN KOREAN

1. Korean has a strong tendency to slice actions minutely for lexicalization.[1] This tendency is tied with the abundance of compound verb constructions in Korean. English, in contrast, rarely uses more than one verb to express a group of simultaneously occurring, coextensive actions. Accordingly, English has not developed a syntactic mechanism of verbal compounding, as illustrated in (1).

(1)		Korean	English
	a.	*chi-e-tul-e-ka*-ta	invade
		chac-a-*ka*-ta	visit
		hunukki-e-*wul*-ta	sob
		ttu-e-*na*-*Ø*-*ka*-ta	leave
	b.	*nem*-e-*ka*-ta	go over
		talli-e-*na*-*Ø*-*ka*-ta	run out
		mek-e-*peli*-ta	eat up
		ca-*Ø*-*cwu*-ta	sleep for (me)

In (la) each Korean compound consists of two or more action verbs, whereas the corresponding English expression is composed of a single morpheme. Thus, for instance, *chyetulekata* 'to invade' is formed from *chi* 'hit', *tul* 'enter', and *ka* 'go'. There is no single Korean morpheme into which the three actions are incorporated. In (1b), while action verbs are compounded in Korean for each expression, English uses an action verb followed by a verbal particle or preposition. An English example which comes close to Korean compounds in meaning is *Try come*! in the child language, used in the Korean sense, *ili o-a-po-a*! It may be speculated that the compounding tendency of Korean has been caused either by the Chinese borrowings that have predominantly been waved into Korean or by the agglutinative nature of the original Altaic languages.

2. For the present discussion, a compound verb is defined as a sequence of two or more verbs between which only the so-called infinitive suffix (*-e*, *-a*, or -Ø) occurs without any pause intervening. Thus, for instance, a sequence of verbs which are intervened by some other element but an infinitive suffix or an infinitive suffix followed by a pause (#) is not regarded as a compound. None of the sentences in (2), therefore, contains a compound verb.

(2) ilcik il-e-na-Ø- {*se* / #} seyswuhay-Ø-ss-ta.
and (then)
'I got up early and (then) washed my face.'

Nol-*ta(ka)* ca-Ø-ss-ta.
while, after
'I went to sleep after playing.'

ku ton-ul kac-*ko* ka-Ø-ss-ta.
and, with
'He went with the money.'

kho-lul kol-*myense* ca-Ø-ss-ta.
while
'He snored while sleeping.'

cwuk-*ki* silh-ta.
to, -ing
'I don't want to die.'

The aim of this paper is to reveal certain basic semantic properties that compound verbs are regarded to be carrying and some syntactic manifestations through which such semantic properties are reflected. For simplicity, discussions will be limited to those compounds which are composed only of action verbs.

3. There are many instances in the real world in which a group of actions are perceived or conceptualized as occurring coextensively as if they were one action. For instance, sentence (3a), which does not contain a compound, shows that the speaker perceives the two actions, *ki* 'crawl' and *ka* 'go', separately. The unnaturalness of the sentence is due to the fact that the only possible manner by which a crab moves is by 'crawling' and that the redundant manner action is expressed separately from the action of 'going'. On the other hand, sentence (3b) is a natural expression, in that the

two actions in the compound are conceptualized as one coextensive, indivisible action.

(3) a. key-ka ki-e- $\left\{\begin{matrix} \text{se} \\ \# \end{matrix}\right\}$ ka-n-ta!

'A crab goes by crawling!'

b. key-ka ki-e-ka-n-ta!

'A crab is crawling away!'

Schematically, (3a) and (3b) are represented as (4a) and (4b), respectively.

(4) a.

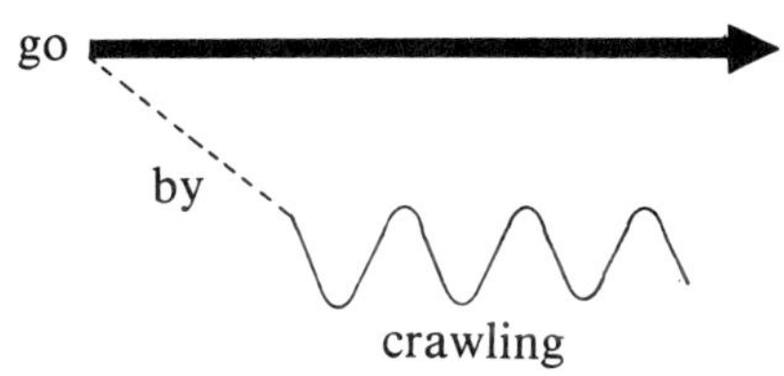

b.

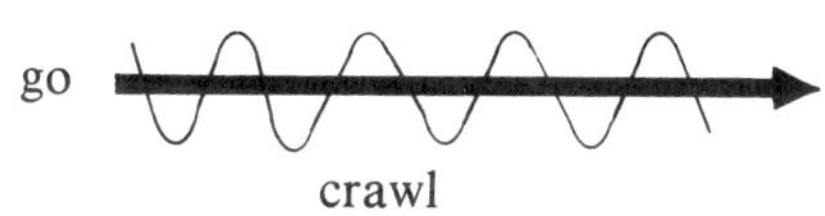

As shown above, the most important function oı compound verbs is to represent the conceptualization of a group of actions as a coextensive whole. Historically, sentence (3b), where a compound occurs, may have been derived from (3a), but synchronically it no longer carries the same semantic content that (3a) does. Similarly, observe sentence (5) where four actions (italic) form a coextensive whole.

(5) com-i os-ul *pha*-Ø-*mek*-e-*tul*-e-*ka*-Ø-ss-ta.
dig eat enter go
'The moths ate into the clothes.'

Since a group of actions are conceptualized as a mutually coextensive whole, compound verbs are frequently idiomatized semantically and (almost) fossilized syntactically. Sentence (6a) is an example where such idiomatization takes place, whereas two actions are separately conceptualized in (6b). Notice the different scopes of negation in the two sentences: in (6a) the scope is *mul-e-ka* whereas in (6b) it is only *mul*.

(6) a. kay-ka koki-lul (an) *mul*-e-*ka*-Ø-ss-ta.
not bite go

'The dog stole (did not steal) the meat.'

b. kay-ka koki-lul (an) *mul*-ko-*ka*-Ø-ss-ta.
'The dog went away with (without) the meat (in its mouth).'

Actions which in their basic meanings, cannot be coextensive, may still be expressed by compound verbs. In this case, the original meaning of non-initial verbs in the compounds are shifted to secondary, more psychological ones, so that again the actions can be conceptualized as coextensively as possible. Observe the sentences in (7) and notice the semantic shifts effected in *peli* 'throw away', *po* 'see', *noh* 'put down', *twu* 'keep', *iss* 'exist', and *cwu* 'give', as they are used as so-called auxiliary verbs. (cf. Sohn 1973a)

(7) ku sakwa-lul *mek-e-peli*-e-ss-ta.
eat finish
'I ate the apple up.'
Iran-ey *ka-Ø-po*-a-ss-ta.
go try/experience
'I have been to Iran.'
ku il-ul *hay-Ø-noh*-a-*twu*-e!
do in advance for later use
'Do the work in advance for later use!'
il-mail-ul *ka-Ø-iss*-ta.
go be in the state of
'He has gone one mile.'
cha-lul *kochi*-e-*cwu*-e-ss-ta.
fix for
'I fixed the car for him.'

4. Our next inquiry is whether the action verbs that enter into compounds can be subclassifiable. Tentative as it may be, four significant subclasses are distinguishable. Using semantic terms, let us call them: activity, direction, motion, and psychological verbs.[2] These four subclasses occur in that order in syntagmatic relations, forming their respective surface slots, as illustrated in (8).

(8)

1. activity	2. direction	3. motion	4. psychological	
talli-e	na-Ø	ka-Ø	po-ta	'to try run
'run'	'appear'	'go'	'try'	out'
il-e	na-ta			'to get up'

'get'	'appear'			
tt-e 'float'	oll-a 'rise'	o-a 'come'	cwu-ta 'for'	'to float up hither for me'
hull-e 'flow'	nali-e 'get down'	ka-ta 'go'		'to flow down'
ttwi-e 'jump, run'	tul-e 'enter'	se-ta 'stand'		'to jump in'
kkul-e 'pull'	an-ta 'carry in arms'			'to hug'

As observed in (8), each subclass of verbs is optional in occurrence, but whenever a psychological verb appears there must be at least one other verb before it. Thus, all psychological verbs are obligatory 'complement' verbs. Notice also that the order among the four slots cannot be changed. Our question is naturally on what principles the order has been or is fixed. In the first place, the semantic scope of verbs is a major factor in the order arrangement. When a verb has the contents of other verbs as its scope, it should be placed after them. This is universal to verb-final languages, just as the order is reversed in SVO languages as in English. Psychological verbs dominate other verbs in terms of scope, and therefore they take the last slot, as we see in the compound, *talli-e-na-Ø-ka-Ø-po-ta* 'to try run out'. The positional alternation between the two psychological verbs, *po* and *peli*, in the sentences in (9) can also be accounted for in terms of their scope.

(9) ku sakwa-lul *mek*-e-*po*-a-*peli*-keyss-ta.
'I will finish up trying to eat the apple.'
ku sakwa-lul *mek*-e-*peli*-e-*po*-keyss-ta.
'I will try eating the apple up.'

If two or more actions cannot be related in terms of their semantic scope, our next recourse is to the principle of 'first action, first', which means that a verb whose denoted action starts prior to the action of another verb must be placed first, however slight the time difference may be.

(10) a. *nay-Ø-mil*-ta[3] 'to push it out' (putting-out starts first)
put-out-push
a'. *mil*-e-*nay*-ta 'to push it out' (pushing starts first)
b. *pha-Ø-mek*-ta 'to bore' (digging starts first)

dig eat

b′. **mek*-e-*pha*-ta

The impossibility of (10b′) is obvious, because 'eating' cannot start before 'digging' in the real world.

When the actions are completely simultaneous, the order of activity-direction-motion should be followed. For instance, *talli-e-na-Ø-ka-ta* 'to run out (run-out-go)' does not denote that running starts first, then appearing, and then going. The actions are totally simultaneous, yet no other order than the above is allowed. This order has certainly been fixed arbitrarily in Korean.[4] The language-specificity of the order can be clearly observed when we compare Korean with English.[5]

(11) putative universal semantic units:
(1) RUN
(2) TOWARD OUTSIDE
(3) (out-going) ACTION
(4) MOVE
(5) AWAY FROM FOCUS

$$\text{Korean: } (1) - \left\{ \begin{matrix} (2) \\ (3) \end{matrix} \right\} - \left\{ \begin{matrix} (4) \\ (5) \end{matrix} \right\}$$

talli na ka

$$\text{English: } \left\{ \begin{matrix} (1) \\ (4) \end{matrix} \right\} - (2)$$

run out

The fact that *go out* is permuted to *out going* without change in meaning in English is another piece of evidence that the order is quite language-specific. One might think that the relative importance among the actions of the three slots has something to do with the order. This, however, may not work, because for instance, *ka* 'go' seems to be the most important in *talli-e-na-Ø-ka-ta* 'to run out' while *nok* 'melt' seems to be more important than *ka* in *nok-a-tul-e-ka-ta* 'to melt into'.

As we have seen, the activity slot may be filled with more than one verb. If there is no discernible real word order between the actions involved, relative importance of the actions comes into the picture. That is, a more important verb comes after a less important one: the former expresses the major action, whereas the latter denotes more or less a manner-type of action in relation to the former. Remember, however, that the actions are still conceptualized as a coextensive whole, as already mentioned. Examples include *twull-e-po-ta* 'to look around', *kalki-e-ssu-ta* 'to scribble', and *kenn-e-ttwi-ta* 'to jump over'. The importance may be tested out as in (12) among others.

(12) { A: ne po-a-ss-ni? | B: ney, twull-e-po-a-ss-e-yo. } 'Did you look?' 'Yes, I looked around.'

* { A: ne twull-e-ss-ni? | B: ney, twull-e-po-a-ss-e-yo. } 'Did you put around?' 'Yes, I looked around.'

5. Let us now briefly look at cooccurrence restrictions that exist among verbs entering into compounds. Detailed selectional restrictions in Japanese auxiliary constructions are tabulated in Makiuchi (1972:196-203 and elsewhere). In the following, we will observe something more fundamental which is assumed to govern cooccurrence restrictions. Observe the expressions in (13).

(13) a. **mek*-e-*na*-ta
eat appear
**kkul*-e-*tul*-ta
pull enter
**ccochki*-e-*nay*-ta
be-chased put-out

b. *mek*-e-*nay*-ta 'to finish up eating'
finish-up
kkul-e-*tuli*-ta 'to pull in'
take-in
ccochki-e-*na*-ta 'to be driven out'

At a glance, the ungrammaticality of the expressions in (13a) seems to be ascribable to the syntactic rule of transitive + transitive and intransitive + intransitive cooccurrences, as evidenced in (13b). If, however, we expand our data as in (14), we will see that the syntactic rule does not necessarily work.

(14) *muccill*-e-*na*-*Øka*-ta 'to crush (the enemy) forward'
crush
Vt Vi Vi
pil-e-*mek*-ta 'to beg for food'
pray eat
Vi Vt

kenn-e-*ttwi*-ta 'to jump over'
cross jump
Vt Vi

It seems to me that a more fundamental principle governing syntactic cooccurrences is a semantic one. That is, only those verbs whose semantic contents can be conceptualized as coextensive are cooccurable. A compound verb is ungrammatical, if this principle is violated, as we saw in (13a). Certain verbs, like psychological ones, have historically undergone semantic shifts to satisfy the above principle and cooccur with other action verbs.

6. One important topic which has not been touched on in this paper, is the possible underlying structure of Korean compound verbs. Partial efforts on various grounds are made in this connection in I. Yang (1972:chapter 3) and Sohn (1973a), among others. Whether one is oriented by generative or interpretive semantics or any other linguistic sophistication, it seems to be imperative to take the above discussions into account in any future postulation of the structures underlying compound verbs.

Notes

1. This paper was presented to the First Winter Workshop of the Linguistic Society of Korea held in Seoul on January 6, 1976. Valuable comments were made by In-Seok Yang, Maeng-Sung Lee, Chung-min Lee, Yong-kun Ko, and others. I do not claim that the analysis presented here is anything close to being definite, in that it was made on the basis of limited observations. Rather, I hope that this paper will encourage further study on the subject.
   The Yale romanization is followed in transcribing Korean expressions.
2. The term 'psychological' is highly tentative. It simply implies that the verbs belonging to this class are all derived from other more objective and concrete verbs by semantically psychologizing or subjectivizing them. Observe the following examples, where the first verb in each compound carries the original, objective meaning and the second one indicates the psychological meaning:

   peli-e-*peli*-e-ss-ta 'I threw it away.'
   throw away-finish

   cal *po*-a-*po*-a! 'Try looking at it closely.'
   see try

   yeki *twu*-e-*twu*-e! 'Put it over here for later use!'
   put for later use

As an alternative, one might want to call them 'modal' verbs in that they are partly related to the speaker or hearer's subjective views, feelings, judgements, or attitudes. For instance, the sentences below carry some sort of the speaker's feeling or presupposition which is associated with the verb *pelita*:

yeyppu-n kkoch-i cwuk-e-*peli*-e-ss-ta.

'(I am sorry that) the pretty flower died.'

yalmiwu-n koyangi-ka cwuk-e-*peli*-e-ss-ta.

'(I am glad that) the hateful cat died.'

3. When the direction verb *na* 'appear' is causativized as *nay* 'put out', it also has the activity meaning and, syntactically, can take both activity and direction slots.
4. A brief survey of Japanese with David Ashworth reveals that Japanese also follows the same order.
5. An interesting semantic and syntactic observation of motion is made in Talmy (1975) with particular reference to English, Atsugewi, and Russian. Since this work was made available to me only after the present paper was completed, Talmy's discussions are not incorporated here.

Reprinted from *Linguistic Journal of Korea* (Linguistic Society of Korea) 1.1:142-150 (1976).

14. CASE INCORPORATION IN ENGLISH VERBS WITH REFERENCE TO KOREAN STRUCTURE

1. The term *incorporation* refers to the process by which a noun is moved into or swallowed up by a verb within a sentence.[1] This process is frequently regarded as existing in such polysynthetic languages as Eskimo or some American-Indian languages. For instance, Chafe (1973:280) discusses the process of incorporation by analyzing the Onondaga sentence that corresponds to *We made a snowsnake for Bill*, where the noun root 'snowsnake' is incorporated into the verb root 'make'.

On the other hand, Chafe (1973:141-2) states that in the English sentences in (1), the noun roots *water* and *skin* are converted into the derived verb roots *water* and *skin* through the addition of particular verbalizer in each case, which has a meaning similar to *apply to* in (la) and *remove from* in (lb).

(1) a. Roger watered the lawn.
    b. Roger skinned the lion.

Chafe thus considers the sentences in (1) a case of derivation rather than incorporation. In this paper, however, the lexical verb *water* will be viewed as incorporating the noun *water* along with the abstract verb GIVE, and the lexical verb *skin* as incorporating the noun *skin* along with the abstract verb REMOVE in the semantic structures of the sentences in (1). Each abstract verb is understood to contain all the meanings except the meaning of the incorporated noun that the surface lexical verb has. For example, GIVE in (1a) has such meanings as *supply with, give to, put on by sprinkling, pouring, hosing,* or *irrigating*, etc. The very existence of an abstract verb triggers an incorporation transformation which will cause a lexical verb to be realized on the surface.

In (1a) the incorporated noun *water* is in the Object case and the noun *lawn* in the Goal case in relation to the abstract verb GIVE. In (1b) the incorporated noun *skin* is in the Object case while the noun *lion* is in the Source case in relation to the abstract verb REMOVE. These remarks thus introduce the notion of (deep) case incorporation in English verbs.

2. The aim of this paper is to observe the pattern of case incorporation in English verbs with particular reference to Korean, which rarely allows such incorporation. In the course of the observation to be made it will be seen that a large number of existing postulations of syntagmatic case relationships in English are based either on surface structures, or on English or Indo-European-influenced configurations of meanings drawn from the whole of conceptual space. Such postulations need to be modified once it becomes obvious that verbs originally thought to be bare predicates are in fact composites of a predicate and one or more arguments or deep cases. It will be further observed that many Korean sentences present complex case relationships on the surface, including multiple subject or object constructions, while corresponding English sentences do not. And such constructions will prove to be largely ascribable to the fact that Korean is resistant to case incorporation.

3. Several commonly-held assumptions of case grammarians relevant to the present discussion will be adopted from the outset. A simple sentence of a language is said to consist, in its underlying structure, of a *Mode* which contains those elements which modify or are related to the sentence as a whole and a *Proposition* which contains a predicate (verb, adjective, etc.) and one or more arguments or noun phrases that are in particular case (or semantic role) relationships to the predicate. These deep cases usually include the Agent, the Experiencer, the Instrument, the Object, the Source, the Goal, the Location, and the Time (cf., Fillmore 1971:42). Case grammarians, however, do not agree on the number and the kind of cases (e.g., sixteen cases in Shroyer 1969, ten cases in Langendoen 1970, and fifteen cases in Nilsen 1973), or on the criteria (i.e., syntactic or semantic) for identifying cases (see Nilsen 1972, 1973 for a full discussion). Nor do they agree as to whether predicates (e.g., Chafe 1973), cases of nouns (e.g., Fillmore 1968, 1971), or semantic or deep-case features (e.g., Lambert 1969, McCoy 1969 and Nilsen 1972, 1973) should be given primacy in determining the nature of predicate-case relationships. For the sake of convenience, Fillmore (1971) will be followed in this paper, while recognizing the importance of the reasons underlying the arguments of the other grammarians cited.

Another important assumption is that such predicate-case propositions are the primitives in language-independent universal grammar from which the surface structures of sentences in individual languages can be derived through various language-specific transformations and syntactic constraints, together with all types of morphological and lexical information. In other words, it is assumed that the same semantic units and structures underlie all human languages. Thus, deep structures are often very different from their corresponding surface structures even in a single language. Naturally, the differences in syntax among unrelated languages are great indeed.

Yet another assumption is that sentences may be embedded under the domination of certain cases. Such embedded sentences may be attached to complementizers, may be nominalized, or may have their predicates raised (Fillmore 1971:38). Furthermore, Fillmore (1971:49) allows his model to introduce decomposition and conflation processes. For instance, he suggests that the verb *kill* in *John killed the rat* is derived from the conflated-clause construct *by doing cause to die.*

A final relevant assumption of case grammar is that the cases exist in a certain hierarchy which is related to subject and object selection, among others. Such a hierarchy is widely discussed in the literature (e.g., Fillmore 1968:33, 1971:37, 42; Shroyer 1969:115; Langendoen 1970:70; Gruber 1970:139; I. Yang 1972:7-8; Nilsen 1973:135-42). For instance, Fillmore (1971:42) orders the subject selection hierarchy as Agent, Experiencer, Instrument, Object, Source, Goal, Location, and Time. Nilsen, however, suggests a significant relationship between subject marking and direct-object marking, stating that a case of high activity quotient, as determined by its semantic (or case) features, has high priority as a subject but low priority as a direct object. Thus, to Nilsen, the direct object-marking hierarchy is exactly the reverse of the subject-marking hierarchy whose order is Agent, Force, Body Part, Instrument, Experiencer, Locative, Goal, Objective, and Material.

4. Universal semantic units which compose a predicate and the associated cases may be ferreted out through observing the various syntactic units of a language, the structuring of such units and various transformational possibilities of such structures, together with intuitive judgments. This may be comparable to internal reconstruction in historical linguistics. Analyzing the verb *water*, into GIVE and the noun *water*, or the verb *skin*, into REMOVE and the noun *skin*, is an example of this sort. On the other hand, more reliable semantic units and their structures may be obtained through the comparison of two or more languages, while concurrently using

the intuitive judgments of the speakers of the languages. If the languages compared are remote both genetically and typologically, so much the better, since the same semantic units and structures are assumed to underlie all human languages. This approach has parallels in historical comparative linguistics. By means of synchronic comparison, the relationships among two or more languages may support or refute hypotheses concerning semantic structures constructed on the basis of a single language. For instance, the Korean sentences in (2) are the most natural translations of (1).

(2) a. Roger-ka ku canti-ey mul-ul cu -ess -ta.[2]
SM the lawn-to water-OM give-PAST-SE
b. Roger-ka ku saca-uy kacwuk-ul peski-ess-ta.
lion-of skin-OM remore-PAST-SE

As has already been indicated, Korean rarely makes use of incorporation. There is no way to combine *water* and *give* into a verb. Even if we delete the object marker *-ul*, which is allowable, the case relation between the noun and the verb remains unchanged; this fact is supported not only by introspection but by such syntactic tests as passivization, adverb insertion beween the noun and verb, free scrambling (e.g., *mul-ul* can be placed before *Roger-ka* or before *canti-ey* in (2a)), etc. The sentences in (2) which are (nearly) synonymous with those in (1) bolster the analysis of the verbs in (1) as a case of incorporation. There is, of course, a problem of synonymity judgment between the sentences of different languages. However, the synonymity problem is a common one and not unique here; efforts to set up universal semantic structures already presuppose the same kind of synonymity problem. Recourse to introspective judgments and syntactic behaviors seems unavoidable in deciding synonymity among the sentences of different languages.

5. Lambert (1969:59) and Nilsen (1973:14, 155) state that case incorporation appears to occur regularly only with the Instrument case. Nilsen (1973:157) seems to ascribe this fact partly to the uniqueness of the Instrument case, that "it is both the controller of the action of the predicate, and at the same time is controlled by another deep case", say, the Agent. As will be seen shortly, it is the claim of this paper that case incorporation occurs extensively with most other cases in English as well. But first Nilsen's (1973:155-73) extensive discussion of Instrumental incorporation into English verbs will be reviewed briefly.

Nilsen (hereafter N) subclassifies the Instrument into the Material,

Natural Force, Body-Part, and Tool cases. He mentions that Material incorporation is limited to verbs that indicate a change in the appearance, taste, texture, etc. (e.g., *dye, pepper, salt, season*), verbs of filling (e.g., *brick*, cane, stuff), 'enclose' verbs (e.g., *board, glass, screen*), and 'cover' verbs (e.g., *asphalt, butter, cement, grass, gravel, oil, paint, sprinkle, paper, water, wax*). Thus, for example, N thinks that the sentences on the right are 'changed' into those of the left in (3).

(3) a. John seasoned the soup. ← John changed the soup with seasoning.
  b. John stuffed the turkey. ← John filled the turkey with stuffing.
  c. John glassed in the sundeck. ← John enclosed the sundeck with glass.

Notice in (3) that the source sentences contain such Material nouns as *seasoning, stuffing*, and *glass*, which are incorporated in the verbs of the derived sentences.

Natual Force incorporation is observable, according to N, in such change of state verbs as *cremate, dam, dampen, turn off, bake, cook, stew. Dam* incorporates the Natural Force, *river, dampen* incorporates *water, turn off* incorporates *electricity*, and the rest incorporate the Natural Force, *heat.* Body-Part incorporation is quite extensive. N states that the verbs *staggered* and *warned* in (4) incorporate the Body-Parts, *legs* and *vocal tract*, respectively.

(4) a. John staggered from the bar past the policeman onto the wharf.
  b. John warned Harry to keep out of the quicksand.

Such verbs as *cry, laugh, nod, observe, blink, scan, read, look at, wink, kiss, sip, whistle, frown, smile, hear, smell, stink, breathe, spit, chatter, pray, speak, taste, lick, eat, chew, bite, gargle, swallow, cough, shrug, slap, jab, punch, grasp, hug, straddle, stand, thumb, step, jump, walk, run, accept, throw* are all found in N's list of examples of transparent or opaque Body-Part incorporation.

N discusses the verbal incorporation of Tool-Instrument in connection with the following semantic classes of verbs: (1) verbs of sound, such as *bang, click, jingle, pop, roar, thud, whistle,* all of which incorporate the nouns referring to the instruments with which the sounds are made; (2) verbs of location such as *box in, corral (in), coup up, fence (in), wall (in), button, bolt, cement, glue, nail, paste, pin, rope, screw, sew, string, tape, wire;* (3) verbs of movement, such as *cycle, boat, drive, fly, skate, bus, canoe, cart, truck, ship, paddle, row, sail;* (4) tool verbs like *chisel, drill, file, hammer, nail, saw, shovel,* and music verbs like *bat, fiddle, play, putt,* cultivation verbs like *bail, bulldoze, chop, mow, plow, rake,* clothing verbs like *belt, boot, bridle, cap, coat, dress, saddle, shoe,* hunting verbs like *club, fire, knife, net, stab, trap,* primping verbs like *brush, hose, iron, mop, paint, shave, sponge, sweep, vacuum, weigh,* and miscellaneous verbs like *lasso, rope, xerox, photograph, project, slice, spoon, steer, lock;* and (5) change of state verbs such as *chalk out, crayon out, ink out, paint out, cut, elbow, gun down, hip, shoot, stab, stone.*

The only instance of non-Instrument case incorporation that N presents is observed in (5).

(5) a. John and the other cowboys *corralled* the entire herd.
    Agent Agent Inst.-Loc. Object
  b. Mary *bottled* the fruit.
    Agent Inst.-Loc. Object

Corralled and *bottled* are said to have the case frame [____ Agent, Instrument, Location, Object] and incorporate both Instrumental and Locative cases in (5). Verbs of this set belong to the class of 'verbs of location' and, according to N, include *box in, can, bag, encase, encircle, house, rope, shelve, tree, wall*, among others. What is not clear in this double case incorporation is what should be the Instrument, if the incorporated case is the Locative *corral* and *bottle?* On the other hand, if *corral* and *bottle* are Instruments, what can be the Location? Since the case frame given above indicates that Instrument and Location are conjunctively specified, we cannot interpret N as discussing disjunctive incorporation. The above discussion is the only instance of double incorporation in N. As will be seen, there is not only conjunctive, but also disjunctive double case incorporation in English verbs. Sentence (5a) would seem to be an instance of disjunctive incorporation. It is ambiguous in at least two ways, which may be related to (6a) and (6b).

(6) a. John and the other cowboys DROVE the entire herd *into a corral.*
  b. John and the other cowboys CONFINED the entire herd *in a corral.*

Obviously this ambiguity, together with the case difference between *into a corral* and *in a corral* in relation to their abstract predicates, supports the interpretation of *corralled* in (5a) as an example of disjunctive double case incorporation. And (5b) would seem to be another example of disjunctive incorporation for those who feel an ambiguity similar to (5a). For those who interpret the sentence uniquely as (6a), i.e., as (7), it is an example of single case incorporation.

(7) Mary PUT the fruit *into a bottle.*

Into a corral and *into a bottle* in the above examples seem to be the Goal case, rather than Location, even in the light of N's case features (1973:121). Thus, (5) shows an instance of Goal incorporation.

6. On the other hand, many other case grammarians do not recognize (or even admit) Instrumental incorporation. For instance, Langendoen (1970:79-84) handles the above-mentioned phenomena as role (or case) deletion, saying that "the roles that may be deleted are precisely those whose lexical content is the most probable, given the meaning of the predicate". Thus Langendoen (hereafter L) views verbs of contact like *kick, kiss, wink, slap, punch,* and *embrace* as associated respectively with such Instruments as *the foot, the lips, the eyelids, the (flat of the) hand, the fist,* and *the arms.* To L, (8a) is nothing more than a sentence with the Instrument deleted, while (8b) has the Instrument on the surface.

(8) a. Maude kicked Melinda.
b. Maude kicked Melinda with her left foot.

This view is diametrically opposed to that of N discussed in Section 5. L regards (8) as in a way paralled to (9) where the verb of consumption *eat* is associated with *food* (his Patient case) and yet appears without the 'Patient' in (9a) and with it in (9b).

(9) a. John is eating.
b. John is eating fried earthworms.

To further support his claim, L provides (10) where both Instrument (*the razor*) and 'Patient/Location' (*the face* (or *the beard*)) are deleted in (10a), while Instrument (*with a rusty knife*) and 'Patient/Location' (*a peach*) appear in (10b). This means that the verb *shave* does not incorporate any case within itself.

(10) a. John is shaving.
b. John is shaving a peach *with* a rusty knife.

Still another set of L's sentences are given in (11).

(11) a. The carpenter hammered the nail into the board.

b. The carpenter drove the nail into the board with a hammer.

c. The carpenter hammered the nail into the board with his shoe.

L argues that (11a) is not to be derived from any deep structure like that underlying (11b) because the two sentences are not stylistic variants. He points out that (11a) "suggests, but does not claim that the carpenter used an actual hammer to drive the nail, whereas" (11b) makes such a claim. Thus, he argues that (11a) is to be derived directly from a deep structure that contains the main predicate *hammer* meaning 'drive in a hammer-like fashion'.

The position taken in this paper recognizes the existence of a wide range of case incorporation in English verbs, including that of the Instrument. Consider the sentences in (11). Producing the sentence in (11a), a speaker must have one of two situations in mind. He either observed the carpenter actually using a hammer or he observed him driving the nail in hammer-like fashion. This means that the verb *hammer* has (at least) two readings: 'Drive (which includes drive, force, shape with, strike repeatedly with, make or fasten with, etc.) + the Instrument *hammer'* on the one hand and 'Drive in a hammer-like fashion' on the other. It is this second reading that L assigns to the verb *hammer*, not the first. It is only because of this second reading that it can be said that (11a) does not claim that the carpenter used an actual hammer. This reading seems to me to have germinated from the first through a process of abstraction or generalization of meaning, something quite common in the evolution of language. One might call such a process an instance of idiomatization involving the growth of new semantic units (for the definition of idiomatization, see Chafe 1973:Chapter 5). Now, with the first reading of the verb *hammer*, it is obvious that the Instrument is incorporated in the verb, which entails that (11a) is, in one reading, derived from a semantic structure containing DRIVE and *a hammer*. Notice that this semantic structure cannot be equated with (11b) which contains the lexical verb *drive* whose meaning is only a member of the meanings of DRIVE. With the second reading of the verb *hammer*, (11a) has nothing to do with Instrumental incorporation. Depending on whether the verb is viewed as a single semantic unit or as a sequence of units (i.e., DRIVE + in a hammer-like fashion), (11a) may be considered either as being derived direcly from a structure containing the predicate *hammer* (as L proposes) or as being derived from a structure that involves the predicate DRIVE + the Manner *in a hammer-like fashion*. In the latter case, one can speak of Manner incorporation.

It would seem that if the Instrument slot is filled with a noun phrase on the surface, the first kind of reading does not apply, simply because no incorporation has taken place. It is clear, therefore, that (11c) has the verb *hammered* with only the second reading. Similarly:

(12) They carpeted the floor with an animal skin.
The door was bolted with a strong metal bar.
The trees were capped with snow.
She combed her hair with a comb.
He covered the table with a cloth.

In the same way, the sentence in (13) may be acceptable only if the verbs are given the second type of reading discussed above.

(13) The carpenter hammered the nail into the board with a large hammer.
The girl combed her hair with a steel comb.
He spaded the garden with John's spade.
The farmer carted the hay to the barn in an old cart.
They boarded the windows of their house with the boards they bought.
We poled the boat through the shallow water with a long pole.
The dog was chained to the fence with a steel chain.

Once we admit Instrumental incorporation, we can account naturally for the relation existing between the paired setntences in (14), which are representative of hundreds of similar sets.

(14) a. The fisherman fastened/kept-from-drifting his boat with an anchor near the shore.
The fisherman anchored his boat near the shore.
b. The airplane attacked/damaged/destroyed the city with bombs.
The airplane bombed the city.

It is a problem whether the sentences in (8) and (10) should be interpreted in a way parallel to (11). Such verbs as *hammer, carpet, brick, bolt, cap, comb, spade* have a clear-cut reading each with a unique instrument incorporated, even if no specific Instrument appears on the surface. This does not seem to be the case with *kick* and *shave*, because *kick* may be associated with *foot, knee, heel, toes,* etc. and *shave* with *razor, shaver, knife,* etc. with about equal frequency. For instance, if a speaker wants to specify the fact that he observed John covering a floor with a carpet, he can say more naturally (15a), but also marginally (15b). This fact clearly indicates that the instrument *carpet* is incorporated in the verb *carpet* in (15a). (15b) is acceptable only if the verb *carpet* is understood not to incorporate the instrument *carpet*. Otherwise, *with a carpet* would be redundant, making the sentence unnatural.

(15) a. John carpeted the floor.
 b. John carpeted the floor with a carpet.

On the other hand, a speaker who wants to specify John's shaving with *a razor, an electric shaver*, or *a knife* should say (16).

(16) a. John is shaving with a razor.
 b. John is shaving with an electric shaver.
 c. John is shaving with a knife.

When the speaker uses the sentence, *John is shaving*, he simply does not specify the instrument. Bender (personal communication) points out as a reaction to L's two sentences in (10) that the normal interpretation of this sentence would be reflexive. Thus, *John is shaving* may be viewed as being derived from *John is shaving himself*, with *himself* optionally deleted, but not from a structure in which both Instrument (*the razor*) an Patient/Location (*the face* (or *the beard*)) are deleted. Deletion of these cases would result in the loss of information. All this means is that none of the above instruments are either deleted or incorporated in the verb *shave* in the sentence *John is shaving*.

In the same way, many of the examples of N's Body-Part incorporation do not appear to be instances of true Instrumental incorporation. Thus, the verb *breathes* in *John breathes* means 'does breathing' and does not incorporate the Body-Part *nose*, in view of the sentence *John breathes through his nose*, in which the Instrument, *his nose,* is specified.

In general, true instances of Instrumental incorporation seem to be related to cognate verbs, i.e., verbs derived from their corresponding nouns, as in *John buckled his belt* (derived from *John FASTENED his belt with its buckle*), and *The carpenter glued the legs to the chair* (derived from *The carpenter JOINED the legs to the chair with glue*). Cognate verbs absorb all the semantic features of the corresponding Instrumental nouns, which seems to be the major force of Instrumental Incorporation.

An incorporated abstract predicate of a cognate verb is largely predictable in the light of the incorporated instrument. In general, the predicate is determined by the use, service, or function of the instrument. For instance, the verb *buckle* incorporates the Instrument *buckle* whose main use is to *fasten with*. Similarly, the verb *spade* incorporates the Instrument *spade* whose main use is *to dig with* or *to cut with*, hence, the predicate DIG.

7. Besides the Instrument, a large number of English verbs incorporate other cases also. The only exceptions are the Agent and the Experiencer which are rarely incorporated into verbs if at all. (No convincing examples have been found.) The fact that Agent and Experiencer do not participate in verbal incorporation may be due either to the priority of these cases in the subject selection hierarchy (see Section 3), or to their animateness, or to both. When considering other grounds, such as idiomatization, Chafe (1973:103-4 and Chapter 15) points out the closer internal coherence of verb and Patient (roughly, Object) configurations rather than those of verb and Agent. As in the case of Instrument, other cases are incorporated in large part into cognate verbs, such as *air, arch, bridge, butter, color,* and *name* (occasionally into semi-cognate verbs like *weigh*).

Due to its wide coverage and wastebasket nature as defined by Fillmore (1971:42), the Object case is most frequently incorporated into verbs. This phenomenon will be examined in this section, and the other cases relegated to Section 8.

Consider first 'ambient' verbs. Chafe (1973:101-2) indicates that no noun need be present in sentences where ambient verbs appear. Thus, he says that the meaning of such sentences as the following seems to involve only predication, "in which there is no 'thing' of which the predication is made".

(17) a. It is hot.
It is fine today.
b. It is raining.
It is snowing.
It dawned.

The adjectives in (17a) are called state-ambient, while the verbs in (17b) are action-ambient. All the adjectives and verbs in (17) when translated into Korean (18) involve a proposition consisting of an Object case (which is realized as the surface subject) and a predicate. As in English, the sentences in (18a) are state, and those in (18b) are action sentences.

(18) a. nalssi -ka tep-ta.

weather-SM hot-SE
onul nalssi-ka coh-ta.
today good-SE

b. pi-ka o-n-ta.
rain-SM come-AM-SE
nwun-i o-ko-iss-ta.
snow-SM come-ing-exist-SE
tong-i the-ss-ta.
dawn-SM break-PAST-SE

In English, the grammatical subject *it* in (17) is considered semantically empty, which may be true. The view that the adjectives and verbs in such sentences involve only predication does not seem to be correct, however. The Object and the related predicate in each sentence in (18) are never fused with each other to form a simple verb on the surface. In order to obtain a common semantic base covering both Korean and English, therefore, it is necessary to consider each adjective or verb in (17) as being derived from a composite of at least an argument and a predicate. The empty subject *it* is required in the sentences in (17) by the syntactic constraint of English that every nonimperative sentence have a surface subject. This syntactic manipulation is necessary because the adjective or verb (e.g., *rains*) has swallowed up the noun (e.g., *rain*) which would otherwise be the subject of the sentence.

To the Korean speaker approaching English, verbs like *rain* and *dawn* do not differ from verbs like *hammer* and *brick* in terms of case incorporation. If the introspections of such speakers concerning these configurations of underlying structure (and others in this paper) should prove definitely different from those of native English speakers, it would probably constitute support for the Whorfian hypothesis and, moreover, would mean that the task of searching for universal semantic units and structures is doomed to deadlock at best.

Next, observe the following set of sentences.

(19) a. He is tall.
b. He is angry.

The Korean counterparts of the adjectives in (19) include an Object case and a verb, as shown in (20). Notice in (20b) that the verb is apparently derived from two verbs through compounding, as indicated in the parentheses. Further, notice that the Object cases are realized as surface subjects.

(20) a. kui-ka khi-ka khu-ta.
he-SM height-SM big-SE
b. kui-ka seng-i na-ss-ta. (←—na-a-iss-ta)
anger-SM occur-exist-SE occur-ST-exist-SE

(19a) would seem to parallel *He has a big nose (kui-ka kho-ka khu-ta).* Thus, *tall* is a composite of the Object *height* and the predicate *big* to Korean minds. There is no single lexical unit in Korean which corresponds to *tall* as a whole. Thus, (20a) represents the meaning more explicitly than (19a). In the same way, *angry* incorporates the concept 'anger'. The same underlying case relationships hold when the adjectives in (19) are used attributively. For instance, the Korean counterpart of *a tall person* is *khi-ka khu-n salam* (*salam* 'person') and that of an *angry person* is *seng-i na-n salam*, where the Object 'height' and 'anger' are retained. Furthermore, as with other obvious case relationships, an adverb freely intervenes between the object and the predicate in (20) as well as in (18), as in *kui-ka seng-i mopsi na-ss-ta 'He is very angry'* (*mopsi* 'very'). The Object may be topicalized and/or delimited, as in *kui-ka khi-man-un khu-ta* (Lit. As for his height, it is big). Surface case scrambling is allowed, as in *khi-ka kui-ka mopsi khu-ta* 'He is very tall'.

If the above observations are on the right track (e.g., the verb *rain* in (17b) is derived from *rain* + FALL and the adjective *tall* in (19a) from *height* + BIG), the next question is how one should handle the deep cases of the meaningful surface subjects (i.e., *he*) in (19) in relation to the abstract predicates, such as BIG. A common practice of case grammarians would directly relate *he* to *tall* and *he* to *angry* because no incorporated Object and abstract predicate would be postulated. Then we may say that *he* is the Object in (19a) and *he* is the Experiencer in (19b) according to Fillmore's definitions. Once these adjectives are viewed as propositions in their own right, however, an Object appears in each sentence in (19) in addition to the Object or Experiencer mentioned above, thus resulting in double Object constructions in deep structure in the case of (19a). This would be a serious breach of Fillmore's one-instance-per-clause principle (Fillmore 1971:38) unless the sentence is considered an instance of clause embedding. There are some reasons to view the sentences in (19) as complex in deep structure with the two predicates 'be in the state of' and a deeper predicate (e.g., BIG). This analysis may be supported by (20b) where a reflex (*-ss*) of such double predicates shows up on the surface (partly due to the process or change-of-state nature of the deeper verb 'occur'). Viewed in this way, therefore,

Fillmore's principle will not be affected. However, it is necessay for other reasons to reinterpret the whole situation. For instance, *he* in (19a) is the Object of the predicate BE IN THE STATE OF (realized partly as *be*)[3] and *height* (more correctly, *his height*) is the Object of the predicate BIG, as roughly shown below (with the nodes, Mode and Proposition pruned).

(21)

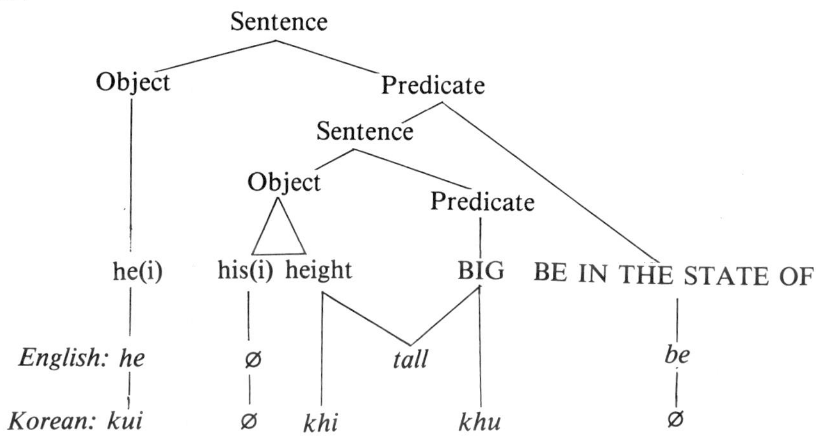

The reason for postulating *his* in the underlying structure is that the relation between *he* and *height* is that of inalienable possession, which will not concern us further here.[4]

Another remark to be made is that *he* in (19b), which would be considered the Experiencer in relation to *angry*, must be treated as the Object in relation to the predicate, BE IN THE STATE OF, in the proposed analysis.

Now let us observe a set of (non-ambient) verbs which incorporate the Object case. First, consider (22).

(22) a. This fish smells.
b. *This fish smells to me.
c. This fish smells terrible to me.

The verb *smell* is expressed in Korean by *naymsay-ka na-n-ta* (Lit. smell occurs) and, accordingly, may be derived from the Object *smell* and the predicate OCCUR (*-n* in *na-n-ta* indicates action). *This fish* seems to be in the Source case in that 'smell' comes out of it. (22b) is not natural, because the action predicate OCCUR, by its very nature, allows neither Goal nor

Experiencer. Then, why is (22c) grammatical? The reason seems clearly that the adjective *terrible* allows an Experiencer, as in *The smell is terrible to me.* Certainly (22c) is a composite of *This fish smells* and *The smell is terrible.* That *the smell* in the second sentence is a noun and refers back to *the smell* incorporated in the verb *smell* in the first sentence is another piece of evidence in support of verbal incorporation of cases. (23) provides more examples of verbs that are parallel to *smell.*

(23) The kimchi *stinks.*
The trees *are budding.*
The music *sounds* too loud to me.
With enough water, the plant will *bloom.*
When a liquid boils, it *bubbles.*

From the viewpoint of Korean structure, all the italicized verbs incorporate an Object (realized as the surface subject in Korean) and an action predicate. The incorporated Objects are *strong smell, buds, sound, blossoms,* and *bubbles*, respectively. The subjects in the sentences in (23) and in the Korean counterparts are all Source cases.

The sentences in (24) also contain action intransitive verbs, but are different from those in (22) and (23) in that the verbs have Agent subjects instead of Source subjects and incorporate an Object which is realized as the surface object when translated into Korean.

(24) a. John coughed.
John lied.
John spoke to the Congressman.
b. He whistled.
He kneeled to pray.
The army camped for the night.
Birds are nesting in that tree.
Those drivers have been trucking for years.

The incorporated predicates of the verbs in (24a) appear as DO verbs in Korean, while those in (24b) have their own unique predicates. For instance, the first sentences in (24a) and (24b) correspond respectively to (25a) and (25b).

(25) a. John-i kichim-ul hay-ss-ta.
SM cough-OM do-PAST-SE
b. kui-ka hwiphalam-ul pul-ess-ta.

he-SM whistle-OM blow-PAST-SE

Notice in particular that *kichim* and *hwiphalam* are followed by the object marker. This fact is closely related to the fact that the subject of the sentences is the Agent, i.e., the instigator of the event.

N (1973:158 *et passim*) considers most of the verbs in (24) as incorporating the Instrument case as has already been noted. For instance, he sets up the case frame for the verb *kneel* as [____ Agent, Instrument], indicating that the Instrument is *knee* and implying that no Object is allowed. What seems to be true, however, is that the Object case, *knee*, instead of being the Instrument, together with the predicate BEND, is incorporated in the verb. This fact is attested by the Korean counterpart *muluph-ul kkwulh-ta* (*muluph* 'knee' and *kkwulh* 'bend, fall on').

The verbs in (22)-(24) are intransitive. Let us examine transitive verbs which incorporate the Object case.

(26) a. We aired the warm room.
The boys stoned the strange dog.
He buttered his bread.
The child is coloring a picture book.
b. The mother dressed her children quickly.
The lady will bill me later.
The new King will benefit all the people.
The lifeguards cautioned the swimmers to be careful.
c. He gapped the board.
They bridged the river.
He blistered his hands in the fire.
d. My father skinned the tree.
I pruned the tree.

In view of the discussion thus far, there is no doubt that all the verbs in (26) incorporate a noun in the Object case. The noun phrases following the verbs in (26a) are in the Goal case, those in (26b) in the Experiencer case, those in (26c) in the Location case, and those in (26d) in the Source case in relation to the respective incorporated predicate and noun. For instance, the verb *air* is regarded as being derived from the predicate PUT and the Object *air,* with PUT comprising such meanings as 'let into', 'let through', 'put into', etc. *The warm room* is the Goal into which the air is put.

All the incorporated Objects in (26) are realized as surface objects in Korean. The Korean sentence which is (nearly) synonymous with the first sentence in (26) is (27).

(27) wuli-ka ku tewu-n pang-ey kongki-lul cipeneh-ess-ta.
we-SM the warm room-to air-OM put in-PAST-SE

Notice the *kongki* 'air' is followed by the object marker *-lul* and *pang* 'room' is followed by the goal marker *-ey*.

Another productive set of transitive constructions where the object is incorporated in the verb is illustrated by the following sentences.

(28) I smelled the fish.
I studied math.
Copy this letter.
John weighed the box.
The Atlantic Ocean bounds the U.S. on the east.
He based his request for re-election on his past performance.

If we do not decompose the verbs in (28), we would say that subjects are all Agents and the surface objects are all deep Objects. Thus, N (1973:158) provides the case frame for the verb *smell* as [_____ Agent, Instrument, Object], with the Body-Part Instrument *nose* incorporated in the verb. As mentioned earlier, body parts of this type are not treated in this paper as instances of case-incorporation but as the nonappearance of a case. In the first sentence in (28), N's Object is of course *the fish* and the Agent, *I*. However, all the verbs in (28) are composed in their underlying structure of a predicate and an Object, i.e., DETECT and *smell,* DO and *study,* MAKE and *copy,* MEASURE and *weight,* FORM and *boundary,* and FORM and *basis*. This analysis is endorsed by the corresponding Korean sentences, which do not allow any incorporation. If this is correct, it will be necessary to modify the commonly-held view that the noun phrase following the verb in each sentence in (28) is the deep Object.

Consider the first sentence as typical of the group. While the incorporated noun *smell* is the Object in relation to the predicate DETECT, the surface object *the fish* is not directly related to DETECT but functions as the Location of the Object *smell.*[5]

(29)

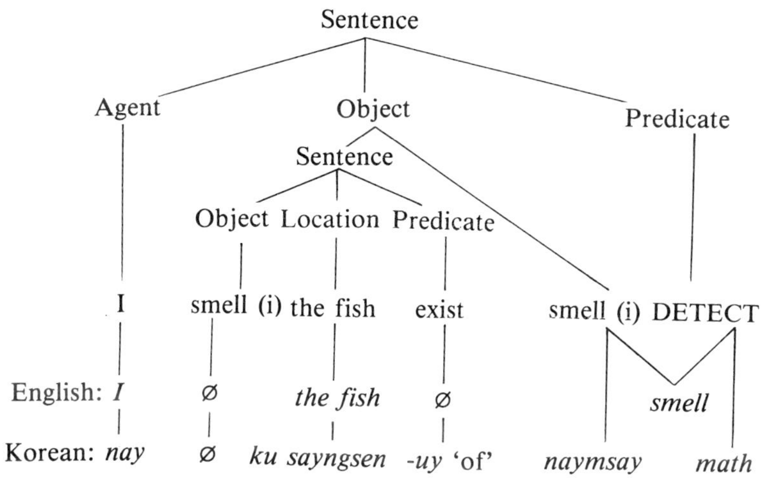

Thus, the sentence in question seems to underlie something similar to the structure shown in (29), where Mode and Proposition nodes are not specified.

The complete Korean sentence is *nay-ka ku sayngsen-uy naymsay-lul math-ass-ta.* If the configuration proposed in (29) is not wrong, it is clear then that *the fish* in the sentence is only remotely related to the main predicate DETECT. This implies that English and Korean segment the same conceptual universe quite differently from each other on their surface levels, and that the view that *the fish* is the Object in relation to the verb *smelled,* is based only on superficial observation.

8. Now let us look briefly at verbal incorporation of the remaining cases. With regard to the Goal case, observe the sentences in (30).

(30) Back the truck away from the door.
Please bundle these newspapers.
Cash this check for me.
The writer dramatized the book.
He boxed the pencils.

The verbs in (30) may be analyzed as 'move to the rear', 'form into a bundle', 'change into cash', 'make into a drama', and 'put into a box', respectively. This is how they are translated into Korean. For instance, there is no way to express in Korean the idea of the verb *back* by a predicate alone, as we see in (31) which is the counterpart of the first sentence in (30).

(31) truck-ul mun-eyse twiccok-ulo ponay-la.
OM door-from rear-to send-SE

While the typical prepositions used for the Goal are *to, into,* and *onto,* Korean normally uses *-ulo* (or *-lo*), which is placed after the case. Locative incorporation may be illustrated by the sentences in (32).

(32) They tented on the old campground.
He was jailed for three years.
She likes to garden.
He banked part of his money every week.

These verbs incorporate the Location case, as we observe in their meanings 'live in a tent', 'confined in a jail', 'work in a garden', and 'deposit in a bank', respectively. Again the incorporation is attested by Korean sentences where the locative marker *-ey* or *-eyse,* 'at, in, on' is postposed to the Location cases (e.g., *tent-eyse sal-ass-ta* 'tented' and *kamok-ey kachi-ess-ta* 'was jailed').

If we define the Time case as 'the point or interval of the time of the state of action' (I. Yang 1972:7), the verbs in (33) may be considered an instance of Temporal incorporation.

(33) a. She timed his speech.
b. He timed his visit to suit her convenience.

Corresponding Korean sentences are given in (34).

(34) a. ku yeca-ka kui kangyen-*uy* sikan-ul cay-ss-ta.
the woman-SM his speech-of time-OM measured
b. kui-ka ku yeca-uy phyenui-ey mac-tolok pangmun-*uy* sikan-ul
convenience-to suit-to visit of
cenghay-ss-ta.
arranged

The appearance of the italicized *-uy* 'of' in the Korean sentence is parallel to its appearance in the sentences in (28) and (29). In (34), *-uy* seems to underlie the embedded predicate BE REQUIRED FOR.

Source incorporation is illustrated by (35).

(35) a. Peanuts shell easily.
b. John shelled oysters.

Here the verb *shell* has the meaning 'be freed from the shell' (35a) and 'take out of the shell' (35b), in which *the shell* is in the Source case.

Consider now two instances of verbal incorporation of entities whose case status is not particularly recognized by Fillmore (1971). These are Manner (36a) and Function (36b).

(36) a. The sail ballooned out in the wind.
He crawfished his way through the tunnel.
Pictures of the children dramatized the need for food.
The horse's shoes clattered on the stones.
He batted the stone with a stick.
The group of dancers circled the leader.
The early settlers braved cold, hunger and violence.
b. She clerks in a department store.

Thus, *ballooned* means 'swelled like a balloon', *crawfished,* 'moved like a crawfish', *dramatized,* 'present in a dramatic way', *clattered,* 'moved with clatters', *batted,* 'hit in a (baseball-) bat-like fashion', *circled,* 'moved in a circle', *braved,* 'fought bravely', and *clerks,* 'works as a clerk', In Korean, these expressions are made only with the Manner or Function shown on the surface. Such manner markers as *chelem* 'like', *-key* '-ly', and (*u*)*lo* 'with' and the function marker -(*u*)*lo*(*se*) 'as' are postposed respectively to Manner and Function noun phrases.

A single verb may incorporate two (or perhaps more) cases, as we see in (37).

(37) a. John bailed his canoe.
b. The boy hosed the sidewalk.

Bailed incorporates the Object *water* and the Instrument *bail,* while *hosed* incorporates the Object *water* and the Instrument *hose. His canoe* in (37a) is the Source and *the sidewalk* in (37b) is the Goal. For instance, (37a) is assumed to have the following underlying structure.

(38)

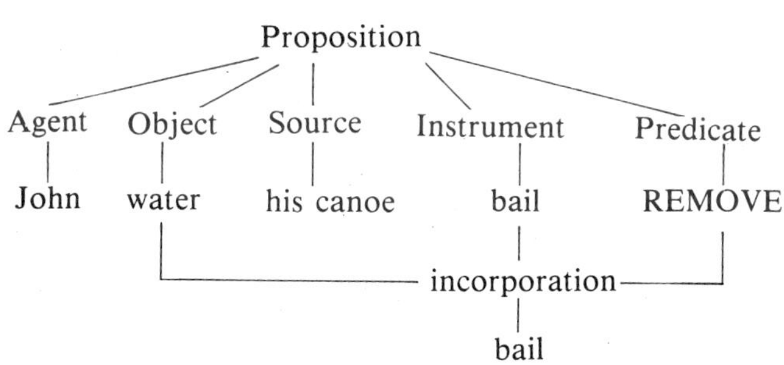

Frequently a verb may incorporate one or another case with different meanings resulting. Examine the sentences in (39).

(39) Panamanian students stoned the United States Embassy.
The cook peppered the meat.
He was bribed to keep silent.

All these sentences are ambiguous in at least two ways depending on the alternate incorporation of the Object and the Instrument in the verb. Thus, *stoned* means either 'threw stones at' or 'attacked with stones', *pepperd,* either 'put pepper on' or 'seasoned with pepper', and *bribed,* either 'given a bribe' or 'influenced by a bribe'. This alternate case incorporation is also fully attested by synonymous Korean sentences.

9. The observations made up to this point highlight the fact that English has a productive mechanism of verbal incorporation of cases, while Korean does not, in general, allow such a mechanism. As a result, surface case relationships in sentences are arranged quite differently between the two languages. This difference is compounded by their basic word order difference (S-V-O in English and S-O-V in Korean), and by the productivity in Korean of such processes as free case scrambling and surface case multiplication. Following are some characteristic differences in surface case relationships between English and Korean for which case incorporation is responsible.

First, many English sentences have fewer surface cases. For instance, (37a) is an example of the structure: Subject-Verb-Object, whereas the corresponding (40) has the case relationship: Subject-Source-Instrument-Object-Verb.

(40)	John-i	caki	canoe-eyse	bail-lo	mul-ul	phe-ss-ta.
	SM	his	from	with	water-OM	dipped

Remember that the order of the surface cases in (40) is completely free, with the verb-final constraint retained. Second, surface cases are frequently quite different. In (37a) *his canoe* is the direct object, but, as we see in (40), *caki canoe* is the source. Similarly, *John married Mary,* where Mary is the direct object, corresponds to *John-i Mary-wa kyelhon-ul hay-ss-ta,* where *Mary-wa* 'with Mary' is the comitative. The occurrence of genitive *-uy* in the Korean sentences corresponding to (28) and (29) is another example. Third, many English intransitive verbs are synonymous with Korean transitive verbs preceded by a direct object. This was observed in (24). Fourth, many English single object constructions correspond to Korean double object constructions. Thus, *I studied math* may be translated as *nay-ka swuhak-ul kongpu-lul hay-ss-ta,* where *swuhak* 'math' and *kongpu* 'study' are direct objects. Fifth, something similar happens in subject position, known as double (or multiple) subject construction. This was observed in (19)-(23). For instance, *This book is interesting* cannot be expressed with a single subject in Korean, i.e., both 'this book' and 'interest' must be the subjects. Accordingly, resistance to case incorporation in Korean contributes, to a considerable extent, to the proliferation of double (or multiple) subject and object constructions.[6] Finally, many ambiguous sentences in which case incorporation takes place are disambiguated in the Korean equivalents. As we saw in (39), the ambiguous sentence, *The cook peppered the meat* is expressed in Korean as both *cook-ka koki-ey pepper-lul che-ss-ta* and *cook-ka koki-lul yangnyem-ul hay-ss-ta* which carry different readings.

10. To recapitulate, this paper represents an attempt to show that case incorporation is a characteristic feature of English, largely attested by comparable Korean structures. Except for the Agent and Experiencer, this incorporation covers not only the Instrument but also all the other cases. It occurs for the most part in cognate or semi-cognate verbs in English. Some existing views on case relationships need to be modified if case incorporation is brought into the picture. And finally, the complexity of surface case marking in Korean, including multiple subject and object constructions, may be ascribable, to a large extent, to the resistance of the language to case incorporation.

One topic which was originally planned but not included is those lexical verbs in English which are equivalent to Korean complementation structures. For instance, the verb *float* (cf., Fillmore 1971:48) is expressed in Korean not only as *ttu-n-ta* (manner) but as *tte-ka-n-ta* (movement), the latter containing two verbs, i.e., the manner 'float' which forms a complement and 'go'. Verbs like *cycle, drive, fly, swim* belong here. On the other hand, such verbs as *amuse, blind, frighten* are expressed in Korean only with a causative verb MAKE and a sentential complement. Time and space have not permitted the elaboration of this topic.

Notes

1. I gratefully acknowledge the corrections and comments made by Byron W. Bender throughout this paper. Final responsibility is mine alone, however.
2. The Yale romanization is followed in transcribing Korean. Abbreviations used are: SM (subject marker), OM (object marker), SE (sentence ending), AM (action marker), and ST (state marker).
3. For a similar treatment of *be* in connection with English aspectual phenomena see Chang (1973b:58-72).
4. The semantic notion of possession is quite complex and remains to be fully explored. For example, see Gruber (1970:42) and Nilsen (1973:35-39).
5. One might even say that *the fish* functions as the inalienable possessor of the noun *smell.* A somewhat similar problem occurred with (20). If one follows Gruber's (1970) broad definition of possession, the two entities in each of *smell of the fish, study of math, copy of this letter, weight of the box, boundary of the U.S.*, and *basis of his request* are all possessively related in view of their close association. However, the relations are not at all of the same kind at a deeper level and cannot be derived from the same type of underlying structure. For instance, *the smell that the fish has* is natural but **the study that math has* is nonsensical.
6. There are many other sources of multiple subject or object constructions. See S. Song 1967; S. Kim 1967; Ree 1969; I. Yang 1972; B. Park 1972; C. Lee 1973a, among others.

Reprinted from *The English Language and Literature* (English Literary Society of Korea) 51-52:431-456 (1974).

15. GOAL AND SOURCE IN KOREAN LOCATIVES WITH REFERENCE TO JAPANESE

0. This paper is dedicated to Professor Sheon Gi Gim in commemoration of his seventieth birthday. My present career owes greatly to his teaching, advice and encouragement.*

1. One area in Korean grammar which, in spite of some ingenious proposals, is far from sufficiently clear is that of locative expressions, typically related to such orientational endings as EY, EYSE, EYSEPUTHE, LO, LOPUTHE, EYKKACI, and EYTA.[1] For instance, Martin and Lee (1969:51) make an efficient distinction between static location, in the sense that something *is* in (on, at) a place, and dynamic location, in the sense that something *happens* in (on, at) a place, to describe the difference, for instance, between (la) and (lb) respectively.[2]

(1) a. John-i cip-EY issta. 'John is at home.'
John-SM home-at is
b. John-i cip-EYSE nonta. 'John plays at home'
John-SM home-at play

Martin and Lee (ibid.:50) further point out that EY is used to indicate the direction 'to', as in (2a), and EYSE to indicate the direction 'from', as in (2b).

(2) a. John-i hakkyo-EY kanta. 'John is going to school.'
John-SM school-to go
b. John-i hakkyo-EYSE onta. 'John is coming from school.'
John-SM school-from come

Static vs. dynamic location and goal vs. source are useful distinctions where the verbs are clearly so definable. There are, however, many verbs whose status is rather ambivalent, hence not easily assignable to the above distinctions. Observe the examples in (3).

(3) a. John-i uyca-EY ancassta. 'John sat on the chair.'
John-SM chair-on sat
b. John-i sewul-EY tochakhayssta. 'John arrived in Seoul.'
John-SM Seoul-in arrived
c. Ssal-i hankwuk-EYSE pissata. 'Rice is expensive in Korea.'
rice-SM Korea-in expensive

The verb *ancta* 'to sit' is certainly neither static nor directional, but its occurrence with EY forces us to call (3a) a case of static location following the above-mentioned distinctions. Martin et al. (1967) list *sewul-EY tochakhata* 'to arrive in Seoul' under the subheading *place, static location.* It seems to me that the verb *tochakhata* 'to arrive' is goal-oriented, if not directional, which means that (3b) is ambivalent between (1a) and (2a). The verb *pissata* 'to be expensive' is a descriptive verb and may not be considered as dynamic in the usual sense, but only EYSE is allowed with it, as in (3c).

In an interesting paper, D. Yang (1973b) proposes to derive the four types of locatives illustrated in (1) and (2) from a single prelexical entity *E,* observing that the four locative concepts are predictable, as is shown in (4).

(4)

	in construction with V	*not in construction with V*
V [−directional]	Inner Location	Outer Location
V [+directional]	Ending Location	Starting Location

Thus, (1a) is a case of 'Inner Location', (1b) 'Outer Location', (2a) 'Ending Location', and (2b) 'Starting Location'. One moot question with regard to Yang's insight that the meaning difference between EY and EYSE is attributable to the underlying constructional difference is how we can define the constructional meanings that are to be responsible for the different locative expressions. Furthermore, it is not entirely clear on semantic as well as syntactic grounds why, for instance, *hakkyo-EY* 'to school' in (2a) is in construction with the verb *kata* 'to go' and *hakkyo-EYSE* 'from school' is not in construction with the verb *ota* 'to come' in (2b) (cf. Gruber 1965:89ff.). As we will see, the concepts of 'ending' and 'starting' do not seem to be particularly limited to 'directional' verbs.

The objective of this paper is to reveal some semantic and syntactic properties associated with Korean Locative expressions in comparison with parallel expressions in Japanese. In particular, I will show that Korean locatives are to be dichotomized into goal and source as against the common practice which trichotomizes them into goal, location, and source, as in English. The usual distinction between goal EY and location EY on the one hand and between source EYSE and location EYSE on the other is not quite well motivated. What I propose is that both EY and EYSE carry semantic contents when they occur in locative expressions, EY locatives consistently referring to goal and EYSE locatives to source, which means that the semantic ranges of EY and EYSE do not overlap at all but are binary and opposite (Sections 2, 3, and 4). I will also discuss -PUTHE (Section 5), LO (Section 6), -KKACI (Section 7), and -TA (Section 8), and clarify some of their basic semantic and syntactic properties. In the course of the following discussion, various correlations between orientational endings and coocccurring verbs, the scopes of EY and EYSE locatives as reflected in syntax, and the properties of different types of verbs will be revealed. Morphological details of the endings (e.g. analysis of EY-SE-PUTHE 'from') are not the concern of this paper.

2. All orientational endings have uniquely definable semantic contents, each containing one or more morphological and semantic units. Let us first observe the ending EY as it occurs in locative expressions.

(5)	a.	hakkyo-EY kanta. school-to go	'(He) is going to school.'
		ttang-EY naylinta. ground-to descend	'(It) is coming down to the ground.'
	b.	uyca-EY ancnunta. chair-on sit	'(He) is sitting on the chair.'
		pyek-EY kitaynta. wall-against lean	'(He) is leaning against the wall.'
	c.	hakkyo-EY namnunta. school-at remain	'(He) is remaining at school.'
		hotel-EY muknunta. hotel-at stay	'(He) is staying at a hotel.'
	d.	cip-EY issta. home-at exist	'(He) is at home.'
		hankwuk-EY manhta. Korea-in plenty	'(It) is plentiful in Korea.'

As illustrated in (5a), the meaning of *goal* is apparent in EY when it occurs with a motional verb in that the 'theme' (in the sense of Gruber 1965) moves from one position, i.e. source, to another, i.e. goal, either horizontally, vertically or along any other dimension. The locative expression in this case is usually called directional or goal, since the theme's referent moves to the locative referent or the ground in Talmy's (1975) terms. Motional verbs include *kata* 'to go', *ota* 'to come', *naylita* 'to move down', *ttelecita* 'to fall', *oluta* 'to ascend', *ponayta* 'to send', *cwuta* 'to give', and *tencita* 'to throw', among others.[3] Goal meaning becomes less distinct with such non-motional action verbs as *ancta* 'to sit', *seta* 'to stand', *kitayta* 'to lean', *tahta* 'to reach', *thata* 'to ride', and *ssuta* 'to write'. EY with such verbs is commonly classed as place or static location, as mentioned above. It is clear, however, that the actions of these verbs are oriented to the locative referent, EY still retaining the goal meaning. In (5b), for instance, the sitting action of the theme ends up with the chair which is the goal or 'ground' of the action. Goal meaning may be even less obvious with verbs like *salta* 'to live', *mukta* 'to stop over', *memuluta* 'to stay', *namta* 'to remain', and *kunmuhata* 'to be employed'. Let us call this class of verbs semi-action verbs for the moment. Even here it is undeniable that the locative referent is the place where the action of the theme ends up, as we observe in (5c). While semi-action verbs are 'processive' in Korean grammar, the following verbs are stative: *issta* 'to exist', *epsta* 'not exist', *manhta* 'to be plenty', *cekta* 'to be few, little', *tumulta* 'to be rare', etc. Notice that these verbs all mean or imply static existence, e.g. *manhta* actually means 'to exist plentifully'. When these stative existential verbs occur with an EY locative, the goal meaning is minimal or not clearly perceivable, since no movement or action is involved (cf. (5b)). The only goal meaning we can possibly discern in this case is that the theme's referent exists at the locative referent as the end result of certain other events. In spite of this opacity of goal meaning, especially with the last group of verbs, I am hesitant to accept the usual bisection of EY into goal EY and location EY for reasons to be discussed shortly. I propose, instead, to set up one and the same EY whose basic meaning in locative expressions is *goal* in the sense that the referent of the EY locative is the place *to* which the motion, action or state of a theme's referent is oriented.

Let us first examine whether there is any ground to favor the bisection. For one thing, there is a scale of various degrees of goal meanings, which militates against the dichotomy. Notice the apparently decreasing degrees of goal meaning in the EY's in (5). As mentioned above, the usual practice is to view only sentences like (5a) as a case of goal and all others as cases of location. As we saw, this practice is not well grounded in that goal-oriented verbs like *tochakhata* 'to arrive', *tahta* 'to reach', *tulta* 'to enter' as well as the verbs in (5b) are improperly to be related to location EY.

Secondly, in Japanese also, *ni* alone covers the continuum with various degrees of goal meaning.[4] It would be too much of a coincidence if homophonous endings for 'goal' and 'location' existed in two different languages. The sentences in (5) are translated as in (6).[5]

(6) a. gakkoo-*ni* iku. '(He) is going to school.'
school-to go
zimen-*ni* oriru. '(It) is coming down to the ground.'
ground-on descend

b. isu-*ni* suwaru. '(He) is sitting on the chair.'
chair-on sit
kabe-*ni* motareru. '(He) is leaning against the wall.'
wall-against lean

c. gakkoo-*ni* nokoru. '(He) is remaining at school.'
school-at remain
hoteru-*ni* tomaru. '(He) is staying at a hotel.'
hotel-at stay

d. uti-*ni* iru. '(He) is at home.'
home-at exist
kankoku-*ni* ooi. '(It) is plentiful in Korea.'
Korea-in plenty

Thirdly, 'goal' EY/*ni* and 'location' EY/*ni* are in complete complementary distribution, i.e. never in contrast, with regard to verbs in both Korean and Japanese (cf. D. Yang 1973b:29). That is, the same verb cannot occur with both endings and accordingly no semantic ambiguity results. Whether it is 'goal' or 'location', or any intermediate variable for that matter, is entirely predictable, once given the verb. This predictability is applicable even when EY is omitted in rapid speech, as in (7).

(7) a. John-i hakkyo kanta. 'John goes to school.'
John-SM school go

b. John-i hakkyo issta. 'John is at school.'
John-SM school exist

All this means that the meaning differences that appear to be due to EY (and to J. *ni*) are in actuality the function of the inherent features of the cooccurring verbs. Then, we have no ground to overtly distinguish the two meanings in EY (and in J. *ni*) in locative expressions. In other words, the semantic scope of EY is unitary, with a continuum of perceptual variables which depend purely upon the kind of verb EY occurs with.

Since now it is clarified that there is a unitary semantic content in EY, it is necessary to make it clear why goal as defined above is to be preferred as the basic semantic content to, say, location (see Gruber 1965:53 for an opposite view with regard to English). In the first place, motional verbs whose semantic content includes movement in any direction always indicate movement *to* (not *from*) the referent of the EY locative. If we take location as basic, the fact that only 'movement to' is allowed and 'movement from' is not cannot be accounted for, unless it is handled in some sort of redundancy rules for semantic features. On the other hand, as we have already observed, goal meaning exists also in other EY locatives however minor it may be. Thus, cooccurrence of EY with a static existential verb can be explained by saying that a theme rests at the goal. Furthermore, as we will see shortly, EYSE which refers to source is semantically opposite to EY in their relation to verbs. Goal (EY) and source (EYSE) are in a natural and symmetrical semantic relation in locative expressions, whereas, say, location and source are not.

Another piece of evidence that in Korean and Japanese 'location' is not basic while the goal feature is persistent in EY/*ni* may be observed in (8).

(8) K. John-un hakkyo {*EY / EYSE} yamcenhata.
John-TM school at gentle

J. John-wa gakkoo {**ni* / *de*} otonasii. 'John is gentle at school.'
John-TM school at gentle

If there is basically a 'location' feature and no goal feature in EY/*ni*, we would have to expect that descriptive verbs like K. *yamcenhata*/J. *otonasii* 'to be gentle', K *kemanhata*/J. *goomanda* 'to be arrogant', K. *pucilenhata*/J. *mamemamesii* 'to be diligent', and K. *pissata*/J. *takai* 'to be expensive' should properly occur with EY/*ni* to indicate the location. The fact that EY/*ni* is rejected may best be ascribed to the existence of a goal feature in each. The above verbs do not denote any physical movement or resting of a theme with regard to a goal point. More will be said about the goal feature of EY later in comparison with EYSE.[6]

3. The orientational ending that is semantically opposite to EY is EYSE, which refers to 'source'. As in EY, the meaning of source is clearly observ-

able in motional verbs, whereas it is less so with other types of verbs. In (9) examples are arranged roughly in the order of apparently decreasing degrees of the source meaning.

(9)	a.	hakkyo-EYSE onta. school-from come	'(He) is coming from school.'
		cipung-EYSE naylinta. roof-from descend	'(He) is coming down from the roof.'
	b.	sewul-EYSE chwulpalhanta. Seoul-from start	'(He) is starting from Seoul.'
		kwumeng-EYSE ppacinta. hole-from come off	'(It) is coming out of the hole.'
	c.	hakkyo-EYSE nonta. school-at play	'(He) is playing at school.'
		cip-EYSE canta. home-at sleep	'(He) is sleeping at home.'
	d.	hakkyo-EYSE issta. school-at exist	'(It) takes place at school.'
		hankwuk-EYSE pissata. Korea-in expensive	'(It) is expensive in Korea.'

Examples (9a) and (9b) illustrate motional verbs. Verbs that belong to (9a) are specifically locomotive in that they imply a goal, which is not the case with the verbs in (9b). This difference may be verified in the examples of (10).

(10)	a.	hakkyo-EYSE cip-EY onta. school-from home-to come	'(He) comes home from school.'
	b.	*sewul-EYSE pusan-EY Seoul-from Pusan-to chwulpalhanta. start	'(He) starts from Seoul to Pusan.'

Since they are still motional, the verbs of (9b) can occur with a directional locative. Thus, for instance, the replacement of EY with LO in (10b) is grammatical with the meaning '(He) is starting from Seoul toward Pusan'. The verbs in (9c) and (9d), on the other hand, represent nonmotional action verbs and descriptive verbs, respectively. Accordingly, it is quite natural that the meaning of source in EYSE is not clearly perceivable with these verbs. It is undeniable, however, that the EYSE locative serves, in our conceptualization, as the place or source from which the activity or state of a theme's referent starts or rises. For instance, the home is the locative source where the action of sleeping takes place or is initiated, as in (9c). Notice especially that the same descriptive verb *issta* 'to exist' occurs with both EY and EYSE (see 5d and 9d). This verb refers to the existence of a physical object in physical space and of a temporal object in temporal space, the former automatically going with EY, usually with a concrete object as the grammatical subject, and the latter occurring with EYSE with an event as the subject. This statement is evidenced in (11).

(11) a. piano-ka hakkyo-EY issta. 'There is a piano at school; *or* The piano is at school.'
piano-SM school-at exist
b. yenghwa-ka hakkyo-EYSE issta 'There is a movie at school; *or* The movie takes place at school.'
movie-SM school-at exist

Existence of an event is equivalent to the occurrence of an event, thus semantically denoting an action, as evidenced in (12).

(12) a. *piano-ka nayil issta. *'There is a piano tomorrow.'
piano-SM tomorrow exist
b. yenghwa-ka nayil iss ta. 'There is a movie tomorrow.'
movie-SM tomorrow exist
Cf. John-i nayil kanta. 'John will go tomorrow.'
John-SM tomorrow go

Thus, an EYSE locative occurring with *issta* indicates a place of source where an event takes place or originates. Other existence-implying verbs like *manhta* 'to be plenty', *cekta* 'to be few, little', etc. behave in a similar way. Incidentally, the foregoing statements regarding (11) and (12) also apply to Japanese existential verbs. Observe the sentences in (13) where the verb *manhta* which contains plurality is taken up as an example.

(13) a. salam-i sewul- {EY / *EYSE} manhta. 'There are many people in Seoul.'
peope-SM Seoul-in plenty
b. yenghwa-ka sewul- {i. EY / ii. EYSE} manhta. i. 'There are many movies in Seoul.'
movie-SM Seoul-in plenty ii. 'Many movies take place in Seoul.'

Notice in (13a) that when concrete objects are the subject, EYSE is not allowed. In the case of an event subject, only when we perceive a group of events like concrete objects can we use EY, with *manhta* meaning static existence.

The verb *pissata* 'to be expensive' in (9d) and many others given in connection with (8) are descriptive but not existential, to say nothing of active or motional. These verbs do not denote the physical orientation of the theme (e.g. *ssal* 'rice') to the locative (e.g. *hankwuk* 'Korea'). They are, therefore, not goal-oriented and cannot occur with EY. These verbs denote a value judgement regarding the theme. Thus, *pissata* is semantically decomposable as 'the price is high', *yamcenhata* as '(his) character is good', etc. where the underlying subjects are abstract nouns. The referent of an EYSE locative is the place of source where the described phenomenon is judged to take place.

From the observation made thus far, it is clear that the ostensibly different degrees of source in EYSE are entirely ascribable to the semantic features of the cooccurring verbs. This fact and the fact that there is a single form EYSE make me again hesitant to accept the commonly held view that in Korean there are source EYSE and location EYSE. One thing which is different between EY and EYSE is that while 'goal' EY and 'location' EY are in complete complementary distribution with regard to verbs, 'source' and 'location' EYSE are not so at first sight, as noticed in (14), where parallel Japanese expressions are given for comparison.

(14) K. John-i uyca-EYSE ttwiessta.
John-SM chair-on/from jumped.
a. John jumped on the chair.'
b. 'John jumped on the chair.'
J. a. John-ga isu-*de* tonda. 'John jumped on the chair.'
John-SM chair-on jumped
b. John-ga isu-*kara* tonda. 'John jumped from the chair.'
John-SM chair-from jumped

With the same verb *ttwita* 'to jump', EYSE is associated with two meanings, i.e. 'location' and 'source'. This fact is attested in the Japanese counterpart, where two different endings (particles) show up. A close examination, however, reveals that there is [$\pm$2nd locus (= $\pm$change of location)] (a term G. Mathias suggested by personal correspondence) in the verb *ttwita* (and J. *tobu*). K. *ttwita*/J. *tobu* having the [+2nd locus] feature occurs with K. 'source' EYSE/J. *kara* and K. *ttwita*/J. *tobu* having the [−2nd locus] occurs with K. 'location' EYSE/J. *de*. Verbs of this class include K. *ketta*/J. *aruku* 'to walk' and K. *tallita*/J. *hasiru* 'to run', among others. Viewed in this way, we are still in a position to claim that 'location' and 'source' are in complete complementary distribution with regard to the semantic features of verbs. Japanese has separately lexicalized the source meaning into *de* and *kara* according to the presence and absence of the syntactic or verbal feature [2nd locus] respectively, although this is not the case in Korean. Thus, the sentences in (9) are translated into Japanese as in (15).

(15) a. gakkoo-*kara* kuru. '(He) is coming from school.'
school-from come
yane-*kara* oriru. '(He) is coming down from the roof.'
roof-from descend
b. souru-*kara* syuppatusuru. '(He) is starting from Seoul.'
Seoul-from start
ana-*kara* nukeru. '(It) is coming out of the hole.'
hole-from come off
c. gakkoo-*de* asobu. '(He) is playing at school.'
school-at play
uti-*de* neru. '(He) is sleeping at home.'
home-at sleep
d. gakkoo-*de* aru. '(It) takes place at school.'
school-at exist
kankoku-*de* takai. '(It) is expensive in Korea.'
Korea-in expensive

As we will see in Section 5, Japanese *kara* also contains the *ablative* feature, while Korean EYSE does not. This means that Japanese *de* and *kara* are separate lexical items with partially overlapping semantic features.[7]

4. Metaphorically speaking, the semantic relation existing between a verb and an EY locative may be described as centripetal force, while the relation between a verb and an EYSE locative may be described as centrifugal force. These forces are multi-directionally operative and not just horizontal or vertical. It has been observed that these forces are perceptually clear when the verbs are motional but not as distinct with other types of verbs.

Viewed from the standpoint of the action of a theme, the EY locative, due to its goal meaning, highlights the final part of the action denoted by a verb without any presupposition as to how and where the action starts, whereas the source meaning in the EYSE locative highlights the starting part of the action denoted by a verb without reference to how and where the action ends. This semantic fact is comparable to the real world situation where, for instance, we can observe the resultant state of a falling stone much more clearly than its source, while we do not fail to see the starting point of an outgoing stone. Since motional verbs are too obvious in this respect, let us take up only non-motional action verbs and observe how the verbal referents are actually realized in relation to goal and source. The examples given in (16) are all minimal pairs.

(16) a. malwu-EY sessta. — '(He) stood on the (Korean-style) floor.'
floor-on stood
malwu-EYSE sessta. — '(He) stood (up) from the (Korean-style) floor.'
floor-at stood

b. nay yeph-EY canta. — '(He) sleeps by my side.'
my side-by sleep
nay yeph-EYSE canta. — '(He) sleeps at my side.'
my side-at sleep

c. tongccok-EY nathanassta. — '(It) appeared in the east.'
east-in appeared
tongccok-EYSE nathanassta. — '(It) appeared from the east.'
east-from appeared

d. ku cip-EY pul-i nassta. — 'The house was on fire.'
that house-at fire-SM occurred
ku cip-EYSE pul-i nassta. — 'Fire broke out from the house.'
that house-at fire-SM occurred

e. san-EYSE phinta. — '(It) blooms on the mountain.'
mountain-on bloom
san-EYSE phinta. — '(It) blooms on the mountain.'
mountain-at bloom

f. sewul-EY santa. — '(He) lives in Seoul.'
Seoul-in live
sewul-EYSE santa. — '(He) is living in Seoul.'
Seoul-in live

The English translations given above are approximations. In some cases like (16e), the difference in meaning between the two sentences is not properly representable in English. Notice in any case that the verbs occurring with EY consistently indicate that the actions denoted by them end up at the places denoted by the associated EY locatives. On the other hand, the same verbs occurring with EYSE consistently indicate that the actions start from the same places. For instance, with EY the verb *seta* 'to stand' simply refers to the end result of the standing action without reference to the place where the theme's referent stood up or without reference to the place where the theme's referent came from. With EYSE, however, *seta* refers to the rising-up action which is initiated from the place denoted by the EYSE locative. For this reason, only the *seta* occurring with EY may be replaced with *naseta* 'to come out' where *na* means 'to be out'. Only the *seta* occurring with EYSE may be replaced with *ileseta* 'to stand up' where *ile* means 'to rise'. Verbs like *salta* 'to live' denote a continuous state of action, hence have no clear starting or ending point in themselves. Due to this inherent nature of such verbs, the two sentences in (16f) look synonymous at first sight with the goal and source features in the two endings reduced to the minimum perceivability. Even here, a linguistically minded native speaker may say that the first sentence is more stative than the second one in which the action of living is more vivid due to the expelling force contained in EYSE. Since I am such a speaker, I gave different translations to the two sentences. What I have said thus far with regard to (16) generally applies to similar Japanese sentences with *ni*, de, or *kara*.

As Martin (1975b:220) points out in connection with Japanese, transitive verbs like *sata* (J. *kau*) 'to buy' behave peculiarly in locative expressions, as illustrated in (17).

(17) a. sewul- {EY / EYSE} cip-ul sassta. '(He) bought a house in Seoul.'
Seoul-in house-OM bought
b. sewul- {*EY / EYSE} chayk-ul sassta. '(He) bought a book in Seoul.'
Seoul-in book-OM bought

Martin's statement that movable objects do not allow J. *ni* applies to K. EY also, as noticed in (17b). On the other hand, locationally fixed objects like *cip* 'house' may occur with both EY and EYSE. With EY, (17a) means that someone bought a house and keeps it in Seoul. In this case, *Seoul* is the goal of the 'keeping' action. The verb *sata* incorporates the meaning 'keep', which may be made explicit by such auxiliary constructions as *satwuessta* or *sa-nohassta* 'bought and keep (it there)'. Aside from an intuitive judgement, existence of the meaning 'keep' is also suggested in the awkwardness of the progressive construction, *sewul-EY cip-ul sakoissta* '(He) is buying and keeping a house in Seoul'. The incorporation of the meaning 'keep' in *sata* is certainly conditioned by the immovability feature existing in the object, which explains the unacceptability of EY in (17b) unless the verb is replaced with *sa-twuessta, sa-nohassta*, etc. Replaceability of EY with EYTA in (17a) further strengthens the view that *Seoul* is the goal in that construction. With EYSE, (17a) simply means that someone's buying a house took place in *Seoul*. In this case, *Seoul* serves as the source of the 'buying' action.

I believe that the foregoing discussions have given some support to my view that the semantic ranges of Korean locatives are divided into two opposing dimensions, i.e. goal and source, typically represented by EY and EYSE, respectively. Before closing this section, let me mention a few words about the multiple scopes of EY and EYSE locatives. From the observations made so far, it is undisputable that EYSE as well as EY enters into direct construction with a verb. Thus, *uyca-EY ancassta* '(He) sat down on the chair' is both syntactically and semantically parallel to *uyca-EYSE ilesessta* '(He) stood up from the chair', *hankwuk-EY kassta* '(He) sent to Korea' parallel to *hankwuk-EYSE wassta* '(He) came from Korea', *sewul-EY tochakhayssta* '(It) arrived in Seoul' parallel to *sewul-EYSE chwulpalhayssta* '(It) started from Seoul', and [*uyca-EY anc-ko*]*issta* '(He) is sitting on the chair' parallel to [*uyca-EYSE ca-ko*] *issta* '(He) is sleeping on the chair'. All these are examples of direct construction between a verb and a locative.

On the other hand, there are cases in which EY or EYSE locatives occur multiply as in (18).

(18) a. John-EY (=hanthey) hocwumeni-EY ton-i issta.
John-at pocket-in money-SM exist
'John has money in his pocket.'

b. mikwuk-EYSE hakkyo-EY taninta.
America-in school-to go
'(He) goes to school in America.'

c. cip-EYSE namu-EYSE tteleciessta.
home-at tree-from fell
'(He) fell from a tree at home.'

d. cip-EYSE-nun malwu-EYSE-man uyca-EYSE canta.
home-at-TM hallway-in-only chair-in sleep
'At home (he) sleeps in a chair only in the hallway.'

One general principle is that a locative with a wider spatial scope must precede one with a narrower space, the latter being properly included in the former in terms of space. See I. Yang (1972:41-58) and Shin (1976:27) in this regard. As we see in (18a), when we have an EY locative as an 'outer' one, the 'inner' one must also be an EY locative. When we have an EYSE locative as an 'outer' one, the 'inner' one can be either an EY or EYSE locative, as we see in (18b) through (18d). Notice also that an EYSE locative used as an 'outer' one always refers to a stage where some other event takes place. Finally, notice that the verb may be in direct construction only with the last locative unless the verb is locomotive and goes into construction with both source and goal (e.g. (19)). This phenomenon may schematically be illustrated as follows:

(18d) cip-EYSE malwu-EYSE uyca-EYSE canta

On the basis of the above observations, a simple explanation can be made on the ambiguity of sentence (19), which is borrowed from D. Yang (1973b:43).

(19) nay-ka maul-EYSE kyohoy-EY kassta.
I-SM village-from/in church-to went
a. I went from the village to the church.
b. In the village I went to the church.

(19a) is a case of direct construction between the verb and both the EYSE and EY locatives, whereas (19b) is a case of direct construction between the verb and only the EY locative with the starting point (e.g. cip-EYSE 'from home') unspecified.

One piece of evidence that D. Yang (ibid.: 42) presents in favor of considering the 'starting location' (EYSE locative) not being in construction with the verb is the fact that it precedes the 'ending location' (EY locative) in such cases as (19a). An alternative solution that I would propose is to ascribe the phenomenon to the fact that in Korean, and probably in human languages in general, the temporal sequence of an action and the corresponding linguistic sequence match each other, other things being equal.

5. In addition to the two basic endings EY and EYSE, three more elements are relevant to locatives, i.e. PUTHE, LO, and KKACI, which will briefly be discussed in this and two following sections. PUTHE is associated only with source and KKACI only with goal, whereas LO is ambivalent between source and goal, being related to source only when it is followed by PUTHE and to goal in default of PUTHE.

(20) a. hakkyo-EYSEPUTHE nolassta. '(He) started to play at
school-from played school.'
b. hakkyo-EYSEPUTHE kelessta. '(He) walked from school.'
school-from walked
Cf. a′. hakkyo-EYSE nolassta. '(He) played at school.'
school-at played
b′. hakkyo-EYSE kelessta. '(He) walked at school.'

As noticed in (20), in addition to the assertion of 'starting (from)', PUTHE has presupposition of separation of the theme's referent from the locative referent. For instance, (20a) presupposes that the theme's referent (e.g. *he*) is no longer at school. The traditional term *ablative* seems to be proper for the semantic content PUTHE carries. Martin (1975b:36) also uses the term ablative to describe J. *kara*. Notice, however, that *kara* incorporates source and direction which are separately lexicalized in Korean. Thus, for instance, *gakkoo-kara aruita* '(He) walked from school' corresponds to *hakkyo-EYSEPUTHE kelessta* (20b) and *hakkyo-LOPUTHE kelessta* '(He) walked from (the direction of) school'.

The use of EYSEPUTHE with locomotive verbs is somewhat unnatural, if not unacceptable, probably because of the redundancy of the ablative feature in this case. LOPUTHE 'from the direction of', to be discussed shortly, is perfectly natural with locomotive verbs, as shown in (21).

(21) a. ?hakkyo-EYSEPUTHE wassta.
school-from came
?'(He) came starting from school.'
b. hakkyo-LOPUTHE wassta. '(He) came from (the direction
school-from came of) school.'

PUTHE does occur by itself in functions other than locative, as in *John-PUTHE nolayhayssta* 'John sang first'. For the discussion of *kara* in such non-locative functions, see for example Inoue (1972) and Martin (1975b:45-46, 205-216).

6. The basic meaning of the ending LO is 'goal direction'. That it is goal is evidenced by the fact that when it occurs with a motional verb, the action of the verb is oriented toward, and not from, the LO locative referent. The fact that it is directional is observed by its inability to occur with nonmotional verbs, as illustrated in (22).

(22) *hakkyo-LO namnunta. *'(He) remains toward the school.'

school-toward remain
*san-LO phinta. *'(It) blooms toward the mountain.'
mountain-toward bloom

The directionality of LO is further observable in the examples in (23) where the source-oriented verbs *ttwita* 'to jump' and *ketta* 'to walk' are unnatural with EY but natural with LO.

(23) a. ?ttang-EY ttwiessta. '(He) jumped to the ground.'
ground-to jumped
a′. ttang-LO ttwiessta. '(He) jumped toward the ground.'
ground-toward jumped
Cf. ttang-EY ttwienayliessta. '(He) jumped to the ground.'
ground-to jump-descended
b. ?cip-EY kelessta. '(He) walked home.'
home-to walked
b′. cip-LO kelessta. '(He) walked homeward.'
home-toward walked
Cf. cip-EY kelekassta. '(He) walked home.'
home-to walk-went

On the other hand, all locomotive verbs and goal-oriented verbs may occur with both EY and LO, which means that the goal feature is persistent in LO.

(24) a. malwu-EY ancassta. '(He) sat on the floor.'
floor-on sat
b. malwu-LO ancassta '(He) sat to the side of the floor.'
floor-toward sat

From the foregoing observation, it is evident that LO has both [+goal] and [+direction], while EY has [+goal] and [−direction].

Probably Japanese *e* is the closest counterpart of LO, although they do not correspond to each other in many cases. Martin (1975b:46) describes J. *e* as target 'to' and direction 'toward', noting that *e* is replaced by *ni* for many speakers. He (ibid.:207) further quotes Isami as saying that "the difference between *e* and *ni* is that *ni* requires 'contact' where *e* merely expresses 'direction', so that if you want to say 'Proceed ahead', you would phrase it *mae e susume* and not *mae ni susume*". In Korean also *aph-EY ka* 'go ahead' and *aph-LO ka* 'proceed ahead' are distinguished. J. *sinbun e deru* 'it appears in the newspaper', however, corresponds only to K.

sinmun-EY nanta, and not to K. **sinmum-LO nanta.*

When LO is followed by the ablative morpheme PUTHE, the goal meaning is suppressed, just as EY loses its goal meaning in EYSE. LOPUTHE thus means ablative direction, as shown in (25).

(25) a. hakkyo-LOPUTHE wassta. '(He) came from (the direction
school-from came of) school.'
b. hakkyo-LOPUTHE kelessta. '(He) walked from (the direct-
school-from walked tion of) school.'

While LO contains goal meaning, LOPUTHE does not seem to have inherent source meaning, although more often than not source is implied in actual speech situations. In the first place, the animate markers *eykey* or *hanthey,* which occur in the goal direction, does not occur in the ablative direction, as in *kim-sensayng-LOPUTHE* (=*uloputhe*) 'from Mr. Kim'. This means that LOPUTHE is indifferent to the nature of locative referents, suggesting that LOPUTHE does not specify that the motion originates in the locative referent. Secondly, the ungrammaticality of (26b) also suggests that source meaning is not inherent in LOPUTHE.

(26) a. hakkyo-EYSEPUTHE nolassta. '(He) started to play at school.'
school-starting from played
b. *hakkyo-LOPUTHE nolassta.

For an extensive discussion on the relation between EY and LO, see D. Yang (1973b:32-36).

7. Korean and Japanese each have a form which denotes 'goal extent', i.e. K. EYKKACI and J. *made,* as illustrated in (27). EYKACCI is analyzed as EY (goal) and KKACI (extent), with EY more frequently deleted assigning its goal feature to KKACI.

(27) K. cip-EYSEPUTHE hakkyo-EYKKACI kelekassta.
home-from school-as far as walked
J. uti-*kara* gakkoo-*made* aruita.
home-from school-as far as walked
'(He) walked from home all the way to school.'

Existence of the extent feature in KKACI/*made* is clearly verified in the examples in (28) in which the action of sitting in (28a) may occur with these endings only when it indicates plurality, i.e. spatial extension of the action, whereas the sentences in (28b) are ungrammatical because the verbs are transient and not compatible with extension.

(28) a. K. *John-un malwu-EYKKACI ancassta.
John-TM hallway-as far as sat
J. *John-wa rooka-*made* suwatta.
John-TM hallway-as far as sat
*'John sat as far as the hallway.'
a'. K. haksayng-tul-un malwu-EYKKACI ancassta.
student-PL-TM hallway-as far as sat
J. gakusei-tati-wa rooka-*made* suwatta.
student-PL-TM hallway-as far as sat
'The students sat as far as the hallway.'
b. K. *sewul-EYKKACI tochakhayssta.
Seoul-as far as arrived
J. *Souru-*made* totyakusita.
Seoul-as far as arrived
*'(He) arrived as far as Seoul.'

One seemingly strange aspect is that, while non-motional action verbs can occur with PUTHE, they cannot occur with KKACI, as shown in (29).

(29) a. hakkyo-EYSEPUTHE wulessta.
school-from cried '(He) started to cry from school.'
b. *hakkyo-EYKKACI wulessta.
school-as far as cried '(He) cried all the way to school.'

Notice, however, that removal of PUTHE and KKACI from (29) still makes the status of grammaticality intact. In other words, the cooccurrence restriction exists between the verb and EYSE or EY, and PUTHE and KKACI have nothing to do with it. The ungrammatical sentence **hakkyo*-LOPUTHE *wulessta* '(He) cried from (the direction of) school' where PUTHE occurs with *wulta* eloquently supports the above statement, because LO cannot occur with *wulta*.

One real difference in cooccurrence is that while LOPUTHE is acceptable LOKKACI is not in locative expressions. As we see in (30), KKACI assumes only mental extent after LO, with the meaning 'even'.

(30) Hakkyo-LOKKACI kelessta. '(He) walked even to school.'
school-as far as walked

8. Before we discuss the nature of TA as occurring in EYTA, let us take a few examples first.

(31) a. kkoch-EYTA mul-ul cwunta. '(He) gives water to the
flower-to water-OM give flowers.'
b. twul-EYTA yel-ul pothaynta. '(He) adds ten to two.'
two-to ten-OM add
c. pap-EYTA ttek-kkaci mekessta. 'In addition to rice,
rice-adding to cake-even ate (he) ate even rice cake.'

There are two general positions in defining the nature of TA. The usual one is meaning-based, defining it as 'shift of location or state', 'placement', 'attachment', 'addition', etc. (e. g. Martin et al. 1967, C. Park 1968:245-7, Chung et al. 1976). I disagree with this position. In the first place, it cannot easily account for the grammaticality of sentences like those in (32a) and the ungrammaticality of those in (32b), which are contradictory to the definitions given above.

(32) a. sewul-EYTA phyenci-lul ssessta. '(He) wrote a letter to
seoul-to letter-OM wrote Seoul.'
hanul-EYTA nalliessta. '(He) flew it to the sky.'
sky-to flew
b. *kkoch-EYTA napi-ka puthessta. 'A butterfly rests on (Lit.
flower-to butterfly attached is attached to) the flower.
*uyca-EYTA ancassta. '(He) sat on the chair.'
chair-on sat
*pang-EYSE malwu-EYTA '(He) went out to the hall-
nakassta. way from the room.'
room-from hallway-to went out

The examples in (32) show that the semantic definitions do not even constitute a necessary condition, let alone a sufficient one.

Secondly, all the sentences in (31) and (32), including those in (32b), are grammatical without TA and retain the same semantic contents. This means that the semantic definitions given are associated not with TA but rather with EY.

Furthermore, the above position may not be able to account for the fact that, in spite of the contradiction in meanings with regard to the grammaticality as in (31) and (32), the native speaker can easily judge the allowance or nonallowance of TA without fail in each sentence. Thus, the meaning-based definition of TA does not capture the simple generalization that the native speaker has internalized.

The second position, which is (more or less) syntactically oriented, is taken by very few authors. For instance, S. Song (1976) calls TA a dative marker, and KEY (1960:154-5, 159) states that there are cases in which TA is attached to an indirect object of a verb or to objects which are enumerated in juxtaposition, to obtain more precise meaning. Admitting that the second position is basically on the right track, I will elaborate the syntactic properties associated with TA below.

When we hear someone saying "sewul-EYTA...", we immediately know that the subject is not the theme but an agent who causes the theme to be oriented to *Seoul,* as in *John-un sewul EYTA kacok-ul twuessta* 'John left (his) family in Seoul'. Needless to say, the causing action is represented by a transitive verb. TA, therefore, appears only when there are (a) an agent which is the subject, (b) a patient which functions as the theme, (c) a goal locative with the ending EY, and (d) a transitive verb which indicates the agent's action to cause the patient to be oriented to the goal locative. Notice that all these are syntactic features and there is no semantic feature inherent in TA. The transitive verbs that can occur with TA are semantically causative, but not all causative verbs can occur with TA. For instance, the verb *cwukita* 'to kill' which is causative semantically as well as morphologically denotes the action of the agent which directly affects the patient, without relating the patient to a third party, i.e. to a goal locative.

Verbs like *cwukita* cannot be compatible with a goal locative even in their intransitive forms, as we see in (33a). On the other hand, when an intransitive verb allows a goal locative, its transitive form also allows a goal locative, and vice versa, as illustrated in (33b, c).

(33) a. *John-i Bill-ul hakkyo-EYTA cwukiessta.
John-SM Bill-OM school-to/at killed
*Bill-i hakkyo-EY cwukessta.
Bill-SM school-to/at died

b. swul-i pyeng-EY namassta. 'Some wine is left in the bottle.'
wine-SM bottle-in be left
swul-ul pyeng-EYTA namkiessta. '(He) left some wine in the bottle.'
wine OM bottle-in left

c. kulim-ul pyek EYTA kelessta. '(He) hung the picture on the wall.'
picture-OM wall-on hung
kulim-i pyek-EY kelliessta. 'The picture is hung on the wall.'
picture-SM wall-on hung

(33) implies that TA has nothing to do with the cooccurrence restriction between a verb and a goal locative. It is the nature of the verb that is responsi-

ble for this and it is EY that is indicative of the goal locative. TA simply appears only when there is a goal locative and the verb is transitive (or semantically causative). Now, when there are a transitive verb and a goal locative, an agent and a patient are automatically presupposed whether they are overtly expressed or understood, e.g. *pyeng-EYTA namkiessta* '(He) left (something) in the bottle'. The reverse is not true, i.e. an agent and a patient do not presuppose a goal locative. All this means that the function of TA is simply to indicate the 'transitivity' of the cooccurring verb which in turn is responsible for the occurrences of a goal locative, an agent, and a patient. It is this simple generalization that the native speaker has internalized. Since the transitive feature is inherent in the verb, it is certainly redundant to specify it in the goal locative, which fact makes TA completely optional. The fact that TA refers to the transitivity of the verb is also verified in (34) where passive and causative constructions are compared.

(34) a. kay-EY (*TA) phal-ul mulliessta. '(He) got his arm bitten
dog-by arm-OM bitten by a dog.'
b. kay-EYTA phal-ul mulliessta. '(He) had a dog bite his
dog-to arm-OM cause to bite arm.'

As mentioned above, TA goes only with an EY (goal) locative, which fact is further verified in (35) where a goal is contrasted with a source, with the same type of transitive verb.

(35) a. mos-ul pyek-EYTA pakassta. '(He) nailed a nail on the
nail-OM wall-on nailed wall.'
b. mos-ul pyek-EYSE (*TA) ppayssta.
nail-OM wall-from pulled out
'(He) pulled out a nail from the wall.'

Incidentally, Japanese does not have any morpheme which corresponds to TA, which fact also suggests that TA does not have its own semantic content.

Let us now briefly look at the type of sentence we saw in (31c). Obviously, EYTA in this case is an idiomatic expression carrying the meaning 'in addition to'. A close observation will show that even here TA carries the transitivity of an understood abstract verb that means POTHAYTA, TEHATA, or KAHATA 'to add' which are all transitive. Thus, the underlying construction of (31c) would be something like (36).

(36) pap-EYTA *POTHAY-se* ttek-kkaci makessta.
rice-to add-and cake-even ate

'In addition to rice, (he) even ate rice cake.'

Notice that (36) is a complex sentence with two predicates. In the first sentence, the agent is understood and the patient is *ttek* 'rice cake' which is deleted in coreference to the subject of the main sentence. The general 'abbreviation' phenomenon including *-se* is discussed in Song (1976), so there is nothing strange here. With the deletion of the verb POTHAYTA and *-se*, their semantic contents are taken over by EYTA, which is idiomatized as 'in addition to'.

Notes

* The research here reported was assisted by a grant awarded by the Joint Committee on Korean Studies of the Social Science Research Council and the American Council of Learned Societies. This paper was presented at the 29th Annual Meeting of the Association for Asian Studies (March 1977, New York City). I gratefully acknowledge John Hinds, Gerald Mathias, and Zino Song for the valuable comments they made on this paper.

1. The Yale romanization system is followed in transcribing the Korean forms. Semantically speaking, a locative expression is understood to refer to mental or physical space at (in, on, to, toward, from, etc.) which the state or action of a theme (cf. Gruber 1965), an object (cf. Leech 1970), or a figure (cf. Talmy 1975) is oriented. Syntactically, it consists typically of a locational noun followed by an orientational ending, which is accompanied by a theme noun and a verb. In transitive constructions, an agent noun exists separately from the theme noun, as in *John-un ton-ul Mary-hanthey cwuessta* 'John gave money to Mary' where *John* is an agent, *ton* 'money' is a theme, *Mary* is a locational noun, and *cwuta* 'to give' is a verb. In this paper, a *locative* stands for a locational noun followed by an orientational ending.

   Phonological realizations of the Korean orientational endings are as follows:

   EY 'at, in, on, to, against, etc.': *eykey* (animate, formal), *hanthey* (animate, informal), *ey* (inanimate)

   EYSE 'at, in, on, from, etc.' : *eykeyse, hantheyse, eyse*

   EYSEPUTHE 'from': *eykeyseputhe, hantheyseputhe, eyseputhe*

   LO 'toward, to the direction of': *eykeylo, hantheylo, ulo* (after a consonant other than *l*), *lo* (elsewhere)

   LOPUTHE 'from the direction of': *uloputhe, loputhe* (both animate and inanimate)

   EYKKACI 'as far as, all the way to': *eykeykkaci, hantheykkaci, (ey)kkaci* (*kkaci* is more commonly used.)

   EYTA 'at, in, on, against, to, etc.': *eykeyta, hantheyta, eyta* (plain); *eykeytaka, hantheytaka, eytaka* (emphasis)

2. Irrelevant morpheme cuts are not made in either the Korean or Japanese expressions. The abbreviations used are: SM = subject marker, OM = object marker, TM = topic marker, and

PL = plural marker.

3. 'Motional' verbs are loosely defined here as any verb whose referent indicates movement of a theme from one place to another (cf. Gruber 1965 for more strict definitions).
4. Along with *ni*, Japanese also has *e*. While *ni* is more productively used in a variety of functions just like Korean EY, the syntactic function of *e* is limited usually to locative expressions. *E* is interchangeable with *ni* in many cases (e.g. Martin 1963b:63). Martin (1975b:36) assumes that 'the dative of direction' *ni* is in complementary distribution with the 'ablative' *e*. We will take up only *ni* for the sake of simplicity.
5. Motional verbs like those in (6a) include *kuru* 'to come', *otiru* 'to fall', *okuru* 'to send', *yaru* 'to give', *ireru* 'to insert', and *nageru* 'to throw'. In Japanese also, verbs belonging to (6b) are usually classed as 'place', as against 'direction' (e.g. Kenkyusha 1974), which include *sizumu* 'to sink', *tuku* 'to reach', *noru* 'to ride', *suwaru* 'to sit', *tatu* 'to stand', *kaku* 'to write', and *oku* 'to put'. Martin (1963b:65) uses the term 'inactive' to refer to such verbs as those which occur in (6c) and (6d), including *sumu* 'to live', *tutomeru* 'to be employed', and *aru* 'to exist'.
6. Both K. EY and J. *ni* have many other functions in addition to locative expressions, such as time, standard, proportion, influence, operation, reference, agent, cause, etc. (cf. Martin et al. 1967 and Kenkyusha 1974). Since EY and *ni* in these functions do not enter into direct constructions with locative verbs, they do not have any distinct goal meaning, although certainly some range of meaning is shared by all the occurrences of EY and *ni*. Shin (1976:26-27) defines EY as 'adherence' to include all the functions of EY. This subject is not the concern of the present paper.
7. A complete coverage of locative expressions would have to include the so-called object marker LUL whose major semantic feature is *dimension* as Kuno (1973:97) correctly points out, e.g. *hanul-LUL nanta* '(It) flies through the sky'. According to Kuno, NP-*o* in Japanese indicates that the motion takes place covering the entire dimension of the NP continually and unidirectionally. I wonder if *undoozyoo-o aruita* '(I) walked around the field' necessarily implies continuity and unidirectionality. Furthermore, Kuno states that NP-*ni* indicates the location at which the motion designated by the verb takes place, as in *sora-ni* tobu 'to fly to the sky' and *sora-de tobu* 'to fly in the sky'. In our conception, *tobu* is a verb with the [±2nd locus] feature. In the first case, it is [+2nd locus] in that the theme's referent moves from a certain place to the sky, whereas in the second case it is [−2nd locus] in that action of the theme's referent takes place within the locative referent.

Reprinted from *Eoneohag* (Seoul National University) 2:73-98 (1977).

16. STRATEGIES OF INDIRECTION IN KOREAN

1. The aim of this paper is (a) to discuss, in this section, some major proposals and issues that are associated with the research on what Heringer (1972) and others call indirect speech acts (or ISAs for short), and (b) to observe, in Sections 2 and 3, the kinds of linguistic devices available in Korean for the strategies of indirection.[1]

Austin (1970) and Searle (1976) make it clear that all utterances not only serve to carry propositional content but perform specific actions through having specific utterance forces. Austin proposes three kinds of acts that are simultaneously performed in saying something: locutionary act (the utterance of a sentence with determinate sense and reference); illocutionary act (the making of a statement, request, offer, promise, etc. in uttering a sentence, by virtue of the conventional force associated with it); and perlocutionary act (the bringing about of secondary, circumstantial, and largely non-conventional effects on the audience by means of uttering the sentence). Although the three kinds of acts are all relevant to the speaker-hearer perspective (and, marginally, to the speaker-referent perspective), the most significant utterance forces in communication are illocutionary ones, which are conventionally linked with various illocutionary force indicating devices of sentences. Thus, the term 'speech acts' frequently refers only to illocutionary acts.

It is due to the sensitive human emotion involved in communication in interpersonal situations that ISAs are called for and performed universally across cultures as strategies to tone down, mitigate or hedge utterance forces, i.e. strategies of indirection. This is precisely because language has two basic functions: transmission of meanings and evoking of emotions. That is, language is a means not only of transmitting knowledge, information and other various meanings through the propositional content, but also of regulating interpersonal relations through performing various types of speech acts.

Stimulated initially by Sadock's (1970, 1971) notions of 'whimperative' and 'queclarative' and Gordon and Lakoff's (1971) 'conversational postulates', linguists and linguistic philosophers such as Heringer (1972), Searle (1975), Van der Auwera (1980) and many others have further developed the notion of indirection in language under the rubric of ISAs. According to Searle (1975), (a) ISAs are those complex illocutionary acts which consist of a 'primary' illocutionary act that is performed through a 'secondary' illocutionary act (of a different type); and (b) the hearer gets to the 'primary' illocutionary meaning through a number of inferential steps on the basis of the literal meaning, the context, the general pattern of speech act performance (à la Searlian speech act theory based on felicity and other conditions), and conversational principles (à la Grice 1975). That is, when the hearer decides that the literal illocution is irrelevant in the given context, he assumes that the speaker is cooperating and that his utterance must have some relevance, i.e. the speaker must have meant something else which is retrievable because it must be related to the literal meaning in one of a finite number of ways. For example, observe the utterances in (1) and (2).

(1) a. Could you open the door?
    b. Open the door.
    c. I order/request you to open the door.

(2) a. SPEAKER A: Let's go to the movies tonight.
    b. SPEAKER B: I have to study for an exam.

In (la), which is a conventionalized ISA form, the primary illocutionary act (a request) is performed through the secondary illocutionary act (a question). While the speech act of request through (la) is an ISA in that the primary meaning is derived from the corresponding literal meaning through inferential steps, (1b) and (1c) are regarded as performing 'direct' speech acts (or DSAs for short) of request. Similarly, in answer to (2a), Speaker B performs the speech act of rejection through making a statement, hence another case of ISAs. In contrast to (la) which is an instance of conventionalized or derived ISAs, (2b) is a case of non-conventional or allusive ISAs.

Heringer (1972), Searle (1975), and other ISA researchers describe the relation between primary and secondary meaning in terms of felicity conditions (or FCs for short), i.e. specifications for appropriate usage. Heringer (ibid.), for example, claims that only those non-direct speech acts which are accounted for in terms of FCs are ISAs. The ISA status of (1a) is confirmed by its being a question about the ability of the hearer to perform the action requested in the speech act, because this ability is claimed to be a FC, i.e. a preparatory condition, for a request.[2] On the other hand, a non-conventionalized form like (2b) would bear no relation to a FC, but expounds a reason for the action (i.e. rejection) performed by the speech act. Heringer would not consider (2b) an ISA, although Searle (1975) calls such utterances ISAs.

In (3) are compared the FCs on requests, warnings, and commissives (promises) à la Searle (1969, 1975). S stands for the speaker and H the hearer.

3)

FCs	**Requests**	**Warnings**	**Commissives**
Propositional content	A future act (A) of H	A future event (E)	A future act (A) of S
Preparatory	1. S believes H can do A	1. S thinks E will occur & is not in H's interest	1. S is able to perform A
	2. It is not obvious that H would do A without being asked	2. S thinks it is not obvious to H that E will occur	2. H wants S to perform A
Sincerity	S wants H to do A	S believes E is not in H's best interest	S intends to do A
Essential	Counts as an attempt to get H to do A	Counts as an undertaking that E is not in H's best interest	Counts as the undertaking by S of an obligation to do A

Based on Anscombre (1977), Diller (1978), Searle (1969, 1975) and others, speech acts (SAs) may be subclassified as in (4).

(4) SA — DSA (= primitive SA) — flat sentence
　　　　　　　　　　　　　　　＼explicit performative
　＼Non-direct — ISA (= non-primitive SA) — derived (= conventional)
　　　　　　　　　　　　　　　　　　　　＼allusive (= non-conventional)
　　　　　＼ironies
　　　　　＼metaphors

The foregoing discussions are intended to present an outline of ISA research. There are, however, many theoretical issues on which scholars differ in their views, the discussion of which is not the purpose of this paper. Suffice it to summarize the most outstanding current issues in (5) (cf. Van der Auwera 1980).

(5) a. Are two layers of illocution (i.e. literal and derived) absolutely required to be present for an utterance to be called an ISA?
b. Is the illocutionary type switch (e.g. request through question) obligatory?
c. What is the relation between ISAs and conversational implicatures? Are the two concepts the same or different? Is one a subset of the other?
d. Is treating ISA phenomena in a Gricean way appropriate? Are Grice's cooperative principle and maxims sufficient for the derivation of ISA meanings?
e. Is referring the accounts of ISA phenomena to felicity conditions (FCs) on SAs correct?
f. Are explicit performative sentences ISAs or DSAs?
g. Are non-conventional (or allusive) non-direct SAs really ISAs?
h. Are conventional formulae (e.g. *Could you* pass the salt?) idioms or implicatures?
i. How are ISAs related to politeness?

Some of the issues presented above are interrelated, so that a solution to one may be applicable to another. Although it is not the intention of this paper to look into these per se, some of them will inevitably be brought up for comments as they become relevant to the discussion of Korean data.

2. In order to see how indirect speech acts are performed in Korean, observe the examples given in (6) through (11).[3]

(6) a. Ssuleyki chiwu-sey-yo.
b. Ssuleyki chiwu-l kes ul myenglyenghay-yo.

(7) a. Ssuleyki com chiwu-sey-yo.
b. Ssuleyki com chiw-e cwu-sey-yo.

(8) a. Ssuleyki com chiwu-si-keyss-eyo?
b. Ssuleyki com chiw-e cwu-si-keyss-eyo?
c. Ssuleyki com chiw-e cwu-si-l swu iss-usey-yo?
d. Ssuleyki com chiw-e cwu-si-l swu iss-usi-keyss-eyo?

(9) a. Ssuleyki com chiw-e cwu-si-ki palay-yo.
b. Ssuleyki com chiw-e cwu-si-myen coh-keyss-eyo.
c. Ssuleyki com chiw-e cwu-si-ess-umyen coh-keyss-eyo.

(10) a. Ssuleyki chiwu-l kes.
b. Ssuleyki chiwu-si-la-ko-yo.
c. Ssuleyki com chiw-e cwu-si-ess-umyen hay-yo.
d. Ssuleyki com chiw-e cwu-si-ess-umyen coh-keyss-nun-tey-yo.

(11) a. Onul ssuleyki cha o-nun nal i-yey-yo.
b. Cip i tto kwucilkwucilhay-ci-ess-kwun-yo.

Ignoring, for the moment, the honorifics used, notice that all the sentences in the examples, when uttered, share the speaker's communicative intention to request the hearer to take out the garbage, the differences appearing in their superficial linguistic forms and associated degrees of utterance forces in the request. It is commonly held that sentences like (6a) and (6b) have a *direct* request force with their exact, literal meaning, the only difference being that (6a) is a DSA of the implicit performative type and (6b) a DSA of the explicit performative type. Both (7a) and (7b) are in an imperative form, but (7a) has a hedging word *com* 'just (lit. a small amount)' and (7b) two hedges, i.e. *com* and the benefactive auxiliary verb *cwu* 'for me (lit. give)'. Through uttering such interrogative sentences as those in (8), one can perform SAs of a request. Notice that the sentences contain hedges like *com, cwu, keyss* 'intend', and *-l swu iss* 'can' as an integral part of the indirect request. All the three declarative sentences in (9), along with the accompanying hedges, can be used to perform a SA of request. (9a) contains the nominalization and (9b) the conditionalization of the propositional content, together with the main verbs that denote (the speaker's) wishes. Notice in (9c) that the conditionalized clause is in the past form, although the action is yet to be taken. The past tense here functions as a hedging device for the utterance to be rendered indirect, i.e. soft. All the sentences in (10) are elliptical ones. Unlike (6b), (10a) is a nominalized clause which lacks the main predicate. As in *No parking* in English, it has a considerably strong force of request, although the force is somewhat indirectly expressed and is not as strong as that of the corresponding sentence with the so-called performative verb of order, i.e. (6b). (10b) consists of a quotative complementation without a main verb of saying; (10c) is not provided with a full-fledged verb in the main clause; and (10d) is merely a conjunctive clause, with the main clause elided altogether. Finally, (11a) and (11b) are cases of allusive or non-conventional ISAs.

In a broad pragmatic definition that a SA which tones down or hedges the illocutionary force of a direct way of saying by means of various linguistic devices is an ISA, all the examples in the above, except perhaps for those in (6), may be called ISAs, though with different degrees of indirection and different kinds of presupposition involved. This broad pragmatic approach to the strategies of indirection seems to be useful in a way, especially in view of the notion of communicative competence, in that the overall linguistic devices in a language that are associated with indirection can be captured in a patterned way and accounted for in terms of the function the language serves (e.g. in terms of politeness strategies).

Narrower definitions of the notion of ISAs are maintained by most ISA researchers, as briefly outlined in the previous section. Probably the most widely held view is the so-called literal force hypothesis (or LFH for short), as described in Levinson (1983:263-264). LFH claims that the notion of ISAs makes sense only if we subscribe to the notion of a *literal force*. i.e. to the view that illocutionary force is built into sentence form in such a way that: (Rule a) explicit performatives have the force named by the performative verb in the matrix clause, as in (6b), and (Rule b) otherwise, the major sentence-types (i.e. the declarative, interrogative, propositive, imperative, etc.) have the forces traditionally associated with them (i.e. stating, questioning, proposing, ordering or requesting, etc.) as in (6a) and other examples (cf. Gazdar 1981, Levinson ibid.). It is claimed that any sentence that fails to have the force associated with it by Rule *a* or Rule *b* has in fact the rule-associated force as its *literal force,* but has an additional, inferred *indirect force.* Thus any usages other than those in accordance with Rule *a* or Rule *b* are said to be ISAs.

Unlike the broader definition that I presented earlier, LFH requires that a sentence must necessarily have two layers or types of illocution for it to be qualified to be an ISA (e.g. a literal statement and an inferred indirect request). According to this standard line, the utterances given in (7), as well as many expressions like those in (12), will not be considered ISAs simply because in them both the literal and inferred force happen to belong to the same illocutionary type.

(12) a. Sensayng-nim un cwumusi-nun kes kath-ayo.
'I think the professor is sleeping.'
b. Nai ka myech i-n ci mul-e po-a-to toy-yo?
'Can I ask you how old you are?'

If the speaker knows that the professor is sleeping and yet utters (12a), it should certainly be an indirect way of saying. Similarly, it is not difficult to imagine that (12b) has two question forces (literal and inferred).

Another point to be made with regard to LFH is that no other hedging devices than the basic sentence-type forms are regarded as relevant to the decision of ISAhood. It seems to me that LFH in which the notion of ISAs is limited to basic sentence-types fails to capture the significant pragmatic and communicative fact that all illocutionary force mitigating devices are essential to the strategies of indirection and politeness in interpersonal encounters.

A final comment on LFH concerns its assumption that the rule-associated force is present as a literal force in any ISA. In actuality, however, many utterances are conventionalized or nearly idiomatized formulae as indirect ways of speaking (e.g. *How about having lunch together?; Would you please open the window?; Why not go now?*↘) In our examples, (10a), (10b), and probably (8a) and (8b) may only be interpreted as requests. Such a unique interpretation will particularly be the case if we introduce proper phonological stress and intonation patterns in uttering sentences. Authors like Van der Auwera (1980) claim that such utterances are nothing but DSAs for request, etc., which is a fatal blow to LFH. This issue does not seem to be a significant one if the notion of ISAs is a relative one and is broadly defined as those SAs which tone down or hedge illocutionary forces.

Needless to say, there are various philosophical and linguistic strengths that LFH and other standard varieties of ISA research have. In view of the aforementioned difficulties associated with them, however, I would like in the following section to present, albeit perfunctorily, the overall linguistic devices for indirection in Korean within the broader definition.

3. On the basis of the data I have encountered, it is proposed, as a working hypothesis, that there are hierarchically structured strategies of communicative indirection, as presented in (13).

(13) Communicative strategies for indirection

1. Linguistic
   - Structural (Conventional)
     - Phonological
     - Lexical
     - Syntactico-semantic
   - Implicational (Non-conventional)
     - Situational
     - Discoursal
2. Non-linguistic (i.e. Non-verbal)

In many cases, the strategies classified in (13) closely interact or 'conspire' to effect various degrees of indirection, as will be seen shortly.

For a number of reasons that do not concern us here, honorifics are not included as a part of Korean indirect speech acts despite the fact that they denote social deictics and thus are crucially functional in the expression of politeness (cf. Cho 1982). Suffice it here to point out that honorifics are grammaticalized or lexicalized elements that denote socio-culturally constrained power and solidarity factors. For instance, one is bound to use the most deferential addressee honorifics to one's adult teacher or social superior even when the most direct speech is required. Therefore, ISAs and honorifics are to be regarded as two different dimensions.

Non-linguistic strategies of indirection are included in (13), since, as an integral part of the human communicative system, gestures, facial expressions and other types of non-verbal behavior are used to tone down illocutionary forces. Bowing while greeting people, nodding while listening, covering one's mouth with a hand while talking, avoidance of eye-contact while apologizing, standing straight when talking to a social superior, and many other non-linguistic expressions function as hedges in communication. In a relatively vertical society like Korea, non-verbal strategies are particularly significant and extensively developed to reflect power and solidarity in interpersonal communication (e.g. Kim 1975, Park 1979, Sohn 1983a).

The most typical and universal phonological devices used for indirection strategies include softening intonation, rhythms, soft voice, and slow speech. Certain intonation patterns in Korean also contribute to indirection, as illustrated in (14) where declarative sentences are rendered to carry an illocutionary force of wondering, negative conjecture, or indirect threatening due only to the characteristic intonation pattern.

(14) a. Nay ka ku yeca lul manna-n-ta. ∼→
'I wonder if it is a good idea to meet her.'

b. Yongho ka cikak ul ha-keyss-ta. ∼→
'I don't think Yongho will come to school late.'

c. Ney ka na lul ttayli-ess-keyss-ta. ∼→
'You hit me—I will do something about it.'

Lexical indirection strategies include: (a) the use of metaphors, which abound in Korean, as in *say pal uy phi* 'blood on a bird's leg' referring to a very small quantity, *kwukmul* 'soup' to favors, *cwuk ssu-ta* 'make porridge' to complete failure, and *sayk ankyeng* 'tinted glasses' to suspicion; (b) the use of euphemistic expressions, such as *kasum* 'chest' for *phyey* 'lung', *hwacangsil* 'make-up room' for *pyenso* 'toilet', *kisa* 'technician' for *wuncenswu* 'driver', *wuli cip salam* 'person in our house' for *na uy che* 'my wife', and *maum ey tul-ta* 'come to my mind' for *cho-ta* 'like, good', and *enu pun* 'which person' for *nwukwu* 'who'; (c) the use of Sino-Korean terms and various loan words, as in *siksa* for *pap* 'meal', *che* for *anay* 'wife', *sengmyeng* for *ilum* 'name', *yenlyeng* for *nai* 'age', *swucok* for *phal tali* 'limbs', and *Mr. Kim* for *Kim-ssi;* and (d) the use of technical terms, such as *hangmun* 'anus' and *paypyen* 'excretion'. As R. Lakoff (1973:199) states regarding technical terms in English, use of such 'indirect' lexical items is intended to divorce the subject from its emotional impact by avoiding direct reference.

As regards syntactico-semantic strategies of indirection in Korean, the following include the most common ones.

(a) Passivization, which usually gives a sense of distance between the speaker and the hearer due to the shading of impersonalization that results from this syntactic process.

(15) a. Siksa ka cwunpitoy-ess-eyo.
'Your meal is ready.'
Cf. Siksa lul cwunpihay-ss-eyo.
'I have prepared your meal.'.
b. Ku pun i olh-ta-ko sayngkaktoy-eyo.
'It is considered that he is right.'
Cf. Ku pun i olh-ta-ko sayngkakhay-yo.
'I think he is right.'

(b) Nominalization or complementation, followed on the surface by a main verb which is a member of a certain determinable set of verbs including cogitatives, the copula, the existential verb, and verbs of wishing. Apart from their literal meanings, such main verbs can also function as a device for indirection to express politeness not to impose on the hearer, while giving him options. Nominalization or complementation is a productive mechanism for ISAs, attesting to the existence of the close tie between syntax and pragmatics. It seems that to nominalize or complementize a sentence is pragmatically correlated with the hedging or toning down of the illocutionary force of the sentence, as if we block the flow of water by means of a dike or surround a house with a fence so that view from outside is deterred. Here, a dike or a fence is comparable to a nominalizer or a complementizer.

(16) a. Ce nun ka-l ke yey-yo.
'I am (probably) going.'
Cf. Ce nun ka-yo.
'I am going.'

b. Key ka nemu yalmiwu-n kes iss-ci-yo?
'She is really nasty, isn't she?'
Cf. Key ka nemu yalmiw-eyo.
'She is really nasty.'

c. Ce-huy nun pyel il eps-nun kes kath-ayo.
'(I think) we are pretty good.'
Cf. Ce-huy nun pyel il eps-eyo.
'We are pretty good.'

d. Ha-l swu iss-ta-ko sayngkakhay-yo.
'(I think) I can do it.'
Cf. Ha-l swu iss-eyo.
'I can do it.'

Similarly, such nominal or complement constructions as *-nun insang i-ta* 'I have the impression that...', *sang siph-ta* 'it appears that...', *moyang i-ta* 'it looks like', and *ko po-n-ta* 'I consider that...' belong here, as long as the underlying communicative intention of the speaker remains the same as the corresponding unhedged utterances.

Indirect questions are asked by means of indirect question complementation, as illustrated in (17).

(17) a. Cikum myech si i-n-ci molu-keyss-eyo.
'I wonder what time it is.'
Cf. Cikum myech si yey-yo. 'What time is it?'

b. Sensayng-nim un encey ttena-si-nun-ci malssumhay-cwu-si-keyss-eyo?
'When are you leaving—Can you tell me?'
Cf. Sensayng-nim un encey ttena-sey-yo?
'When are you leaving?'

(c) Subordination, followed by a member of a determinable set of main clause verbs.

(18) a. Kkok wa cwu-si-myen kamsaha-keyss-eyo.
'I would appreciate it if you could come by all means.'
Cf. Kkok wa cwu-sey-yo.
'Please come by all means.'

b. Koynhi simlye lul kkichi-e tuli-e coysonghay-yo.
'I am sorry to have bothered you.'
Cf. Koynhi simlye lul kkichi-e tuli-ess-eyo.
'I have bothered you.'

(d) Syntactico-semantic euphemization.

(19) a. Yensey ka ettehkey toy-si-ess-eyo?
'How old are you?'
Cf. Yensey ka myech i-sey-yo?
'What is your age?'
b. Sengham i ettehkey toy-sey-yo?
'What is your name?'
Cf. Sengham i mues i-yey-yo?

Notice that the pronouns *mues* 'what' and *'myech* 'how many' are changed to the adverb *ettehkey* 'how', the copula *i* to the inchoative *toy,* and, in one case, the present tense to the past.

(e) Use of softening adverbials or delimiters, as illustrated by *com* 'just', *mue* 'what else', *ina, ilato* 'approximately, or something', *eccenci* 'somehow', *taso* 'more or less', *kuce, kunyang* 'just', *hoksi* 'by any change', *selma* 'possibly', *ceypal* 'please', *kkok* 'surely', *kyonhi* 'for no reason', *cinceng ulo* 'sincerely', and *cengmal* 'indeed'.

(20) a. Com tul-e o-sey-yo.
'Please come in.'
Cf. Tul-e o-sey-yo.
'Come in.'
b. Kuce kuleh-ci-yo, mue.
'I am OK, what else?'
Cf. Kuce kuleh-ci-yo.
'I am OK.'
c. Hoksi cey ka cal moshay-ss-na-yo?
'Did I make a mistake by any chance?'
Cf. Cey ka cal moshay-ss-na-yo?

(f) Main clause or predicate ellipsis, which is illustrated in the sentences in (10). Further examples follow.

(21) a. Ce nun ka-po-a-ya keyss-up-ni-ta man.
'I think I must go now (but).'
Cf. Ce nun ka po-a-ya keyss-up-ni-ta (man ettehkey ha-si-

keyss-eyo?)
'I think I must go now (but what are you going to do?).'

b. Eti lul ilehkey ilccik?
'Where are you (going) this early?'
Cf. Eti lul ilehkey ilccik ka-sey-yo?
'Where are you going this early?'

c. Na nun amu-kes to molu-n-ta-ko.
'I don't know anything about it.'
Cf. Na nun amu-kes to molu-n-ta-ko ha-ci anh-ni?
'Don't I say that I don't know anything about it?'

d. Apeci nun an ka-si-n-ta-nikka.
'I told you that my father is not going.'
Cf. Apeci nun an ka-si-n-ta-nikka tto mut-ni?
'Are you asking again? I already told you that my father is not going.'

In general, the communicative intention of the speaker who uses an ellipsis strategy is to avoid sharp and direct confrontation with the hearer by toning down his assertive or questioning force while giving options to the hearer regarding the final decision or judgement.

(g) Use of modals, such as *keyss* (intention/conjecture), *ci* (suspective) *kwun* (apperceptive), *ka* (indirect question), and *na* (indirect question).[4]

(22) a. Al-keyss-eyo.
'I think I know.'
Cf. Al-ayo.
'I know.'

b. I kes un elma-ci-yo?
'How much is this? (I wonder).'
Cf. I kes un elma-yey-yo?
'How much is this?'

c. Ku pun i ka-si-na-yo?
'Is he going?'
Cf. Ku pun i ka-sey-yo?
'Is he going?'

(h) Use of auxiliary verbs, such as the benefactive *cwu* 'for me (lit. give)' and the verb of try *po* 'try (lit. see)'. Examples of *cwu* were already given.

(25) I kes com capswu-e po-sey-yo.
'Please try this.'

Cf. I kes com capswu-sey-yo.
'Please eat this.'

(i) Use of negative questions.

(24) Te tu-si-ci anh-keyss-eyo?
'Won't you have some more?'
Cf. Te tu-si-keyss-eyo?
'Will you have some more?'

Negative questions sound more polite than their positive counterparts when the propositional content (in this case, 'having some more') is to the advantage of the hearer. If the content is not in the interest of the hearer, a negative question, even though it is an indirect way of questioning, is less polite than the positive one.

(j) Use of utterance introducers, such as *kulssey-yo* 'well', *ce-yo* 'by the way', *kulentey-yo* 'by the way', and *isscanha-yo* 'by the way'.

(k) Use of sentence-type endings. This is the most productive strategy of indirection in Korean. As discussed earlier, most ISA researchers are concerned only with sentence types, which are widely utilized as ISAs in any language due to the basic, distinct and strong illocutionary forces associated with them. For example, as Levinson (1983:264) puts it, the imperative is rarely used to issue requests in English. Declarative and interrogative sentences are widely used instead. Since the space does not allow us to discuss the whole range of the phenomena, only a few examples will be given below, in addition to the ones we have already observed.

(25) a. Mun com tat-keyss-ni? (request)
'Can you close the door?'
b. Kath-i ka-si-l-kka-yo? (proposing)
'Shall we go together?'
c. Ku pun i totwukcil ul hay-ss-keyss-eyo? (negative statement)
'Do you think he did the stealing? — I don't think so.'

(26) a. Chayk com pilli-p-si-ta. (request)
'Let me borrow your book.'
b. Nayli-p-si-ta. (request)
'Let me get off.'

(27) a. Nayil twu si ey chwulpalha-p-ni-ta. (request)
'You are to leave at two o'clock tomorrow.'
b. Yeki nun mos tul-e ka-sey-yo. (request)
'You are not to enter.'

(28) a. Ese o-sey-yo. (welcome)
'Welcome (lit. come quickly).'
b. Annyenghi ka-sey-yo. (farewell)
'Goodbye (lit. go peacefully).'

Implicational or non-conventional strategies of indirection are based on shared knowledge about the real world and specific situational or discoursal contexts as well as on shared ability of rational inference between the interlocutors. Examples of situational indirection were given in (11), while those of discoursal indirection were discussed in connection with (2b). These examples are rather universal across cultures. There are, however, many culture-specific implicatures too. In Korean society, the so-called *nwunchi* 'reading other's mind' is considerably developed due probably to the hierarchical and collectivistic value orientations of the people. ISAs through *nwunchi* are productively performed in all walks of the society (e.g. Kim 1975, Park 1979, Sohn 1983a).

Both developmentally and in actual language use, the strongest motivation for the use of indirect speech acts is no doubt the need for politeness expression, in that politeness is a condition for effective communication as well as for smooth interpersonal relationships, and the function of ISAs is to tone down utterance forces. Strategies of indirection and those of politeness are not the same concepts, however. If a SA is in the interest of the hearer, a DSA may be politer than an ISA. I will not go into this topic here.

Notes

1. This paper is a revised version of the one I presented at the Third International Conference on Korean Linguistics held at Bochum, West Germany, in August 1984. The paper is based on my research in Seoul for one summer month in 1984 under a Korea Research Foundation grant that I received through the Center for Korean Studies of the University of Hawaii.
2. Similarly, the following ISAs are all relatable to and accounted for in terms of the FCs of requests (cf. Dillon 1977:109-111):
   I want you to take out the garbage.
   Can you take out the garbage?
   Are you willing to take out the garbage?
   Are you planning to take out the garbage today?

Do you intend to take out the garbage today?
Are you going to take out the garbage today?
Will you take out the garbage today?

Although Dillon (ibid.) states that the last utterance in the above is not an indirect or "softened" request, I include it here because it is a request through a question and can be relatable to FCs in one way or another.

3. The Yale romanization system will be followed in transcribing Korean expressions.
4. The so-called "double modality" element *ta-n-ta* (e.g. *na nun an ka-n-ta-n-ta* 'the situation doesn't allow me to go') and the use of the past tense in the present or future context (e.g. (9c)) may be grouped with the use of modals. Another case which might be included here is indirect requests of the type illustrated below, where the lack of the infinitive suffix (*-e*) renders the sentence indirect:
   Taum muncang ul pat-a ssu-la. 'Dictate the following sentences.'
   Cf. Taum muncang ul pat-a ss-*e*-la.

Reprinted from *Festschrift for Professor Hyonggi Kim*. 679-697 (1985). Taejon, Korea: Chungnam National University Press.

CHAPTER 3
HISTORICAL AND COMPARATIVE STUDIES

17. THE STATE OF THE ART IN THE HISTORICAL-COMPARATIVE STUDIES OF JAPANESE AND KOREAN

Encompassing most relevant works that have appeared to date, this article examines and evaluates as objectively as possible various old and new hypotheses regarding the genetic affiliation of Japanese and Korean. The first part of the article (Sections 1-6) concerns the works that relate the two languages to Altaic or Austronesian, touching briefly on the Tamil substratum hypothesis at the end. It is observed that the Altaic hypothesis is the most persuasive in view of the data presently available. The second part (Sections 7-8) reviews the works dealing with the relationship between Japanese and Korean. It appears undeniable that the two languages are genetically related sister languages. The article closes with some brief suggestions for future research.

1. The lack of historical records revealing the roots of Japanese and Korean has led many scholars to infer the genetic affiliation of the two languages from various degrees of linguistic resemblances, often bolstered by archaeological or ethnological evidence.[1] Unfortunately earlier written language data that can be employed for comparative work are scarce and cannot be traced far back. Old Japanese has useful written records only from the eighth century onward, for example, *Kojiki* (712), *Nihon Shoki* (720), and *Man'yōshū* (*circa* 759), whereas Old Korean suffers from an extreme paucity of records in that some oldest language fragments are available only in the literature of the eleventh century onward, such as *Kyunyŏ chŏn* (1075), *Kyerim Yusa* (1103-1104), *Samguk Sagi* (1145), and *Samguk Yusa* (1285). Worse still, much of the earlier vocabulary has been either irretrievably lost or obscured by succeeding waves of linguistic

contacts, including a massive influx of Chinese loanwords.

In the lack of any such clear-cut evidence in establishing the genealogy of Japanese and Korean (such as that used, for instance, when designating both English and German as Indo-European), innumerable attempts have been made to relate the two languages to such diverse language families as the Indo-European, the Tibeto-Burman, the Dravidian, the Altaic, or the Austronesian. Many of these attempts are based on accidental lexical resemblances, linguistic borrowings, universal typological features, or anthropological similarities. Many others seem to be on sounder ground, but are methodologically lax or are of insufficient scope.[2]

2. The most persuasive hypothesis yet proposed, in terms of the current data and methodological refinements, is the Altaic one. By this hypothesis Japanese (including the Ryūkyū dialect) and Korean belong to the Altaic language family, which is composed mainly of Turkic, Mongolian, and Manchu-Tungus groups that range widely in the regions to the west and the north of China.[3] Ramstedt (1952, 1957) deals with the entire field of Altaic comparative linguistics, while the linguistic unity among the Altaic languages is quite convincingly demonstrated by Poppe (1960), who reconstructs the proto-Altaic phonology, morphology, and lexicon of some 570 roots based on regular sound correspondences attested among many of these languages and partly on the earlier etymological contributions of Ramstedt and others.[4] According to the Altaic hypothesis, the dominant original Japanese and Koreans were Altaic people who migrated to Japan and Korea, bringing with them the basic elements of their languages.

The first serious Japanese comparative work is that of Boller (1857), who, on the basis of a limited number of phonological correspondences, advanced many reasons in favor of the Japanese relationship to the Altaic. Pröhle (1916-1917), Ramstedt (1924), and others have pushed the frontier forward to a considerable extent mainly in terms of data. In a number of valuable works, Murayama (1957, 1962a, 1962b, 1963, 1966a, 1966b, etc.) has made remarkable contributions to the Altaic hypothesis of Japanese. In particular, Murayama (1957) is an attempt to deal with grammatical elements, relating, for instance, Old Japanese attributive adjective inflection *-ki* to proto-Altaic genitive or general referent marker **-ki* and Old Japanese accusative marker *wo* to Manchu *-be* and proto-Tungus **-wa/*-we*.[5] It has been found that in certain respects Japanese is closer to Manchu-Tungus than to any other languages. The previously mentioned accusative marker correspondence is one example, in that Mongolian and Turkish have nothing comparable. Some other examples include Old

Japanese prosecutive case marker *yuri* 'along, by' which corresponds to proto-Tungus **-duli* consisting of locative **-du* and prosecutive **-li,* Old Japanese *yo* '4' which corresponds to proto-Tungus **dö* '4' (Old Japanese *y-* and proto-Tungus **d-* are a regular correspondence), and Old Japanese *nana* '7' which corresponds to proto-Tungus **nadan* '7'.

Ozawa (1968) attempts to establish etymologies for 214 Japanese lexical items (including 75 nouns and 116 verbs) by comparing them with those in Mongolian languages.

Miller (1971) is probably the most enthusiastic supporter of the Altaic hypothesis of Japanese. He deals rather extensively with certain striking cases of phonological, lexical, and some morphological correspondences among Japanese, Korean, and Altaic languages, looking mainly into the Altaic elements in the Old Japanese texts surviving from the Nara period (710-794).[6] Specifically, he advances evidence relating a total of some one hundred Japanese lexical items with proto-Altaic. In general, Miller is more concerned with establishing phonological correspondences and 'sound laws' obtaining between Japanese and Altaic languages than with the etymological investigation of individual items. He, thus, endeavors to trace the Old Japanese phonemes back to the eighteen different proto-Altaic consonants and eighteen proto-Altaic long and short vowels that Poppe (1960) has reconstructed, demonstrating a total of fifty-eight sets of phonological correspondences. For instance, he points out that p(roto-)-A(ltaic) word-initial **b* and **g* were inherited uniformly as unvoiced in O(ld)J(apanese), pA **b-* and **p-* going in general to OJ *F-* and pA **g-* and **k-* merging in OJ as *k-*; pA **s, *m, *n,* etc. were unchanged in OJ; the Japanese developments of pA **t, *d, *č, *ǯ,* and **ñ* may be grasped in the light of the original Altaic front- and back-vocalism contrast; Japanese materials retain traces of pA quadruple $*l^1$, $*l^2$, $*r^1$, and $*r^2$; OJ *i* corresponds to pA **ï* and **i,* OJ *u* to pA **ü* and **u,* OJ *a* to pA **a, *e,* and **ė,* and OJ *ö* to pA **ö* and **o*; and OJ *o, ï, e,* and *ë* are to be viewed as resulting from secondary developments within Japanese. Furthermore, Miller presumes that the OJ pronouns, interrogatives, numerals, negation, and gerunds were inherited from the original Altaic linguistic unity to a large extent. Thus, for example, he relates OJ 1-person *mï*(nominative)/*wan-u*(oblique) to pA 1-person **bi/*män-* and OJ 2-person *si*(nominative)/*sön-e*(oblique) to pA 2-person **si/*sän-*.

Street and Miller (1975) and Street (1978) have recently launched a long-term project for etymological investigations which, when completed, will be by far more extensive as well as intensive than any attempt hitherto made.

They aim to bring together and compile all the reliable information and data on Old Japanese lexical materials (largely from Omodaka, et al. 1967) with Altaic etymologies.[7]

Regarding Korean, Shiratori (1914-1916) compiled a 595-entry vocabulary comparing Korean and the Ural-Altaic languages and claiming their genetic relationship. Polivanov (1927), noticing the existence of vowel harmony in Korean, proposed the affinity of Korean to Altaic. It is Ramstedt (1928, 1949, 1952-1957), however, who for the first time assigned Korean into the Altaic family in a systematic way.

It has been found by Ramstedt (e.g., 1916) and others that proto-Altaic word-initial **p* had the following development: **p* > *f* >*h* > zero. While Old Mongolian had *p* and Middle Mongolian had *h,* most Modern Mongolian dialects have zero (except Monguor, which retains *f*). In the Manchu-Tungus group, the Goldi, Olcha, and Orok dialects retain the original *p* and Manchu has *f,* whereas Orotschi, Evenki, Lamut, etc. have *h,* and Solon has zero. Turkish has lost the sound (i.e., zero) in general. Korean is regarded as retaining the original *p.*

Miller (1971), a strong defender of the Altaic affinity of Japanese and Korean, includes Korean materials (mainly from Martin 1966) in thirty-six of his fifty-eight sets of phonological correspondences that relate Japanese to the Altaic (pp. 305-306). In a recent historical-linguistic study of some ten Old Korean fragments of the Paekche dynasty which are preserved largely in Japanese sources, Miller (1979) claims that at least six of them have clear-cut Altaic etymologies, and that some show inheritance in Japanese, as in **kuti* 'falcon' (Tungusic *gusi, gosi,* etc.), **togan,* or **togar*(?) 'east' (Old Turkish *toɣar*), **tohel* 'field, land' (pA **topār* 'dust, earth'), **oko-* 'upper, top' (pA **ög-*; OJ *ök-* 'rise'), **ala-* 'lower, bottom' (pA **ala* 'lower or front part'; OJ *ör-* 'to descend'), **omo* 'mother' (pA **əm(ə)-*; OJ *omo* <**ömö*), **sima* 'high, soaring' (OJ *sema*), and **suki* 'village', **sugul* 'village chief' (OJ *suguri*).

Crude as they may be, phonological correspondences between proto-Altaic and Old Korean (in particular, the language of Unified Silla) are presented by K. M. Lee (1976: 16-19) as follows on the basis of the findings made thus far.[8]

VOWELS	1	2	3	4	5	6	7	8	9
proto-Altaic	a	o	u	ï	e	ė	ö	ü	i
Old Korean	a	ɔ	u	i	ä	i	ɔ̈	ü	i

Examples of lexical evidence include: (1) M(iddle) K(orean) *alay* 'below' (<* *al*), Evenki *alas* 'leg', Mongolian *ala* 'groin', Old Turkish *al* 'below; (2) MK *mɔl* 'horse', Manchu *morin,* Mongolian *morin;* (3) MK *ula-* 'long lasting', Evenki *uri-pti* 'previously', Mongolian *urida* 'previously'; (4) MK *ilang* 'ridge', Manchu *irun,* Mongolian *iraɤa,* Chuvash *yə̂ran* (< *ïran*), Tartar *ïzan*; (5) MK *kesk* 'to break', Mongolian *keseg* 'pieces', Turkish *kes-* 'to break'; (6) MK *il* 'early', Manchu *erde,* Mongolian *erte,* Chuvash *ir*; (7) MK *məl* 'water', Manchu *mu-ke,* Evenki *mū,* Mongolian *mören* 'river'; (8) MK *pül-* 'to blow', Manchu *fulgiye-,* Mongolian *üliye-;* and (9) MK *pil-* 'to pray', Manchu *firu-,* Evenki *hiruge-,* Mongolian *irüge-.*

CONSONANTS

proto-Altaic	p b	t d	k g	č ǯ	s	m	n	ŋ	r^1 r^2 l^1 l^2
Old Korean[9]	p	t	k	c	s	m	n	ŋ	l

Examples of Korean *l* correspondences are as follows:

OK 1 < *r^1:	K. *(nun)pola* 'snowstorm', Mongolian *boroɤan* 'rain', Yakut *burxān* 'snowstorm'
OK 1 < *r^2:	MK *ilang* 'ridge', Manchu *irun,* Mongolian *iraɤa,* Chuvash *yə̂ran* (< *ïran*), Tartar *ïzan* (< *ir²an*)
OK 1 < *l^1:	MK *alay* 'below' (< *al*), Evenki *alas* 'leg', Mongolian *ala* 'groin', Old Turkish *al* 'below'
OK 1 < *l^2:	MK *tulh* 'stone' (< *tuluh* <*tïlagu*), Mongolian *čilaɤun* (< *tïla-gūn*), Chuvash *čul,* Old Turkish *taš* (< *tïl²a*)

There are a considerable number of putative cognates which are shared by the Altaic languages and Korean. K. M. Lee (1958) attempts to demonstrate a close affinity between Manchu and Korean based on a total of 236 lexical sets. Hong (1959) presents some lexical correspondences betwen Mongolian and Korean. Observe the following examples for some regular consonant correspondences between Manchu and Korean.

Manchu:Korean	*Manchu*	*Korean*	
h:k	holo	kol	'valley'
	hala	kal	'change'
	halu	kalu	'powder'
	hulan	kul	'cave'
s:h	se	ha-	'to do'
	sonio	hana	'one'
f:p	fatha	pal	'foot'

	fulgiyan	pulk-	'red'
	fulihe	ppuli (< pulhwi < pulɔgu)	'root'
	fusihe	ssi (< psi < pisigu)	'seeds'
m:m	mulu	mœ (< mɔlɔ)	'mountain'
	muke	mul	'water'
n:n	na	nala (< na-lah)	'(M) earth, (K) country'
	ni	ni	'to go'

Some case endings, verbal nominalizers, and other suffixes are also believed to be shared by Korean and Altaic languages. For instance, K. M. Lee (1967:36-41; 1976:20-22) presumes that the Korean subject particle *i* is related to the Altaic third person pronoun or demonstrative *i,* the Korean topic particle *(n)un* to the Mongolian third person possessive particles *inu* (singular) or *anu* (plural), and the Korean directional particle *lo* to proto-Altaic **ru/rü.* He further assumes that the Korean prospective suffix *-(u)l,* modifier suffix *-n,* nominalizer *-m,* and archaic nominalizer *-i* are the reflexes respectively of the proto-Altaic verbal nominalizers **-r, *-n, *-m,* and **-i.* Lee further points out that Middle Korean locative particle *ay/əy* and prosecutive particle *li* (e.g., *ili* 'hither' *tyəli* 'thither') correspond to proto-Altaic dative **a/*e* and prosecutive **li,* respectively.

Scholars like H. K. Kim (1972:227-228) associate the Korean 'person' suffix *-chi* (e.g., *ichi* 'this guy') with Manchu *-či* (e.g., *čagači* 'clerk', *undeči* 'errand boy'), Mongolian *-chi* (e.g., *holdachi* 'merchant', *yamchi 'guide'),* and Turkish *-či* (e.g., *karakči* 'thief', *alači* 'murderer'). The Korean instrumental nominalizer *-kɛ* (e.g., *ccip-kɛ* 'tweezers', *pe-kɛ* 'pillow') is regarded as related to Manchu *-ku,* and so forth (e.g., *chiri-ku* 'pillow', *eli-ku* 'broom'), Mongolian *-ge, -gei,* and so on (e.g., *ger-gei* 'wife', *kügü-ge* 'drum'), and Turkish *-ga, -ke,* and so forth (e.g., *seber-ga* 'broom', *meik-ke* 'knife'). For further evidence, see B. H. Kim (1963), S. N. Lee, et al. (1971), Gim (1968a, 1968b), Hattori (1974), and so on. In terms of the number of seeming cognates, it is safe to say that among the Altaic groups Manchu-Tungus is the closest to Korean, Mongolian comes next, and Turkish is the most remote.

While it is quite true that firm, satisfactory sound correspondences between Korean and Altaic languages or proto-Altaic have not been established in a systematic way, the languages are so similar, not only in many individual items but in various levels of linguistic systems, that we cannot ascribe the similarities merely to accidental correspondence, genuine borrowing, or pure typology. In short, the Altaic origin of Korean is a generally accepted hypothesis that must be further refined and verified.[10]

3. Many typologically shared features have also been pointed out to relate Japanese and Korean to Altaic.[11] Typological relationships are, in general, of secondary importance in comparative work, although they constitute supporting evidence toward the establishment of a genetic relationship, especially when the typological characteristics are exclusively shared among the languages being compared. On the other hand, typological dissimilarities may be employed as supporting evidence to refute a genetic hypothesis, such as one relating Japanese and Korean to Indo-European. Some frequently cited features include the following.

Japanese, Korean, and Altaic languages manifest striking syntactic similarities. The basic word-order common to them is Subject-Object-Verb (SOV). As a consequence, modifiers such as adjectives, adverbs, relative and complement clauses precede the elements they modify, while postpositions occur instead of prepositions. In all these languages, the singular and plural forms of nouns are not strictly distinguished; articles and conjunctions are not developed; no affix exists in adjectives to express the comparative or superative degree; relative pronouns do not exist; sentence-type endings such as statements, interrogatives, propositives and imperatives, are placed at the end of the sentence; and sentences may consist only of a predicate, with the subject and other cases contextually or situationally understood. Further, possession is expressed by an existential verb in these languages, as in Japanese *ni...aru* and Korean *-ey...issta*. For the syntactic parallelism regarding grammatical cases, see J. Sohn (1973).

The morphological structure common to Japanese, Korean, and Altaic languages is agglutinative in that words are formed by the addition of one or more semantically and functionally clear-cut suffixes to an unchanging stem. At the phonological level, vowel harmony is cited as a shared feature. The Altaic harmony is characterized as front-back (or vertical) harmony in that front vowels may co-occur only among themselves and so may back vowels. Middle Korean vowel harmony is horizontal and the agreement is in terms of tongue height. Compare the two harmony systems below.

Mongolian		*Middle Korean*	
Group I (back):	a, o, u	Group I (low):	a, o, ʌ
Group II (front):	e, ö, ü	Group II (high):	ə, u, ɨ
Group III (netural):	i	Group III (Neutral):	i

The neutral vowel *i* occurs with both Group I and Group II vowels. W. J.

Kim (1963) proposes that the horizontal scheme of Korean vowel harmony is the result of a "Great Vowel Shift" from an earlier vertical arrangement similar to those of Altaic languages. Ohno (1971:106-112) points out that there is some evidence that Old Japanese had vowel harmony similar to the Altaic type, although it was much less strict and restricted to word stems, the proposed harmony groups being *u, o, a* (back), *ö* (central), and *i* (high and neutral). Earlier, Shinmura (1911) was unable to assign Japanese to the Altaic for the lack of vowel harmony in Japanese, among other things. Miller (1976:362) and other scholars are still skeptical about the existence of vowel harmony (in Ohno's sense) in earlier Japanese. Another common phonological typology of Altaic, Japanese, and Korean is the lack of *r* or *l* in the initial position of words. Lack of initial consonant clusters is a further common typological feature.

There are a countless number of obvious typological differences too. An example of striking morphological difference is that Altaic nouns and verbs are inflected according to person and number: Turkish *kɨr-ɨl-ma-dɨ-lar-mɨ*? 'Were they not broken?' has the suffix *-lar* '3rd person plural actor' and Turkish *anam* 'my mother' and *anan* 'thy mother' contain *-m* 'my' and- *n* 'thy' respectively (e.g., Ohno 1970:112-113), a pattern that Japanese and Korean do not have.

4. Some tentative attempts have been made for subgrouping within Altaic. Without reference to Japanese, Ramstedt (1957:15) views Korean as the fourth member of the Altaic family, along with Turkic, Mongolian, and Manchu-Tungus. He seems to presuppose that all four language groups are equally related to each other. Poppe (1960:8, 147), also not discussing Japanese, sees in his reconstruction of proto-Altaic indications that proto-Altaic was divided into Old Korean and the language which later diverged into the Chuvash-Turkic unity and the Mongolian-Manchu-Tungus unity.

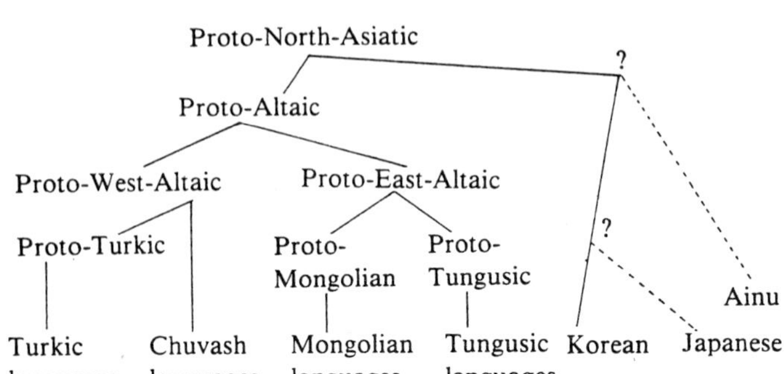

Street (1962:95) places the oldest ancestor of Korean, and probably also of Japanese and Ainu, as a sister to proto-Altaic rather than its daughter, as shown in the preceding page. Poppe, in his foreword to Miller (1971), also indicates this possibility. Martin's (1966) account of the Korean-Japanese relationship and his own research on the Altaic elements in Japanese inspired Miller (1971:44-46) to place Korean, Japanese, and Ryū-kyū quite close to the Manchu-Tungus languages, as represented in his diagram (reproduced below with slight modifications).

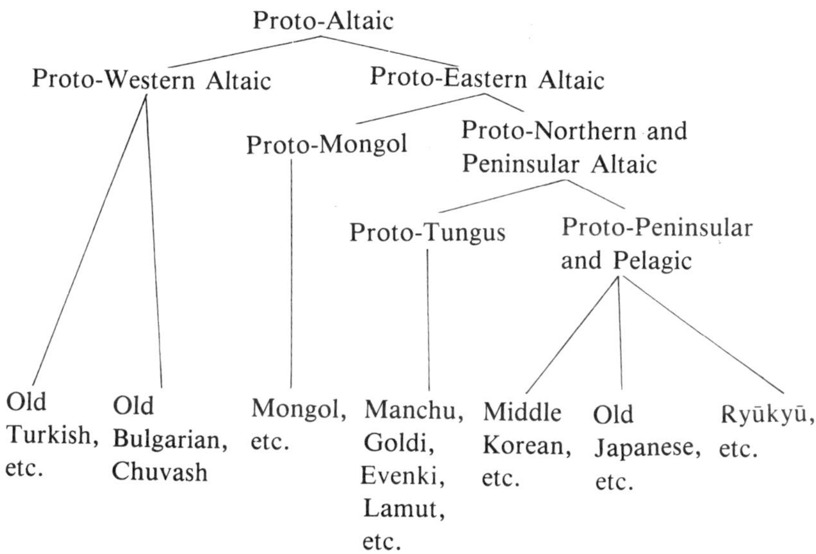

Miller hypothesizes a common heritage for Korean, Japanese, and Ryūkyū. He accounts for the special relationship this groups has with Manchu-Tungus, as evidenced in several important shared features, by positing close geographical association or common habitation for them, thus postulating the unity of Proto-Northern and Peninsular Altaic.

Admitting that it is still premature to theorize on subgrouping in view of the current status of Altaic linguistic scholalrship, Street and Miller (1975:10) prefer to treat West Altaic (Turkic and Chuvash), Mongolian, Tungus, Korean, and Japanese as coordinate descendants of proto-Altaic, which is essentially the same view as that propounded by Ramstedt much earlier.

5. Along with the Altaic hypothesis discussed thus far, there have been suggestions of a genetic affiliation of Japanese, and probably also Korean,

to the Austronesian languages. This Oceanic family embraces over five hundred languages, which are spoken in the great archipelagos of the Pacific and Indian oceans, ranging between Madagascar to the west, Easter Island to the east, Formosa to the north, and New Zealand to the south. Dempwolff (1934, 1937, and 1938) provides a reconstructed sound system for proto-Austronesian, a reconstructed vocabulary of over two thousand words and analysis of sound corréspondences between his proto-Austronesian and eleven daughter languages, furnishing a sound basis for comparative Austronesian linguistics.

Although there is conspicuous disparity in syntax, Japanese shares some obvious phonological and lexical similarities with Oceanic languages: the five vowel system, open syllables, lack of consonant clusters, and quite a few putative cognate sets. Polivanov (1918), Labberton (1924), Whymant (1926), and Matsumoto (1928, 1948) are major precursors of this avenue of investigation. For instance, Polivanov (ibid., 1960) regards Japanese as a hybrid language made up of Altaic, Austronesian, and some undetermined elements.[12] Matsumoto (ibid.) presents, for 113 Japanese lexical items, words from 'Austroasiatic' languages (which include Austronesian) that he thought resembled them in form and meaning and a set of eight sound correspondences based on his lexicon. Izui (1952, 1953), after associating a large number of Japanese words to Austronesian forms and establishing the sound correspondences thereof, speculates that a southern language was already being spoken in Japan when a northern one entered. Ohno (e.g., 1970) has maintained essentially the same view until recently on the basis of the available anthropological, archaeological, and linguistic data. He concludes that an Altaic language came to be spoken in Japan in the Yayoi period some 2,300 years ago, while a southern language had been spoken in the Jōmon period. That is, with the introduction of the Yayoi culture that brought weaving, rice cultivation, bronze tools, and ironware, the language of southern Korea, with its dominant Altaic characteristics, began to be spoken in North Kyūshū and subsequently spread east to Honshū and south to the Ryūkyū islands. Ohno (ibid., 143-144) ascribes the presence of considerable southern elements in the Japanese vocabulary to the assumed fact that the new language was unable to replace all of the native words, although it imposed its grammar on the native language. He further speculates that Korean also had already absorbed quite a few southern words before it was introduced into Japan.

Murayama, originally a strong proponent of the Altaic connections of Japanese, has recently argued that Japanese is to be viewed as a 'mixed language' whose major structural elements consist of Austronesian and Altaic (e.g., Murayama 1969; Murayama and Oobayashi 1973; and Murayama 1974, 1974b, 1976).[13] He rejects, for instance, Shinmura's claim that the Austronesian elements in Japanese are simply loanwords and also the prevalent view (e.g., Kindaichi, et al. 1951) that Austronesian elements constitute a linguistic substratum in Japanese upon which an Altaic superstratum was predominantly imposed. He (1976:419) claims that a much larger portion of the Japanese vocabulary is of the Austronesian origin and there are some phonological, morphological, and syntactic similarities too. Murayama's finder-list (ibid., 432-435) contains seventy-nine proto-Austronesian forms for which he claims to be able to establish Japanese reflexes. Some of these are illustrated in the following.

Proto-Austronesian	*Old Japanese*	
bakul	fako	'basket/box'
bayi	fafa	'mother'
bunga	fana	'flower'
apuị̯	fï	'fire'
papah	fa	'leaf'
put'əg'	fösö	'navel'
putih	futi	'white'
kahuị̯	kï	'tree'
tangan	ta-	'hand'
inum	nömi	'drink'
namnam	namë	'taste'
mata	ma-	'eye'
ivak	iwo	'fish'
vat'a	wata	'ocean'

Murayama also attempts to establish some tentative phonological correspondences between proto-Indonesian and Old Japanese, illustrates the parallelism in verb formation between Indonesian languages and Old Japanese, and points out that at least ten of Martin's (1966) proto-Korean-Japanese forms are shared also by Austronesian languages (Murayama 1974b, 1976). His view of the development of Japanese is that the Austronesian elements encountered, somewhere in the northern part of Kyūshū, a Tungus group of Altaic. In the course of this encounter, the Austronesian elements were grammatically restructured.

Another strong defender of the Austronesian hypothesis is Kawamoto (1972, 1973, 1974, 1977), who attempts to establish the rules of phonological correspondences between Japanese and Austronesian by modifying and further elaborating Izui's (1953). Kawamoto undertakes some morphological comparisons, and collects several hundred Old Japanese words paired with look-alikes in proto-Austronesian or one of its branches, that is, proto-Indonesian, proto-Oceanic, proto-Eastern-Oceanic, or proto-Polynesian. Refuting the Altaic hypothesis of Japanese and Japanese-Korean relationship as unacceptable in view of "the scarcity of lexical cognates and the lack of reliable sound correspondences", Kawamoto (e.g., 1974:127-128) suggests that Japanese is a creolized language formed from a pidgin of an Austronesian language superimposed on a Subject-Object-Verb languages. Kawamoto is undecided whether this SOV language was an Altaic, Ainu, an ancient Asian language, or some other language.

Despite Murayama and Kawamoto's arguments to the contrary, the most reasonable inference to be drawn from the present state of linguistic discoveries is that both Japanese and Korean are basically Altaic, with an Austronesian substratum which is much denser in Japanese than in Korean. For one thing, there is much more convincing evidence, especially in 'quality' items, pointing toward the Altaic hypothesis.[14] Second, the great syntactic and morphological disparity existing between Japanese-Korean and Austronesian makes us skeptical about any proposal that Austronesian is the basis of Japanese and Korean.

6. Very recently, Ohno (1980) has advanced an interesting hypothesis that in Japanese and Korean there is yet another stratum interposing between those of Altaic and Austronesian. It is the stratum of Tamil, one of the four Dravidian languages currently spoken in southernmost India. The original homeland of the Dravidian people was along the Indus River in the north of India. Without attempting to establish rigorous phonological correspondences, Ohno presents a large number of lexical look-alikes between Japanese and Tamil, covering basic verbs, body parts, kinship terms, emotion words, farming and weaving terms, as well as many similar typological features. Based on certain Austronesian, Tamil, and Altaic cultural features, including farming practices, that are found in Japan, Ohno postulates the following linguistic layers in Japanese: (1) An Austronesian language was spoken in Japanese in the early and first stages of the Jōmon period; (2) Tamil people migrated into southern Korea and Kyūshū in the first and middle stages of the Jōmon period (400-300 B.C.); and (3) an Altaic people came to northern Kyūshū from Korea in the Yayoi period, pushing the native Tamil people to the east and south, where more lexical

correspondences between Japanese and Tamil are found.

As already mentioned, Hulbert (1905) noticed much earlier that Korean and Dravidian languages share some grammatical features, and he insisted on their genetic relationship.

7. With regard to the relationship between Japanese (including the Ryūkyū dialect) and Korean, it appears an undeniable fact that they are genetically related, however remote may be their relationship. Notwithstanding skepticism from some quarters (e.g., Haguenauer 1956, Kwon 1962, Kawamoto 1974), a sizable number of shared cognates, partially attested phonological correspondences, and some already obvious uniquely shared morphological, syntactic, and semantic characteristics all bolster the existence of the relationship. Some Korean linguists offer arguments in favor of the supposition that Korean may be more closely related to Altaic languages than to Japanese, but all the evidence so far uncovered appears to indicate that the two languages are closer to one another than to any other languages.

The common origin of Korean and Japanese was proposed as early as 1717 by Arai Hakuseki, a Tokugawa Confucian, and again in 1781 by Fujii Teikan, a precursor of modern archaeology in Japan (Hattori 1974:36; Miller 1967:61-62). But it is Aston (1879) who, for the first time, made a serious comparative study exclusively of Japanese and Korean. He attempted to set up some ten consonant correspondences on the basis of approximately seventy lexical items, as well as by comparing the Chinese sounds borrowed in Japanese with those borrowed in Korean. However, he made no attempt to reconstruct a protophonemic system. Aston also points out similarities in grammatical categories and word-formational characteristics. Later his views were methodologically refined and expanded by such Japanese scholars as Ōya (1889), Shiratori (1897), and Kanazawa (1910). In particular Kanazawa, whose study was partly politically motivated, claimed that Korean and the native language of the Ryūkyū Islands are branches of Japanese. Some of the 146 lexical pairs he presented as cognates are: J. *ba* :K. *pa* 'place'; J. *ha* 'tooth' : K. *ppyə* 'bone'; J. *a* : K. *a* 'I'; J. *na* : K. *nə* 'you'; J. *ka* : K. *kɨ* 'he, she, it'; J. *kachi* : K. *kət* 'to walk'; J. *kah-u* 'to buy' : K. *kap* 'price'; J. *kata* : K. *kyət* 'side'; and J. *kata* : K. *kut* 'hard'. Important contributions to scholarship though they may be, his lexical comparisons are linguistically unappealing as they stand, because they are not based on regular phonological correspondences. He also proposes correspondences in word formation and some fifteen grammatical markers.

Ramstedt (1924, 1949, 1951, 1952, 1957), who contributed greatly to the comparison of Japanese and Korean with Altaic, was very cautious in defending linguistic affinity between the two languages. So have been many other linguists, including Shinmura (1911, 1935), Ogura (1920, 1934), Kōno (1949), Hattori (1974) and B. H. Kim (1976). Their caution arises chiefly from the incompleteness of available evidence. On the other hand, scholars like Ohno (1957, 1970) postulate close relationships between Japanese and Korean, as mentioned earlier.[15]

The most significant breakthrough is no doubt the work of Martin (1966), who systematically compares 320 sets of seeming cognates, reconstructs their hypothetical protoforms (establishing thereby the proto-Korean-Japanese phonemic system), includes suprasegmental features, and provides phonological rules of correspondences. Let us observe some of Martin's obvious consonant correspondences with irrelevant information omitted and Korean transcriptions slightly modified. (In Middle Korean (MK), prime (′) and double prime (″) indicate respectively high and low-rising pitch accents, while in Modern Korean, double prime indicates vowel length. The Japanese and proto-K-J pitch accents are marked on the vowels concerned).

proto-K-J	*K J*	*proto-K-J*	*K*	*J*
*p . .	p p < *hw* < h	*pal(y)i 'bee'	″pəl, *MK* pəli	pati
		*pudye 'brush'	pus < *MK* ′put	pude
		*pɔ́r(a)- 'desire'	pala- < *MK* ′pɔ′la-	OJ por-
		*pataxye 'field'	path < *MK* path	patake
		*pyal 'fire'	pul < *MK* ′pɨl	pi
		*paryɔl 'needle'	panɨl < *MK* palɔl	pári
		*par(a) 'plain'	pəl	pára
		*párya 'stomach'	pɛ < *MK* ′pɔy	pará
*m . .	m m	*myom 'body'	mom < *MK* ′mom	mi
		*mur(ye) 'crowd'	muli? < *MK* ′mul, ′mɨli	muré? < mur(e)-
		*mašu 'measure'	mal < *MK* ′mal	masú
*v . .	p #	*vašyi 'foot'	pal < *MK* ′pal	así
		*válk(a)- 'red'	pulk- < *MK* pɔlk-	aka-
*k . .	k k	*kuma 'bear'	″kom < *MK* ″kom	kumá
		*kani 'crab'	ke < kəy	kani
		*kalǧ- 'hang'	″kəl-	kák(e)-
		*kwat(a)- 'hard'	kut-	kata-

proto-K-J	*K J*	*proto-K-J*	*K*	*J*
		*kašyi 'oak'	kal	kási
		*kes 'thing'	kəs < *MK* kəs	kotó
		*kura 'valley'	kol < *MK* ″kol	kura
*t..	t t	*tɔx- 'arrive'	*tah- *MK* tah-	túk-
		*taxye 'bamboo'	tɛ < *MK* 'tay	take
		*tɔ́rkyi 'chicken'	talk < *MK* tɔlk	tori
		*tɔ́d- 'c̣lose it'	tat- < *MK* tat-	tód(i)-
		*tɔlǧyi 'moon'	tal < *MK* 'tɔl	tukí
		*tɔ́ 'place'	-te < təy < *MK* 'tɔ(y)	-do < -to
		*twɔmbi 'sea bream'	tomi	tápi
*n . .	n n	*nɔ́š- 'carry'	nalɨ- < nɔlɔ-	nos(e)-
		*nɔmpxa 'marsh'	nɨph	numá
		*nYalɔm 'summer'	yəlɨm < *MK* nyə'lɨm, nyə(')lɔm	natú
*d . .	t y	*dyar- 'enter'	tɨl- < *MK* 'tɨl-	yir-
		*dar- 'give'	″tal-	yar-
		*dyoš 'stone'	″tol < *MK* ″tolh	yisí
*c . .	c t	*cyic(yi) 'breasts'	cəc	tití
		*cump- 'pick it'	cup-	tum-
		*cur(u)- 'string'	cul	turú
		*cekyi 'time'	-cək < *MK* cək	tokí
*j . .	c y	*jipye 'house'	cip < *MK* cip	yipé
		*jɔ́rɔ́keb- 'enjoy'	cɨlkəp- < *MK* 'cɨl(')kəp-	yorokób-
*s . .	s s	*syɔš 'flesh'	sal < *MK* 'sɔlh	OJ sisi
		*(a-)sam 'hemp'	sam < *MK* sam	asa
		*sYyima 'island'	″səm < *MK* ″syəm	sima
		*sarya 'new'	sɛ < *MK* 'say	sára
		*salpyi 'spade'	sap < *MK* 'salp	OJ sapi
*. . s . .	l s	*nɔ́s- 'carry'	nalɨ- < *nɔlɔ-	nos(e)-
		*m̉ašu 'measure'	mal < *MK* 'mal	masú
		pYesyi 'star'	″pyəl	posi
		*xeši 'waist'	həli < *MK* hə'li	kosi

As alluded to in the preceding examples, the proto-Korean-Japanese phonemic system that Martin reconstructs is quite rich. Martin's work has provided a new footing not only for Japanese-Korean comparative linguists but for those who attempt to relate Japanese to Altaic, as evidenced in Miller (1971). On the other hand, some alternative solutions to or criticisms of certain aspects of Martin's work have been advanced by Miller (1971), Osada (1972), Mathias (1973), K. M. Lee (1973), Murayama (1974b), and Sato (1974), among others. For instance, one treatment of Martin's which has received much criticism is that of protovowels (e.g., Japanese *a* corresponds to as many as six different Korean vowels); another comment is on Martin's Korean *l* which corresponds to the Japanese *r, t, k,* and *s*; the third is related to the selection of the lexical items that are compared; and the fourth is that its method is too mechanical, with the reconstructions appearing somewhat unrealistic (e.g., Martin's **mp* and **mb* are 'non-Altaic'). K.M. Lee's (ibid.) fundamental criticism is that without introducing other Altaic languages into the comparison of Korean and Japanese as checks, we can neither achieve comprehensive reconstructions, nor guarantee the legitimacy of any reconstruction. Moreover, as K. M. Lee puts it and Martin (1975a) himself admits, the major shortcoming of the work is that the comparisons were based not on the oldest forms of the languages or on reconstructed proto-Korean and proto-Japanese, but largely on the modern or late premodern forms. In spite of such weaknesses, Martin's work is a superb contribution to comparative Japanese-Korean linguistics, and his conclusions are regarded as generally valid. Martin (1968) also looked into several grammatical elements that are likely to have a common origin, for example, subject and genitive particles, infinitive and other suffixes, and interrogatives.

Another strong defender of the kinship of Japanese and Korean is Osada (1972), who claims that both languages belong to a branch of 'Ancient Altaic' while admitting the presence of southern elements in the Japanese language and people. S. Kim (1974) takes up more than 1,270 lexical comparisons between Japanese and Korean, but due to the amateurish method he employs, his work does little to prove the relationship.

Recently Martin (1975a) has claimed that the most striking similarity between Japanese and Korean, which is not shared by any other Altaic languages, is the fact that the accentual systems of the two languages have many common features. Martin maintains that the accent patterns for proto-Japanese and proto-Korean can be reconstructed with reasonable accuracy from some modern dialects as well as from the available philological records dating back to the twelfth century for Japanese and to the fifteenth century for Korean.

8. Needless to say, an extensive search for a set of reliable regular sound correspondences is the surest way to prove the genetic relationship of the languages compared. This task is not an easy one, however, if the two languages diverged long ago, and there have been frequent contacts with other languages since. Forms and meanings constantly change, and loanwords from all sources and substratal elements not only destroy the original sound system but replace native or superstratal words. This is the case with Japanese and Korean, which are assumed to have been separated for several thousand years. For instance Ohno (1957:175) postulates about 2,300 years of divergence, while Hattori (1974:250) estimates at least 4,700 years. Independently of each other, the two languages must have absorbed a large number of external elements through various early language contacts. For instance, see Hattori (1974) for some Ainu elements in Japanese and B. H. Kim (1976) for Giljak elements in Korean. The extensive Tamil elements in Japanese have already been discussed.

K. M. Lee (1976:25) and others place the total number of the plausible Japanese-Korean cognate pairs at around two hundred words and fifteen endings. A portion of these might turn out, upon closer examination, to be either external or mutual borrowings. Nevertheless we cannot deny that the relationship is there. How can we say that the correspondences in so many functors, including J. *i*: K. *i* 'this', J. *i*: K. *i* 'subject particle', J. *ka*: K. *ka* 'question particle', J. *ro*: K. *la* 'command particle', J. *tati*: K. *tɨl* 'plural particle', J. *-i, -mi, -ku*: K. *-i, -m, -ki* 'nominalizers' (e.g., Ohno 1970: 129-131; K. M. Lee 1976:25), and in so many other lexical and grammatical items, could be attributed to mere borrowings or chance resemblance?

Although differing in some details, K. M. Lee (1961, 1963, 1972) and Murayama (1962b, 1963) regard Old Japanese as manifesting a remarkable relationship with the Koguryŏ language that was spoken by those who occupied Manchuria and the northern part of Korea before and around the beginning of the Christian era. There is some linguistic and archaeological evidence to suggest that the Yayoi culture (characterized by rice farming) was brought by the ancestors of Koguryŏ to northern Kyūshū in Japan. According to Lee and Murayama, the extent Korean chronicle *Samguk Sagi* contains some eighty Koguryŏ words which may be compared with thirty-four Old Japanese, thirty-one Middle Korean, seventeen Tungus, and thirteen Mongol and Turkish (Lewin 1976:408). For instance, K. M. Lee (1976:34-35) postulates the following correspondences.

Koguryŏ language	*Old Japanese*	
*i	ir-	'enter'
*mie	midu	'water'
*nua	na	'earth'
*nuami 'sea, pond'	nami	'wave'
*namər	namari	'lead'
*tan, tuan	tani	'valley'
*kuc	kuti	'mouth'
*nanən	nana-	'seven'
*tək	töwo	'ten'
*mir	mi-	'three'
*üc	itu-	'five'
*usaxam	wusagi	'rabbit'

The wall paintings of Takamatsuzuka tumulus (late seventh to early eighth century) opened in 1972 are known to be similar to those found in Koguryŏ graves of the fifth century. It is also generally believed that the combware (comb-marked pots), unearthed in western Japan is related to Korean combware.

K. M. Lee (ibid.) and others assume that the predecessor of proto-Japanese and the language of the Koguryŏ kingdom (37 B.C.-668 A.D.) is the language of Puyŏ, a dominant state in Manchuria before the Christian era. Together with the Han language of those Koreans who occupied the southern part of Korea, Puyŏ is viewed as descended from an early branch of the Altaic family. The Three Kingdoms (Silla, Paekche, and Koguryŏ) succeeded the Han states in the first century of our era, and subsequently Silla conquered the other old Korean states and unified Korea. The other old Korean languages or dialects are assumed to have either become extinct or to have been incorporated into the Silla language, which was essentially the predecessor of modern Korean.

The preceding hypothesis is quite different from what Kōno (1945) envisaged earlier, when he held that Japanese and the Han language were sister languages and posited that the Koguryŏ language was a successor to Manchu-Tungus.

The circumstances observed thus far, call for continued careful etymological investigations, covering not only the material from Japanese and Korean, but that from their neighbor languages as well. At the same time attention must be directed to such hitherto largely neglected areas as the comparison of morphological and syntactic features, which are in general more resistant to change than phonology and vocabulary. Many of the morphological and syntactic similarities uncovered thus far appear to be uniquely shared between Japanese and Korean, or between them and some Altaic languages. These features include the subtle use of case markers, limiters, causative suffixes, honorifics, sentence-final particles and so forth. If we codify a sufficiently large number of uniquely shared innovations, we will have a much stronger ground on which to reconstruct a genetic relationship. The genetic affinity between Japanese and Korean and their relationship to other languages are problems to be tackled from all possible directions.

Notes

1. The present work was supported by the Ministry of Education of the Republic of Korea under its grant to the Center for Korean Studies of the University of Hawaii. I am greatly indebted to Gerald Mathias, who made invaluable comments on an earlier version of this paper. Particular thanks are expressed to Jeannie Sohn for her excellent research assistance.
2. For instance, Lowell (1891) and Parker (1939), noticing the similarities in word order and the pronoun system, propose that Tibeto-Burman and Japanese were originally sister languages. Hulbert (1905) maintains that Korean is related to the Dravidian languages in India in view of such shared syntactic features as word order and the lack of a gender system. Koppelman (1933) and Eckardt (1966) attempt to relate Korean to Indo-European languages, observing certain accidental lexical and anthropological resemblances. Rahder's (1956-1961) etymological dictionary of Chinese, Japanese, Korean, and Ainu lists, for each of his lexical entries, forms from a vast variety of the world's languages, though without following the principles of comparative linguistics. Similarly, Syromjatnikov (1972) attempts to compare Japanese words with those from such languages as Uralic, Altaic, Austronesian, Eskimo, Thai, Khmer, and Indo-European.
3. Altaic is thought to be a linguistic unity spoken sometime during the Neolithic, and its original homeland is assumed to be somewhere in northern or north-central Eurasia (e.g., Miller 1976:341).
4. Street (1974) summarizes and indexes Poppe's reconstructions.
5. Asterisked forms are not attested, but reconstructed either through a comparative method or through internal reconstruction.
6. Miller's Old Japanese data are mostly from Omodaka, et al. (1967), Korean data from Martin (1966), and proto-Altaic data mainly from Poppe (1960). For some criticisms on Miller (1971), see Mathias (1972) and Unger (1973), among others.
7. Street and Miller (1975) and Street (1978) contain a total of thirty-one articles, each dealing

with one Old Japanese lexical item with Altaic etymology. Discussions of the sound correspondences between proto-Altaic and Old Japanese and on the pitch-accent of proto-Japanese are appended to Street and Miller (ibid.).

8. As a result of the fall of Paekche and Koguryŏ, the Silla language became the only dominant Old Korean language used since the latter part of the seventh century. The languages of Silla and Paekche are thought to be closer to each other than they are to the Koguryŏ language which is considered a distinct Altaic.
9. K. M. Lee assumes that the Korean aspirated consonants were Old Korean innovations.
10. For discussions on the state of the art of the comparative study of Korean and the Altaic, see K. M. Lee (1975). On the other hand, there are some scholars who are skeptical regarding the putative affinity, for example, P. Kim (1960) and Kwon (1962).
11. Fujioka (1908) hypothesized a genetic relationship of Japanese to the Altaic on the grounds that they share thirteen out of the fourteen typological features that he considered characterize Altaic languages. The only feature he thought Japanese does not share is vowel harmony. For some Korean-Altaic typological characteristics, see Ogura (1935).
12. Polivanov (1918) noted that the Japanese prefix *ma-* (an emphatic adjective) corresponds to a similar phenomenon in Philippine and Melanesian languages. He (1924) also observed parallelisms between Japanese and Austronesian languages in prenasalization, vowel and consonant systems, existence of bilabial fricatives, lack of vowel harmony, and so forth.
13. Murayama maintains that many Japanese verbal roots are of the Austronesian origin, to which some Altaic affixes came to be attached, hence the notion of *Mischsprache*. For instance, he regards Japanese *abura* 'fat, (cooking) oil' and *abur-u* 'broil, boil' as related to proto-Austronesian **apui* 'fire' to which he believes the Tungus verbal aorist suffix in *-ra* was attached. He also links Japanese *hako* 'box' and Middle Korean *pakuloi* 'basket' to proto-Austronesian **bakul* 'basket'.
14. Miller (1976:314) advocates the importance of the 'quality' of the evidence, saying that uniquely shared innovations are more convincing in anomalous cases within the totality of the lingustic systems being compared. For instance, there are a small number of anomalous Japanese verbs which manifest *-r-* and *-s-* alternation in causative formation (e.g., *tar-u* 'be suficient' vs. *tas-u* 'make sufficient'). Parallel to Japanese, Old Turkish has a similar well established variation, as attested in *tol-* 'be full' vs. *tos-* 'make full' (Miller ibid.:345-346; Miller 1971:134-137). The parallelism in the nominative/oblique forms of proto-Altaic and Old Japanese (already mentioned) and the correspondence between proto-Altaic *dȫ- 'four' and Old Japanese *yö-* 'four' are all examples of 'quality' evidence (Miller 1976:378).
15. Up until now, few Korean linguists have conducted comparative research on Japanese and Korean, except perhaps for S. N. Lee (1955) and S. Kim (1974). Korean scholars' apparent disinterest in this area in the past is often ascribed to political reasons.

Reprinted from *Korean Studies* (University of Hawaii) 4:29-50 (1980).

18. RELATIVE CLAUSE FORMATION IN MICRONESIAN LANGUAGES

1. Introduction

This paper will concern itself with a synchronic comparison of the patterns of relative clause formation of six Micronesian languages: Woleaian (WL), Trukese (TR), Mokilese (MK), Marshallese (MR), Kusaiean (KS), and Gilbertese (GL). These languages are genetically related and distributed from west to east in the Trust Territory of the Pacific Islands.[1]

A relative clause is a sentence embedded in a noun phrase of a larger sentence in such a way that it modifies the head of that noun phrase. A head modified by a relative clause is called the antecedent of that clause. In order for a clause to be relative, its antecedent must be coreferential with an underlying noun phrase of that clause. This noun phrase is either pronominalized or deleted on the surface. For example, (1a) contains the relative clause *re torofi* 'they caught it', whose antecedent is *mal we* 'the bird'. In the conceptual structure of the sentence, as hypothesized in (1b), the relative clause contains *mal we* as the object of the verb. The underlying *mal we* is thought to be deleted obligatorily on the surface due to its correference with the antecedent.

(1) a. WL. I weri mal we re torofi.
I saw bird the they catch-it
'I saw the bird that they caught.'

b.

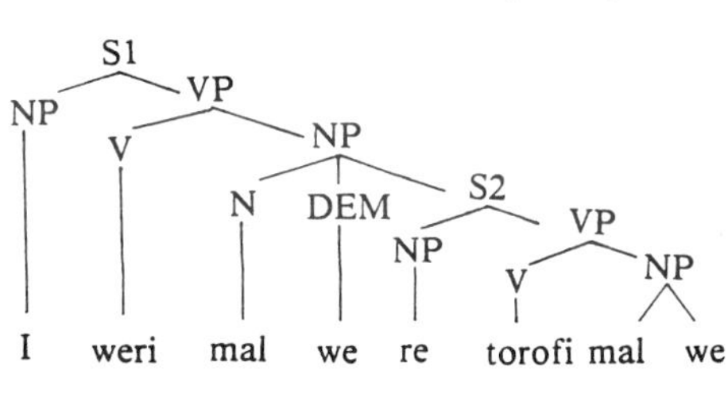

The sentences in (2) also embed a clause (in italics), but we cannot postulate any noun phrase in either embedded clause that is coreferential with any noun phrase in the main sentence. Since the coreference condition is not met, the clauses are not viewed as relative ones. They are complement clauses which are not included in the present discussion.

(2) a. WL. I giula be *re torofi mal we.*
know that they catch-it bird the
'I know that they caught the bird.'

b. GL. I aki atai bukin teraa b'a *e un.*
I not know reason what that he angry.
'I don't know why he got mad.'

Sometimes a relative clause is not dominated immediately by the node dominating its antecedent. In (3), the clause *i be liiy* 'I will kill it' is a relative one in relation to its antecedent *mal we* and a complement in relation to the clause *i tipeli* 'I want it'. Coreference, thus, applies between the object of the highest verb and that of the most deeply embedded verb in (3).

(3) WL. Ye sa weri mal we i tipeli be *i be liiy.*
he prf. see bird the I want-it that I will kill-it
'He saw the bird which I want to kill.'

When an antecedent is modified by a relative clause, its meaning is specified in certain ways. Like adjectives and numerals, the major semantic function of a relative clause is to specify the antecedent in the sense that it restricts the referential range held inherently by the antecedent, regardless of the involvement of the speaker's presupposition. Whether an antecedent is definite or not in the sense of old or new information is not the function of a relative clause but that of certain demonstratives. Some demonstratives (e.g., WL *we,* TR *ewe,* MK *o,* MR *yew,* KS *ah* and GL *are*) definitize their antecedents in addition to specifying them. In (4), for example, the referential ranges of the antecedents (in italics) are considerably specified, but they are not definitized in spite of the presence of their relative clauses (bracketed).

(4) WL. Si be fang ngali shag *semal yaremat* [le ye gach]
we will send to-him just a person that he good
mwaremwar yeel.
lei this

'We (incl.) will award this lei to someone who is good.'

MK Ioar *mehkij* [ma kisai kin johmwehuki].
that something that we habit. sick-with
'That is something we are usually sick of.'

Notice in the above examples that there is no demonstrative. In (5a) on the other hand, the antecedent is definitized by the presence of the demonstrative *kawe* 'those (we are talking about)'. Even if we eliminate the relative clause, the definiteness will not be affected. In (5b), the demonstrative *e* 'this' specifies the antecedent in terms of singular number and closeness to the speaker, but it does not definitize the antecedent.

(5) a. WL. *Yaremat kawe* [re sa kker] ila lai sar skuul.
person those they prf. happy (topic) Cl-my child school
'Those happy persons are my students.'

b. MK. Ngoah mwehuki *armajj-e* [ma mwehu].
I like person-this that he good
'I like this person who is good.'

The discussion in this paper will cover the following topics: some characteristic processes involved in Micronesian relativization in comparison with those of English (Section 2), advocation of the assumption that Micronesian sentences embed not only predicational but also equational relative clauses (Section 3), common syntactic properties involved in Micronesian relative clause formation (Section 4), syntactic differences observable among the languages (Section 5), and a brief conclusion with some allusion to the linguistic subgrouping among the languages compared (Section 6).[2]

2. Processes in Micronesian Relativization

It is a common hypothesis in English relativization that there are three processes involved, i.e., (a) movement to the clause-initial position of the embedded noun phrase which is coreferential with the antecedent, (b) *relative* pronominalization of the preposed noun phrase, and (c) optional deletion of the relative pronoun in certain definable syntactic environments, such as when the pronoun is the object of the embedded verb. Thus, for example, observe the following derivational processes.

(6) I saw the bird they caught.
← I saw the bird which they caught.
← I saw the bird (the bird they caught)
← I saw the bird (they caught the bird)

(7) That person whose books I stole is my teacher.
← That person (his books I stole) is my teacher
← That person (I stole his books) is my teacher
← That person (I stole that person's books) is my teacher

(8) I know the place where he lives.
← I know the place (there he lives)
← I know the place (he lives there)
← I know the place (he lives at the place)

In Micronesian languages, a movement hypothesis is untenable in the first place. There is no evidence, implicit or explicit, that an embedded noun phrase is moved to the clause-initial position. Rather, there is evidence that this is not the case. For simplicity's sake, I will use Woleaian examples only, with the understanding that more or less the same thing applies in the rest of the languages. The three English sentences (6-8) are translated as follows in Woleaian. (Underlying sentences are also given, from which the actual sentences are thought to be derived.)

(9) WL. I weri mal we re torofi.
I saw-it bird the they caught-it
I weri mal we (re torofi mal we)

(10) WL. Yaremat la i pira yaal babiyor ila yaai sensei.
person that I steal-it Cl-his book (topic) Cl-my teacher
← Yaremat la (i pira yaal yaremat la babiyor)
ila yaai sensei Cl-of

(11) WL. I giula biuleiu la ye log *iyang*.
I know-it place that he stay there
← I giula biuleiu la (ye log biuleiu la)

Woleaian has the relative marker *le* 'that' which is comparable to English relative pronouns. *Le* always comes immediately before a relative clause if both appear together. *Le* never appears, however, if the antecedent is modified by a demonstrative, hence the non-appearance of *le* in the above examples.

Now (9) does not tell us whether the embedded noun phrase *mal we* 'the bird' is deleted in its underlying position or deleted after having been preposed in clause-initial position. (10), however, shows an alternation between the construct suffix *-l* 'of' that occurs in the underlying structure and the third person possessive suffix *-l* 'his' that is manifested on the surface. The suffix *-l* 'his' is derived with the deletion of the embedded noun phrase *yaremat la* 'that person' from the construction *yaal yaremat la* 'the general object of that person'. In Micronesian languages, it is a general rule that pronominalization of the construct suffix + noun phrase results in a third person possessive suffix, as observed below.

(12) WL. metal John 'John's eyes' → metal 'his eyes'
silel sar we 'mother of the child' → silal 'his mother'
yaal yaremat la → yaal 'his general object'

In (10) pronominalization occurs because the antecedent and the embedded attribute noun phrase are coreferential.[3] Notice that the pronominalization takes place not in clause initial position but in the place where the underlying *yaal yaremat la* is located, and the pronominalized *yaal* is not moved. In (11) also, the locative pronominalization from *biuleiu la* '(at) that place' to *iyang* 'there' is effected where *biuleiu la* occurs in the underlying sentence, and *iyang* remains there without moving to the front. The evidence provided by (10) and (11) against any movement hypothesis leads us to treat (9) in a parallel manner. That is, the deletion of the embedded phrase *mal we* takes place where it is in the underlying sentence. As noticed in (7) and (8), the non-appearance of such pronominalized phrases as *his books* and *there* and the clause-initial appearance of such relative-pronominalized phrases as *whose books* and *where* certainly justify the movement hypothesis for English. This, however, is not the case with Micronesian languages.

Secondly, there is no evidence in favor of a hypothesis of relative pronominalization in Micronesian languages. English *who, whose, whom, which,* and *where* reflect the syntactico-semantic features of the coreferential embedded noun phrase. Obviously, this fact partly motivates the hypothesis of relative pronominalization in English. On the other hand, there is no indication that Woleaian *le* and the relative markers of the other Micronesian languages in question contain any of the syntactico-semantic features of the embedded noun phrase which is coreferential with the antecedent. Besides, as we have observed, certain embedded noun phrases are pronominalized (not as relative pronouns) and remain on the surface (e.g., *iyang*). So far as such noun phrases are persistent on the surface, there is no input upon which relative pronominalization is to be operative. It seems to me, therefore, that the main function of a relative marker is that of a conjunction and not that of a pronominal at least in present Micronesian languages. It merely conjoins an antecedent and its relative clause. If no ambiguity arises, it is frequently not introduced, as will be seen later. This may correspond to the third process in English, i.e., optional deletion of the relative pronoun.

Thus, the processes relevant to Micronesian relativization are (a) Equi-NP pronominalization/deletion and (b) relative marker insertion/deletion. It would be interesting to discuss whether Equi-NP pronominalization and Equi-NP deletion are to be ordered or not, and whether a relative marker is to be introduced in the underlying structure or through transformation, but such problems will not be touched in the present paper. Incidentally, Schwartz (1971:150-51) points out, based on an observation of a limited number of languages, that VSO and SVO languages have the tendency to move WH-forms to clause-initial position. However, Microensian languages, which fall somewhere between VSO and SVO (but closer to VSO if I am not mistaken), neither have pronominals of the WH sort nor allow any movement of embedded elements, as observed thus far.

3. Are There Equational Relative Clauses?

Two types of major sentences are recognized in Micronesian languages: predicational and equational. A predicational sentence involves a verbal predicate, whereas an equational sentence involves a nominal predicate. Accordingly, the former may have in its verb phrases such elements as tense/aspect morphemes and a predicational marker (or subject marker: SM), which the latter lacks. Observe the following examples and notice the structural differences as well as semantic peculiarities of the two types of sentences.

(13)	*predicational*	WL.	Sar kawe re sa lag iiya?
			Child those they (SM) prf. go where
			'Where have those children gone?'
	equational	WL.	Laumw sar kawe?
			child-your child those
			'Are those children yours?'

Thus, an equational sentence is in general a sequence of two noun phrases, one identifying or predicating the other. The normal order here is that the subject follows the predicate unless the subject is a personal pronoun or focused.

There is no doubt that all the Micronesian languages compared have relative clauses of the predicational type, as we have observed in the examples given thus far. Now the problem is whether the bracketed part of each sentence below may be considered a relative clause with the italicized phrase as its antecedent or simply a noun appositive to the italicized phrase.

(14) WL. Ye gangin *mai kawe* [gelai].
he eat-it breadfruit those food-my
'He ate those breadfruit of mine.'

TR. Aa åni *eney kkewe* [maay].
he-prf. eat-it food-my those b.f.
'He ate those breadfruit of mine.'

MK. Ih kang-la *koanoai* [moai]-*ok*.
he eat-up food-my b.f.-those
'He ate those breadfruit of mine.'

MR. Ye-har kagiy *may kew* [kijėh].
he-prf. eat-pl.obj. b.f. those food-my
'He ate those breadfruit of mine.'

KS. *Oak* [okuh-k] *ah* ac som nuh Kuam.
canoe canoe-my the will go to Guam
'Those canoes of mine are going to Guam.'

GL. *Waa ake* [nima waa akekei] a tabe n nako Kuaam.
canoe those 5 canoe those they are particle going Guam
'Those five canoes will go to Guam.'

To mention the conclusion first, I propose that the bracketed parts in the above examples be treated as equational type of relative clauses with the italicized parts as their antecedents. This proposal is based on the following observations, all of which indicate parallelism between the pattern of predicational clause formation and that of the assumed equational relative formation. For a similar proposal for Ulithian, see Sohn and Bender (1973:4.5.3 & 4.9.4).

First, in all the languages compared, predicational and assumed equational relative clauses take the same position with regard to the antecedent and the demonstrative modifying the antecedent, as illustrated below.

(15) WL. *predication* Ye sa weri *shoabut we* [ye sa tang].

he prf. see-her girl the she prf. cry
'He saw the girl who cried.'

equation Ye sa weri *shoabut we* [laiul].
child-his
'He saw the daughter of his.'

KS. *predication* *Mwet* se [ma eltahl uniyah] *ah* pa Sohn.
man a who they killed the (focus) John
'The man who they killed is John.'

equation *Oak* [luhmkoe] *ah* ac som nuh Kuam.
canoe 5 the will go to Guam
'The five canoes are going to Guam.'

Second, in languages like WL and MR, the relative marker may appear before assumed equational clauses in the same way as with predicational relative clauses. In (16), the relative marker is obligatory in the WL sentence, but optional in the MR case.

(16) WL. *Yaremat ka* [lai] *le* [selimel] ila sar skuul.
person these child-my RM 3-animates (topic) students
'These three children of mine are students.'

MR. Ye-har kagiy *may kew* (mey) [kijėh].
RM
'He ate those breadfruit of mine.'

Kusaiean is an exception in that the relative marker *ma* which may appear before a predicational relative clause is not allowed before an assumed equational clause. Thus, we notice the different degrees of allowance of a relative marker before an equational clause. Probably, the Kusaiean case may be viewed as obligatory deletion (or non-occurrence) of the relative marker in the equational context.

Third, in the languages (e.g., WL and GL) where the set of demonstratives appearing before a (predicational) relative clause are distinct formally from the set of demonstratives appearing elsewhere, only the former set are allowed before an equational clause, as illustrated in (17).

(17) WL. *predication* *kook mwu* [ye gach] 'that coke which is good'

equation *kook mwu* [iuliumemw] 'that coke which is yours'

cf. kook mwuul 'that coke (near you)'

*kook mwu
*kook mwuul ye gach
*kook mwuul iuliumemw

GL.	*predication*	*waa ake* [raoiroi]	'those canoes which are good'
	equation	*waa ake* [nimawaa]	'those canoes which are five'

cf. waa akei 'these canoes here'
*waa ake
*waa akei raoiroi
*waa akei nimawaa

Fourth, in Mokilese, the relative marker may incorporate in itself the antecedent before both predicational and equational clauses, as illustrated below. // marks the subject-predicate boundary.

(18) MK. *predication* Ngoah // *ma* [wahdo mwingehu].
I one-who bring-hither food-that
'I am the one who brought that food.'

equation Rien John jeripeinno // *ma* [pahien
sibling-of girl-that spouse-of
doaksoahn wai wadwadmen].
doctor-of foreign famous-a
'John's elder sister is the (one who is the) wife of a famous American doctor.'

Fifth, in a multiple relative construction in Woleaian where more than one relative clause modifies one and the same antecedent, the relative marker *le* appears before clauses of both predicational and equational types. In (19), the second relative clause is of the equational type, and the third of the predicational type. Notice that both these clauses are preceded by the relative marker *le*.

(19) WL. Ye toar *mele* [i guila] [*le* terel]
it not-exist ANT-the-thing I know-it cause-its
[*le* ye sa wegiteg tipel shoabut we].
it prf. subside feeling-of girl the
'I don't know the way how he could persuade the girl.'

Sixth, in a language where a demonstrative is required in principle if a noun phrase is the antecedent of a (predicational) relative clause, the same constraint seems to apply to the antecedent of an equational type of clause.

(20) KS. *predication* El use *won se* [ma kahskahs oahna
he bring bird a which talk like
mwet uh] *ah*.
man the the
'He brought a bird which talks like a man.'

equation *Kosro ngalnguhl soko* [nuhtik] *ah*
dog one Cl-my the
arlac kuh.
very strong
'This dog of mine is very strong.'

GL. *predication* Bon anne *te b'ai ae* [ti aoaoraki iai]
it's that the thing this this we sick of
'That is something we are usually sick of.'

equation Taiaoka rooko nakou *te um'a ae*
please come to the house this
[um'au].
house-my
'Please come to this house of mine.'

Seventh, in Micronesian languages there are constructions which may be viewed as purely appositive, as illustrated in (21). Such constructions must be handled differently from the assumed equational type of relative clauses. An attempt to handle them within a single frame of apposition would complicate the grammar to a considerable extent in view of the peculiarities in the semantic and syntactic differences between the two sets.

(21) WL. gelai mai 'my breadfruit'
TR. eney maay 'my breadfruit'
MK. koanoai moai 'my breadfruit'
MR. kijėh may 'my breadfruit'
KS. mos nak 'my breadfruit'
oak luhmkoe 'five canoes'
GL kanau mai 'my breadfruit'
nimawaa waa 'five canoes'

Eighth, since we have two major types of simple sentences in all the Micronesian languages as stated in the beginning of this section, it is theoretically reasonable to recognize the same two types of relative clauses, since in theory the underlying structure of a relative clause itself is that of a complete simple sentence.

Finally, if we assume the existence of equational relative clauses, we can simply apply the two processes we have postulated in Section 2, i.e., Equi-NP deletion and relative marker insertion/deletion, to equational relativization. Then, the sentences in (14) are considered to have been derived from the following underlying structures.

(22) WL. ← Ye gangin mai kawe [gelai mai kawe]
TR. ← Aa ȧni eney kkawe [maay eney kkewe]
MK. ← Ih kang-la koanoai [moai koanoai-ok]-ok
MR. ← Ye-har kagiy may kew [kijėh may kew]
KS. ← Oak [luhmkoe oak ah] ah ac som nuh Kuam
GL. ← Waa ake [nimawaa akekei waa akei] a tabe n nako Kuaam

Notice that the deleted embedded noun phrases all take the subject position, i.e., the second position in an equational sentence in the underlying structure. This is the common (probably the only) pattern of equational relativization.[4]

4. Syntactic Aspects in Common

Since the languages compared belong, genetically, to the so-called nuclear group of Micronesian languages, they have many typological features in common with regard to relative clause formation. Some general syntactic aspects shared by the languages have been alluded to in the preceding sections. Some more specific common aspects will be discussed briefly in what follows.

First of all, all the languages have relative clauses of the $[NS]_{NP}$ type, i.e., a relative clause always follows the antecedent. This may be a predominant pattern of the languages of the prepositional type, as implied in "Universal 24" in Greenberg (1966a:90-91).

Another characteristic is that all the languages in question place the relative marker, if it appears at all, immediately before the relative clause. Again, this may be universal to relative clauses of the [NS] type, as pointed out in Schwartz (1971:139-44). The following sentence illustrates this fact.

(23) MK. Ngoah kangla *mwingehu* [*ma* [*koah kihdoahng ngoahi*
ANT RM RC

I ate food that you gave-to me
aio]].
yesterday
'I ate the food you gave me yesterday.'

Thus, the basic structure of a relative clause in Micronesian languages is: ANT + RM + RC. It seems that RM is more closely related to RC than to ANT in that appearance of RM is conditioned by the presence of RC. Besides, as we have seen in (19), the relative marker may be detachable from the antecedent but not from the relative clause. Therefore, the relevant tree would be of the form:

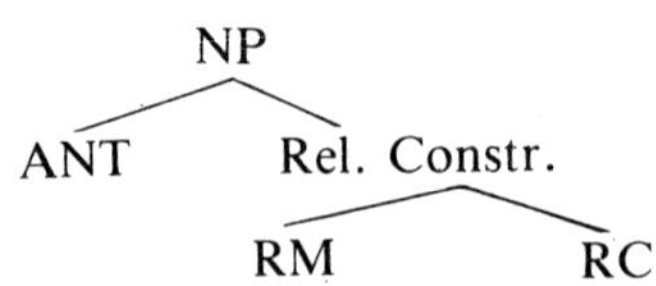

In Woleaian, the relative marker *le* never shows up if there is a demonstrative, which brings up the question as to whether *le* is in complementary distribution with a demonstrative or whether it follows or precedes a demonstrative in underlying structure and is deleted on the surface. It can be said that the position of *le,* even though it is not realized, is still after the demonstrative in view of the evidence from the other Micronesian languages. Ulithian, which is the language most closely related to Woleaian, maintains the relative marker *là* after a demonstrative as shown below.

(24) Ulithian. Ye mommay yengaang le [*là* John ye feoruy].
it good work this that he did-it
'This work which John did is good.'

A third characteristic in common is that relative markers seem to be tending to lose their grounds for existence. As already mentioned, their function tends to be limited to that of conjunction only. And that in many cases, their presence is syntactically redundant—to say nothing of their meaning, if any. Therefore, they frequently do not appear, obligatorily or optionally. They are invariant, not being syntactically or semantically oriented toward the function of either the antecedent or the embedded noun phrase which is coreferential with the antecedent. The fact that a relative marker is semantically (nearly) empty may be illustrated in (25) where the presence or absence of *mey* does not bring in any meaning difference (Bender

1969a:165-67).

(25) MR. Ye-har lew jet libbiqey [(mey) jėyjah].
he-past see some shell which rare
'He found some shells which are rare.'

A fourth characteristic in common is that, while relative markers are losing syntactic significance, demonstratives with their highly developed system are gaining an important role in relative clause formation. A demonstrative provides the antecedent with definiteness and specification of number and deixis, in addition to other features. Since the relative marker does not appear frequently, particularly when there is a demonstrative, a demonstrative occurring with a relative clause takes on the function of relating the clause to the antecedent. In Woleaian and Gilbertese, a preclause demonstrative has a shape different from one with other functions. In these languages, therefore, the function of a demonstrative as a relative marker is even stronger. In languages like Kusaiean, when a noun phrase has a relative clause in it, one of the demonstratives must be used (K. Lee 1975a), as illustrated in (20). Observe the following examples where demonstratives function as if they were relative markers.

(26) WL. *Yaremat we* [re liiy] ila John.
ANT DEM they kill-him
that
'The man whom they killed was John.'

TR. *Ewe mwáàn* [re nniiy] iiy John.
DEM ANT they kill-him he
that person

MK. *Woall-o* [arai kojukdi] ioar John.
ANT DEM they killed (topic)
person that

MR. *L'e-yew* [re-har m̄an-ey] ye-j Jawan.
ANT DEM they-past kill-him he-prog.
person that

KS. *Mwet se* [eltahl uniyah] *ah* pa Sohn.
ANT they killed DEM (topic)
person a the

GL. *Te mm̄aane are* [a tia ni kamatea] bon Tiaon.
ANT DEM they already kill-him was
the man that

A fifth characteristic is that the same pattern of coreference prevails in all the languages compared. That is, the embedded noun phrase which is coreferential with the antecedent may be the subject, direct or indirect object of the verb, object of the preposition, attribute of a noun phrase, or an adjunct (oblique case) in the relative clause. Moreover, basically the same Equi-NP deletion pattern is shared by these languages. That is, the embedded noun phrase in the relative clause is suppressed when coreferential with the antecedent. These facts are illustrated below.

When the subject of an equational relative clause is coreferential with the antecedent, it is deleted without any reflex of it remaining within the clause. The only member of the clause left out on the surface, therefore, is the predicate noun phrase, as discussed in Section 3.

When the subject of a predicational relative clause is coreferential with the antecedent, it is generally deleted. For exceptional cases with MK and KS, see Section 5. In certain languages, the subject (or predication) marker is also deleted, as we will observe in Section 5. The sentence in (27) illustrates the subject deletion common to all the languages compared.

(27) GL. *Aomata akeke* [a kukurei akekei] boni kaiin au
person those they happy there are group my
reirei.
school
'Those happy persons over there are my students.'
← Aomata akeke [*aomata akekei* a kukurei akekei] boni au reirei.

When the direct or indirect object of the verb in a predicational relative clause is coreferential with the antecedent, it is deleted, with the object suffix of the verb, if any, intact. In all these languages, if a relative clause contains both the direct and indirect objects of the verb, the object suffix of the verb always agrees with the indirect object, regardless of the coreferentiality with the antecedent. The sentence in (28) contains only one object, while those in (29a) and (29b) each have two objects, direct and indirect. (29a) illustrates an antecedent being coreferential with the direct object and (29b) an antecedent being coreferential with the indirect object. Notice in (29b) that the object suffix *-y* in *ganney* 'give him' agress with the underlying indirect object in the embedded clause, i.e., *yaremat la*.

(28) WL. Yaremat we [re liiy] ila John.
kill-him

'The man whom they killed is John.'
← Yaremat we [re liiy *yaremat we*] ila John

(29) a. WL. Ye log *seliuw buk* [*le* i be gennag].
it stay 3 book that I will give-you
'I have three books to give to you.'
← Ye log seliuw buk [le i be gennag *seliuw buk*]

b. WL. *Yaremat la* [i be ganne*y* buk we laiu] ila
that give-him tomorrow
merayerai.
friend-my
'That person whom I shall give the books to tomorrow is my friend.'
← Yaremat la [i be ganne*y* *yaremat la* buk we laiu]
ila merayerai

When the object of a verb-like preposition in a relative clause is coreferential with the antecedent, it is deleted, with the object suffix of the preposition intact. The sentences in (30) illustrate this.

(30) TR. *Ewe mettòòch* [John aa mmwus-ááseni] ooch apen.
that thing prf. vomit with-it some apple
'That which John vomited is a piece of apple.'
← Ewe mettòòch [John as mmwus-ááseni *ewe mettooch*]
ooch apen

MR. *Men yew* [ye-kkay ham nahginmėj yakey] ṅey.
thing that it usual our(excl) sickness about-it that
'That is something we are usually sick of.'
← Men yew [ye-kkay ham nahginmėj yak*ey* men yew] nėy

Notice in the above MR sentence that *men yew* is the object of the verb-like preposition *yakey,* which is not related to the embedded main verb *kkay* 'be usual' but to the still more deeply embedded *nahginmėj* 'be sick'. The construction *ham nahginmėj yakey (men yew)* 'our being sick with it (that thing)' is a nominalized clause which functions as the embedded subject. As mentioned in Section 1, coreference is operative between an antecedent and a noun phrase quite deeply embedded. This is a general phenomenon common to the Micronesian languages compared.

When the attribute (or possessor) of a noun phrase is coreferential with the antecedent, it is deleted, with the concurrent change of the construct suffix 'of' to a third person possessive suffix, as discussed in Section 2.

Here are some more examples.

(31) TR. *Enaan mwààn* [*meyi* minefė nėwùn ppwuk] neyiy
that guy that new Cl-his book Cl-my
chóón sukun.
person-of school
'That guy whose book is new is my student.'
← Enaan mwáàn [meyi minefė nėwù*n* *enaan mwààn* ppwuk] neyiy chóón sukun of

MK. Noai jeripeinn-o painki *woall-o* [*ma* jamah-*u*
Cl-my daughter-the marry man-the that father-his
koapwoahpwoa].
rich
'My daughter married that man whose father is rich.'
← Noai jeripeinn-o painki woall-o [ma jeme-*n* *woall-o* koapwoahpwoa] of

KS. *Tuhlihk muhtwahn se* [*ma* Tuhlwen el kihnisyac
girl a that he pinched
niyahl] *ah* tuhngyak.
leg-her the began-crying
'The girl whose leg Tuhlwen pinched began to cry.'
← Tuhlihk muhtwahn se [ma Tuhlwen el kihnisyac niye*n* *tuhlihk mutwahn sac*] ah tuhngyak

The above pronominalization in a relative clause, i.e., construct suffix 'of' + noun phrase (or attribute) → third person possessive suffix, takes place whenever the coreference condition is met irrespective of the function of the head noun of the attribute (i.e., the noun to which the construct suffix is suffixed). In (31), the TR and MK sentences illustrate the case where the head of the attribute (*nėwù-* and *jamah-*) is the subject of each relative clause, while the KS sentence gives an example where the head (*niyah-*) is the object of the verb in the relative clause. In the sentence in (32), the head of the attribute is the adjunct (or oblique case) of the relative clause.

(32) TR. Ina ena *mettòò*ch [si sowu semmwen ree*n*].
that that something we habit. sick at-its
'That is something we are usually sick of.'
← Ina ena mettóóch [si sowu semmwen ree*n* *mettòò*ch] of

When the whole adjunct (or oblique case) is co-referential with the antecedent, there appears a discrepancy among the languages concerned. This will be discussed in Section 5. Except for this and some MK and KS (Section 5) cases, what we have discussed so far with regard to coreference may be formularized as follows, which is considered to apply to all the languages concerned.

Equi-NP pronominalization/deletion (Obligatory Rule)

$$\underbrace{[\mathrm{NP_i}\ [\ldots}_{1}\ \underbrace{\begin{bmatrix} \text{construct suffix} + \mathrm{NP_i} \\ [\alpha\ \text{pl. hum.}] \\ \mathrm{NP_i} \end{bmatrix}}_{2}\ \underbrace{\ldots]_S \ldots]_{NP}}_{3}$$

$$\rightarrow 1 + \begin{bmatrix} \text{3rd per. } \alpha \text{ pl. poss. suffix} \\ \varnothing \end{bmatrix} + 3$$

The syntactic feature [α pl. hum.] is required, because if an attribute is plural and human the third person possessive suffix takes the plural form, and otherwise it takes the singular form, as observed below.

(33)	WL.	metal yaremat we	'the person's eyes'
		→ meta*l*	'his eyes'
		metal yaremat kawe	'those people's eyes'
		→ metaa*r*	'their eyes'

A sixth characteristic in common is that these languages apply the same processes of Equi-NP pronominalization/deletion to both relativization and topicalization or focus. Observe the parallelism between the two sentences in (34).

(34)	*relativization*	WL.	mwal we [ye ffeo yaal buk] 'the man whose book is new' ← mwal we [ye ffeo yaal mwal we buk]
	topic./focus	WL.	Mwal we ila/mele ye ffeo yaal buk. top. foc. 'As for the man, his book is new./ It is the man that his book is new.' ← Mwal we ila/male [ye ffeo yaal mwal we buk]

Finally, the process of adjectivization is similar among the languages compared. A relative clause whose coreferential (or controlled) noun phrase is deleted as the subject and whose main verb is of the descriptive (or adjective) type and is the only member of the clause may optionally be reduced to an adjective construction. The processes involved are (a) deletion of the relative marker, (b) deletion of the predication (or subject) marker or personal pronoun, and (c) movement of the demonstrative modifying the antecedent to the position immediately after the embedded verb. (35) illustrates these processes.

(35) MK. Ngoah mewhuki armajj-e [ma ih mwehu].
like person-this who he good
'I like this person who is good.'
→ Ngoah mwehuki armaj mwehu-e.
this
'I like this good person.'

The above characteristics are certainly not exhaustive. There may be many more yet to be discovered.

5. Syntactic Divergence

Along with a number of syntactic aspects in common among the languages compared, we also notice many syntactic differences among them with regard to relative clause formation. In the following we will limit ourselves to a discussion of relative markers, demonstratives, subject markers (or pronouns), pronominalization, and equational relative clauses.

Obviously, the four languages, WL, MK, MR and KS, each have an invariant word as a relative marker as follows.[5]

(36) WL. le MR. mey
MK. ma KS. ma

Notice the appearance of these relative markers in the sentences in (37).

(37) WL. I tipeli semal yaremat [le ye gach].
want-it 1 person that he good
'I like a person who is good.'
MK. Ngoah mwehuki emen armajjok [*ma* mwehu].
I good-with 1 person-those that good
MR. Yi-keṅahan harmėj r̄et yeṅ [mey ye-ṁṁan].
I-like person kind that that he-good
KS. Nga luhngse mwet se [*ma* wo] uh.
I like man a that good the

All these markers have a common function, i.e., that of conjunction, and their semantic content is negligible. Gilbertese, on the other hand, does not have any word which may be called a relative marker, as observed below.

(38) GL. I tatangiriia aomata akana [a raraoi].
like-them person those they good
'I like those persons who are good.'

In Trukese, *meyi* and *minne* are the words which might be considered the relative markers, although no agreement seems to have been reached among scholars on the status of these words. Dyen (1965: 13-28), for example, calls *meyi* a particle functioning as a noun and *minne* a relative. Goodenough and Sugita (personal communication) call *meyi* a stative marker and view *minne* as a possible relative marker. *Meyi* seems to function like a relative marker comparable to those in (36) in the sentences below.

(39) a. TR. Ese wor pecheriyen John *meyi sine kkapasen*
it-not exist relative-of John one-who know speech-of
Ingenes.
English
'John doesn't have any relative who can speak English.'

b. TR. Nupwen ekkewe semiriit raa nȯ pėnchė, iir *meyi*
when those children they go toilet they ones-who
sowu tėnu̇ pėwu̇u̇r?
habit. clean hand-their
'When the children go to the toilet, do they usually clean their hands?'

c. TR. Wu̇ saani emėn aramas *meyi (aramas) ėėch.*
I like I person one-who good
'I like a person who is good.'

In spite of the above relative-like function, *meyi* has some unique features which are not shared by the relative markers in (36). First of all, *meyi* may not be followed by a predication (or subject) marker or a tense aspect particle. Secondly, a demonstrative may modify *meyi* to make it specific and/or definite, as in (40).

(40) TR. Sipwe niffang eey mwaramwar ngeni iyė ewė *meyi ėėch.*
we-will give this lei to who that one-who good
'We will award this lei to someone who is good.'

Third, *meyi* itself always functions as the subject of the following verb. No other noun is allowed as the subject. For example, *meyi sine kkapasen Ingenes* 'one who knows English' is grammatical but **meyi ewe yaremat sine* 'one whom the person knows' is ungrammatical. Fourth, *meyi* seems to have its own semantic content which is different from conjunctive meaning, i.e., 'one (who)', 'ones (who)', 'one (which)', etc. Since this is the case, it may freely appear as an initial element or the head of a noun phrase.

(41) a. TR. *Meyi wor reey* wúnúngát ppwuk wúpwe ngoanuk.
exist at-my 3 book I-will give-you
'I have three books to give to you.'

b. TR. Ngaang *meyi semmwen.*
'I am sick (or a sick one).'

In (41), *meyi,* together with *wor reey* or *semmwen,* forms the predicate constituent of the equational sentences. From these observations, it seems that *meyi* is a defective noun (or pronoun) which functions as the subject antecedent of a nominalized clause. It is defective in that it does not appear without a following clause. The nominalization of the clause is allowed only when the subject is co-referential with *meyi* and there is no tense-aspect morpheme. In the sentences in (39), it seems to me that the noun phrase preceding *meyi* and *meyi* itself are in apposition rather than in an antecedent-relative marker relation. Thus, *meyi* is not a relative marker.

As for *minne,* Sugita (personal communication) shows its possible function as a relative marker in the sentences below.

(42) TR. *Ewe ààt* [(minne) inan we aa máá-nó] iiy emén
the boy that mother-his that she-prf. die he I
néwun pwiiy we.
son-of brother-my the
'The boy whose mother is dead is a son of a brother of mine.'

TR. Ina *ewe iimw* [(minne) ósun we aa ássinó reen ewe
that the house that roof-its the it-prf. blown by the
tayifuun].
typhoon
'That is the house whose roof was blown off by the typhoon.'

As in the case of the relative markers of the other languages, *minne* may optionally be deleted without any change in meaning, and its major function, at least in the above sentences, is to connect the relative clause with the antecedent without itself having any noticeable semantic content.

Another divergence with regard to relative markers is found in their syntactic uses. The relative markers do not always occur in relative constructions. The pattern of their appearance is different from language to language. In general, MK, MR and KS allow the relative marker to appear in much broader contexts than WL and TR. MK and KS share a similar pattern in the use of the relative marker. Let us observe this more closely in terms of a few relevant syntactic environments.

A relative marker is allowed before an equational clause in MR and WL, but not in the other languages. See Section 3 for the examples. In all the languages but TR and GL, a relative marker may appear before a predicational clause whose coreferential noun phrase may have any function—subject, direct or indirect object of the verb, prepositional object, attribute, or adjunct. In TR, however, the relative marker *minne* may appear only with a clause where the coreferential noun phrase is the attribute of a noun phrase, as we have seen in (42) and (43). Remember that GL does not have a relative marker.

A relative marker may appear with a demonstrative that modifies the antecedent in TR, MK, MR and KS, but not in WL. Observe the sentences in (43).

(43) WL. Sar mwal *la* [(**le*) ye bel mwongo] ila semal
child male DEM he will eat (topic) I
rebiuleiu kaiy.
person-place here
'The boy who is going to eat is one of my neighbors.'

TR. *Ewe* ȧȧt [(*minne*) itan Taro] e mwocen cuuruk.
DEM boy his his name he want see-you.
'The boy whose name is Taro wants to see you.'

MK. Jerimweinn*o* [*ma* pirin ken mwinge] (ih) emen in
boy-that (DEM) that will then eat he 1 of
noai piriennok.
my friend-those

MR. L'adik *yew* [(*mey*) ye-j yiten m̈egay] ye-j m̈ettan
boy DEM he-prog. go eat he part-of
harmėj rañey yitiṙi-h.
people those near-me

KS. Tuhlihk se [*ma* ac mongo] *uh* sie sin mwet tuhlan
child a will eat DEM one of people neighbor

luhk ah.
my the

GL. Te ataei ni mm'aane *ane* [(*) nangi tabe n
the child of boy that (DEM) will -ing of
am'arake] boni kaain rarikiu.
eat is live near-my

In MR and TR, a relative marker is optionally deletable in all cases (see (43) for example). In MK and KS, it is a general rule that the relative marker must appear before a predicational clause if the coreferential noun phrase is the subject. (43) illustrates this. In all the other cases, MK and KS allow it to be deleted optionally. In WL, the relative marker *le* must be introduced, in general, when the antecedent is not modified by a demonstrative, and it is not deletable.

Differences also appear in the use of antecedent-modifying demonstratives. As briefly mentioned elsewhere, WL and GL both have two sets of demonstratives, one set occurring only before a relative clause and the other elsewhere. The former set has both spatial and mental reference of deixis, while the latter has only spatial reference with emphasis of location. For example, WL *ye* 'this' appears only before a relative clause as in *sar ye ye gach* 'this good child', while *yeel* 'this here' elsewhere as in *sar yeel* 'this child here'. In the same way, GL *ae* 'this' appears only before a relative clause, while *aio* or *aei* 'this here' elsewhere. So far as my data indicate, the rest of the languages do not show the same kind of alternation. In Trukese, there are two sets of demonstratives which are formally distinct but without difference in meaning. For example, *ewe* vs. *we* 'that', and *ekkewe* vs. *kkewe* 'those'. The demonstratives with initial *e-* occur only before the noun they modify, whereas those without it only after. In Trukese, if a demonstrative modifies an attributive construction, it necessarily follows it, otherwise it always precedes the modified noun. Thus, the two Trukese sets depend not on the presence or absence of a relative clause but on the morphological structure of the word they modify, as in *ewe mwaan* 'that man (we are talking about)', *waan we* 'that canoe of his', and *waan ewe mwaan we* 'that canoe of that man'.

Still another divergence is found in the position of a demonstrative in relation to the relative clause and its antecedent. Three different sets of relative order between the demonstrative and the rest are observable: (a) demonstrative between antecedent and relative clause, (b) demonstrative before both, and (c) demonstrative after both, as in:

(a) ANT + DEM + RC
(b) DEM + ANT + RC
(c) ANT + RC + DEM

As we discussed in Section 4, the relative order between an antecedent and the relative clause is fixed throughout the Micronesian languages, i.e., ANT + RC. It is DEM which has the freedom of occurrence in different positions. The (a) order is predominant in that a majority of geographically separate languages follow it. WL, MR and GL belong to the (a) order in both predicational and equational relative constructions, as observed below.

(44) *predication* WL. Ye gachiur *shoa ka re gachiuw.*
like-them people these they like-him
ANT DEM RC
'He likes people who like him.'

MR. Ye keṅahan *harmėj r̈et yeṅ ye-yiyaqey yėy.*
like people kind the he-love him
ANT DEM RC

GL. E tangiriia *aomata ane e tangiria.*
like-them people those they like-him
ANT DEM RC

equation WL. Faal pesheemw nge go be buu tog mwo
under feet-your but you will come
reel *imw ye imwei.*
just to house this Cl-my
ANT DEM RC

MR. Jėwij yim yiteq gan *ṁi-yin yiṁėh.*
kind & come to house-this Cl-my
ANT DEM RC

GL. Taiaoka ma rooko nakou te *um'a ae um'au.*
please but come to the house this Cl-my
ANT DEM RC

MK belongs to the (a) order in predicational relative constructions, as illustrated in (45).

(45) MK. Ih kin mwehuki *armaj-koa ma kin mwehuki ih.*
he habit. good-with person the who him
ANT DEM RC

TR belongs to the (a) order only in equational relative clause construction of the type in which the antecedent is an attributive construction. If the antecedent is other than an attributive construction, it belongs to the (b) order, as we will see shortly.

(46) TR. *Wu̇nu̇momw na kkok* e-se pat.
drink-your that coke it-not cold
ANT DEM RC
'That coke of yours is not cold.'

The only member that belongs to the (b) order is TR. Except for the type of equational construction illustrated in (46), this order is the only possible way in both predicational and equational constructions in TR, as shown below.

(47) TR. *predication* Aa saani *ekkewe aramas re pwan*
he-prf. like-him those person they also
DEM ANT RC
saani.
like-him
'He likes people who like him.'
equation A'yitingeni *ekkena nimmėn iik wu̇nu̇kkumw.*
Pass-him those 5 fish beside-your
'Pass him those five fish (which are) near you.'

KS is the language typical of the (c) order, while MK floats between the (a) and (c) orders. In both types of relative constructions, (c) is the only allowable order for KS, as in (48).

(48) KS. *predication* El luhngse *mwet ma luhngse-l uh.*
he like-him person who like-him the
ANT RC DEM
'He likes the person who likes him.'
equation El rahrah elan liye tuhlihk
he anxious he-to see child
muhtwahn se nuhtuhl ah.
female a Cl-his the
ANT RC DEM
'He is anxious to see the daughter of his.'

As mentioned above, MK predicational relative constructions are basically of the (a) order. However, it is possible for a demonstrative (except -*wa* 'that (we know)') to follow a predicational relative clause resulting in the (c) order, although it is less common (Harrison 1976).

(49) MK. Ioar woall-e ma ngoah kapang.
behold man-this that I saw
ANT DEM RC
→ Ioar *woal ma ngoah kapangg-e.*
behold
ANT RC DEM
'It was this man that I saw.'

A further peculiarity with MK is that with the movement of a demonstrative to the end it is common to delete the relative marker *ma* and the subject pronoun of the relative clause if the subject is coreferential with the antecedent. This process looks like an extension of adjectivization discussed in Section 4, although it is not adjectivization itself in that transitive relative constructions are also subject to this process as in (50).

(50) MK. Ngoah kijradki jeripeinn-*ok ma* (*ih*) kin nimen lallal.
I hate-with girl-that that she habit. like talk
'I hate the girl who likes to talk.'
→ Ngoah kijradki jeripein kin nimen lallall-*ok*.

It seems to me that this dual possibility is due to the geographico-linguistic closeness to both the (a) order language (MR) and the (c) order language (KS).

Also differing from the other languages, MK may have two demonstratives, one following the antecedent and the other following the relative clause (*ibid.*), i.e., ANT + DEM + RC + DEM. It seems to me that one of the demonstratives is redundant both syntactically and semantically and therefore it is assumed that one of them will eventually disappear once and for all, rather than remain optionally as it stands now, in view of the fundamental nature of language that tends to eliminate complete redundancy. Observe the double demonstratives in (51).

(51) MK. Ioar *woall-e ma ngoah kapangg-e.*
ANT DEM RC DEM

In MK equational type constructions, the natural order is (c), as illustrated below.

(52) MK. Ih adpwal in kapang *nah jeripeinn-o.*
child-his girl-that

ANT RC DEM
'He is anxious to see the daughter of his.'

The (a) order, *nah-o jeripein,* is totally ungrammatical.

What we have said thus far regarding the position of a demonstrative may be summarized as follows.

order type	predication	equation
(a) type	WL, MR, GL, MK	WL, MR, GL, TR*
(b) type	TR	TR
(c) type	KS, MK**	KS, MK

*Only when ANT is an attributive constr.
**As an optional derivation from the (a) type.

Another divergence among the languages compared may be observable in the deletability of the predication (or subject) marker or the subject pronoun (in MK) in a relative clause in which the subject is coreferential with the antecedent. In WL, TR and MR, deletion of the subject marker is not allowed, as observed below.

(53) WL. Sar ka *re* tangiteng ila re be ttiril mas.
child those they cry (topic) they will fast-of die
'Those children who cry all the time die early.'
TR. Ekkewe semiriit *re* sowu kkechiuw re mȧ mwittir.
those children they habit. cry they die early
MR. Hajriy r̄et yen *ye*-jjagjag yė-mėj m̄ekaj.
child kind that he cry he die early

In MK, KS and GL, deletion of the subject marker (or pronoun) is allowed with different degrees of optionality. In MK, the subject pronoun is obligatorily deleted unless it is coreferential with the *human* antecedent in which case its deletion is optional.

(54) MK. Pahioaio wiahda ew pukohk ma (**ih*) riskihdi
wife-my-that made a basket-those that close-with
skrihnin pahrang.
screen-of wire
'My wife made a basket which is closed with a net.'
MK. Jeriok ma (*arai*) kin joang anjoau ohroj nen
child-those that they habit. cry time all will
pispis ahr mehdi.
quick their die

'Those children who cry all the time die early.'

In KS, the subject marker is obligatorily deleted if the relative marker *ma* is present, while it is optionally deleted if *ma* is absent.

(55) KS. Tuhlihk se $\left\{\begin{matrix} (el) \\ ma\ (*el) \end{matrix}\right\}$ nuhmlah piru ah arlac sruhilac.
child a that he drink-up beer the very drunken
'The child who drank up the beer became very drunken.'

In GL, the subject marker is optionally deleted without restriction.

(56) GL. Anganna iikana (*a*) kaani ma' ngkoe.
give-him fish they near with you
'Pass him those fish near you.'

If the subject of a relative clause is not coreferential with the antecedent, the subject marker must be present in all the languages under discussion.

Divergence among the languages appears in pronominalization too. MK is a language which does not have the paradigm of predication markers. In this language, if the subject of a relative clause is coreferential with the antecedent, that subject, instead of being deleted, is replaced by the corresponding personal pronoun, i.e., the pronoun with the same person and number features. This pronoun functions like a predication marker in other languages and may optionally be deleted as discussed above. KS has a similar pattern (K. Lee, personal communication). One exception in KS is that if the subject is a singular human proper noun the personal pronoun *el* 'he' appears after the noun functioning as a predication marker. If this construction is placed as a relative clause and the subject is coreferential with the antecedent, then the proper noun is not pronominalized but simply deleted as with the other languages except MK. In the rest of the languages, all of which have predication markers, no pronominalization is made in the subject position of a relative clause. The subject is simply deleted as indicated in Section 4. Observe the following MK example, in which *arai* 'they' is a personal pronoun derived through pronominalization.

(57) MK. Ngoah kijradki *jeripeinnok* [ma (arai) kin nimen lallal].
I hate-with girl-those who they habit. like talk
'I hate those girls who are talkative.'
← Ngoah kijradki jeripeinnok [ma *jeripeinnok* kin nimen lallal]

Another difference between MK and the rest of the languages is observable in locative pronominalization. In all the languages but MK, if a locative adjunct (or oblique case) in a relative clause is coreferential with the antecedent, it is replaced by an anaphoric locative pronoun instead of complete deletion. In MK, the adjunct is completely deleted. The locative pronouns used in the above languages (except for MK) have the meaning 'there, about it, at it...' and are very similar to each other in form, which implies that they are related historically to each other. They are as follows.

(58) WL. iyang   KS. we
TR. iye   GL. iai
MR. yiyėy

In the following example sentences, the anaphoric locative pronouns in the relative clauses are italicized. Observe that these pronouns appear exactly where the corresponding locative nouns would have occurred in underlying structures, that is, at the end of the relative clauses, as illustrated in the WL sentence.

(59) WL. Ifa ssengal yaamw giula *biuleiu we* [re mil *iyang*]?
which way-of your know place the they live there
'How do you know the place where they live?'
← Ifa ssengal yaamw giula biuleiu we [re mil *biuleiu we*]?

TR. Ifa wussun oomw sineey *ewe neeni* [re nnomw *iye*])
way-of your know-it the place they live there

MR. Yė-wiy waywėyėn ham̀ jel'ay kajjiyen *yijew*
it-where way-of your know-it location-of there
[re-j jėqėy *yiy*ėy]?
they-prog live there

KS. Kom etuh fuhkah acn se [ma eltahl muhta *we*] ah?
you know how place a that they stay there the

GL. Ko kangara n tia ata te tabo are [a maeka *iai*]?
you now past know the place that they live there

In contrast with the above, the following MK sentence illustrates the lack of locative anaphora.

(60) MK. Imdoahr oamw kidal wijahu [ma arai mine]?
how your know place-that that they stay

If the adjunct in a relative clause that is coreferential with the antecedent is other than a locative expression, it is deleted rather than being pronominalized in all the languages but WL. In WL, it is either pronominalized or deleted, with slight emphasis on the adjunct if pronominalized.

A typical case is where the adjunct is a time expression, as shown below.

(61) WL. I tewai maliuwegili lag yat we [i buu long lan
will-not forget away time the come in in
kalech (*iyang*)].
college at-it
'I will not forget the time when I entered the college.'

TR. Wúsapw ménnúúkóóńó ewe eewin fansowun [wúwa
I-will-not forget the first time I-prf.
toonong nnon ewe kaanech].
enter in the college

MK. Ngoah jehpirin moalkoahla anjoawo [ma ngoah
I will-not forget time-that that
sapda oai doadoakin koahlej].
was-begun my work-of college

MR. Yi-b̄an mel'aql'aq yiyen yew [yi-har d̄eyl'ağ
I not-able forget time that I-past enter in
yilew kahl'ej]

KS. Nga tiyah kuh in muhlkuhnlah pacl se [ma nga som
I not able to forget time a that enter
nuh colege] ah.
to the

GL. Nna aki m'aninga te tai are [ngke i a tia ni
I-will not forget the time that when I past already
mena n te college].
place of the

Finally, divergence is also noticeable in the equational type of relative clauses. I will discuss only one typical case. In an equational relative clause where the antecedent or the coreferential subject and the predicate of the clause are in classifier-classified relation, there are different restrictions among the languages as to which between the classifier and the classified should be the antecedent or the coreferential subject of the clause. It has been assumed that there are equational relative clauses in Micronesian languages and that an antecedent precedes the associated relative clause. Observe the relative constructions below and notice the unacceptability of a classifier or a classified noun as the antecedent (the first noun in each phrase) according to different languages.

(62) WL. Mai kawe [gelai]
breadfruit those Cl-my
'those breadfruit of mine'
*gelai kawe [mai] *or* *gelai [mai] kawe

TR. eney kkewe [maay]
Cl-my
*maay kkewe [eney] *or* *kkewe maay [eney]

MK. koanoai [moai]-ok
Cl-my
*moai [koanoai]-ok *or* *moai-ok [koanoai]

MR. may kew [kijėh]
CL-my
*kijeh kew [may] or *kijeh [may] kew

KS. mos [nak] ah
Cl-my
*nak [mos] ah *or* *nak ah [mos]

GL. mai ake [kanau]
CL-my
*kanau ake [mai] *or* kanau [mai] ake

There are two patterns in the above, one allowing only the classified noun as an antecedent and the other allowing only the classifier noun as an antecedent. To the former belong WL, MR, KS and GL, while to the latter belong TR and MK. No language allows both as an antecedent. It seems to me that these restrictions are related to the constraint that in WL, MR, KS and GL an attributive construction (i.e., N-poss. suffix or N-construct suffix + attribute noun phrase) may not be directly modified by a demonstrative, while in TR and MK it may. In other words, in the former set of languages, an attributive construction and a demonstrative cannot be the sister constituents dominated by the same node, while in the latter they can be. Observe (63).

(63)

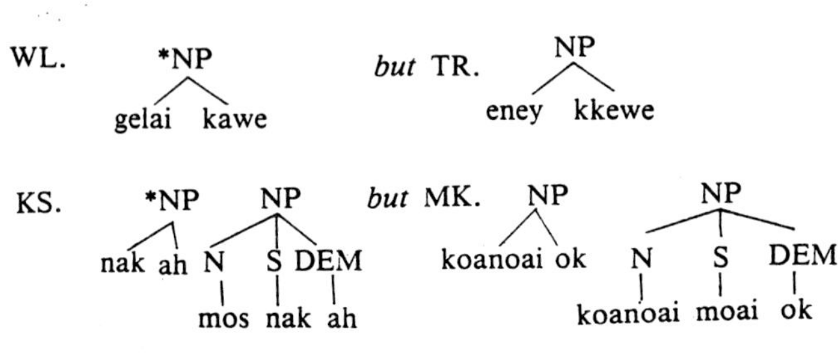

Because of the constraint illustrated in (63), WL **gelai kawe mai,* for example, should be ungrammatical because its underlying structure would be the ill-formed sequence **gelai kawe* [*mai gelai kawe*] in which *gelai kawe* is an unallowable sequence in WL. The same is true with MR, KS and GL. TR *eney kkewe maay* is grammatical since its underlying sequence *eney kkewe* [*maay eney kkewe*] is well formed. The same applies to MK. Incidentally, this may be another justification for the existence of equational relative clauses in Micronesian languages.

6. Conclusion.

The above discussion is far from being complete, but I think I have touched on a number of substantial points. We have observed a number of essential syntactic behaviors commonly shared by all the languages compared. Such behaviors, together with many other unique linguistic features, may characterize the languages as belonging to a subgroup of the Eastern Oceanic family. Alongside this commonality, we have also noticed quite a few differences among the languages of a language-specific nature and which may be relevant to the subgrouping of the languages. These differences can be summarized as follows.

	WL	TR	MK	MR	KS	GL
1. relative marker	+	+	+	+	+	–
2. broad use of relative marker	–	–	+	+	+	–
3. rel. marker before equational clause	+	–	–	+	–	–
4. rel. marker before all types of pred. clause	+	–	+	+	+	–
5. rel. marker/demonstrative cooccurrence	–	+	+	+	+	0
6. optional deletion of rel. marker	–	+	+	+	+	0
7. two sets of demonstrative	+	–	–	–	–	+
8. ANT + DEM + RC in pred. rel. construction	+	–	+	+	–	+
9. ANT + DEM + RC in equat. rel. construction	+	+	–	+	–	+

		WL	TR	MK	MR	KS	GL
10.	DEM + ANT + RC in pred/ equat. construction	−	+	−	−	−	−
11.	ANT + RC + DEM in pred/ equat. construction	−	−	+	−	+	−
12.	extended adjectivization & double demonstratives	−	−	+	−	−	−
13.	deletion of subject marker	−	−	+	−	+	+
14.	subject pronominalization	−	−	+	−	+	−
15.	locative pronominalization	+	+	−	+	+	+
16.	classifier as antecedent in equat. construction	−	+	+	−	−	−

On the basis of the above information, the numbers of both positively and negatively shared features are specified as follows.

	TR	MK	MR	KS	GL
WL	8	4	12	6	10
	TR	5	10	8	8
		MK	8	12	4
			MR	10	8
				KS	6

Or the higher number of shared features can be arrayed as follows:

		KS	10	MK
	8	10	8	
TR	10	MR		
8	8	12		
GL	10	WL		

The above results are somewhat contrary to our common subgrouping of the languages based on lexical cognates. For example, contrary to the common understanding that WL is the closest linguistically to TR, the above chart shows that WL is closer to MR and GL than to TR. On the other hand, as expected, KS and MK are the closest to each other. Since linguistic subgrouping should be based on the overall aspects of phonology, morphology, lexicon, syntax and semantics, I will not attempt to draw any generalization from the above findings of a limited nature.

Notes

1. The selection of the languages depended on considerations of geographical distribution, linguistic divergence, and availability of informants. For example, Ulithian and Ponapean have not been included for comparison, because Ulithian follows more or less the same pattern of relative clause formation as that of Woleaian, and Ponapean that of Mokilese. I gratefully acknowledge B. W. Bender, S. P. Harrison, K. D. Lee, H. Sugita, T. Tawerilmang and Terebata Groves for their kind provision of the language data and their valuable comments on this paper.
2. The following conventions and abbreviations are used in the present paper: relative clause (RC) and relative marker (RM) usually bracketed together; antecedent (ANT) and demonstratives (DEM) usually italicized; prf. = 'perfective' morpheme; habit. = 'habituative' morpheme; Cl = classifier; prog. = 'progressive' tense/aspect morpheme; ← means 'derived form' and → 'derived to'. Most of the spellings of the data sentences that were given to me are retained as they were in the present paper. One change I made is insertion of morpheme boundaries in certain cases.
3. A common Micronesian phrase type is that of attributive construction. An attributive construction consists of a head noun followed either by a possessive suffix or by the construct suffix + a noun phrase. The head noun belongs to a special subclass of nouns including classifiers, inalienable nouns and locative nouns. The construct suffix has the meaning roughly equivalent to 'of' in English. The noun phrase that follows the construct suffix is related to the head noun either as a possessor, an agent, a goal, or a reference and is here called an 'attribute' noun phrase. For example, in WL *waal mwal we* 'that man's canoe', *waa* is the head noun, *-l* the construct suffix and *mwal we* 'the man' the attribute noun phrase.
4. So far I have advocated the assumption that there are equational relative clauses in Micronesian languages from the point of view of comparative evidence. Certain languages appear less convincing than the others in the light of the above nine pieces of evidence, because some of the evidence is simply lacking in such individual languages. Even so, we must admit the existence of strong parallelism common to all with regard to the equational type. For a comparative description of the languages concerned, therefore, it will be much simpler and more consistent than otherwise to view all of them as having equational relative clauses. I do not claim, however, that a description of an individual language, where little motivation could be found on internal grounds, should be based on the same assumption.
5. Notice the similar shapes between MK, MR and KS. With the TR relative marker *minne* as the third witness, there could be a possibility of relating WL *le* to the others. TR *minne* frequently appears in a position where in WL sentences WL *mele* (a focus marker with the 'definite' meaning 'that' occurs. It seems that TR *minne* and WL *mele* may be related etymologically. WL *mele,* which may have been derived etymologically from *mel* 'thing'+ *e* 'this,' may be regarded as a derivational source of WL *le,* i.e., *le* resulting from a reanalysis

of *mele*. One piece of evidence for such a hypothesis is (19) in which both syntactic and semantic relation between *mele* and *le* may be observed. If we are to assumre for any reason that MK and KS *ma* and MR *mey* may be related to the first CV of TR *minne* (Dyen (1965) gives *menne* along with *minne* as relatives), the WL *le* may be related to the second half (*-nne*) in view of the above syllogism. This is, however, highly speculative, and needs further study.

Reprinted from *Oceanic Linguistics* (University of Hawaii) 12.1/2:353-392 (1973).

19. PROTO-OCEANIC REFLEXES IN WOLEAIAN

(with Anthony F. Tawerilmang)

1. General

Woleaian (WOL) is a nuclear Micronesian (MC) language spoken by some 1,400 inhabitants of the atolls of Woleai, Eauripik, Faccaulap, Elato, Lamotrek, and Ifaluk, all located in the Yap District of the Trust Territory of the Pacific Islands. The language used for comparison with Proto-Oceanic (POC) in this paper is the dialect of Woleai Atoll where Tawerilmang came from.[1] POC is the name given to the reconstructed language that comprises what have been traditionally known as the MC, Polynesian, and Melanesian groups, as over against the Indonesian or Western Austronesian. The few sets of POC reconstructions then available (which had generally not included data from MC languages) are collected with slight modifications in Grace 1969, to make a total of 698 POC lexical items.[2]

The aim of this paper is to describe the pattern of phonological evolution from POC to WOL through a comparison of the two sets of vocabulary. It is hoped that the findings presented in this paper will contribute to a larger and more significant undertaking: MC comparative linguistics. This hope is particularly strong in that WOL has been found to be a language which retains POC forms faithfully and consistently in terms of both the number of obvious cognates (see Appendix) and sound (especially vowel) reflexes.

2. Methodology

Since our main concern is the historical development of the phonological structure of WOL, it is imperative at the outset to draw the line between synchronic and diachronic aspects of WOL phonology. Needless to say, all rules are historical products in their origin, i.e. added in the course of time. However, addition of certain rules results in the restructuring of the underlying representations of lexical items, while addition of others has nothing to do with restructuring. Let us call the former type of rules diachronic and the latter, synchronic. For instance, the vowel *a* is obligatorily raised to *e* between two high vowels in WOL. Addition of this rule in the grammar of WOL has not yet been accompanied by any restructuring of relevant lexical items in underlying representations. Thus, the appearance of the alternation between *sila-* and *sile-* in *silasE* 'our (incl.) mother' and *silei* 'my mother' has not caused the underlying form *sila* 'mother' to be changed. On the other hand, the change of POC **t* to WOL *s,* as in POC **tina* 'mother' vs. WOL *sila,* has certainly resulted in restructuring of the underlying representation of relevant lexical items (e.g. **tina* > *sila*). Therefore, POC **t* > WOL *s* is a diachronic rule.

Suppose we directly compare POC **tina* and WOL *sile-* 'mother', as in the form *silei* 'my mother,' ignoring the existing synchronic alternation between *a* and *e* in WOL. We would have to describe the development as **tina* >*sila* >*sile.* This description would overlook the important fact that *sila* and *sile* are automatic alternants produced by a general rule of *a*-raising which currently applies to all forms that meet the given environment (cf. Sohn 1971 and Bender 1973). This rule, which has no exceptions, has nothing to do with the meanings of the lexical items involved, and may be presumed to be internalised by contemporary speakers of WOL. The change **t* >*s,* however, is neither exceptionless nor is it internalised by contemporary speakers. It may once have been a synchronic rule, but is now quite foreign to the native speaker, who does normally not even know of its existence.

Currently, there are two opposing views concerning the occurrence of restructuring. In transformational generative grammar as represented by Chomsky and Halle (1968), it seems that a rule remains synchronic as long as surface forms are derivable predictably from underlying representations even by means of powerful abstract devices. Restructuring is allowed only when no predictability is possible. In natural generative phonology, on the other hand, restructuring occurs much sooner, i.e., immediately upon the addition of a new phonological rule (e.g. Hooper 1974:121). This claim of the natural generativists is an integral part of their theoretical framework, which also includes the general abolishment of rule ordering, establishment of only one level of phonological representation, and adherence to the strong naturalness condition.[3]

Our concept of restructuring falls somewhere between these two extremes. We will not postulate any abstract devices, inasmuch as we believe that such devices are mostly far from the psychological reality of the native speaker. However, we will recognise the existence and importance of deep and surface levels of phonological representation. We will also admit a certain amount of ordering in phonological rules, not only to attain greater simplicity in the statement of the conditions associated with rules but to achieve greater generality in the statement of phonological processes. Let us take an example.

In WOL, we have a productive process called dissimilation, which, operating from right to left, raises *a* to *e* before a low vowel (Sohn 1975a:31-32).[4] Thus, we have the following alternations.

(1)	{ [meramE] [maremalI] }	'moon' 'moon of'
	{ [temai] [tamemamI] }	'my father' 'our (excl.) father'

In the natural generative framework, which admits only one level of phonological representation, the underlying stem of 'moon' would be either *merame* or *marema,* and that of 'father' either *tema* or *tame.* However, there is no way to predict one form from the other. Both forms in each set are derivable only from a third which is never realised on the surface, i.e. *marama* for 'moon' and *tama* for 'father.' If, in this situation, we were to consider both surface forms in each set as lexical representations, we would miss an important phonological generalisation (i.e. the dissimilation process) which is purely phonological and applies without exception. Moreover, to the linguistically unsophisticated native speaker of WOL, the formal difference between *meramE* and *marema* (in *maremalI*), for example, is not recognised, because it comes about entirely automatically, just as in allophonic alternation. We consider an allophonic variation to be a synchronic alternation. Then, there is no reason why we should not also consider purely phonological alternations such as this dissimilation process to be synchronic facts. Both phenomena are governed by the native speaker's unconscious, meaning-disregarding linguistic habits. Insofar as the native speaker of WOL recognises the two forms *meramE* and *marema* as one, it would be unreasonable to treat the dissimilation process as a historical (or diachronic) rule.

A natural corollary of considering it to be a synchronic rule is that we have to admit the existence of two levels of phonological representation. A basic premise of this paper, therefore, is that diachronic rules apply to POC forms and derive the corresponding WOL base forms, which are reconstructable from purely phonological alternations, while synchronic rules apply to WOL base forms to derive the corresponding surface forms. In other words, diachronic rules deal with the patterns of restructuring, while synchronic rules deal with the patterns of currently automatic sound alternations. Based on this premise, we draw a distinction between those processes which are partly or wholly dead and those which are completely active in purely phonological environments. If a certain phonological change were suspended prematurely or were in progress through lexical diffusion, we would consider it to be a diachronic fact, since restructuring in our sense of the term is involved in either case.

Let us go back to our examples. In order to obtain the surface forms from the reconstructed base forms *marama, marama-li, tama-i,* and *tamamami,* we must have three general synchronic rules: prejunctural raising of *a* to *e,* dissimilation, and devoicing of the final post-consonantal simple vowel.

(2)	marama	maramali	tamai	tamamami
pre-junctural raising	e (final)			
dissimilation	e (first)	e	e	e
devoicing	E	I		I
	[meramE]	[maremalI]	[temai]	[tamemamI]

One significant ordering to be imposed on the above rules is that prejunctural raising must apply before dissimilation because the latter requires a surface low vowel (e.g. [a]) as its environment. On the other hand, devoicing does not have to be ordered in relation to the other two rules.

One may naturally ask, then, how we should treat WOL pairs like *b* (= [ƀw]) and *pw, š* and *c, r* and *c, x* and *k,* and *l* and *n.* The members of each pair are in complementary distribution in native vocabulary, in that the first occurs only as a single consonant and the second only as a geminate. Besides, when two of the first members of a given pair meet at a morpheme boundary, they are automatically replaced by the corresponding second member, as in *xx* → *kk.* For instance, notice the alternation between *xaŋi* 'to eat it' and *kkekkaŋi* 'to be eating it.' The only feature that differentiates *x* from *k* is [continuant]. If we take only native vocabulary into account, *x* and *k* are certainly allophonic variants. A flood of recent borrowings (especially from Japanese), however, have caused the WOL system to develop simple *pw, c, k,* and *n* which contrast with the corresponding double or fricative ones. Moreover, some neighbouring languages retain *pw, c, k,* and *n* where WOL has *b, š/r, x,* and *l,* respectively, which fact makes the native speaker sensitive to the phonetic differences between, for example, *x* and *k*. Based on these observations, we will regard the development of *b, š, r, x,* and *l* as historical (or diachronic) facts, while the fortition of for example *xx* → *kk* is regarded as a synchronic process.

Another thorny problem concerns the treatment of semivowels. **w* and **y* have been reconstructed as phonemes in POC, as in **awaŋ* 'mouth' and **yaŋo* 'yellow.' In WOL, *w* and *y* are inserted before syllable-initial vowels in an entirely predictable way (see SR 1 below). In many cases, therefore, it is difficult to tell whether a given semivowel in a WOL form is inherited or has been synchronically epenthesised. However, in the case of *ya:wE* 'mouth,' it is easy to tell that the *w* is an inherited one even without the evidence of POC **awaŋ,* because *w* is never inserted between unrounded vowels. In the case of *yaŋoyaŋo* 'yellow' on the other hand, one might want to set up *aŋo-aŋo* as the base form, because *y* is inserted in the environment #____*a* anyway. To this word correspond two POC forms, **aŋoaŋo* and **yaŋo,* both meaning 'yellow,' which might suggest either *yaŋo-yaŋo* or *aŋoaŋo* as the WOL base form. Some morphophonemic alternations involving the word in question and others, however, lead us to choose *yaŋoyaŋo.* Compare the pairs in (3a) and those in (3b).

(3) a. { yaŋoyaŋO — 'yellow'
   xeyaŋoyaŋo — 'make it yellow' }

{ yateffasE — 'beardless'
   xeyateffesa — 'shave him completely' }

{ yarusa:sa — 'reddish'
   xeyarusa:sa:li — 'make it bloody' }

{ yaŋŋeŋŋawE — 'sloppy'
   xeyaŋŋeŋŋewa — 'make him do things sloppily' }

{ yaŋekuwE — 'mischievous'
   xeyaŋekuwa — 'make him mischievous' }

b. { yalI — 'to fly'
   xa:li — 'make it fly' }

{ yarE — 'to get through'
   xa:ra — 'make it get through' }

{ yaxiyexI	'to think'
{ xa:xiyexi	'to plan'
{ yafE	'to swim'
{ yefa:fE	'to swim vigorously'
{ yalI	'thin piece'
{ rúwa:lI	'two thin pieces'

Notice that in (3a) *y* is retained after the causative prefix *xa-* (*xe-* before *a* by dissimilation), whereas in (3b) *y* does not show up after the same prefix. Further, notice in (3b) that *y* does not occur in the second member of a reduplicated form (e.g. *yefa:fE*) and after a numeral (e.g. *rúwa:lI*). What this means is that the *y*'s in (3a) and those in (3b) differ in historicity. The former are already fossilised, either through inheritance from POC or through later development, while the latter are synchronically epenthesised in the given environments. The WOL base form of 'yellow' should, therefore, be *yaŋo-yaŋo,* and not *aŋo-aŋo.*

A similar phenomenon is observed with *w*. For instance, *w* is epenthetic in *wolɔ:lO* 'to flip' and *wo:rO* 'fence,' in that the former may be derived from *ola-ola* (cf. *wolati* 'flip it') and the latter from *oro-oro*. The above observation leads us to distinguish base-form semivowels which are inherited or historically developed from surface ones which are epenthesised through synchronic processes.

3. Synchronic Phonological Processes

WOL has the following phonological inventory in the native vocabulary. Notice that many sounds are limited to single or double occurrence. This is viewed as largely due to phonological diffusion through linguistic contact with neighbouring languages, and to the internal pressures to maintain structural symmetry (Sohn et al:1976).

(4) Consonants

p	t	c (doubly)	k (doubly)
		š (singly)	x (singly)
pw (doubly)	s	r (singly)	
b (singly)			
	l (singly)		
m	n (doubly)		ŋ
mw			

Vowels

i	u̇	u
e	əə (long)	o
	a	ɔɔ (long)

Semivowels

y w

The major synchronic rules (SR's) operative in WOL are listed below, with relevant examples. Rule ordering is specified where applicable.

SR 1 (semivowel insertion)

$$\emptyset \rightarrow \begin{cases} y \;/\; \begin{cases} \#\_\_\_\bar{V}r \\ \bar{V}r\_\_\_V \end{cases} \\ w \;/\; \begin{cases} \#\_\_\_Vr \\ Vr\_\_\_V \end{cases} \end{cases}$$

(Vr = rounded vowel; $\bar{V}$r = unrounded vowel)

Condition: A semivowel is not inserted before a high vowel (i, u̇, or u) or between two identical simple vowels.

(The semivowel *y* is inserted before a word-initial unrounded vowel or between an unrounded vowel and any vowel. The semivowel *w* is inserted before a word-initial round vowel or between a rounded vowel and any vowel.)

(5) Examples

alu̇su̇ → yalu̇su̇ → yalu̇sU̇ (by SR 7)	'ghost'
ama → yama → yame (by SR 3) → ya:mE (by SR's 7 & 8)	'office'
afi → yafi → ya:fI (by SR's 7 & 8)	'fire'
ate → yate → ya:tE (by SR's 7 & 8)	'chin'
weriai → weriyai → weriyei (by SR 5)	'see me'
ia → iya → iye (by SR 3) → i:yE (by SR's 7 & 8)	'he'
liia → liiya → li:yE (by SR's 3 & 7)	'kill him'
olo → wolo- (by SR 1)	'six'
laloa → lalowa → lalowE (by SR's 3 & 7)	'yesterday'
falu̇a → falu̇wa → falu̇wE (by SR's 3 & 7)	'island'
xasu̇u̇a → xasu̇u̇wa → xasu̇:wE (by SR's 3 & 7)	'build it'
uaa → uwaa → uwa (by SR 7)	'fruit'

SR 2 (*a* rounding)

$$a \rightarrow o \; / \; \left\{ \begin{matrix} o \\ ɔɔ \\ u \end{matrix} \right\} \; C\_\_\#$$

(The simple word-final vowel a is rounded to o after a back rounded vowel followed by a simple or double consonant.)

(6) Examples

bunna → bunno → bunnO (by SR 7)	'heart'
ssooŋa →ssooŋo → sso:ŋO (by SR 7)	'anger'
xotɔɔta → xotɔɔto → xotɔ:tO (by SR 7)	'crack'

When, instead of a consonant, a semivowel occurs between a rounded vowel and *a*, SR 2 does not apply, as in *paxowa # paxowE* 'shark' (by SR's 3 and 7).

SR 3 (prejunctural *a* raising: applies after SR's 1 and 2)

$$a \rightarrow e \; / \; \left\{ \begin{matrix} C \\ G \end{matrix} \right\} \; \_\_\#$$

(The simple vowel *a* is raised to e between a consonant or a semivowel (G = glide) and a word boundary.)

(7) Examples

ita# → ite → i:tE (by SR's 7 & 8)	'name'
afara#→ yafare (by SR's 1 & 3) → yefarE (by SR's 4 & 7)	'shoulder'
mwara#mwarali# → mwaremwarali → mwaremwerali (by SR's 4 & 7)	'lei of'

SR 4 (dissimilatory *a* raising: applies after SR 3)

$$a \rightarrow e \; / \; \_\_(C) \; \left\{ \begin{matrix} a \\ ɔɔ \end{matrix} \right\}$$

Condition: This rule applies from right to left.

(The simple vowel *a* is raised to *e* before a low vowel, i.e., *a* or *ɔɔ*.)

(8) Examples

matamami → matemami → matemamI (by SR 7)	'our (excl.) eyes'
matai → metai	'my eyes'

xammata → xammate (by SR 3) → 'bailer'
xemmate → xemmatE (by SR 7)
xatɔɔlaa → xetɔɔlaa → xetɔ:la (SR 7) 'make it bloom'
xamɔɔa → xamɔɔwa (by SR 1) → xamɔɔwe 'erase it'
(by SR 3) → xemɔɔwe → xemɔ:wE (by SR 7)

SR 5 (assimilatory *a* raising)

a → e / Vh (C)____(C) Vh
Condition: The rule applies across word boundaries.

(The simple vowel *a* is raised to *e* between high vowels, whether or not a simple or double consonant intervenes.)

(9) Examples
maŋi#maŋi → maŋimeŋi → maŋimeŋI (SR 7) 'to think'
itai → itei 'my name'
paaủ#šalủ → paaủšelủ → paaušelỦ (SR 7) 'water provisions'

An allophonic process relevant to SR's 3-5 is that *e* is pronounced with the lips rounded (i.e. [ə]) before or after *ủ*, as illustrated in (10). However, simple [ə] is not a separate phoneme in WOL.

(10) (a) before *ủ*

surface form	pronunciation	
lexỦ	[ləxỦ]	'make it tight'
mmweủ	[mmwəủ]	'broken'
iteủ	[itəủ]	'who?'
faủfeủ	[faủfəủ]	'to weave'

(b) after *ủ*

surface form	pronunciation	
yaủtE	[yaủtƎ]	'current'
xủ:sE	[xủ:sƎ]	'octopus'
pa:ủšelỦ	[pa:ủšəlỦ]	'water provisions'

SR 6 (*i* assimilation)

$$i \rightarrow \left\{ \begin{array}{l} \dot{u} \ / \ \dot{u}\ (C)\_\_\_ \\ u \ / u\ (C)\_\_\_ \end{array} \right\} \ \#$$

(The word-final vowel *i* is completely assimilated to the preceding *ủ* or *u* whether a consonant intervenes or not.)

(11) Examples

alùsùli → yalùsùli (by SR 1) → yalùsùlù → yalùsùlÙ (by SR 7) → 'ghost of'
xattui → xattuu → xattu (by SR 7) 'my finger'
maŋaaxuli → meŋaaxuli (by SR 4) → meŋaaxulu → meŋa:xulU (by SR 7) 'clothes of'

SR 7 (vowel devoicing and shortening)

$$V_i \rightarrow \begin{cases} \text{devoiced} \; / \; \begin{Bmatrix} C \\ G \end{Bmatrix} \;\_\_\_\#\# \\ \varnothing \; / \; V_i\_\_\_\#\# \end{cases}$$

(A simple vowel following a consonant or a semivowel (G = glide) is devoiced before a phrase boundary; a long (geminate) vowel is shortened before a phrase boundary.)

(12) Examples
imwa → imwe (by SR 3) → imwE → i:mwE (by SR 8) 'house'
iiaa → iiyaa (by SR 1) → i:ya 'where?'
iraa → ira 'branch'

SR 8 (vowel lengthening)

$$\varnothing \rightarrow \; : \; / \; \# \; (\{ {C \atop G} \}) \begin{Bmatrix} V\_\_\_ \; (\{ {C \atop G} \}) \; \underset{\circ}{V} \\ V_i\_\_\_V_j \end{Bmatrix} \#$$

($\underset{\circ}{V}$ = voiceless vowel)

Condition: This rule applies only to a noun.
(In a form which consists of only two simple vowels, with one or two simple consonants or semivowels (G = glide), the first vowel is lengthened.)

(13) Examples
faù → fa:ù 'stone'
afi → yafI (by SR's 1 & 7) → ya:fI 'fire'
lamwo → lamwO (by SR 7) → la:mwO 'lagoon'
ia → iya (by SR 1) → iyE ('v SR's 3 & 7) → i:yE 'he'

SR 9 (fortition)

$$\begin{bmatrix} b \\ x \\ \{ {\gamma \atop \check{s}} \} \\ l \end{bmatrix}_a + \alpha \rightarrow \begin{bmatrix} ppw \\ kk \\ cc \\ nn \end{bmatrix}$$

(When doubled, the fricative *b, x, r,* and *š* are plosivised, and the flap *l* is nasalised.)

(14) Examples

bbubbuutoxo → bbubbuutoxO (by SR 7) → ppwuppwu:toxO 'to be coming'
 (cf. bu:togO 'to come')

xxaxxatapaa → xxexxatepa (by SR's 4 & 7) → kkekkatepa 'to be touching it'
 (cf. xettapE 'to touch')

rrorro → rrorrO (by SR 7) → ccoccO 'to decorate'
 (cf. rosi 'decorate it')

rraxo → rraxO (by SR 7) → ccaxO 'to hug'
 (cf. raxomi 'hug it')

ššaššalúúa → ššeššalúúwE (by SR's 1, 3, 4, & 7)
→ cceccalú:wE 'to fill it with water'
 (cf. ša:lU̇ 'water')

llútú → llútU̇ (by SR 7) → nnútU̇ 'to be jumping'
 (cf. lútU̇ 'to jump')

4. Diachronic Rules

The POC phonemic system as reconstructable from Grace 1969 is as follows:

(15) POC Consonants:

p	t		k	ʔ
mp	nt		ŋk	
ŋp				
	d			
	nd			
	s			
	ns			
	nj			
		R		
	l	r		
m	n		ŋ	
ŋm				

POC Vowels:

i		u
e		o
	a	

POC Semivowels:

y w

The following diachronic rules (DR's) show the development from POC forms to WOL base forms. The WOL forms cited are, therefore, all base forms. Ordered rules are marked as such. Unlike synchronic rules, DR's have certain exceptions which may be regarded either as having undergone idiosyncratic changes or as later borrowings from neighbouring languages.

DR 1 (final-consonant apocope)
*C > Ø / ____#

All word-final POC consonants were dropped and no reflexes are found unless protected by a suffix of a certain kind (and hence non-final in the suffixed form).

(16) Examples

*p	*maˀudi(p) < mau̇ru̇	'alive'
	*ˀatop > aso	'thatch'
*t	*laŋi(t) > laŋi	'sky'
	*masaki(t) > mataxi	'sick, pain'
	*ŋkinit > xili-	'to pinch, pluck'
*k	*manu(k) > malu̇	'bird, animal'
*ˀ	*daRa(ˀ) >ccaa	'blood'
	*muta (ˀ) > (m)mwuta	'to vomit'
*s	*manipi(s) > malifi	'thin'
*R	*matudu(R) > masu̇ru̇	'to sleep'
*m	*inu(m) > u̇lu̇	'to drink but u̇lu̇mii drink it'
	*ndanum > šalu̇	'fresh water'
	*onom > olo	'six'
*n	*ˀatun > asu̇	'bonito'
*ŋ	*awaŋ > awa	'mouth'

Notice that *ulumii* 'drink it' retains the final **m* of **inu(m)* because it is followed by an object suffix. This verb belongs to the class of so-called thematic-stem transitive verbs (Sohn 1975a:125-127), in that it retains the thematic consonant *-m* only before a suffix (cf. *u̇lu̇* 'to drink').[5]

DR 2 (*u* centralisation)

* u > u̇ / if not preceded or followed by a POC bilabial consonant

(17) Examples

*ʔatun	>	asu̇	'bonito'
*ndanu(m)	>	šalu̇	'fresh water'
*dua	>	ru̇a-	'two'
*kku	>	kku̇	'nail, toe'
*kuRita	>	xu̇sa	'octopus'
*kutu	>	xu̇su̇	'louse'
*mataku(t)	>	mataxu̇	'afraid'
*matudu(R)	>	masu̇ru̇	'to sleep'
*natu	>	lau̇	'child'
*panua	>	falu̇a	'land, island'
*pituʔu	>	fu̇su̇	'star'
*Ruʔa	>	u̇a	'neck'
*sau(ʔ)	>	tau̇-	'to pull out'
*susu	>	tu̇tu̇	'breast'
*ʔuna(p)	>	u̇la	'fish scale, body hair'
*ʔuda(ŋ)	>	u̇ra	'lobster'

DR 2 does not apply when **u* occurs in the neighbourhood of a POC bilabial consonant, as illustrated in (18).

(18) Examples

	*lumu	>	lumwu	'seaweed, moss'
	*-mu	>	-mwu	'your (singular)'
	*muta (ʔ)	>	(m)mwuta	'to vomit'
	*namu(k)	>	lamwu	'mosquito'
	*pua(ʔ)	>	uaa	'fruit'
	*mpua	>	bbua	'(betel)-nut'
D.	*puko	>	uxo	'net'
	*puŋa	>	uŋa	'ridge pole'
	*mputo	>	buso	'navel'
	*putu	>	utu	'tree sp. Barringtonia'
	*tampu	>	tabu	'taboo'
	*tumpu(ʔ)	>	subu	'to be born'
	*ʔumu	>	umwu	'earth oven'

As we see in **putu > utu,* Dr 2 does not apply to **u* when it follows another *u* which is not subject to DR 2. Similarly, the second **u* remains unchanged in **ŋapulu(ʔ)* > *ŋaulu* 'ten.' **puti* (D. **punti*) > *wisi* 'banana' might be construed as an exception to (18). However, *wisi* may be viewed as having been derived through *usi* > *wisi* where *u* is diphthongised due to the following *i*. A questionable exception is **tau* 'man, person' < *tau* 'practitioner' where the meanings of the two words are only remotely related.

Due to the operation of DR 2, the WOL phonemic system has seen the split of POC **u* into *u* and *ʉ*, thus resulting in the system of six simple vowels.

In addition to the regular shift of **u* to *ʉ* as shown in DR 2, there are some high vowel alternations conditioned by neighbouring vowels. One such alternation is represented in DR 3, which applies fairly widely.

DR 3 (*i* centralisation: applies after DR 2)

*i > ʉ / ____ (C) ʉ

(19) D *anitu > anitʉ (by DR 2) > anʉtʉ > alʉsʉ (by DR's 7 & 14) 'ghost'
*iku > ikʉ (by DR 2) > ʉkʉ > ʉxʉ (by DR 9) 'tail'
*inu(m) > inʉ (by DR's 1 & 2) > ʉnʉ > ʉlʉ (by DR 14) 'to drink'
*liu(R) >liʉ (by DR's 1 & 2) >lʉʉ 'coconut'
*pituʔu > pitʉʔʉ (by DR 2) > pʉtʉʔʉ > fʉsʉ (by DR's 4, 5, & 7)[6] 'star'

One exception is **pitu* >*fisi* 'seven,' which may have been changed in order to avoid homophony with *fʉsʉ* 'star.' The shift **ʔuluŋa* > *ilʉŋa* 'pillow' is a case of change in a direction opposite to DR 3, in that the first **u* changed to *i* (probably by way of *ʉ*) in dissimilation from the second *ʉ*. Some other forms which show irregular high vowel reflexes include **kuli(t)* > *xili* 'skin, bark' where **u* (> ʉ) changed to *i* before *i*, and **maʔudi(p)* > *maʉrʉ* 'alive' and **tuki* > *sʉxʉ* 'to pound' where **i* changed to *ʉ* in assimilation to the preceding *ʉ*. Still other correspondences show mutual assimilation between a POC high vowel and a neighbouring non-high vowel, as illustrated in (20). Notice that if there is an intervening POC consonant, the assimilation occurs only when the consonant is deleted by rules to be specified later.

(20) *au, *aou } əə — *paʔu >fəə 'to tie'; *ndau(n) > šəə 'leaf'

	*paRu	>	(xili-)fəə	'hibiscus'
	*paʔoRu	>	ffəə	'new'
*eu > ɔɔ	*seu	>	tɔɔ	'rake'
*ai > e(e)	*mai	>	me	'and, with'
	*saʔit	>	tee-tee	'to bind'

The above changes are not entirely regular because, for instance, we have **patu > fau̇* 'stone,' **sapu > tau̇* 'to pull out,' and **ʔaRus > au̇ta* 'current,' where **au̯* did not change to *əə* but followed the regular shift given in DR 2. Also, along with **seu > tɔɔ*, we have **kesu > xu̇u̇* 'back of head' where **e* was completely assimilated to the following *u̇*. One might be able to use some kind of rule ordering in the deletion of the consonants involved (e.g. **ʔ, *t, *p, *R, *s*) to provide an account of the vowel changes. In view of the lack of supporting data, however, such a proposal does not seem particularly attractive. In any case, the fusion of vowels added two new long vowel phonemes *əə* and *ɔɔ* to the WOL phonemic system. Remember that these long vowels do not have corresponding short counterparts.

DR4 (glottal stop deletion)

*ʔ > ∅

The POC glottal stop *ʔ has been completely lost in all positions. Deletion of word-final **ʔ* has already been accounted for by DR 1. In (21) are given examples of deletion of initial and medial **ʔ*.

(21)	initial:	*ʔapaRa	>	afara	'shoulder'
		*ʔaro-ʔopa	>	arofa-	'love, like, miss'
		*ʔate	>	ase	'liver'
		*ʔatop	>	aso	'thatch'
		*ʔuda(ŋ)	>	u̇ra	'lobster'
		*ʔumu	>	umwu	'earth oven'
	medial:	*paʔu	>	fəə	'to tie'
		*daʔa(n)	>	raa	'branch'
		*Ruʔa	>	u̇a	'neck'
		*ma-ʔanu	'to be afloat' >	maalu̇	'flood'
		*maʔudi(p)	>	mau̇ru̇	'alive'
		*pituʔu	>	fu̇su̇	'star'
		*saʔit	>	tee-tee	'to bind'
		*tuʔu(d)	>	su̇u̇	'to stand up'

DR 5 (*p* weakening: applies after DR 2)

$$*p > \begin{cases} \varnothing \ / \ \_\_\_\_ \ *u, *o \\ f \ / \ \text{elsewhere} \end{cases}$$

POC **p* has been lost before a POC back vowel, whereas it has shifted to *f* in all other positions, as illustrated in (22).

(22) *p > Ø

	*mapo	>	mɔɔ	'to heal'
	*napo	>	lɔɔ	'wave, surf'
	*pua(ˀ)	>	uaa	'fruit'
D.	*puko	>	uxo	'net'
D.	*puŋa	>	uŋa	'ridgepole'
D.	*punti	>	wiši	'banana'
	*sapu	>	tau̇-	'to pull out'
	*ŋapulu(ˀ)	>	ŋaulu	'ten'

*p > f

*ˀapaRa	>	afara	'shoulder'
*api	>	afi	'fire'
*ˀaro-ˀopa	>	arofa-	'love, like, miss'
*manipi(s)	>	malifi	'thin'
*pada	>	faša	'pandanus'
*pai-	>	fa-	(reciprocal prefix)
*pale	>	fale	'house'
*panua	>	falu̇a	'island, land'
*papine	>	faifile	'woman'
*patu	>	fau̇	'stone'
*pitu	>	fisi	'seven'
*tipi	>	sifi	'girdle, skirt'

One exception to DR 5 is observed in **tupa > supa* 'fish poison' and **Ripa > repa* 'to go close,' where **p* is reflected as *p*. In view of the abundance of reliable examples supporting DR 5, the exception may be ascribed to one of the following: (a) the POC forms may be reconstructed with **mp* rather than **p;* (b) they are not real correspondences; (c) the POC forms were introduced in WOL as borrowings after DR 5 was no longer active; or (d) the shift **p > f* stopped prematurely before **a*. If the last statement was actually the case, we would have to change DR 5 to DR 5′.

DR 5′

$$*p > \begin{cases} \emptyset / \_\_\_ *u, *o \\ p / \_\_\_ *a \text{ (only in certain words)} \\ f / \text{elsewhere} \end{cases}$$

In **pili(?)* > *ffili* 'to select' and **kapi(t)* > *xaffii* 'seize it,' **p* is reflected as *ff*. The transitive counterpart of *ffili* is *filii* lect it,' which explains the former correspondence. The latter, however, has no explanation at present.

In **nsipo* > *tiwe* 'downward' and **tapu* > *tawii* 'conch,' deletion of **p* is followed by an irregular diphthongisation of the following vowel, i.e. **o* > *we* and **u* > *wii*, respectively.

DR 6 (bilabial denasalisation)

$$*mp, *ŋp > \begin{cases} b / \_\_\_ *u, *o \\ p / \text{elsewhere} \end{cases}$$

POC **mp* and **ŋp* seem to have been merged, and then denasalised in WOL to *b* (by way of *pw*) before a back (or rounded) vowel, and to *p* elsewhere. However, a strong case cannot be made for the two POC consonants, because there is only one correspondence available in which **ŋp* occurs, as shown in (23).

(23) $\begin{Bmatrix} *mp \\ *ŋp \end{Bmatrix}$ > b

*mpo-	>	boo	'smell'
*mpua	>	bbua	'(betel)-nut'
*mpule	>	bulo	'white shell, cowry'
*mputo	>	buso	'navel'
*tampu	>	tabu	'taboo'
*tumpu(?)	>	subu	'to be born'
*ŋpoŋi	>	boŋi	'night'
*mp > p			
*mpampa(n)	>	paapa	'board, plank'
*mpaya	>	paa	'bait, worm'
D. *tampi	>	tapiya	'bowl'

Notice in the shift **mpua* > *bbua* that **mp* is reflected as *bb* for reasons not statable at the moment.

DR 7 (*t* weakening)

$$*t > \begin{cases} t / \_\_\_ *a \\ \emptyset / \_\_\_ *u \text{ (only in certain words)} \\ s / \text{elsewhere} \end{cases}$$

POC *t is retained unchanged before the POC low vowel *a. Otherwise it has shifted to s or ø, although predominantly s. The dropping is observed only before POC *u, and that only in a very limited number of words. One can only speculate that the words with the ø reflex have been either influenced by or borrowed from other Trukic (TK) languages, which are regarded as having undergone a second shift of *t, i.e. t > s and s > ø (Sohn et al 1976). This speculation is partly supported by the reflexes of POC **patu* 'stone,' which are *fasu̇* (old form) and *fau̇* (new form). Examples of DR 7 follow:

(24) *t > t

*taŋi(s)	>	taŋi	'to cry'
*tansi(k)	>	tati	'sea'
*tali	>	tali	'rope'
*taliŋa	>	taliŋa	'ear'
*tama	>	tama	'father'
*tano(ˀ)	>	talo	'earth'
*taku	>	taxu̇	'back'
*mata	>	mata	'eye'
*mataku(t)	>	mataxu̇	'to be afraid'
*muta(ˀ)	>	(m)mwuta	'to vomit'

*t > s

*tuki	>	su̇xu̇	'to pound'
*tumpu(ˀ)	>	subu	'to be born'
*tuˀu(d)	>	su̇u̇	'to stand up'
D. *anitu	>	alu̇su̇	'ghost'
*ˀatun	>	asu̇	'bonito'
*kutu	>	xu̇su̇	'louse'
*matudu(R)	>	masu̇ru̇	'to sleep'
*pitu	>	fisi	'seven'
*pituˀu	>	fu̇su̇	'star'
*ˀate	>	ase	'liver'
*ˀatop	>	aso	'thatch'
*mate	>	mase	'to die'
*mputo(s)	>	buso	'navel'
*tika	>	sixa	'bad, angry'
*tina	>	sila	'mother'
*tipi	>	sifi	'girdle, skirt'
*toko(n)	>	soxo	'pole, staff'

*t > Ø

*motu	>	mmweů	'to break off'
*natu	>	laů	'child'
*patu	>	faů	'stone (old form: fasů)'
*patu	>	faů-faů	'to weave'

Exceptions to **t* > *t* are **ta?aki* 'to draw water' > *saaxii* 'extract it' *and* **kuRita* > *xůsa* 'octopus.' Exceptions to **t* > *s* are **putu* > *utu* 'tree sp.: *Barringtonia*' and **kato* > *xato* 'basket.'

DR 8 (dental denasalisation)
*nt, *nd > š

The two POC prenasalised dental stops **nt* and **nd* have merged into the palatal retroflexed fricative *š* in WOL, as shown in (25).

(25)	*nt > š			
	*-nta	>	-ša	'our (incl.)'
	*kinta	>	-xiša	'we (incl.)'
	D. *punti	>	wiši	'banana'
	*nd > š			
	*ndanu(m)	>	šalů	'water'
	*ndau(n)	>	šəə	'leaf'

The reconstruction of POC **puti* for 'banana' is not adequate as far as the WOL (and TK) data are concerned, because **puti* would have to be subject to DR 7 and would result in a wrong reflex. Therefore, **punti* must be the correct reconstruction.

DR 9 (velar spirantisation)
simple *k, *ŋk > x

Simple POC **k* is regularly reflected as *x* in WOL, while POC **kk* remains unchanged. As mentioned earlier, when two *x*'s meet at a morpheme boundary, they become *kk* by a synchronic process. We have only one example of **ŋk* shifting to *x*.

(26)	*k > x			
	*-?aki	>	-axi	'cause or instrument suffix'
	*(dl)iki	>	šixi	'small'
	*ika(n)	>	ixa	'fish'
	*iku	>	ůxů	'tail'
	*kau	>	xəə	'fish hook'

	*kiekie	> xiexie	'pandanus'
	*kinta	> xiša	'we (incl.)'
	*ko(e)	> xo	'you'
	*kutu	> xủsủ	'louse'
	*lako	> laxo	'to go'
	*masaki(t)	> mataxi	'sick, pain'
	*mataku(t)	> mataxủ	'to be afraid'
	*puko	> uxo	'net'
	*toko(n)	> soxo	'staff, pole'
*kk > kk			
	*kku	> kkủ	'nail, claw'
*ŋk > x			
	*ŋkinit	> xili-	'to pinch, pluck, nip'

One aberrant correspondence is **kali* > *kkeli* 'to dig.' The WOL form may have been derived through *kakali* > *xexali* (dissimilatory *a*- raising) > *xxeli* > *kkeli.*

There are a couple of examples in which **k* and **ŋk* correspond to ø. These are **suku* > *tủủtủủ* 'to bathe' and **waŋka(ŋ)* > *waa* 'canoe.' If these are true cognates, DR 9 has to allow for the Ø reflex. At the moment, however, we have no strong evidence to consider them true cognates.

DR 10 (*d* rhotacism)

*d, *r > r

POC **d* and **r* have been merged to *r* in WOL, as illustrated in (27). Notice that there are not many examples of **r* > *r.* In Grace (1969), **(dr)* indicates that some authors reconstructed **d* and others **r* for the same set of correspondences.

(27) *d > r

*-da	> -:ra	'their'
*daŋa(n)	> raa	'branch'
*deŋa	> raŋa	'turmeric, yellow'
*doŋo	> roŋo-roŋo	'to hear'
*dua	> rủa	'two'
*madama>	> marama	'moon'
*matudu(R)	> masủrủ	'to sleep'
*maʔudi(p)	> maủrủ	'alive'
*sida	> ira	'they'
*ʔuda(ŋ)	> ủra	'lobster'

*r > r

*kari(s)	>	xeri	'to scratch, tear'
*raku	>	raxů	'to take a handful, eat clumsily'
*turu	>	sůrů	'post'

*(dr) > r

*(dr)ani	>	rale	'day'
*(dr)odo	>	rošo	'night, darkness'
*si(dr)i(t)	>	siri	'semen, masturbation'

There are exceptions to DR 10, i.e. certain occurrences of **d* (not of **r*) are reflected as *š* in WOL, as in (28).

(28)	*(dr)odo	>	rošo	'night, darkness'
	*pada	>	faša	'pandanus'
	*dudu	>	ůšů-ůšů	'to shake, collect fruit'
	*(dl)iki	>	šixi	'small'

The regular source of *š* is **nd* or **nt,* as we saw in DR 8. From the WOL examples given in (28), we are tempted to modify the reconstructions in such a way that **d* and **(dl)* are rewritten as **nd.*

DR 11 (pharyngeal weakening)

$$*R > \begin{cases} r \\ \varnothing \end{cases}$$

Without statable reasons, the POC pharyngeal *R has either merged with *d and *r to r (cf. DR 10), or been lost as shown in (29). Notice that more examples favour loss.

(29) *R > r

D. *Ratu	>	-rasi	'1,000'
*Ripa	>	(xa)repa	'to go close'
*ʔapaRa	>	afara	'shoulder'
*tiRi 'to urinate'	>	siri	'to masturbate'

*R > Ø

*kuRita	>	xůsa	'octopus'
*ʔaRus	>	aůta	'current'
*ma(R)a	>	maa	'ashamed'
*Ruŋmaʔ	>	imwa	'house'
*waRo	>	yɔɔ	'string, line'
*pawoRu	>	ffəə	'new'
*Ruʔa	>	ůa	'neck'

Here belongs the correspondence **daRa(ʔ)* >*ccaa* 'blood.' The form *ccaa* is assumed to have resulted from **daRa(ʔ)* > *daRa* > *rara* > *rraa* > *ccaa* (by SR 9).

DR 12 (non-high vowel fusion: applies after DR 5 & DR 11)
*ao > ɔɔ

When **a* and **o* met as a result of dropping of the intervening consonant, they fused with each other, resulting in the long vowel ɔɔ. Three examples are found, as in (30).

(30)	*mapo	>	mɔɔ	'to heal'
	*napo	>	lɔɔ	'surf, wave'
	*waRo	>	yɔɔ	'string, rope'

An example parallel to (30) is **mawap* > *mɔɔ* 'to yawn,' where **awa* is reflected as *ɔɔ*.

DR 13 (dental plosivisation)
*ns, *s > t

POC **ns* and **s* are both reflected as *t* in WOL. The two proto phonemes may have been reconstructed erroneously, as Milke has pointed out (Grace 1969). According to him, the two phonemes should be one and the same in POC.

(31) *ns > t

*nsake	>	taxe	'upwards'
*nsama	>	tama	'outrigger'
*nsila(k)	>	tu̇la	'to shine'
*nsiwa	>	tiwa	'nine'
*nsai	>	i-tau̇	'who?'
*ansa(n)	>	ita	'name'
*anse	>	ate	'chin, jaw'
*mansu(rR)	>	matu̇	'full (of food)'
*pinsa	>	fita-	'how many'
*pinsiko	>	fitixo	'flesh'
*tansi(k)	>	tati	'sea'
*s > t			
*sili	>	tili	'to enter'
*sola	>	tola	'coconut blossom'

*susu	>	tůtů	'breast'
*susu	>	titi	'to sew'
*sa?it	>	tee-tee	'to bind'
*sapu	>	taů	'to pull out'
*seu	>	tɔɔ	'rake'
*?asu 'smoke'	>	atů	'appearance of smoke'
*ma-masa	>	mmata	'dry, low tide'
*masaki(t)	>	mataxi	'sick, pain'
*masawa	>	matawa	'strand, sea'

There are some exceptions to DR 13, as shown in (32), where **ns* and **s* are reflected as *s* or *ø*. It might be the case that the WOL words either have undergone irregular shifts due to the influence of TK languages, or are recent borrowings from them.

(32) *s > s

*ŋase	>	ŋase	'weak'
*si(dr)i(t)	>	siri	'semen, masturbation' (cf. **tiRi* 'to spurt, urinate')

*ns, *s > Ø

*nsaŋa	>	aŋa-aŋa	'a measure'
*nsaŋi	>	aŋi	'wind'
*sala(n)	>	ala	'road, path'
*sida	>	ira	'they'
*kesu	>	xůů	'back of head'
*tasimi	>	taimi-	'sharpen (it)'

POC **nj,* which is supposed to be Milke's nasal grade of **s,* is reflected in only one convincing example. This reflex is *ø*, as in **njala(n)* > *ala* 'road' (cf. **sala(n)*).

DR 14 (*l/n* neutralisation)
simple *l, *n > l

POC **n* and **l* are merged as **l* in WOL. The only case in which **n* is retained unchanged is when it is geminate (cf. Sohn et al 1976). On the other hand, when two *l*'s meet at a morpheme boundary, they automatically become *nn* (SR 9).

(33) *n > l

*-na	>	-la	'his, her, its'

*namo	>	lamwo	'lagoon'
*namu(k)	>	lamwu	'mosquito'
*nana(ʔ)	>	lala	'pus'
*niu(R)	>	lu̇u̇	'coconut'
*anitu	>	alu̇su̇	'ghost'
*ndanu(m)	>	šalu̇	'fresh water'
*inu(m)	>	u̇lu̇	'to drink'
*ŋkinit	>	xili	'to pinch, pluck'
*ma-ʔanu 'float'	>	maalu̇	'flood'
*manawa	>	malawa	'to live, breathe'
*manipi(s)	>	malifi	'thin'
*manu(k)	>	malu̇	'bird'
*panua	>	falu̇a	'land'
*tano(ʔ)	>	talo	'earth'

*l > l

*lako	>	laxo	'go, walk'
*laŋi(t)	>	laŋi	'sky'
*laŋo	>	laŋo	'a fly'
*limu (*lumut)	>	lumwu	'sea-weed, moss'
*njala(n)	>	ala	'road'
*sola	>	tola	'coconut blossom'
*tali	>	tali	'rope'
*ŋapulu(ʔ)	>	ŋaulu	'ten'
*taliŋa	>	taliŋa	'ear'
*pale	>	fale	'house'
*ʔuluŋa	>	ilu̇ŋa	'pillow'

DR 15 (velarisation)

$$*m > \begin{cases} mw \;/\; \_\_\_\_ \; *u, *o \\ m \;/\; \text{elsewhere} \end{cases}$$

POC **m* has been split into verlarised *mw* and plain *m*. Velarised *mw,* which occurs only before a POC round vowel, has merged with the POC **ŋm,* a labiovelar.

(34) *m > mw

*-mu	>	-mwu	'your'
*muʔa	>	mmwa-	'front'
*mudi	>	mwiri-	'behind'
*muta(ʔ)	>	(m)mwuta	'to vomit'

*ˀumu	>	umwu	'earth oven'
*komu	>	xumwu	'mouthful, gargle'
*namo	>	lamwo	'sea, lake, lagoon'
*limu (*lumut)	>	lumwu	'seaweed, moss'
*namu(k)	>	lamwu	'mosquito'

*m > m

*maa	>	maa	'to be ashamed'
*ma-ˀanu	>	maalů	'flood'
*mai	>	me	'and, with'
*-mami	>	-mami	'our (excl.)'
*manipi(s)	>	malifi	'thin'
*manu(k)	>	malů	'bird, animal'
*masaki(t)	>	mataxi	'sick, pain'
*masawa	>	matawa	'strand, sea'
*lima	>	lima	'five, hand'
*tama	>	tama	'father'

As mentioned above, POC *ŋm* appears as *mw* in WOL. Examples follow:

(35)	*ŋmalo	>	mwalo	'to submerge'
	*ŋmata	>	mwata	'worm'
	*Ruŋma(?)	>	imwa	'house'
	*ndaŋma	>	šimwe	'head'
	*ŋmane	>	mwaŋea-	'sibling (different sex)'

POC *ŋ is regularly retained unchanged, as shown in (36).

(36)	*yaŋo	>	yaŋo-yaŋo	'yellow'
	*deŋa	>	raŋa	'turmeric, yellow'
	*laŋi(t)	>	laŋi	'sky'
	*paŋu	>	faŋů	'to be awaken'
	*ŋpoŋi	>	boŋi	'night'
	*taliŋa	>	taliŋa	'ear'
	*taŋi(s)	>	taŋi	'to cry'
	*ˀuluŋa	>	ilůŋa	'pillow'

The POC semivowels are retained unchanged, as in (37). Note that there is only one example of **y > y*.

(37) *y > y

*yaŋo	>	yaŋo-yaŋo	'yellow'

*w >w			
*madawa	>	maarawa	'green, raw'
*masawa	>	matawa	'sea, ocean'
*walu	>	wali	'eight'
*awaŋ	>	awa	'mouth'

One exception to (37) is **waRo > yɔɔ* 'string, rope' where **w* has shifted to *y*. Another exception is **mpaya > paa* 'bait' where **y* has been dropped between *a*'s.

Aside from the changes effected by DR's 2, 3, and 12, the POC vowels are consistently retained unchanged, as illustrated in (38).

(38)	*a > a			
	*api	>	afi	'fire'
	*ia	<	ia	'he, she, it'
	*panua	>	falùa	'islands'
	*o > o			
	*kato	>	xato	'basket'
	*onom	>	olo	'six'
	*ŋpoŋi	>	boŋi	'night'
	*i > i			
	*ika(n)	>	ixa	'fish'
	*tipi	>	sifi	'girdle, skirt'
	*taŋi(s)	>	taŋi	'to cry'
	*kinta	>	xiša	'we (incl.)'
	*e > e			
	*anse	>	ate	'chin, jaw'
	*kiekie	>	xiexie	'pandanus'
	*pale	>	fale	'house'
	*mate	>	mase	'to die'

5. Conclusion

We have tried to describe the phonological development of WOL from POC by explicitly distinguishing synchronic from diachronic aspects. Nine synchronic and fifteen diachronic rules have been presented, together with examples of lexical correspondences and some putative exceptions. As may be noted in the Appendix, there are quite a few idiosyncratic sound changes that have not been discussed. Some could be accounted for in light of the phonological environments involved, while others must await further investigation. For instance, there are a few examples of (putative) correspondences in which **n* is reflected as *ŋ: *nuns(iɔ)* > *ŋito* 'squid,' **kani* > *xaŋi(i)* 'food, eat,' **ŋmane* > *mwaŋea-* 'sibling of different sex,' **nipon* > *ŋii* 'tooth,' and **ponu* > *oŋi* 'turtle.' The regular shift is **n* > *l* in all positions, and we have no way to state a quasi-productive rule **n* > *ŋ*, at least for the moment. We have also included a number of questionable cognates (marked with ?) in the Appendix in the hope that they might provide some important clues for future study, which should be conducted in a broader perspective, i.e. within the framework of comparative Micronesian phonology.

Let us conclude by summarising the regular sound correspondences between POC and WOL, as in (39). For the sound environments, see the fuller statements of the rules in Section 4.

(39)

POC	WOL		DR's
Consonants			
*C#	ø		DR 1
*p	ø		DR 5
	f		
*mp, *ŋp	b	(ppw, *when doubled*)	DR 6
	p		
*t	ø		DR7
	s		
*t; *ns, *s	t		DR 13
*nj	ø		
*nt, *nd	š	(cc, *when doubled*)	DR 8
*d, *r; *R	r	(cc, *when doubled*)	DR 10
*R	ø		DR 11
*k, *ŋk	x	(kk, *when doubled*)	DR 9
*kk	kk		
*ʔ	ø		DR 4
*ŋm; *m	mw		
*m	m		DR 15

*l } *n	————	I (nn, *when doubled*)	DR 14
*nn	————	nn	
*ŋ	————	ŋ	
Vowels			
*u	————	u	DR 2
	⟩	ů	
*i	————	i	DR 3
*a	————	a	
*e	————	e	
*o	————	o	
*ao, etc.	————	ɔɔ	DR 12
*au, etc.	————	əə	
Semivowels			
*y	————	y	
*w	————	w	

APPENDIX. POC-WOL

	POC	WOL surface form	WOL base form	Gloss
1.	*-ʔaki	-yaxi- or -axi-	-axi	causative or instrument (affixed to verb)
2. D.	*anitu	yalůsŮ	alůsů	'spirit'
3.	*aŋoaŋo	yaŋoyaŋO	yaŋo-yaŋo	'yellow'
4.	*ʔapaRa	yefarE	afara	'shoulder'
5.	*api	ya:fI	afi	'fire'
6.	*ʔaro-ʔopa	yarofa-	arofa-	'love, like, seek, miss'
7.	*ʔaRus	yaůtE	aůta	'current'
8.	*ansa(n)	i:tE	ita	'name'
9.	*anse	ya:tE	ate	'chin, jaw'
10. D.	*ʔasu	ya:tŮ (*appearance of smoke*)	atů	'smoke'
11.	*ʔate	ya:sE	ase	'liver'
12.	*ʔatop (D. *ʔato)	ya:sO	aso	'thatch'
13.	*ʔatun	ya:sŮ	asů	'bonito'
14.	*awa	ya:wE	awa	'open space, mouth'
15.	*-da	-:rE	-:ra	'their'

16.	*daˀa(n)	ra	raa	'branch, twig'
17.	*ndaŋma	ši:mwE	šimwe	'head, forehead'
18.	*(dr)an(i)	ra:lE	rale	'day'
19.	*ndanu(m)	ša:lU̇	šalu̇	'fresh water'
20.	*daRa(ˀ)	cca	ccaa	'blood'
21.	*ndau(n)	šə	šəə	'leaf'
22.	*deŋa	ra:ŋE	raŋa	'turmeric, yellow'
23.	*(dl)iki	šixI	šixi	'small'
24.	*(dr)odo	ro:šO	rošo	'night, darkness, shadow'
25.	*doŋo, ndoŋo	roŋoroŋO	roŋo-roŋo	'to hear'
26.	D. *doŋo	ro:ŋO	roŋo	'rite, inheritance'
27.	*dua	ru̇wa-	ru̇a-	'two'
28.	*dudu	u̇šu̇:šU̇	u̇šu̇-u̇šu̇	'to shake, collect fruit'
29.	*eno	wolO	olo	'to lie down'
30.	*ia	i:yE	ia	'he, she, it'
31.	*ika(n)	i:xE	ixa	'fish'
32.	*iku	u̇:xU̇	u̇xu̇	'tail'
33.	*inu(m)	u̇lu̇(m)	u̇lu̇(m)	'to drink'
34.	*ka(dr)u	xerixerI	xeri-xeri	'to scratch'
35.	*kai	xa:xa (Ulithi: xai)	xaa-xaa	'tree, wood'
36.	*kali	kkelI	kkeli	'to dig'
37.	*kami	xa:mamI	xaamami	1st pl. excl. pronoun ('we')
38.	*kamu	xa:mi	xaamii	'ye' (2nd pl. pronoun)
39.	*kani	xaŋi ('eat it') xalE ('food')	xaŋii, xala	'eat, food'
40.	*kapi(t)	xaffi ('seize it')	xaffii	'seize, squeeze'
41.	*kari(s)	xeri ('scratch it')	xerii	'to scratch, tear'
42.	*kasup	kkutU	kkutu	'to spit'
43.	*katea	xeta	xetaa	'side of canoe' 'opposite outrigger'
44.	*kato	xa:tO	xato	'basket'
45.	*kau	xə	xəə	'fish hook'
46.	*kau	xa:xa	xaa-xaa	'tree, stalk'
47.	*kawakawa	xawexawE	xawaxawa	'fish sp.' (yellow finned groper)
48.	*kawe	xə:xə	xəə-xəə	'to fasten on with straps'
49.	*ke	i-xa	ixaa	'here'
50.	*kesu	(xapili)xu̇	(xapili) xu̇u̇	'back of head'
51.	*kianto	xiyɔ	xiɔɔ	'outrigger boom'

52.	*kiekie	xiyexiyE	xiexie	'pandanus'
53.	*(ki)ki(t)	xủ:xủ	xủủ-xủủ	'to bite at, squeeze'
54.	*kilala	xủla ('know it')	xủlaa	'to know'
55.	*ŋkinit	xilI	xili	'to pinch, pluck, nip'
56.	*kinta	xi:šE	xiša	1st incl. pronoun ('we')
57.	*ko	xo ('you!')	xo	specifying particle, vocative particle
58.	*ko(e)	xo	xo	'you, thou'
59.	*komu	xumwU	xumwu	'mouthful, gargle'
60.	*kku	kkU̇	kkủ	'claw, nail, toe'
61.	*kuli(t)	xi:lI	xili	'skin, bark'
62.	*kuRita	xủ:sE	xủsa	'octopus (cf. *uRita)'
63.	*kutu	xủ:sU̇	xủsủ	'louse'
64.	*lako	laxO	laxo	'to go, walk'
65.	*laman	la:mwO	lamwo	'sea, lake'
66.	*laŋi(t)	la:ŋI	laŋi	'sky'
67.	*laŋi	?ya:ŋI	aŋi	'wind'
68.	*laŋo	la:ŋO	laŋo	'house-fly'
69.	*laso	?to:lO	tola	'genitals'
70.	*lawas	lela:i	lalaai	'long'
71.	*lima	li:mE	lima	'five, hand'
72.	*limu	lu:mwU	lumwu	'seaweecd, moss'
73.	*lo	lalo, la-	lalo, la-	'in'
74.	*loku	lexủ ('make it tight')	lexủ	'bend, fold'
75.	*lumut	lu:mwU	lumwu	'seaweed, moss'
76.	*ma	me	me	'and, with'
77.	*maa	ma	maa	'to be ashamed'
78.	*ma-ˀanu	ma:lU̇ ('flood')	maalủ	'to be afloat'
79.	*mada	mmašE	mmaša	'fermented, soft, ripe'
		ma:rE ('preserved breadfruit')	mara	
80.	D. *madama	meramE	marama	'moon'
81.	*madawa	ma:rawE	maarawa	'green, raw'
82.	*mai	me	me	'and, with (cf. *ma)'
83.	*mala	(ni)malE ('open space')	(ni)mala	'place'
84.	*malaˀe	malemalE	mala-mala	'village, open space in village'
85.	*manaŋ	ke-malE	ka-mala	'spiritual power'
86.	*ŋmalo	mwalO	mwalo	'to submerge'

87.	*malu	mannU̇	mallu̇	'soft'
88.	*-mami	-mamI	-mami	'our' (excl.)
89.	*manawa	melawE	malawa	'to breathe'
90.	*ŋmane	mwaŋeya-	mwaŋea-	'woman's brother'
91.	*manipi(s)	malifI	malifi	'thin' (cf. *mapini)
92.	*manu(k)	ma:lU̇	malu̇	'bird, animal'
93.	*mapini	malifI	malifi	'thin' (cf. *manipi(s))
94.	*mapo	mɔ	mɔɔ	'to heal (of a wound, sore)'
95.	*maRa	ma	maa	'to be ashamed' (cf. *maa)
96.	*ma-masa	mmatE	mmata	'dry, low tide'
97.	*masaki(t)	metaxI	mataxi	'sick, pain'
98.	*masawa	metawE	matawa	'strand, shore, sea' (cf. *sawa)
99.	*mansu(rR)	ma:tU̇	matu̇	'full (of food), plenty of food'
100.	*mata	ma:tE	mata	'eye'
101.	*ŋmata	mwa:tE	mwata	'worm'
102.	*mata(ʔ)	yematE	e-mata	'raw, new'
103.	*mataku(t)	metaxU̇	mataxu̇	'afraid'
104.	*mate	ma:sE	mase	'to die, death'
105.	*matudu(R)	masu̇rU̇	masu̇ru̇	'to sleep'
106.	*maʔudi(p)	mau̇rU̇	mau̇ru̇	'alive (of plant)'
107.	*mawap	mɔ:(-li xatelU̇)	mɔɔ(-li xatelu̇)	'to yawn'
108.	*moso	mottO	motta	'cooked'
109.	*motu	mmweu̇	mmweu̇	'to break off, broken'
110.	*-mu	-mwU	-mwu	'your' (sing.)
111.	*muʔa	mmwa-	mmwa-	'front'
112.	*mudi	mwiri-	mwiri-	'behind'
113.	*muta(ʔ)	(m)mwutO	(m)mwuta	'to spit, vomit'
114.	*muntu	mwošomwo:šO	mwošo-ošo	'severed, cut short' (cf. *motu)
115.	*-na	-lE	-la	'his, her, its'
116.	*na	lE (immed. fut.)	le	'sign of future tense'
117.	*namo	la:mwO	lamwo	'lagoon'
118.	*namu(k)	la:mwU	lamwu	'mosquito'
119.	*nana(ʔ)	la:lE	lala	'pus'
120.	*napo	lɔ	lɔɔ	'surf, wave'

121.	*natu	la:ủ	laủ	'child, offspring'
122.	*nipi(s)	malifilifI	malifilifi	'thin' (cf. *manipi(s))
123.	*nipon	ŋi	ŋii	'tooth'
124.	*niu(R)	lủ	lủủ	'coconut'
125.	*noRa	lalowE	laloa	'yesterday'
126.	*nua	la-, le-	la-, le-	'inside'
127.	*nuns (io)	ŋi:tO	ŋito	'squid'
128.	*ŋapulu(?)	ŋaulU	ŋaulu	'ten'
129.	*ŋase	?ŋasE	ŋase	'weak, exhausted, lame'
130.	*onom (D. ono)	wo:lO	olo	'six'
131.	*pada	fa:šE	faša	'pandanus'
132.	*pai-	fa-(fe-)	fa-	reciprocal prefix
133.	*paka-	xa-	xa-	causative prefix
134.	*pakiwak	paxowE	paxowa	'shark'
135.	*pale	falE	fale	'house'
136.	*palisi	fatilI	fatili	'grass'
137.	*panua	falủwE	falủa	'land, earth, village'
138.	*paŋ(ou) (n) (D. *paŋu)	faŋU̇	faŋủ	'awaken, arouse'
139.	*pa?oRU	ffə	ffəə	'new'
140.	*papa	fa:-	faa-	'under, downwards'
141.	*mpampa(n)	pa:pE	paapa	'board, plank, flat'
142.	*papine	faifilE (archaic)	faifile	'woman'
143.	*paRa	yefarE	afara	'shoulder' (cf. *?apaRa)
144.	*paRi	faiyE	faia	'stingray'
145.	*paRu	xili-fə	xili-fəə	'hibiscus'
146.	*pat	fa:-	faa-	'four'
147.	*patu	fa:ủ	faủ	'stone'
148.	*patu	faủfeủ	faủ-faủ	'to weave'
149.	*pa?u	fə:-	fəə-	'to tie, bind'
150.	*mpaya	pa	paa	'bait, worm'
151.	*pe-	fa ('which, where')	faa	'where?'
152.	*pi(dr)i	ffišI ('snap')	ffiši	'to fold, twist, sprain'
153.	*pili(?)	ffilI	ffili	'to select, choose, pick up'
154.	*pine	faifilE (archaic)	faifile	'woman'
155.	*pinsa	fita-	fita-	'how many'
156.	*pinsiko	fitixO	fitixo	'flesh'
157.	*pitu	fi:sI	fisi	'seven'

158.	*pituˀu (D. *pituˀo)	fu̇:sU̇	fu̇su̇	'star'
159.	D. *mpo-	bo	boo	'smell'
160.	*ponu	wo:ŋI	oŋi	'turtle'
161.	*ŋpoŋi	bo:ŋI	boŋi	'night'
162.	*ponse	?fatu̇lE	fatu̇la	'paddle'
163.	*pua(ˀ)	uwa	uaa	'fruit'
164.	*mpua	bbuwE	bbua	'(betel) nut'
165.	*puki	wexI ('turn')	wexi	'return'
166.	D. *puko	u:xO	uxo	'net'
167.	*mpule	bulO, ubilI	bulo, ubili	'white shell, cowry'
168.	*mpulu(t)	bilisE	bilisa	'gum, sap, glue'
169.	D. *puŋa	u:ŋO	uŋa	'ridgepole'
170.	*mpu(dr)i(t)	bu̇ru̇wE	bu̇ru̇a	'buttocks, excrement'
171.	*mpuso(s)	bu:sO	buso	'navel' (cf. *mputo)
172.	*puti (D. *punti)	wi:šI	wiši	'banana'
173.	*mputo	bu:sO	buso	'navel, anus' (cf. *mpuso(s))
174.	*putu	u:tU	utu	'free sp.: Barringtonia'
175.	*raku	raxU̇	raxu̇	'take a handful, eat clumsily'
176.	*Ratu	(saŋe)rasI	(saŋe)rasi	'one thousand'
177.	*Ripa	repE	repa	'to go close'
178.	*Ruˀa	u̇:wE	u̇a	'neck'
179.	*Ruŋma(ˀ)	i:mwE	imwa	'house'
180.	*nsanda	?texašE	taxaša	'to rise (sun, moon), to ascend'
181.	*nsai	iteu̇	i-tau̇	'who?'
182.	*saˀit	te:te	tee-tee	'to bind, restrain'
183.	*nsake	taxE	taxe	'upwards, to climb'
184.	*sala(n)	ya:lE	ala	'road, path'
185.	*njala(n)	ya:lE	ala	'road, path'
186.	*nsama	ta:mE	tama	'outrigger'
187.	*nsaŋa	?yeŋa:ŋE	aŋa-aŋa	'a measure, a span'
188.	*nsaŋi	?ya:ŋI	aŋi	'wind'
189.	*sapu	tau̇-	tau̇-	'to pull out, take to pieces'
190.	*sau(ˀ)	tta:wE	ttaawa	'outside, far off'
191.	*-sawa	ta:wE ('channel')	tawa	'strand, shore, sea (cf. *masawa)'

192.	*seu	tɔ	tɔɔ	'to rake, sweep, scratch'
193.	*sida	i:rE	ira	'they'
194.	*si(dr)i(t)	?si:rI	siri	'semen, masturbation'
195.	*sikita	si:xE	sixa	'enmity, hostility'
196.	*siku(n)	u̇:xU̇	u̇xu̇	'tail, tail of fish'
197.	*nsila(k)	ttu̇lE	ttu̇la	'lightning, to shine'
198.	*sili	tilI	tili	'to enter'
199.	*sina(R)	ttu̇lE	ttu̇la	'to shine'
200.	*nsipo	tiwE	tiwe	'downwards'
201.	*nsiwa	ti:wE	tiwa	'nine'
202.	*so(dr)i	sorou (old form) torou (new form)	sorou, torou	'humility toward a chief'
203.	*nsoka	tokatokO	toka-toka	'to stab'
204.	*sola	to:lO	tola	'coconut blossom'
205.	*suku	?tu̇:tu̇	tu̇u̇-tu̇u̇	'to bathe, dive, wash'
206.	*sulu	ttu̇lE	ttu̇la	'torch, glow'
207.	*susu	tu̇:tU̇	tu̇tu̇	'breast, suck'
208.	*susu(dr)	ti:tI	titi	'to sew'
209.	*-nta	-šE	-ša	'our' (incl.)
210.	*taˀaki	sa:xi	saaxii ('extract it')	'to draw water, dig up'
211.	*ta-dawa	xa:rawerawE	xaa-rawarawa	'green'
212.	*tali	ta:lI	tali	'cord, rope'
213.	*taliŋa	taliŋE	taliŋa	'ear, earwax'
214.	*ntalo	?ccelI	cceli	'shore tree; *Calophyllum inophyllum*'
215.	*tama	ta:mE	tama	'father'
216.	*tamole	mwa:lE tamwelU̇ ('chief')	mwale, tamwelu̇	'man'
217.	*tano(ˀ)	ta:lO	talo	'earth, soil'
218.	*taŋi(s)	taŋI	taŋi	'to cry, weep'
219.	D. *tampi	?tapiyE	tapiya	'bowl'
220.	*tampu	ta:bU	tabu	'a ban, taboo'
221.	*tapu-	tawi	tawii	'conch'
222.	*tansi(k)	ta:tI	tati	'sea, salt water'
223.	D. *tasimi	taimi	taimii	'sharpen it'
224.	*tau-	?tau- ('practitioner')	tau-	'man, person'
225.	*tia(n)	siyalE	siala	'belly'
226.	*tido	surO	suro	'to look at'

227.	*tika	sixE ('angry')	sixa	'bad'
228.	*tina	si:lE	sila	'mother'
229.	*tipi	si:fI	sifi	'man's girdle, woman's skirt'
230.	*tiRi	si:ri ('masturbate')	siri	'to spurt, urine'
231.	*tiRo(m)	?sa:rU̇	saru̇	'oyster'
232.	*toka	toxO	toxo	'to arrive, land'
233.	*toko(n)	so:xO	soxo	'staff, pole'
234.	*tolu	seli-	seli-	'three'
235.	*tom(i)	?sorom(i)	sorom(ii)	'to drink, sip'
236.	*topu	?wo:u	ou	'sugar cane'
237.	*tu'a	so:wE	soa	'back, beyond, outside, edge'
238.	*tu(dr)(i)	šu̇	šu̇u̇	'bone, body'
239.	*tuki	su̇xu̇ ('hit it')	su̇xu̇u̇	'to hammer, pound'
240.	*tupa	su:pO	supa	'fish poison'
241.	*tumpu(?)	su:bU	subu	'to be born'
242.	*turu	su̇:r U̇	su̇ru̇	'post, kneel, knee'
243.	*tusu(k)	?ti, xati:ti	tii, xa-tii-tii	'to point, index finger'
244.	*tu'u(d)	su̇	su̇u̇	'to stand up'
245.	*'uda(ŋ)	u̇:rE	u̇ra	'lobster'
246.	*'uluŋa	ilu̇ŋE	ilu̇ŋa	'pillow'
247.	*'umu	u:mwU	umwu	'earth oven, to roast'
248.	*'una(p) (D. *?una)	u̇:lE	u̇la	'fish-scale, body hair'
249.	*upe	u̇:fE	u̇fa	'seedling, seeds'
250.	*uRita	xu̇:sE	xu̇sa	'octopus (cf. *kuRita)'
251.	*'utup	itiitI	iti-iti	'to flood, draw water'
252.	*waka	wexarE	waxara	'root'
253.	*waŋka(ŋ)	wa	waa	'canoe'
254.	*walu	wa:lI	wali	'eight'
255.	*waRo	yɔ	yɔɔ	'string, rope'
256.	*wasa	?ta:wE	tawa	'open sea'
257.	*yaŋo	yaŋoyaŋo	yaŋo-yaŋo	'yellow (cf. *aŋoaŋo)'

Notes

1. In the writing of this paper, the labour was divided in such a way that Tawerilmang provided the Woleaian (WOL) linguistic data, while Sohn was responsible for the analysis. This paper benefited from a comparative Micronesian seminar conducted by George Grace in 1972-73.

   For a synchronic description of the phonology and syntax of WOL, see Sohn 1975.
2. Other POC reconstructions from Grace n.d. are occasionally cited. These are prefixed with a D. (referring to Grace's source, Dyen 1949).
3. G. Lee (1976) makes a strong case for certain kinds of rule ordering in natural phonology.
4. Judging from the description of Marshallese stress in Bender (1975), dissimilatory *a*-raising may be related to alternating stresses in Woleaian. We must defer the study of WOL stress for the future, however.
5. Base forms of some more thematic-stem transitive verbs are given below:

baisii	'untie it'	(cf. bai-bai	'to unite')
bboolii	'pound it'	(cf. bboo	'to pound')
belifii	'snap it'	(cf. beli-beli	'to snap off')
fatoxii	'plant it'	(cf. fato-fato	'to plant')
filetii	'stir it'	(cf. file-file	'to stir')
narii	'taste it'	(cf. na-na	'to taste')
raxomii	'hug it'	(cf. rraxo	'to hug')
tɔɔfii	'rub it'	(cf. tɔɔ-tɔɔ	'to rub')

6. This appears to be a case of idiosyncratic final-vowel shortening, i.e. *úú* > *ú*. This exception may be explained away by reconstructing **pituʔ* for some pre-WOL (or Proto-TK) stage.

Reprinted from *Studies in Micronesian Linguistics,* ed. by Byron W. Bender. 171-199 (1984). Canberra: Australian National University.

20. CONSONANT SHIFTS AND SUBGROUPING IN THE SONSOROL–ULITHI–WOLEAI CHAIN

(*with Anthony Tawerilmang, Issac Langal, and Celestine Yangilmau**)

1. This paper has two interrelated goals: The first is to infer the consonant shifts that have taken place in Sonsorol (S), Ulithi (U), and Woleai (W); and the second is to develop a hypothesis regarding the genetic splits involving the three languages.[1] The discussion of the first goal will proceed by reconstructing a realistic proto-system from the correspondences not only of contemporary lexical items but of attested proto-Oceanic (PO) forms (Grace 1969) wherever necessary. The second goal will be pursued in the context of the causes by which the consonant shifts are assumed to have been initiated and directed, together with reference to unique or shared innovations.

2. Internal and external (e.g., PO) evidence has led us to postulate the following consonantal contrasts which are considered to have been shared by the three languages (and some other languages which are not our concern here) before they diverged.[2] Let us call the system the proto-Ulithic (PU) for the sake of convenience and use asterisks to indicate PU phonemes.[3]

(1) PU Consonant Phonemes

*p		*t	*c	*k
*pw				
	*f	*s		
		*l	*r	
*m		*n		*ng
*mw				

The reconstructions of **p, *f, *m, *mw,* and **ng* are straightforward because of the complete correspondence among the three languages, as illustrated in (2).

(2)

	S	U	W	
*p	_paa_	_paa_	_paa_	'bait'
*f	yaa_f_I	yȧȧ_f_	_yaaf_I	'fire'
*m	_m_a	_m_o	_m_e	'and'
*mw	_mw_angał	_mw_ongoy	_mw_ongo	'to eat'
*ng	_ng_ɨɨngI	_ng_u̇u̇_ng_	_ng_u̇u̇_ng_U̇	'to chew'

PU *_t_ is reconstructed from the correspondences shown in (3).

(3)

	S	U	W	PO	environment
(A)	t	t	t	*t	/__*a
(B)	θ	s	s	*t	elsewhere

Examples of (A)

S	U	W	PO	
_t_ȧringA	_t_aleng	_t_alingE	*_t_alinga	'ear'
maa_t_A	maa_t_	maa_t_E	*ma_t_a	'eye'
_t_ama-	_t_ama-	_t_ema-	*_t_ama	'father'
_t_aarI	_t_ȧȧl	_t_aalI	*_t_ali	'rope'
_t_aatI	_t_ȧȧt	_t_aatI	*_t_ansi(k)	'sea'
mmwu_t_A	mwommwo_t_	mmwu_t_O	*mu_t_a(q)	'to vomit'

Examples of (B)

S	U	W	PO	
θira-	_s_ila-	_s_ila-	*_t_ina	'mother'
θɨɨ	_s_u̇u̇	_s_u̇u̇	*_t_uqu(d)	'to stand'
yarɨθł	yȧlu̇s	yalu̇_s_U̇	*ani_t_u	'ghost'
yaaθE	yaa_s_	yaa_s_E	*qa_t_e	'liver'
maθE	ma_s_	ma_s_E	*ma_t_e	'to die'
xɨɨθł	xu̇u̇_s_	_x_u̇u̇_s_U̇	*ku_t_u	'louse'
fiiθI	fii_s_	fu̇u̇_s_U̇	*pi_t_uqu	'star'
θėrɨ-	_s_ol-	_s_eli-	*_t_olu	'three'
yaaθO	yaa_s_	yaa_s_O	*qa_t_op	'thatch'

One might argue that PU *_s_ or *θ should be reconstructed for the correspondences of (B). As a matter of fact, H. Quackenbush (1970:53) has reconstructed θ from the Sonsorol θ, Satawal _s, y, w, Ø_, Pullap _s, h, y, w, Ø_, and Moen _s, y, w, Ø_. As soon as we extend our horizon, such a reconstruction will turn out to be not well motivated. As we have seen in the above examples, Sonsorol θ and Ulithi/Woleai *s* originally developed from PO **t* as a positional or allophonic variant. We do not know exactly when they ceased to be allophonic and attained separate phonemic status, i.e., whether during the PU period or after it. The fact that Gilbertese has not developed an allophone from PO **t* (e.g., PO **tina* vs. G *tina* 'mother') indicates that the allophonic development of (B) had not taken place in proto-Micronesian. Even Marshallese retains PO **t* faithfully in the form of *j* (e.g., *maj* 'eye', *jine-* 'mother'), the sound quality of which is given in Bender 1969a (pp. xv-xvii). Trukese, which is considered a member of PU, has gone through the process of allophonic development of PO **t*.[4] All this suggests that it is not unreasonable to postulate only **t* for PU covering the correspondences shown in (3A) and (3B). One additional point is that PU **s* is to be established for another more adequate set of correspondences (see below) than the (B) set. In any case, appearance of such forms as S *rutU,* U *llut,* W *nnutU* 'to jump', U *ssar,* W *ssarU̇* 'knife', U *saraw,* W *serawE* 'barracuda', S *faθa* 'alive', S *yaatE,* W *yaatE* 'chin' has caused the original allophones to attain separate phonemic status. Needless to say, such new forms have been introduced either through borrowings or through regular or irregular sound changes in existing forms.

One crucial question to be posed at this point is whether the S θ and U/W *s* were derived independently from PU **t*. We should like to argue that this was not actually the case and that PU **t* first shifted to *s* (which is assumed to be different phonetically from PU **s*) except before **a* during the PU period, and then the *s* later became θ only in Sonsorol, as shown in (4).

(4)	1st shift:	*t	>	s	/ except __*a	in PU
	2nd shift:	s	>	θ		in S

The second shift is an unconditional sound change, i.e., all occurrences of the *s* derived from **t* underwent the shift.

One basis of our argument is that S θ and U/W *s* share exactly the same environment as far as related PO forms are concerned. It is unthinkable for two similar segments in two separate languages to share exactly the same environment (i.e., before all vowels but **a*) in their phonological shifts, one language undergoing **t* > s and the other **t* > θ. The only natural inference is that either *s* or θ was derived from the other as a secondary shift. We can observe a few cases that are strongly suggestive of the derivation of Sonsorol θ from *s,* and not the other way around. In the first place, as we shall see later, Ulithi θ developed from PU **s,* obviously influenced by Yapese which has θ. Exactly the same thing can be said of Sonsorol θ, that it developed from *s*, influenced by Palauan which has θ. Secondly, the fact that no other nuclear Micronesian languages have θ or reflexes of θ suggests that θ is a foreign element which invaded the two western forerunners of Micronesian (i.e., Ulithi and Sonsorol) and, therefore, U/W *s* cannot possibly have been derived from the intruder θ. This is further supported when we take into consideration the fact that migration most probably took place westward. Thirdly, observe the Trukese examples in (5) and compare them with the forms given in (3).

(5)	Tr	PO	
a.	*s*eling	**t*alinga	'ear'
	maa*s*	*ma*t*a	'eye'
b.	ina-	**t*ina	'mother'
	wɨɨ	**t*uqu(d)	'to stand'
	yanɨ	*ani*t*u	'ghost'
	yȧȧ	*qa*t*e	'liver'
	fɨɨ	*pi*t*uqu	'star'
	ėėn	**t*olu	'three'
c.	ȯȯ*s*	*qa*t*op	'thatch'

Note that the weakening process **t* > *s* > Ø is phonetically quite natural. There is no evidence that **t* was first changed to θ, which is different from *t* not only in position but in manner. Note further that the sound environments given in (3) are also applicable to Trukese except for an example in (5c).[5] What this suggests is that Trukese may have diverged from PU and undergone further weakening of **t*. Thus, S/U/W *t* corresponds to Tr *s*, while S θ and U/W *s* correspond to Tr ø. If it is true that Trukese shared a common history with S/U/W in PU, it is apparent that Sonsorol θ is simply a later unique development in Sonsorol. Fourthly, it seems that there was a systematic consonant shift in Sonsorol, which may be called a 'fronting' shift in that **c* went to *s*, **r* went to *l*, and *s* (< **t*) is assumed now to have gone to θ. By the last assumption, the systematic articulatory tendency is captured. Finally, PU **t* regularly corresponds to Palauan θ, as in *maθ* (PO **mata*), *eθam* (PO **tama*) 'father', *ˀaθ* (PO **qate*), and *ˀaθow* (PO **qatop*) 'thatch'. If PU **t* had changed to S θ directly by the influence of Palauan, we would most probably expect S *maaθA, θama-, yaaθE,* and *yaaθO*, respectively, for the above Palauan words. In fact, however, we have S *maatA, tama- yaaθ*E, and *yaaθ*O. That is, θ appears only in the cognates where PU **t* changed to *s* in Ulithi and Woleai. This certainly constitutes further evidence that, first, S θ and U/W *s* did not develop independently from PU **t* and, second, S *θ* developed from *s*.

The reconstruction of PU **c* is motivated by the correspondences illustrated in (6). Notice that Ulithi retains *c* both singly and doubly, whereas Woleai retains it only when it occurs doubly. The Sonsorol form is *s*.

(6)

S	U	W	
*s*aɨ	*c*ėė	*š*ėė	'leaf'
*s*epexi	*c*ipxi	*š*epexi	'kick him'
wii*s*E	yuu*c*	wii*š*I	'banana'
*ss*aa	*cc*aa	*cc*aa	'blood'
*ss*au	*cc*ou	*cc*au	'heavy'

We cannot reconstruct **s* for the above correspondences, not only because **s* has to be reserved for another more adequate set (see 9 below) but because, as we shall see, the Sonsorol *s* is a consonant derived from **c* through the 'fronting' shift. The Woleai *š* might be a possible candidate though. However, the fact that the eastern part of the Trukic chain, such as Fanapanges and Moen, has the stop *c* (E. Quackenbush 1968:59) and the corresponding PO form is a stop (e.g., PO **ndau(n)* 'leaf', PO **puti* 'banana', PO **daRa(q)* 'blood' in Grace 1969) militates against postulating the fricative *š*.

None of the three languages retains a simple **k* in native words, however all of them have *x* and *kk*. The *x* corresponds to the *k* of eastern languages including Trukese, Ponapean, Marshallese, Kusaean, and Gilbertese, to say nothing of the PO, as illustrated in (7). Furthermore, whenever two *x*'s meet at a morpheme boundary, they automatically turn to *kk*. This suggests that the historical development of **k* > *x* occurred very recently, and not as early as PU. From the broader perspective in Section 4, **k* > *x* is viewed as a case of phonological diffusion, with Ulithi as the focal point.

(7)

S	U	W	Tr	Pon	Mar	Kus	Gil	PO	
ii*x*E	ii*x*	ii*x*E	ii*k*	—	ye*k*	ik	ika	*i*k*a(n)	'fish'
*x*iitE	*x*iit	*x*u̇u̇sE	*k*ɨɨs	*k*iis	*k*weyet	*k*oet	—	**k*uRita	'octopus'
mata*x*I	meθa*x*	meta*x*i	mėta*k*	mete*k*	meta*k*	—	mara*k*i	*masa*k*i(t)	'pain'
*kk*angi	*kk*ang	*kk*angI	*kk*ėng	*kk*eng	*kk*ang	—	*kk*a*kk*ang	—	'sharp'
*kk*ɨ-	*kk*u̇-	*kk*u̇-	*kk*ɨ-	*k*ii*k*	—	—	—	**k*u*k*u	'fingernail'

A phenomenon parallel to **k* is observed in the reconstruction of **pw*. In simple form, all the three languages have the fricative *ƀw*, whereas, in double form, Sonsorol and Woleai have the stop *ppw*, but Ulithi still has the fricative *ƀƀw*, as shown in (8).

(8)

S	U	W	
ƀwo	*ƀwo*	*ƀwo*	'to swell'
*ƀw*oongI	*ƀwoong*	*ƀw*oongI	'night'
*pp*wesA	*ƀƀwec*	*ppw*ešE	'white'

Other Trukic languages including Puluwat and those east of it have the stop *pw* even in simple form (E. Quackenbush 1968:59) and the corresponding PO form is a stop (e.g., PO **ŋpongi* 'night' in Grace 1969).

The PU **s* is reconstructed in view of S *t* / U *θ* / W *t* / PO **s, *ns* as illustrated in (9).

(9)

S	U	W	PO	
yaa*t*E	yaa*θ*	yaa*t*E	*a*ns*e	'chin'
*t*ɨɨ*t*ɨ	*θ*u̇u̇*θ*	*t*u̇u̇*t*U̇	**s*usu	'breast'
*tt*aawA	*θθ*aaw	*tt*aawE	**s*au(q)	'far'
ii*t*A	ii*θ*	ii*t*E	*a*ns*a(n)	'name'
mė*t*awA	ma*θ*aw	me*t*awE	*ma*s*awa	'ocean'
taa*t*I	taa*θ*	taa*t*I	*ta*ns*i(k)	'sea'

PU **t* cannot be reconstructed for the above correspondence set, because there is no evidence that Ulithi *θ* has been developed through the process PO **s, *ns* > *t* > *θ*. On the contrary, there is strong indication that U *θ* was directly derived from PO **s, *ns*. For one thing, if PO **s, *ns* developed into U *θ* through *t*, the phonemic opposition between U *t* (< PO **t*) and U *θ* would never have been maintained. The reasons for not taking U *θ* as the PU phoneme are that it is unlikely that Woleai and Sonsorol had *θ* in their history for the above correspondences, and that all the other Trukic and most other Micronesian languages have *t*. The reason for selecting PU **s* is obvious. Certainly PO **s* and **ns* were merged before the PU period, and we cannot think of any phoneme between it and U *θ* or S/W *t*. From the phonetic point of view also, *s* differs by one feature from both *t* and *θ*.

Our next reconstructions are PU **l* and **n*. Woleai has *l* only in single form and *n* occurs only in double form, whereas Ulithi *l* occurs in both single and double forms. Sonsorol *r* corresponds to U/W single *l*, and Sonsorol *nn* to U *ll* and W *nn*.

(10)

S	U	W	
maa*r*i	mȧȧ*l*	maa*l*U̇	'animal'
*r*ɨɨ	*l*u̇u̇	*l*u̇u̇	'coconut tree'
kke*r*I	kke*l*	kke*l*I	'to dig'
si*nn*A	si*ll*	si*nn*E	'his mother'

nnaɨ	lloi	nnėė	'sweet'
mwȧnnE	mwall	mwannE	'sour'

One might propose to reconstruct only *l because the original l and n which are still distinct in Mortlockese are merged anyway in all the three languages. Suppose that we reconstruct only *l, assuming that the original n merged to l in the three languages. Then, it would be easy to account for the r/l/l correspondence and the appearance of U ll, but we would have to have a rule that derives nn from ll for Sonsorol and Woleai. In actuality, this rule should not apply to the original nn, because this nn has existed from the beginning, and was not derived through *nn > ll > nn. For this reason, we have decided to reconstruct both *l and *n for PU, i.e., *l from S r, n / U l / W l, n / Tr l while *n from S r, n / U l / W l, n / Tr n. We cannot reconstruct *r, because it is obviously a recent development in Sonsorol. The fact that when two S r's meet they automatically turn to nn also indicates that S r has been derived from *l rather recently. Examples of *l and *n reflexes are given in (11), in which Trukese examples are mostly from E. Quackenbush (1968: Appendix).

(11)

	S	U	W	Tr	
*l	reewE	leew	leewE	leew	'tongue'
	pparE	ppal	ppalE	ppȧl	'light'
	tȧringA	taleng	talingE	seling	'ear'
*ll	–	ƀwull	ƀwunnO	pwull	'heart'
	nnutU	llu̇t	nnu̇tU̇	llɨs	'to be jumping'
	xinnI	xill	xinnI	xill	'skin of'
*n	rɨɨ	lu̇u̇	lu̇u̇	nɨɨ	'coconut tree'
	rarowA	lalow	lalowE	nanew	'yesterday'
	raawO	laaw	lȯȯ	nȯȯ	'wave'
	saarI	cȧȧl	šaalU̇	caan	'water'
*nn	nnarA	llal	nnalE	nnen	'taste'
	nnatI	llaθ	nnatU̇	nnat	'scaevola'

Our last PU phoneme is *r, which is based on the correspondence S l / U r / W r. Sonsorol l is a later development from *r.

(12)

S	U	W	
leeƀwE	reeƀw	reeƀwE	'beard'
laa	raa	raa	'branch'
xalaxA	xarax	xeraxE	'to crawl'
ɨɨlE	yu̇u̇r	u̇u̇rE	'lobster'

3. The diachronic rules that derive the current consonantal systems of the three languages from the PU system set up in (1) are given in (13). Rules 5 and 6 are ordered. Some of the rules may be collapsed.

(13)

Rule				Environment
Rule 1.	**k*	>	*x*	in single form in S/U/W
Rule 2.	**pw*	>	*ƀw*	in U and in single form in S/W (Rules 2–3)
Rule 3.	**n*	>	*l*	
Rule 4.	**c*	>	š	in single form in W
Rule 5.	**t*	>	*s*	/ except __**a* in PU
	s	>	*θ*	in S
Rule 6.	**c*	>	*s*	in S (Rules 6–7)
Rule 7.	**r*	>	*l*	
Rule 8.	**s*	>	*θ*	in U
			t	in S/W
Rule 9.	**l*	>	*r*	In S

As a result of the above shifts, the three current consonantal systems in the native vocabulary have been developed as shown in (14).

(14) Sonsorol

p		t		k (doubly)	
ƀw (singly) / pw (doubly)	θ f	s		x (singly)	
		l	r (doubly)		
m		n (doubly)			ng
mw					

Ulithi

p		t	c	k (doubly)	
ƀw	θ f	s		x (singly)	
		l	r		
m					ng
mw					

Woleai

p		t	c (doubly)	k (doubly)	
ƀw (singly) / pw (doubly)	f	s	š (singly)	x (singly)	
		l (singly)	r (singly)*		
m		n (doubly)			ng
mw					

*When two *r*'s meet in Woleai, they turn into *cc*, being neutralized with the *cc* that comes from *šš*.

4. Let us observe a few major causes of the consonant shifts. It has been found in our data that sound shifts have been brought about not by one single cause but by the 'conspiracy' of a number of causes, and that one shift has been caused or affected by another shift.

The most significant cause is, no doubt, linguistic contact. Both Yapese and Palauan, which are only remotely related to nuclear Micronesian languages, are predominant lingustic groups that have exercised strong influence on Ulithi and Sonsorol, respectively. The addition of Rules 1 (**k* > *x*), 2 (**pw* > *ƀw*), 5 (*s* > *θ* in S), 6 (**c* > *s* in S), and 8 (**s* > *θ* in U) in (13) is ascribable to the contact with Yapese or Palauan, which have the consonants to which the sound shifts have been directed. Rule 4, which changed PU **c* to the Woleai *š*, seems to have resulted from the Woleaian contact with the languages to the east. Certain phonological diffusions are obviously due to incessant contacts between linguistic communities. This is especially the case with the development of *x, ƀw,* and *n/l* neutralization, which are viewed as innovations that originated in Ulithi and subsequently diffused eastward as far as Woleai and a few neighboring dialects. Notice that in (14) Woleai is the language that shows the most alternations between single and double forms. This may be because Woleai is a battlefield where the easterly movement of Ulithian innovations and the westerly diffusion of Trukic influence collide.

Sound shifts through linguistic contacts seem to have been accelerated by two other causes: genetic linkage and lexical borrowing. Since Yapese is genetically related to Ulithi and Palauan to Sonsorol, they still share quite a few cognates, a fact that has certainly expedited sound shifts, as may be observed in examples such as those in (15).

(15)	U	Yapese	PO	
	θu̇u̇θ	θu̇θ	**s*u*s*u	'breast'
	θaam	θam	**ns*ama	'outrigger side'
	S	Palauan	PO	
	maθE	maθ	*ma*t*e	'to die'
	yaaθE	aθ	*qa*t*e	'liver'
	*ss*aa	ra*s*ė?	da*R*a(q)	'blood'

Lexical borrowing is also regarded as having contributed to consonant shifts. For instance, U *makkaaθ* 'to blackmail' was borrowed from Yapese without change in form. Another example, to which K. Kuroiwa drew our attention, is U *yaθemaxil* 'to endeavor' which was also borrowed from Yapese. Thus, it seems that PU **s* > U *θ* was accelerated by a kind of lexical diffusion (cf. Chen and Wang 1975).

Another important cause of the consonant shifts is structural equilibrium. Certain shifts have been made to fill holes in the system that were opened by other shifts. Others were effected to maintain phonological oppositions with pushing or invading phonemes. Martinet's classical work (1972) depicts this situation in phonology very succinctly. Consider Sonsorol as an example. Obviously, under the influence of Palauan noted above, all the occurrences of *s* (< PU **t*) shifted to *θ*, which would have left the indispensable *s* position open in the system if PU **c* had not shifted to *s*. Conversely, **c* would not have moved to *s*, if *s* had not shifted to *θ*, as evidenced in nearby Tobi where both *s* and **c* are retained intact. This strong 'fronting' force in Sonsorol seems to be correlated with **r* > *l*, which in turn pulled **l* to the vacant *r* position.[6] Similarly, in Ulithi, **s* > *θ* is correlated with the shift **t* > *s*. All this is a natural consequence of man's tendency to attain maximal communicative effect through the functional interdistinction of phonemes and to minimize mental and physical effort through the symmetrical arrangement of phonemes in a system.

Finally, phonetic naturalness underlies all sound shifts. For instance, Rules 1 through 6 in (13) are all weakening processes. Only one feature was changed in most of the rules in (13). This indicates that, if other conditions did not intervene, consonant shifts in our languages have been made by the change of one feature in each shift.

5. We are now ready to propose a subgrouping that includes the three languages. E. Quackenbush (1968:87) presents the following percentages of shared retentions of basic vocabulary: Sonsorol-Ulithi, 78; Sonsorol-Woleai, 69; Ulithi-Woleai, 82. The relevant portion of Bender's (1971:442) lexicostatistical count of 176 items is shown below:

	Sonsorol		
Ulithi	68.8%	Ulithi	
Woleai	59.4%	74.1%	Woleai

These figures reflect the geographical distribution of the three languages as well as the close political and cultural tie existing between the people of Ulithi and Woleai. The very fact that Sonsorol has been extremely isolated until very recently and still is isolated from Ulithi and Woleai makes us hesitate to use the above figures for a genetic subgrouping of the languages.

In the same way, E. Quackenbush's (76) phonological isoglosses drawn among the languages will not be very helpful for our purpose, because we think that some isoglosses have been developed by the wave-like spread of the phonological features from focal points over the already divergent geographical areas. We may even think that certain phonological diffusions are still in progress, which has nothing to do with genetic relationships.

We propose that the earlier split among the three languages was made between Ulithi and Sonsorol/Woleai, and that Sonsorol and Woleai later diverged. Tentative as it may be, we also propose that Trukese developed from the PU along with Sonsorol/Woleai and then was split from the latter. (Other languages like Tobi also belong to the PU, but will not be discussed.) The genetic tree is represented in (16).

(16)

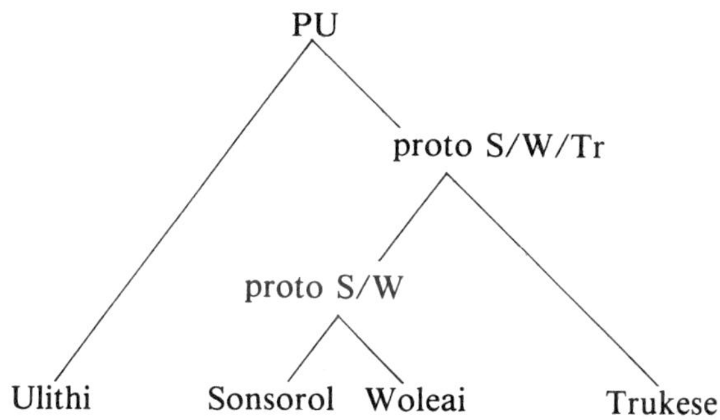

Our first basis for proposing (16) is the shifts associated with PU **s*. PU **s* is reflected as θ in U due to Yapese influence and as *t* in S/W/Tr (e.g., PU **tasi*'sea': U *taaθ*, S/W *taatI*, Tr *saat*). As we have seen, **s* > U θ was direct and not through **s* > *t* > θ. Insofar as this shift was direct and S/W/Tr share the innovation **s* > *t*, no other plausible hypothesis than the proposed one can be made. One might say that the unconditional plosivization **s* > *t* in S/W/Tr is phonetically unnatural. However, when we take into account the fact that the earlier allophonic shift **t* > *s* / except __ **a* in PU left wide open the syntagmatic positions of *t, the shift *s* > *t* was rather natural.

Our second basis for proposing (16) is the development of PU **t*. It was mentioned in connection with (5) that Trukese has undergone further weakening of PU **t,* as in (17).

(17) 1st weakening $*t > \begin{cases} \underline{\underline{t}} \; / \; \_\_ \; *a \\ \underline{\underline{s}} \text{ elsewhere} \end{cases}$ ... in PU

2nd weakening $\left[\begin{smallmatrix} t \\ \underline{\underline{s}} \\ \underline{\underline{s}} \end{smallmatrix}\right] > \left[\begin{smallmatrix} s \\ \emptyset \end{smallmatrix}\right]$ ... in Tr.

The second weakening in (17), which was a Trukese innovation, is evidence that Trukese was split from S/W.[7] Thus, PU **tina* 'mother' is reflected as *ina-* in Tr, whereas U has *sila-*, S, *θira-*, and W, *sila-*.

Our next argument is related to **n* and **l*, which are neutralized in S/U/W and restructured in such a way that only *l* occurs in Ulithi, whereas S *r* and W *l* occur in single form and S/W *n* occurs in double form. Unless we hypothesize a common development for Sonsorol and Woleai, we will be unable to account naturally for the restructuring, especially for the shift **ll > nn* that only took place in Sonsorol and Woleai. We further speculate that the S/W restructuring was caused by contacts with Ulithi (see 18).

(18)

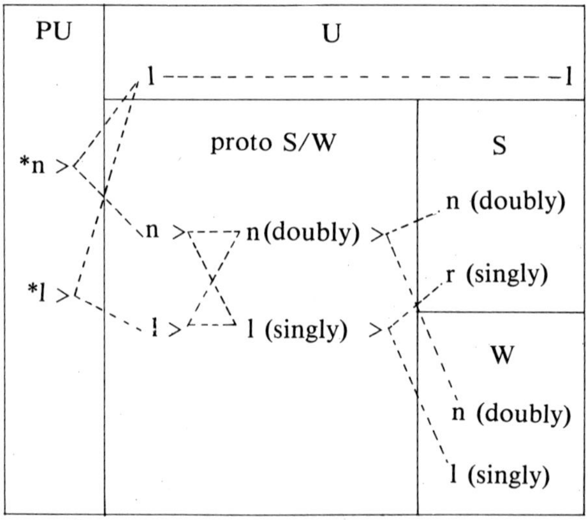

Incidentally, U *l* is a lateral, W *l* is a flap, and S *r* is a resonant. Phonetically, therefore, W *l* is a sort of transitional sound between U *l* and S *r*, another piece of evidence for the closeness between Woleai and Sonsorol. As soon as S *r* shifted to *l* owing to the fronting force, S *l* filled in the *r* position. Furthermore, the parallelism between the morphophonemic alternations *rr* → *nn* in Sonsorol and *ll* → *nn* in Woleai is suggestive of a common history between the two languages.

While **pw* has been completely fricativized to *ƀw* in Ulithi, the fricativization has occurred only in simple form in both Sonsorol and

Woleai. Minor as it may be, the commonality can best be explained by postulating a stage of development shared by Sonsorol and Woleai. This fricativization, together with **k* > *x* and **n/*l* neutralization, is assumed to have originated in Ulithi, and then diffused to proto S/W before Sonsorol and Woleai diverged.

Finally, let us observe the fronting shifts in Sonsorol, i.e., **s* > *θ* and **c* > *s* which were a chained development caused by the Palauan influence. Unlike the case of **l* and **n*, S *ss* does not go to *cc*. Thus, **c* > S *s* is a complete restructuring, with the phoneme *c* completely eliminated from the system. In other words, the forms with **c* were all relexicalized with *s*. Now, the fact that the hole left by **s* > *θ* was filled by **c* leads us to suspect that **c* > *s* may not have been direct, but through **c* > *š* > *s*. The phoneme *c* is different from *s* in two features, [palatal] and [continuant]. If **c* had not already been fricativized, the chained shift might not have been effected so easily. If this was actually the case, it will be easy to believe that Sonsorol and Woleai shared a common development in that Woleai still has *š*, which occurs only in single form.

Notes

* The data for the present study were collected in the summer of 1975, when the authors participated in a Micronesian Linguistics course conducted by Ho-min Sohn for the Micronesian Bilingual Project at the University of Hawaii. The Woleai data were provided by A. Tawerilmang, the Ulithi data by I. Langal, and the Sonsorol data by C. Yangilmau; Ho-min Sohn was responsible for the analysis.

1. The three languages under comparison are spoken in the westernmost part of the Trust Territory of the Pacific. They belong to the Trukic subfamily of the nuclear Micronesian family in the Eastern Oceanic group. The overall phonological and lexical descriptions of the languages of the Trukic subfamily are given in E. Quackenbush 1968 and Bender 1971 and 1973. A synchronic study of Ulithi phonology is presented in Sohn and Bender 1973 and that of Woleai phonology in Sohn 1975a.
2. Since loan words are excluded from consideration in this diachronic study, marginal phonemes that occur only in loanwords will not be taken into account.
3. We may also call it the Proto-Trukic, because we assume that the dialects of Trukese also share the same consonant system.
4. Ponapean also underwent the allophonic development of **t*. Other consonantal evidence, however, precludes including it in PU. For instance, PO **p* is reflected as PU **f* or **ø*, whereas it is reflected as *p* or *Ø* in Ponapean, whose consonant system does not contain *f* (Rehg 1973:32-34). This suggests that Old Ponapean and PU were sisters, as discussed by

Bender (1971: 439). It also leads us to assume that the allophonic split of **t* occurred before the two languages diverged and continued in the two separated languages.

5. Hiroshi Sugita (personal communication) reconstructs the underlying form *ossu-* for the Trukese word *òòs* 'thatch'. If this is the case, (5c) cannot be called an exception.
6. Tobi also shares **r > l,* probably as a result of contacts with Sonsorol (Bender 1971:443). Instead of **l > r,* however, Tobi underwent **l > x,* probably through **l > r > g.*
7. Ponapean underwent the same second weakening. At best, we can speculate that Trukese might have undergone the process through the influence of Ponapean, a case of phonological diffusion from the east, with Ponapean as a focal point.

Reprinted from *Language Sciences* (Indiana University) 44:19-24 (1979).

CHAPTER 4
SOCIOLINGUISTICS AND LANGUAGE PEDAGOGY

21. POWER AND SOLIDARITY IN THE KOREAN LANGUAGE

1. The concept of power is related to vertical and that of solidarity to horizontal closeness and distance.[1] While the former is linked with such notions as non-reciprocal control and submission, the latter has bearing on such notions as reciprocal bonding and alienation. In general, power variables such as kinship, age, achieved or ascribed status and sex function as sociocultural constraints about which individuals have little choice, whereas solidarity variables such as intimacy, ingroupness, and informality may, in large measure, be manipulated as part of a speaker's communicative strategies. If a society is completely egalitarian, the term 'role' would be more suitable than the term power, since the linguistic items of such a society would reflect social characteristics of the speaker, of the addressee, or of the relation between them without any connotation of vertical relationship. Since this is not actually the case with Korean society, we will use the term power à la Brown and Gilman (1960), although we admit that the sex variable in contemporary Korea is role-based to a considerable extent.

In any society, power and solidarity constantly interact like two ends of a seesaw, the former broadening the gap among people vertically and the latter narrowing the gap, closing interpersonal relationships horizontally. Their interactions are reflected not only in linguistic structure but in sociolinguistic usages. For example, the American system of address terms is sensitive to both power and solidarity, as shown in (1) where the terms are arranged in the order of decreasing power and increasing solidarity (cf., Brown and Ford 1964; Buren 1974).

(1) title sequence (Mr. President, Mr. Secretary, Mr. Chairman, etc.)
title alone (Professor, Doctor, Sir, Madam, Ma'am, Captain,

General, Father, Miss, etc.)
title and last name (Professor Martin, Dr. Lukoff, Mrs. Bender, Captain Wehrman, Miss Smith, etc.)
full first name (Albert, Christine, Daniel, Frederick, James, Joseph, Lucille, Samuel, etc.)
nickname (Al, Chris, Dan, Fred, Jim, Joe, Lu, Sam, etc.)
affectionate nickname (Albie, Chrissy, Danny, Freddy, Jimmy, Joey, Lucy, Sammy, etc.)

Notice that the lower in power and the closer in solidarity, the more individual identity is revealed in personal address, which appears to be a sociolinguistic universal. Brown and Ford (1964) and Slobin, et al. (1968) maintain that, in American English, title and last name expresses both deference in the power dimension and distance in the solidarity dimension, while first name denotes both condescension in power and intimacy in solidarity. They further assume that the linkage of deference and distance and of condescension and intimacy in sociolinguistic expressions is universal across cultures.

Power may take precedence over solidarity and vice versa in different societies and in different times. For example, Brown and Gilman (ibid.: 258-61) discuss the use of the familiar pronoun, generically designated as T (e.g., French *tu*, German *du*, Italian *tu*, and 13th-18th c. English *thou*), and the polite pronoun, designated as V (e.g., French *vous*, German *Sie*, Italian *Lei*, and 13th-18th c. English *ye*), in many languages of Europe and India, and present their semantic evolution as they are related to power and solidarity. Brown and Gilman observe that T was originally associated with condescension and intimacy and V with reverence (or deference) and formality (or distance), as shown in the two-dimensional scheme given in (2a). They further observe that, since the last century, solidarity has largely won out over power; thus (2a) has shifted more or less to the one-dimensional scheme as given in (2b) by way of a brief conflicting intermediate stage.

(2) a.

superiors
V
← T → | ← V →
equal & solidary | equal & not solidary
T
inferiors

b.

← T → ← V →
solidary not solidary

Several insightful studies have recently appeared relating the dynamism of power and solidarity in Korean society to the ongoing change in honorific patterns (e.g., M. Lee 1973; Ko 1974; Hwang 1975; Park-Choi 1976, 1978; Suh 1979). In particular, Suh (ibid.) points out that Korean interpersonal relationships on which honorific patterns are based have shifted from the traditional vertical to the modern horizontal structure due largely to the structural change of Korean society, particularly since World War II. As a result, Suh argues, the traditional consciousness of humility has markedly declined; levels of addressee honorification have been simplified; formality has given way to informality to a great extent; and honorifics are being abused due partly to the trend of egalitarian human relationships among Koreans.

The aim of the present paper is (a) to review some major changes in structural regularities and sociolinguistic patterns associated with Korean honorifics and present alternative ways of interpreting or analyzing them, and (b) to propose that, although power variables have undergone significant functional change and have been weakened considerably owing to the changes in social structure and cognitive values, they are still strongly dominant in Korean sociolinguistic reality. This leads to a claim that the present Korean society is a mixture of the traditional vertical social structure with the Western horizontal structure superimposed, as reflected in the sociolinguistic dynamism.

2. A complex lexical, morphological, and syntactic system for marking the speaker's power and solidarity relationship with the addressee or a third-person referent exists in the Korean language—a system usually referred to as honorifics or reverentials.[2] The pattern of addressee honorifics is much more complex and dynamic than that of subject honorifics, which is in turn more varied than that of non-subject referent honorifics, reflecting the socio-cultural intricacy and sensitivity of Korean face-to-face encounters and suggesting that the referent of the syntactic subject of a sentence has much more sociolinguistic significance than the other case referents.[3]

Needless to say, the primary motive for the use of honorifics is attributed to the intricate social and family stratification in traditional Korean society.[4] This stratification was based largely on various ascribed power relationships such as social status, kinship, age, and sex. It has been shown on the basis of fragmentary records that the languages of the Three Kingdoms, which had caste systems, already had honorific patterns (e.g., Huh 1972).

It appears that the honorific system of the Yi dynasty was the most complicated, reflecting the social structure of the time, in which the strata were rigidly institutionalized.

One striking sociolinguistic phenomenon clearly observable in the use of the Korean language is that power variables have significantly weakened and formality has given way considerably to casualness, to such an extent that the paradigmatic linguistic system of honorifics is being simplified and rearranged right in front of our eyes. There are many aspects demonstrating this dynamic, of which the following are of particular relevance to the linguistic system.

First, the highest speech level in the early modern period, represented by the verbal ending *-naita* was used colloquially up until 1945, but now is nothing but a historical relic to the present generation (cf., Choi 1959; M. Kim 1973; Ko 1974; and Suh 1979, among others). The last time I heard this style, together with the now archaic address term *nauli* 'master', was when law violators talked to Korean-Japanese policemen during the Japanese occupation. This speech style is used now only in historical dramas and novels, certain types of extremely deferential or submissive letters, and religious prayers. As a result, the second highest level of speech in the early modern period, represented by the verbal ending *-supnita* (hereafter {P}), has come to occupy the highest level in the current system.

Secondly, the style represented by the verbal ending *-yo* (hereafter {Y}) used to be a variant, along with the style of *-(s)o* ending (hereafter {S}), of the third and last deferential level in the early modern period. With its pleasant and soft sound symbolism, it was mainly used by women and children and seldom by male adults (e.g., Ko 1974; Suh 1979). The {Y} style has gradually acquired, since the turn of the century, a higher speech level and now is used by both males and females extensively. It has become the predominant deferential speech style of female speakers of standard Korean (the Seoul dialect), who rarely use the {P} style. Views are divided regarding the level of {Y} vis-à-vis that of {P}. Many linguists working on Korean (e.g., Martin 1964; M. Lee 1973; Park-Choi (1978) maintain that {Y} is next to {P} in terms of level, while others (e.g., Hwang 1975) consider it to be equal to {P}, the difference being in formality. These differing views seem to reflect the historical shift of emphasis away from power-orientedness. The former position is more appropriate to the generation of the past and older speakers, while the latter position is more representative of the youth of the contemporary generation. Interviews with native speakers have revealed that equivalence in level between {P} and {Y} is maintained more by younger people. Also, the productive use of {Y} over {P} becomes more conspicuous as the speaker becomes younger, as is evidenced in a survey conducted by Park-Choi (1976). The following are some of my observations in support of the view that contemporary Koreans tend to equate {P} and {Y} in power and differentiate them in the solidarity dimension, especially in formality.[5]

The ascension of {Y} to the level of {P} is manifest in the interchangeability of the two styles in one and the same discourse by the same speaker. In (3) are presented the distributions of the two styles based on a tape-recorded discussion between two university professors on the topic of Korean society (the data extracted from Chun 1976:355-50). / indicates a paragraph boundary; y is a structurally obligatory {Y} style while Y is a "discretionary" {Y} style (see below).

(3) a. Prof. LHY (male, questioner, age 51, born in Seoul)
P/P-P/y/y/y-P-P/P/P-P-y/P/Y-y/y-P-P-P-P/y/y/y-P/y/P/y-y-y/P-y-P-y-y-P-P-Y-Y/y/y-P-P-P-P-y-y-y-Y-y-Y/y/y-P-P-y-y-Y-y-y-Y/Y-y/Y-Y-y/Y-P/P-Y-Y-P
Total: 28 {P}'s and 42 {Y}'s

b. Prof. HWK (male, answerer, age 61, born in Pyongyang)
P-Y-P-P-Y-P-Y-y-P-P/Y-y-y/y-Y/P-P-P/P-P-P/P-P-Y-Y-y-P-Y-Y-Y-Y-P-y-P/P-y/y-Y-Y/y-Y-Y-Y-P-y-P/P-Y-P/y/y-P-Y-P-P-P/Y-y-Y-y-Y/P-Y-P-Y-Y-P-Y-y-Y-y-P/y-y-Y-y-y-Y-Y-y/P-y-P-Y-Y-P-P/y/P-y-y-Y/P-y-Y-P-P/y/y-Y-Y-y/y-Y-P/Y-y-y-Y-y-P
Total: 40 {P}'s and 71 {Y}'s

As observed in (3), the ratio between {P}'s and {Y}'s is roughly 5:7 for LHY and 5:9 for HWK. I fail to ascribe the {P}/{Y} switching to variation in power or deference. Nor can I say that either {P} or {Y} should be the unmarked style for the two interlocutors in the given setting. The switching can best be interpreted as stylistic, i.e., a subconscious effort to avoid the monotony which would arise either in the excessive formality in the case of {P} or in insufficient formality in the case of {Y}. In general, {P} appears to be more frequently used when more formality is called for either contextually, topically or interpersonally. Thus, the beginning and end of a paragraph tend to have {P} more frequently than {Y} unless {Y} is structurally obligatory. Other things being equal, a younger adult tends to use {P} more frequently than his older interlocutor in that the former tends to feel more formality.

Using of {Y} is sometimes structurally inevitable because certain sentence endings, such as *-kwun-yo, -ci-yo, -ketun-yo, -lkka-yo, nikka-yo*, and *-ntey-yo*, do not allow {P} to occur with them. In (3), 29 cases of such {Y} endings (represented as y) out of 42 are found in Prof. LHY and 33 out of 71 in Prof. HWK. These endings are more or less indirect speech styles that avoid strong assertion or illocutionary force on the part of the speaker while leaving room for the addressee's judgement or advice (cf., Searle 1975).

Pragmatically, such {P} forms as the propositive *-psita* and the retrospective *-ptita/-ptikka* are less polite than {P} forms in indicative statements or questions (cf., Ko 1974; Cho 1982). Thus, an adult using {P} forms in indicatives usually uses {Y} forms in indirect speech to denote proposition, retrospection, and command, these being more polite than {P} forms in direct speech. On the other hand, two adult friends who use {P} forms in propositives rarely use {P} forms in indicatives. Instead, {Y} forms in direct speech are of common use. All this suggests that {P} and {Y} are bound to be mingled unless people choose to use only {Y} forms consistently as was noted for standard-speaking women. The formality-informality distinction is viewed as neutralized in {Y} in the standard speech of females.

In general, any adult, regardless of his social status, is as happy to be addressed with {Y} as with {P}, unless exceptional formality is called for. In the case of {P}, the addressee would feel formality, whereas in the case of {Y}, he would feel some kind of familiarity, informality, and softness.

As a piece of evidence in support of her claim that {Y} is slightly lower than {P} in the level of deference, Park-Choi (1978:29) advances her observation that, while the most deferential address terms (e.g., deferential kinship term and title + *-nim*) can co-occur with both {P} and {Y}, the occurrence of her second highest address terms (e.g., plain kinship term and plain teknonymy) with {P} is blocked, with only {Y} allowed in this case. We may, however, interpret such cooccurrence restrictions in terms of the degree of formality that the address forms and the speech styles inherently carry. For example, *ape-nim* 'father' is associated with much stronger formality, i.e. psychological distance, etc., than *apeci*, although the vertical power and deference relationship between father and child is normatively constant in Korean society. When {Y} is to be regarded as a less formal variant of {P}, it will be natural to say that a more formal address term occurs with {P/Y}, while a less formal term occurs with {Y}. Such cooccurrence restrictions seem to be somewhat loose in the speech of many speakers, who accept, for example, both *apeci, tanye o-keyss-up-nita* and *apeci, tanye o-keyss-eyo* 'See you, dad', where the informal variant *apeci* occurs with both {P} and {Y}.

Indeed, the use of {Y} by a male to a superior is somewhat inhibitory if the construction in which it occurs denotes directness and has strong illocutionary force. Suppose, for example, that a university male student utters the sentences in (4) to his professor for leave-taking.

(4) a. ??Ce mence ka-yo.
    I first go
  b. ?Ce mence ka-pnita.
  c. Ce mence ka-po-keyss-eyo.
  d. Ce mence ka-po-keyss-up-nita.

Native speakers of Korean would agree that (4a) is next to unacceptable whereas (4d) is the most polite. (4b) is as direct as (4a), but more acceptable owing to the use of {P}. Use of such cogitatives as *-keyss* 'I intend' and of indirect verbs like *-po* 'tries' as hedging devices in (4c) and (4d) allow the utterances to be much politer. Suppose, conversely, that a professor utters the sentences in (5), meaning 'please come in', to a student.

(5) a. Tule wa-yo.
    enter come
  b. ?Tule o-sey yo.
  c. ??Tule o-si-p-siyo.

Notice that (5c) is more unacceptable than (5b) and the only difference between them is the presence of {P} and {Y}, respectively. From (4) and (5), one might conclude that {P} is more deferential than {Y} and, therefore, we should assign them to different speech levels. I would rather like to analyze cases like (4) and (5) in terms of formality. (4a) is impolite and thus not readily acceptable due to the combination of the lack of proper formality required in a student's association with a professor and the direct assertion of an inferior's own behavior to a superior. (4b) contains proper formality but not indirectness. In (4c), hedging is sufficiently expressed so that loosening of formality is allowed. Since one's student should not be treated with formality and deference (i.e., with {P} and the honorific suffix *-si/sey*), (5b) and (5c) are generally unacceptable, the latter being more so. In particular, the fact that (4c) with {Y} sounds more polite than (4b) with {P} seems to mitigate the claim that {P} is inherently more deferential than {Y}. Treating them in the light of the difference in the degree of formality may also be supported by Suh's (1979:209) survey, which shows that {Y} is predominantly used to higher family members and relatives and school senior members, while {P} is more predominant in addressing people in higher occupational ranks and social status. Thus, for example, 58.2% of Suh's subjects use {Y} to their parents as against 39.6% using {P}, whereas 41% of company employees use {Y} to their immediate superiors (i.e., *kyey-cang* 'section chief') as against 57.3% using {P}, and 33.1% of students use {Y} to their professors as against 65.4% using {P}. One's father is as powerful as his immediate superior or professor in Korean society. Yet {Y} is relatively more favored due, in my view, to the solidarity (i.e., informality and intimacy) involved.

Another frequently discussed aspect with regard to the system of speech levels is the destiny of the {S} style (the so-called authoritative or blunt style), represented by the verbal ending *-(s)o*. It was mentioned that the extra-deferential level, i.e., *naita*, etc., which was addressed mainly to the ruling class before the end of World War II has disappeared with the fall of the estate system. The process of the ensuing structural and sociolinguistic shifts involving {P}, {S}, and {Y} may be speculated to be as shown in (6).

(6)

LEVEL	STAGE I		II		III	
					+FORMAL	−FORMAL
I	{P}-mf	>	{P}-m {Y}-f	>	{P}-m	{Y}-mf
II	{S}-mf {Y}-f		{S}-mf		{S}-m	

Where *m* stands for male and *f* female.

In stage I, both {S} and {Y} were variants occupying the level below {P}. In stage II, however, with the gradual exclusive use of {P} by males, {Y} ended up with the only deferential level of female (and child) speakers. In stage III, males started to use {Y}, this time as a casual or informal counterpart of {P}, which appears to have been precipitated by the egalitarian trend in sex.

On the other hand, {S} was unable to climb up because of the existence of {P}. In Early Modern Korean, this style was used not only between equal adults but by a socially higher adult to a lower adult (Ko 1974:75-6). Only the latter usage is current, while the former usage has generally ceased in favor of {P} and {Y}. Along with its co-occurring pronoun *tangsin* 'you', the {S} style, now usually called 'authoritative' or 'blunt' (e.g., Martin and Lee 1969; S. Chang 1973a) and kept alive only among some people in the older generation, is the only style which is rarely reciprocal. All the other styles are both reciprocal and nonreciprocal. The {S} style is now used for the most part by a power-laden adult to a power-less adult, usually between males. While giving {S}, the power-full person usually receives {P}, rather than {Y}, from the male addressee because the context is mostly formal.

Some middle-aged or old husbands use {S} to their wives and receive {Y} because females do not generally use {P}. Aside from the husband-wife relationship, the power associated with the use of {S} is not usually caused by age or kinship but by the differences in achieved status in terms of occupation, rank, wealth, and interests, as well as personality. Although many Koreans still live in an authoritarian moral atmosphere, few Koreans would be happy when addressed with this style, which is high-handed on the part of the speaker and is a strong insult to the hearer if both interlocutors are males. Fighting or emotional resentment caused by the use of this style, which violates the so-called cooperative principle in conversation (Grice 1975), may be viewed as egalitarian resistance against authoritarianism. At best, the {S} style is tolerated if it is used, for example, by an older boss to a younger employee. This power-laden style, together with the pronoun *tangsin,* is doomed to extinction because it is totally dispensed with in the speech of the younger generation and many belonging to the older generation.[6] That it is the only asymmetrical style used mainly by males to denote achieved power indicates that it is extremely insecure both in the linguistic system and in the democratic society of Korea.

It has been observed that a variant of {S}, represented by the ending *-(s)wu*, is used especially by old females and children. This variant does not carry as much power and formality as the *-(s)o* ending does. This ending can partly be equated in functional value with the intimate style (to be discussed below), in that those who do not use the intimate style often employ the *-(s)wu* ending where the intimate style would otherwise be expected. For example, an old female often use *-(s)wu* to an adolescent (e.g., a college student); and a child often uses it to an older sibling or an adolescent.

The low frequency and gradual disappearance of the style represented by the *-ney* ending (hereafter {N}) is also worth mentioning. In the early modern period, this style, in addition to reciprocal use between adolescents, was used non-reciprocally by a higher person to a lower ranking relative or in-law, in inter-age, inter-estate, or inter-position relationships, etc., the condition being that the addressee had to be either an adolescent or adult, but not a child (Ko 1974:71-2). Social estates and positions are no longer determinants of this so-called intimate style. It is hardly ever used by or between present adolescents (Park-Choi 1976; Suh 1979). Instead, {Y}, the 'familiar' style (to be discussed below), or exceptionally the -(*s*)*wu* variant of {S} is used. Pervasive democratic values, avoidance of the formality and hierarchism that {N} denotes, its use only by males, structural insecurity between {P} and {T}, and the existence of a more casual, less expressive counterpart (i.e., the familiar style) are all viewed as having contributed to the low frequency of {N} and its eventual extinction in the younger and new generation. The second person pronoun *caney* which co-occurs with {N} is also doomed to extinction, just as *tangsin* and {S} are.

Finally, the so-called *panmal* (half-talk) or familiar style, represented by the verbal ending *-e* (hereafter {E}), has been extensively diffused. This phenomenon is parallel to the diffusion of {Y} (cf., Suh 1979). This is the style children learn first and use more productively than any other styles. Indeed, {E} has now become a favorite form for everyone when addressing adolescents, as an informal replacement for {N}. In particular, one rarely uses {N} to female adolescents in favor of {E}, and females, young and old, seldom use {N} in favor of {E} either. Those who still employ {N} extensively mix {E} and {N} in one and the same discourse, just as in the case of {Y} and {P}.

Similarly, the {E} style is also extensively employed as an informal or casual counterpart of the plain style, represented by the verbal ending *-ta* (hereafter {T}). The {T} style is used typically between children, by an adult or adolescent to a child, and between two close adult or adolescent friends whose acquaintance was formed during childhood. It is also a style of a higher family member (e.g., parents and older siblings) to a lower member (e.g., children and younger siblings). My own survey has revealed that while the occurrence of {T} is more frequently noticeable than that of {E} in adults' speech toward children, {E} is more predominant than {T} between children, probably due to the formality involved. Like {P} vs. {Y} and {N} vs. {E}, {T} vs. {E} appear alternately in one and the same discourse. Frequency statistics are presented in (7) regarding the use of {T} and {E} by elementary school children in a conversation (data from *Elementary Korean,* 4.1:66-77. 1973).

(7) Hayyeng (female): 5 T's and 13 E's
Swunhi (female): 5 T's and 6 E's
Yengswuk (female): 5 T's and 18 E's
Wungki (male): 16 T's and 20 E's
Hakswu (male): 6 T's and 16 E's

Thus, there is a significant parallelism in {P}:{Y} = {N}:{E} = {T}:{E} not only in terms of formality vs. informality but in their interchangeability in a discourse. They are also parallel in that certain verbal endings allow only {Y} and {E} and not {P}, {N}, and {T}. The two informal styles {Y} and {E} are, thus, structurally more productive and ubiquitous than their distributionally limited formal counterparts. Only in exceptional cases is the {E} style also used interchangeably with {S} or {Y}.

In addition to the above-mentioned relaxation of traditional power and formality as reflected in the linguistic system, there are many other changes in sociolinguistic behaviors which point in the same direction. Some examples follow.

First, as alluded to earlier, a noticeable trend is that the less formal styles, i.e., {Y} and {E}, have gained great popularity, as evidenced in Park-Choi's (1978) survey. The younger the speaker is, the more they are used.

Second, there is a (more or less institutionalized) power relation between husband (higher) and wife (lower) for many older people. Thus, among them, either {Y} ⟷ {S} or {Y} ⟷ {N/E} is a common practice, my own practice belonging to the latter. This power relationship has almost completely been obliterated in the speech of the younger generation who are typically in the {Y} ⟷ {Y} term. Similarly, two adolescent lovers may use either {Y}, {E}, or {T/E} reciprocally.

Third, a traditional sociolinguistic rule of Koreans is that kinship takes precedence over age in power decision. This was strict in the past and still is in rural areas and among some older people. Thus, for instance, a younger adult uses {N/E} to an older adult while receiving {P/Y} simply because the former belongs to the ascending generation in consanguinity or is higher in in-law status (for details, see Park-Choi 1978 for example). This strict power relationship has been losing ground to such an extent that it compromises with age power. Again with much individual variation, a common practice is that a younger person in the ascending generation or higher in in-law status uses a reciprocal style ({P/Y} for adults and {T/E} for non-adults) with an older person in the descending generation or lower in in-law status. For instance, I use {P/Y} reciprocally with my wife's uncles and older brothers who are younger than I. Similarly, the principle of mutual deference (*yangcon*) is widely followed between a younger superior person and an older inferior person such as between a younger boss and an older employee in a company. These persons, due to the strong age constraint, use {P/Y} reciprocally.

Fourth, a strong decline in humbleness is noticeable among young speakers who, for example, tend to use *na* 'I (plain)' instead of *ce* 'I (humble)', *mut-ta* 'asks (plain)' instead of *yeccwu-ta* 'asks (humble)', etc. to their seniors. Suh (1979:192-201) lists examples where Koreans no longer use humble forms in referring to those belonging to their ingroup. Ko (1974:

88) points out that the humble variants *-psyo* and *-pcio* of the {P} level have disappeared.

Fifth, it is quite fashionable, particularly among youngsters, to lower their speech styles, under (overt or covert) mutual agreement, from their initial reciprocal {P/Y} to reciprocal {E} as soon as they become sufficiently intimate. This sometimes happens even between different sexes. One constraint in this case is that the age difference should not be more than two or three years for such an agreement to be reached.

Sixth, the productive use of such address-reference terms as *sensayng* (lit. teacher) to all levels of adults, regardless of their occupation, suggests that Koreans are moving toward egalitarianism. Thus, *sensayng* is frequently used to refer to government employees, storekeepers, barbers, plumbers, etc. as well as to professionals including teachers and professors.

Seventh, *appa* 'dad' and *emma* 'mom', which were used exclusively by children, are now used frequently by adolescents and even adults (especially females) as well, suggesting the prevalence of solidarity.

Finally, as Suh (1979) also mentions, such kinship terms as *hyeng* '(male's) older brother', *ęnni* '(female's) older sister', *halmeni* 'grandmother', and *acwumeni* 'aunt' have now acquired daily usage among non-kin people, frequently even among strangers. This metaphorical extension of family relationship to society appears to be an effort to maintain interpersonal relationships based on family-like solidarity.

3. On the basis of the foregoing discussions, we are able to say that, with the elimination of the variable of *ascribed* social status (as per the abolishment of the estate system) and the introduction of democratic principles and ideals since the end of World War II, the traditional vertical power has been mitigated to a great extent, as reflected in the structural shift in the sociolinguistic usage of honorifics.[7] At the same time, we are unable to say that vertical power has been totally replaced by horizontal solidarity in Korean society, since there is another persistent force to maintain social stratification through the language (and nonverbal behaviors). One fundamental principle seems to be that reciprocal solidarity can permeate into only the relationship of power equals, i.e., between persons of approximately equal age and status at the time of initial encounter. Following are some of the typical structural and sociolinguistic cases attesting to the tenacity of verticalism in Korean society.

First of all, Koreans are still very sensitive to relative age due probably to the fact that respect for age is one of the most important value orientations imbued in their minds. In order to see to what extent this is the case, let us go back to the structural and sociolinguistic changes discussed in Section 2. Based on these changes, I propose to distinguish two separate systems of contemporary Korean addressee honorifics, one applicable to the older (approximately 45 years of age and above as of 1981) and the other to the younger generation, which seems to be correlated with the temporal boundary before and after the end of World War II. While individuals differ greatly, the schemas in (8) may be postulated as basic general patterns. { } is the style the speaker-hearer receives from his interlocutor. In {A/B}, the term A is regarded as +*formal* and the term B −*formal.*

(8) a. *Older generation speakers*

AGE GROUPS	*SP-HR*←→SP-HR			SP-HR←→SP-HR	
				+*power*	−*power*
Adults :	{P/Y}	↔ ↕	{P/Y}	{P/Y} ↔	{S/ }
Adolescents :	{N/E}	↔ ↕	{N/E}		
Children :	{T/E}	↔	{T/E}		

b. *Younger generation speaker*

A. sociolinguistic pattern

Adults :	{P/Y}	↔ ↕	{P/Y}
Adolescents :	{ /E}	↔ ↕	{ /E}
Children :	{T/E}	↔	{T/E}

B. linguistic structure

+Adult :	{P/Y}	↔ ↕	{P/Y}
−Adult :	{T/E}	↔	{T/E}

The patterns in (8) are given as a broad framework applicable to outgroup or distant people or strangers. Between solidarity members, however, even a small difference in relative ages is significant and relative social statuses or occupational ranks also come into the picture in the expression of honorifics, as will be seen shortly. Males use all the styles given in (8), except that, at least in standard Korean, older generation speakers, when they were children, seldom used {N} to adolescents. In certain dialects (e.g., Cenla Province), however, children, male and female, still often use {N} to adolescents and older siblings. As already mentioned, females in standard speech seldom use {P}, {S}, and {N}. It seems to be universal across cultures that females use less expressive and much softer forms than males and have a verbal repertoire more restricted than that of males (e.g., Lakoff 1975; Thorne and Henley 1975; Kramarae 1975; Brown 1976, 1980; Zimin 1981; Peng, et al. 1981; Bak 1983; Ide 1982).

The arrangement given in (8) reflects a number of sociolinguistic facts that the one-dimensional scheme is unable to reveal—formality/informality distinction, reciprocal vs. non-reciprocal usage, ascribed (age) power vs. achieved power, sociolinguistic parallelism in {P}:{N}:{T} = {Y}:{E}:{E}, and coexistence of two distinct systems manifesting the ongoing linguistic change from the older to the younger generation.[8] Above all, the proposed scheme reflects the sociolinguistic significance of age groups and age power. A present-generation Korean passes through three age stages as he grows older—childhood, adolescence, and adulthood—each stage having an influence on speech styles. In childhood, he is addressed with {T/E} and the address terms *ne* 'you', *Homin-a* 'Ho-min!', etc.; in adolescence or pre-adulthood, with {N/E} and the address terms *caney* 'you', *Sohn-kwun* 'Mr. Sohn', *Homin-i* 'Ho-min!', etc.; and in adulthood, with {P/Y} or {S} and the address terms *sensayng-nim, sensayng, tangsin* 'you (blunt style)', *Sohn-sensayng*, etc. This is the case when the speaker belongs to the older generation. If the speaker belongs to the younger generation, on the other hand, the hearer in his adolescence is addressed with {E}, not {N/E}, with the address terms *caney, Homin-i*, etc. dispensed with, and the hearer in his adulthood is not addressed with {S}, *tangsin*, etc. It must be stressed that there is considerable variation from individual to individual, not only as to where borderlines should be drawn between age groups, but as to which styles are to be used in different speech situations. It is widely known among variationists, however, that linguistic variation precedes linguistic change and the dynamic system is not chaotic but moves along similar paths for all native speakers.

In (8a), the asymmetrical relation {P/Y} ⟷ {S/ } is the only nonreciprocal encounter that is not controlled by age disparity but by achieved power.[9] This faltering and unstable relation is phased out in the younger generation system, yielding a more symmetrical and simpler system. Thus, as far as the structure of speech styles is concerned, the most significant power element at present is age, which is still very tenacious in Korean except perhaps in baby talk. It was mentioned that even kinishp cannot override age in contemporary Korean but is, in general, neutralized with age in the form of mutual deference when they are in conflict.

One important sociolinguistic principle in Korean that I would like to advance with regard to (8) is the principle of INITIAL ACQUAINTANCE. (8) applies to the initial acquaintance of dyads. Two reciprocal adults use {T/E}, {N/E}, or {P/Y} with each other, depending on when they first became acquainted with each other. No matter how close they may be, for instance, two adults use {P/Y} if their acquaintance started in their adulthood, unless they agree to use another style, which is very rare especially in the older generation. I use {T/E} to my childhood friends (up to high school), {N/E} to my college-day friends, i.e., to those I first became acquainted with in my college days, and {P/Y} to all friends I became acquainted with during adulthood, regardless of the degree of intimacy.[10]

Age power is so strong and firm that one cannot degrade a person in a higher age-stage even in fighting or insulting; even an adult beggar receives proper linguistic deference commensurate with his age; and even the strongest solidarity would be unable to downgrade a speech style or an address term used to one's senior person. Between ingroup members, even a minute age difference becomes significant. In elementary and secondary schools, for example, a few years of difference causes the use of non-reciprocal styles and address terms, which is, in general, an extension of a sibling relationship to be discussed below.

Age is also significant to a certain extent as a power variable in such typical horizontal societies as America. Thus, an American child usually uses title + last name to an adult while receiving first name. Unlike the Korean case, however, an age difference of less than approximately fifteen years does not generally generate asymmetrical use of address terms. And even if the difference is more than fifteen years or even a generation, age can be neutralized by intimacy solidarity (Brown and Ford 1965; Ervin-Tripp 1971). Moreover, the interlocutors of an adult American dyad of equal status may begin with reciprocal title + last name when the acquaintance is new but may, in several minutes of conversation, advance to reciprocal first name (e.g., Brown and Ford ibid.). This attests to the fact that the adult status is easily overruled by intimacy in American English. This degree of intimacy would never cause any address shift in Korean even between ingroup adults.

Kinship also remains a strong power variable in Korea, although, in recent years, many households have been reduced to nuclear families and terms like *ochon* 'father's cousin' and *yukchon* 'second cousin' are becoming out of use (Cho 1982:176). Korean kinship terms are extremely stratified. Unlike in the English-speaking world, Korean siblings or cousins are on non-reciprocal terms, even between twins. The relationship between them is similar to that between childhood and adolescence/adulthood or between adolescence and adulthood depending on individuals. Thus, for example, such address terms as *hyeng* or *hyeng-nim* 'older brother' ←→ FN-*a* or ZERO are used, the choice of which depends on the sibling's age-stage, social status, solidarity, etc. While the terms *uncle* and *aunt* are sufficient to address parents' brothers, sisters, and their spouses in America, Koreans have many different terms indicating not only parents' older or younger siblings but paternal or maternal and consanguineous or in-law relationships. Thus, for example, the English address term *uncle* corresponds to *khun apeci* (lit. big father—father's older brother), *cakun apeci* (lit. small father—father's younger brother), *samchon* (father's brother—usually, a younger one), *koswuk* (father's sister's husband), *iswuk* (mother's sister's husband), *wesamchon* (mother's brother), etc. Again unlike in American society where progressive parents invite FN address from their children, certain parents-in-law are on FN basis mutually with their children-in-law, etc., no degree of solidarity can neutralize non-reciprocal kinship relationship in sociolinguistic expressions in Korea.

Achieved social status is also strong as a power variable in honorific expressions.[11] This is particularly apparent in the use of address-reference terms and in non-verbal behaviors (inter alia, in gestures). For instance, a younger company president may use LN-PT (e.g., *Kim-kwacang* 'section chief Kim') or LN-*sensayng* to an older subordinate, while receiving PT-*nim* (e.g., *sacang-nim* 'company president'). A carpenter is usually addressed with such terms as *mokswu acessi* (lit. uncle carpenter), LN-*ssi acessi* (lit. uncle Mr. LN) or simply *acessi*. A professor, a medical doctor, or a lawyer would not be addressed in this way. Instead, LN-*paksa-nim* 'Dr. LN', (LN)-*sensayng-nim* 'Mr. LN, sir', etc. are used. There is a strict power relationship between high school students belonging to different grades. A student in a higher grade uses {T/E} to a student in a low grade and receives {P/Y}, and in many cases this sociolinguistic relationship is carried on for life due to the principle of initial acquaintance. The same can be said about military people. As Hwang (1975:186) puts it, such asymmetrical uses of speech styles and address terms governing status distinction rarely change regardless of the degree of intimacy between the speakers and speech situations. Power disparity also occurs between a traffic violator and the police, between a seller and a buyer, between a taxi driver and a passenger, between a convict and a prosecutor, to mention only a few. While Americans do not use such hierarchical professional terms as company president, director, division chief, section chief, etc., Koreans do use them in and out of the working place. While Americans rarely use titles in sequence (Mr. President, Mr. Chairman, and Mr. Secretary are about all), Koreans commonly do, as in *uysa sensayng-nim* 'doctor' and *Kim-paksa-nim* 'Dr. Kim'. While an American superior and a subordinate interact frequently on first name basis, Koreans never allow this. Thus, an American professor and a graduate student often arrive at the use of mutual FN if the relationship becomes close, which is never the case in Korea. The abuse of deferential expressions and the prevalence of the non-reciprocal speech in various organizations and social encounters may be due to the still persistent traditional mental structure based deeply on social hierarchy, coupled with the Western material culture which is received in Korea in the form of mammonism and a 'move-up' mentality.

Sex used to be a strong power variable in the traditional society of Korea. This is no longer the case in the contemporary younger generation. Slight sex power remains among some old generation Koreans, but only in family or kin relationships, as between husband and wife. Parents-in-law usually use {N/E} to their son-in-law but {T/E} to their daughter-in-law, which could be attributed to the difference in the solidarity rather than in the power associated with sex. Cho (1982:6) notices that young people use the reflexive pronoun *caki* 'self' (in the innovated sense: 'you') reciprocally for referring to their lovers, spouses, or close friends of the opposite sex, and that female college students use *hyeng* 'male's older brother' to address a male student, especially on campus. Such innovations point to the tendency of equality in sex in Korean.

In addition to the observations discussed above, there are many cross-cultural cases which attest to the dominance of power over solidarity in Korean. Some of the obvious cases are illustrated below. First of all, while an angry American tends to upgrade address terms (e.g., from first name like *John* to title + last name like *Mr. Smith*), an angry Korean tends to downgrade them (e.g., from *sensayng-nim* to *tangsin* or even to *ne* 'you'). In the American case, Buren's (1974:70) example of scolding his child serves our point, as shown in (9).

(9) Jessie, no.
Jess, don't.
Jessica, don't do that.
Jessica Claire, I've told you a hundred times not to do that.
Jessica Claire Van Buren, stop that this instant.

Notice that the fiercer the scolding, the more fully the proper names are used. All this means that, by upgrading address terms, Americans try to distance the addressee in terms of solidarity. Koreans, on the other hand, try to lower the addressee in terms of power through downgrading of address terms and speech styles. The only case somewhat comparable to the American practice is that an angry speaker often drops the vocative suffix

-(y)a (used to children), as illustrated in (10).

(10) a. Yongho-ya, ne eti ka-ni?
you where go
'Yongho, where are you going?'
b. Yongho, ne cwuk-ko siph-ni?
you die want
'Yongho, do you want me to give you a hard time?'

Another illustrative case is that American college students usually want to be addressed with first name by a close child as well as by a close adult and with title + last name by a distant child or adult. In contrast, a freshman Korean student wants to be addressed with such kinship terms as *hyeng* 'older brother' or *enni* 'older sister' along with {Y} by a close or distant child, and with such address terms as LN-*kwun* 'Mr. LN' or LN-*yang* 'Miss LN' and *haksayng* 'student' along with {N/E} by adults. This again shows that Americans put more importance on solidarity than on power, whereas Koreans put more importance on power than on solidarity.

A third illustrative case is that, while Americans feel that mutual first name use leads to smooth social interactions, Korean adults' most comfortable address terms for daily interpersonal encounters are such high terms as *sensayng-nim*. This reflects Koreans' power-oriented consciousness in contrast with Americans' solidarity-orientedness.

Finally, while Americans are comparatively insensitive to their interlocutor's age or occupational rank, Koreans are eager to know them in their encounters and use different power-based sociolinguistic expressions accordingly. Thus, asking about the addressee's age or rank on initial encounters is allowed in Korean culture. This also suggests the existence of the still persistent power consciousness among Koreans.

The structural shift and sociolinguistic behaviors discussed thus far appear to be sufficient to support the claim that in Korean society, while the consciousness of the traditional vertical power has been relaxed, with ascribed social status eliminated, strong verticalism still remains in age, kinship, and achieved social status. As K. Lee (1977) states, it appears that Koreans still seek peace, happiness, safety, and order in hierarchical relationships, feeling uneasy and insecure in horizontal (colleagial) relationships. In view of Parsons' dominant patterns of social behavior in pre-modern or traditional societies and modern industrialized societies (Koh 1976:139-40), it is undeniable that Korean society still retains considerable degrees of pre-modern, traditional traits (e.g., sentimentality, extensiveness, attribution, particularity, and group-orientedness), even if we allow for the fact that behavioral patterns like group-orientedness of Gemeinschaftlich relations are common traits among Orientals in industrialized societies as well. According to Y. Chang (1976:155), the principle of egalitarianism, in its true sense, still remains an ideal in Korea. There are some historical and sociological correlates in such claims.[12] On the other side of the coin, there are many signs that Korea is in the process of modernization in Parsons' sense in that such modern traits as neutrality of sentimentality, limitedness, achievement, universality, and individual-orientedness are being widely diffused throughout urban Korea. Legally, contemporary Korea is a democratic nation, and democratic values have spread over all walks of life.[13] In particular, the younger generation is more sensitive to them. From the sociolinguistic perspective, as we have seen thus far, we can say that Korean society is moving toward Western egalitarianism, though the process is slow. At this moment, as far as linguists can tell from linguistic evidence, Korean society is standing at the crossroads between pre-modern and modern society.

Notes

1. This paper is a result of a Fulbright-Hays Faculty Research grant that I received in 1978 to conduct a sociolinguistic study on Korean. An earlier version of this paper was presented at the panel on Reflection of Society in the Korean Language, the Annual Meeting of the Association for Asian Studies held in Toronto in March 1981. I would like to thank John Haig for his valuable comments on this paper. In this paper, the system of Yale romanization is followed in transcribing Korean.
2. There are a large number of studies on Korean honorifics, most of which are purely linguistic. Some proposals regarding generative derivation of Korean honorifics include Song (1967), H. Lee (1970), Suh (1972), S. Chang (1973a), C. Lee (1974), Sohn (1974a), and Cho (1982), among others. Only recently has serious sociolinguistic research been conducted, e.g., Martin (1964), Howell (1967), M. Lee (1973), Hwang (1975), D. Lee (1975), Park-Choi (1976, 1978), Lukoff (1977), Suh (1979), and Cho (1982).
3. Brown and Levinson (1978) assume that the mutual knowledge of face and the social necessity to adjust to it in interaction are universal and propose that face saving constitutes a powerful functional pressure on any language.
4. According to C. Kim (1976:57-8), the institutionalized pattern of social strata are of three major types: First, caste (prevalent in ancient societies) in which the positions are defined by such factors as pedigree and religion; second, estate (in the medieval societies) in which social ranks are defined by law; and third, class (in the modern societies) in which

senior/junior and superior/inferior status is determined by individuals' abilities and achievements. Kim roughly equates the stratal system (such as the Silla dynasty's *Kolp'um*) of the Three Kingdoms to the caste system, the system of the Koryo (aristocrats, commoners, and lowlies) and Yi societies (Yangban or Upper estate, Chungin or Middle estate, Sangmin or commoners, and Ch'onmin or lowlies) to the estate system, and the system of the last part of the Yi dynasty on to the class system. In particular, the Yi dynasty's social strata, legally stipulated, were based not only on the traditional social order but on the newly introduced Confucian ideology which placed unprecedented emphasis on detailed and extensive discriminations among people in all spheres of life. Confucianism, which provided the ideology for the foundation of the Yi dynasty, stipulated an ethical code that categorized and regulated five basic types of interpersonal behaviors based mainly on hierarchical human relations, and which stressed the subordinate's unilateral obedience to the superior. These five are: loyalty between king and subject, filial piety between parents and child, distinction between husband and wife, precedence between senior and junior (in terms of age, sex, generation or social status), and confidence between friends (Y. Chang 1976:154).

5. In this paper, the terms formality and informality are used without strict definition, understood simply as relative or scalar concepts. Irvine (n.d.), for example, proposes that formality and informality represent a complex of interrelated factors concerning many facets of a speech event—such as code structuring, code consistency, social identities of participants, and situational emergence of a focus. Roughly, they are regarded in this paper as properties of a communicative code as well as of the social setting. For instance, {P} is said to be formal in that it denotes more psychological distance and is used, in general, in relatively more serious moments or situations than {Y}.
6. Although I have never used {S} in my life, I have once in a while received it, each time to my great resentment even when I received some kind of favor along with it.
7. According to historians and sociologists, the traditional order of estates of the Yi dynasty gradually disintegrated from the 18th century due mainly to the incessant partisan strife of the Yangban estate, disorder in the land system, farmers' desertion of their farms to escape the burden of excessive land rents, and various popular uprisings in the 19th century demanding egalitarianism. Furthermore, certain farmers rose to the Yangban class owing to their accumulated wealth; the government destroyed all registers of public surfs in 1801; commerce and industry began to develop, signalling the emergence of a capitalist society; the neighboring nations (China, Japan, and Russia) intervened in Korea's domestic affairs; and Western influence began to penetrate, all these contributing to the disintegration of the Yi dynasty.
8. The most frequently cited treatment of Korean addressee honorifics is to recognize six different levels of speech in current colloquial Korean according to the six distinct sets of verbal endings (e.g., Martin and Lee 1969; M. Lee 1973; Park-Choi 1978), as shown below:

LEVELS	STATEMENT VERBAL ENDINGS		TERMS OF ADDRESS
I. deferential	-(su)pnita	{P}	sensayng-nim, etc.
II. polite	-(e)yo	{Y}	sensayng-(nim), etc.
III. blunt	-(s)o	{S}	LN-sensayng, tangsin 'you', etc.
IV. intimate	-ney	{N}	LN-kwun, FN-i, caney 'you', etc.
V. familiar	-a	{E}	LN-kwun, FN-i, FN-a,

			caney/ne 'you', etc.
VI. plain	-ta	{T}	FN-a, ne 'you', etc.

Where LN = family name; FN = given name

This one-dimensional description of Korean addressee honorifics, although mnemonically helpful, does not project sociolinguistic aspects relevant to the use of Korean honorifics.

9. Although the *-(s)wu* variant of {S} may be viewed as an informal counterpart of the *-(s)o* ending, I have not included it in (8) separately as a right-hand term of {S/ } because its usage is extremely limited and, unlike {Y} and {E}, it does not cooccur with the *-(s)o* ending in the same speaker's speech in a given discourse.
10. Exceptions to this principle are related to the developmental age change of the addressee. When two childhood friends who have been separated meet again in adulthood, they may either maintain the initial usage or change their honorific terms from the original *ne* 'you' and {T/E} to *caney* 'you' and {N/E}. In the case of a non-reciprocal relationship in terms of age, the principle is strictly observed by a junior person. A person is addressed by his former student with the highest address term (e.g, *sensayng-nim*) and {P/Y} no matter how high the latter's present position is. However, the senior person usually upgrades his former student who is now an adult to a level which still shows the former hierarchical difference, e.g., from FN-*a*, *ne* 'you', and {T/E} to LN-*kwun*, FN-*i*, *caney* 'you', and {N/E}. When a former student becomes one's colleague, a common practice is to use LN + professional title (PT) and {Y} or {S} while receiving LN + PT + *-nim* and {P/Y}. Even many parents do not use *ne* and {T/E} to thier married children. A common practice in this case is to use teknonymy (e.g., *apem-a* 'dad!') or ZERO and {E}. All these attest to the predominance of age power in Korean society.
11. Hierarchical as they may be in this sense, achieved statuses in the present society, of which chances are open to anybody, are transient and may not be strong enough to cause any noticeable chances in the linguistic system, whereas ascribed statuses in the traditional society were so powerful and permanent that they could easily be built into the system.
12. First of all, although Japanese colonization of Korea marked the end of the traditional estate system, the traditional norms regulating the social hierarchy did not disappear as easily and in fact the superior/subordinate role was often utilized in support of the Japanese authoritarian hierarchy. So to a degree, Confucianistic ethics persisted. Secondly, although it is true that after the liberation in 1945, Western culture, with its democratic values and modernization process (embodying such concepts as liberty, equality, individualism, free competition, and social welfare) flooded Korea, the imported culture has been unable to take root at the bottom of the Korean social scale (Koh 1976:131-8). Koh attributes this situation to the fact that Western cultural elements were not derived from the traditional indigeneous culture. Finally, cities, due to their urbanism, are behaviorally a little more modernized than rural areas. Y. Chang (1976:148-58) points out, however, that urbanization in Korea has been affected largely due to migration of the agricultural population since the liberation, and that these migrants have carried with them, in large parts, their rural behavioral patterns of human relations. According to Chang, such relational patterns include personalism (mutual indebtedness or obligation), collectivism (the group over individualism), authoritarianism (social and family stratification), and ritualism (sensitivity to others' evaluation of oneself). Chang (pp. 159-61) further observes that some form of individualism, although not yet fully institutionalized, is rising among the urbanites owing mainly to moral ambiguity in cities, a wide area of activities where the

group is unable to provide guidance, expansion of the zone of impersonalism, and growing egalitarianism.

13. Although age distinction is a tenacious linguistic vestige of traditionalism in the process of de-traditionalism, it does not appear in any way to deter modernization. Rather, many sociologists today seem to recognize that modernization can take place without completely destroying the traditional society including its values such as group-orientedness, which rather can adapt itself to a new society (Koh 1976: 136). Incidentally, the Japanese honorific pattern is not as sensitive to age as that of Korean but favors such other variables as achieved status, group membership, and intimacy (e.g., Martin 1964, Hijirida and Sohn 1983).

Reprinted from *Korean Linguistics* (International Circle of Korean Linguistics) 3:97-122 (1983)

22. CROSS-CULTURAL PATTERNS OF HONORIFICS AND SOCIOLINGUISTIC SENSITIVITY TO HONORIFIC VARIABLES: EVIDENCE FROM ENGLISH, JAPANESE, AND KOREAN

(*with Kyoko Hijirida*)

1. The aim of this paper is to describe, in comparative terms, the structural patterns of honorifics in American English (hereafter, E), Japanese (hereafter, J), and Korean (hereafter, K), and to discuss the functions and interactions of the major cross-cultural variables of power and solidarity with regard to the usages of honorific expressions.[1] In the sociolinguistic discussion, we would like to observe the different degrees of sensitivity to honorific variables that the three linguistic communities manifest.

For our purpose, we define honorific expressions not simply as any forms used to convey the speaker's politeness to the addressee (e.g., R. Lakoff 1972, Neustupny 1978, Brown and Levinson 1978, and Cho 1982), but narrowly as those explicit expressions which have structurally or lexically encoded the speaker's socioculturally appropriate regard toward the addressee or the referent. We regard politeness and deference as two different concepts, although they frequently interlock in linguistic expressions, with honorifics serving to express politeness to a considerable extent. E, J, and K, and all other languages for that matter, have devices other than honorifics to express politeness, e.g., prosodic means, modal elements, softening adverbials, tag forms, cogitatives, indirect speech or conversational implicature, ellipsis, and non-verbal behavior. Hedging devices of this sort can satisfy, for example, R. Lakoff's rules of politeness (1974): not to impose on the addressee (formality), to allow him his options (hesitancy), and to make him feel good (equality). In discussing putatively universal politeness strategies of social interaction in language, Brown and Levinson (1978) have proposed an extensive variety of positive, negative, and 'off-record' strategies. Although a few such strategies (e.g., use in-group identity markers including address forms; give deference; impersonalize the speaker and the addressee; nominalize) could be implemented by means of honorifics (i.e., grammaticalized or lexicalized forms of deference), it will be difficult to consider honorific expressions a proper subset of polite expressions in Lakoff's or Brown and Levinson's sense. For example, the three sentences in (1), which are considered honorific expressions, are all impolite when they are used by an angry speaker who is annoyed by the presence of the addressee.

(1) E. Mr. Smith. Would you please stay out of here.[2]

J. Sensei. Koko o dete kudasai.
sir here go-out for me

K. Sensayng-nim. Yeki lul na ka cwuseyyo.
sir here out go for me

The same expressions become polite when they are used by a thoughtful speaker who feels that the addressee's going out would be advantageous to the addressee himself. Similarly, the sentences in (2), which are all non-honorific expressions, are nevertheless polite when a mother warns her child to take care of himself.

(2) E. Take care of yourself.
J. Ki o tukete ne.
K. Cosimhay-la.

In short, polite expressions are based largely on universal pragmatics and are from an open-ended pattern of language usage that is applicable, in principle, to any speech participants regardless of their age, sex, kinship or social status, whereas honorific expressions are based on a closed, language-specific system consisting of a very limited set of structural and lexical elements with which the speaker indicates his social or interpersonal relationship with the addressee and/or referent.[3] As a linguistic system, however, an honorific system includes as an integral part not only deferential elements but non-deferential ones as well. This paper will be concerned only with honorific expressions and the underlying socio-cultural variables.

In discussing the structural and sociolinguistic aspects of honorifics, we make use of Brown and Gilman's (1960) distinction between power and solidarity, and regard the distinction as two basic dimensions underlying honorific expressions. Although sociocultural variables like sex function as roles, in addition to powers, especially in egalitarian societies, we will limit our observation and discussion mainly to power-related aspects. We would like to tentatively propose, for our purpose, the subdivision given in (3). The scheme is intended to present the eight major cross-cultural variables of interpersonal relationships involved in the choice of different honorific codes, including the choice of address-reference terms. All the eight variables are functional, to different degrees, in the use of the three languages in comparison.

(3)

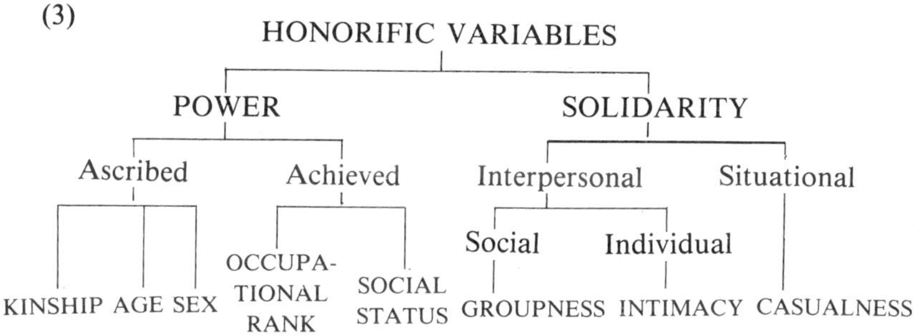

KINSHIP refers to ascending/descending relationship between the speaker and the addressee and/or the referent (e.g., father vs. son), AGE to older/younger (e.g., adult vs. child), SEX to male/female (e.g., James vs. Julie), OCCUPATIONAL RANK to higher/lower (e.g., employer vs. employee or teacher vs. student), SOCIAL STATUS to higher/lower (e.g., senator vs. plumber or customer vs. waiter), GROUPNESS to in-/out-group (e.g., classmate vs. non-classmate or family member vs. non-family member), INTIMACY to intimate/distant (e.g., friend vs. stranger), and CASUALNESS to casual/formal situation (e.g., picnic vs. formal meeting). Although there are monarchic societies where occupational ranks and social statuses are ascribed, the scheme in (3) is meant for democratic societies where ranks and statuses are achieved by way of free competition.

2. In order to see how and to what extent the cognitive cultures of the three societies compare with regard to power and solidarity, let us turn to our first goal of this paper, i.e., the description of the structural patterns of honorifics. J and K may be called honorific languages in view of the fact that relative interpersonal relationships are elaborately encoded in linguistic forms to the extent that speech acts are not performable without taking the notion of honorifics into account. In contrast, English is a typically non-

honorific language which, except perhaps for address-reference terms, has only sporadic cases (mostly euphemistic words) which may be called honorifics. In the following is given a summary of typological comparisons of honorifics.

First, while contemporary E has single, power-free forms of personal pronouns, J and K have rich systems of hierarchical personal pronouns, as in (3), where ## marks very deferential (or humble in 1st person) forms and # average deferential (or humble in 1st person) forms, and D stands for Demonstrative.

(1)

speaker / person	E		J		K	
	MALE	FEMALE	MALE	FEMALE	MALE	FEMALE
1st per	I		##watakusi		##ce	
			----	#atakusi	na	
			#watasi	watasi		
			#atasi	atasi		
			boku	----		
			ore	----		
2nd per	you		anata		tangsin	---- [4]
			anta			
			kimi	----	caney	---- [5]
			omae	----	ne	
3rd per	he/she		#D-kata 'person'		#D-pwun 'person'	
			D-hito 'person'		D-i 'person'	
			kare/kanozyo 'he/she'		D-salam 'person'	
			D-ko 'child'		D-ay 'child'	

Secondly, while *you* in E can be used to any superior or inferior person, both J and K do not have any second person pronoun to refer to a socially superior person. That is, unlike the use of *you* in English and V/T in European languages, J and K do not allow a speaker of a lower status to use any of the second person pronouns toward a higher status addressee, except in such marked cases as when fighting. Asymmetrical use of a second person pronoun is made only by a superior to an inferior and symmetrical use only between non-adults or between intimates. Thus, both J and K lack a second person pronoun of deference (cf., Kurokawa 1972:234, Hwang 1975:35,

Tani 1981). To serve the purpose, J and K employ nominal substitutes extensively, as in J *sensei* 'you' (lit. teacher), *syatyoo* 'you' (addressed to a company president), and *o-taku* 'you' (lit. honorable house) and K *sensayng-nim* 'you' (lit. Mr./Ms. teacher), *sacang-nim* 'you' (addressed to a company president), and *tayk* 'you' (lit. honorable house).

Third, all three languages have extensive sets of address and reference terms that are sensitive to social stratification in terms of power and solidarity. Even here, the E set is much more restricted than those of J and K not only in the number of ranks but also in the number of the social titles allowed to be used for address and reference. For example, in J and K all kinds of professional titles (including even section chief, division chief, bureau director, company president) are used as address terms, whereas in E only military and police ranks and some other limited terms like Doctor, Professor and Father are used for address (for details, see Section 4.1(d) below). In the following are ordered address/reference terms used in the three languages roughly in decreasing deference and/or distance, where ANn = affectionate nickname; FFN = full given name; FN = given name; GT = general title (e.g., *sir, madam* in E; *senpai* (lit. senior), *sensei* 'sir, madam' in J; *sensayng* 'sir, madam' *puin* 'madam' in K); HT, HTa, HTb, etc. = honorific title; KT = kinship term; LN = family or sirname; Nn = nickname; PT = professional title.

(4)

E TERMS	EXAMPLES
Title sequence (HT + PT)	Mr. President, Mr. Chairman, Mr. Secretary
Title alone (PT, KT, GT, HT)	Professor, Father, Colonel, Doctor, mother, grandfather, sir, ma'am, mister, miss
Title & last name (PT + LN; HT + LN)	President Reagan, Dr. Smith, Mrs. Anderson, Mr. Nixon
Last name alone (LN)	Reagan, Smith, Anderson
Full first name (FFN)	Robert, Samuel, Eveline
Nickname (Nn)	Bob, Sam, Eve
Affectionate nickname (ANn)	Bobbie, Sammy, Evie

J TERMS	EXAMPLES
Title sequence (PT + HTa)	syusyoo-kakka 'His Excellency Prime Minister' (old usage)
Title sequence (PT/KT/GT + HTb)	syatyoo-sama 'co. president,' syatyoo-dono (written style), ozii-sama 'grandfather,' oku-sama 'madam'
Full or family name & title (LN (+ FFN) + HTb)	Yamamoto (Minoru)-sama, Yamamoto (Minoru)-dono
Title alone or family name & title (LN + GT)	sensei, Yamamoto-sensei, senpai, Yokoyama-senpai
Full given name & title (FFN + HTb)	Muneo-sama, Yosiko-sama
Title sequence (PT/KT/GT + HTc) + HTc)	syatyoo-san 'co. president,' otoo-san 'father,' ozyoo-san 'miss'
Title alone or family name & title ((LN) + PT/GT)	(Yamamoto) syatyoo 'co. president,' (Hijirida) sensei 'Mr. Hijirida/sir'
Full name or family name & title (LN (+FFN) + HTc)	Yamamoto (Yosiko)-san
Full given name & title (FFN + HTc)	Yosiko-san
Family name alone (LN)	Yamamoto
Full name or family name & title (LN (+FFN) + HTd)	Nakayama (Hiroki)-kun
Full given name & title (FFN + HTd)	Hiroki-kun
Full given name alone (FFN)	Hiroki
Full given name & title (FFN + HTe)	Hiroki-tyan
Affectionate name and title (ANn + HTe)	Hiro-tyan

K TERMS	EXAMPLES
Title sequence (PT + HTa)	taythonglyeng-kakha 'His Excellency President'
Title sequence (PT/KT/GT + HTb)	sacang-nim 'co. president,' halapenim 'grandfather,' sensayng-nim 'sir'
Full name or family name & title sequence (LN (+FFN) + PT/GT + HTb)	Kim (Yongswu) kwacang-nim 'Div. Chief Kim (Yongswu),' Kim (Yongswu) sensayng-nim 'Mr. Kim (Yongswu)'
Title alone (PT/KT/GT)	chakwan 'vice-minister,' emeni 'mother,' pwuin 'madam'
Full or family name & title (LN (+FFN) + PT/GT)	Kim (Yongswu) kwacang 'Div. Chief Kim,' Kim (Yongswu) sensayng 'Mr. Kim (Yongswu)'
Dr. + LN	Dr. Kim
Full name & title (LN + FFN + HTc)	Kim Yongswu-ssi
Family name & title (LN + HTc)	Kim-ssi
Miss/Mr./Mrs. + LN	Miss Yang, Mr. Kim, Mrs. Lee
Full given name & title (FFN + HTc)	Yongswu-ssi
Full or family name & title (LN (+FFN) + HTd)	Kim (Yongswu)-kwun 'Mr. Kim Yongswu,' Kim (Swunhi)-yang 'Miss Kim'
Full given name & title (FFN + HTd)	Yongswu-kwun 'Mr. Yongswu,' Swunhi-yang 'Miss Swunhi'
Full given name & intimate vocative (i)	Homin-i, Yongswu
Full given name & plain vocative (y)a	Homin-a, Yongswu-ya

Fourth, such E honorific titles (HT's) as *Mr., Mrs., Ms.* and *Miss* are used primarily to indicate sex role and marital status and no distinctly hierarchical connotation is involved among the titles. On the other hand, as observed in the above, J and K HT's are hierarchical: J *kakka, sama/dono, san, kun* and K *kakha, nim, ssi, kun/yang,* as listed in the decreasing order of deference.

Fifth, while E has a limited number of the so-called elevated terms (e.g., Levinson 1983:92), J and K have numerous lexicalized nouns and verbs to refer to a superior or distant adult's family members, possessions, and actions. J and K also have some humble expressions to refer to an inferior person's actions. Observe the examples given in (5).

(5)

LANG.	WORD CLASS	DEFERENTIAL	PLAIN	GLOSS
E	noun	Mrs. X	your wife	
		residence	home	
		lady	woman	
		gentleman	man	
		steed	horse	
	verb	dine	eat (a meal)	
		pass away	die	
J	noun	go-hujin/ okusan	kanai	'wife'
		o-taku	ie	'house'
	verb	irassyaru	iru/kuru/iku	'stay/come/ go'
		mesiagaru	taberu	'eat'
		nasaru	suru	'do'
K	noun	puin/samonim	che/anay	'wife'
		tayk	cip	'house'
		ttanim	ttal/yesik	'daughter'
		cinci	pap	'meal'
	Verb	kyeysita	issta	'stay'
		capswusita	mekta	'eat'
		cwumusita	cata	'sleep'
		tolakasita	cwukta	'die'

LANG.	WORD CLASS	HUMBLE	PLAIN	GLOSS
J	verb	ageru/ sasiageru	yaru	'give'
		mairu	iku/kuru	'go/come'
		itasu	suru	'do'
		itadaku	taberu	'eat'
K	verb	tulita	cwuta	'give'
		mosita	taylita	'accompany'
		poypta	pota	'see'

Sixth, while E lacks grammaticalized mechanism for subject honorification, both J and K have productive predicative devices for it. J uses the patterns *o-NV ni naru, o-NV copula* (where NV is a nominalized verb) or the verbal suffix *-(r)areru,* as in *o-yomi ni naru, o-yomi da* and *yom-areru* (a deferential person reads). K employs the productive verbal suffix *-(u)si,* as in *ilk-usi-n-ta* (a deferential person reads).

Seventh, unlike E where no salient mechanism is available to denote addressee honorification, both J and K do have productive suffixes exclusively for this purpose. J uses the verbal suffixes *mas/des,* as in *iki mas-u* '(he) goes' and *hon des-u* '(it's) a book' where the addressee is understood to be a person who deserves the speaker's proper deference. Similarly, K has the verbal suffix *sup/up/p* for addressee honorification, as in *coh-sup-nita* '(it's) good,' *ka-ss-up-nita* '(he) went,' and *ka-p-nita* '(he) goes.'

Eighth, unlike E, where no speech level is grammaticalized in predicates and instead such indirect speech act patterns as *would you...?* and *could you...?* are used for politeness toward the addressee, J and K have systematic addressee honorific levels or 'registers' as determined by sentence enders. Four levels are recognized in J: superpolite, polite, intimate, and plain, as illustrated respectively by statement forms *(de) gozaimas-u, mas-u/des-u,* ZERO, and da. Six levels are distinguished in K: formal deference, informal deference, blunt, familiar, intimate, and plain, as illustrated respectively by statement forms *sup-nita, yo, (s)o, ney, e/a,* and *ta.*

Ninth, only in J, there is a morpho-syntactic pattern *o-NV suru/moosiageru* for non-subject referent honorification, as in *o-mati suru* or *o-mati moosiageru* 'wait for (a superior).'

Tenth, only in J, repetition of addressee honorific suffixes shows added politeness, as in *ik-i mas-en des-i ta des-yoo* 'he didn't go, did he?' (Martin

1975b:1030).

Eleventh, only in J, there is a productive morpheme which may be called the honorific prefix (HP), *o-/go-*, which is prefixed to a noun or a nominalized verb, as in *o-hima* '(your) free time,' *go-ryokoo* 'trip,' and *go-syuzin* 'husband.'

Finally, only in K, there are two honorific case particles: the nominative particle *kkeyse* (for the plain *ka/i*) and the dative-locative particle *kkey* (for the plain *eykey*), as in *Kim sensayng-nim kkeyse Yang sensayng-nim kkey cenhwaha-si-ess-eyo* 'Professor Kim called Professor Yang.'

3. The honorific devices listed in the preceding section systematically combine with one another in sentences and discourses. In order to see how, it is essential to distinguish two main dimensions that are either overtly expressed in sentences and utterances or understood in speech situations: the dimension of referent honorifics (speaker-referent perspective) and that of the addressee honorifics (speaker-addressee perspective). The former concerns the speaker's regard for a referent denoted by a nominal expression that is overt or covert in the propositional content, whereas the latter is associated with the speaker's regard for the addressee in a speech-act situation which is usually reflected in the address term used and other sentential elements.

In J and K, the honorific patterns given thus far are extensively used in the linguistic expression of both perspectives. In actual speech act situations, addressee honorifics are more important and subtle in usage than referent honorifics in view of the subtlety of interpersonal feelings and 'face' involved in face-to-face encounters.[6] Thus, for example, the same person may be referred to as *Kato-san* when he is not an addressee and is talked about as a third person propositional element (i.e., as subject, object, etc.) and as *Kato sensei* when he is an addressee. Similarly in K, a Buddhist monk may be referred to either as *cwung* (when he is referred to as a third person) or as *sunim* (when he functions as an addressee). The syntactic distribution of the two perspectives are illustrated below.[7]

(6) Setting: Speaker: a low ranking male company employee
Addressee: a male division chief of the company
Subject referent: a male bureau chief of the company
Dative referent: the company president

J:

Katyoo,	butyoo	ga	syatyoo	ni	bangohan	o	gotisoo	nasai	masi-ta
div. chief	bureau chief	NM	co. presid.	to	dinner	AM	treated	SH	AH-pst

DATIVE REFERENT HONORIFIC

SUBJECT REFERENT HONORIFIC

ADDRESSEE HONORIFIC

K:

Kwacang -nim,	pucang -nim	kkey -se	sacang -nim	kkey	cenyek	ul	taycep -ha	si	ess-up-ni-ta
div. chief	bureau chief	NM	co. presid.	to	dinner	AM	treat	SH	pst-AH-HIN-ST

DATIVE REFERENT HONORIFIC

SUBJECT REFERENT HONORIFIC

ADDRESSEE HONORIFIC

'Division Chief, the Bureau Chief treated the Co. President for dinner.'

Compared with the expressions in (6), those in (7) are non-honorific, being uttered typically to a child about other children.

(7) J:

Hiroki,	Masao	ga	Hideo	ni	bangohan	o	ogot	ta-yo
		NM		to	dinner	AM	treat	pst-ST

DATIVE REF. NON-HONORIFIC

SUBJECT REFERENT NON-HONORIFIC

ADDRESSEE NON-HONORIFIC

K: Yoin-a, Chelho ka Swunhi hanthey cenyek-pap ul sa ss-e
VOC NM to dinner AM BUY pst-ST

DATIVE REF. NON-HONORIFIC

SUBJECT REFERENT NON-HONORIFIC

ADDRESSEE NON-HONORIFIC

Notice in the foregoing examples that, unlike the case in E, honorifics in J and K spread throughout a sentence, making the honorific sentential form look markedly different from the corresponding plain form. The honorific and non-honorific expressions may have the same truth values, but distinct socio-cultural meanings and connotations. Further notice that addressee (non-)honorifics appear in the outmost layer of a sentence and referent honorifics in the inner layer, with the subject being further out than the dative. Since the addressee is a performative element and has no place in the proposition, its honorific or non-honorific expression may occur as a vocative preceding the proposition with its syntactic reflexes limited to the last part of the predicate, following the referent honorific or non-honorific elements if these are present. The distinction between the perspectives of speaker-addressee and speaker-referent is structurally so tenacious that even when the addressee is coreferential to the subject referent, the two are grammatically differentiated in both J and K, as illustrated in (8), where the italic type indicates subject honorification and the boldface type addressee honorification in the predicates.[8]

(8) J: *Sensei* wa sono hon o *o-yomi-ni nari* **masu** ka?
you TM that book AM HP-read-SH AH Q
K: *Sensayng-nim kkeyse* nun ku chayk ul ilk-*usi*-**p**-**ni**-kka?
you HT HNM TM that book AM read-SH-AH-HIN-Q

'Are you (deferential) reading that book?'

The honorific phenomena of the three linguistic communities are also observed in the discourse level. Suffice it here to illustrate them by way of a simple exchange of leave-taking at night between a high school student and his teacher, say, during a camping trip.

(9) E. Student: Good night, Mr. Smith.

Teacher: Good night, John.
J. Student: Sensei, o-yasumi nasai mase.
teacher HP-rest do-IMP AH
Teacher: Kimi mo yasumi nasai.
you too rest do-IMP
K. Student: Sensayng-nim, Annyenghi cwumu-sey-yo.
teacher-HT peacefully sleep-SH-IMP
Teacher: Ne to cal ca-la.
you too well sleep-IMP

In E, the only difference appears in the use of address terms, i.e., title and last name vs. first name. In J and K, again, the difference appears throughout the whole utterances, showing the phenomenon of so-called 'diglossia' (Ferguson 1959). In fact, as has been alluded to earlier, J and K may be called languages of multiglossia, in that speech forms are multi-layered depending on who one talks to. In J and K, for example, different forms of utterance are used if the addressee is a college student, one's wife or husband, one's peer, or one's senior.

In the use of different 'glossia' or 'registers,' one has to observe a high degree of cooccurrence restrictions among the address term, the subject form, the verbal form, the subject honorific form of the verb, and the addressee honorific form of the verb. Brown and Ford (1964:239) maintain that the usage of T (e.g., French *tu* and 13th-18th c. English *thou*) and V (e.g., French *vous* and 13th-18th c. English *ye*) in some twenty languages studied in Brown and Gilman (1960) follow essentially the same pattern as the FN and TLN, respectively. Thus, for example, reciprocal V begins where TLN begins in the dyad of adult new acquaintances; both reciprocal T and reciprocal FN is an expression of increased intimacy. Such examples of cooccurrence as *Hi, John* vs. *Good Morning, Mr. Grace* also attest to the same generalization. Similarly, observe the examples of J and K cooccurrence sets given in (10), which are applicable when the addressee and the subject referent denote the same person.

(10)

LANG.		ADDRESS FORM	PRONOMINAL SUBJECT 'you'	SH VERBAL ELEMENTS	AH LEVELS
J	(a)	LN-sensei	sensei	honorific verb form	superpolite/ polite
J	(b)	LN-san FN-san	LN-san or anata/anta	honorific or plain verb form	polite/ intimate
J	(c)	FN	kimi/omae	plain verb form	plain
K	(a)	LN-sensayng -nim	sensayng-nim	honorific verb form	formal/infor-mal deference
K	(b)	LN-sensayng	LN-sensayng	honorific or plain form	informal deference
K	(c)	NAME-ssi	NAME-ssi/ tangsin	honorific or plain form	informal def-erence/blunt
K	(d)	FN-(i)	caney	plain form	familiar/ intimate
K	(e)	FN-(y)a	ne	plain form	plain/intimate

The above lexical and morpho-syntactic descriptions of honorific devices in the three languages seem to give some indication that Japan and Korea are typically vertical and hierarchy-laden societies, as compared with American society where only the address-reference terms appear to allude to a mild degree of social hierarchism and otherwise egalitarianism prevails. However, structural descriptions alone are not sufficient to shed light on the reality of each social structure and the detailed function of power and solidarity variables, due, among other things, to the putatively universal sociolinguistic linkage of distance and deference on the one hand and of intimacy and condescension on the other. Thus, for example, structural descriptions alone are unable to show whether the use of TLN or FN in address in a given society is due to power, role, or social distance, unless we observe a variety of sociolinguistic usages of honorifics in relation to such variables as kinship, age, sex, rank, status, groupness, and casualness. This is the main concern of the following section.

4. In a recent paper on address/reference term usages of American English, Japanese, and Korean (Hijirida and Sohn 1983), we have proposed the following scheme, which is meant to indicate the relative sensitivity each

variable receives from the three linguistic communities. 1, 2, and 3 in the scheme indicate ranks of decreasing sensitivity.

(11)

		1	2	3
POWER VARIABLES:	KINSHIP	K	J	E
	AGE	K	J	E
	SEX	J	K	E
	RANK/STATUS	J/K	E	
SOLIDARITY VARIABLES:	GROUPNESS	J	K	E
	INTIMACY	E	J	K
	CASUALNESS	E	J/K	

In order to arrive at the above tentative conclusion, we have observed a variety of contexts for address/reference term usage, with a basic assumption that the lower in power and the closer in solidarity the more individual identity is revealed in personal address and reference. Notably, it has been observed that Americans, due to their relatively weak sensitivity to power, put great importance on intimacy solidarity, that Japanese, on the other hand, put great emphasis on groupness solidarity, and that Koreans on age power. In the following we would like to summarize some of the earlier findings, while adding new observations, in favor of the above scheme.

4.1. Of the three societies under comparison, America is least sensitive to power variables, as evidenced in both the patterns and usages of honorifics. This seems to be due to their egalitarian value orientation. As a result, solidarity variables like intimacy and casualness prevail, although groupness solidarity is the last thing for Americans to give heed to due probably to their strong individualistic value orientation (Sohn 1983a). Americans' weak and Japanese and Koreans' strong sensitivity to power variables is attested to by the following usages.

(a) As for kinship term usages, the three languages share the same practice that non-reciprocal terms are used if the speaker and the addressee/referent are apart by at least one generation (e.g., *father* ↔ FN in E, *otoo-san* ↔ FN in J, *apeci* ↔ FN in K). While less than a difference of one generation is considered equal in E, siblings and cousins are considered unequal in J and K and use asymmetrical terms (e.g., *onii-san* 'older brother' ↔ FN in J, *hyeng-nim* 'older brother' ↔ FN in K). Moreover, while there are American families where parents allow or invite first name usage by their children, this is never the case with Japanese and Korean families. A third case is that, according to an American address system proposed by Ervin-Tripp (1971:18), an alter who is a kin adult of ascending generation is addressed by kinship term (KT) + FN if he or she is older than ego and FN if he or she is younger. In Japan and Korea, on the other hand, KT is maintained whether the alter is older or younger than ego. When the alter is younger, however, FN usually precedes KT, as in *Masao ozi-san* 'uncle Masao' in J and *Yongho samchon* 'uncle Yongho' in K.

Between Japanese and Korean societies, the latter appears to be more strict and conservative in kinship term usages. For one thing, in addressing uncles and aunts, both Americans and Japanese do not distinguish either between father's and mother's side, between older and younger siblings, or between consanguinity and in-law, all of which are more or less differentiated in K. Secondly, even between in-laws in the same generation, Japanese are not as strict as Koreans in kinship term usage. For example, a Japanese informant is addressed by his younger sister's husband (who is two years younger than himself) with FN-*tyan;* in a parallel Korean context, he would be addressed with the kinship term *hyeng-nim* 'older brother.' Finally, some scholars have observed that in post-war Japan speech forms toward senior members in the family have become less polite and many parents tend to converse with their children mutually in informal speech (e.g., Z. Song 1980). This is not the case with Korean parents, who have their children use deferential forms after the children reach school age.

(b) As for age-related usages, again the three languages have one basic commonality: that an adult and a child normally use asymmetrical terms of address (e.g., title + LN [TLN] ↔ FN in E, J, and K). However, there are many sociolinguistic indications that Americans are much less sensitive to the age variable than Japanese or Koreans. For one thing, other things being equal, an elder by at least fifteen years gives FN to his junior while receiving TLN (Brown and Ford 1964:236, R. Brown 1965:68, Ervin-Tripp 1971:18). That is, as in kinship, roughly one generation is a minimum requirement for two Americans to communicate on an asymmetrical basis, otherwise two interlocutors are considered equal as far as age goes. Even here, age can easily be neutralized by kinship, as observed above, or by intimacy, as pointed out by Ervin-Tripp (ibid.), or overridden by achieved status, as will be discussed below.

Age figures much more distinctly in the use of J and K. Even between two stranger or distant children, three or four years of difference may give rise to asymmetrical address term usage (e.g., *onii-san* 'older brother'↔LN in J, *hyeng* 'older brother' ↔ FN in K). Age becomes less significant as dyads are older, especially when their relationship is distant. For example, other things being equal, a person at 60 and a person at 50 would be on equal basis if they are not ingroup members. Among ingroup members, age features delicately. Both in J and K, two or three years of difference causes a boy or girl to be on a non-reciprocal basis with their close juniors. Age-based address terms are never downgraded by any degree of intimacy both in J and K if the age difference is more than four or five years. Sensitivity to age in the use of J and K can also be noticed in the fact that Japanese mothers change the informal verbal endings used to their children to formal *des/mas* forms and Korean mothers similarly raise the plain style to familiar (half-talk) style when their children become adults.

Evidence shows that Koreans are more age-conscious than Japanese. First of all, as claimed in Sohn (1983b), Korean systems of pronominals and speech levels are essentially grammaticalizations of age stages. Thus, a present-day Korean is addressed, as he grows older, by such forms as *ne* 'you' and FN-*(y)a* (in childhood), *caney* 'you,' FN-*(i)* and LN-*kwun/yang* (in adolescence or pre-adulthood), *tangsin* 'you,' *sensayng*(-*nim*) 'you,' LN-*sensayng-nim,* etc. (in adulthood), and *elusin* 'you,' *noin* 'you (lit. old person),' *yengkam-nim* 'you (male only; lit. lord),' *halmeni* 'you (female only; lit. grandmother),' etc. (in senescence). Verbal endings representing different speech levels also go with the appropriate address/reference terms given above. The boundaries between the age groups are so firm, and Koreans' sociolinguistic sensitivity so strong that, for example, an adult, whether he or she is a professor or a beggar, receives proper linguistic deference for his age and a child must be addressed by plain-level forms regardless of his social and family background. As for J, on the other hand, age difference is not built into such honorific patterns as pronouns, address/reference terms, and honorific words and suffixes as strongly as into K patterns. Thus, J polite forms as a polite mode of speech are widely used, frequently even to children, while plain forms are often used to al levels of age groups. Secondly, a younger American boss may use FN to an older employee, while receiving TLN. A younger Japanese boss may address an older employee by such low forms as LN-*kun,* while receiving such high terms as *syatyoo* 'company president.' In Korea, the most socially appropriate and desirable practice between a younger boss and an older employee is that of mutual deference, as in the boss's LN-*sensayng-nim* vs. the employee's PT-*nim*. Unlike the Japanese practice, for example, LN-*kwun* is totally unacceptable. Finally, Koreans are enormously sensitive to the ages of those with whom they are associated, even distantly. Probably any Korean knows the ages of his or her friends no matter how many there are and, in the case of equal age, who was born first. Frequently, a Korean reveals his or her age on the initial encounter and does not hesitate to ask a new acquaintance about his or her age. Moreover, a younger Korean adult often asks an older person to lower his or her speech level in an effort to establish a more congenial asymmetrical power relationship based on age. In short, Japanese appear to be not as sensitive to age as Koreans in their sociolinguistic behavior.

(c) Aside from inherent sex roles (e.g., use of *Mrs., Miss, madam,* etc. as compared with *Mr., sir,* etc.) and the universal assumption that females use more polite speech than males, sex, as a power variable, does not seem to be very significant in contemporary Americans' consciousness, as judged from the sociolinguistic perspective (cf., R. Lakoff 1975, Kramer 1975, Kuno 1977, Kramarae 1981, and others). Although power in sex seems to have been weakened in Japan and Korea considerably ever since the end of World War II, sociolinguistic evidence shows that sex is still power-laden in these two societies to a significant extent, especially in the older generation.

First of all, while there is no sex distinction in the use of E pronouns, the Japanese female, as observed earlier, does not usually use low-level, power-laden personal pronouns *boku, ore* 'I' or *kimi, omae, kisama, temme,* etc. 'you' which are restricted to the male speaker. As also observed the same pronouns *watasi* and *atasi* 'I' in J are deferential when used by a male and not deferential when used by a female (Mochizuki 1980 and Ide 1982). We would interpret this fact as indicating that, although females are generally politer than males, Japanese females may be in the lower social status than males in Japan and therefore must use humbler forms of first person pronouns to attain the male's level of politeness. The fact that only females may use the honorific title *sama* or *san* after a professional title, as in *syatyoo-san* 'co. president,' points to the same generalization. The Korean female uses the humble form *ce* 'I' much more frequently than the male and does not usually use such power-laden forms as *tangsin* (except to one's husband) and *caney* 'you' and the corresponding verbal endings (e.g., *(s)o, ney*).

Secondly, asymmetrical address terms are generally used between husband and wife in both J and K. As observed by Pusavat (1981) and Russell (1981), the most common address pattern between Japanese spouses is that husbands call wives by names (mainly FN), *omae, kimi,* or the power-laden interjection *oi* 'hey,' while wives call them by child-centered kinship terms (*otoo-san, otoo-tyan, too-san, too-tyan, papa* 'father') or *anata/anta* 'you.' Similarly, many Korean husbands in the old generation call their wives by *caney* 'you,' *eyi* 'hey,' *emma-ya* '(child's) mother,' etc. while receiving *tangsin* 'you,' *appa* '(child's) dad,' etc. Notice here that, in addition to some obvious asymmetrical pronouns, the presence of the child-addressee vocative suffix *ya* in *emma-ya* and its absence in *appa* reveal the hierarchical power relationship. Furthermore, different speech levels are generally used by both Japanese and Korean couples, as illustrated in a Japanese wife's deferential utterance to her husband, *itte irassyai-mase* 'good-bye,' which is never used by a husband and a Korean wife's deferential form to her husband, *tanye osey-yo* 'good-bye,' which is hardly used by a husband even in the younger generation.

Finally, although it seems to be a universal fact that more polite and less assertive speech is used by females than males (cf., R. Lakoff 1975, Thorne and Henley 1975, P. Brown 1976 and 1980, Kramarae 1981, Zimin 1981), it is true that American female speech is not as salient as those of Japanese and Koreans, as pointed out in such works as Hwang 1975, Pusavat 1981, Cho 1982, Reynolds 1982, Bak 1983, and Hijirida and Sohn 1983.

Between Japan and Korea, the former appears to be more power-conscious with regard to sex. Unlike J, even many older generation couples in Korea tend to use symmetrical address terms (*yepo* 'honey' and *tangsin* 'you') if not reciprocal speech levels. While sex-based asymmetry is distinctly noticeable in both younger and older generations in Japan, younger generation Koreans do not, in general, seem to be conscious of power in sex as much as the older generation, especially in cities, as attested by their wide use of reciprocal speech levels. Moreover, Japanese female speech is more clearly differentiated from male speech than the Korean counterpart (Hijirida and Sohn 1983).

(d) Rank/status-based power relationship is reflected to varying degrees in the asymmetrical use of honorifics in all three societies, as between an employer and an employee (e.g., TLN ↔ FN in E; PT ↔ LN-*san* in J; PT-*nim* ↔ LN-PT in K), between a teacher and a student (e.g., TLN ↔ FN in E; *sensei* ↔ LN-*kun* in J; *sensayng-nim* ↔ LN-*kwun* in K) and between a congressman and an electrician (TLN ↔ FN in E; *sensei* ↔ LN-*san* in J; PT-*nim* ↔ LN-*sensayng* in K). Despite the fact that rank or social status generally takes precedence over age in the determination of asymmetrical use of honorifics in E (e.g., Brown and Ford 1964:267), J and K reflect much stronger power-sensitivity than E in many ways. For one thing, as mentioned earlier, both J and K have an open ended set of professional titles (PT's) that are used as address terms, while the E usage is limited to military and police ranks plus some professional titles, as illustrated below. In the use of address terms by a lower to a higher person, J forms, when used by a female, may be followed by an honorific title *sama* or *san,* or, with a military rank, by *dono* and K forms must be followed by the honorific title *nim*. LN may also accompany the professional titles.

(12)

E	J	K	gloss
Mr. Chairman	gityoo	uycang	'chairman'
Mr. Secretary	daizin	cangkwan	'minister'
Colonel	taisa	taylyeng	'colonel'
Father	sinpu	sinpu	'Father'
Professor	sensei	kyoswu	'professor'
______	sensei	sensayng	'teacher'
Doctor	sensei	sensayng	'M.D.'
______	______	paksa	'Ph.D.'
______	sensei	uywen	'congressman'
______	syatyoo	sacang	'co. presid.'
______	katyoo	kwacang	'div. chief'
______	kenzi	kemsa	'prosecutor'
______	kootyoo-sensei	kyocang-sensayng	'principal'
. . .	. . .	. . .	

Secondly, while, in E, intimacy overrules rank or social status, as will be discussed shortly, this does not hold in J and K unless the dyads have grown together from childhood or used to be classmates. Finally, both Japanese and Koreans, being extremely status-conscious, are eager to give and receive power-laden titles in daily interpersonal encounters. Various non-verbal behaviors such as exchanges of name cards showing one's status or rank and interactional gestures (e.g., bowing or scratching one's head to show deference or humility) all indicate the Japanese and Korean's consciousness of rank/status-based hierarchism. There seems to be little difference between J and K in this respect.

4.2. The relatively weak power-consciousness of Americans seems to have caused them to develop strong sociolinguistic sensitivity to such solidarity variables as intimacy and casualness, although, due to their egalitarian tradition, not many cases are found where given sociolinguistic expressions are ascribable exclusively to groupness solidarity.[9] In many situations, solidarity variables take precedence over power variables in America. Although intimacy and casualness prevail in Japan and Korea as in any society, their sociolinguistic reflection is by and large limited to power equals or socially inferior persons, which fact indicates that power generally precedes solidarity in the two societies as far as intimacy and casualness variables go. Due probably to their long Confucian tradition of valuing collectivism or interrelatedness among people, groupness is reflected strongly in J and, to a lesser degree, in K also. Let us observe some concrete cases where the three solidarity variables are responsible.

(a) As for groupness, one case where groupness seems to function in E is when two newly introduced colleagues observe reciprocal FN from the very beginning. TLN is more appropriate between two out-group persons at the initial encounter, although they move fast to the mutual FN. J, on the other hand, has many structural and sociolinguistic characteristics that are attributable to in-and out-groupness. For one thing, unlike E or K, there is a large set of plain kinship terms (e.g., *titi* 'father'), along with deferential terms (e.g., *otoo-san/sama* 'father'), which are used exclusively for reference to in-group members. Secondly, while an American secretary who addresses her boss with FN refers to him by TLN when talking to an outsider, probably to show psychological objectivity and formality, and a Korean secretary who addresses her boss with PT-*nim* refers to him by the same term when talking to an outsider, a Japanese secretary who addresses her boss with PT-*san* due to rank power refers to him by PT or LN alone when talking to an outsider, unless the outsider is a family member of the boss in which case she uses PT-*san*. This reflects the Japanese's strong sensitivity to relative groupness. Thirdly, finer age grades are sociolinguistically significant within in-group members. Finally, certain expressions are used only to an in-group member: an in-group boss's use of *kimi* 'you' and LN-*kun* even to an older employee; use of names (LN or FN) without any title (e.g., between two high school students); use of less polite first person pronouns; limited use of *desu/masu;* different function of donatory verbs; etc. (Martin 1964; Kurokawa 1972; Kuno 1973:Ch.9; Neustupny 1978; Pusavat 1981; E. Shinoda 1981).

In K, finer age grades are significant within in-group members; address terms may be downgraded among in-group members, either mutually or unilaterally; intimate and familiar levels of speech are more frequently used among in-group members; etc.

(b) As for the intimacy variable, E is the most sensitive to it, in that, unlike in J and K, it overrules other variables to a large extent. Use of Nn to one's parents (in certain young families) or to one's parents-in-law or distant relatives illustrates the precedence over kinship. Two adults' mutual advancement from TLN to FN within a few minutes after their initial encounter and a child's use of FN to his neighbor college student are cases where intimacy overrules age. Reciprocal use of Nn between a professor and a graduate student when they become close is an example of intimacy superceding occupational rank. For example, our survey with University of Hawaii students has revealed that, in the 40 dyad pairs each consisting of a professor and an undergraduate student, 10 pairs are mutually on the FN basis, while 30 pairs are on TLN ↔ FN. Dyad pairs including graduate students show a much higher rate of reciprocal FN usage. The tendency of Americans to upgrade address terms (from FN to TLN) toward a person they are angry at, structural differentiation of FN into FFN, Nn, and ANn in E and the productive use of them all reflect the extreme sensitivity Americans have toward the intimacy variable.

Due to relative emphasis on power variables, the sociolinguistic domain of intimacy in J and K is limited to in-group power equals (childhood friends, hierarchically equal club members, class mates, intimate activity friends, co-workers, colleagues, etc.) and superior persons toward inferiors.. Even here, the degree of intimacy must be very high in order to attain linguistic differentiation. In our survey with Japanese faculty members at the University of Hawaii, we have observed that use of *sensei* 'you' or *anata* 'you' between colleagues depends on intimacy alone, unless the speaker is a female and the addressee is a male in which case only *sensei* is used. For example, an elderly female professor uses *sensei* even to a young female graduate student who is also a lecturer, while using *anata* to another elderly female professor. It was also observed in the same survey that some Japanese adults, especially females, use mutual or asymmetrical FN-*san* if in-group intimacy is considerably deep. Speakers of standard K hardly allow such LN to FN dynamism, due to their strong age-consciousness. At most, Korean university colleagues may use LN-*sensayng-nim,* LN-*sensayng,* or rarely LN-*hyeng* (lit. older brother).

(c) Although all three linguistic communities use different modes of speech depending on the degree of casualness/formality of the speech act situation, E seems to be the most vulnerable to the variable. For example, many American graduate students switch their usual TLN to FN to address their professors in a party or a picnic, whereas Japanese and Korean students never change their speech styles to their professors no matter how informal the situation is. On their first encounter, Americans easily move from TLN to the FN basis, while in Japan and Korea even colleagues are mostly on formal terms forever regardless of the situation.

The fact that the most commonly used pattern of nominal address for Americans is Nn, as compared with LN-*san* for Japanese and LN-*sensayng-nim* for Koreans, also points to the Americans' relatively strong sensitivity to casualness. Americans strive to reach informal and comfortable relationships with others for smooth social interaction, whereas Japanese and Koreans seem to be more comfortable on formal terms. This suggests pragmatism for Americans and formalism for Japanese and Koreans in their value orientation.

4.3. Although cross-cultural honorific variables have been discussed separately thus far, they frequently interact or collaborate with each other in the determination of a specific honorific level in a given situation.[10] For example, use of TLN, FFN, or Nn to one's boss in America may be caused by the interaction of OCCUPATIONAL RANK and such other variables as relative AGE difference, degree of INTIMACY, and CASUALNESS of the situation.[11] A young Japanese boss's use of *kimi* 'you' and LN-*kun* to an older subordinate while receiving PT-(*san*) can be accounted for in terms of the collaboration of the two variables OCCUPATIONAL RANK and GROUPNESS. A younger Korean boss's being on mutual deferential terms with an older subordinate may be attributable to the collaboration of AGE and OCCUPATIONAL RANK.

Our survey with University of Hawaii students demonstrates the phenomenon rather clearly. Each student gives one or more reasons or variables for using FN or TLN to address a particular professor, as shown below, where each set of reasons is for each use of TLN or FN and the number in parentheses after an answer indicates the repetitions of the same answer.

(13) REASONS FOR USING TLN (60 dyad pairs)

.respect (4)
.different sex (female addressee) (2)
.age
.achievement (6)
.social status (7)
.personality (2)

.personality mostly (most uncomfortable course I ever took)
.formality (8)
.formality, "I don't like him!!"
.status, formality (2)
.age, personality
.age, formality (3)
.age, respect
.age, respect, experience
.age, sex difference (female addressee), social status
.age, personality, formality
.achievement, personality, social status
.achievement, formality, paternalistic attitude
.achievement, different sex (male addressee), age, status (he has a Ph.D. from a well-known university and is my teacher), personality (his language usage creates distance), formality
.age, formality, profession
.age, achievement, position
.age, achievement, formality (3)
.age, achievement, social status, respect, formality (3)
.age, formality, asked to be called "Professor/Mr. LN"
.formality (I did not know him well enough to call him by FN), nationality (I didn't want to offend him by being too informal)
.I was introduced by full name, and I responded with Dr. LN
.he called me Mr. LN
.seemed reserved
.he is a kind of formal and reserved—hard to get to know as an individual
.did not get to know them well

REASONS FOR USING FN (30 dyad pairs)

.friendly
.personality (5)
.young age (2)
.informality of the class
.informality, personality
.young age, personality (2)
.asked to be called by FN (3)
.informal, friendly; she introduced herself by FN
.told to use FN, age and personality

.I was introduced by first name (6)
.same sex (female), and asked to be called by FN
.after working with him closely on some research
.she is pretty informal
.she is very informal and approachable; age didn't matter
.he is pretty informal, supportive; he's 40 or 41 but somehow acts younger
.because my friends who work for him called him "FN"
.because I don't know him well

REASONS FOR AVOIDANCE OF DIRECT ADDRESS (4 dyad pairs)

.personality (pompous)
.informality, social interaction, personality
.personality, positive attitude toward students (2)

Most American professors surveyed used FN to both undergraduate and graduate students, with the exception that, in four dyad pairs, all of which include a graduate student, both the professor and the student are mutually on the TLN basis.

In contrast to the American practices, Japanese and Korean students address their professors only by TLN (LN-*sensei* in J and LN-*sensayng-nim* or LN-*kyoswu-nim* 'prof. LN' in K), the only distinctive variable being RANK. Japanese students may receive LN-*san*, LN-*kun*, LN, or FN, depending on the degree of relative AGE, SEX, and the degree of INTIMACY. Korean students may receive LN-*sensayng* (only when he is a graduate student of an age similar to the professor), MR./Miss LN, LN-*kwun/yang*, or FN (-*i*), depending on relative AGE, SEX, and INTIMACY.

Time and space do not allow us to go into a detailed analysis of the survey. Suffice it here to mention, by way of a conclusion, that the survey, as well as our other structural and sociolinguistic observations, support the claim that American society is much more egalitarian, individualistic, and pragmatic, as compared with Japanese and Korean societies whose people are, despite the process of democratization, stil imbued with relatively strong hierarchism, collectivism, and formalism in their value orientations.[12]

Notes

1. An earlier version of this paper was presented at the Annual Meeting of the Linguistic Society of America on December 28, 1982 at San Diego. We want to thank John Haig for his valuable comments. The research was partly supported by an Instructional Improvement grant (to Kyoko Hijirida) and a Center for Asian and Pacific Studies (CAPS) fellowship (to Ho-min Sohn) of the University of Hawaii. The CAPS also provided a travel grant to Hijirida to present the original version at the above-mentioned LSA meeting.
2. One might suspect that in (1E) the polite modal *would* (as compared to *will*), the softening directive adverbial *please* and the indirect request by means of the question form (as compared to a 'command') are honorific expressions. We are inclined to view them as politeness devices since they do not bear any socio-hierarchical connotation. Compare the following utterances:

   Open the window.
   Please open the window.
   Will you open the window?
   Would you open the window?
   Would you mind opening the window?

   Although the above expressions become increasingly politer as we move down, all of them can be used by a child to an adult or vice versa depending on contexts. Similarly, a socially superior person can use any of them to a socially inferior person. On the other hand, a janitor may not use any of them to the company president. In short, unlike address/reference terms which are considered honorific, expressions like *would* and *please* are relevant to politeness, but not to honorification.
3. Several other languages of the world such as Javanese, Ponapean and Tibetan are reported to have honorific systems comparable to those of J and K (e.g., Goodenough 1965, Uhlenbeck 1970, Soenjono 1974, and Hayashi and Minami 1974).
4. One exception to male use of the blunt pronoun *tangsin* is its reciprocal use by some older generation couples, in which case the pronoun has the connotation of affection.
5. In certain dialects of Korea, *caney* is used also by females in the older generation to refer to one's older sister, younger sister-in-law, and son-in-law, as well as to young adults in the neighborhood.
6. With regard to J, Harada (1976) points out that in subject honorifics the subject referent is required to be socially superior to the speaker, whereas in addressee honorifics the addressee should be either socially superior or equal to the speaker. The same is generally true with K. As for the notion of face or public self-image, Brown and Levinson (1978) assume that, although the content of face is culture-specific, the mutual knowledge of face and the social necessity to adjust to it in interaction are universal and propose that face saving constitutes a powerful functional pressure on any language.
7. The following abbreviations are used for grammatical terms:

   AH = addressee honorific
   AM = accusative marker
   HIN = addressee honorific indicative

HNM = honorific nominative marker
IMP = imperative ending
HP = honorific nominal prefix
NM = nominative marker
pst = past tense
Q = question ending
SH = subject honorific
ST = statement ending
TM = topic marker
VOC = vocative marker

8. For a variety of proposals regarding syntactic or discoursal derivation of J and K honorifics, see Prideaux (1970), Uyeno (1971), A. Shinoda (1973), and Harada (1976) for J, and S. Song (1967), H. Lee (1970), Suh (1972, 1984), S. Chang (1973a), C. Lee (1974), and Sohn (1974a, 1979) for K, among other works.
9. The lack of collectivism of Americans is also attested to by their general verbal and non-verbal communicative behavior. For example, they pass by strangers saying 'Good Morning,' 'Hello,' or 'Hi' or at least smiling to them. Japanese and Koreans greet only acquaintances, guests and hosts.
10. In view of the collaborative, scalar, and situation-dependent nature of the variables, we find it extremely difficult, if not impossible, to determine neat precedence hierarchies among honorific variables for each society (for some proposals in this regard see Martin 1964, Ervin-Tripp 1971, Brown and Gilman 1974, Hwang 1975, D. Lee 1975, Park-Choi 1978, Ishikawa, et al. 1981).
11. The following diagram in Buren (1974:69) illustrate how power and solidarity variables inseparably interlock in the determination of an address term in a given social context.

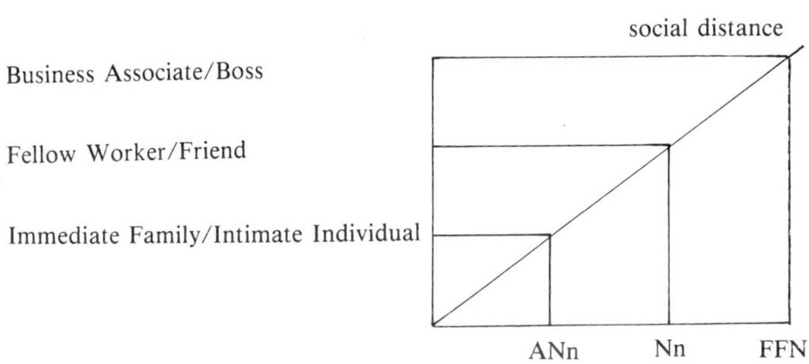

12. For an extensive sociolinguistic comparisons of Americans' and Koreans' value orientations, see Sohn (1983a).

23. INTERCULTURAL COMMUNICATION IN COGNITIVE VALUES: AMERICANS AND KOREANS

1. Introduction

Despite the revolutionary advances in modern communication technology, our understanding of the human dimension in communication is still relatively limited. This is particularly the case with intercultural communication, where the causes of communication interference or failure, as well as of misunderstandings, are due to differences not only in linguistic structure and usage, but in the underlying cognitive culture.[1] Culture-bound miscommunication arises from the tendency for people to encode or decode a message from the framework of their own cultural background including the system of culturally conditioned perceptions by which they select, organize and interpret the given stimuli (e.g., Klopf and Cambra 1981). Various tacit or subtle cues that tell the people of one culture how to communicate may not apply to another culture. The degree of miscommunication is therefore proportional to the extent of cultural variance. Intercultural communication becomes successful to the extent that the communicative means, verbal or nonverbal, function as a set of *shared* expectations between the interactants, since understanding the cognitive frames of reference underlying each other's communicative acts is crucial to an understanding of what each other says and does.

In intercultural communication, therefore, the interactants must know not only the form-function relation of the foreign language used and the social constraints on how certain things are said, but also the basic values and other cognitive aspects of acceptable behavior in each other's society. The aim of this paper is to show how communicative patterns differ from society to society due to underlying differences in cognitive culture; our method will be a comparison of contrasting patterns of communication inherent in the culture-specific value orientations of Americans and Koreans.

The communicative and cultural differences between Americans and Koreans may be broadly regarded as typifying Western and Eastern societies, respectively.

I have used a comparative perspective not only because members of various cultures may categorize experience and environment in different ways, but because no culture-related generalization is distinctively significant unless it is compared cross-culturally. For example, we cannot generalize that Koreans are hot-tempered if there is no comparison with some other societies whose members are less hot-tempered or are generally placid. I have chosen values for observation rather than such other cognitive aspects as world view or ways of thinking, ideals, assumptions, ethos, attitudes, postulates, prejudices, etc., partly because other cognitive aspects are correlated with values in one way or another, and partly because values seem to play the most pivotal role in intercultural communicative encounters.

The approach adopted here is partly a sociolinguistic one, in that it is a study of *language,* both verbal and nonverbal, in relation to society, and partly that of the sociology of language, in that it is also a study of *society* in relation to language (Hudson 1980:4-5). As noted by Brown and Levinson (1978:60), patterns of message construction, or simply of language usage, are crucial parts of the expressions of social relations; thus, discovering the principles of linguistic, prosodic, and kinesic usage is generally coterminous with discovering the principles out of which interactional social relationships are constructed.

Whether verbal or nonverbal, language has two interrelated and mutually-complementary functions: the function of transmitting knowledge or information, and that of establishing and reinforcing interpersonal relationships. The cognitive values of a society are intricately reflected mainly in this second function of language. Referentially equivalent linguistic forms and expressions across cultures may have different social or connotative meanings due largely to value differences. These facts suggest that not only linguistic competence in the target language, but also a thorough grasp of the socio-cultural backgrounds of the language, be they perceptual, conceptual, or emotive, is essential to successful intercultural communication. It is often said that cultural barriers are more difficult and time-consuming to overcome than linguistic barriers.

Defining culture as "all those historically created designs for living... which exist at any given time as potential guides for the behavior of men," many recent anthropologists claim that culture is a structured system of patterned behavior (e.g., Lado 1968:111). Using this perspective, I would like to investigate the structured systems of value orientations underlying communicative patterns of Americans and Koreans.

The concept of 'value' or 'value orientation' has been used in many different ways. C. Kluckhohn, et al. (1951) observe that the one feature common to all the usages is the idea of *oughtness,* which is detached from personal preference or choice. In the same vein, F. Kluckhohn and Strodtbeck (1965) define value orientations as complex but patterned principles that give order and direction to human acts and thoughts as these relate to the solution of common human problems. Thus, the cultural values of a society are ubiquitous, orienting the everyday modes of behavior, including communicative patterns, of the members of the society.

In discussing the two societies' value orientations, it is inevitable that we make some broad generalizations, taking only the dominant traits into account while ignoring countless minor differences. Despite individual and regional variations, a majority of the members of each society do act in their daily life according to their society's culturally prescribed patterns and rules of behavior. For instance, an American male who forgets to kiss his wife when parting from her at the airport will be in trouble when he returns, and a Chinese visitor who compliments his hostess on her beauty is likely to be considered immoral (Hsu 1981:2). In the two societies under comparison, the vague set of values usually associated with the middle class is regarded as typical and dominant.

2. Universality

Although our main concern is sociolinguistic differences, let us briefly touch on the universals in communication that are assumed to be shared by all rational human beings in all cultures. That is, human nature does not differ fundamentally in different societies; rather, it is traditions, conventions, and experiences that vary from culture to culture. There are therefore both universality and distinctiveness in human behavior, the former usually existing as broad abstract principles and the latter as culturally specific details. In addition, universality often provides a reference model for distinctiveness. Being a pattern of human behavior, communication is no exception.

Linguists, linguistic philosophers, social psychologists, social anthropologists, and scholars in speech communication have recently proposed a variety of what are often called universal pragmatic principles for human beings to follow in language use for effective communication across cultures. For instance, Grice (1975) advances Quality, Quantity, Relevance and Manner Maxims of Cooperation; these stipulate, respectively, that the speaker must be sincere and speak the truth, that the speaker must say as much as and no more than is required, that the speaker's contribution to a conversation must be relevant, and that the speaker must be perspicuous and avoid ambiguity and obscurity. As Lakoff (1973), Brown and Levinson (1978), and Cho (1982) point out, Grice's maxims will serve with maximum efficiency the purpose of one of the functions of language mentioned earlier, transmission of knowledge or information. However, they must be violated in many contexts if interpersonal relationships are to be established and reinforced. Such is especially the case with societies, such as Korean society, in which holistic values (to be discussed below) are cherished.

Lakoff (1973) proposes such rules of politeness as: (a) Do not impose on the addressee; (b) give him his options; and (c) make him feel warm and friendly. It seems that all human languages have some mechanism to express politeness in Lakoff's sense (i.e., softening intonation, use of modal elements such as past or future forms, softening adverbials, tag forms, cogitatives, ellipses, indirect speech or conversational implicature, polite nonverbal behavior, etc.). Hedging devices of this sort are effective and polite in normal contexts. If the speech act is to the benefit of the addressee or the speech situation is a critical one, direct expressions with a high degree of illocutionary force, such as imperative, are frequently more effective and more polite

Viewing sociolinguistics as applied pragmatics and rebutting the doctrine of cultural relativity in interaction, Brown and Levinson (1978:61-63) claim that superficial cross-cultural diversities can emerge from underlying universal pragmatic principles and are satisfactorily accounted for only in relation to them. They maintain that linguistic strategies are *means* satisfying communicative and face-oriented *ends*. While listing numerous 'face-threatening acts' (FTAs), they (ibid.:65) present the framework of politeness strategies given below. In this framework, they assert, the more an act threatens the

Circumstances determining choice of strategy:

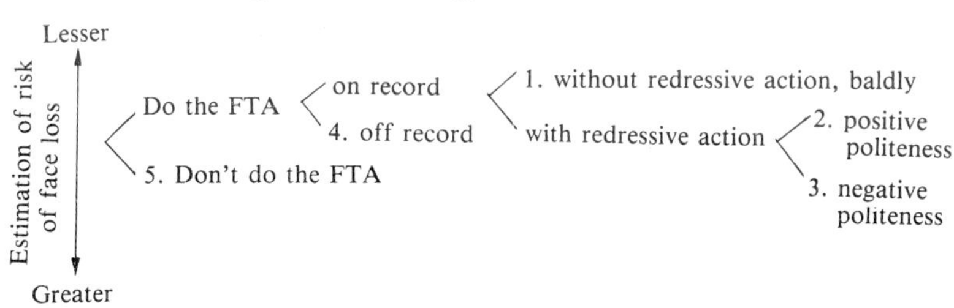

speaker's or the addressee's face, the more the speaker will wish to choose a higher-numbered strategy to afford payoffs of increasingly minimized risk.

The bald-on-record strategy (1) involves performing an act in the most direct, clear, unambiguous, and concise way possible, as stated in Grice's maxims (ibid.:74, 99-106). The circumstances for this strategy include cases when the FTA is used for great urgency, desperation, or efficiency; or in the addressee's interest; or where the speaker is vastly superior in power to the addressee, as shown in such examples as "Help!", "Watch out!", "Excuse me!", "Come in!", or "Bring me wine, John!"

Positive politeness is oriented toward the positive face or self-image that the addressee claims for himself. Brown and Levinson (ibid.:106-134) present fifteen positive politeness strategies designed to claim common ground, to convey that the speaker and the addressee are cooperators, and to fulfill the addressee's desire for something. In the following, some strategies in this category are illustrated.

Notice, attend to addressee (his wants, needs, interests, goods)
Eg.: "Your blouse is very nice, did you make it yourself?"
Exaggerate (interest, approval, sympathy with addressee)
Eg.: "What a fantastic garden you have!"
Use in-group identity markers
Eg.: "Bring me your dirty clothes to wash, *honey (darling, Johnny).*"
Seek agreement
A: "I had a flat tire on the way home."
B: "Oh my!, a flat tire!"
Presuppose/raise/assert common ground
Eg.: A: "Oh this cut hurts awfully, Mom."
B: "Yes, dear, I know it does."
Be optimistic
Eg.: "Look, I'm sure you don't mind if I remind you to do the dishes tonight."
Include both speaker and addressee in the activity
Eg.: "Let's have a cookie, then." (i.e., *me*)
"Let's get on with dinner, eh?" (i.e., *you*)
Give gifts to addressee (goods, sympathy, understanding, cooperation)

Negative politeness is oriented toward partially satisfying the addressee's negative face, i.e., his basic desire to maintain his freedom of action, his freedom from imposition, his territory, and his self-determination. Ten negative politeness strategies are given, as illustrated below (ibid.:134-216).

Be conventionally indirect
Eg.: "Can you pass the salt?"
Question, hedge
Eg.: "Won't you open the door?"
"I suppose that Harry is coming."
"I rather think it's hopeless."
Be pessimistic
Eg.: "You don't have any manila envelopes, do you by any chance?"
Give deference
Eg.: "Excuse me, sir, but would you mind if I close the window?"
Apologize
Eg.: "I'm sure you must be very busy, but..."
Impersonalize speaker and addressee
Eg.: "One shouldn't do things like that."
(cf., "You shouldn't do things like that.")
Go on record as incurring a debt
Eg.: "I'd be eternally grateful if you would let me escape."

An off-record communicative act is an act that cannot be interpreted as expressing one clear communicative intention. The speaker resorts to this act when he wishes to avoid responsibility for his act, leaving it up to the addressee to decide how to interpret it. Fifteen strategies are given, some of which are illustrated below (ibid.:216-232). (C.i. denotes communicative intention.)

Give hints
Eg.: "What a boring movie!" (C.i.: "Let's leave.")
"It's cold in here." (C.i.: "Shut the window.")
Give association clues
Eg.: "Are you going to the market tomorrow?...I'm quite sure the market is opened tomorrow." (C.i.: "Give me a ride to the market.")
Understate
Eg.: A: "What do you think of Harry?"
B: "Nothing wrong with him." (C.i.: "I don't think he's very good.")
Be ironic
Eg.: "John's a real genius." (C.i.: "John is stupid.")
Use metaphors
Eg.: "Harry's a real fish." (C.i.: "He drinks/swims/is cold-blooded like a fish.")
Use rhetorical questions

Eg.: "What can I say?" (C.i.: "Nothing, it's so bad.")
Be vague
Eg.: "Perhaps someone did something naughty."
Be incomplete, use ellipsis
Eg.: "Well, if one leaves one's tea on the wobbly table..."

All of the above putatively universal pragmatic principles and politeness strategies are applicable, in general, to the parallel communicative acts of Koreans. However, they are far from sufficient to allow an intercultural communicator to achieve successful communication, unless he is also aware of cross-cultural differences. For example, the principles and strategies discussed thus far do not explain why Americans treat everyone more or less equally in speech acts, while Koreans are overly helpful and courteous to some people but act with no regard for others; why an angry American tends to upgrade address terms, as from "John" to "Mr. John Smith" when addressing someone with whom he is angry, whereas an angry Korean tends to downgrade address terms and speech levels; why, unlike Americans, Koreans cannot use a second person pronoun when addressing a social superior; and why American adults most commonly use nicknames like "Bob" and "Liz", while Korean adults most frequently use the deferential speech style for smooth daily social interaction. None of the aforementioned principles or strategies can explain why, unlike an American, a Korean finds it either very impolite or extremely awkward to say "Thank you" immediately after someone praises his wife or son, when an inferior family member does something for him, or when someone invites him to dinner or gives him a gift. Further, none of the pragmatic principles can explain why Americans and Koreans are so different in their nonverbal behavior. These and hundreds of other differences are regarded not as random, unrelated facts, but as arising from something systematically different in the two people's consciousness, i.e., the difference in their systematic patterns of value orientations.

3. Value Difference

3.1. Value Systems of Americans and Koreans

Various claims advanced regarding Americans' value orientations are boiled down to individualism, equality, confrontation, competitiveness, achievement, a future-time orientation, doing (rather than being), informality, impermanence, and depersonalization (cf., Stewart 1972). As for Koreans', some authors propound that contemporary as well as traditional Koreans stress roughly the opposite of the American values. Others note that Koreans' values have undergone drastic change toward Western values since the end of World War Two due to the structural change of Korean society from the traditional vertical to modern horizontal form (see Sohn 1983b for these opposing views). To present the conclusion first, despite the fact that contemporary Koreans, especially the younger generation, have been much westernized in their behavior, and many intellectual, social and political leaders have been educated in Western culture, traditionalism is still persistent in a slightly dilute form in the consciousness of most Koreans. Its presence is reflected in the communicative patterns of Koreans.

It is true, as some social anthropologists have experienced, that the value system of a society is difficult to grasp not only because it fluctuates with time, space, and social class, but because it would be a tremendous, if not totally impossible, task to statistically measure (through interviews, questionnaires, or some other means) a society's value orientations. At the moment, we can only speak about the values of a society in relative terms, compared with those of some other societies, as they are deduced from the members' general communicative patterns. Viewing a society's values as describable only in terms of degree rather than in absolute terms, I would like to tentatively propose that the five partly interlocking dimensions (or scales) of value orientations given below serve as a framework for the purpose of this study. It is assumed that the terms on the right-hand and the left-hand sides are the broad value categories for the two ends of each scale on which any society (or part of it) may be located. Under each value category we can subsume many more specific values. For example, privacy, freedom, independence, personal preference, self-fulfillment, initiative, and self-motivation may fit the category of individualism. Kinship, age, sex, power, and social status may fit the category of hierarchism.

ATOMISTIC-MECHANISTIC VALUES	Americans	Koreans	HOLISTIC VALUES
A. INDIVIDUALISM			COLLECTIVISM
B. EGALITARIANISM			HIERARCHISM
C. CONFRONTATION			INDIRECTNESS
D. PRAGMATISM			FORMALISM
E. RATIONALISM			EMOTIONALISM

The terms 'atomistic-mechanistic' and 'holistic' are borrowed from Yoshikawa (1982), who uses them to denote two opposing world views, i.e., those of Americans and Japanese, that he assumes are connected to the current left- and right-brain theory.

Of the five value dimensions, the first two seem to be basic while the others are more or less derivative. These two dimensions seem to mark the most characteristic distinctions between the West and Asia in general, and between Americans and Koreans in particular.

The above diagram demonstrates that in the value orientations reflected in their communicative patterns, Americans are more individualistic, egalitarian, confrontational (i.e., direct), pragmatic, and rationalistic than Koreans, whereas Koreans are relatively more collectivistic, hierarchical, indirect, formalistic, and emotionalistic than Americans. The remainder of this study will be devoted to the elaboration of this hypothesis.

3.2. Individualism—Collectivism

Numerous socioanthropological studies have shown that the American character contains a decidedly individualistic bent, i.e., a general preference for noninvolvement, noninterference, privacy, a sense of resistance to regimentation, and a lack of a strong sense of familial duties and obligations. Let us examine some linguistic, sociolinguistic, and communicative aspects from a comparative perspective.

a) At the lexical level, observe the frequently used Korean terms given below in comparison with the English translations:[2]

> *kohyang* 'native place, hometown', *kacok* 'family', *pumo* 'parents', *casik* 'children', *chinkwu* 'friend', *wuceng* 'friendship', *hyoto* 'filial duty', *unhyey* 'gracious favor', *inyen* 'connection', *yemlye, simlye* 'concern', *milyen* 'regret, attachment', *conkyeng* 'respect', *yeyuy* 'decorum', *cheymyen* 'face', *puthak* 'request for favor', *ceng, inceng* 'feeling, love', *kyemson* 'modesty', *tekthayk* 'indebtedness', *toli* 'morality', *uyli* 'moral obligation', *ungsek* 'playing on another's affection', *nwunci* 'reading others' mind'

English-Korean bilinguals will quickly note significant differences in connotative and social meaning between the Korean terms and their English equivalents. All the Korean terms carry the sense of deep human interrelatedness and interdependence in addition to the inherent denotative meanings. For example, in his study of the concept of *kohyang,* Goldberg (1979:90) states that "*kohyang...* is the place of one's ancestors, of one's kin and neighbors; it is the place from which one derives one's identity." As for the concept of *hyoto* 'filial duty', Szalay and Fisher (1979:69) report that this concept is generally unknown and relatively meaningless to Americans. For Koreans, it refers to a particular relationship between parents and their children, a relationship that involves an attitude of sincerity and respect as well as the virtues of loyalty, obedience, service, and sacrifice. The term *chinkwu* 'friend' is used only for deep and long-lasting friends who are around the speaker's age and with whom the speaker uses an extremely intimate speech style on a reciprocal basis. It is not only the connotation that differs between the Korean terms and their English counterparts. The Korean terms are extensively verbalized in daily utterances, while the English equivalents are either very infrequently used or seem rather unnatural in many cases, as illustrated below:

A: *Yocum ettehkey cinayseyyo?*
'How are you?' (Lit. 'How are you living these days?')
B: *Tekthayk ulo kulek celek cinayciyo.*
'So so.' (Lit. 'I am living so so thanks to you.')

On the other hand, terms like *kayincwuuy* 'individualism', *sali* 'self-interest', *caconsim* 'self-esteem', etc. have strong negative connotations in Korea, which are associated as they are with selfishness and egocentricism. Korean does not yet have proper terms for such English concepts as 'privacy', 'self-concept', and 'identity'.

b) Syntactic differences are also suggestive of different values. As K. Kim (1975) points out, Americans put the given name first and the family name second, and write a mailing address in the order of the personal name followed by gradually larger units. The Koreans' practice is a mirror image of American practice, with given name placed at the end. Another structural difference is that while English noun phrases, including personal nouns and pronouns, must be expressed in sentences, Korean personal nouns and pronouns (especially 'I' and 'you') are generally not expressed whenever they are situationally understood. This linguistic habit of Koreans may have contributed to the weakening of the illocutionary force related to individual identity or individualism. Still another frequently cited difference is that his strong 'we-feeling' usually prompts a Korean to say "our country" instead of "my country," "our school" instead of "my school," "our house" instead of "my house," and "our wife" instead of "my wife". Using "my" would give an impression that the speaker is strongly egocentric and therefore arrogant. Some Koreans prefer to use "we" instead of "I" in certain contexts, as in *Wuli nun swul ul cohahayyo* 'I (lit. we) enjoy drinking liquor.' That is, unlike the practice in strongly individualistic Western cultures, where the *I* exists independently of others, *I* in Korean is not outstanding in communication.

c) Observe some common greetings and leave-takings below:

English:
"How are you?" "Good morning." "Good evening." "Good night." "Hi, John." "Bye." "Have a nice weekend." "Have fun." "See you again." "Welcome!"
Korean:
Annyenghaseyyo? 'How are you?' (Lit. 'Are you peaceful?')
Eti kaseyyo? (Lit. 'Where are you going?')
Eti kassta oseyyo? (Lit. 'Where are you coming from?')
Ettekhey naosiesseyo? (Lit. 'On what business did you come out?')
Cinci capswusiesseyo? (Lit. 'Did you eat your meal?')
Annyenghi kaseyyo. 'Bye.' (Lit. 'Go peacefully.')
Ese oseyyo. 'Welcome.' (Lit. 'Come quickly!')

Although conventionalized, as Cho (1982:188-189) and others point out, many of the Korean expressions are considered too personal to be accepted by Americans. This disparity can be attributable to Americans' emphasis on privacy (derived from individualism) and Koreans' emphasis on mutual involvement and concern (derived from collectivism).

d) Tied to this absence of privacy is a tendency for Koreans to ask questions about things that Americans would consider personal, such as marriage, salary, age, and the value of the addressee's belongings. Koreans' interest in others' private life is apparently due to the deep-rooted collectivism through which they can attain favorable interpersonal communication.

e) It has long been observed that Korean (and Japanese) *yes/no* answers to negative questions are opposite to those of English, as shown below:

English: A: "Didn't you go?" B: "No." (B did not go.)
Korean: A: *An kasiesseyo?* B: *Aniyo.* ('No'; B did go.)
English: A: "Didn't you go?" B: "Yes." (B did go.)
Korean: A: *An kasiesseyo?* B: *Ney.* ('Yes'; B did not go.)

Notice that English *yes/no* is based on B's own action, whereas Korean *yes/no* is determined by agreement or disagreement with the content of A's question. Here we may conjecture, as some Japanese scholars have done regarding to the parallel pattern of Japanese, that the American communication pattern is *me* oriented, while the Korean pattern is *other* oriented.

Americans' individualism and Koreans' collectivism are also reflected in a variety of daily nonverbal patterns, as illustrated below:

a) In various nonverbal actions, Americans maintain strict privacy even toward family members, whereas Koreans wish to be involved in each other's actions. For instance, I have heard that in her honeymoon with a young bright American professor, a well-bred Korean lady, following the traditional Korean way, offered a towel with two hands to her husband when he had finished washing his face. To her surprise and dismay, this American grew angry and snatched the towel away from her, saying that he did not wish his freedom and privacy impinged upon by her.

b) Unless invited out, Americans follow the custom of dutch treat in paying restaurant bills, whereas in Korea, one person usually pays the entire bill.

c) In drinking, Americans fill their own glasses and do not pass an empty glass to others, whereas Koreans fill each other's glasses and pass an empty glass around.

d) Americans strictly follow the custom of knocking before entering someone's room, whereas Koreans still frequently violate this imported social rule. (The traditional custom of coughing before entering a room is disappearing in Korea.)

e) Koreans frequently visit relatives, friends, or other acquaintances without prior appointment or notice, as Americans seldom do.

f) Americans keep about an arm's length of personal space around themselves (M. Park 1979). Koreans do not avoid bodily contact and often prefer close proximity while engaged in conversation. At a dinner table, an American asks his neighbor to pass the salt to avoid the latter's spatial privacy; saying "Can you pass the salt" is conventionally indirect and considered polite in America. A Korean will reach over and take the salt himself, because Koreans are insensitive to the concept of spatial privacy, and because asking a stranger or superior to do something is considered rude in Korea.

The American is encouraged to be independent from childhood. As Stewart (1972:56, 1979:4) points out, the American locus to decision-making is in the individual, with motivation arising from within him and responsibility for his decisions and actions devolving upon him. Thus, the expression "Who is responsible?" is a common daily question in America, but has no exact equivalent in Korean. In the case of group decision making, Americans express their individual opinions and exert fair influence, usually adopting the majority rule.[3]

On the other hand, due to the Korean's strong ties to his immediate family, organization, or community, decisions in Korean society are usually made by the head of the group or reached by consensus.[4] Due to the stress on relations among individuals rather than on the individual himself, saving face has become very important to Koreans, and dependency on others is still regarded as a virtue for many Koreans. This is evidenced, for example, in frequent utterances of old Korean parents who take pride in being dependent on their children (M. Park 1979). Unlike the situation in the United States, where one must learn to "stand up for his rights" in handling various affairs and defend his rights when they are threatened, in Korea *unhyey,* favors graciously given and willingly returned, provide a much smoother and more harmonious way of handling things in various relationships in society (Kalton 1979:11-12). Koreans' daily conversations frequently relate to what is going on with relatives, friends, and other acquaintances, including snatches of gossip. As M. Park (1979) puts it, Koreans are generally more concerned with how others think of them than with how they regard themselves. Probably for this reason, Koreans, unlike individualistic Americans, are very sensitive to fashion as it pertains to clothing, housing, shopping, furniture, children's education, etc. The whole Korean people appear to move as a single, massive unit. In Korea, both family and social relationships of all sorts are characterized by a deep awareness of interrelatedness.

Collectivism in Korea has engendered group consciousness in terms of the relative in-group and the relative out-group, with the family as the basic in-group unit. This concept of groupness is much stronger in Korean language and cognitive culture than in American English and American culture where groupness seems to function marginally at best, everyone being treated more or less equally whether he is an in- or out-group member. The Japanese exhibit even more group consciousness than Koreans (Hijirida and Sohn 1983). Due to this consciousness, different communicative patterns are used for different levels of groups, as illustrated below:

a) Unlike the case in English, only two or three years of age difference between in-group members may be significant enough to call for asymmetrical address terms and speech levels between the group members.

b) Use of honorifics is relaxed between Korean in-group members, from a moderate to an extreme degree, depending on the degree of in-groupness. For example, two adult friends who grew up from childhood speak to each other like two children, with no honorific terms, while two colleagues still use generally polite forms.

c) Many verbal expressions are allowed only to in-group members. The 'blunt' pronoun *tangsin* 'you' and the address term *yepo* 'hello' are polite only between husband and wife. 'Insulting' utterances like *Ne way kulehkey musikhani?!* 'Why are you so ignorant?' are acceptable between two close friends. There are many nonverbal behaviors acceptable only among in-group members.

d) Americans are willing to talk to strangers or people they don't know well. Koreans tend to be indifferent and avoid talking to strangers or out-group members while eager to talk to close acquaintances. Similarly, Americans smile and offer greetings to anybody who passes by, saying "Hi" or "Good Morning". whereas Koreans never smile to strangers but greet only their acquaintances.

e) Although competition among out-group members is as keen as in America, competition among in-group members is restricted due to the existing seniority-juniority relationship determined by relative age, graduation years, employment years, etc.

f) Americans usually make numerous friends consequent to the activities they pursue, but rarely enter into close friendships. Koreans tend to have fewer, but much closer friends.

Unlike Americans, Koreans tend to feel uneasy and alienated without the feeling of belonging and therefore strive to be included in groups. There is an unusually strong family tie in Korea, which also extends to and is reflected in social life.

Koreans' communicative patterns reveal that their collectivism is somewhat similar to that of the Japanese. Lebra (1976:25) propounds that "the Japanese concern for belonging relates to the tendency toward collectivism, which is expressed by an individual's identification with the collective goal of the group to which he belongs. Collectivism thus involves cooperation and solidarity, and the sentimental desire for the warm feeling of *ittaikan* ('feeling of oneness') with fellow members of one's group is widely shared by Japanese".

There is evidence that individualism has permeated urban Koreans to a great extent. Many Koreans show a sense of aloofness, noninvolvement, or self-centeredness in certain social contexts in Seoul, especially in their communicative interaction with outsiders. Possibly because of Korea's unique history, Koreans appear to be less collectivistic than Japanese but less individualistic than Americans, as evidenced in their linguistic and other communicative behavior (e.g., Hijirida and Sohn 1983).

3.3 Egalitarianism—hierarchism

Egalitarianism is associated with the concept of equality or symmetrical distance and closeness among people that gives an irreducible value to their humanness, while hierarchism is regarded here as a concept of power, i.e., asymmetrical, vertical distance and closeness, that is related to such notions as non-reciprocal control or submission. Power includes such variables as kinship, age, and sex, as well as social status in its broad sense.

Although Americans have modified their concept of egalitarianism during their history, and have sometimes unduly violated it, it is undeniable that egalitarian values underlie Americans' social relationships (Stewart 1972:50-53). In an encounter between two Americans of unequal status, both strive to reach an informal, comfortable relationship as quickly as possible by establishing an atmosphere of equality, as evidenced in such communicative patterns as the following:

a) In communicative interaction, a superior and an inferior will use first names as terms of address in many settings (Mead 1963:7-8, Brown and Ford 1964, Buren 1974:68, Hijirida and Sohn 1983). For example, a professor and a graduate student may use reciprocal title + last name at their initial stage of acquaintance. Sooner or later, the professor usually starts to use the student's first name to show friendship. As their intimacy grows, the student may also use the professor's first name. The same is true with a superior and an inferior in a company setting. Such reciprocal usage of address terms never occurs in comparable Korean contexts.

b) As mentioned above, American use of deferential and plain forms of address and reference, as well as of other politeness-sensitive lexical items, is determined to a large extent by the dimension of solidarity (i.e., intimacy-distance) rather than by the hierarchical dimension (i.e., deference-condescension), while the opposite is true of Korean usage (Hijirida and Sohn 1983). Thus, for example, an angry American tends to upgrade address terms toward the addressee to psychologically distance him or her in terms of solidarity (e.g., from "Bea" to "Miss Beatrice Smith"). In a similar situation, a Korean would downgrade his address terms in order to distance him or her in terms of power hierarchy.

c) That there are American families, especially in the younger generation, where parents allow or invite first-name forms of address by their children indicates that egalitarianism permeates even kin relations.

d) In all levels of discussions, Americans freely express their disagreement to their seniors or superiors. Such is not the case among Koreans.

e) An American boss often comes to his subordinate's office to discuss business, or he will sometimes offer the subordinate a cup of coffee before initiating a conversation.

f) Stouffer et al. (1949) points out that even the typical American soldier derives his will to fight from a sense of loyalty to the other men in the immediate group rather than to authority.

In spite of the strong egalitarian value orientation, Americans also manifest a certain degree of hierarchism in all walks of their life. For example, observe the cases listed below, which are also applicable to Koreans.

a) Hierarchism is most distinctly shown in the structure and usage of the terms of address and reference, as between an adult and a child or between a teacher and a student (e.g., Mr. + last name↔first name). Thus, such terms may be arranged as follows in the order of decreasing power: title sequence (e.g., "Mr. President"), title alone (e.g., "professor", "sir", "madam"), title + last name (e.g., "Professor Smith"), last name alone (e.g., "Smith"), full first name (e.g., "James"), nickname (e.g., "Jim"), and affectionate nickname (e.g., "Jimmy"). For details, see Brown and Ford (1964), Buren (1974), Ervin-Tripp (1971), Hijirida and Sohn (1983), etc.

b) While there is nothing to prevent a superior from using "we" to include someone in an inferior social position, it is often impolite for an inferior to use it to include a social superior. Thus, a student would say "Professor Smith and I discussed the problem" instead of "We discussed the problem" (Kuno 1977:312). Similarly, an inferior person cannot usually say "Let's go (eat, sleep, ...)" to a superior.

c) The second member of the following pairs encode greater respect to the addressee or referent: "like" vs. "care for", "eat" vs. "dine", "man" vs. "gentleman", "give" vs. "bestow", "bit" vs. "piece", "book" vs. "volume", "Hi" vs. "Good Morning", "will/do you" vs. "would you", etc. (cf., Brown and Levinson 1978:186). Observe, for example, "Good Morning, Mr. Smith" (vs. "Hi, John"), "We look forward very much to dining (vs. "eating") with you" and "Excuse me, but would you (vs. "do you") mind if I open the window?"

d) Such suggestive expressions as "had better" and "should" are not used as main verb auxiliaries to one's superior. Thus, for example, we can use "You had better do this at once" or "You should do this at once" to equals or subordinates, but not to superiors, to whom "I suggest that you do this at once" or "Don't you think that you should do this at once" would be more appropriate (Kuno 1977:323).

Although the above cases attest to the existence of Americans' value of hierarchism, the degree is much lower than that of Koreans. Evidencing the low degree of hierarchism in Americans' consciousness, even an extremely low degree of solidarity or intimacy can override power in many sociolinguistic situations, as shown in earlier illustrations.

There is ample evidence that Korean society is still deeply imbued with traditional hierarchism despite Korea's having been a constitutional democratic nation for some forty years. The claim that Koreans are much more hierarchical than Americans is supported by the following facts.[5]

a) The inventory of American terms of address and reference, which is the only systematic honorific pattern, is much smaller than that of Korean (Hijirida and Sohn 1983). For example, the set of American title sequences include "Mr. President", "Mr. Secretary", and "Mr. Chairman", at most, whereas Korean title sequences constitute an open set, which is used for both address and reference terms, including *taythonglyeng kakha* (lit. 'His Excellency President'), *cangkwan-nim* (lit. 'Mr. Minister'), *kwacang-nim* (lit. 'Mr. Division Chief'), *kyeycang-nim* (lit. 'Mr. Section Chief'), *sacang-nim* (lit. 'Mr. Company President'), *kisa-nim* (lit. 'Mr. Driver'), *paksa-nim* (lit. 'Mr. Ph.D.'), *son-nim* (lit. 'Mr. Guest'), *hyeng-nim* (lit. 'Mr. Older Brother'), etc. American siblings are considered to be equals and address each other on a first name basis, whereas Korean siblings are unequal and on nonreciprocal terms (e.g., *hyeng-nim* 'older brother'↔first name). Koreans have no expressions equivalent to Americans' "This is my brother" or "This is my sister." Either "This is my older brother/sister" or "This is my younger brother/sister" must be used. In addressing uncles and aunts, Americans make no distintions based on whether a relation is on the father's or the mother's side of the family, whether he is older or younger than the parent, or whether he is consanguineous or an in-law. All of these distinctions are reflected in Korean. In America, an elder by approximately fifteen or more years gives first name to his junior while receiving title + last name (Brown and Ford 1964:236, R. Brown 1965:68, Ervin-Tripp 1971:18), whereas in Korea a few years' difference is significant among in-group members.

b) In English, there is no hierarchical connotation among such titles as "Mr.", "Mrs.", and "Miss". In Korean, titles are hierarchical as in *kakha* 'his exellency', *-nim* 'Mr., Mrs., Miss (deferential)', *-ssi* 'Mr., Mrs., Miss (neutral for adult)', *-kwun* 'Mr. (for lower adult or pre-adult)' *-yang* 'Miss', and the vocative suffixes for intimate pre-adults (-(*i*)) and for children (-(*y*)*a*).

c) Korean, unlike English, has hierarchical personal pronouns (e.g., *ce* 'I (humble)', *na* 'I (plain)', *tangsin* 'you(bulunt—for adult)',*caney* 'you (familiar)', *ne* 'you (plain)'), as well as terms denoting a social superior's family member, possession, action, or manner, and a social inferior's humble action (e.g., *samo-nim, puin* 'wife (deferential)' vs. *che, anay, manwula, cip-salam* 'wife (plain)', *taky* (def.) vs. *cip* (plain) 'house', *ttanim* (def.) vs. *ttal* (plain) 'daughter', *kyey* (def.) vs. *iss* (plain) 'stay', *cwumu* (def.) vs. *ca* (plain) 'sleep', *capswu* (def.) vs. *mek* (plain) 'eat', *annyenghi* (def.) vs. *cal* (plain) 'well', *tuli* (humble) vs. *cwu* (plain) 'give', *mosi* (humble) vs. *tayli* (plain) 'accompany'). Similarly, certain terms cannot be used to describe one's seniors, e.g., *yamcenhata* 'gentle', *chakhata* 'dependable', *kwiyepta* 'cute', and *kkamccikhata* 'clever'. The expression *swukohata* 'thank you' is not used to one's seniors; *komapta, kamsahata,* or *coysonghata* is used instead.

d) Korean even has an honorific-plain distinction in two case particles (nominative *kkeyse* (def.) vs. *ka/i* (plain), dative-locative *kkey* (def.) vs. *eykey/hanthey* (plain) and a verbal suffix (*u*)*si* to denote subject honorification.

e) Korean has six different speech levels for addressee honorification that are reflected in verbal suffixes: formal deference (e.g., *-supnita*), informal deference (e.g., *-eyo*), blunt (e.g., *-so*), familiar (e.g., -ney), intimate (e.g., *-e/a*), and plain (e.g., *-ta*), as illustrated below:

Annyenghi cwumu-si-psio. (Formal deference)
Annyenghi cwumu-si-eyo. (Informal deference)
Cal ca-o. (Blunt)
Cal ca-key. (Familiar)
Cal ca. (Intimate)
Cal ca-la. (Plain)
'Good night.' (Lit. 'Sleep well.')

f) Unlike the use of *you* in English and V/T in European languages, Koreans may not use any of the second person pronouns to a superior person or a stranger adult, except in such exceptional contexts as in a fight. Instead, nominal substitutes like *sensayng-nim* (lit. 'teacher'), *emeni* 'mother', and *sacang-nim* 'company president' occur in the pronominal place. Pronouns are used only by a socially superior person to a social inferior, or between two intimate friends.

g) Unlike the standard practice in American English, a superior is never downgraded in address or reference by intimacy solidarity. At most, Korean adults of equal status in terms of age and rank may proceed mutually, for example, from *Kim sensayng-nim* to *Kim sensayng* to *Kim hyeng* (lit. 'Older Brother Kim'), as their intimacy grows. On the other hand, an angry Korean tends to downgrade address terms from *sensayng-nim* 'sir, you (lit. 'Mr. Teacher')' to *sensayng* 'you (lit. 'Teacher')' to *tangsin* 'you (blunt)' to *ne* 'you (plain)', etc. as his anger intensifies. In this way the speaker insults the addressee by downgrading his relative status. Slight upgrading of address terms and speech styles is also observed among in-group young people when they try to distance the addressee based on solidarity.

h) In all levels of private conversations, meetings, and discussions, only a person in a socially superior position is assertive and expressive while his socal inferiors usually just listen, occasionally expressing agreement in the junctures in the speech of the social superior. The inferiors seldom oppose the superior's views or opinions, unless very indirectly. Thus, in American academic circles, young newcomers frequently attempt to establish themselves by aggressively attacking the established views of older authorities, whereas a Korean must wait his turn rather than challenge his seniors' views. In Korea, such expressive acts as jokes and compliments are not generally allowed to be performed toward one's seniors.

i) Koreans are extremely status conscious in daily human interactions, as reflected in their communicative patterns. They are eager to receive and give titles denoting status, rather than names with general title like *Kim-sensayng-nim* 'Mr. Kim'. One recent innovation I have noticed is that people like storekeepers and bellboys call male strangers *sacang-nim* (lit. 'Mr. Company President'). Very frequently, a Korean retains for life the highest professional title he has ever held. Moreover, strangers meeting for the first time exchange name cards listing in detail their professional positions; they thereby exchange information about each other's social standing.

j) While Americans have no distinctive gestures indicating hierarchism, Koreans have many hierarchy-sensitive gestures (K. Kim 1975, M. Park 1979). A Korean boss usually calls his subordinate through a receptionist or an errand girl; at a dinner table, a lower-ranking person must wait until a higher-ranking person sits down and starts eating, while the reverse does not hold true; one does not smoke in the presence of a social superior; when drinking with a social superior, the subordinate hides his glass and turns away from the superior; in giving to or receiving from a social superior or distant equal, a Korean uses both hands or the right hand, with the left hand supporting it; in greeting a social superior (though not an inferior) a Korean must bow; a Korean must rise when an obvious social superior appears on the scene, and he cannot pass in front of an obvious social superior. All social behavior and actions are conducted in the order of seniority or ranking; as the saying goes, *Chanmul to wi alay ka issta* 'There is order even to drinking cold water.' Filling wine glasses, eating, entering a room, seating, etc. are all done strictly in this order.

As for the age variable, Americans and Koreans take opposite points of view. While Americans pay no particular respect to age, although an adult and a child use asymmetrical terms of address (e.g., Mr. + last name vs. first name), Koreans view age as one of the primary criteria for showing deference and in the choice of honorifics and speech styles, as well as in nonverbal behavior (e.g., Sohn 1983b). Indeed, seniority counts in all aspects of Korean social life—even in a promotion or the election of a chairman or president. While among out-group members in Korea only three major stages of age (childhood, adolescence, and adulthood) are socially and linguistically significant, within an in-group of relatives, club members, neighbors, or students, even two or three years' difference in age is significant enough to engender sibling-like asymmetrical modes of communication. Furthermore, unlike Americans who often do not know the ages of even their closest friends, Koreans are keenly sensitive to the age of those with whom they associate even distantly. Probably any Korean is sensitive enough to know the ages of his or her friends no matter how many he or she has. A Korean frequently reveals his or her age on the initial encounter and does not hesitate to ask a new acquaintance about his or her age, as mentioned above. One important social rule of communication is that a much younger Korean should ask an older addressee to lower the speech level if the latter is a prospective in-group member. This is an effort to establish a more congenial asymmetrical power relationship based on age.

Although it is frequently argued that women's speech is characterized as less assertive and more subservient to men's, the concept of sex-related power appears to have been losing ground in both the United States and Korea and have been replaced by sex roles to a considerable extent, particularly among Americans. Aside from inherent sex roles (e.g., use of "Mrs.", "Miss", "ma'am", etc. vs. "Mr.", "sir", etc.) and the universal assumption that females use more polite speech than males, the sex variable does not seem very significant in the United States (cf., R. Lakoff 1975, Kramer 1975, Kuno 1977, Kramarae 1981, Bak 1983, etc.).

Sex was a significant power variable in traditional Korea, and it still is among many Koreans of the older generation. For example, many older-generation spouses, and even young spouses in conservative areas, use non-reciprocal speech styles, as illustrated below:

Wife: *Tangsin i ka-po-seyyo.*
'Why don't you go there?'
Husband: *Caney ka ka-po-a.*
'You better go there.'

In this example, the wife used a higher pronoun (*tangsin*) and a deferential level (*yo* style), whereas the husband used the familiar pronoun *caney* and an intimate level (*a*). One may still use expressions like *Yeca ka cayswu epsi* 'Gosh! I am unlucky because of a female!' or *Amthalk i wulmyen cip an i manghanta* 'When a hen crows, the house is doomed', where replacing of *yeca* 'female' with *namca* 'male' and *amthalk* 'hen' with *swusthalk* 'rooster' will not be acceptable as socially appropriate utterances. In general, however, symmetrical communicative patterns are used by the younger generation, especially in Seoul.

Some communicative evidence shows that Koreans are far more sensitive to status difference, whether occupational or social, than Americans. In Korea, communicative asymmetry is observed between members of the hierarchy of a public or private organization and between people of different social statuses, as between a person in a socially recognized professional field (e.g., a professor, a doctor, a lawyer, a politician, a company executive, or a high-ranking government or military officer) and a person who is not in such a field. Observe the following examples, where *A.* denotes an American and *K.* denotes a Korean.

A. student: "Good night."
A. teacher: "Good night."
K. student: *Sensayng-nim annyenghi cwumuseyyo.*
'Good night.' (Lit. 'Sleep peacefully, Mr. Teacher.')
K. teacher: *Kulay, ne to cal ca-la.*
'Good night.' (Lit, 'O.K., you too. Sleep well.)
A. division chief: "John, can I see you for a minute?"
A. section chief: "Oh, sure, Bill."
K. division chief: *Kim-kyeycang, na com poa-yo.*
(Lit. 'Section Chief, see me for a while.')
K. section chief: *Ney, kwacang-nim.*
(Lit. 'Yes, Mr. Division Chief.')

As regards American English, Brown and Ford (1964:236) maintain that the nonreciprocal address patterns are generated by a difference of occupation and a difference of age, and that status takes precedence over age in the determination of deference. However, solidarity, especially intimacy, takes precedence over social status in many cases, as already alluded to, leading to establishment of a reciprocal first-name basis between social superiors and inferiors in the United States.

In short, Americans' interpersonal relations are typically horizontal; Americans function most effectively on the level of equality. Hierarchism, on the other hand, is ubiquitous in Koreans' daily interpersonal communication. A Korean is extremely sensitive to the status he holds in relation to others in terms of kinship, age, rank, power, sex, wealth, etc. This does not mean that Koreans do not have symmetrical interaction. Egalitarianism exists between two power equals, e.g., classmates, activity friends, co-workers, colleagues of equal rank, strangers, etc. Two adults who do not belong to the same group tend to be on equal basis regardless of their age or status difference. No communicatively significant power distinction is noticed nowadays, for example, between a taxi driver and his fare, who use *kisa-nim* (Lit. 'Mr. Driver/Engineer') and *son-nim* (Lit. 'Mr/Mrs./Miss Customer) as terms of address.

Confucianism, which provided the ideological basis for the founding of the Yi dynasty in Korea, is regarded as the strongest source of Korean hierarchism. Confucianism stipulated the ethical code that categorized and regulated the five basic types of interpersonal behavior, based mainly on hierarchical human relations, and stressed the subordinate's unilateral obedience to the superior. The Five Relationships of Confucianism are loyalty between king and subject, filial piety between parents and child, distinction between husband and wife, precedence between senior and junior (in terms of age, sex, generation or social status), and confidence between friends (Y. Chang 1976: 154). Indeed, as K. Lee (1977) states, Koreans still appear to seek peace, happiness, safety, and order in hierarchical relationships, feeling uneasy and insecure in horizontal relationships.[6] Indeed, Koreans tend to relate better to people of higher or lower status than to people of the same status in many social settings. It seems that the principle of egalitarianism, in its true sense, still remains an ideal in Korea.

3.4. Confrontation—Indirectness

Our sociolinguistic evidence reveals that in contrast to Americans' emphasis on confrontation, directness, and frankness, Koreans are rather indirect in communicative behavior. Not only in interpersonal encounters but in all manner of problem solving, Americans prefer to face the people, facts, and situations involved directly and intentionally, with a self-assertive attitude, and get to the source of a problem (Stewart 1972:52). Similarly, Barnlund (1979:100) observes that the ability to articulate ideas and feelings is highly respected among Americans in that the American social system rests upon articulation and discussion as the primary mode of inquiry, learning, negotiation, and decision making. On the other hand, as among Japanese (Lebra 1976), indirectness is conspicuous in various communicative interactions and social exchanges among Koreans. Some specific examples are given below:

a) While Americans have a variety of address terms for spouses (e.g., "Darling," "Honey," "John"), Koreans have not developed particular address terms. A Korean wife may use a ZERO term to her husband until she has had a child, when she may use the child-centered term *appa* 'dad'. Some older people use *yepo* (Lit. 'Look here').

b) While Americans are willing to introduce themselves to each other whenever they meet for the first time, many Koreans tend either to avoid introduction or approach people by way of an introduction through a friend and convey their messages through the channel of food or drink—a pattern which is what Yoshikawa (1982) calls indirect-intermediated interpersonal communication.

c) Americans frequently say "I disagree," "I have a different view on that," or "I cannot agree with you" in meetings, regardless of rank or status difference. Such expressions are avoided in Korean meetings unless the speaker feels animosity toward the addressee. That is, any open and direct disagreement implies hostility in Korea.

d) While Americans prize frankness and outspokenness, silence is prized in Korea, as such sayings as demonstrated by proverbs that are still in use (K. Kim 1975, M. Park 1979): *Ip ulo manghanta* 'You shall perish by your mouth'; *Mal i manhumyen ssul mal i cekta* 'One who does much talking says little'. It is considered a virtue in Korea not to openly express one's opinions or feelings, but to show humility by remaining silent. Americans often say "I love you," but Koreans hardly use such expressions, for love is conveyed nonverbally. Even in conversations, long silences are not only tolerated but often appreciated in Korea. Most Americans feel uncomfortable and rush in to fill the gap in the conversation when a silence lasts longer than 0.3 seconds (Hatch 1983:xiv). This is why Koreans often perceive Americans as talkative, while Americans often perceive Koreans as morose and unfriendly.

e) Closely related to the above is the fact that Koreans value *nwunchi* 'reading other's face, mind, and feeling (Lit. 'eye measure')'. In daily interactions, many communicative intentions of Koreans are conveyed and understood through *nwunchi* or intuitive communication. Conversational implicature appears more keenly developed among Koreans than among Americans, both in verbal and nonverbal interaction. Observe the dialogue given below, where *c.i.* denotes communicative intention:

Setting: A division chief (*kwacang*) and an employee (Mr. Kim) around

5:00 p.m. at their office

Kwacang: *Nalssi to cwup-ko cholcholhan-tey.*
'It's cold and I'm kind of hungry.'
(C.i.: "Why don't you buy a drink or something to eat.")

Mr. Kim: *Kwacang-nim, yakcwu han can hasi-ci-yo.*
'Section Chief. How about having a glass of liquor?'
(C.i.: "I will buy liquor for you.")

Kwacang: *Muel kulay. Nwatwuci.*
'It's Ok. Don't bother.' (C.i.: "I will accept your offer if you repeat it.")

Mr. Kim: *Sicanghasil theyn-tey naka-si-ci-yo.*
'You must be hungry. How about going out?'
(C.i.: "I insist upon treating you.")

Kwacang: *Kulaypol-kka?*
'Shall I do so?' (C.i.: "I accept.")

There is a saying to the effect that one who has ready *nwunci* will rise in the world ahead of others.

f) The so-called 'expressive' acts (Searle 1976) in Korean, such as thanking, apologizing, congratulating, and offering condolences, do not seem to be as expressive as in English, not only in the latitude of the forms, but in the frequency of use and the expressive intensity. Thus, for example, use of "Thank you" is quite limited among Koreans, as illustrated earlier. While Americans most frequently acknowledge a compliment (e.g., "That's a nice watch") with "Thanks," Koreans are most likely to deny the positive evaluation (e.g., "Oh, no. It's nothing"). Similarly, an outsider's praise of a person's family member, as of his wife's beauty, must be answered with a strong denial of the content of the praise. A Korean who answers "Thank you," as an American would, will be considered insolent and unmannered. When an American introduces his wife in public, he often says "This is my lovely (pretty, beautiful) wife", which is never the case with Koreans. Apologies are used much less frequently in Korea than in America, as are congratulations. The same word *chwukhahanta* 'congratulations' is used for someone's birthday, Christmas, child-birth, engagement, success, etc. In condolences in Korea, silent language may be more appropriate. At best, one can say "How sad you are" or "I have no words to express..." As observed at the end of the above dialogue, a Korean should not be enthusiastic about an invitation or a gift from another. He should decline it mildly at first, accepting it only after it has been offered repeatedly. If an offer is not repeated, it is usually considered insincere, or the person making the offer is thought stingy at best.

g) Directness in America and indirectness in Korea are also observable in their use of "yes" and "no". In contrast to Americans' emphasis on definitive verbal message, Koreans try to avoid making negative responses as much as possible if the negation is judged as causing even the slightest loss of the addressee's face. Instead of saying no, one uses such expression as *Kulsseyyo* 'Well', *Elyepkeyssnunteyyo* 'I think it's going to be difficult', *konlanhanteyyo* 'I am in a difficult situation', *Twukopopsita* 'Let's wait and see', *Kwenchanayo* 'It's OK', or silence, as illustrated below:

A: *Kyelhonhasiesseyo*? 'Are you married.'
B: *Kulsseyyo*. 'Well.' (C.i.: "No.")
A: *Phathi ey kkok oseyyo*. 'Please come to the party.'
B: *Com elyepkeyssnunteyyo*. 'It'll be a little difficult.'
(C.i.: "I won't be able to go.")
A: *Cha han can tusiciyo*? 'How about a cup of tea?'
B: *Kwenchanayo*. 'It's OK.' (C.i.: "No, thanks.")

It is considered impolite for a Korean to say no to someone's face, as such an act is often interpreted as a rejection of the other person as a friend; as the saying goes, *Myencen paktay moshanta* 'We cannot treat someone negatively in his presence'. As K. Kim (1975), M. Park (1979), and others have pointed out, Americans' "yes" and "no" are to be taken at face value, whereas Koreans' "yes" does not necessarily signal agreement, but means more or less the same as "I see" in many settings, while their "no" to an offer is given purely out of courtesy in many cases. Koreans understand such responses as being related to the value of harmony, humility, and saving each other's face, whereas Americans would be more likely to judge such responses as uncooperative or even unfriendly.

h) While modesty, an aspect of indirectness, is negligible in American culture, it is highly valued in Korea. As Klopf and Park (1982:50) put it, "Westerners feel that one's achievements should be broadcast to the world and that one's feelings should be asserted". In contrast, modesty or humbleness is a key in Korean communicative acts. Cho (1982:155-157) observes superficially illogical but pragmatically well-formed cases in Korean:

Mas un epsci-man manhi tuseyyo.
'The food doesn't taste good, but help yourself.'
Amukes to anici man patacwuseyyo.

'This is nothing good but please accept it.'

Such expressions can also be accounted for in the light of Koreans' prizing humbleness (an aspect of indirectness) as a social virtue.

i) Various forms of nonverbal behavior manifest the two differing values vividly—American couples' open expression of their love vs. Koreans' suppression of their passion, Americans' *frank* vs. Koreans' *humble* gestures (bowing, shuffling in a doorway while urging another to enter first; handing things to others with two hands), Americans' opening of a gift in front of the giver vs. Koreans' opening in his absence, etc. While Americans do not do things that they do not wish to do, Koreans frequently do or do not do things simply to save *cheymyen* 'face'.

In intercultural communication between an American and a Korean, the American frequently feels that the Korean is too indirect and does not "come to the point", while the Korean tends to find the American to be tactlessly abrupt and straightforward (Kalton 1979:13).

3.5. Pragmatism—Formalism

In a survey of 173 Korean professors who studied in the United States, Chung (1976) asked them what the most important spiritual foundation of American culture is. The responses turned out as follows: pragmatism (77 professors), Christianity (46), pioneer spirit (34), compromise spirit (12), and others (4). On this basis, Chung claims that Americans highly value the real over the ideal, the concrete over the abstract, and practicality over formality, and that in its historical development, American society has grafted pragmatism onto the root of Christianity. Similarly, Stewart (1972:74) claims that the American is a pragmatist in that he acts so as to get things done, and he will put any workable idea into practice without adhering to coherent personal philosophies and systematic ideologies. Furthermore, Americans are said to prefer to pursue their social life under conditions that minimize incurring social obligations. Indeed, Korean immigrants to the United States are initially struck by Americans' informality and friendliness, their search for convenience and practical benefit, and their clear distinction between work and play.

Related to Americans' pragmatism is F. Kluckhohn's (1963) insistence on American predominance of *doing* (that is, "getting things done", "keeping busy", "being active") and of achievement and visible accomplishments. Contemporary Koreans, especially in urban areas, are also strongly doing- and achievement-oriented, although still constrained by seniority to a large extent. While younger Koreans seem to pursue pragmatism to a certain extent, the older generation tends to conform to a formalistic and conservative tradition in which, for example, junior members are not supposed to be promoted above senior members. Some specific communicative patterns that attest to American pragmatism and Koreans' relative formalism are given below:

a) Americans' most commonly used pattern of nominal address for smooth social interaction is the nickname, as compared with Koreans' (family name) + *sensayng-nim*. Single syllable nicknames like "Jim," "Bob," "Liz", and "Bea" are terms with which the speaker feels most comfortable, friendly, and intimate, but the terms lack the connotation of affection, childishness, or femininity carried by such affectionate nicknames as "Jimmy" and "Bobbie" (cf., Buren 1974). Americans' predominant use of first names, including nicknames, names without titles, and personal pronouns reflect the pragmatic American value orientation. Koreans, on the other hand, avoid using an adult's given name in favor of his title alone, his family name + title, or teknonymy (e.g., *Yongswu apeci* 'Yongswu's father', *apem-a* '(child's) dad' (referring to one's own son). Given names are not used even between a husband and wife, or between colleagues, male or female. Koreans tend to avoid using personal names to superiors in favor of their occupational titles. All these indicate the formalistic Korean value orientation.

b) Americans' dynamism and Koreans' staticism in code switching are also worth mentioning. The surprising degree of facility with which American adults agree on a mutual first-name basis, and the extreme difficulty with which Korean adults change their speech styles, are attributed to differences in the values under consideration. An American professor and colleague who used to be his student can easily use a symmetrical speech style; i.e., they can place themselves on a first name basis. In a parallel setting in Korea, asymmetry is maintained for life. My own survey shows that quite a few American students, especially graduate students, who use title + last name when addressing their professors either in class or in the office, switch to first-name terms either in church or at picnic. Such code switching never occurs among Koreans. An American lady divorcee usually is called "Miss," while such is never the case with a Korean woman.

c) In general, the so-called expressive acts like greetings, leave-taking, thanks, and apologies are simpler in English than in Korean, as already mentioned. "Hi, John" is good enough as a morning greeting to an American colleague, whereas a more lengthy speech act is appropriate in a

Korean setting, as in *Kim-sensayng-nim ilcik naosiesskwunyo* 'Mr. Kim, you came out early'.

d) Older Americans shrink from telling their age because they wish to leave the impression that they are still active and doing things energetically, so that they will not be excluded from their pragmatic society. Korean counterparts are willing to reveal their ages so that they will be treated as senior members of a formalistic society.

e) It has been pointed out that Koreans speak little while eating, whereas Americans enjoy eating and talking at the same time; American table manners are generally casual compared with Koreans'; American gifts are usually simple and inexpensive and given from a superior to an inferior, while the reverse is generally true among Koreans; and unlike Americans, Korean guests rarely appear without bringing gifts.

f) It seems to me that Americans' rarely forming deep and lasting friendships can also be attributable to their pragmatism. C. Kluckhohn (1954:96) observes that friends and membership groups change easily as Americans shift status or locale, and that Americans' social life lacks permanence, personal attachment, or depth. As Glenn (1966) has said of Russians, Koreans expect to form a deep bond with another person and assume the "obligation of almost constant companionship," due probably to their conservative values, as well as to their emotionalism.

g) American culture does not attribute particular meaning to place of birth, family occupation, political views, education, or ways of dressing, whereas all of these are particularly important in Korean social life.

In short, the average American considers formality pompous and unnatural, while formality and conservatism are still shared by average Koreans despite the fact that they have imported various elements of material, behavioral, and spiritual culture from the United States for the past four decades. The Confucian emphasis on regard for others has led traditional Koreans to be excessively sensitive to the concept of *cheymyen* 'face' and *yeyui* 'decorum; the rules of proper and polite behavior'.

3.6. Rationalism—Emotionalism

Americans' ideal of "fair-play", their noninvolvement in emotional issues, and their strict distinction between public or official vs. private or personal affairs are well-known. Americans stand up for their fair share and are concerned with fairness toward others too. In this connection, Stewart (1979:5) states as follows: "The stuff of rationalism turns out to have a typical American flavor, eventually derived from the assumption that the world is mechanistic and the things worthy of effort are material... The American's tendency is to be means-oriented toward the world... he conceives of the technological goal of the material world in terms of problems which a rational problem-solver can solve."

Due probably to their rationalism and individualism, Americans tend to be moderately kind to everybody without becoming deeply involved with anyone. This gives the impression to Orientals that Americans are impersonal in their relations with others, and that Americans' human interactions, even between close friends, take the form of business transactions.[7]

While Americans tend to be impersonal in their interpersonal relations, the Korean people may be characterized largely as emotional or affective, owing probably to their collectivistic consciousness. In most social interactions among Koreans, emotion plays a major role. Without personalization, human relationships can hardly proceed smoothly in Korea. This fact is clearly evidenced in daily language expressions and nonverbal behaviors. Below are some typical communicative patterns in support of this claim.

a) Many such words of daily usage as those given at the outset of Section 3.2 have deep emotional connotation in addition to their denotative meanings, attesting to Koreans' value of emotionalism. For example, *ceng,* one of the most frequently used emotion-related words, is a combination of such dictionary translations as 'feeling', 'emotion', 'love', 'affection', 'sentiment', and 'sympathy'. There are many stative verbs which show the speaker's deep compassion or sympathy toward the addressee or a third person, such as *sepsephata* 'sad, sorry,' *pulssanghata* 'sorry, pitiful,' *anssulepta* 'sorry, sad (dialectal)', *akkapta* 'pitiful, sad to say', etc. (for an extensive list, see K. Kim 1978).

b) A large number of daily expressions and proverbs are based on emotionalism, as illustrated below:

Cal puthakhapnita.
'Nice to have met you.' (Lit. 'I hope you will look after me.')
Hanpencwumyen ceng epsta.
'Affection cannot be had by giving only once.'
Cal com pwacwuseyyo.
'Please give me special consideration.'
Ceng ttelecil soli haci maseyyo.
'Don't talk about anything that may hurt our affectionate relationship.'
Ttacici malko cektanghi haseyyo.
'Don't be analytical. Do it in an approximate way.'

Phal i an ulo kwupci pakkulo kwup-na?
'The wrist bends toward inside, not toward outside.'
Inceng meli epsnun salam 'A person with no humanity'.
Milyen ttaymuney 'Beacuse of one's attachment to...'
Tem ulo cwuseyyo. 'Please give it to me as a favor.'
Kwukmul epse! 'You won't get any favor from me!'

c) While Americans tend to view people in fragments, Koreans tend to evaluate a person as a whole. Thus, an American observes good and bad points in another; by contrast, once he judges that he cannot accept another's attitudes and feelings in totality, a Korean tends to refuse to talk any further.

d) While Americans tend to reach certain decisions on the objective merits of each case, Koreans frequently put great weight on personal factors as well. Whether you know someone or not makes a great deal of difference in Korean social life and interpersonal communication. Such concepts as *senpay* 'senior', *hwupay* 'junior', *susung* 'teacher', ceyca 'student', *chinchek* 'relative', and *anun pun* 'acquaintance' mean much and contribute greatly to smooth communicative interaction.[8]

Due to the emotionalism and personalism of Koreans, people act rather coldly with no regard for others in a situation when no acquaintance is involved. Due also to personalism, Koreans frequently confuse public and private matters.

e) In many interpersonal communication settings, Koreans follow the so-called affective communication style, as opposed to Americans' typical 'instrumental' communication style. That is, a Korean must always read the other person's feelings and choose his words to avoid hurting the other's feelings. In the same vein, Koreans are deeply interested in others' business and want to know what is happening to others.

f) Extensive use of kinship terms among non-kin may be attributed not only to collectivism but also to emotionalism. *Emeni* 'mother' is used in addressing one's friend's mother. Similarly, *hyeng-nim* 'older brother,' *enni* 'older sister,' *acessi* 'uncle,' *acwumeni* 'aunt,' *halapeci* 'grandfather,' and *halmeni* 'grandmother' are common address terms to non-kin.

g) In general, Koreans have negative feelings toward an analytical attitude in communication: they favor tacit understandings or handling things *cektanghi* 'approximately.' Thus, such words as *ttacita* 'bring out exactly' and *thasancek* 'calculating' have a strong negative connotation. Americans make extensive use of written contracts even in minor transactions, but Koreans proceed on the basis of unwritten understandings in many such cases.

h) Many kinds of nonverbal behavior among in-group members seem to reveal emotionalism, such as one person's paying for everybody's food and drink (as opposed to going dutch), two females walking hand in hand, putting more food on a guest's dish without asking, filling a companion's wine glass, exchanging wine glasses, repeatedly urging more food or drink on a guest or friend, or frequent exchange of gifts to maintain emotional bondage.[9]

4. Overview and Conclusion

Parsons presents dominant patterns of social behavior in premodern or traditional societies and modern industrialized Western societies as follows (from Koh 1976:139-140):

Premodern societies

a. Sentimentality (pursuing emotional satisfaction)
b. Extensiveness (investing one's whole personality in all objects)
c. Attribution (attaching importance to automatically accorded status)
d. Particularity (treating objects with discrimination, as in cliquism and favoritism)
e. Group-orientedness (acting for the interests of the group)

Modern societies

a. Neutrality of sentimentality (favoring discipline and calculativeness)
b. Limitedness (paying limited interests to meet only the need)
c. Achievement (valuing activeness and ability)
d. Universality (treating objects impartially based on a general standard)
e. Individual-orientedness (acting for one's individual interests)

Viewed from this perspective, American society is typically modern, whereas Korean society is in transition, retaining both premodern and modern traits (Sohn 1983b). Legally, contemporary Korea is a democratic nation, and democratic values have been spreading through all walks of life. In particular, the younger generation is more sensitive to such values, as evidenced in their behavior and their considerable reduction in linguistic honorific usage and nonverbal communication (e.g., Hwang 1975, Park-Choi 1978, Suh 1979, Sohn 1983b). Conflicts between traditionalism and modernism are a social reality in contemporary Korea.

On the other hand, Americans are also affected by cultural change.

Stewart (1972:75-78) observes that young Americans have deplored the depersonalized and alienating aspects of the American self, and that the typical American tends now to be more willing to place himself in the hands of the group (e.g., an organization) to which he belongs than was the American of a generation ago. This is an obvious sign of the world societies gradually narrowing the differences of their cultural traits, including their value systems.

The value dimensions discussed thus far in relation to communicative patterns can be understood with reference to the respective societies' roots in their traditions, in that different value orientations that shape societies differently have been formed by different traditions of cognitive culture. As Kalton (1979:3) and others have pointed out, the common Western individualism and egalitarianism are drawn from the traditional Greek, Judaic, and Christian views that each person, living in relation to God, has an inviolable dignity in terms of self-reliance, independence of thought and judgement, freedom, and equality. This tradition of Americans, together with their unique experience in the New World, reflected in such concepts as pragmatism, seems to be responsible for the system of American values as it stands at present.

It is well known that in the East, Confucianism deeply influenced the whole East Asian cultural sphere including Korea. With the decline of Korean Buddhism by the sixteenth century, Neo-Confucianism, containing the moral and social doctrine of the Five Relationships mentioned above came to dominate the intellectual and spiritual life of the people (e.g., Kalton ibid.:4). Thus, the Confucian approach stresses filial duty, respect for others, harmony, social hierarchism, and a keen awareness of what each other does or should do. Indirectness, formalism, and emotionalism seem to have arisen inevitably from such collectivism and hierarchism.

The fact that people in the world contact with one another much more frequently than ever means that there are more chances for communicative conflicts. Different communication patterns too often bring about cross-cultural miscommunication due to underlying value differences. No successful intercultural communication can be attained unless cross-cultural communicators are willing to positively understand, appreciate, and affirm the culture with whose representatives they communicate, and unless they adopt appropriate value-bound expressions, verbal or nonverbal, when using a foreign language as a medium of communication. For instance, the most important strategies in communicating with Americans are to honor the inviolability of individualism and egalitarianism, whereas the most desired strategies in interacting with Koreans are to use the language of collectivism and hierarchism.

Living in the age of cultural pluralism, with the world shrinking day by day, the general public is now required more strongly than ever to attain comprehensive and conscious awareness of internationalism and global cooperation in all aspects of life, and to become multicultural members of the larger human community.

Notes

1. The research reported here, which was initiated with a small grant awarded by the University of Hawaii Center for Korean Studies in 1982, was conducted mainly in Korea in the summer of 1983 under a U.S. Office of Education Fulbright-Hays Faculty Research Abroad Award. The initial version of this paper was presented at the International Convention on Crosscultural Communication: Encounters and Conflicts held in Seoul, July 28-31, 1983. I would like to extend my deep appreciation to the Hankuk University of Foreign Studies for the assistance and accommodation provided to me, notably to Professors Dong-Sun Kim, Young-Jo Kim, Sang-Ki Lee, Ki-Hong Kim, Yeun Kyu Chung, Young-Soo Yae, Kyu Chul Cho, Soon-Ham Park, and In-Seok Yang.
2. The Yale romanization system is followed to transcribe Korean expressions in this paper.
3. Due to the individualistic orientation, competition is a basic emphasis in American culture and is known as the primary method Americans have of motivating the members of a group (Potter 1954:59-60).
4. It is still common practice for parents to choose their children's spouses even in cities.
5. For some interesting sociolinguistic studies of Korean honorifics, see Martin (1964), D. Lee (1975), Lukoff (1977), etc.
6. A similar situation is reported with regard to Japanese society (Lebra 1976:76-78).
7. A Korean who has lived in America for an extended period of time would perceive Americans very friendly at the initial stage of their association but rather cold at their later stage because, in spite of their long acquaintance, Americans hardly change their attitude. In this connection, it has been pointed out by scholars that American rationalism makes human relationship rather mechanical.
8. Kalton (1979:14) has made an interesting observation in this regard: "...Americans would probably say that ability counts most but connections help; the Korean approach is more likely to be that connections weigh heavily but ability is also necessary. Thus blood relationships, friendships, and school ties are of great importance in Korean society, and it is frequently difficult for one to 'get his foot in the door' as an outsider with no established relationships or connections".
9. Due probably to Confucian teaching that there should be a strict distinction in their social

life between male and female, average Koreans seem to feel much more comfortable among the people of the same sex.

Reprinted from *Language and Linguistics* (Hankuk University of Foreign Studies) 9:93-136 (1983).

24. SYNTACTIC AND SEMANTIC INTERFERENCE FOR KOREAN ADULT ENGLISH LEARNERS

1. The most significant and basic dimension that the everoincreasing Asian immigrants in this country must cope with for successful adaptation is their linguistic assimilation.[1] The strenuous efforts of the federal and local governments toward the implementation of improved educational programs and services for limited English speakers have not changed the reality that little is known about the English learning process by Asian immigrants.

It is only recently that emphasis in second language learning has been shifted from the teacher-centered view to the analysis of the learner's language (e.g., Corder 1967). In particular, error analysis is viewed as input to general linguistic as well as psycholinguistic theory, the assessment of language learning processes and strategies, teaching methods, materials development, and the design of improved curricula (cf. Richards 1974a; Schumann and Stenson 1974).

What this paper attempts to do is to present a cross-sectional analysis of the syntactic and semantic errors a Korean adult immigrant has made in English with particular reference to errors caused by interference as compared with developmental errors. Following Mackey (1970:195), interference, which is characteristic of the message as against the code, is here defined as the use of elements or features of one language while speaking or writing another. Developmental errors are those which do not derive from transfers from another language (e.g., Richards 1974). On the basis of the findings that have resulted from the case study, a modest proposal will be made toward the end of this paper with regard to the future direction of the teaching of English to Asian immigrants. To my knowledge, not a single work is available at present which deals with errors Korean adult immigrants make in learning English as a second language. My pioneer study, therefore, although I believe it has covered most major points, is somewhat rudimentary and leaves much to be desired.

The corpus is composed of a small sample of 280 incorrect English sentences that the informant produced in daily life during the period from January through early April 1978. Repeated sentences, errors made by slip of the tongue, and mere failures to memorize an element are excluded from the data. Also Hawaiian pidgin English patterns like "no more nothing" and "our company no need people who speak good English" are not included. Thus, the corpus consists of competence errors and rather persistent performance errors.

The informant is a 42 year old female who came to Honolulu seven years ago with the background of a minimum ability in spoken English and a totally negligible English grammar. Shortly after she arrived in Honolulu, she attended evening English classes at the University of Hawaii for a total of approximately 120 hours over 14 months. In addition, two years ago, she attended state-sponsored community night classes for a total of some 30 hours. She is a full-time worker at a place where only English is spoken. At home she currently uses both English and Korean with four English speaking children and her husband.

The objective of second language acquisition is to attain the maximum communicative competence in the target language, i.e. the knowledge of vocabulary, phonology, syntax, semantics, pragmatics, non-verbal communication, and a variety of socio-cultural rules and attitudes. The present paper is limited to syntax and semantics, which probably have the most significant implication in the teaching of English to Korean adult immigrants.

2. Two major hypotheses are associated with second language learning: one is that of contrastive analysis and the other, which is new but has irresistible force, is that first language (L1) acquisition is the same as second language (L2) acquisition (hereafter, L1 = L2). The gist of the former is that the learner tends to use his L1 features in his L2 speech, and where L1 and L2 structures are different, he makes errors. Thus this hypothesis advances a transfer or interference theory which is based on the acceptance of learning as habit formation. The proponents of this hypothesis include Fries (1945), Lado (1968), and others. For them, language teaching should emphasize intensive drills of the L2 features which contain the new habit. For the last two decades or so, contrastive analysis has been the most powerful mechanism in the teaching of second languages, in that it was believed to predict the difficulties of the learner most effectively.

The L1 = L2 hypothesis, supported most strongly by Dulay and Burt (1974) but also by Ravem (1968, 1974) and others for children and by Bailey, et al. (1974) for adults, basically maintains that the learner actively organizes the second language speech and makes generalizations about its structure just as in learning the language as his or her mother tongue. In other words, second language learning is a creative process like first language acquisition. Therefore, L2 learners make the same kinds of errors that L1 learners make. This new interest in comparing L2 acquisition with L1 acquisition is indebted to the vigorous research on L1 acquisition since the sixties.

In a perceptive study of syntactic development in children learning English as a second language, Dulay and Burt (Ibid.) hypothesize that children's errors are not dominated by transfer from or comparison with their mother tongue, but their organization of L2 relies on their dealing with L2 as a system. They interpret most of what have been treated as errors by interference as overgeneralizations. They advance an active mental organization theory, assuming that human beings have innate mental organization to exercise a set of universal utterance-producing strategies applicable to both L1 and L2. Bailey, et al. (Ibid.) claim similar things for adult learners.

Authors like Richards (1974a, 1976) and Richards and Sampson (1974) who are also error analysis pioneers do not rule out cases of interference, although they put much more weight on intralingual and developmental errors as far as syntax is concerned.[2] Richards (1974a:172), for example, states that numerous studies of L2 acquisition "have tended to imply that contrastive analysis may be most predictive at the level of phonology, and least predictive at the syntactic level." According to Richards, intralingual and developmental errors reflect the learner's over-generalization, ignorance of rule restrictions, incomplete application of rules, and false concepts hypothesized.

The bulk of the rest of this paper will be devoted to the discussion of most of the major errors that appear in the informant's sentences, trying to identify them either as interference or developmental errors or both.[3] The major areas that are related to the analysis include word order (See. 3), ellipsis (4), articles (5), prepositions (6), questions (7), tense (8), verb groups (9), number (10), comparatives (11), and residuals (12). Section 13 will conclude the paper with some practical suggestions.

3. Word order is frequently quoted as a strong piece of evidence in support of the hypothesis that the learner does not make errors that reflect transfer of L1 structure onto L2 structure (e.g. Price 1968, Milon 1972, Dulay and Burt 1974:180). For instance, Price's research shows that

English-speaking children followed Welsh word order in the early state of their learning Welsh NP constructions. Similar things can be said about Koreans learning English. Despite the drastic difference in word order typology between English and Korean, the informant rarely fails in arranging words in the right order. Compare the informant's sentences in (1) with those corresponding hypothetical sentences which reflect the Korean order (2).

(1) a. Man is smart than lady.
b. I saw that book at our house one or two month before I start to read.
c. If you start to check my English mistake before, I could learn correct English earlier.

(2) a. Man lady than smart is.
b. I that book read-to start one or two month before our house at saw.
c. You before my English mistake check-to start if, I earlier correct English learn could.

It is true, as observed in (1), that the informant has internalized the intricate English order of elements. Early mastery of the word order does not mean that there was no interference from Korean. For instance, in the very early stage of learning, the informant made frequent errors in the basic word order, using the Korean subject-object-verb sequence. Besides, the corpus contains sentences like those in (3), where minor errors in word order are attributable partly or wholly to the Korean order.

(3) *I and my children* are all right.
Anyway, *every my mistake*, write down!
You wanna wear *this my ring*?
The paper said about *our this year's fortune.*
This blanket doesn't *much help you.*
He doesn't know *'opulence' meaning.*
Japanese tourist wear *this kind of material clothes.*

Now, what makes the English word order so early acquired? My own explanation is as follows. English is an SVO language, whereas Korean is an SOV language. Consonant to Greenberg's (1966a) implicational universals, modal elements precede the verb stem in English but follow it in Korean; adverbials and relative or complement clauses come after the modified element in English but come before it in Korean; and adjectives, determiners, and possessives appear before the modified word in both languages, to mention the most important grammatical relations. In other words, English and Korean are mirror images in many cases. Since such universal implications no doubt reflect natural conceptualization and production processes, the learner who has internalized the basic SVO relation tends more to follow the implied order of grammatical relations than to introduce the mother tongue order which is unnatural in that it is against the implications. An additional reason for the speedy mastery of the English word order may be that the order of elements, especially the subject and direct and indirect objects, is functional in changing meanings, whereas all the cases in Korean are distinguished by means of case markers, thus allowing free order scrambling.

In short, the L2 word order acquisition does not verify that interference is not operative.

4. Ellipsis of situational or contextually predictable cases is a frequently observed type of error.

(4) a. Today was really tired.
You guys, don't finish your dinner yet?
b. He advised how to go China.
Whenever he saw wrong thing, he cannot stand.
c. You know how could do, yeah?
d. Green trees send their fresh aroma.
You have to patient until I send a carriage.

(4a) is the ellipsis of the subject, (4b) that of the object, (4c) both the subject and object, and (4d) oblique cases. It is no doubt that the extensive elliptic phenomena are due to the interference from Korean which allows free deletion of any nominal elements that are recoverable situationally or in the discourse context, unless the elements are to be contrasted, exhaustively listed, or delimited. Thus, while neutral cases like those given in (4) are deleted, certain elements are unnecessarily inserted, as in 'If you hungry, you eat first!' where the second *you* is inserted in order to exhaustively list it in accordance with the Korean pattern.

5. Another productive type of error is observed in the use of articles. Some 40 out of the 280 sentences are associated with article errors, most of which are the omission of 'the' or 'a/an', as illustrated in (5a) and (5b) respectively. (5c) contains the occurrences of unnecessary articles.

(5) a. You put the paper in machine hole.
Both books are same quality.

Your clothes was best.

b. Kim Il-han was really talented and smart scholar.
He made promise with them.
He was looking for singer.
My husband received letter from him few days ago.

c. That's *the* my point.
Your brother loves you. You are *the* nice brother, too.
If we sustain *the* certain life style, we need 5% income increase every year.
That's not *a* my pen.

Errors in the use of articles in English, for example, are intralingual and developmental (Richards 1974a:186-7) in that both those learning English as the mother tongue and those learning it as a second language make similar mistakes. French (1949:9) and Aguas (1964) [quoted from Richards 1974a: 76-7] illustrate common article mistakes by rational analogy, which is the case even when the mother tongues (Burmese and Tagalog) are similar to the English pattern. Dulay and Burt (1974:108-120) observe that omission of functors in L2 acquisition is similar to that in L1 acquisition, and functors are learned relatively late. All this means that we cannot rule out the possibility that developmental errors sometimes avert the pressure of the mother tongue.

Due to their syntactic and semantic complexity, learning of articles is probably the most vexing to Korean adults, who, no matter how long they have lived in the U.S. as an adult, rarely have a native-like control of them. Semantically, the Korean topic (*nun*) and focus (*ka*) markers only partially overlap with English definite (*the*) and indefinite (*a*) articles in that *nun* and *the* are related to old information and *ka* and *a* to new information. The partial overlapping only confuses the learner because of the mismatching of the other semantic and syntactic differentiations. Incidentally, Korean topic and focus markers overlap almost completely with those of Japanese both in syntax and semantics. An adult Korean learning Japanese has no problem whatsoever in acquiring the Japanese *wa* and *ga,* which give tremendous difficulty to Westerners. For the same reason, I suspect that a learner whose mother tongue has an article system similar to the English one will have no difficulty in acquiring English articles relatively early. To the extent that the above discussion is not false, errors in article acquisition do not falsify interference theory, although it is true that such errors are largely developmental.

6. The next set of errors concern the use of prepositions, where the syn-

tactic and semantic interference of Korean are conspicuous. Observe the examples in (6).

(6) a. Everybody complain the toothbrush.
He pounded door.
I believe you everything.
b. Please trash this paper *to* there.
Then you should pay *to* me.
She doesn't marry *with* him.
I know *with* them.
When he announce *about* his departure, she was really feel sad.
c. You guys are different *with* people in Korea.
Hawaii's crime extortion was started *from* 1960.
He feels kind of hostility *about* China.
When you take a trip, you have to be careful *about* your friends.
Also anyway, this year is good *to* you.

The sentences in (6a) illustrate the omission of a preposition in the places where one is needed. The omission can easily be ascribed to the fact that, in the corresponding Korean sentences, the relation is that of a transitive verb and its object. For instance, the verb *complain* is first associated with *pulphyenghata.*[4] While *complain* does not have transitivity, thus requiring *about* to govern an object, *pulphyenghata* is used as a transitive verb. The sentence 'I believe you everything' is translated as a double object construction in Korean, hence the omission of *in* before *everything*. The sentences in (6b) are the cases opposite to those in (6a). Similarly, (6c) illustrates the use of wrong prepositions due to the informant's association of certain English prepositions uniquely with certain Korean prepositions at the early stage of her learning. Such syntactic and semantic associations of the paired items must be conditioned by the frequency of their occurrences. Thus, for instance, *with* in 'You guys are different with people in Korea' is due to the informant's association of the Korean comitative particle *kwa* with *with*. The verb *taluta* 'to be different' must occur with *kwa* in Korean.

Richards (1974a:176) points out that intralingual analogy seems to be a major factor in the misuse of prepositions, as in *he said to me* vs. *he asked to me* and *go with him* vs. *follow with him*. This is only partly true. As we have seen, analogy operates only when there is no intrusion of other features from the mother tongue or when the mother tongue feature is the same as the analogical direction. The informant accepted *he asked to me* as natural whereas she immediately rejected *follow with him*. No doubt, the last sentence is not in the bounds of the Korean pattern, as shown in (7).

(7) a. Ku-pun i na *eykey* mal-hay-ss-ta.
he NM me to said
Ku-pun i na *eykey* mul-ess-ta.
he NM me to asked
b. Ku-pun *kwa* ka-kela.
he with go
Ku-pun (*ul*) ttalaka-kela.
he AM follow

7. Ravem (1974), Richards (1974a:187), and Dulay and Burt (1974:116) maintain that certain types of error in the use of English questions are typically intralingual and developmental in that they are similar to L1 developmental errors. Observe the informant's sentences in (8).

(8) I am the informant?
You don't wanna job?
You guys going to the library tomorrow?
Why you do silly things?

At first glance, the omission of inversion in (8) may be attributed entirely to transfer from Korean, in which, due to its SOV order, sentence types are determined by sentence-final endings without any inversion transformation involved. Ravem (Ibid.), however, reports his Norwegian speaking son's absence of the auxiliary-subject inversion in English, although Norwegian does require it. Obviously, the learner's initial strategy is to minimize grammatical redundancy. That is, rising intonation is sufficient in yes-no questions and *wh-* words are sufficient for *wh-* questions.

The informant is slowly learning the inversion in some frequently used expressions like "Shall we go?", "Do you know that?", "Did you see that?", and "Where did you go?". This phenomenon agrees with one of the L1 = L2 hypotheses that base structures are learned first and then transformational processes are increasingly acquired (Dato 1970; Dulay and Burt 1974:108). Even here, I suspect that the substratum of Korean considerably hinders the inversion in view of the length of time the informant has been exposed to English and her degree of English proficiency including the mastery of the basic ordering of elements.

In contrast to matrix question sentences, the embedded sentences in the indirect question have a regularly inverted construction, as shown in (9).

(9) Do you remember where *did I* put the airgram?
Daddy asked *did you guys* go.
I asked you where *did you* get this.
She ask poet's wife what *is your purpose*.

Dulay and Burt (Ibid.:120) attribute sentences like (9) to 'the pervasiveness of a syntactic generalization', saying that, if a principle like the transformational cycle has been acquired, its use in structures where it should not apply will result in developmental mistakes. But how can we account for the lack of inversion in (8) where it is required and the inversion in (9) where it is not required? As I mentioned above, the strategy of minimum redundancy seems to prevail in (8), whereas some other motivating factors appear to be involved in (9). I advance the conjecture that the informant subconsciously tends to manifest the question meaning in the embedded sentence, which leads to hypercorrection. Another more plausible conjecture is that the informant is partly affected by the Korean structure in which a type of question ending is maintained in indirect questions. The interference is apparent particularly in the last sentence in (9), where *your* actually refers to the poet's wife. In Korean, the distinction between direct and indirect question is not so clear-cut. Thus, Korean allows a direct quotation pronoun with indirect quotation verb endings. Further support for the interference hypothesis comes from embedded imperatives like "I told you that don't watching T.V.!"

8. Errors in the use of tense expressions are quite extensive. In particular, the sequence of tense is hard for the informant, as in (10a and b), and she frequently uses the present tense form for the past even in simple sentences (10c). Sometimes the past tense is used with infinitives (10d) and not infrequently the verb *be* is used for tense marking (10e).

(10) a. This morning Mr. Conrad *sees* me and he waved hands to me.
I asked my husband that your family *will come* to Hawaii.
b. When I was in Korea, I *hear* about Pearl Buck wrote about story about Korea.
When he finished his works and he *return* to home.
Do you know the restaurant which recently *open?*
c. She *shake* hands with me.
I *walk* around in Liberty House and then I *return* to my work.
d. They have to *went* to school.
Did you *ate* your lunch?
She didn't *brought* queen to her house.

e. *Isn't* it look good?
I *am* still love you.
I *was* really envy you.
Was Junghan wake up?

The sentences in (10a) reflect the corresponding Korean structure. Korean uses the simple present tense in the first clause of a coordinate construction, i.e. *sees* rather than *saw*. Korean does not have a syntactic rule of tense agreement between the matrix verb and the embedded verb, i.e. *will* rather than *would*. Unless the rules involved in such errors, especially the syntactic agreement, are taught to the informant, I predict that she will continue to produce such errors.

On the other hand, most other tense marking errors in (10) seem to be purely developmental, i.e. not traceable to Korean. Had the informant followed the syntax of Korean, she would have produced the correct English forms in (10b) and (10c). Notice that in (10b) at least one element in each sentence always specifies the past, e.g. *was, finished, recently*. Also in (10c), the previous discourse context always made it clear that the sentences were intended for past events, hence a case of redundancy reduction. The informant has not learned the syntactic constraint that an infinitive cannot carry tense, as we observe in (10d), where hypercorrection or overgeneralization is also noticed. The examples in (10e) may be a case of faulty comprehension of distinctions in English, as advocated by Richards (1974a). Thus, *was* is falsely interpreted as a marker of the past tense, and *is* as that of the present. We may also invoke the strategy of analogy. For instance, the informant uses *was envy* by analogy with *will envy, did not envy,* etc. Also it may be pointed out that tense marking in Korean applies to both verbs and adjectives in a parallel way. Thus, the grammaticality of *was happy* may easily lead the learner to create *was envy*. Incidentally, the informant has not internalized the rule associated with the use of *do* and *be,* which is a hard rule for a Korean to learn from scratch due to the underdifferentiation in Korean.

9. In connection with tense, quite a few errors are found in the use of verb groups in general. Observe the passive errors in (11).

(11) a. It's supposed to *be boiled* already.
Hawaii's crime extortion *was* started from 1960.
My husband *is recovered* his health little by little.
She *was* really *welcomed* him.
b. Junghan will gonna *confusing*.

They *surprised;* they *disappointed.*
I was *confusing.*

Korean has passive constructions but their semantic ranges only partially overlap with those of English. Thus, the first three sentences in (11a) may all be expressed in the form of passives, as in *sicak-toy-ess-ta* 'started' where *toy* has a kind of passive meaning. The last sentence in (11a) is apparently the result of using *was* as a simple past tense marker in the informant's 'approximate system' (Nemser 1964) or interlanguage (Selinker 1974). In English, emotional verbs like *interest, confuse, surprise,* and *disappoint* are used as passives in relation to the experiencer, which is not the case with the corresponding verbs in Korean. This semantic asymmetry seems to be the major factor that leads the informant to make errors like those in (11b).

English perfectives are entirely foreign to Koreans. For this reason, I have come across very few cases where a perfective construction is used. The informant uses either the present form of the verb, the past form, or an ungrammatical coinage, as observed in (12).

(12) You guys, don't finish your dinner yet?
You certainly become dumb!
Kimchi become salty.
Oh, how many years I passed here!
I didn't send letter over a year, but many times I thought about you.
Is Junghan came?

One rule the informant has developed in the use of verb groups is the replacement of a verb stem with an *-ing* form (13). Dulay and Burt (1974: 117) handle a similar sentence ('Now we will talking about...') under Unique Goofs, in that it does not reflect L1 (Spanish), nor is it found in L1 acquisition data in English.

(13) I have to shopping today.
Are you gonna jogging today?
I will looking for syrup.
Shall we playing ping-pong?
Can I watching T.V.?
Are you gonna hiking?
When we shopping, maybe we will see our colleagues.
If you don't accompany my song, how can I singing?

The use of *-ing* forms erroneously may be partly due to the frequent use of such gerunds as *shopping, jogging,* and *hiking* in the context of Korean expressions. Frequency of the pattern (interference), wrong semantic segmentation and lack of knowledge of the syntactic constraint regarding gerunds and infinitives (developmental), naturally lead the informant to use the pattern with a structure which requires a verb stem. Upon request, the informant analyzed *have to* as *hay-ya-han-ta* 'must do' in the context 'I have to shopping today', apparently having internalized *shopping* as a noun. The Korean expression calls for a noun, but the English expression calls for a verb. Sentences like 'I will looking for syrup' may be due to the analogy with 'He is (was) looking for syrup.'

A parallel case is the omission of a *be* verb before an *-ing* form of a verb or before an adjective, as we see in (14). This may be accounted for in terms of the redundancy suppression strategy and verb/adjective equivalence in Korean.

(14) That's why you watching movie too much.
Queen wearing just a normal clothes.
You hungry now?
I familiar with them.
You have to patient until I send a carriage.

10. One of the areas where the informant is much affected by Korean is number in nouns. In Korean, plurality is usually not specified by its marker *tul* unless there is a demonstrative before the noun in which case it is obligatory. This phenomenon is clearly reflected in the informant's sentences.

(15) a. Man is smart than lady.
There's no much car today.
Most of hearer think that I said correctly.
One of our lady saw it.
They have two boy.
He always write poem.
b. Those servants lock all door.
All of those students went to school.

Notice in the two sentences of (15b) that *servants* and *students* are plural forms after the demonstrative, which is exactly the case in the corresponding Korean translation.

The constraint that only the verb in the present tense whose subject is singular receives the ending *-s* is annoying to both L1 and L2 learners equally.

(16) Nobody use your brush.
Japan have enough rice.
Maybe Seunghan know it.
The kimchi become salty.

As Duskova (1969) points out, omission of the *-s* is due to the generalization or the heavy pressure of all other endingless forms.

The informant is beginning to feel the *-s* attachment rule from scratch, occasionally applying it to a wrong form by way of hypercorrection, as in 'What does mangoose means?' and by way of reverse overgeneralization, as in 'He heard about lots of things happens at queen's palace'.

11. Errors in comparative constructions include omission of *-er* (17a), omission of *more* before *than* (17b), use of *more* before one syllable adjective (17c), omission of *the* in the superlative (17d), and hypercorrection (17e).

(17) a. Man is *smart* than lady.
If you brush your teeth *early* than then...
That time bride was older than bridegroom, two or three years *old*.
b. He loved Kitty than Kitty's sister.
c. Queen Min was *more* smart and talented than Kojong.
d. Your clothes was best.
e. Then you have to find a person who speak *more worse* than I.

All the sentences in (17) correspond to the comparative pattern of Korean in which the comparative postposition *pota* 'than' is sufficient and *te* 'more' must be used when *pota* is not present. The lack of *the* in (17d) is simply one of the cases of the article deletion already mentioned. Lexical comparatives like *worse* and *better* seem to be recognized as simple adjectives, hence (17e) and sentences like 'This is better than before one'.

12. In addition to the above major types of error, there are a large number of sporadic syntactic and semantic errors that are attributable more often to the intrusion of Korean features but also to developmental strategies such as redundancy suppression, hypercorretion, analogy or overgeneralization, wrong semantic association, wrong syntactic hypotheses. Time and space do not allow me to go into discussion of them. Suffice it here to present some examples in (18).

(18) You can eat anything what you want.
We want to walk cross to God.

They change the coin.
When I checked you, you never cover your blanket.
I will cook my best.
Morning time take a walk is good.
Both books are same quality.
How can machine answer our fortune?
They feel love each other.
His personality is liberalism.
That time was chilly and winter.
We have to pretend as a brother and sister.
After a little bit of take rest, let's play again.
Welcome to come.

13. A rough count of the errors of the sentences in the corpus, taking the foregoing discussion into account, shows that slightly over 50% are attributable to the interference of Korean and the rest to putatively universal language acquisition strategies, analogical extension of syntactic and semantic elements within English, or incomplete learning of rules. It has been apparent from the present case study, that contrastive analysis would predict only about half of the errors, rather than most of them as has been claimed by the hypothesis. Dulay and Burt (1973) report that only 3% of the errors made by children are traceable to their mother tongue. The result of my analysis indicates that there is a striking difference between child and adult learners as against Bailey, et al. (1974). Thus, the L1 = L2 hypothesis cannot be supported in the case of adults. (The contrastive analysis hypothesis does not make the child-adult distinction.)

It is strongly suggested that, for their successful linguistic assimilation, limited English speaking adult Asians be taught, along with the other aspects, the syntactic and semantic rules of English that cover the types of errors discussed in this paper. Since it was shown that a large number of the errors are related to the system of the mother tongue, it is imperative that the structural and semantic differences between the two languages be gradually introduced and clearly taught in a systematic manner. This is particularly the case because English and Asian languages are different to the extreme degree, unlike English and such Indo-European languages as Spanish, German, and French. Developmental errors also can easily be prevented or corrected through precisely stated rules. Simple pattern practices not only make the learner feel bored but frequently leave him with 'a patchwork of unfruitful, partial generalizations'. Unlike the foreign language learning situation, immigrants are surrounded by English speakers with whom they can practice their rules through daily exposure. It is lamentable that the informant, after seven years of learning English, has not been taught such a simple rule that only a verb stem form can come after *to*.

Drawing on several areas of research, Lenneberg (1967) takes a stand for the distinction between adults and children in language learning. For instance, the finding that a deaf person who regains his hearing after puberty cannot master a spoken language, which is not the case with a child, indicates a biological limitation in adults. Ritchie (1973: 3) contends that the child's linguistic theory is universal in scope, highly restrictive and specifically linguistic, whereas the adult's theory fails in all these. Certainly a child can acquire any language as a native tongue in a relatively short period of time, which an adult cannot. How then can we expect an Asian adult to construct so many intricate rules by himself from scratch? It is known that adults are more rule-oriented, and this characteristic must be fully utilized in the teaching/learning of English. Furthermore, an extensive knowledge of rules is indispensable for effective reading and writing. Teaching/learning materials, teaching techniques and procedures should take account of the syntactic and semantic rules discussed above.

Notes

1. The research reported here was supported by a University of Hawaii Research Administration grant. The travel to New York for presentation at the 2nd National Conference on Asians in America and Asian Americans (May 12-13, 1978) was supported by the University of Hawaii President's funds and the Asian American Assembly for Policy Research. I gratefully acknowledge the assistance of Barbara Mori provided in the analysis of the data. I also thank Dong Jae Lee for helpful comments.
2. Authors like Mackey (1969:108-112), who are not involved in error analysis, also point out that not all errors in L2 are due to the structure of the mother tongue. Incomplete learning, analogy within the target language, social and psychological influences, etc. are enumerated as factors that cause error.
3. Dulay and Burt (1974:155) set up a separate category called unique goofs which, according to them, are assignable neither to 'interference-like goofs' nor 'L1 developmental goofs'. I have no reason why I cannot consider them simply developmental.
4. Korean expressions are transcribed by the Yale romanization system. The abbreviations are NM = a nominative marker, AM = an accusative marker.

Reprinted from *Bilingual Education for Asian-Americans: Problems and Strategies,* ed. by J.H. Koo and T.N. St. Clair. 111-129 (1980). Hiroshima: Bunka Hyoron Co.

25. PATTERNS OF AMERICAN STUDENTS' COMPOSITION ERRORS IN KOREAN

1. The aim of this paper is to observe and establish, albeit tentatively, the main areas of weakness in the written Korean of American university students.[1] This will be done by presenting a distribution of the errors made by students among various linguistic levels and categories, discussing the nature of the errors and advancing speculations regarding the causality of the errors. Being a cross-sectional analysis, this study will not deal with the students' developmental aspects, such as the determination of a hierarchy of difficulty and developmental paths of acquisition.

Compositions by twenty-two students for two semesters are used as data. All the subjects have English as a native language and have learned Korean for at least two years in a formal environment. The data is composed of the students' pattern tests, translation tests, and free compositions on various topics of their choice. The reason for choosing students at the advanced level is to observe and determine what the most tenacious problems students generally have are even after their linguistic ability is considerably mature.[2]

Although the main concern of this paper is an analysis of students' errors, the approach I would like to advocate regarding the analysis of the problems associated with foreign language teaching and learning is essentially an integrative one, encompassing all the three representative approaches currently available: descriptive analysis, contrastive analysis, and error analysis. Descriptive analysis is concerned with a description of various aspects of the target language within the traditional, structuralistic, or generative framework, its ultimate goal being to describe the linguistic and other communicative competence a native speaker possesses. Needless to say, descriptive analysis, linguistic or sociolinguistic, is most essential, both in quality and quantity, for language education and has been pursued most productively. Despite its enormous contribution, however, descriptive analysis alone has been found insufficient for foreign language teaching and learning. For one thing, the native speaker's communicative competence is quite different from that that a non-native learner of the language would have. By definition, descriptive analysis does not accommodate the description of such differences. As a result, the language learner easily falls into a variety of pitfalls, because he frequently tends to be guided by his competence of native language patterns in the learning process. Furthermore, as will be observed in Korean data, certain areas of the target language structure are far more difficult to learn than others. In many cases, descriptive analysis fails to notice such difficult areas without the help of contrastive or error analysis, and is thus unable to discuss them in sufficient detail. Besides, recent descriptive analyses, especially generative ones, are frequently either too formal or too abstract to adapt to textbooks and classroom situations.

The goals of contrastive analysis are, by and large, pedagogical and the approach largely concentrates on superficial differences between languages. Much of the work on contrastive analysis has been done under the assumption that a linguistic comparison of two languages can predict areas of the learner's difficulty and thus explain the errors that speakers of the first language will make in learning the target language (e.g. Fries 1945, Lado 1957, Stockwell and Bowen 1965, Stockwell and Martin 1965, and Banathy, Trager, and Waddle 1966). Thus, most, if not all, errors are assumed to stem from interference between the structures of the first and target languages. As Wardhaugh (1974) and others challenge and the data dealt with in this study will verify, contrastive analysis has serious limitations in that errors are due not only to the differences between the two languages but also to target-language rule deviance, which has nothing to do with linguistic or sociolinguistic interference from the first language. A more drastic position against contrastive analysis, which I am not inclined to subscribe to, is taken by such authors as Wolfe (1967), who claim that all natural languages are very similar in deep structures, that the rules of the way in which a language relates its deep structures to its surface structures and phonetic representations are unique, that the learner must internalize such idiosyncratic rules of the target language, and therefore that superficial contrastive statements can be of no help in the learning task. Needless to say, the language learner must internalize the underlying patterns of the target language and the rules to map them onto the corresponding surface forms and vice versa. This is precisely the reason why descriptive analysis is essential for language learners. This does not mean, however, that contrastive analysis is of little or no help, because, as will be shown in the present data, errors are caused, to a considerable extent, by structural and socio-cultural interference from the first language, and such errors are prevented or corrected most effectively through contrasting the linguistic systems and sociolinguistic patterns of the two languages.

A relatively new approach called error analysis or the study of learners' interlanguage has recently arisen as an alternative or supplement to the contrastive analysis hypothesis which, with its narrow view of interference, ignores the intralingual effects of learning, among other factors. This approach, which grew out of transformational-generative theory, which reveals insights into the deep level of linguistic structure and the notion of language as a rule-governed system, maintains that second language learning is a creative process of constructing an 'interlanguage' system in which the learner is testing hypotheses about the target language from such sources as the learner's limited knowledge of the target language itself, knowledge about the first language, knowledge about the communicative function of language, and knowledge about human beings and the universe (H. Brown 1980:162). Richards (1974) defines the field of error analysis broadly as the area which deals with "the differences between the way people learning a language speak, and the way adult native speakers of the language use the language." Within the error analysis framework, the error is regarded largely as a rule violation concerning the target language alone. One limitation error analysis has is that the learner tends to avoid the patterns and structures that pose difficulty for him. Although pattern, translation, and other tests allow us to elicit errors of this type to a certain extent, the range of areas that error analysis can examine is far more limited than that descriptive or contrastive analysis can.

As specific forms of linguistic analysis, contrastive analysis, especially the (weak) version that aims to account for observed errors in terms of linguistic differences, and error analysis are similar in that both attempt to account for observed facts based on the learner's errors in using the target language. Differences in the two approaches are in their focus in accounting for the data observed. Contrastive analysis is concerned with points of interference from the learner's first language, whereas error analysis deals with errors only in terms of the learner's formulation of the target language system. As will be observed in the Korean data, both approaches are essential; they are not incompatible but complementary to each other and contribute, together with descriptive analysis, to the solution of a variety of problems related to students' errors.

2. Students' errors may be looked at from three dimensions: (a) the linguistic levels, categories, and subcategories to which errors belong, (b) the manners in which errors are made, and (c) the possible sources of errors. As for the linguistic levels for error analysis, Rogers (1984), for example, establishes syntax, morphology, lexis, orthography, and complete transfer of English expressions, in her study of German students' written errors in English. H. Brown (1980:170-172) proposes four levels: phonology or orthography, lexicon, grammar, and discourse. A recent breakthrough in research related to second language acquisition is the shift of emphasis from the study of the aquisition of linguistic forms and meanings and structural rules to the study of the so-called communicative competence, which includes not only linguistic abilities but interactional social abilities of language use (e.g., Hymes 1967). Studies of the latter abilities, which are still in the fledgling stage, are usually subsumed under such rubrics as sociolinguistics, linguistic pragmatics, discourse analysis, and conversational analysis. The results of the present study lend support to the validity of this new emphasis in that the given data can be analyzed exhaustively only when both linguistic and interactional aspects are taken into account. Although the level of discourse per se is not directly related to the present study where individual students' compositions are analyzed, sociolinguistics and pragmatics are relevant to a certain extent, and thus will be included in the list of the linguistic levels to be dealt with in this paper. The other levels are orthography, lexicon, morphology, and syntax.

As for the manners in which errors are made, Brown (1980:169) presents four processes following standard mathematical categories: addition (e.g. *do* addition in *does can he sing?*), omission (e.g. definite article omission in *I went to movie*), substitution (e.g. *I lost my road*), and ordering (e.g. *I to the store went*). All such processes are observed in our data and will be discussed in terms of relevant linguistic elements.

With regard to the sources of errors, the observation that the degree of the learner's errors does not necessarily correspond to that of divergence between the two languages in question is partly attributable to the existence of multiple sources of the learner's errors (e.g. Selinker 1974, Richards 1974, Wardhaugh 1974). Selinker (ibid.) identifies five processes as central to second language learning: (i) language transfer (if fossilizable items, rules and subsystems occurring in interlanguage performance are a result of the native language), (ii) transfer of training (if they are a result of identifiable items in training procedures), (iii) learning learning strategies if they are a result of an identifiable approach by the learner to the material to be learned), (iv) communication strategies (if they are the result of an identifiable approach by the learner to communication with native speakers of the target language), and (v) over generalization or reorganization of linguistic materials (if they are the result of a clear overgeneralization of target language rules). Selinker claims that these five processes force fossilizable material upon the surface structures of the learner's interlanguage.[3] Similarly, Richards (1974), based essentially on Selinker's classification, advances multiple sources of the learner's errors as follows: (i) interference or language transfer, (ii) learning strategies such as overgeneralization and analogy, (iii) performance errors such as those caused by memory lapses, fatigue, confusion, and strong emotion, (iv) markers of transitional competence such as those caused by a natural and developmental sequence in the second language learning process, (v) strategies of communication and assimilation such as the learner's attempt to make his learning task easier or to communicate in the target language without having completely acquired necessary grammatical forms, and (vi) teacher-induced errors. Brown (1980:172-181), while assuming it an impossible task to enumerate all hundreds of possible sources of errors, presents four major sources as follows: (i) interlingual transfer from the native language, (ii) intralingual transfer including overgeneralization, (iii) context (classroom and social) of learning, and (iv) communicative strategies such as avoidance, prefabricated patterns (as in 'tourist survival' language), cognitive and personality styles, appeal to authority (e.g., asking a native speaker for help), and switch to one's native language.

Since the Korean data dealt with in this study is limited to compositions made in formal situations, not all the sources discussed above are applicable. Three major sources, i.e., interlingual transfer (interference), intralingual transfer (overgeneralization, etc.), and teacher-induced errors, however, are extensively observed in the data collected. In general, as Brown (ibid.) and others have noticed, the early stages of second language learning are characterized by a predominance of interlingual transfer from the first language, but as the learning process advances, more and more intralingual transfer is manifested. Following this general developmental pattern, the present data shows that intralingual transfer is more widespread than interference, especially in morphology and syntax, while interference is still considerably tenacious in orthography and other levels. Teacher-induced errors are particularly noticeable in the syntactic data of the translation and pattern test results.

In the following are discussed the errors in orthography (Sec. 3), lexicon (Sec. 4) morphology (Sec. 5), syntax (Sec. 6), and sociolinguistics and pragmatics (Sec. 7) in terms of the three dimensions mentioned in this section.

3. Errors in Orthography

In identifying orthographic or spelling errors, only phonological ones are taken into account. Thus, such morphology-related errors as *nwu.kwu.ka* (for nwu.ka) 'who' and *kal.e ip.ta* (for *kal.a ip.ta*) 'to change clothes', such lexical errors as *hays.pich* (for *hays.pyeth*) 'sunshine', and such syntactic errors as *onul.ey.nun* (for *onul.un*) 'as for today' are not included.[4] Phonology-based errors seem to be of four general kinds: (a) graphic mismatch, (b) phonemic transcription, (c) wrong pronunciation of words, and (d) wrong graphic association of sound features. Graphic mismatch, which is rather rare, occurs when the writer knows the exact pronunciation, yet uses aberrant symbols or spellings, as illustrated in (1). In the following, correct spellings are given in parentheses.

(1) esp.e.yo (eps.e.yo) 'do not exist'
mis.ey (mith.ey) 'at the bottom'
ttwu.e.ka (ttwi.e.ka) 'to run'
pich (pic) 'debt'
nakk.cey (nak.cey) 'failure'
kath.a.cwu.ta (kac.ta.cwu.ta) 'to bring'
soyp.key (swip-key) 'easily'
ppalk.an (ppal.kan) 'red'
wi.sa (uy.sa) 'doctor'
o.lay.tong.an (o.lays.tong.an) 'for long'
aph.toy (aph.twi) 'background'
kas.i (kath.i) 'together'
wi.kwuk (woy.kwuk) 'a foreign country'
ces (cec) '(mother's) milk'
eh.tte.key (e.tteh.key) 'how'
aph.a.yo (a.pha.yo) 'sick'
an.i.la (a.ni.la) 'not only it is'
pa.ta.ka (pa.tas.ka) 'seaside'
han.kwan (han.kwen) 'one volume'
mac.hi.anh.ta (mac.ci.anh.ta) 'not correct'
hwi.sa (hwoy.sa) 'company'

It is observed that the students at the third-year level have already mastered the 'morphophonemic' spelling system of Korean rather thoroughly, and hardly made errors that reflect the observance of pure 'phonemic' principles. The examples given in (2) are about all the errors of this type that are found.

(2) man.i (manh.i) 'much'
u.mak (um.ak) 'music'
tta.wi.ey (tta.wi.uy) 'of what not'
hwi.pal.lywu (hwi.pal.ywu) 'gasoline'
sul.phe.cyess.e.yo (sulph.e.cyess.e.yo) 'became sad'
myech.sal.im.ni.kka (myech.sal.ip.ni.kka) 'How old is he?'
ka.yep.ta (ka.yeps.ta) 'pitiful'
sam.payk.ssek (sam.payk.sek) '300 *soks*'
cip.ap (cip.aph) 'front of a house'

As for the third (c) and fourth (d) kind of phonology-based orthographic errors, it is hardly clear from the data whether an error is caused by a wrong pronunciation of the word or by a wrong graphic association of phonemic features. For example, the wrong spelling *yang.hwa* for *yeng.hwa* 'movie' or *si.ham* for *si.hem* 'exam' may be due either to the subject's wrong pronunciation of the word or to his association of an approximate sound of *e* with the symbol *a*. In either case, the fact seems to be that the subject has failed to distinctly perceive or produce the two sounds represented by *e* and *a*. In the following, therefore, I will present the recurrent patterns of errors without attempting to make a distinction between the two kinds of error.

Consonant errors are of the following types.

(3) *p* for *ph* or *pp:*
pa.lu.thi (pha.a.thi) 'party'
ko.pass.ta (ko.phass.ta) 'was hungry.'
pi.kon (phi.kon) 'fatigue'
pal.li.key (ppa.lu.key) 'fast'
pal.pwu.li (pal.ppwu.li) 'toes'
pal.kan (ppal.kan) 'red'
pap.seng (phap.ssong) 'pop. song'
ko.pul.kka (ko.phul.kka) 'will be hungry?'
ko.pi (kho.phi) 'coffee'
pwun.te.le (ppwun.te.le) 'not only'
ki.pu.ki (ki.ppu.ki) 'being happy'

ph for *p* or *pp:*
phil.li.ta (pil.li.ta) 'to borrow'
yet.phe.yo (yey.ppe.yo) 'pretty'
phay (pay) 'stomach'
phun (ppwun) 'only'

pp for *p:*
ppi.sal (pi.ssal) 'expensive'
ppa.ppun (pa.ppun) 'busy'

(4) *t* for *th* or *tt:*
kyo.tong (kyo.thong) 'traffic'
kal.tey.ni (kal.they.ni)
tay.o.nan (thay.e.nan) 'to be born'
tas.u.lo (thas.u.lo) 'due to'

'since I will go'

te (tto) 'again'

twi.e.ka (ttwi.e.ka) 'to run'

th for *t:*

the ssan (te ssan) 'cheaper'

hap.kyek.han.they.ta (hap.kyek.han.tey.ta) 'in addition to his passing'

ko.than.han (ko.tan.han) 'tired'

pwu.thay (pwu.tay) 'military unit'

(5) *c* for *ch:*

cin.kwu (chin.kwu) 'friend'

cil.nyen (chil.nyen) 'seven years'

cwung.pwun-hi (chwung.pwun.hi) 'enough'

cen.cen.hi (chen.chen.hi) 'slowly'

to.cak (to.chak) 'arrival'

cap.cay (cap.chay) 'chop suey'

cwu.ess.ta (chwu.wess.ta) 'was cold'

meng.ceng.han (meng.cheng.han) 'stupid'

cayk (chayk) 'book'

cwi.chik (chwi.cik) 'employment'

co.tay (cho.tay) 'invitation'

ce.nye (che.nye) 'maiden'

sim.ceng (sim.cheng) 'Shimchong'

khim.ci (kim.chi) 'kimchee'

ch for *c* or *cc:*

chong.si.kyey (cong.si.kyey) 'alarm clock'

chal (cal) 'well'

cwi.chik (chwi.cik) 'employment'

chak.nan (cak.nan) 'mischievousness'

toy.chi (twe.ci) 'pig'

che.nyek (ce.nyek) 'evening'

cho.pan (co.pan) 'breakfast'

chil.mwun (cil.mwun) 'question'

sal.chi.ta (sal.cci.ta) 'to gain weight'

(6) *k* for *kh* or *kk:*

man.kum (man.khum) 'as much as'

ken.nyeng (khe.nyeng) 'far from being'

mi.ku.le.wun (mi.kku.le.wun) 'slippery'

sek.ess.ta (sekk.ess.ta) 'mixed'

key (kkey) 'to (someone)'

ceng.seng.kes (ceng.seng.kkes) 'sincerely'

kk for *k:*

ye.le.kka.ci (ye.le.ka.ci) 'many kinds'

han.kka.wun.tey (han.ka.wun.tey) 'center'

mek.ki.ta (mek.i.ta) 'to feed'

co.kki.ccim (co.ki.ccim) 'a kind of cooked fish'

kkay.ta (kay.ta) 'to clear up'

cwuk.ki.ta (cwuk.i.ta) 'to kill'

(7) *s* for *ss:*

sek.ess.ta (ssek.ess.ta) 'rotted'
swu.ley.ki (ssu.ley.ki) 'garbage'
sa.ta (ssa.ta) 'cheap'
nal.si (nal.ssi) 'weather'
ppi.sal (pi.ssal) 'expensive'
pap.seng (phap.ssong) 'pop song'

(8) *n.* for *nn; nn* for *n; m* for *mm:*

ma.na.ta (man.na.ta) 'to meet'
kan.nan.han (ka.nan.han) 'poor'
ken.nyeng (khe.nyeng) 'far from being'
e.ma (em.ma) 'mom'

(9) *l* for *ll*; *ll* for *l*:

ma.la.se (mal.la.se) 'dried, so'
nol.a.o.la (nol.le.o.la) 'to come to play'
kel.e.yo (kel.lye.yo) 'to take'
ta.la.ko (tal.la.ko) 'to give'
ki.wul.li.ta (ki.wu.li.ta) 'to pay attention to'
il.le.nan (il.e.nan) 'rising'
pwu.less. ta (pwul.less.ta) 'called'
o.la.ka (ol.la.ka) 'to climb'
nol.ass.ta (nol.lass.ta) 'was amazed'
wul.ess.ta (wul.lyess.ta) 'rang'
col.lop (col.ep) 'graduation'
pal.li.key (ppa.lu.key) 'fast'

Errors in vowels and semivowels are of the following types.

(10) *e* for *o*; *o* for *e*:

mek (mok) 'neck'
se.cwu (so.cwu) 'Korean whisky'
cel.ep (col.ep) 'graduation'
te (tto) 'again'
hwang.hel (hwang.hol) 'hallucination'
kop (kep) 'scare'
kyel.sok (kyel.sek) 'absence'
e.mo.ni (e.me.ni) 'mother'
ol.kwul (el.kwul) 'face'
tay.o.nan (thay.e.nan) 'to be born'
a.po.ci (a.pe.ci) 'father'
e.lay (o.lay) 'for long'
pap.seng (phap.ssong) 'pop. song'
ttek.ttek.han (ttok.ttok.han) 'smart'
e.cen (o.cen) 'before noon'
to (te) 'more'
col.lop (col.ep) 'graduation'
mok.ul (mek.ul) 'to eat'
tto (te) 'more'
um.sik.com (um.sik.cem) 'restaurant'
te.lo.we (te.le.we) 'dirty'

(11) *e* for *u*; *u* for *e*:

sse.ta (ssu.ta) 'to use'
mwu.sen (mwu.sun) 'what kind of'
ne.me (ne.mwu) 'too much'
pwu.lel.they.ni (pwu.lul.they.ni)
se.twu.le.ta (se.twu.lu.ta) 'to hurry'
ta.len (ta.lun) 'other'
ke.ne.li.ta (ke.nu.li.ta) 'to lead'
key.e.lu.ta (key.u.lu.ta) 'lazy'

'as I will call'

sup.sup.han (sep.sep.han) 'sorry'	e.ttun (e.tten) 'some kind of'
nu.mwu (ne.mwu) 'too much'	si.phu.leh.key (si.phe.leh.key) 'dark blue'

(12) *u* for *wu*; *wu* for *u*:

um.cik.i.ta (wum.cik.i.ta) 'to move'	hum.chi.ta (hwum.chi.ta) 'to steal'
han.sul (han.swul) 'one spoonful'	swi.u.ni.kka (swi.wu.ni.kka) 'easy, so'
ttung.ttung.han (ttwung.ttwung.han) 'fat'	nun (nwun) 'eye'
ku ppun (ku ppwun) 'only that'	ku pun (ku pwun) 'he'
sul (swul) 'liquor'	ku.lum (kwu.lum) 'clouds'
na.ppwun (na.ppun) 'bad'	kkakk.wu.myen (kkakk.u.myen) 'if you cut'
swul.ley.ki (ssu.ley.ki) 'garbage'	mek.wul (mek.ul) 'to eat'
kwu.li.we (ku.li.we) 'longing for'	phyeng.hwa.swu.lep.ta (phyeng.hwa.su.lep.ta) 'peaceful'
e.nwu (e.nu) 'which'	me.mwu.lwu.ta (me.mwu.lu.ta) 'to stay'
kwu.man.twu.ta (ku.man.twu.ta) 'to stop doing'	ka.wul (ka.ul) 'autumn'
nul.e.ttwu.li.ta (nul.e.ttu.li.ta) 'to hang down'	

(13) *o* for *wu*; *wu* for *o*:

ssa.ol (ssa.wul) 'to fight'	wun.thong (on.thong) 'totally'
cheng.swu (cheng.so) 'cleaning'	

(14) *ey* for *ay*; *ay* for *ey*:

cey.mi (cay.mi) 'interest'	sey.kka.mah.key (say.kka.mah.key) 'pitch-dark'
chil.key.wel (chil.kay.wel) 'seven months'	sey.to.lok (say.to.lok) 'until dawn'
twu.ccey (twu.ccay) 'second'	cap.chey (cap.chay) 'chop suey'
say.kwan (sey.kwan) 'customs'	cay.il (cey.il) 'first'
pel.lay (pel. ley) 'worm'	cay.tay (cey.tay) 'military discharge'
cay.cwu.to (cey.cwu.to) 'Cheju Island'	sil.lyay (sil.lyey) 'rudeness'
o.kayss (o.keyss) 'will come'	swu.lay.ki (ssu.ley.ki) 'garbage'

(15) a for *e*:

si.ham (si.hem) 'exam'	chin.cal (chin.cel) 'kindness'

col.ap (col.ep) 'graduation' ywu.an (ywu.en) 'dying will'
yang.hwa (yeng.hwa) 'movie' kkay.ass.ta (kay.ess.ta) 'cleared up'

(16) semivowels:
cwu.ess.ta (chwu.wess.ta) 'was cold' swi.e.yo (swi.we.yo) 'easy'
ttwu.e.kass.ta (ttwi.e.kass.ta) 'ran' kel.e.yo (kel.lye.yo) 'to take'
toy.chi (tway.ci) 'pig' to.chi (to.chwi) 'intoxication'

The error patterns presented in (3) through (16) are attributable to the following three types of confusion: (a) confusion between lax [−tense, −aspirate], aspirated [+tense, +aspirate], and tensed [+tense, −aspirate] consonants; (b) confusion between single and double nasals and laterals; and (c) confusion regarding vowel features. These confusions appear to be caused, by and large, by phonological interference from English. i.e., by the mismatch in sound patterns between the two languages.

The three series of Korean consonants are all phonemic; they are voiceless except that the lax stops *p*, *t*, *c*, and *k* become voiced allophonically between voiced sounds. In English, on the other hand, the two features [tense] and [aspirate] are not significant, being functional merely for allophonic variations, while the feature [voice], which is not significant in Korean, is phonemic in English. Observe the following phonological mismatches between the two languages, as illustrated by *p*- and *s*-series.[5]

(17)
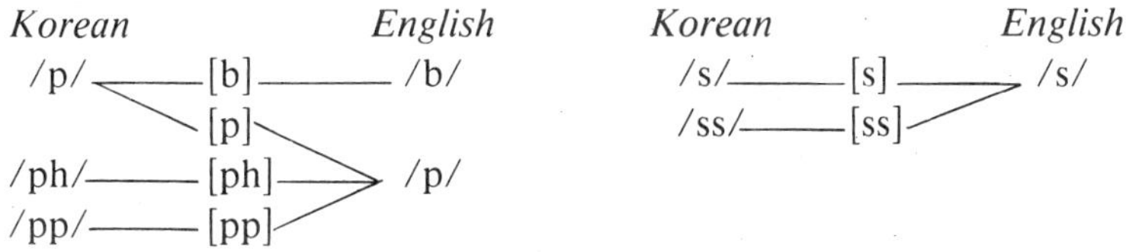

As for the confusion in the use of double and single *m*, *n*, and *l*, it seems to be due to the fact that English sound patterns do not allow significant double consonants to occur within words. Thus, even doubly spelled nasals or laterals are pronounced singly, as in *summer, summit, flannel, tunnel, pill, billow,* and *ellipsis.* English speakers have difficulty in perceiving and producing the difference between a single phoneme and the corresponding double one in Korean.

The confusions related to vowels are also attributable to the mismatch in sound features. The quality of Korean *ay* is somewhere between the qualities of English *e* in *end* and *a* in *ant*. English /o/ hardly occurs without being followed by [w] quality, which fact seems to cause English speakers to perceive the monotonous Korean *o* wrongly as Korean *e* (/ə/) or sometimes even as *wu* (/u/) and vice versa. Similarly, phonetic closeness and free variation between English [ə] (equivalent to Korean *e*) and [ʌ] (equivalent to Korean *a*) in such words as *just, but,* and *mother* may be responsible for the occasional confusion between Korean *a* and *e*. English /ɨ/ (equivalent to Korean *u*) occurs rarely if at all, hence the confusion between *u* and *wu* or between *u* and *e*. Students' errors in vowels may be schematized as in (18).

(18)

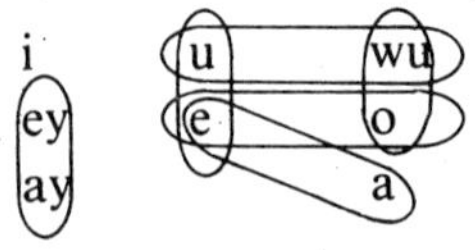

It has been observed that interference or language transfer from English is the strongest in the area of phonology, as reflected in students' spelling errors.

4. Errors in Lexicon

This section will be limited to the errors made in regard to content words and their meanings, with the discussion of function words (particles) and affixes relegated to Sections 5 and 6.

A sporadic, trivial, and largely transient set of lexical errors includes mistakenly used terms many of which are non-sensical, as illustrated below. (Correct forms are given in parentheses.)

(19)

cwung.i (cwung) 'monk'	yey.ki (ay.ki) 'child'
ko (ha.ko) 'and'	thong.hwa (thong.kwa) 'passage'
ma.twung (ma.lwu) 'floor'	i.cum.tong.an (yo.cum) 'these days'
na.ta (nah.ta) 'to give birth to'	mi.cci.ta (mwukk.i.ta) 'to be tied'
ttu.li.ta (ttu.ta) 'to open eyes'	wul.um.ha.ta (wul.ta) 'to cry'
swip.ta (swi.ta) 'to rest'	ay.ceng.ha.ta (sa.lang.ha.ta) 'to love'
cung.ka.hay.ci.ta (cung.ka.ha.ta) 'to increase'	cec.e.ci.ta (cec.ta) 'to get wet'
ppal.li.key (ppa.lu.key) 'fast'	hung.pwun.na.ta (hung.pwun.ha.ta) 'to get excited'
kkok (kot) 'soon'	

A more significant and widespread set of lexical errors includes those words which are either used erroneously or fail to be used in various syntactic constructions. Observe, for example, the incorrect sentence in (20a), whose correct counterpart is given in (20b).

(20) a. Nam.ca ka khun ka.pang ha.ko ki.cha.pang.an ey tul.ess.e wass.up.ni.ta.
b. *E.nu* nam.ca ka khun ka.pang *ul tul.ko yek tay.hap.sil* ey tul.e wass.up.ni.ta.
'A man with a big bag entered the waiting room of a railroad station.'

Notice in particular that the erroneous use of *ha.ko* 'with' to mean 'carrying' in (20a) is obviously due to the English usage of the word 'with'. The Korean particle *ha.ko* does not have the meaning of 'carrying'. The other errors in the example sentence are largely developmental, reflecting the student's immaturity in the learning process. In the following are presented lexical errors under several categories. In the examples given, the lexical items in question are italicized.

4.1. Errors in nouns

Students frequently choose wrong nouns in given constructions. In many cases, the nouns chosen share certain definitional or associated semantic components with the correct forms, as illustrated in (21).

(21) a. na.ppwun *cil* (*cis*) 'bad *behavior'*
b. nuc.un ka.wul *ha.lwu ey* (ka.ul *e.nu nal*) *'one day* in late autumn'
c. *hays.pich* (*hays.pyeth*) ey nwup.u.ni.kka (nwu.wu.ni.kka)
'when we lay down in *the sunshine'*
d. 20 pwun.kan ey (uy) *hywu.ka* lul (*hywu.sik* ul) ha.ca.ma.ca
'as soon as we took *a rest* for twenty minutes'
e. chwi.hal *mwu.lep ey* (chwi.hal *ttay*) wun.cen.ha.myen
'if you drive *when* you are drunk'
f. I sey.sang *a.mwu.kes* (*mwu.es; e.nu.kes*) po.ta.to noph.i ka cey.il mwu.se.we.yo.
'I fear height more than *anything* else in this world.'
g. Yel.sim.hi kong.pwu.ha.myen si.hem ul hap.kyek.ha.nun *phen* (*pep*) i.ta.
'It's *a rule* that if you study hard you will pass the exam.'
h. Hang.sang nong.tam ul han *tays.ka* lo (*thas* ulo) cey chin.kwu.tul un na lul mi.we.hay.yo.
'*Due to* my telling jokes all the time, my friends don't like me.'

Students produce many sentences where appropriate nouns are missing.

Frequently, such missing words are due to interference from English. Observe the following examples.

(22) a. Ha.nu.nim ey (ha.nu.nim *ttus/myeng.lyeng* ey) uy.ha.ye Yey.swu ka ci.kwu ey wass.ta.
'Jesus came to the earth following God's *will/command.'*

b. Na.mwu ey (na.mwu *wi* lul) chye.ta po.ass.e.yo.
'He looked *up* the tree.'

c. Cey.pi.tul un ma.tang ey (ma.tang *wi* lul) han pa.khwi tol-ass-ta.
'The swallows made a circle *above* the yard.'

d. Ai.tul lo (ai.tul *kyeth* ulo) ci.na.kap.ni.ta.
'They pass *by* some children.'

e. E.ma. han.they (em.ma *mal* ul) cal tul.e.la.
'Listen to your mother carefully.'

f. Mop.si twu.lye.wun kyeng.wu ey.nun (*o.cum i*) ma.lye.we.ci.ki il.sswu.yey.yo.
'If you are very scared, it's common that you feel like using the bathroom.'

Notice in (22b, 22c, 22d) that English prepositions are reflected as nouns in Korean and in (22e, 22f) that English does not have words that correpond to *mal* 'words' and *o.cum* 'urine'. In cases like these, students tend to leave out the nouns in expressing Korean sentences.

4.2. Errors in verbs

Verbs are either action or descriptive. Examples of errors regarding the use of action verbs are given in (23).

(23) a. Hwa.mwul.yel.cha nun Se.wul ey (lo) swi.ci anh.ko *hyang. hay*ss.ta (*tal. ly*ess.ta).
'The train *headed* for Seoul without stopping.'

b. Un.hayng ey ton ul *pat.*u.lo (*chac.*ule) kass.ta.
'I went to the bank to withdraw some money.'

c. ka.nung.ha.myen hen la.ti.o lul *hoy.pok.ha.*ko (*swu.li.ha.* ko)...
'I will *fix* the old radio if possible, and ...'

d. sen.sayng.nim i ce ey.key cil.mwun ul *mwul.e pol swu iss.* ki cen ey (*ha.si.*ki cen ey)
'before the professor *asks* me a question'

e. Ai lul thong.ha.ye pwu.mo ka coh.un ci *pol* (*al*) swu iss.e.yo.

'Through their children, we can see whether the parents are good.'

f. Il ul *chac.a ka*.ta.ka (*chac*.ta.ka) *phi.kon.ha*.ko (*ci.chi*.ko) mal.ass.up.ni.ta.
'While *looking for* a job, he got completely *exhausted.*'

g. Ku nun *hayng.pok.hal* (*hayng.pok.hay.cil*) sayng.kak man ha.myen.se so.cwu lul ma.syess.e.yo.
'Thinking only about *becoming happy,* he drank the *socwu* liquor.'

h. Pak i cwu.leng cwu.leng *cal.a.na*ss.e.yo (*yel.lye*ss.e.yo).
'Gourds were *hanging* in clusters.'

i. Nay.il un hak.kyo ey an.*ta.nil* swu (an.*ka*l swu) eps.e.yo.
'I must *go* to school tomorrow.'

j. Ppo.ppo *pat.a.cwu*.nun (*pat*.un) cuk nwun i mak ping.ping tol.a.yo.
'My eyes spun when I *received* a kiss.'

k. Pi ka ol.kka.pwa *kek.ceng.ha.ko mal*.ass.ta (*kek.ceng i toy*.ess.ta).
'I was *worried* that it would rain.'

As noticed in the examples, some errors are due to the poor knowledge about the semantic components inherent in the verbs involved. In (23a), for example, *hyang.ha.ta* 'to leave toward' does not have a 'locomotion' component, thus being unable to occur with *swi.ci anh.ko* 'without stopping'. Similarly, *ca.la.na.ta* 'to grow' in (23h) cannot occur with *cwu.leng cwu.leng* 'in clusters'; *ta.ni.ta* 'to commute' in (23i) which has a 'bi-direction' component cannot occur in the given context. Some other errors appear to be due to interference from English. Choices of such verbs as *pat.ta* 'to get' (23b), *hoy.pok.ha.ta* 'to recover' (23c), *mwul.e po.ta* 'to ask' (23d), and *po.ta* 'to see' (23e) seem to have been prompted by the acceptability of the English translations in parallel English contexts. Still other errors are caused by the immature knowledge about syntactic selectional restrictions. For example, *phi.kon.ha.ta* (descriptive verb) and *ci.chi.ta* (action verb) have approximately the same meaning, yet only the latter is acceptable because the auxiliary verb *mal.ta* 'to end up with' requires its cooccurring verb in the complement to be an action verb. (23g) is another such case, where *sayng.kak.ha.ta* 'to think' requires the preceding verb to be of an action type. As in some other examples, (23j) is a case of overgeneralization. Finally, (23k) seems to be a case of teacher-induced errors, in that the student was asked to make a sentence using *ko mal.ta.*

A rather productive error pattern is that students use intransitive verbs in the context where transitive verbs are called for, and vice versa. I agree with John Haig (personal communication) who thinks it is interlingual transfer due to the fact that English uses many verbs in both transitive and intransitive contexts, e.g., *open, walk*, and *speak*. Also, two inchoative verbs *toy.ta* 'to become' and *ci.ta* 'to get to be' are easily confused. These are illustrated in (24).[6]

(24) a. Si.hem ul *kkuth.na* (*kkuth.nay*) ki ey.nun ne.mwu si.kan i cek.e.yo.
   'We have too little time left to *finish* the exam.'

b. Hwa lul *na*.kin (*nay*.kin) hayss.ci.man pwul.hap.li.ha.ci nun anh.ass.e.yo.
   'Although I *got mad,* I was not unreasonable.'

c. Seng.kong.*toy*.ko (seng.kong.*ha*.ko) nakk.cey.*toy*.nun (nak.cey.*ha*.nun) kes un no.lyek ey tal.lye.iss.up.ni.ta.
   'Whether you *succeed* or *fail* depends on the efforts you make.'

d. Sa.ko. ka na.se sang.che lul *ip.hin* (*ip.un*) thas ulo cwuk.ko mal.ass.e.yo.
   'He *got* injured in the accident and ended up dying.'

e. Kyeng.cey seng.cang.lywul i yen.phyeng.kywun 9% *i.lwuk. hay*ss.ta (*i.lwuk.toy*ss.ta).
   'As for the rate of economic growth, 9% has been *achieved.*'

f. Ku pwun i *ci.lwu.hay.ha.*myen (*ci.lwu.hay.ci.*myen) na.mwu lul kkakk.kon.hay.yo.
   'When he *gets bored,* he usually cuts wood.'

g. *Khu.key toyl* (*khe.cil*) mok.cek ulo 'in order to *grow tall*'

h. E.mi kay.kwu.li uy pyeng.sey nun cem.cem sim.hay *tway*ss. up.ni.ta (*cy*ess.up.ni.ta).
   'The mother frog's sickness gradually *became* worse.'

i. Ca.tong.cha lul ppal.li wun.cen.ha.ni.kka *celm*.un kes (*celm.e cin* kes) kath.a.yo.
   'Since I drive fast, I feel like *being young.*'

Non-use or partial use of certain action or existential verbs is also observed very extensively. Observe the examples in (25).

(25) a. nac.cam ul (nac.cam ul *ca.ki*) si.cak.hal ttay.ma.ta
   'Whenever I began to *take* a nap'

b. Pakk ey *kal* (*na.kal*) mwu.lyep ey pi ka wass.e.yo.

'Around the time when I was going *out,* it started to rain.'

c. Son.nim i o.myen pang.cwung (pang.ka.wun.tey) ey anc. nun (anc.a *iss*.nun) kes i mwe.yo?
'When guests come, what *is sitting* right at the center of a room?'

d. Ku ca.tong.cha ka ku pwuni ka.ci.nun (ka.ci.ko *iss*.nun) ca.tong.cha ey mos.ci anh.key coh.a.yo.
'That car is no less good than the one he *has.*'

e. Kum.ton ulo ka.tuk ka.tuk tul.ess.up.ni.ta (tul.e *iss*.up.ni.ta).
'It *is filled* with gold money.'

f. Ku.nyang ka.myen e.ttay.se kkoch ul ta sa.ko (sa *ka.ci.* ko) kass.ess.ni?
'You could have gone there without *buying* flowers.'

(25a) is a case where cognate verbs are left out. The other examples represent instances where significant helping or auxiliary verbs are left out. Many Korean verbs seem to "slice" the universe of action more minutely than English verbs do and usually do not contain the state resulting from an action as their definitional semantic component.

Errors in the use of descriptive verbs are of the following kind.

(26) a. *kyel.ceng.cek.in* (*kyel.tan.cek.in*) sa.lam 'a decisive person'

b. Ton ul 10 pwul ilh.e.se *se.wun.hay*.yo (*ek.wul.hay*.yo).
'I feel distressed because I have lost $10.'

c. Nayng.myen uy mas i na.ppun.tey.ta.ka naym.say.ma.ce *him i iss*.e.yo (*na.ppa*.yo; *tok.hay*.yo).
'Cold noodles don't taste good. Moreover, the smell is *strong.*'

d. We.nak *ka.nung.ha.nun* (*nung.lyek.iss.nun*) tey.ta.ka *ki.swul. ta.wun* (*ki.swul.iss.nun*) sen.swu ip.ni.ta.
'He is a very *able* player. In addition, he is *skillful.*'

e. *Kong.san.cwu.uy ceng.pwu ey pi.ha.ye min.cwu.cwu.uy ceng. pwu ka ha.nul na.la in kes mo.yang.i*.yey.yo (*kath*.a.yo).
'Compared with a communist government, a democratic government *seems* to be a paradise.'

f. O.nul ey.nun (o.nul un) an.kay kkin nal.si (nal.ssi) *iss*.up.ni.ta (*i*p.ni.ta).
'It *is* foggy today.'

g. Mal ul tha.ko iss.u.ni.kka kyeng.ma uy ki.swu *iss*.nun kes (*in* kes) kath.a.yo.

'Since I am riding horseback, I feel like being a jockey.'

h. Sayng.cen pap ul kwulm.un sa.lam tus.i (sa.lam *in* tus.i) pap ul mek.ess.up.ni.ta.
   'He ate rice as if he were a person who had starved for life.'

(26a, 26b, 26e) illustrate wrong choices of descriptive verbs, which is a phenomenon quite common even among advanced students. Errors in (26c, 26d) are caused by English influence. Similarly, errors in (26f, 26g) are due apparently to American students' confusion between the existential verb *iss* and the copula *i* which both correspond to 'be' in English. (26h) also represents another frequent pattern, where the copula is left out due probably to its low communicative content and the existence of a Ø allomorph.

Another common lexico-syntactic error pattern is associated with the use of psychological or emotional verbs. Confusions are between psychological verbs, which take first person subjects in declarative sentences, and their *ha*-attached counterparts, where the 'auxiliary' verb *ha* means 'shows the sign of' and which are used with non-first person subjects. Clearly, it is an interlingual transfer error in that English does not have such a distinction.

(27) a. Ku pwun un ip.wen.han tus.i *pwul.an.ha*.ko (*pwul.an.hay ha*.ko) iss.ess.e.yo.
   'He was *uneasy* as if he were hospitalized.'

b. Ku i nun mayk.cwu lul coh.a ha.ki nun khe.nyeng *silh*.e.yo (*silh.e hay*.yo).
   'Far from liking it, he *hates* beer.'

c. Kim.sen.sayng un a.i.tul i pa.ta ey ka.ko *siph*.e.se (*siph.e hay*.se) pa.ta lo kal kyey.hoyk ip.ni.ta.
   'Mr. Kim plans to go to the sea, since his children *want* to go there.'

d. Yek.sa kyo.kwa.se lul ilk.e pon cuk *silh.e hayss*.e.yo (*silh*.ess.e.yo).
   'After I read the history textbook, I did*n't like* it.'

e. So.nyen.tul un pwu.mo.nim i po.ko *siph.e hay*.se (po.ko *siph*.e.se) thong.kok.hayss.ta.
   'The boys cried, *missing* their parents.'

4.3. Errors in adverbials

As for adverbial-related errors, students not only use wrong adverbials, as in (28), but also leave out essential ones, as in (29).

(28) a. Mok.cek.ci ey *cik.cep.cek ulo* (*cik.cep; kot.cang*) kass.ta.

'We went to our destination *directly.*'

b. *Pa.po.key* (*pa.po.su.lep.key*) ton ul ssu.ta.ka nun ka.nan.hay toy.keyss.kwun.yo (ka.nan.hay ci.keyss.kwun.yo).
'If I use money *in a silly way,* I am sure I will become poor.'

c. *O.lay.tong.an* (*o.lays.man ey*) pwu.mo.nim pwass.u.ni.kka ki.ppul tta.lum i.ta.
'Since I saw my parents *after a long time,* I feel extremely happy.'

d. Swu.ep i *el.ma.na* (*phek*) hon.tong.ha.ni.kka (hon.tong.toy.ni.kka)...
'Since the class is *extremely* confusing, ...'

e. Sin.mwun ul ilk.ul ttay ey *che.um ulo* (*che.um*) mwu.sun ki.sa lul ilk.e.yo?
'When you read newspapers, which column do you read *first*?'

f. Tal i *el.manna* (*phek*) a.lum.tap.kwun.yo!
'How beautiful the moon is!'

(29) a. Swul i.la.nun swul ul (*ta*) ma.syess.e.yo.
'I drank *all* kinds of liquor.'

b. Sa.cin i.la.nun sa.cin ul (*mo.twu ta*) pwass.e.yo.
'I saw *all* the pictures.'

c. Kim.chi la.ko.nun (*cenhye*) coh.a.ha.ci anh.a.yo.
'I don't like kimchee *at all.*'

4.4. Errors in Sino-Korean collocations

Although infrequent, students often mix Sino-Korean and pure Korean in lexical collocations. Errors are also found in the use of Sino-Korean numerative compounds. These are illustrated in the following.

(30) a. *pang.cwung* ey (*pang ka.wun.tey* ey) 'at *the center of the room*'

b. *ney.nyen toyn kkuth* ey (*sa.nyen hwu* ey) 'at *the end of four years*'

c. han il to (*ha.lwu* to) 'even *a single day*'

d. *i.sip.sam.tal* man.ey (*i.sip.sam.kay.wel* man.ey) 'after 23 months'

e. *sam.kay.pan.nyen* (*sam.nyen.pan; sam.kay.nyen.pan*) 'three and a half years'

5. Errors in Morphology

The majority of morphological errors are associated with verbal endings. Only some sporadic occurrences of errors are observable in other word classes such as nouns. Most of the errors are due to choosing wrong allomorphs. Morphological errors are classified into the following several types, most of which are quite productive. From this section on, syllable boundaries (dots) will not be marked. Instead, relevant morpheme boundaries will be marked by hyphens.

5.1. Use of wrong modifier endings

This is the most frequently occurring pattern, of which there are several sub-types as shown in the following.

(31) a. pihayngki ka khu-*nun* (khu-*n*) panmyen ey 'while planes are big'
keyulu-*nun* (keyulu-*n*) haksayng 'lazy student'
cilwuha-*nun* (cilwuha-*n*) tey 'since it is boring'
pwucokha-*nun* (pwucokha-*n*) kes 'insufficient thing'
chincelha-*nun* (chincelha-*n*) hayngtong 'kind act'
singsing anha-*nun* (singsing anha-*n*) sayngsen 'stale fish'

b. ton i eps-*un* (eps-*nun*) cwucey ey 'in the miserable situation that he does not have any money'
chayk i eps-*un* (eps-*nun*) chay 'without having a book'
toyl swu iss-*un* (iss-*nun*) kes 'the thing that can be done'

c. masi-*lul* (masi-*l*) man han 'drinkable'
sihem chi-*ul* (chi-*l*) swu issnun 'can take a test'
Phalah-*ul* (phala-*l*) kes ita. 'It will be blue.'

d. hankwuk ey *ka-ss-nun* (ka-*n*) kipwun 'the feeling that I went to Korea'
sako ka na-ss-*nun* (na-*n*) kes 'the fact that there was an accident'
pwul-ul khy-ess-*nun* (khye-*n*) swunkan 'the moment that I turned on light'

e. tu-*n* (tul-*ess-ul*) ttay 'when I heard it'
nemwu masi-*n* (masy-*ess-ul*) mangceng 'although he drank too much'

Examples in (31a) share the error that descriptive verbs are suffixed with the present modifier ending form *-nun* on the analogy of the form that action verbs take. In (31b), on the other hand, students use the descriptive verb ending form erroneously for the existential verbs, which happen to share the same ending form with action verbs. Errors in (31c) illustrate cases where wrong allomorphs of the prospective modifier ending *-l* are used. Errors in (31d) are examples where the wrong past modifier ending *-ss-nun* is used on the analogy of such constructions as *ka-ss-nun tey* '(I) went there but' and *ka-ss-nun ci* 'whether (he) went'. Finally, (31e) presents exceptional cases where certain time or other nouns allow the preceding verb to take only *tense* + *-(u)l,* not *-nun* or *-(u)n.*

5.2. *l*-related errors

Verb stem-final *l* behaves like a vowel in certain morphological contexts and gets deleted in certain other constructions. Verb stem-final *lu* loses *u* before an infinitive suffix and the remaining *l* gets doubled compensatorily. Students without knowledge of such rules tend to make errors, as shown in (32).

(32) a. congsikyey ka wul-*umyen* (wul-*myen*) 'when the alarm clock rings'
pil-*umyen* (pil-*myen*) 'if (we) pray'
kamki ka tul-*umyen* (tul-*myen*) 'if (we) catch a cold'.
b. *no*-myen (*nol*-myen) 'if (we) play'
no-kon (*nol*-kon) hay-yo '(he) usually plays'
c. kamki *tul*-un (*tu*-n) haksayng 'a student who has caught a cold'
ttwinol-un (*ttwino*-n) ai 'a child who played around'
al-asey-yo (*a*-sey-yo) '(he) knows'
cenhwa lul *kel*-usey-yo (*ke*-sey-yo) 'please call (me)'
d. mok i *malu*-ese (*mall*-ase) 'since (I am) thirsty'

Notice in particular that (32b) is a case of overgeneralization by analogy with such correct forms as those in (32c).

5.3. Errors related to the infinitive suffix

Students frequently leave out the infinitive suffix (*a, e,* or *ye*) after a verb stem. Some students even insert the suffix where it is not needed. These are illustrated in (33).

(33) a. kippu ci-n-ta (kipp-*e* ci-n-ta) '(I am) getting happy.'
kenkangha ci-n-ta (kenkangha-*ye* ci-n-ta) '(I am) getting healthier.'
al po-ta (al-*a* po-ta) 'to inquire about'
kyothong i nuli cy-ess-e-yo (nuly-*e* cy-ess-e-yo) 'The traffic has become slow.'

maykcwu lul kaci o-ki lul (kaci-*e* o-ki lul) cal hay-ss-ta
'It's good that we have brought beer.'
kyengcey ka nappu ci-n (napp-*a* ci-n) thas ulo
'because the economic situation has become worse'
kochi tala-ko (kochi-*e* talla-ko) 'to fix it for him'

b. sihemchi-ss-nun tey (sihemchi-*e*ss-nun-tey) '(I) took an exam, but'
sihem ul ci-ya (chy-*e*ya) ha-nta '(I) have to take an exam.'
isaha-ss-e-yo (isaha-*ye*ss-e-yo) '(I) have moved.'

c. ppang ul kacy-*e*-ko (kaci-ko) ka-ss-e-yo '(He) took the bread.'
ka pw*a*-nun kes (ka po-nun kes) 'our going and seeing'
hay po-ko mos hay pw*a*-nun kes (po-nun kes) 'whether (you) try or not'

5.4. Copula-related errors

There are two sub-patterns involved here: (a) use of the wrong copulative allomorph (*i* or *Ø*) and (b) use of *i-n-ta* instead of the correct form *i-la* in quotative constructions.

(34) a. yeca *i*-myen (yeca-myen) 'if she is a woman'
khulisumasu *i*-la-n (khulisumasu-la-n) 'what is called Christmas'
ywukkwun yeca *i*-la-ko-nun (yeca-la-ko-nun) 'as for the Army women'
pothong-yey-yo (pothong *i*-yey-yo) '(It's) normal.'
etten-n umsik-la-to (umsik *i*-la-to) 'any food'
mwusun sihem-la-to (sihem *i*-la-to) 'any exam'

b. ku sosik i sasil *i-n-ta*-nun kes (sasil *i-la*-nun kes)
'the fact that the news is true'
ku kes i te coh-un kes *i-n-ta*-ko (coh-un kes *i-la* ko) sayngkak-hay-ss-ci-man
'although (I) thought that it was better'
onul un welyoil i-n-ta-nikka (welyoil i-la-nikka)
'I told you today is Monday.'

5.5. Errors in irregular verbs

Only one error is found with regard to *t*-irregular verbs (35a). All the others are related to *p*-irregular verbs (35b).

(35) a. umak ul *tut*-umyen (*tul*-umyen) 'when (I) listen to music'
b. hays pich ey *nwup*-unikka (hays pyeth ey *nwuw*-unikka)

'when (I) lay down in the sun'
ttukep-ul taylo (*ttukew*-ul taylo) 'extremely hot'
pankap-ul ttalum i-ta (*pankaw*-ul ttalum i-ta) 'only happy'
mikkule-myen (*mikkulew*-umyen) 'if it's slippery'
mikkule-se (*mikkulew*-ese) 'since it's slippery'
elyee-se (*elyew*-ese) 'since it's difficult'
swiu-nikka (*swiw*-unikka) 'because it's easy'

5.6. Errors in case particle allomorphs

Only the following four cases are found. Notice that all of them belong to the same pattern.

(36) wenswungi *kwa* (wa) na 'the monkey and I'
yeca *kwa* (*wa*) namca 'women and men'
hankwuk maykcwu *kwa* (*wa*) mikwuk maykcwu 'Korean beer and American beer'
hankwuk wuncenswu *kwa* (*wa*) mikwuk wuncenswu 'Korean drivers and American drivers'

5.7. Other sporadic errors

Some morphological errors are either not recurrent or unique to certain individuals. The following are about all that are found.

(37) *ce* (*cey*) ka 'I (as subject)'
nwukwu *nwu* ka (nwukwu *nwukwu* ka) 'who and who (as subject)'
nay nun (*na* nun) 'as for me'
seys pyeng (*sey* pyeng) 'three bottles'
kongpwuha-*sup*-nita (kongpwuha-*p*-nita) '(I) study.'
phyenciha-*sup*-ni-ta (phyenciha-*p*-nita) '(I) write a letter.'
kamsaha-*p*-ci-man (kamsaha-ci-man) 'thank you but'
Kukcang ey *anh*-ka-p-nikka (*an*-ka-p-nikka)? 'Aren't you going to the movies?'
Ne ilk-ki-n way ilk-*uni* (ilk-*ni*)? 'Why are you reading?'

As has been observed thus far, morphological errors are the least vulnerable to interference. This seems to be particularly true because English and Korean rarely share any morphological characteristics. That is, their morphological structures are so dissimilar to each other that there are few things that may be confused by language transfer. Most of the errors observed are cases of overgeneralization in its broad sense.

6. Errors in Syntax

Errors in syntax are the most frequent, varied, and extensive. They may be grouped under word-order, case markers and delimiters, tense, negation, clause conjunction, nominalization, and complementation. Among these, case marking errors and wrong uses of conjunctive endings recur most frequently.

6.1. Word-order

Despite the difference in basic word order between English (SVO) and Korean (SOV), advanced students in Korean rarely make mistakes in syntagmatically arranging words, unless the sentence structure in question is of a complex embedding type. The following are about all that are found.

(38) a. *Ta sikkwu-tul* (*sikkwu-tul ta*) mek-ki eynun umsik i ceksup-ni-ta.
'The food is not enough for *all the family* to eat.'
Cikum *an kongpwuha-l* swu (*kongpwu an ha-l* swu) eps-eyo.
'I cannot but study now.'
Ku haksayng i *mos kongpwuha-n* thas ulo (*kongpwu mos ha-n* thas ulo) nakceyha-ko mal-ass-up-ni-ta.
'The student failed because he *didn't study hard.*'
Swulyen i *paltal mwuchek toy*-ess-ta (*mwuchek paltal-toy*-ess-ta).
'The training *improved a lot.*'
Seys-pyeng socwu lul (*socwu sey-pyeng* ul) masy-ess-ta.
'I drank three bottles of *socwu.*'
Isanghan mal ul *acwumeni uy tongney nun cip ey* pwuthe (*tongneys cip acwumeni lo* pwuthe) tul-ess-ta.
'She heard a strange story from a woman of a neighboring house.'
76 nyen 5 wel 9 il seki (*seki 76 nyen 5 wel 9 il*)
'May 9, 1976 A.D.'

b. Hungpwu nun *mwukk-in tali ey* (*tali ey mwukk-in*) hengkeph ul po-ass-ta.
'Hungpwu saw a piece of cloth *tied around its leg.*'
Manul kwa sswuk un ssu-ko maywe-se *elyew-un mek-ul* ppwun tele (*mek-ki elyew-ul* ppwun tele) yang mace cek-eyo.
'Garlic and mugwort were not only *hard to eat* because they were bitter and hot, but also small in quantity.'
Seysikan kitali-n ci man ey (*kitali-n ci seysikan* man ey) na nun

cip eyse (ey) tol-a ka-ss-eyo.
'I went back home *after I waited for three hours.'*
Etten yein ul ep-un ai-tul lo (*ai lul ep-un etten yein-tul* kyeth ulo) cina ka-p-ni-ta.
'They pass by *some mothers with children on their back.*'
Pwuin un cip ey iss-ten (*cip ey iss-ten pwuin un*) namphyen ul poca maca acwu nol-ass-up-ni-ta.
'As soon as *his wife, who had remained in the house,* saw her husband, she was very amazed.'

Errors in (38a) occur in simplex sentences, whereas those in (38b) involve sentence embedding. In simplex sentences, placement of adverbials in wrong positions is the most common.

6.2. Case markers and delimiters

Errors in case marking are the most frequent in occurrence among the syntactic categories. Errors are made most often by using wrong case particles but sometimes even by using a case particle where a delimiter is called for or vice versa, as shown in (39). Notice that the nominative particle *ka/i* and the accusative particle (*l*)*ul* are most frequently confused.

(39) *Errors in the use of case particles*
a. (*l*)*ul* instead of *ka/i* (45 times)
(*n*)*un* 'as for' (5)
to 'also' (4)
Ø (4)
ey 'at, to' (2)
b. *ka/i* instead of (*l*)*ul* (26 times)
(*n*)*un* (9)
to (3)
Ø (2)
c. *ey* instead of (*l*)*ul* (14 times)
eyse 'at, from' (10)
(*u*)lo 'to' (6)
ka/i (4)
Ø (4)
eykey 'at, to (human)' (2)
d. *eyse* instead of *ey* (5 times)
e. (*u*)*lo* instead of *ey* (2 times)
f. (*n*)*un* instead of *ka/i* (7 times)

Ø (3)
(*l*)*ul* (2)

g. Ø instead of (*l*)*ul* (16 times)
ka/i (12)

Sentences illustrating (39) are given in (40), where (40a) through (40g) match with (39a) through (39g) respectively.

(40) a. Nwun i o-nun kwangkyeng *ul* (*i; un*) alumtaw-eyo.
'The sight of snowing is beautiful.'
Hwa ka na-myen nwunmwul *ul* (*i*) na-o-p-ni-ta.
'When I get angry, I cry.'
Os *ul* (*i*) cec-umyen chwuw-e ci-kon ha-p-ni-ta.
'You usually feel cold when your clothes get wet.'
Cha *lul* (*ka*) kocang i na-ss-ese (na-se) pesu lul tha-ko wa-ss-eyo.
'Since my car was broken, I came by bus.'
Menimeni hay-to kongpwuha-nun kes *ul* (*i*) ceyil cwungyoha-p-ni-ta.
'No matter what you say, studying is the most important thing.'
Socwu *lul* (*nun*) swul cwung uy swul i-ta.
'*Socwu* is the best of all liquors.'
Ku say *lul* (*nun*) yeyppu-ko soli *lul* (*ka*) acwu alumtaw-eyo.
'The bird is pretty and its voice is very beautiful.'
Na nun yakha-ciman etten cimsung *ul* (*to*) iki-l swu iss-eyo.
'I am weak but I can beat any animals.'
Socwu *lul* (Ø) nama masi-p-si-ta.
'Let's drink *socwu* or something.'
Say uy wulum soli *lul* (*ey*) hancham kwi lul kiwully-ess-eyo.
'I listened to the bird singing for a while.'

b. Hwahak tung yelekaci kwamok *i* (*ul*) paywu-p-ni-ta.
'I learn many subjects including chemistry.'
Na nun socwu *ka* (*lul*) ceyil coh-a hay-yo.
'I like *socwu* best.'
Na nun tali *ka* (*lul*) cacwu tachi-p-ni-ta.
'I get my legs hurt frequently.'
Apeci nun ai-tul *i* (*ul*) tayhakkyo ey ponay-ki wiha-ye ton ul cekumhay-yo.
'My father saves money in order to send his children to college.'

Etten salam *i* (*un*) nuc-umyen tally-eyo.
'Some people run if they are late.'
Na nun i seysang etten umsik pota *ka* (*to*) Cajun umsik ceyil coh-ayo.
'I like Cajun food more than any food in the world.'
Kaps *i* (*Ø*) mace pissa-yo.
'Even the price is high.'

c. Hakkyo *ey* (*lul*) colepha-n cuk kipwun i coh-ayo.
'I feel good because I have just graduated from school.'
Holangi nun namwu wi *ey* (*lul*) po-ass-ta.
'The tiger looked up the tree.'
Na nun haypyengtay *ey* (*eyse*) halwu congil swi-ci anh-ko ilhay-ya hay-yo.
'As for me, I must work all day without rest in the Marine Corps.'
Ceypi ka namccok *ey* (*ulo*) nal-a ka-ss-eyo.
'The swallow flew toward the south.'
Cwumal *ey* (*i*) toy-myen swul ul masi-kon ha-p-ni-ta.
'When the weekend comes, I usually drink liquor.'
Nayil *ey* (*Ø*) tungsan ul hay-yo.
'We are going hiking tomorrow.'
Mek-ko mos mek-nun kes un anay *ey* (*eykey*) tally-e iss-ta.
'Whether I can eat it or not depends on my wife.'

d. Na nun cip *eyse* (*ey*) tol-a ka-ss-eyo.
'I went back home.'

e. Sinmwun ul ilk-ul ttay cheum *ulo* (*ey*) mwues ul ilk-eyo?
'When you read a newspaper, what do you read first?'

f. Toklip kinyem-il i-lan mikwuk *un* (*i*) toklipha-n nal i-p-ni-ta.
'Independence Day is the day when America became independent.'
Mikwuk salam *un* (*Ø*) hankwuk salam *un* (*Ø*) ha-l kes epsi kongpwuhay-ss-eyo.
'Regardless of whether they were Americans or Koreans, everybody studied.'
Cemcayngi uy mal i-la-myen khong *un* (*ul*) phath i-la hay-to mit-sup-ni-ta.
'If a fortune-teller says that a yellow bean is a red bean, people just believe it.'

g. Na nun i seysang eti pota to Louisiana (*lul*) ceyil coh-a hay-yo.
'I like Louisiana more than any other place in the world.'
Hanca nun swuhyo (*ka*) manh-un tey-taka paywu-ki ka elyew-eyo.
'Chinese characters are not only numerous but hard to learn.'

The fact that English does not have any marker (except for word order) for nominative and accusative cases seems to be responsible for the extensive confusion between the two cases in Korean. It may also be construed as reflecting English speakers' weak sensitivity to the transitive/intransitive distinction, as pointed out by John Haig (personal communication). Misuse of the other particles is also attributable to syntactic or semantic interference to a considerable extent. Unfortunately, space does not allow a detailed explication.

Notice also in the examples that the two delimiters (*n*)*un* and *to* are frequently confused with the nominative or accusative particle. This is obviously due to students' underlearning of syntactic and semantic properties of these delimiters and/or their rules of usage. For example, (*n*)*un* has both topic and contrastive meanings and usually does not occur with indefinite question words or in embedded sentences. Other than these two, students hardly misused delimiters.

6.3. Tense

Depending on where in a sentence an error is made, one can recognize three types in errors in tense: errors in main clauses, errors in embedded clauses, and errors in conjunctive clauses. These three types are illustrated in (41).

(41) Manwula ko (hako) yengkam i cwumwu-si-*n* tey (cwumwu-si-*nun* tey) totwuk i wa-*ss-ese* (wa-*se*) matwung ey (malwu mith ey) swum-*ess-ess*-ta (swum-*ess*-ta).

'When an old couple was sleeping, a thief came in and hid under the floor.'

In (41), use of the past modifier ending *-n* instead of the present ending *-nun* is a case of an embedded clause error, use of the past suffix *-ss* instead of the present Ø in *wa-se* is a case of a conjunctive clause error, and use of the past perfective *-ess-ess* instead of the simple past in *swum-ess-ta* is a case of a main clause error. The main clause type is further illustrated in (42), the embedded type in (43), and the conjunctive type in (44).

(42) Ku yeca nun cal sayngki-p-ni-ta (sayngky-*ess*-up-ni-ta).
'She is good-looking.'
Ce nun swuyengha-le ka-n cuk mwul i ttattusha-p-ni-ta (ttattushay-*ss*-up-ni-ta).
'I went to swim, and the water was warm.'

(43) Thanksgiving i-lan hananim ey tayha-n kamsaha-*n* (kamsaha-*nun*) nal i-p-ni-ta.
'Thanksgiving is a day when we thank God.'
Cha lul pha-*l* (pha-*n*; pha-*nun*) tey-taka cip mace phal-ayo.
'He not only sold (*or* is selling) his car but is selling his house.'
Komap-ta-ko ha-*n* (ha-*l*) kyelul to eps-i ka pely-ess-eyo.
'He went away without my having chance to thank him.'

(44) Ku ai nun sensayng-nim i kaluchi-nun hywungnay lul nay-*ss*-ko (nay-ko) iss-kwun-yo.
'The child is mimicking the teacher's teaching.'
Cip ey ka-nun kil ey cha lul (ka) kocang i na-*ss*-ese (na-se) pesu lul tha-ss-eyo.
'On my way back home, my car broke down. So I took a bus.'
Hankwuk salam ul pwa-*ss*-unikka (po-nikka) hankwuk ey ka-ss-nun (ka-n) kipwun i-p-ni-ta.
'Since I meet Koreans, I feel like being in Korea.'
Cwi ka cheum sewul ey wa-*ss*-*te*-ni (o-ni) maywu khu-ko pokcap ha-p-ti-ta (pokcap-hay-ss-eyo).
'When the mouse came to Seoul for the first time, he found that Seoul was big and crowded.'

The last example in (44) illustrates cases where the retrospective tense suffix is misused. Tense errors are not very many. A total of 33 are found in the collected data.

6.4. Negation

In addition to the word order errors that we have observed in (38), the following sentences in which negation is improperly used are found.[7]

(45) I seysang ey yocum amwuto mit-ul swu *anh*-ayo (*eps*-eyo).
'Nowadays you can't trust anybody in this world.'
Wuncenha-l swu *mos ha-l* (*eps-ul*) cengto lo kil i mikkulew-eyo.
'The road is so slippery that we cannot drive.'

Ton i (ul) pilly-e cwu-l swu mos ha-n (*eps*-nun) kes un twu mal ha-l kes to eps-eyo.
'Needless to say, I cannot lend money to him.'
Ku ke-l kiekha-l swu *mos hay*-yo (eps-eyo).
'I cannot remember it.'
Cilwuha-n thas ulo socwu lul *mos masi-ci anh*-ayo (*an masi-l swu eps*-eyo).
'Since I am bored, I cannot but drink *socwu.*'
Na nun nayngmyen uy mas ul sih-e ha-ki ey *mos* (*an*) mek-ki-lo maum mek-ess-eyo.
'As I don't like the taste of cold noodles, I made up my mind not to eat them.'
Kongpwuha-ci *anh*-ul (*mos ha*-l) cengto lo umak i sikkulew-eyo.
'The music is so noisy that we can't study.'

Use of *mos* instead of *eps* 'does not have' in (45) is clearly overgeneralization in the target language in that some students who have learned *mos* as 'cannot' use it even in *ha-l swu eps-ta* 'cannot (lit. has no way to do).'

6.5. Clause conjunction

Errors related to clause conjunction are numerous and varied. Most of the errors are found in the use of wrong conjunctive endings that are related semantically to the correct ones in one way or another. Descriptive analysis of such errors would shed light on semantic theory in general and on Korean semantics in particular. Time and space constraints do not allow me to go into it here, however. Suffice it here to present some examples.

(46) a. Use of -(*u*)*u chay* instead of *-ess-ciman,* -(*e*)*se,* -(*u*)*myense,* or -(*u*)*n tey/-ess-nun tey*
Pwuncwuha-*n chay* (pwuncwuhay-*ss-ciman*) camsi swi-ess-eyo.
'Although I was busy, I took a rest for a while.'
Kochung kenmwul ey oll-a ka-*n chay* (oll-a ka-*se*) naylye-ta pwa-ss-eyo.
'I went up a tall building and looked down.'
Wuncen ul mos ha-l cwul al-*un chay* (ha-l cwul mol-*umyense*) cha lul wuncenhay-ss-eyo.
'He drove a car, though he does not know how to drive.'
Ku hwanca uy kenkang i napp-a ci-*n chay* (napp-a cy-*ess-nun tey*) uysa ka kolphuha-le ka-ss-e.

'The patient's health is getting worse, but the doctor went out to play golf.'

Kusalam un khamkhamha-*n chay* (khamkhamha-*n tey*) kong-pwuha-ko iss-eyo.

'That person is studying in the dark.'

b. Use of-*nun/(u)n panmyen ey* instead of *-ciman, -(u)l ppwun ani-la,* or *-ko*

Pihayngki ka khu-*nun panmyen ey* (khu-*ciman*) te ppall-i ka-yo.

'An airplane flies fast though it is big.'

Na nun keyulu-*nun panmyen ey* (keyulu-*l ppwun ani-la*) ha-l maum i eps-eyo.

'I am not only lazy but don't feel like doing it.'

Sosel ul ilk-*un panmyen ey* (*ilk-ko*) yenghwa lul po-ci ma-sey-yo.

'Read novels and don't watch movies.'

c. Use of *-ki ey* or *-killay* instead of *-ki ttaymwun-ey* or *-(e)se*

Ku twul un salangha-*ki ey* (salangha-*ki ttaymwun ey*) kyelhonha-ki lo maum mek-ess-eyo.

'Because they are in love, the two have made up their mind to get married.'

Chinkwu ka wa-ss-*killay* (wa-ss-*ki ttaymwun ey;* wa-*se*) kongpwu mos hay-ss-eyo.

'Since my friends came, I couldn't study.'

d. Use of -(*u*)*nikka instead of -(e)se* and -(*e*)*se* instead of -(*u*)*nikka*

Ku phathi ey (ka) sikkulew-*unikka* (sikkulew-*ese*) ilccik ttena-ss-eyo.

'The party was noisy, so I left early.'

Ku kes i coh-un tey-taka kaps i ssa-*se* (ssa-*nikka*) sa-p-si-ta.

'Let's buy that, because it is not only good but cheap.'

e. Use of *-ko* instead of *-ciman* or *-nun tey*

Ku yoksimcangi halapeci ka (nun) ayki lul (ka) toy-ss-*ko* (toy-ss-*ciman*) tangsin i (un) ton-pellay toy-keyss-eyo.

'That greedy old man became a child, but you would become a money grubber.'

Etten nulk-un pwupwu nun (ka) ca-*ko* (ca-*nun tey*) totwuknom i malwu mis (mith) ey swum-ess-ta.

'An old couple was sleeping and a thief came in and hid under the floor.'

f. Use of *-nun/(u)n cwucey ey* instead of *-nun tey* or *-(e)se*
Kyothong i pwulpyenha-*n cwucey ey* (pwulphyenha-*n tey*) etteh-key cha lul seywu-keyss-eyo?
'Now that the traffic is heavy, how can we park the car?'
Mwusikha-*n cwucey ey* (mwusikhay-*se*) cisi lul cal mos ttala-yo.
'He is ignorant, so he cannot follow the instructions properly.'

g. Use of *-(e)se* instead of *-ko* and *-ko* instead of *-(e)se*
Cemsim ul taycen eyse mek-*ese* (mek-*ko*) ...mokcekci ey ka-ss-ta.
'After we had lunch at Taechon, we proceeded to our destination.'
Pakk ey na-ka-*ko* (na-ka-*se*) mek-ula-ko ha-ko siph-ci anh-ayo.
'I don't want to ask him to go out and eat.'

h. Use of *-(e)se* instead of *-(u)ni* or *-nulako*
Sayngcwi nun Sewul ey (ul) kwukyenghay-*se* (kwukyengha-*ni*) khu-ko pokcaphay-ss-ta.
'When the mouse saw Seoul, he found that it was big and crowded.'
Ku-pwun un ai-tul sicwunghay-*se* (sicwungha-*nulako*) pappu-p-ni-ta.
'She is busy taking care of her children.'

i. Use of *-teni* instead of *-nun tey*
Ku pwun ul umsikcom (umsikcem) eyse po-ass-*teni* (po-ass-*nun tey*) cikum eti ey iss-eyo?
'I saw him at the restaurant. Where is he now?'

6.6. Nominalization

With one exception, as given in (47a), errors in nominalization are all related to *ki*-nominalization, as illustrated in (47b) where the nominalizer *ki* is left out and in (47c) where wrong complementizers are used instead of *ki*.

(47) a. Yeyppu-n yeca ey piha-ye (yeyppu-n yeca *i-m* ey piha-ye) chincal (chincel) ha-ci anh-ayo.
'Compared with her beauty, she is not kind.'

b. Cham nappu-n ene haksayng ttaymwun ey (ene haksayng *i-ki* ttaymwun ey) mayil kongpwuha-ci anh-umyen an toy-p-ni-ta.

'Since I am a terrible language student, I must study every day.'

Na nun nayngmyen ul mek-umyen thoha-nun (thoha-*ki* ka) il-sswu i-p-ni-ta.

'Whenever I eat cold noodles, I throw up.'

c. Ssal sampayk-sek ul tuli-*la-ko* (tuli-*ki* lo) yaksokhay-ss-eyo.

'He promised that he would give him 300 *soks* of rice.'

Chayk ul ilk-*taka* khenyeng (ilk-*ki* nun khenyeng) nol-ass-up-ni-ta.

'Far from reading a book, he just played around.'

Tulek un wuncenha-n *kes* un (wuncenha-*ki* ka) swi-eyo (swiw-eyo).

'It's easy to drive a truck.'

Errors are also found in not observing the selectional restrictions between the nominalized verb and the cooccurring predicate. Observe (48a) where the predicate *ccak i eps-ta* 'has no comparison' requires the nominalized verb to be of a descriptive type and (48b) where the predicate *wiha-ta* 'in order to' requires the nominalized verb to be of an action type.

(48) a. Cey ayin un *cwuk-ki* (e.g., *pwulssangha-ki*) ccak i eps-kwun-yo.

'My wife is extremely pitiful.'

Chevy catongcha nun *coh-a ha-ki* (*coh-ki*) ccak i eps-eyo.

'Chevy cars are very good.'

b. *Hayngpokha*-ki wiha-ye (*hayngpokhay ci*-ki wiha-ye) ihon-hay-ss-eyo.

'I got divorced in order to be happy.'

Kenkangha-ki wiha-ye (*kenkanghay ci*-ki wiha-ye) umsik ul mek-ess-ta.

'I ate food in order to recover.'

6.7. Complementation

The most frequently recurring errors in complementation are found in the use of *kes* 'that, the fact' complementizer. (49a) shows cases where *kes* is called for, whereas (49b) illustrates cases where *kes* is abused.

(49) a. Nuc-key o-n *cuk* (o-n *kes un*) cenhwa pat-ass-ki ttaymwun i-p-ni-ta.

'It was because I had to receive a phone call that I was late.'

Tangsin i kananha-ki nun hay-ss-una (ha-na) hwumchi-*ki* nun

(hwumchi-nun *kes* un) an toy-yo.
'Although you are poor, you shouldn't steal.'

b. Kohyang sacin ul po-myen po-l swulok *tola ka-nun kes* (*kohyang i*) kulip-sup-ni-ta.
'The more I look at the picture of my hometown, the more I miss it.'

Phyenci *ponay-n kes* (*ponay-nun*) taysin ey cenhwa lul kel-usey-yo (ke sey-yo).
'Instead of sending a letter, why don't you call him?'

Wuli to aph ulo wucwusen ul tha-ko tal ey ka-l *kes* (*ci*) to molu-ci-yo.
'Who knows whether we too can get on a spaceship and go to the moon before long.'

Often the quotative *ko* and the non-quotative *ko* are confused, as shown in (50).

(50) a. Alumtap-*ko* (alumtap-*ta-ko*) yekye-se anay hanthey ku kkoch ul cwu-ess-eyo.
'Thinking that the flower was pretty, I gave it to my wife.'

b. Chengkaykwuli kath-i toy-*n-ta-ko* (toy-*ko*) siph-ci anh-umyen emi mal ul chal (cal) tut-ci anh-umyen an toy-yo.
'If you don't want to become like a green frog, you must listen well to your mother.'

Some other complementation-related errors include the following.

(51) 300 sek tuli-keyss-nun (tuli-keyss-*ta* nun) yaksok ul hay-ss-ta.
'He made a promise that he would offer 300 *soks.*'

Tongyang salam kwa seyang salam un mwusen (mwusun) umsik ul mek-nun cem i (mek-*nun ka ha*-nun cem i) tall-a-yo.
'Orientals and Westerners differ in what they eat.'

Cilwuha-myen cilwuha swulok (cilwuha-*l* swulok) phikonha-ki man hay-yo.
'The more I feel bored, the more I feel tired.'

Ku say nun po-ki coh-*key* phun man (coh-*ul* ppwun man) ani-la wul-um soli to alumtaw-eyo.
'The bird is not only pretty but its voice is good.'

7. Errors in Sociolinguistics and Pragmatics

Many of the students' sentences are syntactically well-formed and semantically acceptable, yet turn out to be still unnatural. Such sentences are, by and large, those violating either (a) socio-cultural rules of speaking (i.e., errors in sociolinguistics) or (b) conventions of sentence usage, speech act principles, or situation-bound or other presuppositions (i.e., errors in pragmatics).

7.1. Errors in sociolinguistics

The majority of the students' compositions under investigation are 'non-interactional' writings that contain few aspects that are sensitive to speech participants or speech situations. However, some errors are observed in the use of honorifics and other culture-bound expressions. In particular, students tend to neglect to observe the rules of agreement that hold among the honorifics in a given sentence or discourse, suggesting that Americans are much less conscious of social stratification than Koreans are. (52) presents examples in which honorific agreement is not observed.

(52) *Cey* mom ey un ulo mantu-n ton ul (i) katuk-hi tul-e iss-*ta*.
'My body is filled with silver money.'
Caney ton pelley toy-l kes i-*eyo*.
'You will become a money grubber.'
Kwulum sai ey iss-nun tal ul pwa-*la*. Alumtap-kwun-*yo*.
'Look at the moon between the clouds. It's beautiful.'
Pwusan ey ka-nun kes i etteh-*ni*? Kyengpwukosoktolo ey (lo) ka-myen culkew-ul ke-yey-*yo*.
'How about going to Pusan? It will be fun to go on the Seoul-Pusan expressway.'

Tangsin i pay ka pwule-l (pwulu-l) they-ni chenchen-hi mek-*ela*.
'You must be full now. Eat slowly.'
Camkkan iss-taka nawa-se mwue-l *mek*-usey-*yo*.
'Come out after a while and have something to eat.'
Kicha ka swi-ci anh-ko Sewul ccok ey ka-*si*-ess-up-ni-ta.
'The train went to Seoul without stopping.'

Use of certain expressions is culturally constrained. For example, words like *ttokttokha-ta* 'smart', *yengliha-ta* 'bright', and *kwiyep-ta* 'cute' cannot be used with a subject whose referent is socially superior to the speaker. Observe the following examples.

(53) Apeci ka *ttokttokha-l tay lo ttokttokhay-yo* (aco hyenmyeng-ha-sey-yo).
'My father is very smart.'

Imkum-nim eykey cenkwuk ey iss-nun pongsa lul canchi ey *chotayha-la-ko* (*chotayhay talla-ko*) pwuthakhay-ss-eyo.
'She asked the king to invite all the blindmen in the country to a party.'

Manwula ko yengkam i (*halapeci wa halmeni* ka) cwumwu-si-n-ta.
'An old couple is sleeping.'

Enu nal Simcheng un isangha-n *malssum* (*mal*) ul tul-ess-ta.
'One day, Shimchong heard strange words.'

Cinhulk ey iss-nun toychi (twayci) toy-n cengto lo kipp-ess-eyo.
'He was as happy as a pig in the mud.'

The last example may not be proper in Korean contexts. Perhaps, *nwun o-nun nal kangaci chelem* 'like a puppy on a snowing day' may be more acceptable.

Although letters would manifest many sociolinguistic errors, students' free compositions did not include any letters. The following is the romanized version of a note an American student left in my mail box while I was away. The note should serve to illustrate sociolinguistic errors made in letter writings.

(54) Sen Ho Min sensayngnim:

Sillayhapnita. Nay ilum "X" ssi ipnita. Mi phal kwun ywukkwun cwungwi iessupnita. Samkaypanyen tayhanminkwuk ey salessupnita. Cikum, na nun mwullihak ul hwa chenmwunhak ul UHM tayhakwen ey kongpwuhasupnita. Cham nappun enehaksayng ttaymwun ey mayilmayil kongpwuhaci anhumyen antoypnita. Na hako tangsin hako kasi hankwuke "summer session" ul malhako siphsupnikka?

Tangsin ttaymwuney office ey epsun phenci lul haysupnita. Nay kumyoil tolaokayssupnita. Sensayngnim, tangsin uy sikan ttaymwun ey, taytanhi kamsahapnita.

There are a number of sociolinguistic errors in the note. *Sillyeyhapnita* 'excuse me' or a politer form *sillyeyhakeyssupnita* is a discourse opener in a spoken situation, not in a written context; the title *ssi* 'Mr., Mrs., Miss' is used to refer to a non-speaker and never used for the speaker or writer himself, even when addressing to a socially lower person; *nay* and *na* 'I, my' should be changed, respectively, to the honorific counterparts *cey* and *ce;* the blunt form *tangsin* 'you' should be changed to the deferential form *sensayngnim; na hako tangsin hako kasi* 'you and I together' or a much politer counterpart *ce hako sensayngnim hako kathi* implies an equal status, hence inappropriate; *malhako siphsupnikka*? 'do you want to talk about?' is very blunt especially since the event is for the benefit of the writer himself; *epsta* 'do not stay' must be changed to the honorific form *an kyeysita, phyenci* 'letter' to *kulwel, haysupnita* 'write' to *tulipnita,* etc.; *coysonghapnita* 'I feel guilty' is better than *kamsahapnita* 'thank you'; and a lower or equal person usually puts *tulim* 'respectfully submitted' following his name at the end of a letter.[8]

7.2. Errors in pragmatics

It seems to me that pragmatic errors may be grouped into three general sets: (a) violations of conventional sentence usage, (b) violations of presuppositions, and (c) violations of pragmatic principles (e.g., Grice 1975). The first set includes the following.

(55) Hopak kkoch kath-un panmyen ey *coh-un meli ka iss*-eyo (*meli ka coh*-ayo).
  'While she looks like a squash flower (i.e., ugly), she has good brains.'
 Cey ka mal i eps-ul cengto lo (*malha-l swu eps-ul* cengto lo) kyengchi ka alumtap-sup-ni-ta.
  'The scenery is indescribably beautiful.'
 Kippu-n ci swunkan man ey (*kippu-ca maca; kippu-ki ka mwusep-key*) sulph-e cy-ess-eyo.
  'Moments after I felt happy, I became sad.'
 Chayk ul cheum *o-pwun say ey ilk-nun swunkan ey* (*o-pwun tongan ilk-ess-ul ttay*) coh-ass-eyo.
  'The book was good during the first five minutes of reading.'
 Twu salam uy wiha-n (*twu salam i iss-ul*) pang hana nun elma i-p-ni-kka?
  'How much is a room for two?'
 Naka-se *po-l il ul ha-lye-ko* hay-yo (*il ul po-lye-ko* hay-yo).
  'I am going to go out to do something.'

Presuppositional violations seem to be of two kinds: sentence-bound and situation-bound. (56a) illustrates the former and (56b) the latter.

(65) a. I cha nun *coh-ul taylo coh-ayo* (*aco coh-ayo*).
  'This car is very good.'
 Cf. Naymsay ka tokhal-l taylo tokhay-yo. 'It smells extremely bad.' Sakwa ka ssek-ul taylo ssek-ess-eyo. 'The apple is as

rotten as rotten can be.'

b. TV lul *kku-n chay* (*kku-ko; khye noh-un chay*) ca-ko iss-eyo.
'He is sleeping with the TV off.'
Kuleh-key kongpwuha-*taka nun* (kongpwuha-*myen*) sihem ey hap-kyekha-keyss-eyo.
'If you study that hard, I think you will pass the exam.'
Cey anay nun alumptap-ki ccak i *eps-kwun-yo* (*epse-eyo*).
'My wife is very beautiful.'
Pilok *paykmancangca ka toy-ci anh-ul* mangceng (*kananha-l* mangceng) hwumchi-ci anh-ayo.
'Although I am not a millionaire, I don't steal.'

The form *-ul taylo,* while occurring rather freely with any action verb as long as the meaning is compatible, occurs with a descriptive verb usually with a negative connotation. In (65a), however, it occurs in a positive sense, hence unnatural. The patterns *-(u)n chay* and *-taka nun* require the event in which they occur to be unusual, unexpected, or undesirable from the speaker's point of view. In (65b), their occurrence in 'normal' contexts make the sentences sound unnatural. The form *-kwun* denotes the speaker's exclamation as a result of confirming an event 'here and now.' Therefore, use of this form to describe one's own wife's beauty is quite unnatural unless the context 'here and now' is given. In addition, the sentence also violates the Korean social rule that praising one's own wife in front of others is considered culturally inappropriate. The last example in (65b) is marginally acceptable, when the presupposition that people normally steal when they are not millionaires holds.

The last set of pragmatic errors includes cases where such pragmatic principles as Grice's quality, quantity, relevance, and manner are violated. These are illustrated in (66). Violation of politeness principles was illustrated partly in (54).

(66) a. Chwiha-ki nun kosaha-ko an chwihay-ss-eyo.
'Far from being drunk, I was sober.'

b. Cey os ul (i) cec-umyen pakkwu-ki ka ilsswu i-p-ni-ta.
'I make it a rule to change clothes when they get wet.'

c. Yocum i seysang *an* ey (i seysang ey) amwu salam ina mit-ul swu eps-nun tey-yo.
'I cannot trust anybody in the world.'

d. Hankwukmal 401 kongpwuha-ki pota nun 302 ka *elyew-ess-ci anh*-ass-eyo (*te swiw*-ess-eyo; *tel elyew*-ess-eyo).

'Korean 302 was less difficult to study than Korean 401.'

e. *Ka pwa-nun kes ul thongha-ye* (*ka po-ko*) ku yenghwa ka coh-ta-nun kes ul al-ass-eyo.

'Only when I went to see the movie did I realize that it was good.'

f. *Cenhwa kel-ki lul* (*cenhwa lul*) thongha-ye ku pwun un tachy-ess-ta-nun kes ul al-ass-up-ni-ta.

'Through a phone-call, I knew that he got hurt.'

g. A: Nalssi ka coh-ta-ci-yo? 'I heard that the place has nice weather.'

B: *Ku ppwun man ani-p-ni-ta,* tewe-yo (*Kulen tey,* tewe-yo).
'Not only that. It's hot out there.'

The examples in (66) are related mostly to the quantity and partly to the relevance or manner principle (or maxim). A person is either drunk or not, but not in between; therefore, the first part (i.e., ...*kosaha-ko* construction) in (66a) is redundant, unless it is followed by such emphatic adverbials as *cenhye* 'at all'. (66b) provides hardly any new information; besides, use of *il sswu* 'common practice' makes the sentence sound odd. In (66c), *an* 'inside' is totally redundant. (66d) seems to violate the manner maxim. While (66e) and (66f) both violate the quantity maxim, (66g) appears to go against the maxim of relevance.

Both sociolinguistic and pragmatic errors reveal that students tend to be guided by their mother tongue in many instances, especially when they are still not familiar with conventional usages. There are also many errors whose sources are attributable either to overgeneralization or teacher-inducement.

8. The patterns of American students' common composition errors that we have observed thus far provide us with some important theoretical and pedagogical implications. From the theoretical point of view, the error patterns would function as significant data for or against various old or new hypotheses on linguistic universals and language typology. The error data should be useful to those who are working not only on core linguistic levels but also on such closely related areas as language acquisition theory, sociolinguistics, and psycholinguistics. Pedagogically, we have observed where advanced American students' patterned weaknesses in Korean occur. The error patterns, therefore, should function as significant data not only for reinforcement and remedial purposes but for teaching material development.

In this paper, I have focused mainly on the identification of common error types, while allocating only a small portion of space to the descriptive analysis of the errors, which would deserve a separate paper.

Notes

1. This is a revised and expanded version of a paper which I presented under the same title at a conference on Korean sociolinguistics and language teaching sponsored by and held at the University of Southern California in February 1985. I should like to thank Nam Kil Kim, the conference organizer and chairman, for the generous invitation and John Haig, who has provided me with valuable comments.
2. Many of these students received their initial training in Korean from the Defense Language Institute in California.
3. Selinker maintains that fossilizations are phonological, morphological, and syntactic forms in the speech of a speaker of a second language that do not conform to the target language norms even after years of instruction in and exposure to the standard forms.
4. In transcribing Korean forms, the Yale romanization system will be observed. Dots stand for boundaries between graphic syllable blocks.
5. English words like *boy*, *keep, peak, happy*, *speak*, and *sun* illustrate the phonetic qualities of the English phonemes given in (17).
6. It may be more appropriate for examples like those in (24) to be dealt with under syntax. They are presented in this section along with errors in other action verbs for convenience's sake.
7. In connection with errors in negation, some students are not familiar with the notion of negative polarity. Thus, patterns like the following are noticed where the negative polarity item *-lakonun* (lit. 'something called') occurs with a positive predicate:

    Makkelli-*lakonun* (makkelli *nun*) masi-ko siph-eyo.
    'I want to drink *makkelli*.

    Cf. Makkelli-lakonun cenhye masi-ko siph-ci anh-ayo.
    'I don't want to drink *makkelli* at all.'
8. With the sociolinguistic and other errors corrected, the sample note can be rewritten as follows:

    Son Ho Min sensayngnim

    Cey ilum un "X" ipnita. Miphalkwun ywukkwun cwungwi lo samnyenpan hankwuk eyse salassnun tey, cikum un UHM tayhakwen eyse mwullihak kwa chenmwunhak ul kongpwuhako issupnita. Ene ey caynung i epsnun haksayng iki ttaymwun ey mayil yelsimhi kongpwuhaci anhumyen an toykeyssupnita. Kulayse hankwuke summer session ey tayhayse alko siphese chaca wassuna, sensayngnim kkeyse office ey an keysiki ttaymwun ey ilehkey kulwel ul tulipnita. Kumyoil ey tasi chaca poypkeyssupnita. Sensayngnim kkey phyey lul kkichye tulye coysonghapnita.

    "X" tulim.

BIBLIOGRAPHY

Aguas, E.F. 1964. *English Composition Errors of Tagalog Speakers.* Ed.D. dissertation, University of California, Los Angeles.

Anscombre, J. 1977. "La problématique de l'illocutoire dérivé" *Language et Société* 2:17-41.

Aston, W.G. 1879. "A comparative study of the Japanese and Korean languages." *Journal of the Royal Asiatic Society of Great Britain and Ireland,* New Series 11. <A shortened Japanese version appears in Ikeda and Ohno 1973, pp. 353-376>.

Austerlitz, R., Chin-W. Kim, S.E. Martin, S.R. Ramsey, Ho-min Sohn, Seok Choong Song, and E.W. Wagner. 1980. "Report of the workshop conference on Korean Romanization." *Korean Studies* 4:111-125.

Austin, J.L. 1970. *Philosophical Papers.* Oxford: Oxord University Press.

Bach E., and R. Harms, eds. 1968. *Universals in Linguistic Theory.* New York: Holt, Rinehart, and Winston.

Bailey, C.-J.N. 1970. "Toward specifying constraints on phonological metathesis." *Linguistic Inquiry* 1:347-349.

Bailey, N., C. Madden, and S. Krashen. 1974. "Is there a 'natural sequence' in adult second language learning?" *Language Learning* 24.2.

Bak, Sung-Yun. 1977. "Topicalization in Korean." *Working Papers in Linguistics* (University of Hawaii) 9.2:63-88.

______. 1978. "Double subject constructions in Korean." MS.

______. 1981. *Studies in Korean Syntax: Ellipsis, Topic and Relative Constructions.* Ph.D. dissertation, University of Hawaii.

______. 1983. "Women's speech in Korean and English." *Korean Studies* 7:61-75.

Banathy, B., E.C. Trager, and C.D. Waddle. 1966. "The use of contrastive data in foreign language course development." In Valdman (1966, pp. 27-56).

Barnlund, D.C. 1979. "Verbal self-disclosure: Topics, targets, depth." In Smith and Luce (1979, pp. 83-101).

Befu, H., and E. Norbeck. 1958. "Japanese usages of terms of relationship." *Southwestern Journal of Anthropology* 14:66-86.

Bender, B.W. 1967. "Some Micronesian word lists." (Mimeo). University of Hawaii.

______. 1968. "Marshallese phonology." *Oceanic Linguistics* 7.1:16-35.

______. 1969a. *Spoken Marshallese.* Honolulu: University of Hawaii Press.

______. 1969b. "Vowel dissimilation in Marshallese." *Working Papers in Linguistics* (University of Hawaii) 1:88-96.

______. 1971. "Micronesian languages." In Sebeok, et al. (1971, pp. 426-465).

______. 1973. "Parallelisms in the morphophonemics of several Micronesian languages." *Working Papers in Linguistics* (University of Hawaii) 5.8:1-16.

______. 1975. "Stress in Marshallese." MS. University of Hawaii.

______. ed. 1984. *Studies in Micronesian Linguistics. Pacific Linguistics* C-80. Canberra: Australian National University.

Benton, R.A. 1968. *Substitutes and Classifiers in Trukese.* M.A. thesis, University of Hawaii.

Bierwisch, M., and K.E. Heidolph, eds. 1970. *Progress in Linguistics.* The Hague: Mouton.

Biggs, B. 1965. "Direct and indirect inheritance in Rotuman." *Lingua* 14:383-445.

Binnick, R.I. 1970. "Studies in the derivation of predicate structures, part II." *Papers in Linguistics* 3:519-601.

Boller, A. 1857. "Nachweis, dass das Japanische zum ural-altaischen Stamme gehört." *Sitzungsberichte der philos.-histor. Classe der kais* (Akademie der Wissenschaften, Wien) 33:393-481.

Bouma, L. 1973. *The Semantics of the Modal Auxiliaries in Contemporary German.* Janua Linguarum. Series Practica 146. The Hague: Mouton.

Brown. H.D. 1980. *Principles of Language Learning and Teaching.* Englewood Cliffs, NJ: Prentice-Hall.

Brown, P. 1976. "Women and politeness: A new perspective on language and society." *Reviews in Anthropology* 3:240-249.

______. 1980. "How and why are women more polite: Some evidence from a Mayan community." In McConnell-Ginet, Boker, and Furman (1980, pp. 111-139).

______, and S. Levinson. 1978. "Universals in language usage: Politeness phenomena." In Goody (1978, pp. 56-289).

Brown, R.W. 1965. *Social Psychology.* New York: Free Press.

______, and M. Ford. 1964. "Address in American English." In Hymes (1964, pp. 234-244).

______, and A. Gilman. 1960. "The pronouns of power and solidarity." In Sebeok (1960, pp. 253-276). Also in Fishman (1970).

Buren, H.V. 1974. "The American ways with names." *Topics in Culture Learning* (East-West Center, Honolulu) 2:67-86.

Chafe, W.L. 1970 (=1973). *Meaning and the Structure of Language.* Chicago: University of Chicago Press.

______. 1976. "Givenness, contrastiveness, definiteness, subjects, topics, and point of view." In Li (1976, pp. 27-55).

Chang, Suk-Jin. 1973a. *A Generative Study of Discourse: Pragmatic Aspects with Reference to English. Language Research* 9.2. Supplement.

______. 1973b. "Sisang uy yangsang: 'kyeysok' 'wanlyo' uy sayngsengcek kochal." *Language Research* 9.2:58-72.

Chang, Yun-Shik. 1976. "The urban Korean as individual." In Chun (1976, pp. 147-161).

Chen, M.Y., and W.S-Y. Wang. 1975. "Sound change: Actuation and implementation." *Language* 51.2:255-281.

Cho, Choon-Hak. 1975. "The scope of negation." (1975b, pp. 63-80).

______. 1982. *A Study of Korean Pragmatics: Deixis and Politeness*. Ph.D. dissertation, University of Hawaii.

Choi, Hyun Bae. 1959 (= 1965). *Wuli Malpon*. Seoul: Cengum-sa.

Chomsky, N. 1964. *Current Issues in Linguistic Theory. Janua Linguarum* 38. The Hague: Mouton.

______. 1965. *Aspects of the Theory of Syntax*. Cambridge, Mass: MIT Press.

______, and M. Halle. 1968. *The Sound Pattern of English*. New York: Harper and Row.

Chun, Shin-Yong, ed. 1976. *Korean Society*. Korean Culture Series 6. Seoul: International Cultural Foundation.

Chung, In Seung, et al., eds. 1976. *Hankwuke Taysacen*. Seoul: Hyenswu-sa.

Chung, Man-deuk. 1976. "Hankwukin uy mikwuk insik." In *Hanmiin uy Sangho Insik*. Daegu, Korea: Keimyung University Press.

Cole, P. 1975. "The synchronic and diachronic status of conversational implicature." In Cole and Morgan (1975, pp. 257-288).

______, ed. 1978. *Syntax and Semantics 9: Pragmatics*. New York: Academic Press.

______, and J. Morgan, eds. 1975. *Syntax and Semantics 3: Speech Acts*. New York: Academic Press.

Cook, Eung-Do. 1968. *Embedding Transformations in Korean Syntax*. Ph.D. dissertation, University of Alberta.

______. 1971. "Korean verbal affixes: A generative view." *Journal of Canadian Linguistics*, RCL 16.2:81-91.

Corder, S.P. 1967. "The significance of learner's errors." *IRAL* 5:161-170.

Corum, C., T.C. Smith-Stark, and A. Weiser, eds. 1973. *Papers from the Ninth Regional Meeting of the Chicago Linguistic Society*. Chicago: University of Chicago, Department of Linguistics.

Dahl, Ö. 1970. "Some notes on indefinites." *Language* 46:33-41.

Dato, D.P. 1970. *American Children's Acquisition of Spanish Syntax in the Madrid Environment*. U.S. Office of Education, Institute of International Studies Final Report, Project No. 3036.

Davidson, D., and G. Harman, eds. 1972. *Semantics of Natural Language*. Dordrecht: D. Reidel Publishing Co.

Davison, A. 1978. "Negative scope and rules of conversation: Evidence from an OV language." In Cole (1978, pp. 23-45).

Deck, N.C. 1933-34. "Grammar of the language spoken by the Kwara'ae people of

Mala, British Solomon Islands." *Journal of the Polynesian Society* 42:33-48, 133-144, 241-256, and 43:1-16.

Delattre, P., A.M. Liberman, F.S. Cooper, and L.J. Gerstman. 1952. "An experimental study of the acoustic determinants of vowel colour: Observations on one- and two-formant vowels synthesized from spectrographic patterns." *Word* 8:195-210.

Dempwolff, O. 1934. *Vergleichende Lautlehre des austronesischen Wortschatzes,* I. Berlin-Hamburg. 1937. II, ibid. 1938. III, ibid.

Diller, A. 1978. "La forme en -rais dans les actes indirectes de langage." *In Actes de la Session de Linguistique de Bourg-Saint-Maruice.* Paris: Conseil Scientifique de la Sorbonne Nouvelle.

Dillon, G.L. 1977. *Introduction to Contemporary Linguistic Semantics.* Englewood Cliffs: Prentice-Hall.

Dodson, C.J., E. Price, and L.T. Williams, eds. 1968. *Towards Bilingualism.* Cardiff: University of Wales Press.

Dulay, H.C., and M. K. Burt. 1973. "Should we teach children syntax?" *Language Learning* 23:245-258.

______. 1974. "You can't learn without goofing." In Richards (1974a, pp. 95-123).

Dunbar, E.N. 1973. *How to Say 'Give' and 'Receive' in Japanese: A Preliminary Study.* M.A. thesis, University of Hawaii. *Working Papers in Linguistics* (University of Hawaii) 5.11.

Dušková, L. 1969."On sources of errors in foreign language learning." *IRAL* 7:11-36.

Dyen, I. 1949. "On the history of Trukese vowels." *Language* 25:429-436.

______. 1965. *A Sketch of Trukese Grammar.* New Haven: American Oriental Society.

Eckardt, A. 1966. *Koreanisch und Indogermanisch.* Heidelberg: Julius Groos.

Ervin-Tripp, S.M. 1971. "Sociolinguistics." In Fishman (1971, pp. 15-91).

Ferguson, C.A. 1959. "Diglossia." *Word* 15:325-340.

Fillmore, C.J. 1968. "The case for case." In Bach and Harms (1968, pp. 1-90).

______. 1971. "Some problems for case grammar." *Working Papers in Linguistics* (Ohio State University) 10:245-265. Also in *Monograph Series on Language and Linguistics* 24:35-56. Georgetown: Georgetown University press.

______, and D.T. Langendoen, eds. 1971. *Studies in Linguistic Semantics.* New York: Holt, Rinehart, and Winston.

Firbas, J. 1966. "On defining the theme in functional sentence analysis." *Travaux Linguistiques de Prague* 1:267-280.

______, and K. Pala. 1971. "Review of Osten Dahl, *Topic and Comment: A Study of Russian and General Transformational Grammar.*" *Journal of Linguistics* 7:91-101.

Fishman, J.A., ed. 1960. *Readings in the Sociology of Language.* The Hague: Mouton.

______, ed. 1971. *Advances in the Sociology of Language.* The Hague: Mouton.

French, F.G. 1949. *Common Errors in English.* London: Oxford University Press.

Fries, C.C. 1945. *Teaching and Learning English as a Foreign Language.* Ann Arbor: University of Michigan Press.

Fujioka, K. 1908. "Nihon go no ichi." *Kokugakuin Zasshi* 14.8. Also in Ikeda and Ohno (1973, pp. 334-349).

Gazdar, G. 1981. "Speech act assignment." In Joshi, Webber, and Sag (1981).

Gim, Sheon Gi. 1968a. "Han, il, mong tane pikyo yenkwu." *Hangeul 142.*

______. 1968b. "A comparative study of numerals of Korean, Japanese, and Altaic languages." *Myongji University Journal* 1.

Givón, T. 1972. "Forward implications, backward presuppositions, and the time axis of verbs." *Syntax and Semantics* 1:29-50. New York: Seminar Press.

______. 1978a. "Definiteness and referentiality." In Greenberg (1978, pp. 291-330).

______. 1978b. "Negation in language: Pragmatics, function, ontology." In Cole (1978, pp. 69-112).

Glenn, E.S. 1966. *Mind, Culture, Politics.* Mimeo.

Goldberg, C.N. 1979. "Spirit in place: The concept of kohyang and the Korean social order." In McCann, Middleton, and Shultz (1979, pp. 89-101).

Goodenough, W.H. 1965. "Personal names and modes of address in two Oceanic societies." In Spiro (1965, pp. 265-276).

Goody, E., ed. 1978. *Question and Politeness: Strategies in Social Interaction.* Cambridge: Cambridge University Press.

Gordon, D., and G. Lakoff. 1971. "Conversational postulates." *Papers from Seventh Regional Meeting* (Chicago Linguistic Society). Also in Cole and Morgan (1975, pp. 83-106).

Grace, G.W. 1969. "A Proto-Oceanic finder list." *Working Papers in Linguistics* (University of Hawaii) 2:39-84.

______. n.d. "Some Trukese cognates (from Dyen 1949)." Mimeo. University of Hawaii.

Grammont, M. 1950. *Traité de Phonétique.* Paris: Delagrave.

Greenberg, J.H. 1966a. "Some universals of grammar with particular reference to the order of meaningful elements." In Greenberg (1966b, pp. 73-113).

______, ed. 1966b. *Universals of Language.* Cambridge, Mass: MIT Press.

______, ed. 1978. *Universals of Human Languages 4: Syntax.* Stanford: Stanf University Press.

Grice, H.P. 1975. "Logic and conversation." In Cole and Morgan (1975, pp. 41-58).

Gruber, J.S. 1965 (=1970). *Studies in Lexical Relations.* Ph.D. dissertation, MIT. Indiana University Linguistics Club.

Gundel, J.K. 1974. "The role of topic and comment in linguistic theory." Indiana University Linguistics Club.

______. 1978. "Stress, pronominalization and the givenness distinction." *Working Papers in Linguistics* (University of Hawaii) 10.2:1-13.

Haguenauer, C. 1956. *Origines de la Civilisation japonaise, Introduction à l'Étude de la Préhistoire du Japan, première Partie.* Paris: Imprimerie Nationale.

Hahn, Kyung-Ja Park. 1979. *Development of Negation in One Korean Child.* Ph.D. dissertation University of Hawaii.

Haig, J. 1979. "Real and apparent multiple subject sentences." *Papers in Japanese Linguistics* 6:87-130.

Halliday, M.A.K. 1967. "Notes on transitivity and theme in English." *Journal of Linguistics* 3:199-244.

Harada, S.I. 1976. "Honorifics." In Shibatani (1976b, pp. 499-561).

Harrison, S.P. 1976. *Mokilese Reference Grammar.* Honolulu: University Press of Hawaii.

Hatch, E. 1983. "Foreword." In Wolfson and Judd (1983, pp. ix-xviii).

Hattori, S. 1974. *Nihongo no Keitoo.* Tokyo: Iwanami Shoten.

Hayashi, S., and H. Minami. 1974. "Sekai no keigo." *Keigo Kooza* 8. Tokyo: Meiji Shoin.

Heringer, J.T. 1972. "Some grammatical correlates of felicity conditions and presuppositions." *Working Papers in Linguistics* (Ohio State Univ.) 11:iv-110.

Higa, M. 1972. "The use of the imperative mood in postwar Japan." In Lebra (1972).

Hijirida, K., and Ho-min Sohn. 1983. "Commonality and relativity in address-reference term usages." *Language Research* 19.2:139-168.

Hinds, J. 1976. *Aspects of Japanese Discourse Structure.* Tokyo: Kaitakusha.

Hockett, C.F. 1955. *A Manual of Phonology. IJAL* memoir 11.

Hong, Ki-mun. 1959. "Cosene wa monggoe wauy kwankyey." *Cosen Emun* 6:77-82.

Hooper, J.B. 1974. *Aspects of Natural Generative Phonology.* Indiana University Linguistics Club.

Hornby, P.A. 1971. "Surface structure and the topic-comment distinction: A developmental study." *Child Development* 42:1975-1988.

Householder, F.W. 1959. "On linguistic primes." *Word* 15.2:231-239.

______. 1964. "Three dreams of modern Greek phonology." *Papers in Memory of George C. Pappageotes.* Supplement to *Word* 20.3. (Special Publication 5).

______. 1967. "Distinctive features and phonetic features." In *To Honor Roman Jakobson: Essays on the Occasion of His Seventieth Birthday* 2:941-944. The Hague: Mouton.

______, and R.L. Cheng. 1971. "Universe-scope relations in Chinese and Japanese." *The Hawaii Language Teacher* 13:34-50. Also, Indiana University Linguistics Club (1980).

Howard, I. 1972. *A Directional Theory of Rule Application in Phonology.* Ph.D. dissertation, MIT. *Working Papers in Linguistics* (University of Hawaii) 4.7.

Howell, R.W. 1965. "Linguistic status markers in Korean." *The Krober Anthropological Society Papers* 33:91-97.

______. 1967. *Linguistic Choice as an Index to Social Change.* Ph.D. dissertation, University of California, Berkeley.

______. 1968. "Linguistic choice and levels of social change." *American An-*

thropologist 70:553-559.

Hsu, F.L.K. 1981. *Americans and Chinese.* Honolulu: University Press of Hawaii.

Hsu, R. 1969. *Phonology and Morphophonemics of Yapese.* Ph.D. dissertation, University of California, Berkeley.

Huddleston, R. 1974. "Further remarks on the analysis of auxiliaries as main verbs." *Foundations of Language* 11:215-229.

Hudson, R.A. 1980. *Sociolinguistics.* Cambridge: Cambridge University Press.

Huh, Woong. 1972. *Cwungsey Kwuke Yenkwu.* Seoul: Cengum-sa.

Hulbert, H.B. 1905. *A Comparative Grammar of the Korean Language and the Dravidian Languages of India.* Seoul: Methodist Publishing House.

Hwang, Juck-Ryoon. 1975. *Role of Sociolinguistics in Foreign Language Education with Reference to Korean and English Terms of Address and Levels of Deference.* Ph.D. dissertation, University of Texas, Austin. Seoul: Kwang-moon-sa.

Hyman, L.M. 1975. *Phonology.* New York: Holt, Rinehart, and Winston.

Hymes, D., ed. 1964. *Language in Culture and Society.* New York: Harper and Row.

______. 1967. "On communicative competence." MS. University of Pennsylvania.

Ide, S. 1982. "Japanese sociolinguistics: Politeness and women's language." *Lingua* 57:357-385.

Ikeda, J. and S. Ohno, eds. 1973. *Ronshuu, Nihon Bunka no Kigen 5: Nihon Jin-shuuron—Gengogaku.* Tokyo: Heibonsha.

Im, Hong-Bin. 1972. "Kwuke uy cwuceyhwa yenkwu." *Kwuke Yenkwu* 28.

______. 1974. "Cwukyek cwungchwullon ul chacase" *Munpep Yenkwu* 1:111-148.

Inoue, K. 1972. "*Agent* and *Source* in Japanese." *Papers in Japanese Linguistics* 1.2:195-217.

______. 1974. "Innovating uses of Japanese honorifics and polite forms." *Papers in Japanese Linguisitics* 3:19-41.

Irvine, J.T. n.d. "Formality and informality in speech events." A sociolinguistics working paper (no. 52). Southwest Educational Development Laboratory. Austin, Texas.

Ishikawa, A., et al. 1981. "Address terms in modern Japanese: A sociolinguistic analysis." *Sophia Linguistica* (Sophia University, Tokyo) 8/9:129-141.

Ivens, W.G. 1931. "A grammar of the language of Kwara'ae, North Mala, Solomon Islands." *Bulletin of the School of Oriental Studies* 6 (part 3):679-700.

Izui, H. 1952. "Nihongo no keitoo ni tsuite josetsu." *Kokugogaku* 9.

______. 1953. "Nihongo to nantoo shogo, keifu kankei ka, kiyo no kankei ka?" *Minzokugaku Kenkyuu* 17.2

Jackendoff, R.S. 1972. *Semantic Interpretation in Generative Grammar.* Cambridge, Mass: MIT Press.

Jacobs, R.A., and P.S. Rosenbaum. 1970. *Readings in English Transformational Grammar.* Waltham, Mass.: Blaisdell.

Jespersen, O. 1924 (= 1955). *The Philosophy of Grammar.* London: George Allen and Unwin.

Jorden, E.H. 1962. *Beginning Japanese.* 2 vols. New Haven: Yale University Press.

Josephs, L.S. 1972. *Selected Problems in the Analysis of Embedded Sentences in Japanese.* Ph.D. dissertation, Harvard University.

Joshi, A.K., B.L. Webber, and I.A. Sag, eds. 1981. *Elements of Discourse Understanding.* Cambridge: Cambridge University Press.

Kalton, M.C. 1979. *Korean Ideas and Values. Philip Jaisohn Memorial Paper 7.* Elkins Park, Penn: Philip Jaisohn Memorial Foundation.

Kanazawa, S. 1910. *Nikkan Ryookokugo Dookeiron.* Tokyo: Sanseidoo.

Karttunen, L. 1971. "Implicative verbs." *Language* 47:340-358.

Kawamoto, T. 1972. "Nihongo to nantoogo to no on'in taioo shian." *Nara Kyooiku Daigaku Kiyoo* 21.1:1-21.

______. 1973. "Nihongo to nantoogo to no on'in taioo: hosoku to shuusei." *Nara Kyooiku Daigaku Kiyoo* 22.1:1-22.

______. 1974. "Agreements and disagreements in morphology between Japanese and Austronesian (chiefly Melanesian) languages." *Minzokugaku Kenkyuu* 39.1:113-129.

______. 1977. "Toward a comparative Japanese-Austronesian I." *Bulletin of Nara University of Education* 26.1:23-49.

Keenan, E.L. 1976. "Towards a universal definition of 'subject'." In Li (1976, pp. 303-333).

Keiler, A.R., ed. 1972. *A Reader in Historical Comparative Linguistics.* New York: Holt, Rinehart, and Winston.

Kempson, R.M., and R. Quirk. 1971. "Controlled activation of latent contrast." *Language* 47:548-572.

Kenkyusha. 1974. *A New Japanese-English Dictionary.* Tokyo.

Kim, Bang Han. 1963. "Altai-e ey issese uy pochwungpep ey kwanhan kochal." *Tonghwa Munhwa* (Seoul National University) 1.

______. 1976. "Hankwuke kyeythong yenkwu uy munceycem." *Eoneohag* (Seoul National University) 1:3-24.

Kim, Chae-Yun. 1976. "Social strata." In Chun (1976, pp. 57-72).

Kim, Chin-W., ed. 1977. *Papers in Korean Linguistics.* Columbia: Hornbeam Press.

Kim, Choong-bae. 1978. "The Romanization of Korean: Problems and suggestions." *Linguistic Journal of Korea* 3:71-85.

Kim, Hyun Kyu. 1972. *Kwukehak Kaylon.* Seoul: Ilcokak.

Kim, Ki-hong. 1975. "Cross-cultural differences between Americans and Koreans in nonverbal behaviors." In Sohn (1975b, pp. 5-18).

______. 1978. *The Language of Emotion of Americans and Koreans.* Ph.D. dissertation, Keimyung University.

Kim, Min-Soo. 1973. *Kwuke Munpepnon.* Seoul: Ilcokak.

Kim, Nam-Kil. 1975. "The double past in Korean." *Foundations of Language*

12:529-536.
Kim, Po Gyom. 1960. "Gehört die koreanische Sprache zur altaischen Sprachfamilie?" *Journal of Korean Cultural Research Institute* (Ewha Woman's University) 2.1:115-175.
Kim, Sa Yop. 1974. *Kodai Choosengo to Nihongo.* Tokyo: Koodansha.
Kim, Soon-Ham Park. 1967. *A Transformational Analysis of Negation in Korean.* PH.D. dissertation, University of Michigan.
______. 1970. "Kyekmunpep ey ipkakhan kwuke uy 'kyep cwue' ey tayhan kochal." *Language Research 6.2:11-32.*
Kim, Wan Jin. 1963. "Kwuke moum cheykyey uy sin kochal." *Cintan Hakpo* 23.
Kimball, J.P., ed. 1975. *Syntax and Semantics 4.* New York: Academic Press.
Kindaichi, K., et al. 1951. "Nihongo no keitoo ni tsuite." *Kokugogaku* 5:9-36.
Kiparsky, P. 1968. "Linguistic universals and linguistic change." In Bach and Harms (1968, pp. 171-202).
______, and C. Kiparsky. 1970. "Fact." In Bierwisch and Heidolph (1970, pp. 143-173).
Kisseberth, C.W. 1970. "On the functional unity of phonological rules." *Linguistic Inquiry* 1:291-306.
Klein, E.F. 1979. "Romanization of Korean: problems, experiments, suggestions." In McCann, Middleton, and Shultz (1979, pp. 174-199).
Klopf, D., and R. Cambra. 1981. *Personal and Public Speaking.* Denver: Morton Publishing Co.
Klopf, D., and Myung-Seok Park. 1982. *Cross-cultural Communication: An Introduction to the Fundamentals.* Seoul: Hanshin Publishing Co.
Kluckhohn, C. 1951. "Values and value-orientations in the theory of action." In Parsons and Shils (1951, pp. 388-433).
______. 1954. "American culture—a general description." In Williams (1954).
Kluckhohn, F.R. 1963. "Some reflections on the nature of cultural integration and change." In Tiryakian (1963).
______, and F.L. Strodtbeck. 1965. *Variations in Value Orientations.* New York: Row, Peterson.
Ko, Yong-kun. 1974. "Hyentay kwuke uy conpipep ey tayhan yenkwu." *Language Research* 10.2:66-91.
Koh, Yong-Bok. 1976. "Traditionalism and de-traditionalism." In Chun (1976, pp. 129-145).
Kokuritsu Kokugo Kenkyuujo. 1957. *Keigo to Keigo Ishiki.* Tokyo: Shuei Shuppan.
Koo, John H. 1975. "On the phonemic principle and romanization of Korean." In Sohn (1975b. pp. 121-126).
Koono, R. 1945. "Choosen hoogengaku shikoo—kyoogokoo." *Keijoo Teikoku Daigaku Bungaku Kaironsan* 11.
______. 1949. "Nihongo to choosengo no nisan no ruiji." *Jinbun Kagaku no*

Shomondai. Tokyo: Seki Shoin.

Kopplemann, H. 1933. *Die eurasische Sprachfamilie, Indogermanische, Koreanisch und Verwandtes*. Heidelberg: Winter.

Kramarae, C. 1981. *Women and Men Speaking: Frameworks for Analysis*. Rowley, Mass: Newbury House.

Kramer, C. 1975. "Sex-related differences in address systems." *Anthropological Linguistics* 17.5:198-210.

Kuno, S. 1972a. "Functional sentence perspectives: A case study from Japanese and English." *Linguistic Inquiry* 3:269-320.

______. 1972b. "Evidence for subject raising in Japanese." *Papers in Japanese Linguistics* 1.1:24-50.

______. 1973. *The Structure of the Japanese Language*. Cambridge, Mass: MIT Press.

______. 1977. "Eigo ni okeru keigo." In *Keigo: Iwanami Kooza Nihongo* 4. Tokyo: Iwanami Shoten.

Kuroda, S.-Y. 1965. *Generative Grammatical Studies in the Japanese Language*. Ph.D. dissertation, MIT.

Kuroiwa, K. 1973. "Report on the Yap Outer Islands Orthography Committee Meeting." (Mimeo). University of Hawaii.

Kurokawa, S. 1970a. "Preliminary analysis of relative honorifics." *The Hawaii Language Teacher* (The Hawaii Association of Language Teachers) 11.1.

______. 1970b. "Speaker evaluation of some honorifics: A brief survey." *Journal-Newsletter of the Association of Teachers of Japanese* 6.3.

______. 1972. "Japanese terms of address: Some usages of the first and second person pronouns." *Papers in Japanese Linguistics* 1.2:228-238.

Kusanagi, Y. 1972. "Time focus within the Japanese tense system." *Papers in Japanese Linguistics* 1:52-68.

______, ed. 1976. *Japanese Linguistics and Language Teaching* (Proceedings of the 1st Japanese Language Festival at the University of Hawaii).

Kwahakwen Enemunhwa Yenkwuso (KEY). 1960. *Cosene Munpep* 1. Pyongyang: Kwahakwen Publishing Co.

Kwon, Hyongmyong. 1962. *Das koreanische Verbum vergleichen mit dem altaischen und japanischen Verbum. Zur Typologie des Koreanischen*. Munich: privately printed.

Labberton, D.V.H. 1924. "Preliminary results of researches into the original relationship between the Nipponese and the Malaypolynesian languages." *Journal of the Polynesian Society* 33.4.

Lado, R. 1957 (=1968). *Linguistics across Cultures*. Ann Arbor: University of Michigan Press.

Lakoff, R. 1970. "Tense and its relation to participants." *Language* 46:838-849.

______. 1972. "Linguistics and natural logic." In Davidson and Harman (1972).

______. 1973. "The logic of politeness: Or, minding your p's and q's." In Corum,

Smith-Stark, and Weiser (1973).
______. 1974. "What you can do with words: Politeness, pragmatics and performatives." Berkeley Studies of Syntax and Semantics (Department of Linguistics, University of California at Berkeley).
______. 1975. *Language and Women's Place.* New York: Harper and Row.

Lambert, D.M. 1969. *The Semantic Syntax of Metaphor: A Case Grammar Analysis.* Ph.D. dissertation, University of Michigan.
Langdon, M. 1976. "Metathesis in Yuman languages." *Language* 52:866-883.
Langendoen, T.L. 1970. *Essentials of English Grammar.* New York: Holt, Rinehart, and Winston.
Lebra, T.S. 1976. *Japanese Patterns of Behavior.* Honolulu: University Press of Hawaii.
Lebra, W.P., ed. 1972. *Transcultural Research in Mental Health, Vol. 2 of Mental Health Research in Asia and Pacific.* Honolulu: University Press of Hawaii.
Lee, Chungmin. 1973a. *Abstract Syntax and Korean with Reference to English.* Ph.D. dissertation, Indiana University. Seoul: Pan-Korea Book Corp. (1974).
______. 1973b. "Presupposition of existence of theme for verbs of change (in Korean and English)." *Foundations of Language* 9.4:384-388.
Lee, Dong Jae. 1975. "Some problems in learning Korean second person pronouns." In Sohn (1975b, pp. 19-32).
Lee, G. 1976. "Rule limitation in phonology." MS. University of Hawaii.
Lee, Hee Sung. 1975. *Say Kotung Munpep* Seoul: Ilcokak.
Lee, Hong-Bae. 1970. *A Study of Korean Syntax.* Ph.D dissertation, Brown University. Seoul: Pan-Korea Book Corp.
Lee, Hyun-Bok. 1979. "A critical appraisal of the revised romanization system." *Mal* 4:145-164.
Lee, In Mo. 1971. *Kocen Kwuke uy Yenkwu.* Seoul: Senmyeng Munhwasa.
Lee, Keedong. 1970. "On the so-called auxiliary verbs in Korean." MS. University of Hawaii.
______. 1975a. *Kusaiean Reference Grammar.* Honolulu: University Press of Hawaii.
______. 1975b. "Lexical causatives in Korean." *Language Research* 11.1:17-24.
______. 1976a. "Arguments against lexicalization: With reference to deadjectival clauses in Korean." *Linguistic Journal of Korea* 1.1:237-255
______. 1976b. "Auxiliary verbs and evaluative viewpoints." *Linguistic Journal of Korea* 1.2:47-69.
Lee, Ki-Moon. 1958. "A comparative study of Manchu and Korean." *Ural-Altaische Jahrbucher* 30:104-120.
______. 1963. "A genetic view of Japanese." Choosen Gakuhoo 27:94-105.
______. 1961 (=1967). *Kwukesa Kaysel.* Seoul: Mincwung Sekwan.
______. 1972 (=1976). *Kayceng Kwukesa Kaysel.* Seoul: Mincwung Sekwan.
______. 1973. "Hankwuke wa ilpone uy ehwi pikyo ey tayhan caykemtho."

Language Research 9.2:1-19.

______. 1975. "Remarks on the comparative study of Korean and Altaic." *Proceedings of the International Symposium Commemorating the 30th Anniversary of Korean Liberation.* Seoul: National Academy of Sciences.

Lee, Kyu-Tae. 1977. *Hankwukin uy Uysikkwuco.* 2 vols. Seoul: Munli-sa.

Lee, Maeng-Sung. 1973. "Variation of speech levels and interpersonal social relationship in Korean." *Festschrift for Dr. Chong-Soo Lee,* 109-142. Seoul: Samhwa Publishing Co.

Lee, Soong-Nyong. 1955. "Hanil yange uy ehwi pikyo siko." *Hakswulwen Hakpo* 1.

______, et al. 1971. *Kwuke Pangenhak.* Seoul: Hyengsel-sa.

Leech, G.N. 1969 (=1970). *Towards a Semantic Description of English.* Bloomington: Indiana University Press.

Lehman, W.P. 1962. *Historical Linguistics: An Introduction.* New York: Holt, Rinehart, and Winston.

______. 1976. "From topic to subject in Indo-European." In Li (1976, pp. 445-456).

Lester, M. 1974. "Bilingual education in the United States, the Pacific and Southeast Asia." *Topics in Culture Learning* (East-West Center, Honolulu) 2: 137-146.

Lenneberg, E.H. 1967. *Biological Foundations of Language.* New York: John Wiley & Sons.

Levinson, S.C. 1983. *Pragmatics.* Cambridge: Cambridge University Press.

Lewin, B. 1976. "Japanese and Korean: The problems and history of a linguistic comparison." *The Journal of Japanese Studies* 2.2:389-412.

Li, C.N., ed. 1976. *Subject and Topic.* New York: Academic Press.

______, and S.A. Thompson. 1976. "Subject and topic: A new typology of language." In Li (1976, pp. 457-489).

Lowell, P. 1891. "A comparison of the Japanese and Burmese languages." *Transactions of the Asiatic Society of Japan* 19.

Lukoff, F. 1977. "Ceremonial and expressive uses of the styles of address of Korean." In C.-W. Kim (1977, pp. 269-296).

Lyons, J. 1968. *Introduction to Theoretical Linguistics.* Cambridge: Cambridge University Press.

Mackey, W.F. 1969. *Language Teaching Analysis.* London: Longman.

______. 1970. "Interference, integration and the synchronic fallacy." *Georgetown University Monograph Series of Languages and Linguistics* 23:195-227.

Magretta, W.R. 1977. *Topic-comment Structure and Linguistic Theory: A Functional Approach.* Ph.D. dissertation, University of Michigan.

Makiuchi, M. 1972. *A Study of Some Auxiliary Verbs in Japanese.* Ph.D. dissertation, University of Illinois.

Malone, J.L. 1971. "Systematic metathesis in Mandaic." *Language* 47:394-415.

Marino, M. 1973. "A feature analysis of the modal system of English." *Lingua* 32:309-323.

Martin, S.E. 1952. *Morphophonemics of Standard Colloquial Japanese*. Language Dissertation 47. Baltimore: Waverly Press.

______. 1954. *Korean Morphophonemics*. A Special Publication of the Linguistic Society of America. Baltimore: Waverly Press.

______. 1963a (= Forthcoming). *Korean Reference Grammar*. MS.

______. 1963b. *Essential Japanese*. Rutland, Vermont and Tokyo: Charles E. Tuttle.

______. 1964. "Speech levels in Japan and Korea." In Hymes (1964, pp. 407-412).

______. 1966. "Lexical evidence relating Japanese to Korean." *Language* 42:185-251.

______. 1968. "Grammatical elements relating Korean to Japanese." *Proceedings of the 8th Congress of Anthropological and Ethnological Sciences*. B.9:405-407.

______. 1975a. "Problems in establishing the prehistoric relationships of Korean and Japanese." *Proceedings of the International Symposium Commemorating the 30th Anniversary of Korean Liberation*. Seoul: National Academy of Sciences.

______. 1975b. *A Reference Grammar of Japanese*. New Haven: Yale University Press.

______, and Young-Sook Lee. 1969. *Beginning Korean*. New Haven: Yale University Press.

______, Young-Sook Lee, and Sung-Un Chang. 1967. *A Korean-English Dictionary*. New Haven: Yale University Press.

Martinet, A. 1972. "Function, structure, and sound change." In Keiler (1972, pp. 139-174).

Masuoka, T. 1979. "Double-subject constructions in Japanese." *Papers in Japanese Linguistics* 6:219-236.

Mathias, G.B. 1972. "Review of Miller 1971." *Harvard Journal of Asiatic Studies* 32:284-289.

______. 1973. "On the modification of certain proto-Korean-Japanese reconstructions." *Papers in Japanese Linguistics* 2.1:31-47.

______. 1977. "Musing around and about neutral description statives." M.S. University of Hawaii.

______. 1978. "'Subject' and 'topic' in Korean, Japanese, and English." *Korean Linguistics* 1:128-145.

Matsumoto, N. 1928. *Le Japonais et les Langues austro-asiatiques: Étude de Vocabulaire comparé. Austro-Asiatica 1*. Paris: Librarie Orientaliste Paul Geuthner.

______. 1948. "Nihongo to nanpoogo to no kankei." *Minzokugaku Kenkyuu* 13.2:1-10.

McCann, D.R., J. Middleton, and E.J. Shultz, eds. 1979. *Studies on Korea in Tran-*

sition. Occasional Papers 9, Center for Korean Studies of the University of Hawaii.

McCawley, J.D. 1971. "Tense and time reference in English." In Fillmore and Langedoen (1971, pp. 96-113).

______. 1978. "Conversational implicature and the lexicon." In Cole (1978, pp. 245-259).

McConnell-Ginet, S., R. Boker, and N. Furman, eds. 1980. *Women and Language in Literature and Society*. New York: Praeger.

McCoy, A.M.B.C. 1969. *A Case Grammar Classification of Spanish Verbs*. Ph.D. dissertation, University of Michigan.

McIntire, M.L. 1972. "Terms of address in an academic setting." *Anthropological Linguistics* 14.7:286-291.

Mead, M. 1963. "The factor of culture." In Torre (1963, pp. 3-22).

Mikami, A. 1960. *Zoo wa Hana ga Nagai*. Tokyo: Kuroshio Shuppan.

______. 1970. *Bunpoo Shooron Shuu*. Tokyo: Kuroshio Shuppan.

Miller, R.A. 1967. *The Japanese Language*. Chicago: University of Chicago Press.

______. 1971. *Japanese and the Other Altaic Languages*. Chicago: University of Chicago Press.

______. 1976. "The relevance of historical linguistics for Japanese studies." *The Journal of Japanese Studies* 2.2:335-388.

______. 1979. "Some Old Paekche fragments." *The Journal of Korean Studies* 1:3-69.

Milon, J. 1972. "A Japanese child learns English." Paper presented at TESOL Convention. March 1972.

Mio. I. 1958. *Hanasikotoba no Bunpoo*. Tokyo: Hosei Daigaku Shuppankyoku.

Mochizuki, M. 1980. "Male and female variants for 'I' in Japanese: Cooccurrence rules." *Papers in Linguistics: International Journal of Human Communication* 13.3:474-498.

Monane, T.A. 1976. "The interplay of language and cultural perceptions: Universals and specifics." In Kusanagi (1976, pp. 73-90).

Munkyopu (MOE). 1959. "Hankul uy Roma-ca phyokipep." Ministry of Education, Republic of Korea.

______. 1978. "Kwuke uy Roma-ca phyokipep kayceng sian." Ministry of Education, Republic of Korea.

Muraki, M. 1970. *Presupposition, Pseudo-clefting, and Thematization*. Ph.D. dissertation, University of Texas, Austin.

Murayama, S. 1975. "Vergleichende Betrachtung der Kasus-Suffixe im Altjapanischen." In *Studia Altaica, Festschrift für Nikolaus Poppe*, 126-131. Wiesbaden.

______. 1962a. "Etymologie des altjapanischen Wörtes *irö* 'Farbe, Gesichtsfarbe, Gesicht." *Ural-Altaische Jahrbücher* 34:107-112.

______. 1962b. "Nihongo oyobi kookurigo no suushi—Nihongo keitoo mondai ni yosete." *Kokugogaku* 48:1-11.

______. 1963. "Über einige japanische Kulturwörter altaischen Ursprungs." In *Aspects of Altaic Civilization*, 227-233. *Ural and Altaic Series* 23. Bloomington: Indiana University Press.

______. 1966a. "Mongolische und Japanische — ein Versuch zum lexikalischen Vergleich." In *Collectanea Mongolica, Festschrift für Professor Dr. Rintchen, zum 60. Geburtstag,* 153-156. *Asiatische Forschungen* 17. Wiesbaden: Otto Harrassowitz.

______. 1966b. "Gengogakuteki ni mita nihon bunka no kigen." *Minzokugaku Kenkyuu* 30.4.

______. 1969. "About the origin of the Japanese language." *Proceedings of the 8th International Congress of Anthropological and Ethnological Sciences* 3:477-481.

______. 1974a. *Nihongo no Gogen*. Tokyo: Koobundoo.

______. 1974b. *Nihongo no Kenkyuu Hoohoo:* Tokyo: Koobundoo.

______. 1976. "The Malayo-Polynesian component in the Japanese language." *The Journal of Japanese Studies* 2.2:413-436.

______, and T. Oobayashi. 1973. *Nihongo no Kigen*. Tokyo: Koobundoo.

Na, Jin Suk. 1971. *Wuli Mal uy Ttaymaykim Yenkwu*. Seoul: Kwahak-sa.

Nakane, C. 1970. *Japanese Society*. Berkeley: University of California Press.

Nemser. W. 1974. "Approximate systems of foreign language learners." In Richards (1974a, pp. 55-63).

Neustupny, J.V. 1978. *Post-Structural Approaches to Language: Language Theory in a Japanese Context*. Tokyo: University of Tokyo Press.

Newmeyer, F.J. 1980. *Linguistic Theory in America*. New York: Academic Press.

Nilsen, D.L.F. 1972. *Toward a Semantic Specification of Deep Case*. Janua Linguarum, Series Minor 152. The Hague: Mouton.

______. 1973. *The Instrumental Case in English*. Janua Linguarum, Series Minor 156. The Hague: Mouton.

Niyekawa, A.M. 1977. "Code switching in a stable relationship: An analysis of a Japanese TV drama." In *Proceedings of the Symposium on Japanese Sociolinguistics*. 1977 Summer Institute of the Linguistic Societv of America at the University of Hawaii.

NLRI (The National Language Research Institute of Japan). 1981. *Sociolinguistic Survey in Tokyo and Osaka*. Tokyo: Sanseidoo.

Ogura, S. 1920. *Kokugo oyobi Choosengo no tame*. Keijo: Utsuboya Shosekiten.

______. 1934. *Choosengo to Nihongo. Kokugo Kagaku Kooza* 4. Tokyo: Meiji Shoin.

Oh, Choon-Kyu, 1971. *Aspects of Korean Syntax: Quantification, Relativization, Topicalization and Negation*. Ph.D. dissertation, University of Hawaii.

______. 1972. "Topicalization in Korean: NUN vs. KA comparable to Japanese WA vs. GA." *Papers in Lingustics* 4:624-659.

Ohno. S. 1957. *Nihongo no Kigen.* Tokyo: Iwanami Shoten.

______. 1970. *The Origin of the Japanese Language.* Tokyo: Kokusai Bunka Shinkookai, <English version of Ohno 1957.>

______. 1975. *Nihongo o Sakanoboru.* Tokyo: Iwanami Shoten.

______. 1980. "Nihongo no ruutu wa Tamil-go da." *Shuukan Asahi* 2.15:16-22; 2.22:22-27; 4.11:150-155; and 4.18:26-30.

Okada, M. 1963. *Keigo, Honorific Speech in Japanese.* Far Eastern Publications, Minor Series J.5. New Haven; Yale University Press.

Omodaka, H., et al., eds. 1967. *Jidaibetsu Kokugo Daijiten, Joodaihen.* Tokyo: Sanseidoo.

Ooishi, H. 1975. *Keigo.* Tokyo: Chikuma Shoboo.

Ooya, T. 1889, "Nihongo to choosengo to no ruiji." *Tokyo Jinrui Kagaku Zasshi* 4.37.

Osaka, N. 1972. *Genshi Nihongo Kenkyuu, Nihongo Keitooron e no Kokoromi.* Kobe: Kobe Gakujutsu Soosho 2.

Ozawa, S. 1968, *Kodai Nihongo to Chuusei Mongurogo—Sono Jakkan no Tango no Hikaku Kenkyuu.* Tokyo: Kazama Shoboo.

Palmer. F.R. 1968. *A Linguistic Study of the English Verb.* Miami Linguistic Series 2. Coral Gables: University of Miami Press.

Park, Byung-Soo, 1972. *A Study of the Korean Verb Phrase and Noun Phrase Complementation with Special Attention to the Verb HA.* Ph.D. dissertation, University of Pittsburgh.

______. 1973. "On the multiple subject construction in Korean." *Linguistics* 100:63-76.

Park, Chang-Hai. 1968. *An Intensive Course in Korean I.* Seoul: Yonsei University Press.

Park, Myung-Seok. 1979. *Communication Styles in Two Different Cultures: Korean and American.* Seoul: Hanshin Publishing Co.

Park, Nahm-Sheik. 1977. *Variables in Sentential Readability with Special Reference to EFL/ESL for Korean Learners.* Ph.D. dissertation, Georgetown University.

Park-Choi, Young-Soon. 1976. "Kwuke kyengepep uy sahoyenehakcek yenkwu." *Kwuke Kwukmunhak* 72/73:47-65.

______. 1978. *Aspects in the Development of Communicative Competence with Reference to the Korean Deference System.* Ph.D. dissertation, University of Illinois, Urbana.

Parker, C.K. 1939. *A Dictionary of Japanese Compound Verbs, with an Introduction on Japanese Cultural and Linguistic Affiliations with the Yangtze-Malay-Tibetan-Pacific Quadrilateral.* Tokyo: Maruzen Co.

Parsons, T., and E.A. Shils, eds. 1951. *Toward a General Theory of Action.* Cambridge, Mass: Harvard University Press.

Passin, H. 1966. "Intra-familial linguistic usage in Japan." *Monumenta Nipponica:*

Studies in Japanese Culture (Sophia University, Tokyo) 21.1/2:97-113.

Patterson, B.S. 1972. *A Study of Korean Causatives.* M.A. thesis, University of Hawaii. *Working Papers in Linguistics* (University of Hawaii) 6.4.

Peng, F. 1973. "La parole of Japanese pronouns." *Language Sciences* 25:36-39.

______, et al. 1981. *Male/Female Differences in Japanese.* Tokyo: East-West Sign Language Association.

Polivanov, E.D. 1918. "Odna iz japono-malajskich parallelej." *Izvestija Rossijskoj Akademii Nauk*, Ser. VI. 12. 18:2283-2284.

______. 1927. "K voprosu o rodstvennyx otnošenijax korejskogo i 'altajskix' jazykov." *Izvestja Akademia Nauk,* SSSR, Ser. VI, XXI. 15-17:1195-1204. Moscow.

______. 1960. "Predvaritel'noe soobščenie ob etimologičeskom slovare japonskogo jazyka." *Problemy Vostokoved'enija* 3:174-184.

Poppe, N. 1960. *Vergleichende Grammatik der altaischen Sprachen, Teil 1, Vergleichende Lautlehre.* Wiesbaden: Otto Harrassowitz.

Potter, D.M. 1954. *People of Plenty: Economic Abundance and the American Character.* Chicago: University of Chicago Press.

Price, E. 1968. "Early bilingualism." In Dodson, Price, and Williams (1968, pp. 17-77).

Prideaux, G.D. 1970. *The Syntax of Japanese Honorifics.* The Hague: Mouton.

Pröhle, W. 1916-1917. "Studien zur Vergleichung des Japanischen mit den uralischen und altaischen Sprachen." *Keleti Szemle* 17:147-183.

Pusavat, Y. 1981. "Address terms of married mates in contemporary Japan." Paper presented at the 1981 Conference of Asian Studies of the Pacific Coast held in Honolulu.

Quackenbush, E.M. 1968. *From Sonsorol to Truk: A Dialect Chain.* Ph.D. dissertation, Unviersity of Michigan.

Quackenbush, H. 1970. *Studies in the Phonology of Some Trukic Dialects.* Ph.D. dissertation, University of Michigan.

Rahder, J. 1956. *Etymological Vocabulary of Chinese, Korean, and Ainu, I, Monumenta Nipponica, Monograph* 16. Tokyo. 1959-1960. II and III, *Journal of Asiatic Studies* 2.1 and 2 (Seoul). 1960. IV, *Orbis* 10.1 (Louvain).

Ramstedt, G.J. 1924. "A comparison of the Altaic languages with Japanese." *Transactions of the Asiatic Society of Japan.* Second Series 7.

______. 1949. *Studies in Korean Etymology.* Helsinki: Suomalais-Ugrilainen Seura.

______. 1951. "Two words of Korean-Japanese." *Journal de la Société Finno-Ougrienne* 55:25-30.

______. 1952. *Einführung in die altaische Sprachwissenschaft, II, Formenlehre.* Helsinki: Suomalais-Ugrilainen Seura.

______. 1957. *Einführung in die altaische Sprachwissenschaft, I, Lautlehre.* Helsinki: Mémoires de la Société Finno-Ougrienne 104.1.

Ravem, R. 1968. "Language acquisition in a second language environment." *IRAL*

6.2.

______. 1974. "The development of *wh*-questions in first and second language learners." In Richards (1974a, pp. 134-155).

Ree, Joe Jung-No. 1969. *Some Aspects of Korean Syntax.* Ph.D. dissertation, Indiana University.

Rehg, K.L. 1973. "On the history of Ponapean phonology." *Working Papers in Linguistics* (University of Hawaii) 5.8:17-55.

Reynolds, K.A. 1982. "Female Speakers of Japanese." MS. Stanford University.

Richards, J.C., ed. 1974a. *Error Analysis: Perspectives on Second Language Acquisition.* London: Longman.

______. 1974b "Error analysis and second language learning strategies." In Schumann and Stenson (1974, pp. 32-53).

______. and G.P. Sampson. 1974. "The study of learner English." In Richards (1974a, pp. 3-18).

Riesenberg, S.H., and S. Kaneshiro. 1960. "A Caroline Islands script." *Bureau of American Ethnology Bulletin* (Smithsonian Institute, Washington) 173:269-333.

Richie, W.C. 1973. "Constraints on adult-acquired syntax." *Orange Papers: Syracuse Studies in Linguistics* 1.2

Rogers, M. 1984. "On major types of written error in advanced students of German." *IRAL* 22.1:1-39.

Ross, J.R. 1967. "Auxiliaries as main verbs." Indiana University Linguistics Club.

______. 1970. "On declarative sentences." In Jacobs and Rosenbaum (1970, pp. 222-272).

Russell, H. 1981. "Second person pronouns in Japanese." *Sophia Linguistica* (Sophia University, Tokyo) 8/9:116-128.

Sadock, J.M. 1970. "Whimperatives." In Sadock and Vanek (1970).

______. 1971. "Queclaratives." In *Papers from the Seventh Regional Meeting of the Chicago Linguistic Society.*

______. 1975. *Toward a Linguistic Theory of Speech Acts.* New York: Academic Press.

______, and A.L. Vanek, eds. 1970. *Studies Presented to Robert B. Lees by His Students.* Edmonton: Linguistic Research Inc.

Saint-Jacques, B. 1971. *Structural Analysis of Modern Japanese.* Vancouver: University of British Columbia Press.

Sato. P.T. 1974. "Origin of Korean *l* that corresponds to Japanese *t.*" *Papers in Japanese Linguistics* 3.1:203-232.

Schane, S.A. 1972. "Natural rules in phonology." In Stockwell and Macaulay (1972, pp. 199-229).

______. 1973. *Generative Phonology.* Englewood Cliffs, N.J.: Prentice-Hall.

Schumann, J.H., and N. Stenson, eds. 1974. *New Frontiers in Second Language*

Learning. Rowley, Mass: Newbury House.

Schwartz, A. 1971. "General aspects of relative clause formation." *Working Papers on Language Universals* (Stanford University) 6:139-171.

Searle, J.R. 1969. *Speech Acts: An Essay in the Philosophy of Language*. Cambridge: Cambridge University Press.

______. 1975. "Indirect speech acts." In Cole and Morgan (1975, pp. 59-82).

______. 1976. "The classification of illocutionary acts." *Language in Society* 5.1:1-14.

Sebeok, T.A., ed. 1960. *Style in Language*. Cambridge, Mass: MIT Press.

______, et al., eds. 1971. *Current Trends in Linguistics 8*. The Hague: Mouton.

Selinker, L. 1974. "Interlanguage." In Richards (1974a, pp. 31-54).

Semiloff-Zelasko, H. 1973. "Glide metathesis." *Working Papers in Linguistics* (Ohio State University) 14:66-76.

Shibatani, M. 1973. "Lexical versus periphrastic causatives in Korean." *Journal of Linguistics* 9:281-298.

______. 1975. "On the nature of synonymy in causative expressions." *Language Research* 11.2:267-274.

______. 1976a. "Relational grammar and Korean syntax." *Language Research* 12.2:241-251.

______, ed. 1976b. *Syntax and Semantics 6: The Grammar of Causative Constructions*. New York: Academic Press.

______. 1977. "Grammatical relations and surface cases." *Language* 53.4:789-809.

______, and C. Cotton. 1976/77. "Remarks on double-nominative sentences." *Papers in Japanese Linguistics* 5:261-278.

Shin, Changsoon. 1975. "Kwuke uy 'cwue muncey' yenkwu." *Munpep Yenkwu* 2:131-170.

______. 1976. "Kwuke cosa uy yenkwu." *Kwuke Kwukmunhak* 71:1-41.

Shinmura, I. 1911. "Kokugo keitoo no mondai." *Taiyoo* 17.1. Also in Ikeda and Ohno (1973:325-333).

______. 1935. "Kokugo keitooron." *Kokugo Kagaku Kooza* 4. Tokyo: Meiji Shoin.

Shinoda, A. 1973. "Classification of Japanese speech levels and styles." *Papers in Japanese Linguistics* 2.1:66-81.

Shinoda, E. 1981. "Donatory verbs and psychological distance in Japanese." *Sophia Linguistica* (Sophia University, Tokyo) 8/9:142-151.

Shiratori, K. 1897. "Nihon no kogo to choosengo to no hikaku." *Kokugakuin Zasshi* 4:4-12.

______. 1914-1916. "Choosengo to Ural-Altai-go to no hikaku kenkyuu." *Shiratori Kurakichi Zenshuu* 3. Tokyo: Iwanami Shoten (1970).

Shroyer, T.G. 1969. *An Investigation of the Semantics of English as a Proposed*

Basis for Language Curriculum Materials. Ph.D. dissertation, Ohio State University.

Shuy, R.W., and R.W. Fasold. 1972. "Contemporary emphasis in sociolinguistics." In Smith and Shuy (1972, pp. 1-13).

Sievers, E. 1901. *Grundzüge der Phonetik zur Einführung in das Studium der Lautlehre der indogermanischen Sprachen.* Leipzig.

Silva, C.M. 1973. "Metathesis of obstruent clusters." *Working Papers in Linguistics* (Ohio State University) 14:77-84.

Slobin, D.I., S.H. Miller, and L.W. Porter. 1968. "Forms of address and social relations in a business organization." *Journal of Personality and Social Psychology* 8.3:289-293.

Smith, A.G. 1951. "Guide to Woleai Spelling." (Mimeo). Department of Education, Office of the High Commissioner of the Trust Territory of the Pacific.

Smith, D.M., and R.W. Shuy, eds. 1972. *Sociolinguistics in Cross-Cultural Analysis.* Georgetown: Georgetown University Press.

Smith, E.C. and L.F. Luce, eds. 1979. *Toward Internationalism.* Rowley, Mass: Newbury House Publishers.

Soenjono, D. 1974. "Honorifics in generative semantics: A case in Javanese." *RECL Journal* (English Language Teaching in Southeast Asia) 4.1:86-97.

Soepomo, P. 1968. "Javanese speech levels." *Indonesia 6.* Ithaca: Cornell University Press.

Sohn, Ho-min. 1969. *An Outline of Ulithian Grammar.* Ph.D. dissertation, University of Hawaii.

______. 1971. "*a*-raising in Woleaian." *Working Papers in Linguistics* (University of Hawaii) 3.8:15-36. Also in this volume.

______. 1973a. "A re-examination of 'auxiliary' verb constructions." *Working Papers in Linguistics* (University of Hawaii) 5.3:63-88. Also in this volume.

______. 1973b. "Coherence in Korean 'auxiliary' verb constructions." *Language Research* 9.2:239-251.

______. 1974a. "Modals and speaker-hearer perspectives in Korean." *Papers in Linguistics* 7.3/4:493-520. Also in this volume.

______. 1974b. "Case incorporation in English verbs with reference to Korean structure." *The English Language and Literature* 51/52:431-456. Also in this volume.

______. 1975a. *Woleaian Reference Grammar.* Honolulu: University Press of Hawaii.

______, ed. 1975b. *The Korean Language: Its Structure and Social Projection.* Occasional Papers 6, Center for Korean Studies of the University of Hawaii.

______. 1975c. "Retrospection in Korean." *Language Research* 1.1:87-103. Also in this volume.

______. 1979. "Honorific patterns in Japanese and Korean." In *Festschrift for Dr. Tae Sik Synn*, 57-106. Daegu, Korea: Keimyung University Press.

______. 1980. "Theme-prominence in Korean." *Korean Linguistics* 2:2-19. Also in this volume.

______. 1983a. "Intercultural communication in cognitive values: Americans and Koreans." *Language and Linguistics* (Hankuk University of Foreign Studies) 9:93-136. Also in this volume.

______. 1983b. "Power and solidarity in the Korean language." *Korean Linguistics* 3:97-122. Also in this volume.

______, and B.W. Bender. 1973. *A Ulithian Grammar*. Canberra: Australian National University Press.

______, and B.W. Bender. 1984. "Surface and deep contrasts in Ulithian phonology." In Bender (1984, pp. 201-213). Also in this volume.

______, and A. Tawerilmang. 1976. *Woleaian-English Dictionary*. Honolulu: University Press of Hawaii.

______, A. Tawerilmang, I. Langal, and C. Yangilmau. 1977. "Consonant shifts and subgrouping in the Sonsorol-Ulithi-Woleai Chain." *Language Sciences* 44:19-24. Also in this volume.

Sohn, John J. 1973. *A Study of Grammatical Cases of Korean, Japanese, and Other Major Altaic Languages*. Ph.D. dissertation, Indiana University.

Song, Seok Choong. 1967. *Some Transformational Rules in Korean*. Ph.D. dissertation, Indiana University.

______. 1976. "On an abbreviation phenomenon in Korean." *Linguistic Journal of Korea* 1.2:70-88.

______. 1977. "Causes of confusion in descriptions of Korean causatives." Paper presented at the 1977 Linguistic Society of America Symposium on Korean Linguistics. Honolulu.

Song, Zino. 1980. "The use of speech levels in Japan and Korea: From a sociolinguistic point of view." *Korean Linguistics* 2:77-89.

Spiro. M.E., ed. 1965. *Context and Meaning in Cultural Anthropology*. New York: Free Press.

Stewart, E.C. 1972. *American Cultural Patterns: A Cross-Cultural Perspective*. Chicago: Intercultural Press.

______. 1979. "Orientation to action." In Smith and Luce (1979, pp. 1-22).

Stockwell, R.P. and J.D. Bower. 1965. *The Sounds of English and Spanish*. Chicago: University of Chicago Press.

Stockwell, R.P. and R.K.S. Macaulay, eds. 1972. *Linguistic Change and Generative Theory*. Bloomington: Indiana University Press.

Stockwell, R.P. and J.W. Martin. 1965. *The Grammatical Structures of English and Spanish*. Chicago: University of Chicago Press.

Stouffer, S.A., et al. 1949. *The American Soldier*. Princeton: Princeton University Press.

Street, J.C. 1962. "Review of Poppe 1960." *Language* 38:92-98.

______. 1974. "On the lexicon of proto-Altaic: A partial index to reconstructions."

Madison, Wisconsin: the author.

______. 1978. *Altaic Elements in Old Japanese* (draft version), Part 2. Madison, Wisconsin: the author.

______, and R.A. Miller. 1975. *Altaic Elements in Old Japanese* (draft version), Part 1. Madison, Wisconsin: the authors.

Suh, Cheong-Soo. 1972. "Hyentay kwuke uy taywupep yenkwu." *Language Research* 8.2:147-166.

______. 1974. "Hanil yang kwuke uy kyengepep pikyo yenkwu." *Swuto College Anthology* 5.

______. 1979. "Sahoykwuco pyentong kwa hankwuke kyengepep uy chwui." *Sengkok Nonchong* 10:186-219.

______. 1984. *Contaypep uy Yenkwu*. Seoul: Hanshin Publishing Co.

Suk, Kyong-Jing. 1975. *Speech-act and Syntactic Regularity: A Study of Sentence Ender in Korean*. Ph.D. dissertation, University of Texas, Austin.

Suzuki, T. 1973. *Kotoba to Bunka*. Tokyo: Iwanami Shoten.

Syromjatnikov, N.A. 1972. "Drevnejaponskij jazyk." Moscow.

Szalay, L.B. and G.L. Fisher. 1979. "Communication overseas." In Smith and Luce (1979, pp. 57-82).

Talmy, L. 1975. "Semantics and syntax of motion." In Kimball (1975, pp. 181-238).

Tani, S. 1981. "Gendaigo ni okeru 'anata'." In *Kiyoo* 4:15-29. Tokyo: Inter-University Center for Japanese Language Studies Administered by Stanford University.

Tawerilmang, A.F., and Ho-min Sohn. 1984. "Proto-Oceanic reflexes in Woleaian." In Bender (1984, pp. 171-199). Also in this volume.

Teng, Shou-Hsin. 1974. "Double nominatives in Chinese." *Language* 50:455-473.

Thompson, L.C. and M.T. Thompson. 1969. "Metathesis as a grammatical device." *International Journal of American Linguistics* 35:213-219.

Thorne, B. and N. Henley, eds. 1975. *Language and Sex: Difference and Dominance*. Rowley, Mass: Newbury House.

Tiryakian, E.A., ed. 1963. *Sociological Theory, Values and Sociocultural Change: Essays in Honor of P.A. Sorokin*. New York: Free Press.

Tokieda, M., ed. 1958. *Bunpoo Kakuronhen*. Tokyo: Meiji Shoin.

Torre, M., ed. 1963. *The Selection of Personnel for International Service*. Geneva: Federation for Mental Health.

Tsujimura, T. 1958. "Taiguugo-hoo." In Tokieda (1958, pp. 323-344).

______. 1968a. "Keigo." In *Encyclopedia Japonica* 6:462. Tokyo: Shogakukan.

______. 1968b. *Keigo no Siteki Kenkyuu*. Tokyo: Tokyodo.

Uhlenbeck, E.M. 1970. "The use of respect forms in Japanese." In Wurm and Laycock (1970).

Ultan, R. 1971. "A typological view of metathesis." *Working Papers in Language Universals* (Stanford University) 7:1-44.

Underhill, R. 1972. "Metathesis vs. gemination in Greenlandic." *Papers in Linguistics* 4:299-311.

Unger, J.M. 1973. "Review of Miller 1971." *Papers in Japanese Linguistics* 2.1:155-169.

Uyeno, T.Y. 1971. *A Study of Japanese Modality—A Performative Analysis of Sentence Particles.* Ph.D. dissertation, University of Michigan.

Vachek, J. 1966. *The Linguistic School of Prague.* Bloomington: Indiana University Press.

Valdman, A., ed. 1966. *Trends in Language Teaching.* New York: McGraw-Hill.

Van der Auwera, J. 1980. *Indirect Speech Acts Revisited.* Bloomington: Indiana University Linguistics Club.

Wardhaugh, R. 1974. "The contrastive analysis hypothesis." *In Schumann and Stenson* (1974, pp. 1-19).

Webb, C. 1976. "The status of metathesis as a phonological process." *Proceedings of the Sixth California Linguistics Association Conference* (April 30-May 1, 1976), 77-89. San Diego State University.

Whymant, J. 1926. "The oceanic theory of the origin of the Japanese language and people." *Transactions of the Asiatic Society of Japan*, 2nd Series 3.

Williams, R.H., ed. 1954. *Human Factors in Military Operations. Technical Memorandum* ORO-T-259. The Johns Hopkins University Operations Research Office.

Wolfe, D.K. 1967. "Some theoretical aspects of language learning and language teaching." *Language Learning* 17:173-188.

Wolfson, N., and E. Judd, eds. 1983. *Sociolinguistics and Language Acquisition.* Rowley, Mass: Newbury House Publishers.

Wurm, S.A., and D.C. Laycock, eds. 1970. *Pacific Linguistic Studies in Honour of Arthur Capell.* Series C, No. 13. Canberra: Australian National University.

Yamanasi, M. 1974. "On minding your p's and q's in Japanese: A case study from honorifics." In *Papers from the Tenth Regional Meeting of the Chicago Linguistic Society,* 760-771.

Yang, Dong-Whee. 1973a. *Topicalization and Relativization in Korean.* Ph.D. dissertation, Indiana University.

______. 1973b. "Inner and outer locatives in Korean." *Language Research* 9.1:27-45.

______. 1974. "On the notion of topic (I) and (II)." *Journal of Korean Cultural Research Institute* (Ewha Woman's University) 23:469-509 and 24:209-236.

______. 1975. "Semantic constraints I: Causativization." *Language Research 11.2: 243-248.*

Yang, In-Seok. 1971. "Double modality in Korean." *Language Research* 7.1:23-36.

______. 1972. *Korean Syntax: Case Markers, Delimiters, Complementation, and Relativization.* Ph.D. dissertation, University of Hawaii. Seoul: Paykhap-sa.

______. 1973. "Semantics of delimiters." *Language Research* 9.2:84-121.

______. 1974. "Two causative forms in Korean." *Language Research* 10.1:83-117.

______. 1976. "Semantics of Korean causation." *Foundations of Language* 14.1: 55-87.

Yoshikawa, M. 1982. "Japanese and American modes of communication and implications for managerial and organizational behavior." Paper presented at the 2nd International Conference on Communication Theory: Eastern and Western Perspectives. Yokohama, Japan. July 1982.

Zimin, S. 1981. "Sex and politeness: Factors in first and second-language use." *International Journal of Sociology of Language* 27:35-58.